THE CORNELL BOOK OF CATS

THE CORNELL BOOK OF CATS

A Comprehensive Medical Reference for Every Cat and Kitten

BY THE FACULTY, STAFF, AND ASSOCIATES
CORNELL FELINE HEALTH CENTER
COLLEGE OF VETERINARY MEDICINE
CORNELL UNIVERSITY

Edited by Mordecai Siegal

VILLARD BOOKS · NEW YORK
1989

Grateful acknowledgment is made to E. P. Dutton for permission to reprint
two charts and four lists from *First Aid for Pets* by Robert W. Kirk,
D.V.M. Copyright © 1978 by Robert W. Kirk, D.V.M. Reprinted by permission
of the publisher, E. P. Dutton, a division of Penguin Books, U.S.A., Inc.

Pen-and-ink drawings of the cat breeds by Cynthia Holmes-Harwood.
Anatomical illustrations by Ernest W. Beck, reprinted from
*The Feline: A Veterinary Aid in Anatomical Transparencies with Supplemental
Color Illustrations* with permission from Solvay Animal Health, Inc.

LIBRARY OF CONGRESS CATALOGING-IN-PUBLICATION DATA

The Cornell book of cats: a comprehensive medical reference for every
cat and kitten / by the faculty, staff, and associates, Cornell Feline Health
Center, College of Veterinary Medicine, Cornell University; edited
by Mordecai Siegal.
p.   cm.
Includes index.
ISBN 0-394-56787-0
1. Cats—Diseases.   2. Cats–Health.   I. Siegal, Mordecai.
II. Cornell Feline Health Center.
SF985.C67   1989
636.8′089.6—dc20   89-40195

Manufactured in the United States of America
Designed by Beth Tondreau Design / Jane Treuhaft
9 8 7 6 5 4 3 2
FIRST EDITION

Quality Printing and Binding by:
Arcata Graphics/Halliday Lithograph
Circuit Street
West Hanover, Mass. 02339 U.S.A.

*To all veterinarians with a special interest in
feline medicine and surgery, in appreciation for your
knowledge, expertise, and dedication, which have
vastly improved the health and welfare of cats.*

Contents

Contributors

This book represents the work of twenty-eight authors. They are:

JEFFREY E. BARLOUGH, D.V.M., Ph.D., is Assistant Professor in the Department of Microbiology, Immunology and Parasitology, College of Veterinary Medicine, Cornell University. He earned his D.V.M. at the University of California, Davis, and a Ph.D. in veterinary virology at Cornell University. He is a Diplomate, American College of Veterinary Microbiologists.

MARGARET BARR, D.V.M., is a Ph.D. candidate in the Department of Microbiology, Immunology and Parasitology, College of Veterinary Medicine, Cornell University. She is a contributor to *Feline Health Topics* and *Perspectives on Cats,* both Cornell University publications. She earned her B.S. at the University of the South, and a D.V.M. at Auburn University.

DWIGHT D. BOWMAN, Ph.D., is Assistant Professor of Parasitology in the Department of Microbiology, Immunology and Parasitology, College of Veterinary Medicine, Cornell University. He earned his B.A. in biology from Hiram College and M.S. and Ph.D. degrees in parasitology from Tulane University.

DOROTHY F. HOLMES, D.V.M., Ph.D., is Senior Research Associate in the Department of Microbiology, Immunology and Parasitology, College of Veteri-nary Medicine, Cornell University. She earned her D.V.M. and Ph.D., in veterinary microbiology, from Cornell University.

JOHNNY D. HOSKINS, D.V.M., Ph.D., is Professor in the Department of Veterinary Clinical Sciences, Louisiana State University. He was Acting Assistant Director of the Cornell Feline Health Center in 1985–86. He earned his B.S. and D.V.M. from Oklahoma State University and a Ph.D. in veterinary pathology and clinical sciences from Iowa State University.

KATHERINE A. HOUPT, V.M.D., Ph.D., is Professor of Veterinary Physiology and the Director of the Behavior Clinic, Department of Physiology, College of Veterinary Medicine, Cornell University. She earned her B.S. in veterinary science from Pennsylvania State University and V.M.D. and Ph.D. degrees from the University of Pennsylvania.

LINDA SUSAN JORGENSEN, D.V.M., has a small-animal internal-medicine practice in Redwood City, California. She is a contributor to *Feline Health Topics* and *Perspectives on Cats.* She earned her D.V.M. from the University of California, Davis. She performed her internship and residency in small-animal internal medicine at the College of Veterinary Medicine, Cornell University. She is a Diplomate, American College of Veterinary Internal Medicine.

ROBERT W. KIRK, D.V.M., is Professor Emeritus of Small Animal Medicine and former Department Chairman, College of Veterinary Medicine, Cornell University. He earned his B.S. from the University of Connecticut and D.V.M. from Cornell University. He is a Diplomate, American College of Veterinary Internal Medicine and American College of Veterinary Dermatology.

JUNE KIRVAN-TUTTLE, A.A.S., B.S., is Editor/Communication Specialist for the Cornell Feline Health Center, Department of Microbiology, Immunology and Parasitology, College of Veterinary Medicine, Cornell University. She is the editor of *Perspectives on Cats* and *Feline Health Topics.* She earned an A.A.S. in animal science from S.U.N.Y. at Delhi and a B.S. in agricultural journalism from The Ohio State University. She is a member of the Cornell Editors' Guild and Agricultural Communicators in Education.

DONALD LEIN, D.V.M., Ph.D., is Associate Professor of Theriogenology and Pathology and the Director of the Diagnostic Laboratory, College of Veterinary Medicine, Cornell University. He received his D.V.M. from Cornell University and his Ph.D. in pathology from the University of Connecticut.

PATRICK L. McDONOUGH, Ph.D., is Section Chief of the Microbiology Laboratory and Instructor in the Department of Pathology of the School of Veterinary Medicine, Tufts University. He earned his B.S. in biology from Albright College and his M.S. and Ph.D. degrees from Cornell University.

N. SYDNEY MOISE, D.V.M., M.S., is Assistant Professor of Medicine in the Department of Clinical Sciences at the College of Veterinary Medicine, Cornell University. She earned her B.S. and D.V.M. degrees from Texas A & M University, and an M.S. in veterinary microbiology from Cornell University. She is a Diplomate of the American College of Veterinary Internal Medicine and the American College of Veterinary Cardiology.

MARK L. MORRIS, JR., D.V.M., M.S., Ph.D., is a partner of Mark Morris Associates, president of Theracon, Inc., and Adjunct Associate Professor of Medicine at the College of Veterinary Medicine, Cornell University. He received his D.V.M. from Cornell University and M.S. and Ph.D. degrees from the University of Wisconsin. He is a Diplomate, American College of Veterinary Nutrition.

SUSAN A. MORRISON, D.V.M., is a small-animal practitioner in Weymouth, Massachusetts. She is a contributor to the *Feline Information Bulletin.* She earned her D.V.M. from Cornell University.

DREW M. NODEN, Ph.D., is Professor of Anatomy in the Department of Anatomy, College of Veterinary Medicine, Cornell University. He earned a B.A. in biology from Washington and Jefferson College and his Ph.D. in zoology from Washington University.

DALE D. OLM, D.V.M., is small-animal practitioner for the Behavior Council Clinic at the Manhattan Veterinary Group, and Bergh Memorial Animal Hospital of the A.S.P.C.A. in New York, N.Y. He earned his B.A. and M.S. in chemistry from the University of Connecticut and his D.V.M. from Cornell University.

ELIZABETH ALLISON OLTENACU, Ph.D., is Associate Director for Academic Programs and Associate Professor in the Department of Animal Science, College of Agriculture and Life Sciences, Cornell University. She earned her B.Sc. in agricultural science from the University of Edinburgh, Scotland, her M.S. and Ph.D. in animal science from the University of Minnesota.

ROY V. H. POLLOCK, D.V.M., Ph.D., is Assistant Professor of Medical Informatics, and Director of the Center for Medical Informatics, Department of Clinical Sciences, College of Veterinary Medicine, Cornell University. He is the editor of the *Cornell Animal Health Newsletter.* He earned his B.A. from Williams College and his D.V.M. and Ph.D. in veterinary virology from Cornell University.

RONALD C. RIIS, D.V.M., is Associate Professor of Medicine and Chief of Comparative Ophthalmology Service in the Department of Clinical Sciences, College of Veterinary Medicine, Cornell University. He earned his B.A./B.S. from South Dakota State University and M.T./A.S.C.P. and D.V.M. from the University of Minnesota and an M.S. in veterinary medicine from Cornell University. He is a Diplomate, American College of Veterinary Ophthalmologists.

JOHN EDWARD SAIDLA, D.V.M., is Assistant Director of the Cornell Feline Health Center and Feline Extension Veterinarian, College of Veterinary Medicine, Cornell University. He is the associate editor of the *Cornell Animal Health Newsletter.* He earned his D.V.M. from Auburn University.

DANNY W. SCOTT, D.V.M., is Professor of Medicine in the Department of Clinical Sciences, College of Veterinary Medicine, Cornell University. He earned his B.S. and D.V.M. from the University of California, Davis. He is a Diplomate, American College of Veterinary Dermatology.

FRED W. SCOTT, D.V.M., Ph.D., is Professor of Veterinary Virology in the Department of Microbiology, Immunology and Parasitology, and the Director of the Cornell Feline Health Center, College of Veterinary Medicine, Cornell University. He earned a B.S. in chemistry from the University of Massachusetts and a D.V.M. and Ph.D. in virology from Cornell University. He is a past president of the American Association of Feline Practitioners. He is a Diplomate, American College of Veterinary Microbiologists.

SANG J. SHIN, D.V.M., is Associate Professor of Microbiology and Director of the Microbiology Laboratory, Diagnostic Laboratory, College of Veterinary Medicine, Cornell University. He earned his B.S. in microbiology from the University of Southwestern Louisiana and a D.V.M. from the Seoul National University, Korea. He is a Diplomate, American College of Veterinary Microbiologists.

MORDECAI SIEGAL is an author and journalist, and a member of the Feline Advisory Council, Cornell Feline Health Center, College of Veterinary Medicine, Cornell University. He is vice-president of the Empire Cat Club. He is the author of nine published books concerning behavior, nutritional needs, medical care, training, breed descriptions, and human/animal bonding. His articles and monthly columns on pets appear regularly in national magazines, and he frequently appears on the broadcast media.

BRIAN A. SUMMERS, B.V.Sc., M.Sc., Ph.D., is Associate Professor of Pathology (Neuropathology), Department of Pathology, College of Veterinary Medicine, Cornell University. He has a B.V.Sc. from the University of Melbourne, an M.Sc. in veterinary pathology from the University of London, and a Ph.D. in pathology from Cornell University. He is a Diplomate, American College of Veterinary Pathologists.

CORISSE N. VAUGHAN, D.V.M., is a small-animal practitioner at the Colonial Animal Hospital in Springfield, Virginia. She is a contributor to *Feline Health Topics.* She earned her B.S. and D.V.M. from Cornell University.

MAURICE E. WHITE, D.V.M., is Associate Professor of Medicine in the Department of Clinical Sciences, College of Veterinary Medicine, Cornell University. He is a Diplomate of the American College of Veterinary Internal Medicine and the American Board of Veterinary Practitioners. He is editor of *The Cornell Veterinarian.* His research involvement is with computer-assisted veterinary diagnosis and information management. He is an ambulatory clinician in the Veterinary Medical Teaching Hospital. He earned his D.V.M. from Cornell University.

LEO A. WUORI, D.V.M., is Senior Extension Associate and Special Consultant for fund-raising for the Cornell Feline Health Center, Department of Microbiology, Immunology and Parasitology, College of Veterinary Medicine, Cornell University. He earned his D.V.M. from Cornell University.

THE CORNELL BOOK OF CATS

EDITOR

Mordecai Siegal

ASSOCIATE EDITORS

Jeffrey E. Barlough, D.V.M., Ph.D.

Victoria Blankenship-Siegal

June Kirvan-Tuttle

John Edward Saidla, D.V.M.

Fred W. Scott, D.V.M., Ph.D.

ILLUSTRATOR

Cynthia Holmes-Harwood

PHOTOGRAPHERS

Vickie Jackson

Mordecai Siegal

David W. Tuttle

Preface

Robert D. Phemister, Dean
College of Veterinary Medicine
Cornell University

A photo, circa 1900, of Dr. James Law, shows the first dean of the College of Veterinary Medicine at Cornell seated on the porch of his Ithaca, New York, home with a litter of kittens playing at his feet. It is a heartwarming photo. It is also an early indication of the college's concern for the health and well-being of all animals. From its establishment in 1894, the College of Veterinary Medicine at Cornell University has pursued its mission of animal care through teaching, research, and service. As a result, programs have been built that educate today's veterinarians, investigate zoonotic diseases, preserve the health of companion animals, and serve agriculture by attending to the health, reproduction, and diseases of food-producing animals and horses.

The college proudly points to its role in research that has improved animal health. For example, college faculty members have developed vaccines for canine infectious hepatitis, canine distemper, parvovirus, duck hepatitis, and Marek's disease in chickens. In recent years, faculty members have contributed to what is known about such diseases as progressive pneumonia in sheep, muscular dystrophy in dogs, and strangles and influenza in horses. In the search for new or improved diagnostic tests, work progresses on better tests for Lyme disease, canine brucellosis, giardiasis, and osteoarthritis. Clinical treatment of patients in the College's Veterinary Medical Teaching Hospital complements this work, thanks to the availability of specialists and the latest in diagnostic and therapeutic technology.

The college has been successful in improving animal health because of its ability to attract outstanding faculty from the finest academic institutions and research facilities around the world. Our graduates also exert a strong impact on animal health. Eighty students are admitted annually to the four-year Doctor of Veterinary Medicine degree program. They are among the best-qualified applicants in the country. Upon graduation they are well prepared as veterinarians to enter any of the many fields open to them in private practice, research, industry, government, and academics.

In the tradition of James Law and the College of Veterinary Medicine he established, the Feline Health Center works to improve the health of cats. The center develops methods to prevent or cure feline diseases and provides continuing education to veterinarians and cat owners. Work at the center has established vaccine recommendations for panleukopenia and viral respiratory diseases, identified several feline skin diseases, developed the ELISA test for detecting coronavirus antibodies, and isolated three new viruses in cats. Today, Feline Health Center staff look for ways to understand and combat feline infectious peritonitis, hyperthyroidism, heart disease, feline leukemia, and the newly identified feline immunodeficiency virus. Some of the work of the Feline Health Center is included in *The Cornell Book of Cats*. We hope this book becomes a helpful reference for all cat owners, in the Cornell tradition of working to improve animal health.

Foreword

by Fred W. Scott, Director
Cornell Feline Health Center

WHY *THE CORNELL BOOK OF CATS?*

The Cornell Book of Cats is the realization of an idea that has smoldered for several years: an information book on the health and care of cats for the owners of pet cats, and for cat-health workers. In the course of their work at the Cornell Feline Health Center, the faculty and staff had been developing numerous information pieces for both veterinarians and cat owners, and the idea of putting this information into a book for the general reader appeared to have merit. *The Cornell Book of Cats,* then, is the culmination of efforts by many persons to bring that idea to fruition.

WHAT IS THE CORNELL FELINE HEALTH CENTER?

The Cornell Feline Health Center is a veterinary medical specialty center devoted to improving the health and welfare of cats throughout the world. The Feline Health Center is located within the College of Veterinary Medicine at Cornell University in Ithaca, New York.

The College of Veterinary Medicine at Cornell University is one of twenty-seven veterinary colleges in the United States, and is the only veterinary college in the State of New York. Dr. James Law, a Scottish veterinarian, was one of the original faculty of Cornell University. The first Doctor of Veterinary Medicine (D.V.M.) degree in the United States was awarded in 1876 to Dr. Daniel E. Salmon, who became the first director of the Bureau of Animal Industry, currently known as the U.S. Department of Agriculture.

The concept of a feline medical specialty center began in 1973 as part of a long-range planning effort at the College of Veterinary Medicine at Cornell. In reviewing the present and anticipated future of veterinary medicine, and more specifically veterinary medicine as it is related to cats, it became obvious that if many of the serious disease problems of the cat were to be solved, a concerted effort would have to be applied to do it. Since a number of experts in various fields of small-animal medicine were on the faculty of the College of Veterinary Medicine already it seemed appropriate to draw these individuals together for the particular benefit of cats and, less directly, cats' owners. A proposal was made to Dr. George Poppensiek, the then Dean of the College of Veterinary Medicine, who enthusiastically approved the concept, and subsequently guided the proposal through the appropriate channels. The Board of Trustees of Cornell University, in February 1974, approved the formation of the "Cornell Feline Research Laboratory." The name was subsequently changed to "Cornell Feline Health Center," to more accurately depict the efforts and goals of the Feline Center.

The initial staff of the Feline Health Center consisted of a part-time director and a part-time secretary, with several veterinarians on the college faculty agreeing to serve as participants in their areas of expertise. These participants held full-time appointments in other areas of the college, and received no special remuneration for their efforts on behalf of the Feline Health Center. As time went on, full-time staff were added, including secretarial staff, an editor, a feline extension veterinarian, and various research scientists, graduate students, and technicians.

At the outset, there were no funds available to support any of the Feline Health Center's activities, and there did not appear to be any hope of obtaining support for them from the state, Cornell University, or the College of Veterinary Medicine. It became clear quickly that if such a center was to be successful, an active fund-raising effort would have to be mounted. So with a concerted effort over several years, the Cornell Feline Health Center has successfully developed an active fund-raising program to support its various activities.

....

PURPOSES OF THE CORNELL FELINE HEALTH CENTER

The purposes of the Cornell Feline Health Center are (1) to find ways of preventing and curing diseases of cats; (2) to educate veterinarians and cat owners about feline health; and (3) to aid veterinarians when new or unknown feline diseases occur. In short, the faculty and staff of the Feline Health Center are dedicated to improving the health and welfare of cats.

Research is the cornerstone to providing better health care for cats. Veterinarians must have specific information with which they can make intelligent decisions on the best treatment and prevention regimes for cats. New vaccines and specific treatment protocols do not just appear—they require dedicated effort, often over several years. The Cornell Feline Health Center is dedicated to obtaining that information about diseases of cats and cat health management that will enable the private practitioner to maintain healthy and happy pet cats. Research is designed for the overall benefit of cats, not for the benefit of humans. Often, however, information gained about the feline disease under investigation will provide information that can also be applied to similar human diseases.

Faculty and staff of the Feline Health Center are involved with numerous areas of research. Some of these areas include:

1. *Infectious diseases.* Investigations of infectious diseases have been aimed at developing accurate diagnostic tests, improved treatments, and effective vaccines. Over the years almost every infectious disease of cats has been studied. Many of the current vaccination and treatment procedures conducted daily in veterinary clinics across the United States have been influenced by these studies at Cornell.

2. *Nutrition.* Scientists have studied the basic nutritional requirements of cats in order to advise owners on the proper nutrition and feeding of cats. Once the normal nutritional state is understood, the relationship between nutrition and disease can be established.

3. *Behavior.* Scientists with expertise in behavior have studied both the normal and abnormal behavior patterns of cats and ways of dealing with cats when abnormal behavior does occur.

4. *Reproduction/genetics.* Normal and abnormal reproduction of the cat has been studied, including the normal hormonal status before, during, and after pregnancy. The etiologies of many reproductive, neonatal, and congenital diseases have been clarified.

5. *Dermatology.* Numerous skin diseases of the cat have been identified and characterized by the participating faculty of the Feline Health Center.

6. *Internal medicine.* Several naturally occurring systemic diseases of cats have been identified and characterized by participating members of the Feline Center. Feline patients referred to the Cornell Veterinary Medical Teaching Hospital provide a wealth of information that enables clinicians to better understand the disease involved, and hence to better treat the condition.

Research accomplishments over the years by the Feline Center have been numerous. Some of these include:

1. Clarification of the role of maternal immunity in kittens as it affects vaccination against feline panleukopenia.

2. Aid in the development of respiratory vaccines against feline herpesvirus and feline calicivirus.

3. First isolation and characterization of feline reovirus as a cause of respiratory disease.

4. First isolation and characterization of feline rotavirus as a cause of enteritis in young kittens.

5. First identification of feline astrovirus as a cause of enteritis.

6. Identification and characterization of "kitten mortality complex" as a major cause of kitten loss in catteries.

7. First isolation of feline infectious peritonitis (FIP) virus in the laboratory.

8. Characterization of the role of antibodies and macrophages in the pathogenesis of FIP.

9. Attenuation of FIP virus to establish an experimental FIP vaccine.

10. First isolation and characterization of feline herpesvirus-2 as a cause of urinary disease and urolithiasis.

The Feline Health Center is dedicated to providing information about feline diseases and feline care to veterinarians and owners. This is accomplished through many means, including publications, seminars and short courses, and electronic media.

Scientific information obtained from research is first published in peer-reviewed scientific journals, so that the information is available to all veterinarians and the entire scientific community. Several publications are produced by the center to provide information to veterinarians and cat owners. These are discussed below.

The Feline Health Center also benefits from the guidance of the Feline Advisory Council, which also serves as a vital link with the public at large. The council is made up of approximately twelve individuals from all over the United States, and includes clinicians, breeders, scientists, writers, and owners.

CONSULTATION AND DIAGNOSTIC SERVICE

The Louis J. Camuti Diagnostic and Consultation Service was established in the early 1980s as a living memorial to the late Dr. Camuti, who conducted a house-call feline practice in New York City for over fifty years. This service has been gradually developed as funds became available. The key position for this service is the feline extension veterinarian, who handles and coordinates the interactions between the veterinarians and cat owners and the staff of the Feline Health Center.

There is close interaction between the Feline Consultation and Diagnostic Service and the Diagnostic Laboratory at the College of Veterinary Medicine, with the feline extension veterinarian coordinating this interaction. As new diagnostic tests are developed by the staff of the Feline Health Center, this information is passed on to the Diagnostic Laboratory, where these tests are put into routine operation.

The Veterinary Medical Teaching Hospital within the Department of Clinical Sciences serves as a referral clinic for special problems in feline medicine and surgery. Clinicians refer cases to this hospital for special care, and the cooperative efforts of the clinical staff, the research staff of the Feline Health Center (armed with the latest information about the particular condition), and the staff of the Diagnostic Laboratory provide an impressive combined effort to give the sick cat the best chance possible.

STAFF OF THE CORNELL FELINE HEALTH CENTER

The core staff of the Feline Health Center is composed of a director, an assistant director, an editor, secretarial staff, research staff, graduate students, and technical support staff. The dedication and diligent work of this core staff have played a major role in the success of the Feline Health Center. Special mention should be made of the exceptional work of June Kirvan-Tuttle, editor, without whose exemplary efforts *The Cornell Book of Cats* would never have come to fruition.

Approximately thirty faculty members and staff of the College of Veterinary Medicine and College of Agriculture and Life Sciences compose the participating staff of the Feline Health Center. This group of dedicated individuals makes up an impressive list of experts in feline medicine and surgery. Many of these participating staff members are leading experts in their particular area of specialty. Many of them have contributed to *The Cornell Book of Cats;* publication is due in large part to their efforts.

Facilities of the Cornell Feline Health Center are incorporated into the College of Veterinary Medicine. There is a group of offices and laboratories for the central or core staff of the Cornell Feline Health Center, and participating members have their own offices and laboratories within several departments in the college. The Veterinary Medical Teaching Hospital and the Diagnostic Laboratory are key facilities for carrying out the mission of the Feline Health Center. Extensive additions to the College of Veterinary Medicine are being developed at the time of this writing. These new facilities will greatly benefit the college and the center.

EXOTIC FELINES

While the primary mission of the Cornell Feline Health Center is to improve the health and welfare of domestic cats, information is obtained by the center that will help exotic and endangered species of felines as well. Exotic cats are susceptible to most of the same diseases as the domestic cat. The faculty and staff of the Feline Health Center have worked with veterinarians from several zoologic facilities to assist in the diagnosis and treatment of special conditions. For example, a special project for several years has been to provide part of the laboratory and diagnostic support services for a long-term study of the Florida panther. Information obtained from these studies has helped wildlife veterinarians in their efforts to save this endangered species of exotic cat.

PUBLICATIONS

Feline Health Topics is a scientific publication sent to all small-animal veterinarians in the United States four times a year. This newsletter provides practical information that veterinarians can utilize in their practices.

Perspectives on Cats is published four times a year as a newsletter to provide basic feline health-care information for cat owners. This newsletter is sent to all members of the Cornell Feline Health Center.

Feline Information Bulletin is published periodically, usually once a year, to review the latest information about a particular disease.

Client Information Brochures are published by the Feline Health Center on a variety of topics. These are sold to veterinarians to provide information about particular diseases or basic cat care for their clients. They are designed to facilitate education of clients while saving time for the busy practitioner. After reviewing the brochure, the client can then further discuss the topic with the veterinarian if necessary.

Symposium Proceedings are published from time to time. An in-depth, week-long "Feline Specialist Seminar," co-sponsored by the American Association of Feline Practitioners, is held annually at Cornell for veterinarians interested in improving their skills in feline medicine.

International Publications. Publications from the Cornell Feline Health Center are sent to individuals in several foreign countries. In addition, *Feline Health Topics* is translated into Japanese by a commercial Japanese company and made available to small-animal veterinarians in Japan. Periodically, excerpts from *Feline Health Topics* are translated into several European languages and disseminated throughout Europe by Dr. Marian Horzinek of the University of Utrecht, the Netherlands.

Electronic Media (computer programs) are being developed for veterinarians as a form of continuing education and as diagnostic tools. These media put the clinician in instant contact with the latest information about a particular disease and with a recognized expert in the particular area in question.

FUND-RAISING

Since the center does not receive financial support directly from the state, college, or university, it is the cat owners themselves and their veterinarians who play a key role in keeping the Feline Health Center in operation.

Contributions from owners and veterinarians are a vital part of the overall support of the Feline Health Center.

Bequests are especially appropriate ways of saying "Thank you" to one or more special feline companions. Bequests are usually invested through the Development Office of Cornell University, and only the income received from those investments is used to support the Cornell Feline Health Center. Thus, a bequest or a living trust ensures long-term and even indefinite support for feline studies.

Research grants and contracts are obtained by the research scientists at the Feline Health Center whenever possible. These may be from governmental funds, private foundations, or commercial companies.

Memberships in the center are available for both cat owners and veterinarians. These memberships enable individuals to become partners of the Cornell Feline Health Center, and together, with such support, we can continue the effort to eliminate or prevent all diseases of cats.

In Memoriam programs provide an especially meaningful way for a veterinarian to recognize the loss suffered when an owner must part with a special feline companion. The thoughtful contribution by the veterinarian is acknowledged to the owner by the Cornell Feline Health Center and helps the owner to work his or her way through that difficult period of grief following the loss.

WHAT DOES THE FUTURE HOLD?

The future of cats as pets and the future of feline medicine could not be brighter. The cat has surpassed the dog as the more popular pet in the United States and in several other countries, and in metropolitan areas cats are especially popular as apartment pets.

Cats are receiving better and better veterinary care as more information is becoming available to provide new vaccines for serious diseases, and new and more effective treatments are gradually being developed, all of which contributes to their health and longevity.

The future of the Cornell Feline Health Center is also bright. The center has an excellent staff, and there are many outstanding participants who lend their expertise to improving the health of cats everywhere. Support from the veterinary profession and the cat-owning public continues to grow and to provide the base support to keep the program on course. Therefore, the faculty and staff of the Cornell Feline Health Center takes this opportunity to extend a hearty "Thank you" to all those who have supported the center's efforts over the years, through encouragement and financial means.

Introduction

by Mordecai Siegal, Editor

The image of the *public* cat is that of a mysterious animal, aloof, independent, and possessed of an unknowable secret, a luxurious pet sleeping on velour pillows, dining on gourmet food, and adding a dash of status and a statement of individuality to its owners. But the *private* cat is an endearing animal capable of accepting affection and returning it in kind, like any other pet. Cats have once again come into the social consciousness, not as Egyptian deities, nor as consorts of the devil, nor as the familiars of witches, but as cherished companion animals and creatures of rare grace and beauty.

If the cat has a secret it is this: Throughout its long history with humans as god, devil, and friend, the cat is what it has always been, simply a cat. It has 245 bones and thirty teeth, and is the keenest hunter of rodents in the animal kingdom. Human perceptions notwithstanding, the reality of cats exceeds the legend of cats. However, they are as vulnerable to the processes of nature as any other living organism. The natural cat is an attractive, alluring animal that requires our help and good intentions if it is to survive in the human environment.

Cats have nutritional requirements based on their own unique needs in order to grow, reproduce, function normally, and cope with stress. When a cat falls from a great height, it is likely to be injured. Its body is defenseless against physical trauma. If it is exposed to viruses, bacteria, or fungi, it is likely to become ill. The invasion of internal or external parasites will disrupt normal body functions and most certainly will cause discomfort, pain, or sickness without veterinary treatment. Cats, like all animals, are susceptible to hundreds of diseases, disorders, and potential medical threats. Many of these disorders are defeated by the animal's own immune system; many are not. It is essential for caring cat owners to have a grasp of the medical realities of their special friends. With knowledge comes the ability to take the correct action.

It is upsetting when a cat gets sick. The intelligent solution, of course, is to get professional veterinary care. Quite often, however, cat owners leave the veterinarian's office unable to understand or retain the details of their animal's medical condition, and this impairs the ability of the cat owner to give a sick cat the care it needs. An owner's inability to grasp the substance of a cat's medical condition can be stressful to him and, indirectly, harmful to the cat.

The Cornell Book of Cats is a reference book of uncommon depth. It offers the caring cat owner and the animal professional alike a sophisticated source of medical, nutritional, and behavioral information. Written by the faculty, staff, and associates of the College of Veterinary Medicine at Cornell University, it is a project of the Cornell Feline Health Center. It represents a major body of knowledge for those with a need to understand the medical disorders of cats.

The Cornell Book of Cats cannot help the reader diagnose an illness or treat a sick cat. This book cannot, nor should it, attempt to replace professional veterinary care. Its purpose is to impart to the conscientious cat owner medical information about the diseases and disorders that harm the feline body and its various systems. We have given to those who care about cats a wealth of medical information, derived from one of the world's leading institutions of veterinary medicine, which has a time-honored tradition of providing instruction, research, and service to cats and those who care for them.

We have assembled this book in the belief that a well-informed cat owner helps the veterinarian provide the best possible medical care. It is our goal to help cats live longer, happier lives. A happy cat enjoying the glow of good health is a pleasing, aesthetic presence, providing us with a window through the wall that separates us from the wild side.

As a member of the Feline Advisory Council of the Cornell Feline Health Center, I was overwhelmed by the positive response to my suggestion for this book. There was no way to know that such a project had long been the desire of those who have the responsibility of stewardship for the Cornell Feline Health Center. The encouragement and enthusiasm from my fellow council members provided much of the incentive to proceed down the long, unknown path to completion. This book exists because of the work of a dedicated team of scientists, educators, doctors, writers, and editors. For this author and editor, *The Cornell Book of Cats* will always be the benchmark of excellence for a life spent creating books about animals.

Acknowledgments

T*he Cornell Book of Cats* has become a reality because of the hard work, generosity, and dedication of many who joined in its creation with their skills, talents, and special considerations. It is with gratitude and admiration that the editor and the Cornell Feline Health Center acknowledge the assistance so generously given by the scientists, educators, veterinary practitioners, health-care specialists, professionals in the cat world, and cat lovers who involved themselves in this project. *The Cornell Book of Cats* represents the efforts of a great many who support the meaningful work of the Cornell Feline Health Center.

For their advice and valuable assistance, we wish to thank: Alexander deLahunta, D.V.M., Ph.D., Professor of Veterinary Anatomy, Chairman, Department of Anatomy, College of Veterinary Medicine, Cornell University; Herbert F. Schryver, D.V.M., Ph.D., Associate Professor of Pathology, College of Veterinary Medicine, Cornell University; and John C. Semmler, Assistant Dean for Public Affairs, College of Veterinary Medicine, Cornell University.

We would also like to thank the members of the Feline Advisory Council of the Cornell Feline Health Center for their enthusiasm and approval: George W. Abbott, D.V.M.; Joan M. Arnoldi, D.V.M., M.S.; Jane Bicks, D.V.M.; Joan Blackburn; Roger Caras; Marjorie Cornell; Hazel Lindstrand; Mark L. Morris, Jr., D.V.M., Ph.D.; Theodore A. Rude, V.M.D.; Ellen Sawyer; Barbara S. Stein, D.V.M.; and Joan Wastlhuber.

We are grateful for the tireless efforts and invaluable help from the following staff members in their various capacities at the College of Veterinary Medicine, Cornell University: Gwen Frost, Karen Havekost, Sheryl Thomas, secretaries for the Cornell Feline Health Center; Sue Hubert, secretary, Veterinary Medical Teaching Hospital, College of Veterinary Medicine, Cornell University; Barbara Van Arkel, former secretary, and Helen Bell, secretary, Diagnostic Laboratory, College of Veterinary Medicine, Cornell University.

A special note of gratitude is extended to: Thomas Dent, executive director, Cat Fanciers Association, Inc., for reviewing those chapters concerning the sources, selection, and breeds of cats. His thoughtful comments and suggestions were invaluable; to Gene Phillips, director, The Cat Fancier's Data Center, for his assistance as a source of important information regarding the sources, selection, and breeds of cats; to Miles Freitag, president, Solvay Animal Health, Inc., for his generosity in allowing the use of his company's anatomical drawings, titled "The Feline," "The Eye," "Internal Ear," and "External Parasites," in this book; and to Dr. Frederick Born for the development of those drawings; to Joan Wastlhuber, president, Robert H. Winn Foundation, CFA judge, and member of the Feline Advisory Council, Cornell Feline Health Center, for her valuable counsel concerning the accuracy of the breed illustrations appearing in these pages; Gwen Northrup, secretary, Ragdoll Fanciers' Club, for her kind advice; Mel Berger, literary agent, and to Phil Liebowitz, attorney, of the William Morris Agency, whose expertise and persistence made this book possible. And to Fran Lebowitz, assistant to Mr. Berger, for her kind support; to Peter Gethers, editorial director, Villard Books, for his vision, wisdom, and sensitivity. And to editor Alison Acker, for her infectious enthusiasm and dedicated efforts in behalf of this project.

We would also thank John Turner, for the generous use of his communications and computer skills and equipment; Lisa Bressler of Rinkurl Cattery, for her kind assistance; Les Lone, alumnus, Cornell University, for his support and devotion to the concept of this book; Richard Katris (Chanan Photography), photographer, for his generous assistance; Lowe's, Inc., for the use of several of their photographs; Karen Redmond for her help with photographs from Cornell University; and Marlene Luyster, for two photographs of her beloved "Sunny," CFA "Cat of the Year"— 1977–78 (Gr. Ch. Jama Kats Midnight Sun, a Copper-eyed Black Persian male).

And to the following cats and their owners for allowing themselves to appear in this book, by way of the portrait photography of Vicki Jackson: GRC ANGKOR ROSE SHANTUNG OF OFFSHORE (Chocolate Point *Siamese*), owner: Diane Dagley; GRC ZIEGFELD'S INDIAN PRINCESS (Tortoiseshell *Persian*), owner: William Pine; GRC KITJIM'S BEAUTY PATCH (Silver Patched Tabby and White female *Scottish Fold*), owner: Kitty Angell; CH CHEVRA RAINBOW BRITE (Brown Mackerel Tabby and White *Turkish Angora*), owner: Frances Chabala; KARRERA'S SULTANHISAR (Auburn and White male *Turkish Van*), owners: Marla and Dan Dunrud; GRC EBONFYRE'S ALEXIS OF KIMERON (Lilac Point female *Balinese*), owner: Sandy West; GRC AUSTRIANA ARIANE OF MAR-CHU (Sable female *Burmese*), owners: Mary Reich and Erika Graf-Webster; GRC SCATTERGOLD WAVING BEAUTY (Brown Tabby female *Devon Rex*), owners: Leroy and Betty Held; GRC ZAYNZALBAR CHICLET OF ORCADIA (Bronze female *Egyptian Mau*), owner: Virginia Luke; GRC WITAYASAT MS. J. C. PEEPERS OF PETLAR (female *Korat*), owners: Peter Greuel and Larry Jones; GRC LUPRACAN MUS FLOWER DRUM SONG (McTorbie/White female *Manx*), owner: Pam DelaBar; GRC PURRICOON'S ARTHUR COONAN DOYLE (Brown Mackerel Tabby male *Maine Coon*), breeders/owners: Herb and Brooke Berger; TORVMYRA'S SAGRES (male *Norwegian Forest*), agented by Louise Clair; CO-MC TRIBBLE OF CLACRITTER (Tortoiseshell female *Cymric* kitten), owners: Leslie Falteisek and Jeanie McPhee; GRC LEMEAUX'S APOLLO (Red male *Abyssinian*), owners: Bill and Pat Garner; GRC THORNWOOD'S LEE A. IAKINKA (Red Tabby male *American Wirehair*), breeders/owners: Wayne and Shirley Field; CAROCATS ENCHANTRESS (Silver Tabby female *American Shorthair*), owners: Carol and Michael Rothfeld; CRC HENRIJEAN KEMO SABE (Seal Point male *Birman*), breeders/owners: Eugene and Paula Boroff; GRC ROAD TO FAME RETURN TO SHAWNEE (female *Bombay*), owner: Nikki Horner; GRP, GRC NW JEDI BLUSUN OF VEGAMAR (Blue *British Shorthair*), owners: Gail and Mark Alsager; GRC FRENCHEON'S CLAUDE OF JACQUELNJIL (Blue male *Chartreux*), owner: Jill Rasmussen; GRC ALSACE Y. LESTAT (Lynx Point Blue male *Colorpoint Shorthair*), owners: Pam DelaBar and Barbara Baylor; GRC FENWAY FINESSE (Blue female *Cornish Rex*), breeder/owner: Nancy T. Dodds; DAJENS FRIDAY THE 13TH (Ebony male *Oriental Shorthair*), owner: Erma Jenei; GRC SATTERLEE PAYDAY OF PAKU (Blue male *Exotic Shorthair*), owners: Kurt and Pat Anderson; GRC BUNDASH'S CLASSIC DUSTY ROSE (female *Havana Brown*), owners: Wallace and Lynne Guinn; GRP, NW MERRACAT'S MOTO SITEBOI OF KARLETON (Red and White *Japanese Bobtail*), owners: Jerry and Eve Russell; JASMEEN'S BLUE ANGEL (Blue Lynx Point female *Javanese*), owner: Shirley O. Cox; GRC OCIVILLE'S CHOCOLATE SURPRISE OF KAYZIE (Chocolate spotted female *Ocicat*), owner: Kaye Chambers; GRC ROXANASTASIA LEGACY II (male *Russian Blue*), owner: G. W. Hester, H. Schneider-Hester, and Pam Anderson; GRC JUBILATION PIKKKU POYKA (Sepia Agouti male *Singapura*), owner: Mary Tichenor; GRC ZARPA'S LAKOTA (Ruddy male *Somali*), breeders/owners: Dick and Nell Foster; GRC SPIELZEIT TRAUMEREI (Natural Mink *Tonkinese*), owners, Bruce and Fran Nickerson; SGC AMENOPHIS CLONE (Black and White female *Sphynx*), owners: Phillippe and Aline Noël; PATRIOT JULIA OF SYCODELICFUR (Brown Mackerel Tabby female *American Curl*), owner: Cassandra Harris; GRC BILBAR TOO GOOD TO BE TRUE (Blue Point female *Himalayan*), owners: Bill and Irene Carlisle; SHAMUS O'FLYNN (*Snowshoe*), owner: Mary McGarry; SGC HOOSIER DOLLS MARSHALL (*Ragdoll*), owner: Monte Stuart; and CH RAIN RIVER'S LITTLE NEMO (Chocolate male *Oriental Longhair*), breeders: Robin Radlein and Bob Smith, owners: Robert, Ruth, and Robin Radlein.

P A R T   I
....

Acquiring a Cat

CLEOPATRA: . . . Do you think that the black cat can have been my great-great-great-grandmother?

CAESAR: *(staring at her)* Your great-great-great-grandmother! Well, why not? Nothing would surprise me on this night of nights.

CLEOPATRA: I think it must have been. My great-grandmother's great-grandmother was a black kitten of the sacred white cat; and the river Nile made her his seventh wife. That is why my hair is so wavy.

—George Bernard Shaw, *Caesar and Cleopatra*

Origins, Sources, and Selection

ORIGINS OF THE CAT

There is nothing easier to acquire than a cat. Anyone can do it. But finding the right cat and learning to live with it is another matter. Since the beginning of recorded history the feline has wandered through society, mewing to be let in and then out again. It is the behavior of a finicky species that through the ages has chosen to enjoy the comforts of mankind but on other occasions to satisfy its ancient birthright in the netherworld of the wild. To be fair, the domestic cat has not always left the human heart and hearth voluntarily: In the Middle Ages it was driven out, because it was believed to be associated with devil worship, witchcraft, and evil spirits. The popularity of cats runs in cycles, possibly because it is the last of the domestic animals to surrender its wild and lusty inclinations. The demure house cat of today, with its delicate, reserved manner, its loving behavior, and its playful nature, can, if necessary, revert to its wild state instantly and reveal a side of its untamed nature few pet owners ever witness.

But even in "civilization" the issues of sex and property bring out the furious side of the feline personality. It will fight to mate or fight for its proprietary rights to a territory. And when hungry, almost any cat is capable of catching its own dinner. Darting and fluttering animals automatically trigger its hunting instincts, and then the cat at prey performs a prehistoric drama that raised its curtain 53 million years before the Great Ice Age. Despite its gentle behavior toward people and its touching preference for the human home, this species is still one of nature's most perfect hunters.

The ancestor of the cat was the *Miacis,* a vanished genus of early carnivores that appeared in the Eocene Epoch, approximately 54 million years ago. The *Miacis* was an early mammal with a low skull, a long, slender body, a lengthy tail, and short legs. It is believed to have lived in trees, preying upon small animals for food. Like cats of today, it possessed retracted claws that extended from the paws when fighting, hunting, running, and tree-climbing. The *Miacis* is generally accepted as the com-

mon ancestor of such carnivores as raccoons, civets, bears, hyenas, dogs, and cats. The early cats that descended directly from this primitive carnivore are shrouded in the veil of extinction. They consisted of various species of two separate lines. One line, *Hoplophoneus,* produced the massive *Smilodon,* a formidable, prehistoric sabertooth cat. All traces of this line are now extinct. The second line, *Dinictis,* produced several smaller cat species with greater agility and intelligence than the *Smilodon.* Many researchers consider this line to be the ancestor of all cat species of today, including the domestic cat.

Today's "great cats" (lions, tigers, jaguars, leopards, pumas, cheetahs) and the smaller wild cats are among the most ferocious of all the animals living in nature. Their adroit hunting skills (stalk, ambush, pounce) are precise, pitiless, and near perfect. So how, then, can those fierce hunters, totally dedicated to satisfying their hunger, be related to the pussycats we stroke and pamper? The domestic cat is the most prolific house pet in the United States, totaling more than 58 million. Where did it come from, and at what moment in time did it walk out of the deserts and forests to sleep at the foot of man?

It is impossible to determine the origin of the family of cat species (Felidae), including the domestic cat. With only the most meager fossil evidence dating back to the Pliocene Epoch, two to five million years ago, researchers believe that the species of the *Dinictis* line are the ancestors of today's cat family. Based on the evidence of coat pattern and color, size, behavior, and geography, the domestic cat, many research-

ers feel, is the descendant of *Felis libyca,* the African wild cat, and to a lesser degree, *Felis silvestris,* the European wild cat. However, there is disagreement among scientists concerning the origins of the cat.

The first real evidence of the domestication of the cat appeared in the recorded history, murals, and artifacts of ancient Egypt between 1600 and 1500 B.C. Egyptian cats were proclaimed to be sacred animals, however, long before they were domesticated (2500–2200 B.C.). There is speculation that the cat's unique ability to hunt and its appetite for rodents, which destroyed Egyptian grain, were greatly rewarded, leading ultimately to the status of a god. It was then that the cult of the cat began, with temples dedicated to cats and laws protecting them, as well as the artistic expressions of appreciation and devotion that we can still see today. In ancient Egypt, cats were worshipped, cherished, and adored.

The first known cat deity was Bast, the goddess of Bubastis, the ancient city of the Nile Delta, which became important to the pharaohs of the nineteenth dynasty (1320–1200 B.C.). Bast (also Bastet, Bash, Pasht), the Egyptian goddess of fertility and of the home, was also a symbol of fruitfulness and beauty, and was depicted in small statues and amulets with the head of a cat and the body of a woman. Statuettes were carried showing her with a small basket and sistrum (a musical instrument), which were carried in processions in honor of the goddess. She was revered with great affection until Egyptian priests incorporated her into the official religion of the New Kingdom (1567–1085 B.C.). She was then viewed as a goddess of war because of the similarity in appearance to the lioness. However, her cat identity remained with most Egyptians who revered cats with great affection. They considered cats to be supernatural and endowed with mysterious qualities relating to the moon and the stars. But eventually the cat became a participant in Egyptian family life, jumping off its symbolic pedestal and walking freely among the ordinary. Egyptian paintings clearly portray the cat in Egyptian homes. This was the age of glory in the checkered history of the domestic cat.

The remains of cats have been uncovered in Etruria (present-day Tuscany) from the Etruscan culture, which predates the Roman Empire. Etruscan art, principally painted vases, depicts cats in domestic settings playing with humans. It is the first suggestion of cats kept as pets on the European continent.

Ancient Greek and Roman art also displays cats on

vases, marble reliefs, coins, and sculptures. Their poetry and manuscripts refer to cats frequently as objects of amusement and affection, although historians feel that cats were mostly appreciated as predators of rodents. There is evidence that cats also lived in domesticity in India and throughout Asia about the same time; they are referred to in ancient Sanskrit writings that predate the birth of Christ. And in China Confucius is said to have enjoyed cats.

Long before the earth was circumnavigated, wild cats were distributed throughout the world. They were found everywhere except in Australia and the Antarctic, where migration may have been prevented by environmental barriers of water, climate, or altitude. Various species of felids probably migrated onto the American continents before continental drift (the displacement of land masses) separated them from the Eastern Hemisphere during the Jurassic Period, between 190 and 140 million years ago. Geologists speculate that North America was originally part of Europe, and South America was part of Africa. According to one theory, Antarctica, Australia, Madagascar,

India, and southeast Africa were originally close together, separated only by narrow water boundaries.

It is only logical to assume that cats entered society in Asia the same way they did in Egypt. Domestic cats were eventually seen throughout North Africa, Asia, and most of Europe. The distribution of these much-admired animals went unnoticed, without so much as a footnote in recorded history. Historians and scientists can only speculate that the sweep of invading armies (Persians, Greeks, Romans), along with merchant seamen, adventurers, and colonials, distributed cats throughout the known world. It must have been these travelers who set in motion the incredible saga of humans and their cats.

The New Egyptians

Human involvement with cats hardly appears at all on the pages of history. When it does, it is treated as a trivial preoccupation falling somewhere on the scale of importance between stamp collecting and obscure spectator sports. But the huge number of cats lovingly accepted as house pets has been growing steadily throughout the twentieth century, with a dramatic increase within the past decade. Negative attitudes of the past toward cats are less prevalent. Typical of such past sentiment is the entry for the domestic cat in *The Fieldbook of Natural History* (New York: 1949): "**Do-**

mestic Cat . . . Known to be a disease carrier . . . Cannot be trusted. Probably loved, hated, or tolerated by most persons but not economically valuable; however, cats do eat many destructive rodents such as rats and mice." This is contrasted with the opening statement from *The Good Cat Book* (New York: 1981): "The feline presence is an important one and must not be dismissed with a nonchalant shrug. Your cat does much more than chase mice and eat your food. He is the mortal enemy of empty rooms. Soft, warm, needful, all cats, but especially yours, gives far more than he takes. That is what makes him good." Times have changed and cats have flourished in the last half of the twentieth century.

The increase in the cat population and the cat's elevation to member-of-the-family status have run parallel with significant social conditions—population increases, development of rural areas, the decline of family farms, and the trend toward apartment living—conditions that may or may not be related to the newfound prosperity of the domestic cat. However, that relationship must tiptoe into the equation somewhere between theory and fact.

The cat is no longer thought of as a farm animal, relegated to the barn, catching its share of mice. It has become a highly pampered companion, satisfying the personal needs of modern living. Its perceived independence, contrasted with its playful nature, is once again greatly admired. A cat is beautiful to look at. It is almost always allowed in condominium apartments, even where dogs are restricted. It is easier to care for than a dog. Like microwave cooking and frozen gourmet dinners, it embodies the word "convenience." Its needs are flexible and adaptable to the demanding schedules of busy men, women, and children who

still require a touch of nature's grandeur in a high-tech society. We are the "New Egyptians," and we have rediscovered the cat. Inadvertently, a new situation has been created that is novel even for the cat: The hunters are now the hunted. There is now a constant search among the uninitiated for beautiful, well-behaved, healthy cats. The question of where to look is an important one for those who are hunting for the best cat possible; we "New Egyptians" have no granaries with which to lure them out of the desert. Those who have their hearts set on owning a cat are best served by learning something about sources and selection.

A GUIDE TO CAT SOURCES

It's easy to get a cat. Kittens are everywhere, and many of them are free. Acquiring a cat over the back fence may be the most common source of kittens, but it is not the only place to get one, nor is it necessarily the best. A new cat in your life is going to become a family

for getting a cat are to enjoy it as a companion, to compete in cat shows, or to breed it as part of a carefully planned line of purebred cats. It is safe to assume that the vast majority of cats are acquired by those who simply want a pet. No matter what kind of cat you want, or for what reason, there are many sources for them. Following are the most important sources available; but bear in mind that catteries, pet shops, shelters, and pounds are only as good as the people or the administrative bodies regulating them. They may be excellent, adequate, inadequate, or worse. Only an informed, knowledgeable purchaser can tell the difference and make the correct choice.

Catteries

Some kittens purchased from a cattery are more expensive than anticipated by pet owners, because of the time and expense involved in creating a line of cats that meet the breed standards set down by the various national cat associations. Producing beautiful, healthy, happy kittens is a costly hobby, and most breeders become involved for the sheer love of it. Catteries are an important source when looking for a kitten most likely to possess the physical and behavioral qualities expected of its breed. However, some catteries are better than others, while some are not at all satisfactory.

A cattery, in most instances, is an establishment whose name is enrolled in a national cat organization such as the Cat Fanciers Association (CFA) or the American Cat Association (ACA). It is devoted to the housing and breeding of purebred cats. Most catteries are set up in the homes of cat breeders. The cattery may occupy a section of a house, an apartment, or a separate building devoted exclusively to cats. A cattery depends more on the quality of its animals and the reputation of its owners than on its physical arrangement. Pet quality, breeding quality, or show quality kittens and cats are for sale at catteries. Litters of kittens are produced on a limited basis.

A good cattery is devoted to hygiene, knowledgeable care, and concern for feline health and behavior in addition to the genetic quality of its animals. Effective immunization regimens must be maintained. Veterinary attention is a vital aspect of cattery operations. The experienced cattery operator understands that distance between cats dilutes infectious agents and reduces chances of exposure to harmful organisms; physical barriers such as cages, fences, and walls pre-

member and may be with you for perhaps fifteen years. The possibility of getting a cat that has the best opportunity for long life and good health is greatly influenced by the source of the animal, and acquiring a healthy cat of sound temperament and emotional stability does not have to depend on luck alone. The beauty of a cat is also a consideration. There are more than forty separate cat breeds to choose from, in addition to the many variations of mixed breeds.

Impulsively accepting the first kitten that is offered to you is not necessary. There are many opportunities to choose one that will be suitable and appealing. When looking at the kitten in front of you, try to envision it as the cat it will grow into. The ability to choose, and choose intelligently, makes all the difference.

The first step is to become familiar with the important sources for cats and to understand the options available. Where to look for a new cat should be determined by what kind of cat is desired, how much money one is willing to spend, and, most important of all, the reason for wanting a cat. The best reasons

vent "nose-to-nose" contact of cats. Lack of air flow is an important factor in the spread of disease. A room containing numerous cats where humidity is high and there is no exchange of filtered or new air for old presents the probability of contagion. Fresh air is ideal with ten to fifteen exchanges per hour, and air-conditioning or some other form of circulating air is necessary.

Good sanitation is important for the health of the animals as well as for the aesthetics of the cattery. Swept floors should be mopped with a one-part-bleach-to-thirty-two-parts-water (1:32) solution and then rinsed with clear water. Litter pans should be washed daily with soap and water, adding fresh litter afterward, and should be scooped clean frequently. All walls, doors, windowsills, ceilings, light fixtures, and fans should be washed with the 1:32 bleach/water solution once a week. Although hygiene practices vary, you should not be confronted with an unpleasant odor when entering a cattery. Good sanitation, however, is not the only criterion for evaluating a cattery.

Those who produce purebred cats that meet breed standards are likely to be involved in cat shows, because the hobby aspect of this activity is not *breeding* cats; it is *showing* cats. A cattery need not win First Place ribbons to produce outstanding cats. However, cats entered in shows are exposed to the scrutiny of many breeders, exhibitors, show judges, and other knowledgeable cat people. Breeders lose credibility if they consistently show cats of poor quality. Competing at cat shows is a form of "show-and-tell" for breeders. The quality of their cats reflects the quality of their breeding programs and the management of their catteries.

Cat shows require their entrants to be pedigreed cats that are registered with the cat association sponsoring the show. Such cats must be in good health and come from respected breeding lines. They must also be of sound temperament and measure up to the established standard for their breed if they are to compete in shows and bring prestige to their catteries.

A cat of "show quality" may cost hundreds or even thousands of dollars. Show cats are the result of years of effort to meet the standards of perfection set down for their particular breed. To produce such cats requires a knowledge of genetics, mating, "queening," nutrition, and behavior. Breeders who develop important show cats rarely sell them or their kittens to those with no intention of showing them. It is a matter of pride and purpose that breeder/exhibitors want their cats to be "campaigned," which means competing in cat shows along a national circuit. "Campaigners" hope to win Champion and Grand Champion

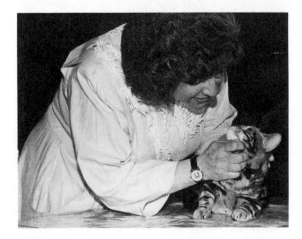

titles for their cats and they compete for national ranking. There is no guarantee, however, that a show-quality kitten will ever become a champion, no matter what the cost.

However, not every kitten in a litter meets the strict standard for its breed and therefore will not be shown. These animals are usually referred to as "pet-quality" kittens and will be sold (at a reduced price) as companions. Pet-quality kittens are healthy, beautiful animals with a slight imperfection, and breeders are usually quite fussy about the homes in which they place them. They try to evaluate a prospective purchaser and determine if that person will be good to the cat and provide a proper home. Most require that the owners agree to neuter the animal.

When selecting a cattery from which to purchase a kitten, it is sensible to ask if the cattery owner is also an exhibitor. This is a fair question. Anyone buying a kitten should insist on a health guarantee on a money-back basis.

One of the advantages of purchasing a kitten from a cattery is the opportunity to see it interact with some or all of its littermates. How a kitten behaves is an

important aspect of selection. Much can be learned about a kitten by observing its parents. It is quite likely that one or both will be available. (*See* "A Guide for Selecting a Cat," page 13)

A cattery must house its animals in adequate cages large enough for comfortable movement. Anything less is inhumane and unacceptable. Light, ventilation, resting shelves, climbing poles, and room to move about are necessities for all cats, including males at stud. A cattery that does not offer these basic necessities of life may be creating cats with potential behavior problems.

Finding a good cattery is not as difficult as it sounds. The best method is to attend cat shows. There, one can find many exhibitors with catteries who are willing to answer questions after they have met their obligations in the show ring. Catteries can also be found in the classified ads of cat magazines, which are available on newsstands and by subscription. Catteries from all parts of the United States and Canada advertise in these magazines. Current cat publications offering breeder ads, in addition to cat show information, are *Cats Magazine, Cat Fancy Magazine, Cat Fanciers' Almanac* (CFA), *I Love Cats,* and *Cat World.*

An interesting method for locating purebred kittens is the use of a computerized data-base service. Currently, there is only one such service devoted to catteries of specific breeds and their delivery dates for litters of purebred kittens. The Cat Fancier's Data Center (CFDC) 77 Essex Avenue, Montclair, New Jersey 07042, is the only service currently available. Many breeders of purebred cats, with catteries throughout the United States and Canada, subscribe to CFDC for an annual fee. A constant flow of new and updated

information is fed into the CFDC computer. Those seeking show-quality or pet-quality kittens may contact the CFDC. There is no fee for those seeking to purchase a kitten.

Pet Shops

In the past, browsers and customers would enter a pet shop to watch a window full of puppies vying for attention. This reflected a time when dogs were the primary companion animal throughout the United States and Canada and were considered more commercially valuable than most other animals. A recent survey has revealed that cats are now the most preferred pets; that the cat population has doubled since 1972, surpassing the dog population in 1985. Consequently, many pet shops have changed their marketing strategy and sell kittens and the things they need in greater quantities than ever before. Kittens are now frequently seen in window displays, and pet shops are becoming a significant source of kittens for prospective pet owners.

Some pet shops are owned and managed by those who breed their own cats and maintain them until they are sold. Many other shops obtain their kittens from local breeders or from various commercial sources. Kittens in pet shops may be purebred (with or without registry papers) or mixed-breeds, which are often referred to as domestic shorthairs or longhairs (and are unregistrable). A purebred kitten is eligible to be registered if both its parents were registered by a national cat association. However, both sound and unsound house cats have been purchased from pet shops. The same can be said of catteries and shelters.

Some pet shops do not sell cats, but rather serve as an unofficial shelter and clearing house to give away unwanted kittens and stray cats. This service has important humane connotations, despite the fact that (good) business considerations are involved. The astute shopkeeper creates cat-owning customers, who then purchase all their supplies at that establishment.

For the vast majority of pet owners, it is of no significance whether a kitten is purebred or not. Many who seek the pleasures of a companion animal are not concerned with the cat's genetic history, bloodlines, or registered pedigree, even though these may have a bearing on inherited health factors. Obtaining a kitten from a pet shop is a satisfactory option if the animal is in obvious good health, has no apparent behavior problems, and is maintained in a clean, pleasant environment. If the source of the kitten is of little or no importance to the prospective pet owner, then a pet shop is a practical option.

When obtaining a kitten from a pet shop one should be concerned about the shop itself. It should be well lit, clean, cheerful, odor-free, and obviously

hygienic. One cat pan should be available for every two cats. The pans should be cleaned once a day with fresh litter, and should have little fecal matter in them at any time. No more than one cat should be in a single enclosure unless it is of generous proportions. It is potentially unhealthy, unsanitary, and behaviorally damaging to place large numbers of kittens together in window displays. One sick cat can quickly spread its illness to the others. Separation is especially important to prevent the spread of internal or external parasites. The housing together of many kittens can also encourage the formation of aggressive or shy behavior. Sales personnel and others handling the cats should be gentle, affectionate, knowledgeable, and careful. Handling a cat incorrectly can be dangerous for both the animals and the humans.

Pet shops are magnetic attractions for those who are entertained by the look or the antics of animals on display. They offer prospective pet owners the convenience of location and availability. Many pet shop purchases are made on impulse, and that can be a disastrous mistake whether a pet is acquired from a breeder, a shelter, or a shop. Acquiring a kitten should be a choice based on careful consideration and planning and not on reacting to one's own emotional responses or need for instant gratification. Many pet shops are beautiful to walk through and try to create a visual impact on their potential customers. Many displays are designed to attract the attention of children, so that they will influence their parents to make an impulse purchase. It is far less disastrous to impulsively buy a goldfish than a puppy or a kitten.

When acquiring a kitten from a pet shop it is advisable to understand your desires and limitations. It is critical that you understand the needs of a cat and your willingness to satisfy them. Long-haired cats require grooming and combing on a regular basis. Oriental breeds such as the Siamese are quite "talkative" and need more personal relating than many others. Abyssinians are high-energy, active cats that are demanding and affectionate. Educate yourself about cat breeds and cat care. Cats require medical care, personal relating, sound nutrition, hygienic surroundings, an occasional bath, grooming, and a clean toilet area. Be certain you are willing and able to provide the needs of a cat for the next fifteen years. Salespeople at pet shops know how irresistible a kitten or puppy is once it's in a customer's arms. Just say "no" if the kitten is not the kind you wanted or if you have any doubts. (*See* "A Guide for Selecting a Cat," page

13.) Education, investigation, and determination are the necessary elements for choosing the right cat.

Once you understand what you want, and are willing to make the commitment, it is possible to find the right cat at a pet shop. Also on sale at pet shops are repellents, plant protector sprays, litter-box additives, cat-litter scoops, travel carriers, feeding dishes, treats, catnip, cat toys of every description, and many other essential grooming tools and products that novice cat owners are sure to need.

Animal Shelters

A shelter is the most important animal source one can use. It affords cat lovers a wide range of choice plus the opportunity to provide safety and comfort for a homeless animal. The possibility of obtaining a delightful cat or kitten from one of the thousands of animal adoption agencies is excellent. Adopting a pet from an animal agency saves its life. There are simply not enough homes for the surplus of cats and dogs that are lost, abandoned, or born unwanted.

Homeless animals fortunate enough to make it to a shelter spend the remainder of their lives waiting to be adopted or euthanatized. Animal shelters bring people and cats together, fulfilling the needs of each. They are often the safest, most efficient, economical source for acquiring healthy, endearing kittens and cats. Their good works reward humans with the pleasures and delights of cat ownership while affording the opportunity to do something kind for an animal in need.

Many full-service animal shelters are fully staffed

with skilled professionals and expert workers, including veterinarians, veterinary technicians, administrators, animal handlers, peace officers, humane-educational specialists, et cetera. There are also many volunteer rescue organizations with caring workers that are unfunded, unchartered, and, in some cases, unlicensed. Although it is impossible to assess the quality of their efforts in general terms, it can be said that their work is often effective.

Some shelters are time-honored philanthropic associations, underwritten by well-managed investment portfolios, bequests, and wealthy donors. They may also receive funding from local or state governments in exchange for animal-control services. Others rely solely on the contributions made by adopters. Many shelters and humane societies are affiliated with or recognized by national organizations such as the Humane Society of the United States or the American Humane Society; they can be found in the Yellow Pages under the listing "Animal Shelters" or "Humane Societies." The larger establishments such as the Society for the Prevention of Cruelty to Animals (SPCA) of San Francisco, the MSPCA (Boston), ASPCA (New York City), or the Hamilton County SPCA (Cincinnati) are full-service organizations offering adoptions, veterinary service, information and education, animal abuse investigations, and animal control. They provide their respective areas with essential animal services and have become indispensable to their communities.

The privately funded and independently operated Tree House Animal Foundation in Chicago functions in a unique fashion. It has pioneered new programs that have had a direct impact on the stray-animal and

pet ownership problems that exist today. Their humane programs include emergency medical aid; operation of their innovative, cageless Tree House Adoption Center; a pet-owner counseling program; humane education and information services; assistance to low-income pet owners facing temporary financial emergencies; and a spay/neuter program to help curb pet overpopulation.

A cat will be admitted to Tree House if it is injured, abused, sick, pregnant, or a stray. After appropriate medical and socializing attention, the cat is permitted to enter the general cat population, which lives in a cageless environment comprising climbing trees, window perches, tunnels, cubes and benches, plus many comfortable cat beds. Although cats may live at Tree House forever, the goal is to find suitable homes for them.

To understand a shelter's policies one must become familiar with local animal laws and conditions. A nongovernment animal shelter, operating under the legal restrictions placed upon it by legislation, is often prohibited from collecting stray animals off the streets. In some communities, shelters are even prohibited from accepting lost or abandoned animals. That responsibility may be reserved by statute as the work of a government agency, such as a city dog pound or a private animal agency commissioned by a city, town, or county.

The American Society for the Prevention of Cruelty to Animals (ASPCA) in New York City is typical of this arrangement. In addition to its adoption programs, veterinary hospital, animal shelter, humane-education efforts, and cruelty investigations, the ASPCA is com-

missioned by the City of New York to carry out animal-control policies, which include dealing with injured, lost, stray, and abandoned animals from the streets. No other animal agency or shelter in that city may do so. The ASPCA employs a team of uniformed animal-control officers, whose function is to investigate violations of the various animal laws of New York City. They are empowered to issue citations and summonses. The ASPCA also administers the licensing of dogs for the city.

Other private shelters in New York City may only accept unwanted animals from their owners. Even with these restrictions, the Humane Society of New York and the Bide-a-Wee Home Association, like hundreds of other adoption agencies throughout the country, accept unwanted cats and dogs from their owners by the thousands each year. The animals are given medical attention, neutered when possible, fed, housed, and cared for until proper homes can be found.

Many who have adopted cats from shelters have described the experience as pleasant, exciting, interesting, and always laden with emotions. The purrs and meows of a cat being taken home in its crisp new travel carton can only be interpreted as the sound of pleasure and gratitude.

Veterinary Hospitals

A frequent source for acquiring cats and kittens is the veterinarian. In thousands of clinics, private practices, and animal hospitals throughout the country, it is a daily occurrence for cats to be placed in new homes. Veterinarians have traditionally served their communities and their clientele as go betweens for those who must find new homes for their pets and those who are looking for pets. Many animal hospital and veterinary office bulletin boards have notices about kittens and cats in need of a family. It is an important source to consider when acquiring a new pet.

A GUIDE FOR SELECTING A CAT

Selecting a cat is not difficult. It has little or nothing to do with purebred cats as opposed to mixed-breed cats. No one breed or mixed-breed is smarter, healthier, cleaner, or more lovable than the other. In this respect, all cats are equal. Whether to purchase a purebred or a mixed-breed cat is only a matter of aesthetic preference and economic consideration. The correct approach for selecting a cat is not to consider which is best, but which is best for you, your home, and your life-style. Do you want a cat that requires a great deal of personal interaction, or one that prefers a greater degree of solitude? There are breeds that are very active, and there are some that sleep much of the time. Is that a plus or a minus? Some cats need to be groomed often, particularly the longhair breeds such as Persians, Birmans, and Ragdolls.

Whether to live with a male or female is of no significant importance if the cat is to be neutered or spayed. Unneutered (whole) male cats must be mated on a frequent basis if they are to remain emotionally sound. Whole male cats past puberty "spray" powerfully odorous, sexually scented urine against walls, windows, and vertical objects when they are sexually aroused or in need of expressing their territorial rights. A whole male cat will roam if given the opportunity and will fight with other males. (*See* Chapter 4: Feline Behavior, and Chapter 5: Misbehavior.)

Unspayed females experience estrus ("heat") at least twice a year and perhaps more frequently. A female in estrus is little understood by the novice cat owner. The behavior of a female in estrus is meant to attract a male cat and involves intense vocalization and sexually oriented body language. It can be puzzling or even frightening to witness for the first time. Inexperienced owners are mistakenly convinced their cat is ill. During estrus the female cat secretes an odorous fluid intended to attract whole male cats for the purpose of mating. (*See* Chapter 9: Reproductive Physiology, and Chapter 10: Mating.)

If the purpose of living with a cat is companionship, then have your veterinarian spay a female (ovario-

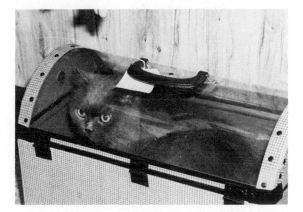

hysterectomy) between six and eight months of age or sometime before the first estrous cycle, and neuter (castrate) a male between six and eight months of age. (*See* Chapter 36: Surgery and Postoperative Care.) This will prevent undesirable sexual behavior and unwanted pregnancies.

Choosing a cat should be based only on aesthetic preference, cost, and the behavior and health of a specific cat. (*See* Chapter 2: The Breeds, for profiles of the existing cat breeds.)

The Healthy Cat

After settling the questions of breed, cost, source, and gender, it is essential to select a cat in good health. This consideration requires simple discernment when examining a litter of kittens or an individual. Because all kittens are appealing, it is difficult to remain objective and uncover medical problems when they exist. Although the pedigree of a purebred cat is useful, it cannot tell you the current state of health of the kitten sitting before you. A vaccination record is far more helpful. Most kittens should receive their first vaccination at eight weeks of age and the second at twelve weeks. If there is any question about exposure to feline panleukopenia (FPV), a kitten can be

vaccinated as early as four weeks of age. Ask for a written record of vaccines given, their dates, and their type. Save this record for your veterinarian. (*See* Appendix B: Vaccinations.)

When examining a kitten for health, the most obvious aspect is the coat. It should be downy, lustrous, and without clumps or mats. Under the coat, the skin should be smooth, showing no scaly areas or sores. A kitten's skin should also be free of minuscule debris, appearing as a salt and pepper mixture, which indicates flea eggs and blood specks. Active fleas may or may not be apparent. Bald or bare patches of skin are signs of ringworm or mange.

Healthy eyes should be clear with no excessive watering; no ulcers on the surface, which appear as small indentations; and no whitish scars from previous medical conditions. Look for any abnormalities, including soreness or swelling. A blue-eyed kitten with a white coat may be deaf. (*See* Chapter 13: Genetics, page 116.)

Examine the nose. It should be cool and slightly damp. If the nostrils exude a discharge, it could indicate the presence of infection. Sneezing, coughing, and runny nose are signs associated with various illnesses, especially upper respiratory infections.

Ears should be clean with no unpleasant odor. Excessive dirt or a dark, waxlike substance indicates ear mites. Mites usually cause head-shaking and rubbing of the ears with the paws (but can easily be eliminated).

Kitten teeth should be white and clean with the upper incisors meeting the bottom incisors evenly. Incisors are the twelve small teeth in the front of the mouth, which are present by the fourth week. At six weeks of age all twenty-six baby teeth are present. (Adult cats have thirty teeth.) Look for pink gums and mouth tissue; a pale color is a sign of anemia, which could be caused by internal parasites.

A bulging stomach may indicate the presence of internal parasites (worms) or a nutrition problem. A bump on or near the navel of a kitten can be an umbilical hernia and may require medical attention.

Important signs of parasitic infestation or sickness can be found in the anus or vulva areas. Signs of worms and diarrhea are apparent with tapeworm segments and stains of feces. Look for secretions, irritated tissue, and hair loss, which may indicate chronic diarrhea or possible virus infection such as feline enteric coronavirus. Chronic diarrhea is the most common

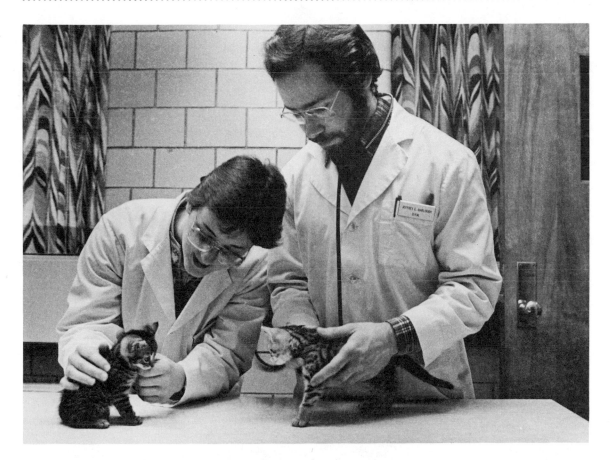

medical problem in young kittens. Diarrhea, coughing, sneezing, and running nose or eyes are also common problems.

A sound kitten stands straight and tall. The legs should have a linear quality. A kitten's walk should be bouncy, uninhibited, and effortless. Stilted movement warrants closer examination for lameness.

When you are examining eight- to twelve-week-old kittens, prefer ones that appear to be in good proportion. This means that the individual components of their bodies create a total look that is pleasing and harmonious. Kittens at this age should weigh between two and three pounds, no more or less. Those that are too portly or too slender may have health or behavior problems. This criterion becomes apparent after one has examined many litters of kittens.

Of all the aspects to consider when selecting a kitten, none is more important than temperament, emotional stability, and acceptable behavior. A playful yet calm and stable disposition is the ideal to look for in a kitten. A reserved kitten is different from a shy one. Some breeds hold themselves aloof from strangers and take a wait-and-see attitude before making direct contact; but that is not the same as shyness, which may be a behavior deficiency. The shy cat is abnormally afraid of anything unfamiliar and tries to avoid humans, other animals, or change of any kind. Shyness is expressed by escape behavior, cringing, cowering, and, when all else fails, by defensive aggression. Kittens that are not curious, energetic, playful, and anxious to greet you may either be ill or have a behavior problem. Of course, kittens can also be tired when being viewed and may simply be in need of a nap.

Kittens that have been handled by humans on a regular basis early in life have been socialized. This means they should be more adaptive to interacting with humans. If they have been allowed to remain with their mother and littermates for a minimum of ten weeks, they are likely to adjust easily to other cats. The transference of genetic characteristics plays an important role in cat behavior, too. If possible, observe the kittens' mother. If she is at ease with strangers, congenial, outgoing, and friendly, it is likely that her kittens will be the same, providing external influences do not change them. (*See* Chapter 13: Genetics.)

When observing a litter of kittens, kneel to floor level and notice which ones are curious about you, are friendly toward you, and want to rub up against you. Lift them in your arms, one at a time, to see if they are at ease with you. A normal kitten will either thrash about playfully or settle in and purr. A normal kitten should follow you about when it is set down on the floor once again. Try playing with it. A friendly, outgoing kitten will respond to something dangled in front of it, such as a string or peacock feather, or to something rolled, such as a ball or empty spool.

There is more to feline health than clear eyes and a glossy coat. A happy, self-assured kitten that delights in the company of humans is likely to enjoy good health and long life.

No matter how healthy or normal a kitten appears, it is always possible for it to have a medical problem that is not apparent. It is essential that a new kitten be given a complete veterinary examination soon after it arrives in its new home. The first examination could be the most important one of its life. If buying an expensive purebred, have a written understanding that if a veterinarian finds the cat to be unhealthy, defective, or incubating an infectious disease, it can be returned and the purchase price refunded.

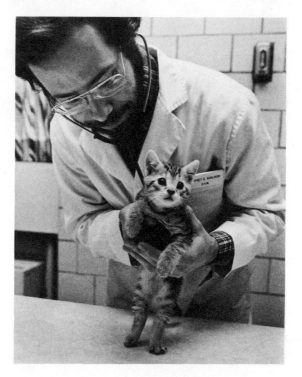

The Breeds

WHAT IS A PUREBRED CAT?

The registered breeds and varieties of domestic cats that regally adorn human upholstery are beyond the boundaries of taxonomy, the science of classifying plant and animal organisms. A *taxon* is a unit of biological classification, arranged in descending order. Although there are many conflicting approaches to the subject, the most accepted classifications of animal taxa are *kingdom, phylum, class, order, family, genus, species* and *subspecies.*

The term *breed* is not used as a separate classification in the science of taxonomy. Cats in general are identified as various species, divided into three groups or genera: *Panthera, Acinonyx,* and *Felis.* For example, the lion is classified as *Panthera leo,* the cheetah as *Acinonyx jubatus,* and the domestic cat as *Felis catus* (formerly *Felis domestica*). Within each group are the various *species.* A species is a scientific grouping of living organisms with similar traits, distinguished by the ability to breed successfully with one another. The minimum taxonomic category is *subspecies,* which is

a subdivision of a species, usually determined by geographical distribution. *Felis catus,* or the domestic cat, has no subspecies classification. The many varied breeds of the domestic cat are interesting variations of the same species.

The term *breed* began as a verb form from Middle English *(breden)* and Old English *(bredan)* meaning to nourish, to keep warm, possibly with warm *breath* or by *breathing* upon. Its use as a noun grew out of breeding domestic animals. A litter of kittens, puppies, piglets, et cetera—were collectively called a brood, and the individual offspring were casually referred to as breeds. As farmers and herdsmen began utilizing genetics—the science of heredity—the term *breed* was then used to distinguish a specific type within a species and came into common usage, even among educators and researchers. Charles Darwin applied the word's modern usage in *The Origin of Species,* in 1859. Eventually, *breed* came to mean a division of a species with separate and distinctive characteristics that were genetically pre-

LONGHAIR CATS		SHORTHAIR CATS		
American Curl	Norwegian Forest Cat	Abyssinian	Cornish Rex	Oriental Shorthair
Balinese	Oriental Longhair	American Curl Shorthair	Devon Rex	Russian Blue
Birman	Persian	American Shorthair	Egyptian Mau	Scottish Fold
Cymric	Ragdoll	American Wirehair	Exotic Shorthair	Siamese
Himalayan	Somali	Bombay	Havana Brown	Singapura
Javanese	Turkish Angora	British Shorthair	Japanese Bobtail	Snowshoe
Kashmir	Turkish Van	Burmese	Korat	Sphynx
Maine Coon Cat		Chartreux	Manx	Tonkinese
		Colorpoint Shorthair	Ocicat	

dictable and consistently reproducible. Human intervention is necessary to recreate purebred cats. Those involved in breeding purebred animals circumvent the process of natural selection and decide which animals will mate, based on their genetic patterns. It is an activity pursued by those with an interest in maintaining and preserving the unique qualities of the various breeds that have been developed within each species of domestic animal. Still, taxonomists and other scientists prefer the designation *strain* or *race* when speaking of a type or variety of a species.

To the cat breeder, a purebred cat comes from a traceable line of mutual ancestry. Such cats possess genetically governed variants, consistently producing similar traits and characteristics in their offspring as a result of a controlled breeding program. The offspring of purebred cats must be registered with a cat association if they are to authenticate their purebred status.

Cat breeders and others involved in animal husbandry use the science of heredity to eliminate, add to, or emphasize specific physical or mental characteristics of breeds. Cattle with more muscle and less fat have been developed. Horses are bred for type, size, speed, stamina, et cetera. Male and female cats are often selected for breeding because they possess a body structure or coat or overall appearance that represents a concept of excellence for their particular strain (or breed). Some animals are bred for characteristics that help them perform a demanding task. For example, the American Quarter Horse was developed to gallop fast for short distances while being able to stop abruptly and anticipate the erratic movement of cattle. It became the rancher's "right-hand man."

The great differences of size and type among dog breeds are the most striking examples of selective breeding. It is difficult to imagine that the Chihuahua

and the St. Bernard are members of the same species. Here, those practicing selective breeding have conspired with the demands of nature as dictated by geographic differences and the consistent uses and activities of the dogs. The result has been the broad range of physical and mental differences among the dog breeds. Although differences among the various cat breeds are not as radical, they are pronounced. One need only observe the Persian next to the Siamese to see the contrast in appearance and temperament. Among serious breeders and exhibitors in the Cat and Dog Fancies, the primary goal is to develop, improve, and preserve the various established breeds and their standards.

WHAT IS A MIXED-BREED CAT?

The majority of pet cats are mixed-breeds. They are the result of random matings of various cat breeds or of other mixed-breed cats. They almost never resemble the standard of any cat breed. They are usually not registered, have no pedigree (record of ancestors), and are not considered purebreds. Owners of such cats have no interest in these matters. In the United States, they may be referred to as house cats or alley cats. In Great Britain, they are sometimes called moggs. However, the Cat Fancy has gone to great lengths to acknowledge the desirability of *all* cats by allowing household pets to be registered (by some cat associations) and by encouraging a Household Pet Competition for ribbons and prizes in most cat shows. To qualify for entry, household pets must be neutered (except for kittens); have all of their physical properties (except for a tail in the case of an unregistered Manx); and may not be declawed. Unlike purebreds, they are not judged according to a written standard but on the basis of physical condition, cleanliness, presentation, temperament, and attractive or unusual appearance. Throughout the world, cats of unknown lineage comprise the vast majority of house pets and most of them are mixed-breeds. They are, without a doubt, the most popular cats of all.

PUREBRED-CAT ASSOCIATIONS

Purebred cats must be registered with a national cat association and have a traceable lineage through a verified pedigree to authenticate their status. The registration papers and pedigree support a breeder's assertions regarding breed, parentage, and cat-show attainments of a particular cat. These qualify it for showing and breeding according to the rules of the various cat associations, so long as it is a breed recognized by the association of choice. No breeder will use a nonpedigreed, unregistered cat in a breeding program. Exhibitors may not enter such cats in championship competition. Mixed-breed cats or nonpedi-

greed cats are primarily companion animals with no need for papers.

Those who prefer purebred cats are either attracted to the look and the personality of a breed as a pet or have an interest in showing cats. Whatever the reason, the interest in purebred cats grows larger each year, with a constantly expanding Cat Fancy. In the United States and Canada, there are seven organizations that register purebred cats, maintain pedigrees, create and support breed standards, and sanction cat shows and the judges who preside over them. These national organizations include: American Cat Association (ACA); American Cat Fanciers' Association (ACFA); Canadian Cat Association (CCA); Cat Fanciers' Association (CFA); Cat Fanciers' Federation (CFF); The International Cat Association (TICA); and the United Cat Federation (UCF).

The Cat Fanciers' Association, Inc., is the largest cat registry in the world, with close to six hundred affiliate clubs in the United States, Canada, and Japan. It generates over three hundred cat shows a year, which attract a total of almost seventy thousand entries. The oldest organization in the United States is the American Cat Association, which continues to register purebred cats with over forty member clubs. It was formed as the Beresford Cat Club of Chicago in 1897, and became the ACA in 1904. In 1906, several members of the ACA left that organization over a rules dispute and formed their own national registry, the Cat Fanciers' Association. CFA began with five member clubs in 1906, but grew into the largest cat association anywhere. The International Cat Association (TICA) is a relatively new organization, with growing influence in the United States, offering the established cat associations their greatest challenge ever. Still, CFA is con-

sidered to be the feline counterpart of the American Kennel Club in terms of size and prestige.

For purebred enthusiasts, the choice is large and varied. However, it is important to understand that no two cat associations accept or register all of the existing breeds. For example, CFA, at this writing, registers thirty-one breeds, but there are at least forty-one breeds accepted by one or more of the seven cat associations. Each breed is allowed a specific variety of coat colors and patterns in its official standard, which means that there may be dozens of different-looking cats of the same breed. For example, the Persian comes in fifty-one coat colors and color combinations approved by the Cat Fanciers' Association. In contrast, CFA allows the Bombay to be shown only in solid black. These rules are outlined by every cat association in a set of *breed standards*. A breed standard is a precise, written description of a breed. The standard, according to CFA literature, "is an abstract aesthetic ideal."

PUREBRED TYPES

According to CFA literature, cat breeds can be divided into three types: *natural, man-made,* and *spontaneous mutation*. Natural breeds such as the Persian, Russian Blue, Turkish Angora, and others were created by nature but refined and stabilized by cat fanciers through selective breeding. Man-made breeds, or hybrids, such as the Exotic Shorthair and Bombay, were created by cat breeders who skillfully combined existing breeds. Spontaneous mutations, such as the Manx and Scottish Fold, are the consequence of unex-

plainable deviations in genetic code. These resulted in the lack of tail in the Manx and the tightly folded ears, bent forward and downward, of the Scottish Fold.

Before a new breed or color is accepted for championship competition by the various cat associations, it must meet strict requirements. CFA, for example, requires a minimum of ten breeders working with the breed. They must demonstrate to the board of directors that the new breed is sufficiently distinct from existing ones and free from genetic or health complications. Once the breed is accepted for registration, it may be shown in noncompetitive *Miscellaneous Classes* at shows. When a standard for a new breed has been approved by the board, and one hundred cats of the new breed have been registered, it is eligible to compete in *Provisional Classes*. Finally, after a total of twenty-five different cats have been shown in all seven regions of CFA throughout the United States, the breed is eligible, upon board approval, to take its place in the show ring as a fully approved breed with championship status.

Body Types

Purebred cats have two extreme body types: the *foreign* and the *cobby*. The foreign (or oriental) type is often described in breed standards as "svelte," "slim," "lithe," "elegant," "fine-boned," and "with tapered lines." In most breeds of foreign type, the body is slim, almost tubular in shape, and "serpentine," with a firm musculature. It is typified by the Siamese, which is ideally a sleek, lightly built cat. *Cobby* refers to a heavy, low-lying, short-legged, compact, broad-

chested body. It is typified by the American Shorthair, Burmese, Chartreux, British Shorthair, and Persian. There are some breeds slightly less cobby than other cobby breeds, such as the Russian Blue, while a few are somewhere between foreign and cobby types, as typified by the Abyssinian. These types are referred to as "modified" or "moderate."

Coat Types

Purebred cats are seen in many coat types. Color, length, and texture have more influence on the selection of a breed than any other visual aspect of the cat. The feline coat is its primary aesthetic attraction. Many consider the cat's fur to be the most glamorous part of its body. Although show cats are divided into Longhair Breeds and Shorthair Breeds, there are some variations within those two categories.

Hairless Cats. Although no cat is totally hairless, the Sphynx, an extremely rare breed, comes closest. The cat is not bald. Thin, short hairs grow tightly packed on the ears, muzzle, and tail. It has no whiskers or eyebrows.

Shorthair Cats. Shorthair cats may have a single or double coat. Single coats should look polished and satiny. Double coats should appear thick, full, and plush. A single coat is usually a fine fur (sometimes glossy), which clings close to the body and is found on such breeds as Siamese, Bombay, Burmese, and Oriental Shorthair. A double coat consists of long

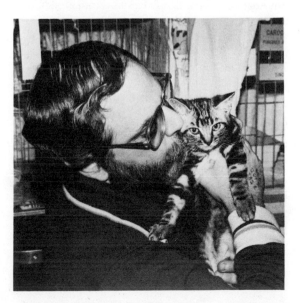

guard hairs that display the primary coat color, and a thick, downy undercoat, most of which grows on the underside of the torso. Some of the shorthair breeds with double coats are Chartreux, Manx, Russian Blue, and American Shorthair.

There are two unusual variations of shorthair coats. They are the *wirehair coat* and the *curly* or *Rex coat*. Both coat types were the result of spontaneous mutations in kitten litters, which were then carefully nurtured for generations into stabilized, established breeds. The wirehair coat can be seen in the American Wirehair, which is similar to the American Shorthair, except for its springy, tight, and bent-over fur. The curly or Rex coat is allowed by the CFA only in two separate breeds. They are the Cornish Rex and the Devon Rex. Although similar in type, the Cornish Rex coat has no guard hairs but has greater density than the coat of the Devon Rex. It curls, waves, or ripples. The coat of the Devon Rex is also wavy but it is longer, with less density than the Cornish.

Longhair Cats. The length of the coat of longhair cats varies from two to six inches, depending upon the breed and the part of the body. For example, Persians have long, thick coats of fine texture, which fall away from the body. The ruff (similar to the mane on a lion) is substantial and flows from behind the head into a frill along the chest and between the forelegs. Some longhair breeds, such as Persians, have a double coat.

Another type of longhair coat belongs to the Turkish Angora. Its coat is medium long on the body and longer at the ruff. The tail has a full brush (that is, plumelike or bushy). The Turkish Angora's fur is silky with a wavy tendency and very fine with a satiny sheen.

CORNISH REX

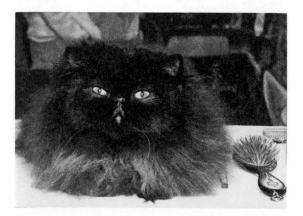

The Somali's longhair coat is somewhat different. It is of medium length except on the shoulders, where it is slightly shorter. The breed is double coated, which means it has a thick, short undercoat with a top coat of long hair, which is, in the case of the Somali, extremely fine and soft to the touch.

Yet another type of longhair coat can be found on the Maine Coon Cat. Its coat is heavy and shaggy, shorter on the shoulders and longer on the underside and britches (haunches). It has a frontal ruff, though not as pronounced as on the Persian. Its lengthy tail sustains long and flowing fur, and its hair texture is silky and smooth.

Coat Patterns

Tabby Patterns. There are four accepted tabby coat patterns: *Classic, Mackerel, Spotted,* and *Ticked.*

Classic Tabby refers to dense, clearly defined markings on the body that are darker than the ground color. They are unbroken on top and swirled on the sides, with rings on the tail and bars on the legs. The face is barred with upward-pointing lines, forming the letter M on the forehead.

Mackerel Tabby refers to dense, clearly defined vertical stripes going around the body. The stripes are narrower than those of the Classic Tabby. The legs are striped with bracelets and the tail is barred. The head is also barred, the bars forming the letter M on the forehead. In some examples of this pattern, the stripes resemble those of a tiger.

Spotted Tabby refers to broken stripes appearing as spots.

Ticked Tabby refers to darker bands of color on each hair-tip.

Tabby patterns come in prescribed colors, depending on specific breed standards, which include Blue-patched Tabby, Blue Tabby, Brown-patched Tabby, Brown Tabby, Cameo Tabby, Cream Tabby, Patched Tabby and White, Red Tabby, Silver-patched Tabby, Silver Tabby, and Tabby and White. (*Patched* refers to Tabby with red patches. It is called a "torbie.")

Self. The self coat pattern is a coat of solid color. Each hair is consistently the same color from its tip to its root and is the same on all parts of the body.

Tipped or Tipping. The tipped coat is one which has contrasting colors at the hair ends. Lightly tipped cats are referred to as *Chinchillas,* medium tipped cats are referred to as *Shaded* and heavily tipped cats are *Smokes.*

Van (Piebald). This is an almost white coat with patches of color on the head, tail, or legs.

Bi-color. Bi-color is a solid-color coat with patches of white.

Parti-color. Parti-color is a coat pattern with two separate colors.

Tortoiseshell. This represents a black coat color with patches of red (orange). It is often referred to as a "tortie."

Calico. The Calico pattern is a tortoiseshell coat with white.

Cameo. The Cameo pattern has a white undercoat with red hair-tips.

BREED DESCRIPTIONS

LONGHAIR CATS

American Curl	Norwegian Forest Cat
Balinese	Oriental Longhair
Birman	Persian
Cymric	Ragdoll
Himalayan	Somali
Javanese	Turkish Angora
Kashmir	Turkish Van
Maine Coon Cat	

AMERICAN CURL

The American Curl has been accepted by the CFA as one of its most recent breeds in the Miscellaneous Class. This experimental breed was first reported as a spontaneous mutation by Joe and Grace Ruga of Lakewood, California, owners of the foundation cat, Shulamith, from which all pedigreed American Curls descend. As in the Scottish Fold, the distinctive feature of the breed is the unusual formation of the ears. On this breed the ears are firm to the touch, erect and open, curving up in a gentle curl. The body is "semiforeign," not cobby, and medium in size. The coat is "moderately long and flowing with a minimal undercoat so it lies flat, not bushy." The texture is silky with a lustrous sheen. American Curls are also being developed with shorthair coats. (*See* "Shorthair Cats," page 28.)

BALINESE

The Balinese was developed in the United States as a separate breed after it appeared as a spontaneous, longhair mutation of the Siamese cat. It has a long, svelte, foreign-type body, with a wedge-shaped head. It is like the Siamese in every way except that its hair is longer and its voice is softer. Its coat colors are Seal Point, Chocolate Point, Blue Point, and Lilac Point. The eyes are deep, vivid blue. (*See* "Javanese," page 25.)

BIRMAN

Considered an ancient breed, it was smuggled out of Burma circa 1919 and developed into a recognized breed in France. Its body is long and stocky with a rounded head and Roman-shaped nose. Its coat is medium-long to long, and silky. This sweet-natured cat is the only breed that shows white "gloves" (fur) on its four paws. Birman colors are the same as the traditional Siamese point colorings: Seal Point, Blue Point, Chocolate Point, and Lilac Point.

CYMRIC

Pronounced *Kim'rik,* this breed is a spontaneous mutation derived from another spontaneous mutation. The Cymric is a long-haired Manx. The two breeds are virtually identical except for the Cymric's medium-long, double coat. Like the Manx, it should be completely tailless if a perfect specimen, although it is seen with three varieties of tail: the "rumpy," no tail at all; "stumpy," with a tail stump of one to five inches; and "longie," with a complete tail.

HIMALAYAN

CFA registers this man-made breed as Persian (with point coloring). Other cat associations accept it as a separate breed. It was produced by crossing Siamese (for color) with Persians (for type). It has a cobby body with a long, fine coat. Its colors include Seal Point, Blue Point, Chocolate Point, Lilac Point, Flame Point, Cream Point, Tortie Point, Blue-cream Point, Seal-lynx Point, and Blue-lynx Point. In solid colors of Chocolate or Lilac, it is registered as the Kashmir by some cat associations other than CFA. (*See* "Persians," page 26.)

JAVANESE

The Javanese (like the Balinese) is a Siamese with long hair. The difference between a Javanese and a Balinese is the wide variety of coat colors allowed the Javanese by CFA (excluding the four traditional Siamese point colors). Its CFA color standards are identical to those of the Colorpoint Shorthair. Its body type is foreign (Siamese) with fine bones and firm muscles. Coat type is long, fine, silky, without a downy undercoat. CFA accepted colors are Red Point, Cream Point, Seal-lynx Point, Chocolate-lynx Point, Blue-lynx Point, Lilac-lynx Point, Red-lynx Point, Chocolate Tortie-lynx Point, Red-lynx Point, Chocolate Tortie-lynx Point, Blue-cream Lynx Point, Lilac-cream Lynx Point, Cream Lynx Point, Seal Tortie-lynx Point, Seal-tortie Point, Chocolate-tortie Point, Blue-cream Point, and Lilac-cream Point.

KASHMIR

(*See* "Himalayan," page 24, and "Persian," page 26.) A solid-color Himalayan is called the Kashmir by some cat associations. The CFA classifies it as a division of the Persian breed.

MAINE COON CAT

The Maine Coon Cat is considered a native American breed that occurred "naturally" in the northeastern areas of the United States and in northeastern Canada. Its transition from farm and backyard cat to show cat was a long, difficult journey. It has a medium to large, muscular, broad-chested body. Some fanciers believe it is the largest of all the pure breeds. The coat should be heavy and shaggy, shorter on the shoulders and longer on the underside and britches, and long and flowing on the tail. Maine Coon Cat coat colors and patterns include a wide range of solids, parti-colors, tabbies, and other colors. The traditional Maine Coon Cat appearance consists of a brown tabby pattern with a long, shaggy coat and tail, creating a slight resemblance to a raccoon.

NORWEGIAN FOREST CAT

Although similar in appearance to the Maine Coon Cat, the Norwegian Forest Cat is a separate breed. Its body is cobby, with longer hind legs than front legs,

which make the rump higher than the shoulders—a characteristic that differentiates it from the Maine Coon Cat. All colors are permitted except the four Siamese (or Himalayan) colors. References to the "Norsk Skogkatt" have appeared in Scandinavian poetry, legends, and writings for hundreds of years. It was recognized and shown in Oslo long before World War II, but has only recently been accepted in the Miscellaneous Class of the CFA where it is registrable but not yet eligible for cat shows. Some American cat associations other than CFA have recognized it for competition, but the breed is rare in the United States.

Other Colors. CFA-recognized colors are Ebony, Blue, Chestnut, Lavender, Cinnamon, Fawn, Red, and Cream.

ORIENTAL LONGHAIR

The Oriental Longhair is a man-made breed. Created in the early 1980s and first recognized in 1984 by The International Cat Association (TICA) as a nonpointed Balinese, it was quickly given separate breed status. Accepted by most associations, it was included in the CFA's Miscellaneous Class (registrable but not eligible for competition) in 1988. The Oriental Longhair is a long-coated Siamese with no color points. Because of its longer coat it appears to have softer lines and less of an extreme Siamese look than its cousin, the Oriental Shorthair. TICA recognizes five color divisions: Solid, Tortie, Tabby, Shaded (including Shaded and Smoke colors), and Parti-color. TICA-recognized colors are Black, Blue, Chocolate, Frost, Cinnamon, Fawn, Red, and Cream. CFA recognizes six color classes: Solid, Smoke, Shaded, Tabby, Parti-colors, and

PERSIAN

Considered an ancient, "natural breed" by many, the Persian can also be classified as a modern breed because it is the result of selective breeding begun in the late nineteenth century. The history of the Persian is unrecorded before 1520 and its origin can never be proven. It may stem from Angora cats from Turkey, which were crossed with other longhairs from Persia (now Iran), Afghanistan, Burma, China, Russia, France, Italy, and England, until the modern type was developed. Persians are among the most popular cats in the world and win many of the prizes at important cat shows. The Persian body is of cobby type, low on the legs, deep in the chest, equally massive across shoulders and rump, with a short, well-rounded middle piece. Persians are large or medium in size. The coat must be long and thick, standing off from the body,

with fine texture. The ruff (mane) should be immense and continue in a deep frill between the front legs. The breed is seen in fifty-one separate colors and color combinations. CFA divides Persian colors into six divisions for showing. They are: Solid Color Division; Shaded Division; Smoke Division; Tabby Division; Parti-color Division; and Himalayan Division. CFA's Himalayan Division of the Persian is recognized as a separate breed by other cat associations. Solid chocolate and solid lilac colors are also considered a separate breed, the "Kashmir," by other cat associations, but are registered by CFA as Persians of the Solid Color Division, Other Solid Colors Class (OSCC).

RAGDOLL

This longhair breed is a hybrid created in California in the 1960s. It was achieved by crossing a white Persian with a Seal Point Birman, and possibly other breeds. This controversial breed is recognized by several cat associations but not by the CFA. An extremely

gentle and easy-to-handle breed, Ragdolls are big cats with broad chests and large hindquarters. The "china blue" eyes of the Ragdoll are large, oval, and wide-set on a bias. It is seen in three patterns: Color Point, Bi-color and Mitted (white paw tips). Ragdoll colors are Seal, Blue Chocolate, and Frost; some have white spotting.

SOMALI

The Somali is a long-haired variant of the Abyssinian. The breed began appearing in the 1960s and was recognized by CFA in 1978. The original Somalis came from matings between shorthair Abyssinians with a recessive gene for long hair, which is carried in some Abyssinian bloodlines. The body is a lengthy type, similar to the Abyssinian: medium long, lithe, and graceful, between the extremes of the cobby and the svelte. The coat is medium in length, but long enough to accommodate two or three dark bands of ticking. Somalis are expected to carry the Abyssinian colors: Ruddy, Red, or Blue (blue-gray). Its distinctive tail is bushy, almost foxlike.

TURKISH ANGORA

The true Angora was near extinction in the early twentieth century, as it was being replaced by Angoras crossed with Persians. One of the oldest longhair breeds and long fancied in Turkey, it was first seen in Europe during the Renaissance. Its name is taken

from the Turkish city of Ankara. The Turkish Angora is radically different from its relative, the Persian. It has a long head and medium-size body. Its torso is long and lithe, with a lightly framed chest. The body coat is medium-long, long at the ruff, with a full brush on the tail. The coat is silky with a wavy tendency, very fine and lustrous. While the solid white Turkish Angoras are best known, the breed comes in all colors.

TURKISH VAN

This is a natural breed, native to eastern Turkey, and is a working cat from the remote, snowy region of Lake Van. It was brought to England in 1955 and was officially recognized there in 1969 by its Governing Council of the Cat Fancy (GCCF), and by the Fédération Internationale Féline de l'Europe (FIFE), which represents twelve countries on the European continent. In the United States, the Turkish Van is recognized by TICA and ACFA and has recently been

accepted in the Miscellaneous (noncompetitive) Class by the CFA. Its body is long, broad, muscular, and deep-chested. The Turkish Van is one of the largest breeds of domestic cat, with males weighing from twelve to eighteen pounds and frequently more. The coat should be long, soft, and silky. The tail, or "brush," is foxlike and strongly ringed. Coat color should be a pure chalk-white, and its colored markings confined to the head and tail, with one or more random body markings in the shoulder or rump areas. They are allowed any color markings and white.

SHORTHAIR CATS

Abyssinian	Havana Brown
American Curl Shorthair	Japanese Bobtail
American Shorthair	Korat
American Wirehair	Manx
Bombay	Ocicat
British Shorthair	Oriental Shorthair
Burmese	Russian Blue
Chartreux	Scottish Fold
Colorpoint Shorthair	Siamese
Cornish Rex	Singapura
Devon Rex	Snowshoe
Egyptian Mau	Sphynx
Exotic Shorthair	Tonkinese

ABYSSINIAN

Although the Abyssinian resembles cats depicted in ancient Egyptian artwork, its exact origins are uncertain. The breed was developed in England in the late 1800s, allegedly from ticked cats brought from North Africa. An English military command brought some of these cats from Abyssinia to England in 1868 after the Abyssinian War. The "Aby" is fancied for its wild look, its desert colors, its lithe body, its quickness, and its very spirited personality. The breed came to the United States at the turn of the century. Its body is the lengthy type, medium-long, lithe, and muscular. It strikes a balance between the cobby and svelte. Its coat is soft, silky, fine in texture, but dense and with a lustrous sheen. It is medium in length but long

enough to accommodate two or three dark bands of ticking.

....

AMERICAN CURL SHORTHAIR

(*See* "American Curl," page 23.) The American Curl Shorthair is identical in every way to the American Curl (Longhair), with the following exceptions: The interior ear furnishings extend beyond the outer edge of the ear; the coat is short and should lie flat but not close; hair on the tail should be the same length as on the body, and the hair texture is soft.

....

AMERICAN SHORTHAIR

The American Shorthair is America's own breed. Its progenitors were farm cats and house cats that were large-boned, short-coated working cats. Some naturalists believe them to be the original domestic cat. They are descended from basic European working cats. These everyday cats came to North America on the same ships with the first European settlers in the seventeenth century. Today's purebred cat still bears some resemblance to the typical house cat with its solidly built, cobby body, short coat, and genial temperament. When the breed first became registrable, it was commonly referred to as a Shorthair. For many years, and in several cat associations, it was registered as the Domestic Shorthair. In 1966 its breed designation became the American Shorthair. The American Shorthair differs from all common cats in that it has been bred to meet breed standards, which keep it strong, muscular, intelligent, and lively, with a distinctive physical image. The breed displays a short, thick, even coat, which is hard in texture and seen in thirty-three colors and patterns. Its most striking appearance is in the Classic Tabby coat in silver, red, or brown.

....

AMERICAN WIREHAIR

A spontaneous mutation of the American Shorthair, the American Wirehair is best known for its unusual fur, which is crimped, hooked, or bent, reminiscent of a lamb's coat. Its guard hairs are especially springy;

even its whiskers are bent or curly. The first known American Wirehair was "Council Rock Farm Adam of Hi-Fi," born in 1966 in Verona, New York. The standard calls for a medium to large body, which should be cobby, compact, and muscular. The Wirehair is seen in the same colors as the American Shorthair.

BOMBAY

The Bombay is a hybrid, resembling a house-size panther. It was created by Nikki Horner of the Shawnee Cattery, in Louisville, Kentucky, in 1958. It is the result of many generations of crossing the sable Burmese with black American Shorthairs. It is a medium-sized cat, muscular, somewhat cobby, with a surprisingly solid feel to its body. The mature Bombay must be jet black down to the hair roots.

BRITISH SHORTHAIR

The British Shorthair resembles the American Shorthair, but differs somewhat because of the introduction of Persians into its lines by English breeders after World War I. Although this practice is no longer acceptable, its influence on the current look of the breed remains pronounced. British Shorthairs have broader heads with a rounder shape and more developed cheeks than the American Shorthair. The neck is short and stocky with a hint of Persian about it. The body is huskier than the American Shorthair's, and the coat is plusher. CFA accepts nineteen colors and patterns in this breed.

BURMESE

The Burmese is a hybrid breed developed by Dr. Joseph Thompson in 1930 from one cat imported from Burma. "Wong Mau" is the foundation cat for almost every pedigreed Burmese in North America. This original cat was bred with a Siamese, "Tai Mau." This mating led to the breed now seen. A medium-sized cat, its body is muscular, compact, with a rounded chest. Although related to the Siamese, it must not resemble that breed in any way. Until recently the only Burmese color accepted by CFA was Sable Brown. Champagne, Blue (gray), and Platinum were allowed but only as the Malayan division of the Burmese. Other cat associations considered the Champagne, Blue, and Platinum to be Other-Color Burmese or Malayans.

CHARTREUX

One of the older natural breeds, these French cats are believed to have existed before they lived with the Carthusian monks in their mother house, "Le Grand Chartreux," in the seventeenth century. Their bodies are powerful and massive and they may weigh as much as fourteen pounds, with wide shoulders and a stocky neck. Their short coats are dense, velvety, and glossy. The Chartreux standard permits any shade of blue-gray from ash to slate, with the hair-tips lightly brushed with silver. The preferred tone is a bright, unblemished blue with an overall iridescent sheen.

COLORPOINT SHORTHAIR

The Colorpoint Shorthair appears to be a Siamese with colors other than the traditional Siamese point colors (i.e., Seal Point, Chocolate Point, Blue Point, and Lilac Point). Most cat associations in the United States and in other countries accept Colorpoint Shorthairs as Siamese. CFA, however, accepts them as a separate breed, partly because traditional Siamese breeders do not wish to permit any colors other than the four traditional ones and partly because cats were

crossed with American Shorthairs to introduce the new colors. CFA accepts these cats but only as a separate, hybrid breed. Complicating the issue further is the Oriental Shorthair, which is another nontraditional version of the Siamese. It does not have color points on the extremities of its body, but has a solid color over the entire body. Therefore, the Siamese is a cat of foreign type, which is pointed (has dark coloring on the extremities) in four traditional colors and accepted by all associations; the Colorpoint Shorthair is a CFA breed with colors other than the Siamese colors on the points, but is registered as a Siamese by the other cat associations; and the Oriental Shorthair, which is not a pointed cat but has a solid color or tabby pattern, is accepted by all associations. The body of the Colorpoint Shorthair is svelte, medium-sized, and tubular. The coat is short, fine-textured, and glossy, lying close to the body. Colorpoint Shorthair colors are Red Point, Cream Point, Seal-Lynx Point, Chocolate-Lynx Point, Blue-Lynx Point, Lilac-Lynx Point, Red-Lynx Point, Seal-Tortie Point, Chocolate Tortie Point, Blue-Cream Point, Lilac-Cream Point, Seal Tortie-Lynx Point, Chocolate Tortie-Lynx Point, Blue-Cream Lynx Point, Lilac-Cream Lynx Point, and Cream Lynx Point.

CORNISH REX

The Cornish Rex is a spontaneous mutation that was discovered in 1950 on a farm in Cornwall, England. The foundation cat for this breed was "Kallibunker." The breed is named for the Rex rabbit, which is known for its velvety fur and curly whiskers. A mutation from a white domestic shorthair, the Cornish Rex

features a longer, slimmer, more agile body than that of its ancestors. The cat has a small, narrow head, punctuated by large, oval-shaped eyes that slant slightly upward, and a Roman nose. The most striking aspect of this breed is its coat with deep even "waves" over the entire body, head, legs, and tail. The fur is very fine and soft, short but very dense. The Cornish Rex is accepted in most American colors and coat patterns. The Cornish Rex and its cousin the Devon Rex have much in common. However, they are genetically incompatible. These similar, but separate, breeds are different, and, when mated to each other, do not produce curly- or wavy-coated kittens.

DEVON REX

The Devon Rex, a mutation similar to the Cornish Rex, appeared ten years later, in Devon, England. The foundation cat was "Kirlee," a black male. The Devon is a cat with a medium-fine frame, well covered with soft, wavy fur, with a more relaxed wave to its coat and less of a pattern to the waves than the Cornish Rex. Its coat is longer and somewhat less curly than the coat of the Cornish. The Devon head is a short wedge with a nosebreak as well as a whisker break. The Devon Rex is seen in most American and British colors and coat patterns. (*See* "Cornish Rex," above.)

EGYPTIAN MAU

The Egyptian Mau is one of the rarest registered breeds in North America and is not often seen at cat shows, despite the fact that it is accepted by all associations for championship competition. The breed has been clearly identified in ancient Egyptian artworks. It is the only naturally spotted domestic cat. The conformation is often described as a balance between the compactness of a Burmese and the slim elegance of a Siamese. Its medium-length body is muscular, with the hind legs longer than the front, giving the Mau the appearance of standing on tiptoes when upright. The coat is silky and fine in texture but dense and resilient to the touch. It is long enough to allow two or more bands of ticking, separated by lighter bands. The coat pattern of the Mau is distinctive: It must have good contrast between its pale ground color and deeper markings; the forehead is etched with a dark M; the cheeks are barred with "mascara" lines that begin along the outer corner of the eye and continue across the cheek; the chest is ringed with "necklaces"; and random spots dot the coat. The Mau pattern is accepted in Silver, Bronze, and Smoke.

EXOTIC SHORTHAIR

Exotic Shorthairs are hybrids. Although they were originally created by crossing American Shorthairs with Persians, this outcross is no longer permitted by CFA. These cats are of definite Persian type but with short-haired coats. They have been accepted for registration and championship competition by CFA since 1966. Their standard is based upon the Persian standard for type. They have massive heads, short noses, cobby bodies, heavy bones, and short tails. The breed is accepted in most of the Persian colors and coat patterns.

HAVANA BROWN

The Havana Brown was originally crossbred in England, circa 1950, by mating a black Shorthair with a Chocolate Point Siamese. The breed was later produced in the United States by crossing Russian Blues or black Shorthairs with Chocolate Point Siamese. Named for the rich tobacco color of Cuban cigars, the Havana Brown is a solid brown cat, from its pure brown whiskers to its tail. The body is medium in length, firm, and muscular, and stands with a level back. Although the original English Havana was of

foreign body-type, the American Havana Brown is not. It has a distinctive profile with a long face, rounded muzzle, and wide-set, round-tipped ears. The mahogany-colored coat is smooth and should be one solid color from the hair-tip to the skin (if the cat is to compete in cat shows). The nose and paw pads should have a rosy color to them, complementing the cat's coat hue.

JAPANESE BOBTAIL

This is a natural breed of a type that has been seen in ancient paintings and carvings from Japan. Bobtails are considered to be the indigenous cats of Japan and are believed to bring good luck to households in which they reside, if they wear the most popular and traditional coat colors of jet-black and red-orange irregular spots on a snowy-white background. Their most recognizable feature is their bunnylike bobbed tails. Their bodies are medium-sized, with long, lean, and elegant torsos, but not tubular (that is, not foreign in type). There is no inclination toward flabbiness or cobbiness. The coat should be medium in length, soft and silky, but without a noticeable undercoat. Japanese Bobtail colors are White, Black, Red, Black and White, Red and White, Mi-Ke (Tricolor—black, red, and white) and Tortoiseshell (black, red, and cream).

KORAT

The Korat is a rare, ancient, natural breed from Thailand. It is greatly loved by the Thai people, who regard it as a "good luck" cat. The foundation stock stems from a male and female imported to the United States in 1959. The breed was recognized by CFA for championship competition in 1967. It is a medium-sized cat characterized by its semicobby body, medium bone structure, and heart-shaped head. It has a single coat with short, fine, glossy hair lying close to the body. It is seen only in solid silver-blue, tipped with silver—the more silver tipping the better.

MANX

The Isle of Man, situated in the Irish Sea, is the home of the unique cat breed known for its tailless body. This breed is considered to be a spontaneous mutation. Although generally identified by the complete lack of a tail, the Manx is actually seen in three varieties of tail: "rumpy," no tail at all; "stumpy," a tail stump of one to five inches; and "longie," a complete tail. Only the tailless Manx, however, is accepted for show. The Manx is stout in appearance, medium in size, with sturdy bone structure. It is broad-chested and surprisingly heavy when lifted. It has a round look. It has a short, dense double coat, with a plush undercoat and harder overcoat, with glossier guard hairs. The breed is seen in most colors and coat patterns.

OCICAT

The Ocicat is a hybrid breed created by crossing Siamese and Abyssinians. It was the unexpected result of a breeding experiment in 1964 by CFA breeder Virginia Daly. The outcome was kittens with spotted tabby coats bearing a striking resemblance to the wild ocelot. Although the breed was accepted for CFA registration in 1966, it was not advanced to championship status until 1987. The current Ocicat is a large, well-spotted, agouti cat (each hair has bands of color) of moderate body type. (*See* "Body Types," page 21.) It possesses a solid, long-bodied torso, with substantial

ental Shorthair and the Siamese are almost identical except for color. The Oriental Shorthair body is long, svelte, and tubular (of foreign type). The coat is short, fine-textured, and glossy, and lies close to the body. Coat color—the cat's reason for being—must be solid (self) or tabby-patterned. The entire coat, as well as each hair, must be of a uniform solid color. The breed is accepted in almost all solid colors. (*See* "Colorpoint Shorthair," page 31.)

bone and muscle development. It is always seen as a spotted tabby, with all hairs banded except on the tip of the tail. The coat pattern includes an intricate tabby "M" on the forehead. Spots are scattered across the shoulders and hindquarters, extending as far as possible down the legs. Ocicat colors are: Tawny (brownspotted tabby), Chocolate, Cinnamon, Blue, Lavender, Fawn, Silver, Chocolate Silver, Cinnamon Silver, Blue Silver, Lavender Silver, and Fawn Silver.

ORIENTAL SHORTHAIR

The Oriental Shorthair was conceived in the 1950s by English breeders who wanted a Siamese-type cat with a self-colored (solid color) coat. This hybrid was created by crossing the Siamese with various Shorthairs, including the Russian Blue. It was a by-product of the efforts to create a solid-colored brown Siamese, which ultimately became the Havana Brown. (*See* Havana Brown, page 33.) The breed was accepted by CFA for registration in 1972 and entered championship competition in 1977. The standards for the Ori-

RUSSIAN BLUE

When applied to the coat colors of cats, the term "blue" refers to various shades of gray, from pale (bright) to dark (almost steel-blue gray), that are essentially a "dilute" pigmentation from black to gray. This natural breed is very old, but was first seen and later shown in England in the 1880s. In the 1960s the Russian Blues became popular show cats. They have a fine-boned, long, firm body that, without being tubular in appearance, is considered to be a modified foreign type. (*See* "Body Types," page 21.) Their bodies are covered with a double coat, which stands out because of its density. The coat must be short, fine, and plush, with a soft, silky quality. The Russian Blue color must be an even, bright blue shade throughout the coat. Lighter shades of blue are preferred with silver-tipped guard hairs contributing a silvery, lustrous appearance.

and created the foundation stock for all authentic Scottish Fold cats. In addition to its unusual ears, the breed is characterized by a softly rounded head, a short, muscular body, and a thick, sometimes marbled short-haired coat, which is dense and resilient. The Scottish Fold comes in a wide variety of colors and color patterns similar to those of the American Shorthair.

SCOTTISH FOLD

One of the more recent mutations, this breed was developed from Scottish cats after its unusual ear formation first appeared. The cats' ears are folded forward and downward on the head. The first such cat was a white female named Susie, discovered in a litter of normal-eared kittens by William and Mollie Ross in 1961 at a farm near Dundee, Scotland. The Rosses were given one of two folded-eared kittens from Susie's first litter. They bred her to a normal-eared male

SIAMESE

It is impossible to single out the wild or natural species from which this breed is descended. However, many consider it to be a natural breed. The true origin of the Siamese is Asian, possibly from Siam or Burma. Legends indicate the Siamese originated in Siam as prized possessions of ancient kings and priests of Siam and were trained to guard the royal palaces and temples. The first cats exported from Asia

sailed from Bangkok to London in the latter part of the nineteenth century. Shortly afterwards they reached American shores where, by the turn of the century, they began to appear in cat shows. Second only to the unpedigreed house cat, the Siamese is considered to be the most popular cat breed in America. Their brilliant blue eyes and "pointed" (darker) facial mask, ears, tail, and legs have earned them the great favor they enjoy. Once stocky and round-headed, they have been meticulously bred to create the sleek, elegant cats seen at today's cat shows. Siamese cross-breeding has resulted in many of the currently popular breeds, such as the Balinese, Havana Brown, Himalayan, and Tonkinese. The ideal Siamese is a medium-sized, svelte, refined cat, with long tapering lines and a tubular body that is muscular but lithe. The head must be a tapering wedge with a long and straight nose that is a continuation of the forehead with no break. The Siamese possesses a short, fine-textured, glossy coat that lies close to the body. Siamese cats are accepted by CFA in only four classic colors: the Seal Point, with seal-brown, almost black points and a fawn-colored body; the Blue Point, with deep silver or slate-blue points and a grayish body; the Lilac Point, with pinkish-gray points and a glacial white body; and the Chocolate Point, with milk-chocolate points and a pale ivory body. The crossed eyes, kinked tails, and round heads of the past are regarded as flaws in today's show ring, though some fanciers prefer round heads.

Considered a natural breed, the Singapura was imported into the United States in 1975 from Singapore. This rare breed was accepted for CFA registration in 1982 and for championship competition in 1988. It is a small cat bearing a ticked coat pattern similar to that of the Abyssinian. Both breeds resemble a miniature cougar. All other characteristics of the Singapura are different from those of the Abyssinian. Its coat standard requires that barring be present on the inner front legs and back knees. The body should be small to medium-sized, moderately stocky and muscular. The coat should be fine, very short, lying very close to the body. Singapura color must be dark brown ticking on a warm, ivory ground color. Muzzle, chin, chest, and underside should be the color of unbleached muslin. Each hair must have at least two bands of dark ticking separated by light bands.

SNOWSHOE

The Snowshoe is a hybrid cross of Siamese and an American Shorthair bicolor. The origin of this breed can be traced to Dorothy Hinds Daugherty of Philadelphia, Pennsylvania, in the late 1960s. Her two Siamese cats produced three females with unique, striking bicolored points. Because of their white feet, they were given the name Snowshoes. As a result of promotional efforts in the late 1970s, the Snowshoe has grown in popularity throughout the United States and was advanced to CFF championship status in May 1983. The breed standard calls for a medium-sized, Himalayan-patterned cat, with white feet and a white muzzle. The point color may be either blue or seal, with a light-shaded body color. The white markings

SINGAPURA

should go up to the ankle on the forelimbs and up to the hock on the hindlimbs. The coat should be medium-coarse, short, glossy, and lying close to the body.

SPHYNX

The Sphynx is the result of spontaneous mutations appearing in several types of cats. After many years and various attempts to stabilize it in breeding programs, it was accepted for championship competition by The International Cat Association (TICA). It is basically a hairless cat with very large ears set evenly on the head. It has a semiforeign body type, which appears as a combination of the Devon Rex and the Cornish Rex. The body should be dense, bulky, and heavy, with surprising weight for its appearance. Although not fat, the cat should give the impression that it has just eaten a full meal. The shoulders must be well developed and strong with the elbows turning out slightly, as on the bulldog. There are few or no whiskers showing on the muzzle. There is no coat, only warm skin with a smooth, soft feel. Small amounts of hair are allowable on the bridge of the

nose, behind the ears, on the feet, and on the upper part of the tail. The Sphynx is allowed in all colors and coat patterns that appear as skin pigmentation rather than hair.

TONKINESE

The Tonkinese is a hybrid breed. It was achieved by crossing a Siamese to a Burmese. It was first accepted by the Canadian Cat Association (CCA) in 1978, although the breed has been experimented with since the 1950s. The breed was accepted by various other cat associations in the mid-1970s and was approved for registration by CFA in 1978. It was accepted for CFA championship competition in 1984 and never fails to attract attention at cat shows. The Tonkinese body is medium in length, striking a balance between the foreign type and the cobby, compact body type. Its coat is medium-short in length, close-lying, fine, soft, and silky, with a lustrous sheen. Its most outstanding feature is its coat color. Unlike that of the Siamese, the Tonkinese's point color does not contrast sharply with its ground coat color. The Tonkinese ground coat is always a dilution (lighter shade) of the same, darker point color. Tonkinese colors are Natural Mink (medium brown body and dark brown points), Champagne Mink (buff-cream body and medium brown points), Blue Mink (soft, blue-gray body and slate blue points), Honey Mink (golden-cream body and light to medium, ruddy brown points), and Platinum Mink (pale, silvery gray body with pewter-gray points).

Pediatrics

The smallest feline is a masterpiece.

—Leonardo da Vinci

Kittens and Disorders

PLANNING FOR KITTENS

Producing normal healthy kittens begins many months before the expected breeding time. Cats are seasonally polyestrous, and although some breeds and some individuals may cycle all year, the majority do not. In the northeastern United States, breeding activity usually begins in January or February and continues in cycles lasting anywhere from twelve to twenty-two days. By September, virtually all females will stop cycling until the following February. Most females will have their first litter between twelve and twenty-four months of age. (*See* Chapter 9: Reproductive Physiology.) Before the breeding season commences, all breeding queens should be well exercised, free of intestinal parasites, and up to date on their appropriate immunizations. They should be fully nourished and in a relative state of "gain."

The social hierarchy of the cat world must be catered to in planning and carrying out the actual breedings. At least four matings with the male are desirable. Queens ovulate only after copulation. Pregnancy often can be diagnosed by careful abdominal palpation about seventeen to twenty-five days into gestation; radiographs (X rays) are diagnostic at forty to forty-five days.

A pregnant queen should not be overfed. If she is usually housed with many other cats, she should be isolated for the final six weeks of pregnancy. A queen can experience a false pregnancy, or can resorb fetuses, especially if she is old, if she feels overcrowded or disturbed, is unable to make a nest, or if a strange male is present. In extreme situations she may abort and ingest her fetuses.

A nest box should be provided for the queen. If she feels secure, "queening" is generally a swift and easy process. The first kitten usually appears within an hour of the onset of labor; the entire litter may be delivered within twenty-five minutes to four to six hours. A dark vaginal discharge indicates placental separation; this only persists for two or three days after delivery, unless there is a problem. Once labor has commenced, the queen should not be disturbed except to check

occasionally that all is well. (*See* Chapter 11: Pregnancy and Parturition.)

NEWBORN KITTENS

The new family should be left alone in warmth, quiet, and solitude. Constant crying, kittens squirming around the nest box, and restlessness of the queen are signs of trouble. Young kittens have a normal rectal temperature of 92°–96°F during the first few days. By one week it is usually up to 98°F (when the kittens develop the ability to shiver). Umbilical cords drop off at two to three days and eyes open at around six to twelve days. (*See* Chapter 4: Feline Behavior.)

Female kittens weigh in at about 100 grams (3.5 ounces) and gain approximately 15 grams (over half an ounce) per day. Thus, they will double their birth weight by seven days and triple it by twenty-one days (males gaining even faster). Large quantities of breast milk are needed, and this is stressful for the lactating mother. If a supplemental food source (e.g., milk replacer) can be provided by three weeks of age, it will lessen the need for milk production and may shorten the time to weaning.

CARING FOR ORPHAN KITTENS

It is possible to encounter neonatal or young kittens with no queen to nurse them or care for them. If a breeding queen dies after giving birth, rejects her offspring, is unable to feed all of her young, or has a mammary disorder such as mastitis, human intervention becomes necessary if the kittens are to survive. The task of "substitute queen" requires meticulous attention to details and accurate record-keeping. A simple logbook will track the progress of each kitten and provide helpful data if one begins to fail.

Kittens should be weighed at birth on a gram scale (newborns usually weigh between 90–110 grams [3.15–3.85 ounces]), and then on a daily basis for the first two weeks. When properly fed, they will usually double their weight within the first week. In addition to food, warmth is essential to the well-being of newborn kittens. A consistent environmental temperature of 90–94°F is recommended for the first two weeks, then 75–80°F for the third week. A temporary incubator, using a standard household sixty-watt bulb placed approximately two and a half feet above the kittens, will maintain the desired temperature.

When the queen licks her kittens, she is not only cleaning them but also stimulating them to urinate and defecate. Massaging or stroking the kitten's anal area with a warm, damp cotton ball will provide the same stimuli. Continue the massages for three weeks or until the kittens are capable of urinating or defecating on their own.

Milk Substitutes

COW'S MILK. Cow's milk is sometimes erroneously thought to be a substitute for queen's milk. However, analysis of cow's milk shows that the calcium-to-phosphorus ratio and lactose levels are too high, and the energy, protein, and fat levels are too low to sustain a growing kitten. Adding egg yolk (enriched cow's milk) increases the protein and fat to more reasonable levels, but the calcium level remains four times greater and the phosphorous level two times greater than those of queen's milk. Enriched milk is an unsuitable substitute for the long term, though it can be used temporarily until a more appropriate milk replacer is obtained.

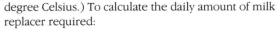

HUMAN BABY FORMULA. When commercial, human baby formula is made up at twice the recommended concentration, it can be used on a short-term basis for kittens. The percentage of nutrients in baby formulas is similar to that of cow's milk, except that the lactose level is lower. However, baby formula provides less than 50 percent of the protein and fat that growing kittens require.

COMMERCIAL FELINE FORMULAS. The best substitutes are commercial products such as KMR (PetAg, Inc.), Havolac (Haver Co.), or Veta-Lac (Vet-A-Mix, Inc.), which have been specifically formulated to closely match the nutrients found in queen's milk.

Feeding

Obviously, intake is limited by the size of the stomach. Also, excessive fluid intake must be avoided because a newborn kitten's kidneys are functionally immature and have a very limited capacity. Numerous feedings throughout the day, usually every four hours, will prevent overloading the digestive system and kidneys. The number of feedings can be decreased, and the intake per feeding can be increased accordingly, as the kitten matures.

The daily intake of food is based on the kitten's energy requirement. According to one study, kittens need 380 kilocalories per kilogram at birth and by four weeks of age only 250 kilocalories per kilogram. (A kilogram is 1000 grams, or 2.2 pounds. A kilocalorie, a term often shortened to calorie by the nonscientific community is the amount of heat required to raise the temperature of one kilogram of water one

degree Celsius.) To calculate the daily amount of milk replacer required:

1. Divide the kitten's weight in grams by 1000 to determine the weight in kilograms.
2. Multiply the answer from Step 1 by 380 (kilocalories). The result provides you with the daily number of kilocalories needed to sustain the newborn kitten.
3. Find the caloric value of the formula on the label. Divide the amount needed by the kitten by the caloric value of the milk replacer. Multiply the answer by the quantity of formula (in milliliters) that supplies the specified caloric value.
4. Take the total for the day and divide it by the number of feedings per day.

EXAMPLE

Kitten's weight: 100 grams (3.5 ounces)
Formula's caloric value: 88.5 kilocalories/100 milliliters (3.4 ounces)
Step 1: 100 grams ÷ 1000 = 0.1 kilogram (kg.)
Step 2: 0.1 kg. × 380 kcal. = 38.0 kcal. needed per day
Step 3: 38 ÷ 88.5 = 0.43
0.43 × 100 ml. = 43 ml. formula needed per day
Step 4: 43 ÷ 6 (feedings per day) = 7.1 ml. per feeding (2⅓ teaspoons)

Some milk replacers provide a feeding chart, which eliminates the need to do any calculations. If KMR is used, do not exceed five milliliters (1 teaspoon) of formula per feeding of newborn kittens for the first week. Thereafter, slowly increase the amount per feeding.

Formula should not be fed to a weak and hypothermic kitten. Instead, a dilute (5 percent) dextrose solution (sugar water) and lactated Ringer's solution (a sterile, salt-water solution for injection) should be given orally as directed by a veterinarian. Also, the kitten's body temperature should be gradually increased in a warm environment (85°–90°F). Formula can be fed after the kitten's rectal temperature is over 90°F.

When preparing formula, make up only enough for a forty-eight-hour period and divide it into individual feeding portions. These portions can be stored in the refrigerator. Before feeding, warm the formula to about 100°F. While warming the formula, sterilize the feeding utensils in boiling water for fifteen minutes to destroy harmful bacteria or viruses. All handlers should wash their hands before feeding or handling the kitten(s).

Kittens that did not receive colostrum (first milk) should be vaccinated against rhinotracheitis, calicivirus, and panleukopenia at four weeks of age.

Special animal-feeding bottles are available at various pet stores. These bottles have been designed to meet the needs of nursing kittens. Yet sometimes the nipple openings are too small. So, if the liquid doesn't drip slowly from the nipple, enlarge the hole slightly. Never force formula by squeezing the bottle while the nipple is in the kitten's mouth. The liquid may be aspirated (inhaled into the lungs), causing aspiration pneumonia, which could be fatal. A medicine dropper can also be used, though the volume will be greatly reduced, making feedings more tedious and time-consuming.

The kitten should be fed in an upright position to help it avoid aspirating any fluid into its lungs. Bottle-fed kittens must be burped after feeding because of the air they inhale during feeding. Stomach-tube feeding eliminates this step; however, other problems are associated with tube feeding.

The greatest danger in tube feeding is choking by directly dispensing fluid into the lungs. Despite the drawbacks, tube feeding is considered the most reliable method for feeding kittens unable to suckle or that need immediate nourishment. Tube-fed kittens should be housed in separate compartments to prevent them from sucking on each other's tails, ears, feet, et cetera.

A small catheter (premature infant size or 5 French) and syringe work well for tube feeding. The catheter can be purchased in most drugstores and the syringe can be obtained from a veterinarian. Before passing the tube down the kitten's esophagus, carefully mark the tube for the proper length. This is done by measuring the tube from the last rib, behind which the stomach is located, to the opening of the mouth. Tape can be used to mark the section of catheter that reaches to the mouth. This mark indicates the point at which the tube reaches the correct position in the kitten's stomach. Lubricate the tube with warm water or formula before inserting it into the kitten's throat. While the kitten is in an upright position, with its head tilted slightly up, insert the tube along the roof of the mouth. If the kitten begins to gag or you feel resistance, remove the tube and try again. Continue to pass the tube until you reach the mark on the tube. Then slowly administer the formula over a two-minute period. Each week remeasure the tube from the last rib to the tip of the mouth; the length will increase as the kitten grows.

A kitten has received an adequate supply of food when its abdomen feels full, but not distended. Within three weeks kittens can learn to drink fluid from a dish. The weaning process can be started when kittens are three to four weeks old by adding small amounts of commercial cat food to the formula.

Feeding problems usually encountered by inexperienced handlers are overfeeding or underfeeding. A sure sign of overfeeding is diarrhea. The intensity of the problem is indicated by the color and consistency of the stool. The color can range from yellowish to grayish. A grayish diarrheic stool indicates a more severe problem, and may signal impending dehydration. Failure to gain weight, excessive crying, listlessness, and shivering occur when a kitten is underfed.

The best criteria by which to determine if the kitten is being properly fed are a steady weight gain of ten grams or one-third of an ounce per day and a normal stool (firm and yellowish). The number of stools usually approximates the number of feedings per day.

WEANING KITTENS FROM BREAST MILK

See "Kittens," Chapter 7: Feeding Cats.

KITTEN DISEASES AND MORTALITY

The overall mortality of kittens, up to one year of age, averages 24–30 percent, including stillborns at 10 percent and malformations at 6 percent. Of those dying, 6 percent die in the first 24 hours; 8 percent die between 1–7 days; 5 percent die between 7–42 days; 4 percent die between 42–180 days; 1 percent die between 180–360 days. The most common causes are: fading kitten syndrome; kitten mortality complex; bacterial infections; parasitisms; and other infectious diseases.

Kitten Mortality Complex

During 1977 and 1978, many cat breeders and their veterinarians consulted the Cornell Feline Health Center to report alarming reproductive failure in queens, and kitten mortality. These and other second-hand reports were strikingly similar. Everyone's story was the same: convincing evidence that a specific disease complex, termed *kitten mortality complex* (KMC), was occurring throughout the country. Kitten mortality rates in certain extensively studied catteries ranged from 40 to 80 percent during peak periods of kitten loss. Apparently a new disease existed whose etiology was and still is unknown.

KMC is characterized by three main problems: reproductive failure, kitten mortality, and various diseases in the queen. Reproductive failures include lack of conception (evidenced by repeated breedings), fetal resorption (disintegration of the fetus within the uterus) between four and six weeks of gestation, abortion (usually during the last two weeks), stillbirths, and congenital malformations. These malfor-

mations have included skull defects (open-top fontanelles), cleft palates, "open stomach," heart defects, and *atresia ani* (incomplete extension of the colon to the anus).

Kitten mortality is usually manifested by the *fading kitten syndrome,* wherein kittens either are born weak and die within a few hours or appear healthy and then become depressed and anorectic (having no appetite), eventually dying of starvation or secondary bacterial infections. Perhaps the most dramatic expression of kitten mortality is in acute congestive cardiomyopathy (heart failure). These kittens suddenly are unable to breathe, become cyanotic (bluish discoloration of the skin due to reduced hemoglobin in the blood), and die within a few hours. Postmortem and histologic (microscopic study of tissues) examinations reveal hugely dilated and thin-walled hearts with acute muscle fiber degeneration, usually accompanied by fluid-filled thoracic (chest) cavities and lungs. A small percentage of kitten mortality is due to *feline infectious peritonitis* (FIP). (*See* Chapter 29: Viral Diseases.)

In the queens, respiratory disease and uterine infections, such as endometritis (inflammation of the mucous-membrane lining of the uterus) or pyometra (pus within the uterus), are both common and highly consistent findings in the catteries experiencing KMC. (*See* Chapter 12: Reproductive Disorders.) The respiratory disease is usually chronic and mild, involving the upper respiratory tract, with sneezing as its most common sign. Watery ocular and nasal discharges may also occur, and the cat seldom becomes seriously ill. Many queens (up to 40 percent of the queens in some catteries) have vaginal discharges; further examination usually reveals endometritis or pyometra. Other reported problems include queens and older kittens with intermittent and usually low-grade fevers, acute congestive cardiomyopathy, and cardiovascular disease.

Although the exact cause of KMC is not known, many feline viruses can cause reproductive failure, fetal malformations, neonatal kitten death, and various other diseases in the adult such as *feline viral rhinotracheitis* (FVR). (*See* Chapter 24: Respiratory System and Disorders.) Most catteries affected by KMC routinely vaccinate against FVR, *feline panleukopenia virus* (FPV), and *feline calicivirus* (FCV). It must be remembered that kittens should be vaccinated twice, preferably at eight and twelve to fourteen weeks of age, to provide full protective immunity. Although most catteries experiencing KMC have been found negative for *feline leukemia virus* (FeLV), any cattery having reproductive and kitten-mortality problems should be FeLV-tested. If cats are found to be positive, a proper course of action must be quickly followed either to isolate or to eliminate the FeLV-positive animals. Many other factors, such as uterine bacterial infections, taurine deficiency, toxoplasmosis, genetic factors, toxic chemicals, and nutrition, also may play a role in this disease complex.

Many, if not all, catteries have some cats that are feline infectious peritonitis (FIP) antibody–positive, and therefore FIP virus has been incriminated as the etiologic agent of KMC. Research has involved studying the transmission of FIP virus from queens to their kittens, particularly to determine whether or not the virus can be transmitted *in utero* to the developing fetus. If it can be transmitted, this would be strong evidence that FIP virus is somehow involved in KMC. At the present time, the relationship between the virus and KMC is not completely understood. It is also important to note that the great majority of catteries have FIP antibody–positive cats, both those which are experiencing KMC and those which have had no problems whatsoever.

Based on the number of cases of KMC reported to the Cornell Feline Health Center, KMC seems to have peaked in incidence in 1978. There are catteries that still experience these same reproductive and kitten-mortality problems, and we continue to receive reports of new cases of KMC in previously unaffected catteries. However, KMC seems to have run its course for the most part. In the absence of any cures for KMC, this may offer some reassurance for cat breeders. In the meantime, the Cornell Feline Health Center continues to explore this extremely frustrating disease.

Omphalophlebitis (Navel Ill)

Bacterial infection of the veins of the umbilical cord stump (*omphalophlebitis,* or *navel ill*) can result from trauma to the cord or from insufficient care by the queen. Signs include a darkening of the skin around the umbilical stump, sometimes with the active production of an odorous pus. Thorough cleansing of the stump with an antiseptic solution is recommended. The attending veterinarian may also prescribe an antibiotic, especially if secondary signs (fever, malaise, inappetence) resulting from systemic spread of the causative bacteria, are evident.

Toxic Milk Syndrome

Mastitis (mammary gland inflammation) in queens can be the result of infection with any of a number of bacteria, but streptococci and staphylococci are the most prominent. Affected animals become febrile and may refuse food; infected glands appear red, swollen, and painful. (*See* Chapter 12: Reproductive Disorders.) Kittens nursing infected glands may become infected themselves, manifesting signs such as fever, lethargy, depression, bloating, and diarrhea. Such kittens should be removed from the queen and fed on another nursing queen or given milk replacer. Veterinary attention should be sought immediately. Antibiotics may need to be given to the kittens, as well as to their mother. In addition, surgical drainage procedures may be necessary to reduce swelling in the affected glands, especially if an abscess has developed.

Skin Diseases

Young kittens are susceptible to a number of skin problems, including mange and ringworm (*see* Chapter 17: Skin and Disorders), flea infestation (*see* Chapter 19: External Parasites), and bacterial dermatitis.

The latter condition, caused by various bacteria, occurs on the head, belly, and chest of kittens. It consists of a pustular (pimply) reddening of the skin. The condition is thought to be caused by overzealous licking and biting by the mother. Antibiotic therapy, either topical or systemic, may be advised by the veterinarian.

Hemolytic Disease of the Newborn

This is a relatively rare condition in cats. Antibodies in the queen's colostrum destroy the kitten's red blood cells, resulting in a profound anemia. The effect is usually seen within one or two days of birth and can be rapidly fatal. Severe depression, jaundice (yellowing of the mucous membranes), and respiratory difficulty may be seen. Kittens suspected of having this condition require immediate veterinary attention; the prognosis is guarded to poor.

Contagious Streptococcal Lymphadenitis (Strangles)

This bacterial disease, caused by steptococci, is occasionally seen in young kittens. Clinical signs include swelling of the lymph nodes of the head and neck with more generalized signs of fever, malaise, and inappetence (resulting from spread of the causative bacteria). Treatment involves the use of antibiotics and, if needed, surgical drainage of abscessed lymph nodes. The prognosis is guarded.

Viral Diseases

Young kittens are susceptible to a number of virus infections, some of which (panleukopenia, feline leukemia virus) are contracted *in utero*. Panleukopenia acquired before birth or just after birth can produce changes in the cerebellum (portion of the brain concerned with motor function, balance, and coordination), intestinal tract, and bone marrow. Affected kittens may have lowered resistance to other infections, diarrhea, and a wobbly walk. Feline leukemia virus infection can produce so-called "fading kittens," or other signs. Young kittens also are susceptible to infection with respiratory disease agents (herpesvirus [Rhinotracheitis], calicivirus, and the bacterial agent *Chlamydia*), which can produce signs ranging from mild conjunctivitis (inflammation of the eyelids) to life-threatening pneumonia. (*See* Chapter 29: Viral Diseases, and Chapter 24: Respiratory System and Disorders.)

Parasitic Diseases

Acute *toxoplasmosis,* a disease caused by the protozoan parasite *Toxoplasma gondii,* may occur in young kittens, producing a rapidly fatal illness. Cats are the natural hosts for *Toxoplasma gondii* and, in most cases, are resistant to its disease-producing effects. Under certain conditions, however, the parasite can cause fever, pneumonia, diarrhea, depression, and neurologic abnormalities. The prognosis is very poor in such cases. (*See* Chapter 31: Internal Parasites.)

There are other parasites that more frequently cause disease in young kittens such as roundworms, coccidia, and *Giardia.* These are much more common problems than toxoplasmosis and, in general, are much easier for the veterinarian to treat. (*See* Chapter 31: Internal Parasites.)

KITTEN BEHAVIOR

See "Critical Social Development Periods in Kittens," Chapter 4: Feline Behavior.

Feline Behavior

We should be careful to get out of an experience only the wisdom that is in it—and stop there: lest we be like the cat that sits down on a hot stove-lid. She will never sit down on a hot stove-lid again—and that is well; but also she will never sit down on a cold one anymore.

—Mark Twain, *Following the Equator*

Feline Behavior

Cats make excellent pets. Despite the feline reputation for aloofness and independence, many owners can attest to the mutual strength of the human/companion-cat bond. An understanding of cats, their origins, and their natural behavior can help deepen our appreciation of our pets. When feline misbehaviors threaten to rupture the bond between owner and cat, application of our knowledge of cat behavior can help stabilize the relationship.

DOMESTICATION OF THE CAT

We will never really be certain how cats became domesticated. The available archaeological evidence indicates that cats began residing with humans approximately six thousand to ten thousand years ago. The cat from which the domestic cat originated is believed to be the North African wild cat, *Felis libyca* (also known as *Felis sylvestris-libyca* and *Felis catus libyca*). Those cats that deigned to share their

territory with people may have done so because the humans' caches of food attracted rodents, a favorite feline prey. Cats probably chose to live with humans, rather than being captured and deliberately tamed as dogs and other farm animals were; humans may have tolerated the cats' presence because of their value as rodent killers. Perhaps for these reasons there has been much less selective breeding of cats than of other domesticated animals. One need only compare the differences between Pomeranians and Great Danes, or between Clydesdale horses and Shetland ponies, to appreciate clearly how little the feline anatomy has been altered. In fact, there was little selective breeding of cats until just a few hundred years ago.

Behavior can also be modified by selection. The most significant behavioral change resulting from domestication of cats is the species' greater tolerance of human contact. This aspect of behavior can also be strongly influenced by experience.

Once cats were accepted by humans (and vice versa), they soon spread from their home in North Africa to the remainder of the world. Crossing the vast ocean distances aboard sailing vessels, cats became valued members of the crew by killing rats and mice and thus protecting the cargo and ship's supplies. Today, cats can be found on every continent except Antarctica.

SOCIAL BEHAVIOR AND ORGANIZATION

Cats are fairly fluid in the organization of their social structure. In a rural setting, cats have territories that can be as large as three acres per female or thirty acres per male. In cities, densities can be as high as ten cats per acre. In general, the dominant tom's territory encompasses the females' territories. Although he will not hunt on the females' territories, he will repel other males. Cats may share a general "core area," but most of their hunting and other activity takes place within exclusive territorial boundaries. Repeated use of territory—and presumably repeated marking of territory—is necessary to maintain this exclusiveness.

Cats characteristically display brief bursts of activity (one to two hours' total activity, distributed over twenty-four hours), and are more active during the day than at night. Caged cats spend ten hours per day sleeping. Ordinary sleep lasts three times longer than dream sleep. To date, no one has investigated the sleeping and activity patterns of house cats.

Farm cats spend approximately 40 percent of their time asleep, mostly during the night. The rest of the farm cat's time is variably divided into resting (22 percent), hunting (14 percent, though this will vary from cat to cat), grooming (15 percent), traveling (35 percent), and feeding (2 percent). Urban cats are most frequently seen—and presumably most active—at night, between the onset of darkness and dawn.

Aggression

SOCIAL AGGRESSION. When two cats approach each other with aggressive intent, they walk on tiptoe, slowly lashing their tails about their hocks, turning their heads from side to side, and making direct eye contact. These threatening gestures may be sufficient to intimidate the subordinate cat, so that it slinks off. Evenly matched rivals, however, will continue to approach. They will walk slightly past one another, and then one cat will suddenly spring, seeking a grip at the nape of the opponent's neck. The latter cat immediately throws itself on its back for protection. The two adversaries will lie on the ground, belly to belly, as they claw, yowl, and bite at each other. After a few moments, one cat, usually the initial attacker, jumps free. The other cat may adopt a defensive posture, attack, or run away. The victor usually pursues the vanquished.

When placed together in a home or a laboratory or on a farm, cats—essentially a solitary species—form dominance hierarchies. Aggressive activity may persist, however. Cats may "divide up" a house: one's territory may encompass the first floor, the other's territory the second floor. Roommates—of the human variety, that is—may find that the two cats belonging to one person will gang up on the single cat belonging to the other. Urine spraying in the house, especially on vertical surfaces, may be triggered by the introduction of strange new cats.

SEXUAL AND TERRITORIAL AGGRESSION. Aggression directed by one sex partner toward the other is seen most clearly when the tom bites the nape of the female's neck before mounting. He may be testing her, for only a female cat in full estrus would submit to such a bite. Immediately after copulation, the female may turn on the male, hiss, and strike out at him with her claws. Antagonistic interplay among males competing for access to an estrous female has provided inspiration for many a cartoon sequence, while serving as an annoyance to both pet and homeowner.

Cats are considered to be a "nonsocial" species because they do not live in groups as adults. The crowding experienced in an urban setting thus creates many territorial disputes, with fighting among intact males being a very common problem. Many toms are repeatedly presented to the veterinarian for treatment of bite wounds and abscesses, the result of aggressive behaviors. Castration is approximately 90 percent effective in eliminating roaming and fighting, although the disappearance of either roaming or fighting may not necessarily be associated with a decline in the other.

PREDATORY AGGRESSION. The tall posture of the cat engaged in territorial or sexual aggression is to be contrasted with the stalking posture of predatory aggression. The cat on the hunt carries its body as close to the ground as possible. Ever so slowly it steals forward toward its quarry, taking advantage of any natural cover. The closer the stalking cat gets to its prey, the more slowly it advances. Almost inevitably the cat will pause before leaping to attack, only the tip of the tail moving as it lies in wait. Some cats make a chattering sound at the same time. Usually two or three quick bounds separate the stalker from its prey. When attacking a larger animal, cats try to bite the nape of the neck, in order to sever the spinal cord.

Predatory aggression is not easy to elicit in cats that have not been taught to hunt. Kittens raised with a mother that has killed rodents in their presence will kill at their first opportunity; kittens raised alone seldom do. Apparently, kittens learn to direct various innate predatory behavior patterns toward whatever prey their mother gathers for them. She does not allow them simply to eat the prey; she lets the prey go, and then catches it again. If the kittens attempt to catch or eat the prey, the mother will compete with them for it. In this way, the kittens are introduced to hunting behaviors, learning both by observation and participation. The types of prey brought to the kittens by their mother may influence the range of prey species they will seek as adults.

One behavioral characteristic that is distasteful to some humans is the feline propensity for playing with prey, both before and after it is dead. A cat will catch a mouse, then let it go and catch it again. After the mouse is dead, the cat may toss it into the air with its paws and leap upon it. The precise function of this behavior is unknown; it may stimulate appetite or, perhaps, reflect a displacement behavior. Truly hungry cats rarely play with their prey; they consume it as soon as it is dead and they have "recuperated" from the predatory effort.

······················

COMMUNICATING

The Voice of the Cat

Cats possess an extensive vocabulary that may not be recognized by every pet owner. Feline vocalizations can be divided into low- and high-volume sounds and strained intensity patterns.

The *purr* is the easiest low-volume feline sound to recognize. Purring is associated with rapid contractions of the muscles of the larynx and the diaphragm.

Purring only occurs in the presence of another cat or person; it may be a submissive signal. Other low-volume calls are the request or greeting call—which can vary from a coax to a command—and the acknowledgment or confirmation call—a short, single murmur with a rapidly falling intonation.

Louder calls are the *demand,* which can also be a begging demand; the *bewilderment cry;* the *complaint;* the milder *mating call;* and the *wail of anger.* The *growl* and *hissing* are signs of defensive aggression. Cats that hiss at one another are frightened, but will attack if avoidance is not possible. The growl may be given by both contestants throughout a cat fight (*caterwauling*). Other intense cries include the *refusal cry,* which is low and discontinuous; *spitting,* an involuntary cry; the *cry of pain;* and the *snarl.* The male *mating cry* may also be intense, and the *two-syllable call* of the estrous female is so characteristic that estrus itself is sometimes referred to as "calling."

Body Language of the Cat

POSTURE. A cat carries its tail high when greeting or investigating, or when frustrated. The tail is depressed and the tip is wagged when the cat is stalking. When the cat is walking or trotting, the tail is held out at a 40° angle to the back, but as the cat's pace increases, the tail is held lower. A relaxed cat usually stands with its tail hanging and its ears pointed forward. When the cat's attention is attracted, the tail is raised and both ears are pointed forward and held erect. Raising of the tail might be considered a greeting signal.

Aggressive Cat. The aggressive cat walks erect on tiptoe with the head down. Because the cat's hind legs are longer than its front legs, it appears to be slanting downward from rump to head. Its tail is held low but arched away from the hocks and the hair begins to stand on end. The ears are held erect and swiveled so that the openings point to the side. Whiskers are rotated forward and claws are protruded.

Frightened Cat. The body language of a frightened cat differs from that of an aggressive cat. The frightened cat crouches, with ears flattened against its head. It salivates and spits. The pupils of the eyes dilate, while the pupils of an aggressive cat constrict. The light-colored iris of the cat's eye makes an especially prominent signal of mood. The eyes of a frightened or excited cat appear red, because the retinal vessels can be seen through the dilated pupils. Contrary to popular belief, the body language and expression of the traditional "Halloween cat" indicate fear as well as aggression; the hissing cat with arched back, erect tail, flattened ears, and hair standing on end corresponds to the fear-biting dog. Such a cat is fearful, but will demonstrate aggression if its "critical distance" is invaded. One clue to the frightened cat's emotions is that the hind feet appear to be advancing

while the front feet retreat; the paws are gathered close together under the body.

GAPE, OR FLEHMEN. Adult cats exhibit a unique behavior and facial expression, the gape or Flehmen, at the odor of foreign cat urine. The components of the behavior are the approach, sniffing and licking of the urine, flicking the tip of the tongue repeatedly against the palate behind the upper incisor teeth, withdrawing the head from the urine, and opening the mouth and licking the nose. This gape response is not seen in kittens less than five weeks of age, but can be elicited by the age of seven weeks. The response serves to transfer urine to the vomeronasal organ, which is a sense organ located between the mouth and nasal cavity above the hard palate. Cats probably use this organ to identify the sex of the urine donor.

Perception

In order to understand how cats communicate we need to know what they can perceive.

SMELL. Smell is a very important means of feline communication. The most common method of signaling involves scent marking with urine, anal sac secretions, or skin gland secretions.

Urine Marking. Male cats scent-mark by spraying urine. Cats defend only a small home range; spraying by tomcats is a means of marking that territory and of suppressing the sexual behavior of other young toms. This normal behavior can be a significant problem for pet owners.

Anal Secretions. Cats are well known for the fastidious covering of their feces; however, cats do use anal sac odors for communication. Two strange cats investigating each other spend a considerable amount of time circling one another, attempting to smell in the perianal area. If the cats are not overly antagonistic, they will eventually permit each other to smell.

Skin Secretions. Bunting behavior (rubbing the side of the head against an object or person) may also be a form of feline olfactory communication, in that glandular secretions from the cat's face are deposited on the object being bunted. When a cat twines itself around the leg of a chair or a person, it is also transferring odors, in this case from tail glands, the same glands that become infected in the syndrome *stud*

tail, a dermatitis of the tail. (*See* Chapter 17: Skin and Disorders.)

VISUAL ACUITY. Communication in cats depends on their ability to perceive messages. A reflective layer within the eye, the *tapetum,* functions to intensify any incoming light. Cats can discriminate illumination at one-fifth the light threshold of humans, but their *resolving power* (ability to distinguish two points from one) is only one-tenth that of humans. Siamese cats usually do not have the normal *binocular vision* (ability to focus both eyes on an object) that other cats do. (*See* Chapter 18: Sensory Organs and Disorders.)

A question often put to a behaviorist is whether animals have color vision. Color vision is well developed in fish and primates, but not generally in other mammals. Many mammalian species that have *cones,* the retinal cells involved in color perception, apparently do not normally use them. Cats have two types of cones that should absorb green and blue light; however, it is very difficult to teach cats to discriminate among colors, although they learn other visual discriminations with ease. So, cats do have some sense of color vision, but do not use it often.

AUDITORY ACUITY. In hearing, as in vision, cats appear to perceive more than humans do. The human ear can detect 8.5 octaves, while the feline ear can detect 10. The absolute upper limit of hearing in cats is 60 to 65 kHz (*kilohertz* = kilocycles per second). Thus cats can perceive the ultrasonic calls of rodents as well as of their kittens. Because they can hear ultrasound, ultrasonic rodent repellers could be stressful to cats. But cats, despite their mobile ear structure, can only discriminate between sounds that are at least 5° apart, while humans can distinguish sounds that are only 0.5° apart. When two sounds originate close together in front of a human being, the person is able to hear two separate sounds; a cat in a similar situation cannot. Without their external ears, which funnel sounds down to their eardrums, cats would not be able to hear nearly so well as they do.

MATING BEHAVIOR

Only selected aspects of feline mating behavior will be discussed here. For a full discussion of this subject, *see* Chapter 9: Reproductive Physiology; Chapter 10: Mating; and Chapter 11: Pregnancy and Parturition.

Catnip

The catnip plant *(Nepeta cataria)* elicits estrus-type behaviors, and there has been continued debate as to whether this represents a release of sexual behaviors or whether catnip is simply a nonspecific pleasure-inducer. Estrous behavior is similar—but not identical—to catnip-induced behavior. Catnip also stimulates play-fighting and eating behaviors. Catnip does *not* induce vulvar presentation, vocalization, or foot treading, and cats in estrus do not head-shake as do cats exposed to catnip. In addition, male cats respond to catnip in an identical manner to the female. The body-rolling and head-rubbing behaviors characteristic of both the estrous and catnip-induced states can be induced in males and females by an extract of tomcat urine. *Nepetalactone* (the chief constituent of catnip) may be similar to one of the substances in tomcat urine, to which most cats respond, but to which estrous females may be particularly sensitive.

Nursing

To locate their mother newborn kittens probably sense the heat generated by her, as well as her mobility and responsiveness. Once they are in contact with her, the blind and deaf kittens apparently rely on their sense of smell and, probably to a greater extent, tactile sensations to find the nipple. Generally, most kittens are suckling within an hour or two of birth.

Kittens ambulate by pulling themselves along with their forelimbs and paddling with the weaker hindlimbs. As they crawl forward they turn their heads from side to side. When they encounter the nipple, they pull their heads back and lunge forward with open mouths. Eventually the nipple is secured in the mouth. The position of the mother facilitates the kittens' locating her mammary region.

By the second day, most litters will have established a *teat order* that is usually—but not always—followed. Despite what one might think, the larger kittens do not always acquire the best-producing glands. Once the teat order is established, the kitten can use the presence of its siblings on either side to help guide it to the proper nipple, though sometimes the kittens hinder rather than facilitate each other's progress. Kittens massage the breast with treading motions

of their tiny paws. Treading is one readily recognizable behavior of cats that persists into adult life; presumably it is pleasurable in itself or reflects a pleasurable situation—comfort or security while snugly ensconced within an owner's lap.

The feline nursing period has been divided into three stages. In stage 1 (days 1 to 14), the mother initiates nursing; in stage 2 (days 14 to 21), both mother and kittens initiate nursing; in stage 3 (days 22 to 35), the kittens initiate nursing.

Nursing kittens probably represent a tactile pleasure to the mother at first. However, as kittens grow older and their feeding demands become more persistent, the female develops an approach-avoidance type of behavior toward her kittens; she discourages their attempts to suckle from the third week onward by moving away from them. Another ploy of the mother is to lick the kittens vigorously, thus preventing them from nursing.

Feline "retrieval" behavior is quite different from the canine form. The mother retrieves her kittens in response to auditory, rather than visual, clues. The more a kitten vocalizes, the more apt is the mother to retrieve it. She usually picks the kitten up by the scruff of the neck, though occasionally she grasps the skin at the back of the skull or even the kitten's whole head. Queens are able to lift and even jump several feet while carrying a large kitten. In fact, the peak of kitten-carrying occurs when the offspring are three weeks of age. (Picking other cats up by the scruff is an effective means of establishing dominance, even over an adult cat, probably because the cat is being treated like a kitten.)

Grooming

Grooming plays an important role in feline maternal behavior, as it does in most other species. Mothers lick their kittens frequently. In particular they lick the *perineum* (anogenital area) in order to stimulate the kitten to urinate and defecate. In common with most carnivores, female cats ingest the kittens' urine and feces for several weeks postpartum, thereby keeping the nest clean.

Acceptance of Kittens

At the time of parturition, queens will accept kittens that are not too much older than their own. Maternal behavior persists in cats so that a queen whose kittens were removed at birth will accept a kitten—or even a baby squirrel—weeks later.

CRITICAL SOCIAL DEVELOPMENT PERIODS IN KITTENS

Critical periods of social development have not been as well defined in cats as they have been in dogs, but they undoubtedly exist. A litter of kittens that is born in a cranny inaccessible to humans will hiss, when handled by humans, at two or three weeks of age, whereas another litter from the same mother, if handled daily, will not react fearfully. Handling kittens each day for the first month may improve the kittens' learning ability.

The reaction to weaning varies with the age of the kitten. Kittens weaned at twelve weeks of age do not cry upon separation, even though they have been living on their mother's milk alone. Kittens weaned at six weeks will cry for a day or two. Those weaned at two days and fed by dropper may cry for a week.

A cat that never had the opportunity to play as a kitten will not respond to the appropriate play signals as an adult. Kittens have genetic information adequate to form the neurologic connections in the brain necessary for social behavior; however, the complex connections necessary for play form only if a cat has had the proper play experience during its "sensitive" or "critical" period as a kitten.

Sleep

Sleep in kittens displays a developmental pattern. Although the percentage of time kittens are awake remains constant as kittens mature, the percentage of "dream" or rapid eye movement (REM) sleep decreases, while that of quiet sleep increases. Muscle twitching, which is characteristic of dream sleep, also decreases with age. Also sleep cycles are much shorter in kittens than in adult cats.

Neurological Development

The neurological development of the cat is reflected in the locomotion of the kitten. At first it drags itself by the forelimbs, but later the pushing movement of

the hindlimbs grows stronger. The eyes open at seven days of age (ranging from six to twelve days); orienting responses to auditory stimuli develop a day or two before.

Visual acuity, or the ability to see, improves sixteen-fold between two and ten weeks of age. Adult cats and dogs will respond to a silhouette of their own species as they would to an actual animal. Adult cats apparently are threatened by silhouettes and will exhibit *piloerection* (hair standing up) toward a silhouette on its first presentation. Five-week-old kittens show no piloerection, and six-week-old kittens show very little, but eight-week-old kittens demonstrate the adult response to silhouettes.

Kittens can make ultrasonic vocalizations, which are perceived by the mother. As kittens mature, they become more proficient at finding their way back to their home ground. They also vocalize less when placed on a cold surface (thirty cries per minute at one day of age versus seventeen cries per minute at fifteen days). Once their eyes have opened, the kittens use visual cues to find the nest; prior to that, they use their sense of smell. Very young kittens will become less active and less vocal when placed on a warm rather than cool surface, but this calming effect of thermal stimuli is lost after the first week. Being left alone induces most of the vocalizing (four cries per minute) at three weeks of age; younger and older kittens vocalize less. The response to physical restraint remains unchanged (five cries per minute) throughout development.

Play

Play in kittens is first seen at the beginning of the third week. This is approximately the same time at which the mother begins the process of weaning by repulsing her kittens' attempts to nurse. Play in kittens begins with gentle pawing at one another. As kittens improve their coordination, biting, chasing, and rolling replace simple pawing. One kitten is usually in the belly-up position (lying on its back with all four legs held in a semi-vertical position). Social play increases from four to eleven weeks of age, and then declines relatively rapidly. At first, three or more kittens may play together, but by eight weeks almost all play is between pairs of kittens. A reliable sign of play is the arched back and tail; but a definite "play signal" has not been identified in cats.

PLAY PERIODS. There are usually four play periods a day. Kittens nine weeks of age spend almost an hour a day playing. Most kitten play-bouts begin with a pounce and end with a chase. In between, the kittens frequently face off, hunching forward with tails arched out and down. They may bat at one another. Kittens also assume a vertical stance in play, rearing back on their hind legs, sometimes standing up by extending and stretching the legs. Various exotic leaps are also seen. Kittens are much more apt to paw, rather than bite, at one another (as puppies do). The common occurrence of pouncing, stalking, and chasing behaviors in feline play suggests that this play is rehearsal for hunting. During play-bouts, there may be one chase per minute. Play may occupy 9 percent of the kitten's total time and only 4–9 percent of its energy expenditure, indicating that play may be important but it is not energetically costly.

PREDATORY PLAY. The mother plays an active role in the development of her kittens' predatory behavior. Not only does she attack and eat prey in front of her kittens, but she also vocalizes to attract the kittens' attention to it. These behaviors occur when the kittens are four to eight weeks of age. After that time, the mother defers to the kittens, in that she rarely kills and almost never eats the prey. The kittens are more apt to interact with the prey if the mother has just been interacting with it than if a littermate has, indicating that the mother's influence is greater. Kittens also learn other tasks better from observing their mother than from observing another cat.

There is a marked increase in predatory activity around eight weeks of age. At this time most kittens will kill and eat mice and more of their behavior is directed toward potential prey than toward playing with one another. Once the prey is dead and eaten, the kittens return to playing with one another, indicating that the motivation to play is still present but overridden by the motivation to hunt. By two months of age, those kittens that will be frightened rather than aggressive toward prey (and other cats) can be identified; these kittens are reluctant to explore their surroundings and to relax with humans in a new environment. This is unfortunate, because while some people prefer that their pet does not hunt, and many wish that it should be less aggressive to other cats, almost all owners want their cat to be friendly, even in unfamiliar surroundings.

SEXUAL PLAY. Elements of sexual behavior are not seen in kitten play. Males play more with objects than females do; however, females with male littermates play with objects more than females without male littermates. Because cats are solitary creatures for much of their adult lives, play may be more important for intraspecies socialization in cats than it is in other species.

SOLITARY PLAY. Kittens frequently chase small rolling objects or even a moving string wiggled by an owner. They particularly like to bat at suspended objects, such as window-shade pulls or tassels. Many of the pounces and face-offs of social play may be performed alone by kittens with "imaginary" playmates, a mirror, or their own shadow. Solitary play persists in many adult cats. Playfulness is a factor for which breeders should select, because it enhances the pleasure a cat gives to its owner as well as to itself. Social play may also occur between species. Cats will often play with dogs with which they are familiar. Interspecies play consists mostly of chases by the dog and elaborate pounces by the cat.

DECLINE OF PLAY. Several factors may contribute to the decline of play in kittens. Juvenile and young adult cats, for example, begin to sleep more during the day. Older cats tend to spend more time sitting quietly but alertly. Male kittens show sexual activity by four and a half months of age and will attempt to mount and bite the scruff of females; the females will reject these attempts until they themselves reach sexual maturity a few months later. Young feral cats may also devote more time to finding their own prey.

EATING BEHAVIOR

Defense of Body Weight

Cats gain and lose body weight in cycles of several months' duration. Food intake may decrease when the set point of body weight of the cat falls during a portion of the eating cycle (time when appetite regulates intake to maintain a lower body weight). Loss of appetite and weight loss (several hundred grams [0.5 pound] or more) on the part of the cat may produce distress on the part of the owner, but this loss is normal unless the lack of appetite is persistent or other signs of disease are present.

Cats can eat for calories. For example, they increase their food intake if the water content of their canned cat food is increased. And because cats consume more when their food is diluted with water, their total water intake is increased. This may be advantageous in certain clinical situations where an increase in water consumption is beneficial, such as feline urologic syndrome.

Food intake decreases in hot weather and increases in cold weather; this is a reflection of behavioral thermoregulation. Some spayed cats may become obese, but the low rate of obesity among cats in general is good evidence that this does not occur often. Castration of male cats may also lead to an increase in body-fat content, but this has not been studied thoroughly.

Cats increase their food intake when treated with the hormone *progesterone,* or with *benzodiazepine* tranquilizers (e.g., Valium). Valium often is used clinically to stimulate appetite.

Palatability

Cats are notoriously finicky eaters, which is a reflection of the strong influence of palatability on their food intake. Most cats prefer fish to meat, as is commonly recognized, but they also prefer novel diets to familiar ones. Cat food manufacturers undoubtedly take advantage of both these feline preferences. If a new diet is not more palatable than the usual one, a cat will, after a few days, begin to favor the old familiar food. And one peculiarity of cats (including exotic cats, such as lions) is their indifference to table sugar (sucrose).

Meal Patterns

Cats eat many small meals, as many as twelve per day, when given free access to food, both in the light and in the dark. One might argue that this intake pattern is not natural; a carnivore should eat large meals at infrequent intervals. Yet the caloric intake per meal is approximately equal to that contained in one mouse. A feral cat with good hunting skills might easily catch twelve mice (or three rats) per day. (*See* Chapter 7: Feeding Cats.)

....
INTELLIGENCE OF THE CAT

Everyone wants his or her favorite animal species to be the smartest, and there is no exception where cat owners are concerned. Certainly cats are intelligent; they have been smart enough to identify a species, humans, that will feed them, buy them large bags of kitty litter, and provide them with the best in medical care. They are also intelligent enough to be able to survive on their own in both urban and rural surroundings.

"Objective" tests of intelligence, in which species are compared, are as likely to be biased as are human intelligence tests. For example, jumping an obstacle is easy for a horse, but a cat would be more likely to climb over it. Similarly, a cat would find it much eas-ier to manipulate a string than would a horse or even a dog. Dexterity may be confused with intelligence. Maze-learning is relatively independent of an animal's anatomical constraints, yet cats do not do well under such conditions; in fact, their performance is inferior to that of both dogs and large farm animals. Their memory for which box contains food or which door leads to freedom is better, but still they perform less satisfactorily than dogs.

Learning

Cats learn to "operate" on their environment (a form of learning called *operant conditioning*) in order to escape from puzzle boxes. They can also learn to pull strings to which a piece of food is attached, selecting the string attached to a morsel of meat from among several others. Cats can also be "classically" condi-

tioned, that is, taught to blink or to salivate in response to a tone (conditioned stimulus) paired with an unconditioned natural stimulus (a puff of air in the case of the blink, or the appearance of food in the case of salivation), because they must operate on the environment in order to receive the reward. Neurosis can also be produced in cats by requiring them to discriminate between two very similar stimuli.

Discrimination

The cat's ability to learn discrimination has been used to great advantage by psychophysicists in studying vision. For example, color vision can be studied by teaching cats to discriminate between two symbols, and then to discriminate further between the symbols when they differ in no characteristic except color. Cats can, in fact, make this discrimination—but only after 1,400 trials. As mentioned earlier, cats do have color vision; however, even when brightness is controlled, the color stimulus must be large (a big object) before a cat is able to make any use of the hue.

Rewards

Unlike dogs, cats will not usually perform in order to be reunited with a person; however, cats will perform for food rewards. But feline finickiness can interfere even with the reward value of food. In general, cats will work harder for food rewards if the experimenter is the person who feeds them in their home cages as well as in the learning situation. Kittens will learn more quickly when the reward is freedom to explore a room than when the reward is food.

Problem Solving

Cats are able to form *learning sets,* a skill once thought to be confined to primates. Learning set, or learning to learn, refers to an underlying principle by which a variety of related problems can be solved. For example, cats can learn to solve a problem such as choosing an object on the left when identical black squares are the stimulus, and then learn much more quickly on the next problem to choose the object on the left when white triangles are presented. After four problems the cats' errors fall to 36 percent of the original errors, and only 58 percent of the number of trials originally necessary are needed—thus, they have learned to learn.

Cats seldom show "insightful" behavior; that is, they do not learn to move a lightweight box under a suspended piece of fish in order to reach the fish. Captured feral cats learn discrimination more quickly than do cage-reared cats. These findings indicate that varied environments or experience may lead to an increased learning ability in cats.

Imitation

Learning by observation or imitation occurs in cats. Cats watching another cat press a bar or jump a barrier to obtain food can learn to press the bar or jump the barrier much faster than cats who did not observe a trained animal. Cats can also be misled, however. If cats watch another cat obtain food simply by approaching but not pressing a bar, they will learn to bar-press for food more slowly than nonobserving cats.

Misbehavior

Cats are generally thought of as "problem-free." They are easily housebroken and not especially dangerous, as dogs may be. Cats are often selected as pets because they do not demand as much time or personal involvement as dogs. Often, cat owners are unpleasantly surprised to discover that their feline pet does misbehave.

Feline misbehavior may take several forms. The cat may eliminate (urinate or defecate) in an inappropriate place, scratch the furniture, or be aggressive to another cat or—more rarely —to humans. Less commonly, the cat may be destructive or may meow incessantly. Such behaviors are not abnormal for cats, but they may be disconcerting or expensive for the cat's owner.

Inappropriate elimination is the most common feline behavior problem presented to the Cornell Feline Health Center staff. Other common problems include aggression among cats living in a household and rejection of the tom by an estrous queen. These latter two problems may be related to failure of a cat to adequately socialize as a kitten. Kittens usually are removed from the mother at six weeks of age, long before the peak of playful interactions at eleven weeks. Cats that have remained with other kittens for longer than six weeks may be more tolerant of other cats when adult, including courting toms.

Playful behavior itself can be a behavior problem, particularly if it occurs in the middle of the night. This is most likely to happen when the kitten has been alone, and probably asleep, for most of the day, and thus has had little opportunity to play. Subsequent gentle punishment may inhibit the kitten's play; more likely the kitten will simply move out of range and continue to race about, knocking over objects. A regularly scheduled play period in late evening is the best solution for this problem. Cat toys also help. One solution is to have two kittens. This usually solves the immediate problem, but two cats that play together as kittens may still become incompatible as adults. (*See* "Aggressive Behavior," page 65.)

HOUSE SOILING

Moving to a new home can elicit one of the most common forms of feline misbehavior—house soiling. In a recent survey of cat owners, 24 percent reported that their cats did not use the litter box. Of fifty-nine behavioral cases presented to Cornell University's Small Animal Clinic from 1979 to 1985, thirty-eight involved spraying or inappropriate urination, ten involved inappropriate defecation, and eleven involved both urination and defecation. Interestingly, both sexes were equally represented; however, there were distinct differences in the sexual representation of the problems presented. Under normal circumstances cats are fastidiously clean in their elimination habits, therefore some underlying cause(s) for such misbehavior must exist.

Causes of House Soiling

Feline urologic syndrome (cystitis, urethritis, urethral blockage), commonly referred to as FUS, accounted for a significant number of the cases. Signs associated with FUS include inappropriate urination and passing of bloody urine. The aversion to the litter box results from the association with painful urination or an urgency to urinate. (*See* Chapter 22: Urinary System and Disorders.)

Territorial marking by urine spraying (depositing urine on vertical surfaces) is common in intact male and female cats. The frequency increases with hormonal changes during the breeding season. However, spraying can also occur in neutered cats of either sex. Usually a neutered cat's spraying is associated with conditions of overcrowding and/or aggressive behavior toward other cats.

Moving to a new home, a change in the owner's schedule, or the addition of a new cat, dog, or person to the household may be sufficient to initiate problems. Although these environmental stresses often cannot be altered by the owner, recognizing them can lead to a solution that will compensate for the change in the household routine. Stress may result also from placing the litter box too close to a cat's food and water, since cats do not like to eat in the same area in which they eliminate. Positioning the litter box in a busy kitchen or in a laundry room may be convenient for the owner, but may encourage a sensitive cat to seek a quieter, less congested spot. One owner moved her cats' litter box from the floor to a dresser in order to prevent her dog from getting into the litter. Subsequently, one of the cats stopped using it.

Treatments

Litter Box Hygiene. To reestablish consistent use of the litter box, it should be made as attractive to the cat as possible. Cleanliness and accessibility are essential. The litter box should be cleaned daily. The entire contents should be replaced at least once or twice a week. When rinsing the litter box, vinegar or lemon juice can be used to neutralize any remaining urine

odor, which may be as offensive to the cat as to the owner. Cleaning products containing ammonia should not be used because they will intensify the urine odor. Strongly perfumed products may deter the cat from using the litter box.

Litter Box and Litter. The number of litter boxes should be increased to at least one box per cat, preferably more. This can be of particular benefit in multi-cat households, where one cat may be prevented from using the community litter box by another cat, or where a cat simply prefers not to eliminate in the same area as another. Some owners have observed that their cats will use one box exclusively for defecation and another for urination. Some cats just prefer larger boxes; others prefer to perch on the edge of the box; a box with a platform built around the outside can make these cats more comfortable when using the box. Providing different sizes and types (covered and uncovered) of litter boxes in several locations can be of tremendous help in eliminating bad habits.

If a recent change in litter material has occurred, the material formerly used can be reintroduced in an attempt to thwart soiling. Offering several types of material in the different litter boxes, such as sand or soil, alfalfa pellets, clay (scented and unscented), sawdust, paper, or corncobs, can help bypass an aversion to a specific substance. If a cat has been eliminating on rugs, placing a small section of carpeting in the litter box or attached to the rim may be helpful, since some cats prefer a material other than the plastic interior of a litter box to scratch while making burying

movements. It is important to remember that cats are creatures of habit; relatively minor changes can create confusion. Sight, smell, shape, and, to some degree, color, are daily stimuli that elicit either a positive or negative response from cats.

Retraining. In cases of overcrowding, some cats require more time alone with the owner. The time can include grooming or permitting the cat to sleep on the owner's lap. Such tender loving care or stroking has helped some cats that appear to be sensitive to competition from other cats in the household. Another solution is to decrease the number of cats in the house by finding a new home for one or more of them, or by providing greater access to other parts of the house.

Even after the above steps have been taken, some cats may still require retraining to the litter box. Confinement to a small room or a cage with a litter box can assist in this process. Cats are strongly inhibited from elimination in confined areas because they do not like to soil their sleeping quarters. Once the cat begins to use the litter box consistently again, it may be allowed access to increasingly larger areas of the house.

Placing the litter box on top of a favorite elimination site, and then slowly moving it to a more desirable location, has also been advocated. A different approach involves retraining cats in a manner similar to that used for house-training dogs: after feeding, cats are brought to the litter box and praised for using it.

Punishment can produce a negative response. Physical or harsh vocal punishment can result in a cat's avoidance of its owner. Occasionally, spraying the cat with water or making a loud noise when the cat is caught in the act of soiling has helped to discourage use of a specific spot. However, the usual result of this is that the cat inappropriately eliminates only when

the owner is not present and/or the cat learns to avoid the owner altogether. Other methods are usually more effective.

If a cat is spraying, it is particularly important first to resolve the initiating causes, such as overcrowding or exposure to unaltered tomcats. Because a cat first sniffs an area before actually spraying it, use of an odoriferous repellent may discourage the cat from moistening a wall or drape. However, this may result only in the cat's selecting a new location. Owners are encouraged to have spraying tomcats or queens neutered, thus reducing their natural inclination to mark territory. A tranquilizer (such as Valium) or a synthetic progestin (Ovaban) can be prescribed to reduce spraying. Unfortunately, progestins can have potentially serious systemic side effects. (*See* Chapter 12: Reproductive Disorders.) As a last resort, the cat's sense of smell can be eliminated. This does not affect appetite and can save the life of a cat that would otherwise be euthanatized.

WITHDRAWAL

A change in the cat's environment is not always followed by inappropriate elimination. Another response may be withdrawal from the owner. In one such case, a cat was taken from a suburban setting, where it was free to roam out of doors, and relocated in a high-rise apartment. This cat had always been an affectionate pet, but now ignored the owner for weeks after the move. The owner boarded the cat for two weeks; on its return to the apartment the cat again became affectionate. The stress of boarding may have been responsible for the cat's sudden adaptation to the new, less stressful apartment.

AGGRESSIVE BEHAVIOR

Aggression, reflecting misbehavior of psychological origin, occurs in cats in two major forms: aggression toward humans and aggression toward other cats. Pathological causes can be varied.

Aggression Toward Humans

Aggression directed at humans can be subdivided into *predatory/playful* and *irritable* aggression. The predatory type of aggression is preceded by stalking and pouncing and is usually centered on the feet of a walking person. If a cat is young and has no other kitten with which to play, the aggression probably represents play. In such cases, biting and scratching are usually inhibited. However, if the owners have not reprimanded the cat for biting too hard in play, it may not have learned to inhibit its bite. Playful aggression should be redirected toward swinging toys. The owner may swing a toy from a string and praise the cat verbally for attacking it, but punish the cat for biting at people's feet. The best way to punish the cat is to startle it. Water guns or aerosol water sprays are very effective; even a loud noise, like a whistle, can be used. Punishments such as these are best because the cat does not associate the action with the owner directly. A similar strategy of startling the attacking cat is used for true predatory aggression; toys and rewards are obviously not used.

Irritable aggression is usually manifested while a cat is being stroked. The cat, particularly if it is a male, may display aggression by applying to the stroker's hand the nape-bite of copulation. If a verbal reprimand does not suffice, the cat's nose may be lightly flicked with the thumb and forefinger. The owner should also pet the cat more gently and for shorter periods of time.

Aggression Toward Other Cats

Aggression among cats living in the same household is the most common feline-aggression problem. If a new adult cat is introduced into a household, aggression should be expected; however, aggression can also occur among cats that have lived together peacefully for years. In some cases, a physical change or a change in odor can precipitate the aggression. For example, if one cat has been hospitalized at the veterinary clinic, it may be attacked when it returns, either because it is weak or because it smells strange.

To treat aggression among cats, the animals are first physically segregated in different parts of the house. At feeding time, the cats, together with their food, are placed in separate cat carriers or cages kept at either end of a room. Each day the containers and their contents are moved closer together. As a result each learns that it will be rewarded with food only in the presence of the other. When the cats can eat in their containers side by side, with no hissing or growling, it is safe to place them together again.

A similar method involves feeding the cats on

either side of a solid barrier, such as a door. The door is replaced by a clear plastic barrier. The barrier is then further modified so that visual and olfactory stimuli are added gradually.

Diazepam (Valium, a tranquilizer) has been used by veterinarians to treat aggression in cats, sometimes successfully—most often when fear is the root cause of the aggression. In other cases, aggression may actually be accentuated by diazepam therapy. Progestins (female reproductive hormones) may also modify aggressive behavior.

Because of the relatively common occurrence of inappropriate elimination and aggression among cats in multiple-cat households, prospective cat owners should be advised to have only a single cat. It is only during the cat's developmental play period—from four to eleven weeks of age—that companions are advisable.

Aggression Secondary to Underlying Disease

There can be underlying pathological as well as psychological causes of aggression in cats. *Meningiomas* (tumors of the membrane covering the brain), *feline ischemic syndrome* (constricted or obstructed blood vessels in the brain), *rabies,* and *toxoplasmosis* have all been associated with development of aggressive behavior. Sudden onset of such behavior is generally a poor prognostic sign. The aggression is usually well directed; in one case, for example, a cat with toxoplasmosis attacked dogs, but only when she was with her kittens.

· · · · · · · · · · · · · · · · · ·
DESTRUCTIVE BEHAVIOR

As a general rule, cats develop destructive behavior problems much less frequently than do dogs. Feline destructive behavior appears to fall into three main categories: clawing and scratching, wool-sucking, and plant eating.

Clawing and Scratching

Clawing or scratching misbehavior is believed to represent grooming behavior, because during the process old layers of the claw are loosened and often shed. It may also be a means of marking, greeting, getting attention, and of letting off steam. Whatever

the motivation, it is an undesirable behavior if a plush new sofa or draperies are targeted for a clawing. Many cats are declawed to eliminate the problem, but bad scratching habits can also be prevented from developing in the first place. If kittens are encouraged early on to use a scratching post, they usually will not abuse furniture or wall hangings. A good scratching post should be covered with some loosely woven material —not a firm rug—because the purpose of the post is to allow the cat to hook its claws into the fabric. Because cats scratch most often after awakening, the post should be placed near the cat's usual sleeping quarters. The best teacher for a kitten is its mother, so kittens should be obtained from queens that regularly use a scratching post.

Wool-Chewing

Wool-sucking or wool-chewing is a behavior problem that occurs with greater frequency in Siamese and Burmese cats than in other breeds. It should be differentiated from non-nutritive suckling that many early-weaned kittens display. Wool-chewing may or may not be related to early weaning. Free-ranging feral cats are weaned at approximately six months of age; most domestic kittens are weaned earlier.

Wool-sucking is usually not presented as a clinical problem until a cat is an adult. The behavior is characterized by chewing with the molars on cloth. The material chewed is usually wool, but in the absence of wool the cat may select other materials: synthetics, cotton, and even upholstery. Such cats do not chew on raw wool, preferring knitted or loosely woven fabrics. The behavior is sporadic, but gaping holes in cloth (garments, bedspreads, etc.) can be produced in a matter of minutes.

Wool-chewing seems to be related to feeding, because the behavior can be stimulated by fasting and inhibited by access to plants, bones, or food. There is no evidence of a nutritional deficiency; rather, wool-chewing appears to represent a craving for fiber or indigestible roughage. For this reason, treatment is aimed at supplying plant material that is safe for the cat to eat, and by offering wool, such as an old wool sweater or sock. In order to teach the cat to differentiate between things it is allowed to eat and those it is not, a wool object can be doused with cologne and a solution of hot pepper sauce. The cat will learn to associate the aroma of cologne with the unpleasant pepper taste, and thus avoid objects that smell of the cologne. Then articles of clothing, blankets, and other fabrics can be sprayed with cologne alone to deter the cat. In severe cases, in which the owner is considering euthanasia, feeding a cat a raw chicken wing per day is recommended. Although there is a potential danger to the cat in eating chicken bones, one should keep in mind that many cats kill and eat birds regularly without suffering ill effects.

Plant Eating

Cats often eat grass. This behavior has been observed in free-ranging, prey-killing cats as well as in those eating canned or dry diets. It is not surprising, therefore, that cats may also eat house plants. Plant eating can have serious consequences because many house plants are poisonous. (*See* Chapter 39: Procedures for Life-Threatening Emergencies, for a complete list of poisonous plants.) Regardless of whether the plants or the cat are at risk, the behavior is an undesirable one.

When an owner observes a cat eating a plant, the cat often is punished or frightened away. As a consequence, however, the cat (like the destructive dog) is apt to misbehave in the owner's absence. A better solution is to provide the green plants that the cat apparently needs and desires. Plants that are safe for cats to chew on can be purchased at pet suppliers. While the cat is learning that it is allowed access to one source of greenery, the decorative plants can be moved out of its reach. Later, the cat can be taught to discriminate between the plants it must not eat and those it may. A water gun can be used to punish the cat and aid in the discrimination process, but this practice depends on the presence of the owner; the cat would have to be separated from the plants in the owner's absence. Another method is to spray the leaves of the plant with a hot pepper solution.

ABNORMAL SEXUAL BEHAVIOR

Reluctance of a male to mate with a female is usually the result of the female's being nonreceptive and aggressive toward his advances. Inexperienced males may be especially intimidated by the aggressive responses of a female that is not in heat (nonestrous). In the laboratory, only one tom in three will consistently copulate with fully receptive queens. It is not surprising, therefore, that many visits to the tom may be necessary before successful breeding takes place. Estrous females may indicate a mate preference by actively rebuffing one male or staying near another.

Masturbation occurs in pet cats, including free-roaming, sexually active tomcats and castrated males. Usually a furry toy or shoe is the object chosen to mount. Male cats may mount other males or even kittens.

Modifying Unwanted Male Sexual Behavior

Castration is a widely accepted procedure for modifying sexual behavior in male cats. Prepubescent castration (before six to eight months of age) generally eliminates sexual behavior. Some owners object to a "feminized" male and so delay castration until a cat is twelve or fourteen months old, or after the first serious fight-induced abscess. The effectiveness of castration in eliminating sexual behavior depends on a cat's previous sexual experience. Thus, owners are advised to restrict access of their male cats to females until after surgery, unless they do not mind a pet's continued sexual interests.

Castration seems to be effective in reducing or eliminating fighting, roaming, and spraying. Most cat owners interviewed two years after having their cats castrated reported a rapid or gradual decline in fighting, roaming, and spraying. Ten percent of cats continue to spray, roam, or fight. The failure of surgery to eliminate these behaviors completely in all cats is probably due to the learned components of the behaviors.

ABNORMAL MATERNAL BEHAVIOR

There are few maternal behavior abnormalities in cats; in fact, the efficiency of feline reproduction is a much more pressing problem. Occasionally a queen may reject her litter of kittens, but this happens much less frequently than in other species.

Infanticide

Cannibalism by the queen, although rare, does occur, usually at parturition (birth) or shortly thereafter. An inexperienced queen eating the placenta and umbilical cord just does not know when to stop and accidentally eats the kitten.

Very rarely tomcats have also been known to kill kittens, usually kittens that are not their own.

Mismothering

Cats sometimes care for one another's kittens and will nurse communally. An interesting variation on this occurred in a newly spayed cat that stole the kittens of another cat in the household. The problem was easily solved by shutting the natural mother in a room with the kittens. This case illustrates that maternal behavior is independent of ovarian hormones and may be stimulated by a dramatic decline in estrogen and progesterone levels, which occurs after spaying as well as at parturition.

Because cats learn to socialize almost exclusively as kittens, orphan kittens should probably be placed with the litter of another lactating queen, if possible. The nutritional—but not the social—requirements of orphan kittens will be met if they are artificially fed. (*See* "Caring for Orphan Kittens," Chapter 3: Kittens and Disorders.)

Sometimes older kittens will show sucking abnormalities. They may suck on one another, on a human finger, on cloth, or on wool. Occasionally this behavior can be associated with early weaning, but more commonly there is no immediately obvious explanation. The sucking is usually not injurious to the kittens' health and may gradually diminish with age.

ABNORMALITIES OF INGESTIVE BEHAVIOR

Obesity

Obesity is the result of the most common behavioral problem, overeating. The cause, simply put, is an intake of energy that exceeds output. Therefore, obesity is most often observed in a lethargic animal fed a highly palatable diet. (*See* Chapter 8: Diseases of Dietary Origin.)

Anorexia

A much more difficult clinical problem is *anorexia* (inappetence), which is seen often in cats. Anorexia is most commonly encountered in hospitalized cats or in healthy cats that are placed in a boarding kennel. In a hospital situation, a moderately sick cat may seriously compromise its health by refusing to eat. Although a cat can be maintained by intragastric (tube) feeding, it is far more beneficial to the animal to reinstate voluntary feeding, because food taken orally stimulates gastric and intestinal secretions much more than does food given by stomach tube.

The benzodiazepine tranquilizers, particularly Valium, are often used to stimulate the appetite of an anorexic cat.

Nutrition

Or take a cat, nourish it well with milk
And tender meat, make it a couch of silk,
But let it see a mouse along the wall,
And it abandons milk and meat and all,
And every other dainty in the house,
Such is its appetite to eat a mouse.

—Geoffrey Chaucer, from "The Manciple's Tale," *Canterbury Tales*

Feline Nutritional Requirements

The nutritional needs of cats differ from those of other domestic animal species. It is generally agreed that the domestic cat, *Felis catus,* is most closely related to the African wild cat, *Felis libyca,* and to a lesser degree to the European wild cat, *Felis silvestris.* Domestic cats have evolved with some of the specialized characteristics associated with desert animals, such as the ability to concentrate urine and to conserve water. The relatively short digestive tract of the cat promotes rapid passage of ingesta through the system. Therefore, the cat needs highly digestible foods to supply enough nutrients for growth, reproduction, and maintenance.

Feline metabolism is uniquely adapted to a diet high in protein and fat. Because cats are strict carnivores, their taste preferences differ from those of herbivores (cattle, for example) and omnivores (dogs, humans). Cats prefer a high-protein diet that incorporates certain *amino acids* (nitrogen-containing compounds, the chief structural components of protein) and *peptides* (short chains of amino acids); for this reason, meat extracts (commonly referred to as digests) are appealing to feline taste buds.

Cats adapt rapidly to food availability. The eating habits of many domestic cats have been modified from one meal every twenty-four to forty-eight hours, common in their wild relatives, to as many as eight to sixteen small meals within a twenty-four-hour period. This adaptation is a result of the common feeding practice of making food available to pet cats continuously. A cat's water intake usually coincides with its food intake. Water is a particularly important need when dry cat foods are being consumed.

The cat's normal nutritional needs include proteins, fats, minerals, vitamins, and water. These nutrients are required to build various structural body tissues; to support chemical reactions, such as anabolism (the body's conversion of simple substances to complex compounds) and catabolism (the body's breakdown of complex molecules, such as protein and fat, to simpler compounds); to transport substances in, around, and out of the body; to supply energy for growth, reproduction, and maintenance; and to provide diet palatability. Basic minimum nutritional requirements for cats have been established by the subcommittee on feline nutrition of the National Research Council (NRC). It is these standards that are used by pet food manufacturers for formulating cat foods. (*See* "Eating Behavior," Chapter 4: Feline Behavior.)

PROTEIN

Dietary protein serves as a source of amino acids. Amino acids are used to form various hormones, enzymes, and body secretions, and are the major components of body protein tissue. The metabolism of protein also provides an energy source. Kittens require at least one and a half times more protein than adult cats for growth and development, and adult cats require the proportional equivalent of three to four times the protein required by humans or dogs. The large quantity of ingested protein is used primarily for maintenance rather than for growth. Studies show that diets consisting of 19 percent protein are sufficient, if individual amino acid contents are carefully controlled.

The quality of protein consumed is particularly important. The sources should be a combination of meat, fish, and poultry to avoid the deficiencies incurred from a diet of all red meat, all organ meats, or all tuna fish. All animals need twenty-two different amino acids; however, many of these are synthesized by the body in adequate amounts, so that additional dietary supplementation is not needed. Those amino acids that the body can produce are known as the *nonessential* amino acids. The *essential* amino acids required by cats include arginine, histidine, isoleucine, leucine, lysine, methionine, phenylalanine, taurine, threonine, tryptophan, and valine. Of these, arginine, leucine, threonine, methionine, and taurine appear to be the most critical in practical cat diets.

Arginine

Cats are unable to synthesize arginine from its precursor amino acid, *ornithine*. Arginine is needed for con-

verting ammonia into a less toxic substance, *urea.* When the diet is deficient in arginine, toxic levels of ammonia accumulate in the blood. One study showed that deficient cats can lapse into a coma, after experiencing vomiting, excessive salivation, muscle spasms, *ataxia* (incoordination), *apnea* (cessation of breathing), and *cyanosis* (bluish discoloration of the skin from lack of blood oxygen). These are classic signs of *hyperammonemia* (high levels of ammonia in the blood). While arginine is a critical amino acid in feline diets, it is of little concern, since arginine is present in most proteins used in practical cat diets. It would be a concern if a cat were eating a low-protein, homemade diet composed mainly of cereal proteins.

Leucine

Kittens require more of this amino acid than species such as the dog or pig. The reason for this is not known.

Threonine

A threonine-deficient diet results in neurological problems, evidenced by lameness, incoordination, and loss of balance. These signs can appear as early as the fifth day of feeding a threonine-deficient diet. All signs disappear once the diet contains adequate threonine.

Methionine

The cat's requirement for methionine is much higher than that of other mammals, and it is often the limiting amino acid—that is, the one most likely to be lacking in practical cat diets. It is thought that methionine and cystine together may act, to a limited extent, as precursors for the synthesis of taurine. Studies have shown that methionine is essential for growing kittens as well as for adult cats.

Taurine

Taurine is not further metabolized by the body and is eventually excreted in the urine. Problems arising from taurine deficiency include eye lesions *(central retinal degeneration), dilated cardiomyopathy,* and reduced reproduction in queens and growth in kittens. Total blindness can occur within two years if the condition is not remedied. Recent studies have shown that one form of feline heart disease—dilated cardiomyopathy—will develop when the diet contains inadequate amounts of available taurine. Improvement is often noticeable by the fourth day of supplementation. However, dietary taurine supplementation will only help the specific form of feline heart disease related to the diet deficiency. The canning process appears to influence the dietary taurine requirement. Canned cat foods must contain a higher level of taurine in dry matter than dry foods. As a result, most canned cat foods contain added taurine. Currently 1,000 and 2,500 ppm (parts per million) of taurine are recommended for dry and canned cat foods respectively.

Effects of Food Processing on Amino Acids

Even if the essential amino acids are provided in a diet, it does not necessarily mean that they will be absorbed and utilized by the body. Several factors involved in food processing can render amino acids ineffective. These include excessive heat in the presence of sugars and fats; exposure of proteins to strong alkaline solutions; and oxidization of proteins when stored with polyunsaturated fats.

CARBOHYDRATES

Sugars and starches make up this class of nutrients. Although carbohydrates usually make up about 40 percent of commercial dry diets, they are not a dietary necessity for the cat. Many canned cat foods contain less than 10 percent carbohydrates. Carbohydrates are included in cat foods as a source of energy and to provide structure for the particles of dry cat foods. However, cats can be maintained exclusively on a diet in which the energy source is derived from fat and protein. The protein and fat are then metabolized into glucose and other energy-supplying compounds.

Cats have a relatively high potential for digesting carbohydrates because of the activity of an intestinal enzyme, *disaccharidase.* This enzyme hydrolyzes (splits) disaccharides (a class of compound sugars) into sucrose, lactose, and maltose. *Lactose* (milk sugar) intolerance may occur in mature cats. In such cases there is a deficiency of the enzyme *lactase* (which breaks down lactose), resulting in inadequate digestion of lactose and subsequent diarrhea.

Excess carbohydrate is stored in the body as *glycogen* (animal starch) and fat. The primary side effect of excessive food intake is obesity.

FATS

Dietary fat is a good source of energy for cats. It also supplies essential fatty acids *(linoleic* and *arachidonic acids);* acts as a carrier of fat-soluble vitamins (vitamins A, D, E, and K); and gives palatability to food. Through evolution, cats have lost the ability to desaturate polyunsaturated fatty acids that are derived from vegetable oil; they cannot convert linoleic acid into arachidonic acid. Therefore, arachidonic acid is available to cats only from animal sources of food. Cats are able to digest and absorb high levels of dietary fat and rely on a high-fat diet to supply most of the essential fatty acids.

Adult cats require 10 percent fat in their diets; kittens require a minimum of 17 percent. Reported signs of essential fatty acid deficiency include a greasy and flaky hair coat, growth retardation, weight loss, impaired wound healing, and an increased susceptibility to infection.

MINERALS

Surprisingly little quantitative data are available concerning the dietary mineral requirements of cats. It appears, however, that certain minerals, such as calcium, phosphorus, sodium, potassium, magnesium, iron, copper, zinc, and iodine are critical for cats' health. Based on information available for other animal species, it is assumed that certain other minerals —chlorine, manganese, sulfur, cobalt, selenium, molybdenum, fluorine, chromium, silicon, tin, nickel, and vanadium—also are essential for cats.

Minerals help to maintain the body's *acid-base* (electrolyte) *balance,* tissue structure, and fluid balance, and serve as components of enzymes and organic compounds. Mineral requirements are all interrelated—an excessive dietary quantity of one mineral may bind another mineral, preventing its utilization and causing a deficiency. Excessive dietary quantities of certain minerals may also have direct detrimental effects on cats. Supplementation with readily available mineral supplements is likely to be more harmful than beneficial and is a main cause of mineral imbalances in cats.

Calcium and Phosphorus

These are the two major minerals involved in bone and tooth formation (magnesium and fluoride are also involved, but to a lesser extent). In addition, calcium is also involved in the mechanism of blood clotting and in nerve impulse transmission. Phosphorus is important in many other metabolic processes, particularly those related to energy generation and transfer. For cats a calcium-to-phosphorus ratio of 1:1 up to 2:1 is satisfactory for the absorption and utilization of both.

The most common mineral imbalance is caused by feeding an all-meat or all–animal tissue diet, which is deficient in calcium. The body, in an attempt to supply the necessary calcium to maintain the calcium level in the blood, removes calcium from the skeleton. Classical signs of calcium deficiency include bone disease (mineral loss from the bone causing thin deformed bones) and locomotor disturbances. (*See* "Nutritional Secondary Hyperparathyroidism," Chapter 21: Musculoskeletal System and Disorders.)

An excessive amount of calcium causes slow growth and decreased thyroid function. Excessive amounts of phosphorus promote kidney damage.

Magnesium

This mineral aids in bone growth, deposition of minerals at the necessary sites in the body, and metabolic reactions. A dietary level of 400 milligrams per kilogram per day (0.04 percent) is the minimum requirement suggested by the NRC. A greater amount is recommended during lactation. Experimental diets deficient in magnesium have resulted in poor growth of kittens, muscular weakness, irritability, convulsions, inappetence, and calcium deposition in soft tissues. Most cat foods contain more than the needed amount. Diets with excessive quantities of magnesium (above 0.1 percent by weight, i.e., more than 20 milligrams of magnesium/100 kilocalories of metabolizable energy) have been implicated in the formation of urinary struvite crystals and calculi, one of the main causes of the lower urinary tract disease of cats commonly referred to as feline urologic syndrome (FUS). (*See* Chapter 22: Urinary System and Disorders.)

Potassium

Potassium is found in high concentrations within body cells. Potassium is particularly important for proper muscle function and for electrolyte (ion) balance. When a deficiency occurs—whether induced by diet, diarrhea, kidney disease, or diuretics (drugs that increase urine flow)—a cat may appear lethargic, inappetent, and incoordinated. A severe deficiency can result in heart failure. (See "Hypokalemic Polymyopathy," Chapter 21: Musculoskeletal System and Disorders.)

Sodium and Chloride

These two minerals help to maintain the body's fluid and electrolyte balance. Indiscriminate use of table salt to provide sodium and chloride is a dangerous practice because of its potential negative effects on heart and kidney function. Sodium and chloride deficiencies are extremely rare in cats; however, the signs of deficiency include weight loss, hair loss, and dry skin.

Iron and Copper

These two minerals prevent anemia. Iron is present in red blood cells in the form of hemoglobin, which carries oxygen to the cells. Copper is required for normal iron metabolism and aids in other functions as well, including the production of *myelin* (the substance forming the sheath around certain nerve cells), *melanin* (skin pigment), and connective tissue. Anemia is the most profound clinical sign if either of these two minerals is lacking. Bone abnormalities may also occur with copper deficiency.

Zinc

Zinc is present in trace amounts but is widely distributed throughout the body. Certain tissues, including the pancreas, bones, teeth, skin and male reproductive tissues, contain a significant portion of total body zinc. Zinc is important in the metabolism of nucleic acids (the genetic material), carbohydrates, proteins, and fats. Excessive amounts of calcium in the diet can bind zinc in an insoluble complex, preventing its absorption and thus making it inaccessible for the body to use. However, a naturally occurring zinc deficiency is rare in cats. Signs of a zinc deficiency include emaciation, production of defective sperm, general debilitation, and retarded growth.

Manganese

Manganese, a trace mineral, is required by several enzyme systems and is important for reproduction and proper bone formation.

Cobalt

Cobalt, a trace mineral, is an integral component of vitamin B_{12} and is important in the production of hemoglobin. Other functions have not yet been identified.

Iodine

Iodine, as a component of thyroid hormones, plays an important role in proper thyroid function. Thyroid hormones regulate the overall rate of body metabolism. Iodine deficiency is manifested by *goiter* (enlarged thyroid gland), *hypothyroidism* (decreased thyroid function), lethargy, hair loss, and abnormal calcium metabolism.

Other Trace Minerals

The roles of other trace minerals—selenium, sulfur, fluorine, molybdenum, tin, silicon, nickel, vanadium, and chromium—in maintaining the health and well-being of cats have not been thoroughly investigated. However, it is thought that most or all of these trace elements are of importance, based upon the need for them in other animal species.

VITAMINS

Vitamins are categorized as either *fat-soluble* or *water-soluble*. Deficiencies of the fat-soluble vitamins (vitamins A, D, E, and K) should be considered in cases of pancreatic insufficiency, chronic diarrhea, or other fat-absorption problems. Excessive medication with mineral oil or petrolatum-containing (petroleum jelly) hairball remedies may prevent absorption of fat-soluble vitamins.

Several vitamins are unstable; their destruction may

be promoted by light, heat, oxidation, moisture, fat rancidity, or combination with certain minerals. Sufficient amounts of these vitamins are required in the diet to ensure that minimum daily requirements are met. Routine vitamin supplementation of a complete and balanced quality cat food incurs additional expense, is unnecessary, and may cause toxicity. Vitamin supplementation is only recommended during periods of reduced food intake, such as illness or increased loss of body fluids due to diarrhea or increased urination.

Fat-soluble Vitamins

Vitamin A (retinol). Cats lack the enzyme to convert beta carotene to retinol in the wall of the small intestine. Thus, they are completely dependent on rich dietary sources of vitamin A, such as organ meats (including liver). A deficiency of vitamin A in the diet can result in retarded growth, inappetence, weight loss, ocular infections, night blindness, incoordination, and brain damage. Excessive consumption of vitamin A can be just as harmful, producing *cervical spondylosis* (a degenerative disease of the neck vertebrae) and loss of teeth. Limb joints and bones may also be affected. This condition may be reversible by reducing the quantity of vitamin A in the diet. (*See* Chapter 21: Musculoskeletal System and Disorders.)

Vitamin D. The metabolism of calcium and phosphorus (and probably magnesium) is dependent upon vitamin D. Bone deformities may occur, most notably *rickets* in kittens, when the diet is deficient in vitamin D. However, bone deformities in cats are much more commonly caused by feeding all-meat, all-liver, or all-kidney diets than by feeding a diet deficient in vitamin D. Overdosing with vitamin D is just as damaging for cats as it is for humans. There is one documented case wherein a cat was receiving excessive amounts of vitamins D and A to treat a skin condition. The cat gradually lost weight and died. Upon necropsy (autopsy of an animal), it was discovered that the aorta, carotid arteries, and adrenal glands were heavily calcified, and that calcium was also deposited in the stomach wall and parathyroid glands—changes resulting from the overzealous vitamin supplementation.

Vitamin E (tocopherols). Vitamin E acts as an antioxidant, protecting fats in the diet and in the body from oxidation. It helps to maintain the structure of muscle cells. *Steatitis* ("yellow fat" disease) occurs in cats when the diet is lacking vitamin E. This problem is further aggravated if the cat is consuming a diet consisting primarily of cat foods containing red tuna or a diet that is high in polyunsaturated fats. The fatty deposits that are found in the soft tissues of steatitis cases are yellow-orange in color and very firm. If steatitis is untreated, death will ensue. Other disease problems that may result from a lack of vitamin E include inflammation of the heart and skeletal muscles. Excellent dietary sources of vitamin E include egg yolk and liver.

Vitamin K. Cats, like other mammals, need vitamin K, which aids in the clotting of blood. However, a dietary source of vitamin K is not necessary since adequate amounts are produced by intestinal bacteria. Exceptions may occur in cases of chronic intestinal disease and when oral antibiotic therapy is given for long periods of time (more than four weeks).

Water-soluble Vitamins

Vitamin B_1 (thiamine). Vitamin B_1 is essential for the metabolic processes involved in utilization of carbohydrates for energy. When thiamine is lacking in the diet, neurologic disorders may result. These disorders develop in three progressive stages, each with specific signs:

Stage 1 (occurs within one to two weeks): loss of appetite, vomiting, weight loss, and a "weaving" motion of the hindlimbs.

Stage 2: sudden and marked appearance of neurologic signs, including circling, dilation of the pupils, and an inability to stand.

Stage 3: the terminal stage, characterized by progressive weakness, collapse, and death.

All signs of thiamine deficiency are alleviated after administration of the vitamin.

Thiamine is a heat-sensitive compound—an important point that must be kept in mind by formulators of commercial cat diets. Thiamine also can be destroyed *in the body* when raw fish (e.g., herring, carp) containing the enzyme *thiaminase* (which destroys thiamine) is eaten. Good sources of thiamine include lean pork, chicken, beef, kidney, liver, egg yolk, peas, potatoes, milk, and whole-grain cereals.

Vitamin B_2 (riboflavin). Certain microorganisms resident within the digestive tract of most animals help to synthesize this vitamin and thus make it available to the host. It is not known to what extent this holds true for cats. Deficiencies of riboflavin do not occur in ordinary diets, despite the fact that riboflavin loses its potency when exposed to light. Deficiencies seem to occur in cats following a period of excessive riboflavin demand (such as lactation), or as a result of severe microbial infection occurring during a kitten's growth period. Signs of riboflavin deficiency include inappetence, weight loss, hair loss, and reduced fertility. Cats that are chronically deprived may develop *cataracts* (lens opacity in the eye).

Vitamin B₆ (pyridoxine). This vitamin acts as a *cofactor* (required constituent) for enzymes involved in protein metabolism. Dietary deficiency of vitamin B_6 results in weight loss, anemia, convulsions, kidney disease, and the formation of *calcium oxalate* crystals and calculi in the urinary tract. This condition appears similar to the feline urologic syndrome, but is caused by calcium oxalate rather than struvite (magnesium ammonium phosphate) crystals and calculi. Dietary sources of vitamin B_6 include fish, liver, legumes, milk, whole wheat, wheat germ, and yeast.

Niacin (nicotinamide). Cats, unlike other species, are unable to synthesize niacin from the amino acid *tryptophan,* and thus must rely completely on their dietary intake in order to meet their daily requirements.

Signs of niacin deficiency include inappetence, oral lesions, drooling of a thick, odoriferous saliva, diarrhea, emaciation and, if untreated, death within twenty days. If a niacin deficiency occurs, then other B vitamins probably are also deficient in a cat's diet. That is because the dietary sources of the B vitamins are similar.

Raw meat represents an excellent source of B vitamins. However, a diet of raw meat (especially raw pork or lamb) is *not* recommended for house cats because of the possibility of ingesting *Toxoplasma* tissue cysts. (*See* Chapter 31: Internal Parasites.) Other good sources of niacin include brewer's yeast, cereals, wheat germ, and rice.

Pantothenic acid. A cat's requirement for this vitamin is low when compared to that for other vitamins. The likelihood of a deficiency of pantothenic acid is very remote because the normal diet can provide more than adequate amounts. If a deficiency does occur, signs that may be seen include inappetence and weight loss.

Folacin (folic acid). Intestinal microorganisms are capable of synthesizing a portion of the folic acid required in the form of *folate.* Kittens on a folic acid–deficient diet stop growing and develop anemia.

Pregnant cats require additional amounts of folic acid because a considerable quantity of folates are transferred across the placenta to the fetuses.

Biotin. Biotin is synthesized in the intestine. *Avidin,* a constituent protein of raw egg white, can interact with the synthesized biotin to render it unavailable to the body. Indeed, eggs are a good source of protein, fat, and vitamins. However, eggs should be cooked before being fed to cats. A deficiency of biotin is evidenced by dried secretions around the eyes, nose, and mouth, scaly skin, bloody diarrhea, and emaciation.

Vitamin B₁₂ (cyanocobalamin). Vitamin B_{12} is involved in the synthesis of nucleic acids (genetic material) and in red blood cell production. Signs of a deficiency, which has only been seen in cats eating diets containing all vegetable protein, can include inappetence, weight loss, and anemia. In kittens, a vitamin B_{12} deficiency may be manifested by retarded growth.

Choline. Choline mobilizes fat from the liver and contributes to the synthesis of *methionine* (an amino acid). It is also involved in stimulation of nerve cells. Choline is present naturally as a base component of *lecithin* (a fatty acid–containing constituent of cells). Choline deficiency can cause *hepatic lipidosis* (buildup of fat in the liver) and a poor growth rate. Choline in lecithin is found in organ meats, eggs, soybean oil, and yeast.

Vitamin C (ascorbic acid). Cats normally synthesize vitamin C from glucose, so there is no need to supplement the diet. (An exception is made in the case of severe infection, which may impair the body's ability to synthesize vitamin C. In such cases, supplements should be given.) Vitamin C is sometimes recommended as a means of acidifying the urine to prevent *feline urologic syndrome.* (*See* Chapter 22: Urinary System and Disorders.) Since vitamin C is water-soluble and rapidly excreted in the urine, it must be given five to six times daily to be effective, which makes it impractical as a urine acidifier.

WATER

Although water is not usually thought of as a nutrient, it is in actuality the most essential component of nutrition for the growth and maintenance of all living organisms. Living cells cannot exist without a continuous supply of water. An animal is capable of losing most of its body sugars and fats, 50 percent of its stored protein, and more than half of its body mass, and still surviving. If 10 percent of its total body water is lost, however, an animal will experience severe metabolic changes; loss of 15 percent of its body water is incompatible with life.

Water functions in virtually every life process. It is a solvent, a transporter, a catalyst in body chemistry, and a vital component of body constituents. Water constitutes nearly 70 percent of an animal's body and is distributed throughout it.

Because cats evolved as desert animals, they can withstand acute dehydration much better than either dogs or human beings. Cats are able to concentrate their urine to a greater extent, thus conserving more water within the body. Not even cats, however, can withstand long-term dehydration.

Under normal conditions, water is lost from the body during respiration, urination, defecation, lactation, and perspiration. These deficits must be replenished in amounts equal to the loss. Water is obtained from solid foods and liquids, and by chemical oxidation (production of energy). Metabolic water is derived from oxidation of hydrogen during metabolism. The amount of water consumed is influenced by body losses due to environmental conditions (e.g., hot weather), illness (diarrhea, vomiting, excessive urination), or increased consumption of salt. Despite their heritage and habits, cats should be given access to fresh, clean water at all times.

Feeding Cats

F ood is the essence of life, providing the necessary energy and other nutrients required for growth, reproduction, and maintenance of body tissues. Properly feeding a cat is an important responsibility. This chapter provides some perspective and practical guidelines to using the information in Chapter 6: Feline Nutritional Requirements.

Pet food manufacturers have placed great emphasis on cat food development over the past decades, because of the proliferation of cats and the millions who have chosen them as household pets. As a result, the number of varieties and brands of cat foods in the marketplace can present a complicated set of decisions for the novice and experienced cat owner alike. Feline nutritional requirements demand that the caring cat owner learn how and what to feed cats.

CAT FOODS

There are three basic forms of commercial cat food available to nourish cats: dry, semi-moist, and canned. These products differ in water content, nutrient levels, and caloric density. These differences are primarily attributed to the water and nutrient content of the food, the ingredients used, and the requirements of the various forms. Forms of cat foods are compared on an "as is" and dry-matter basis in Table 1. Dry matter is calculated after the removal of all moisture from a cat food.

Dry Foods

Although referred to as dry, these foods actually contain from 7 to 12 percent moisture. Cereals, animal protein meals, fish meal, soybean meal, and vitamins

TABLE 1.

NUTRIENT CONTENTS OF CAT FOOD

	DRY		SEMI-MOIST		CANNED RATION		CANNED GOURMET	
	As Is	Dry	As Is	Dry	As Is	Dry	As Is	Dry
Water	10%	—	35%	—	75%	—	77%	—
Protein	31%	34%	23%	36%	10%	41%	12%	53%
Fat	11%	12%	10%	16%	4%	14%	6%	27%
Ash	7%	8%	5%	7%	3%	12%	2%	10%
Carbohydrates	41%	46%	27%	41%	8%	33%	3%	10%
approximate kcal*/lb.	1600		1300		460		550	
approximate kcal per oz.	100		80		29		34	

* Kcal is the abbreviation for *kilocalorie*, or the "large" calorie that is the unit used to measure metabolic energy and the energy value of food. One kilocalorie is the amount of heat required to raise the temperature of one kilogram of water one degree Celsius (centigrade). The custom in nonscientific circles is to shorten the term *kilocalorie* to just *calorie*; however, scientifically, the term *calorie* is the unit used to measure the amount of heat needed to raise the temperature of one gram of water one degree Celsius. In this book the terms *calorie* and *kilocalorie* are used interchangeably to mean the large calorie.

and minerals are combined, cooked by extrusion (forcing through an opening), and dried to about 10 percent moisture. The resulting chunks are then coated with fat to increase palatabilty and energy content. If digest (meat extract) is used, it is sprayed or dusted on the exterior of the fat-coated particle.

The primary advantages of dry cat foods include lower cost and convenience for ad libitum (free-choice) feeding. A secondary benefit is that chewing dry food reduces the buildup of dental tartar, thus maintaining healthier gums and teeth. Dry foods are usually less palatable than the wet forms for most cats. However, cats are creatures of habit, and those cats accustomed to eating dry foods often prefer them to wet foods.

Dry cat foods may predispose a cat to *feline urologic syndrome* (FUS). Studies conducted in the United States and Denmark have shown that the risk of FUS is six to seven times greater when cats are fed dry foods exclusively. This may be attributed to the higher magnesium content in those dry foods fed, and perhaps the lower moisture content. Studies have shown that urine pH (the measure of the acidity or alkalinity of a solution) is affected by food. When dry food is continuously available on a free-choice basis, the urine pH is less acid for a longer time period than when a cat is meal-fed. This more alkaline urine is a conducive environment for the formation of urinary crystals or calculi, usually composed of struvite, which may lead to a partial or total obstruction of the urethra. FUS is a serious and potentially life-threatening medical condition. (*See* Chapter 22: Urinary System and Disorders.)

Semi-moist Food

These foods are more appealing to the human visual and olfactory senses. The food is formed into pieces resembling tidbits of meat. Meat by-products, poultry viscera, soybean meal, cereals, cereal by-products, and preservatives, such as propylene glycol and acids to prevent spoilage and humectant chemicals to maintain moistness, are the primary ingredients.

The cost is midrange between that of dry and canned food. Semi-moist foods provide a greater water intake than dry cat foods.

Canned Food

Canned foods are quite popular, despite their higher cost. They are highly palatable to cats, which can be beneficial for finicky eaters, but a liability for obesity-prone cats. Canned foods also provide a good dietary source of water, since approximately three-quarters of canned food is water.

Gourmet canned foods are usually sold in small cans (three or six ounces). Initially these foods featured organ meats (e.g., kidney, liver) or fish as their primary food ingredient. Now they are composed of a wide variety of ingredients, with poultry viscera (poultry by-products) being a major one. These foods may or may not be nutritionally balanced. It is important to read the label on all cat foods for a statement of nutritional adequacy.

SELECTING CAT FOOD

To get the best nourishment, the nutrition information on the package label should be read carefully. Pet food manufacturers are required by law to supply certain nutrition information to the consumer.

The section labeled *guaranteed analysis* lists the minimum amounts of protein and fat and the maximum amounts of fiber and water. The actual percentages may vary 1 to 2 percent from the stated guarantees. This section may list the ash or other nutrient contents of the product. Ash is the mineral portion (including calcium, phosphorus, and magnesium) of the diet. A certain level of minerals is necessary for the cat's normal metabolism (*see* Chapter 6: Feline Nutritional Requirements), but the ash content of dry and semi-moist foods is directly correlated with their magnesium content. There is no correlation between the ash and magnesium contents of canned foods.

Unfortunately, the caloric content is not required on the label. Since animals eat to satisfy their energy requirement, you need to know the approximate caloric content to estimate the initial amount to feed. Table 2 provides one method to estimate the caloric content of cat foods.

The approximate nutrient content of various forms of cat food is shown in Table 1 on both an "as is" and

METHOD FOR ESTIMATING
TABLE 2. **CALORIES IN CAT FOOD**

NUMBER OF CALORIES PER GRAM OF NUTRIENT

Protein	3.5	Moisture	0
Fat	8.7	Ash	0
Fiber	0	Carbohydrate	3.5

PROCEDURE:

1. Multiply the percent of each nutrient on the cat food label by the amounts listed above.
2. Total the amount calculated in step 1.
3. Divide the total in step 2 by 100.
4. Multiply the result in step 3 by 454.

EXAMPLE:

"Guaranteed Analysis" on label of dry cat food:

Crude Protein	min. 30%	Ash	max. 6%
Crude Fat	min. 8%	Moisture	max. 10%
Crude Fiber	max. 4.5%	Carbohydrate	41.5%*

* (Usually is not listed, but is calculated by adding up the other nutrients and subtracting from 100.)

Step 1: Protein: 30 x 3.5 = 105
Fat: 8 x 8.7 = 69.6
Fiber: 4.5 x 0 = 0
Moisture: 10 x 0 = 0
Ash: 6 x 0 = 0
Carbohydrate: 41.5 x 3.5 = 145.25

Step 2: 105 + 69.6 + 0 + 0 + 0 + 145.25 = 319.85

Step 3: 319.85 ÷ 100 = 3.2 calories per gram of food

Step 4: 3.2 x 454 = 1452 calories per pound of food (90 calories per ounce)

dry-matter basis. Note that there is a difference between the two forms of canned cat food. Since all the nutrients are in the dry matter, a cat must eat enough food to meet its nutrient requirements. A cat eating canned food will be consuming, for example, far more protein than is needed, since these foods are higher in protein on a dry-matter basis than dry foods. A cat eating dry food will be eating more carbohydrates, which are required to form the particles (pellets) of dry food.

The average, active adult cat needs about thirty-six kilocalories (definition in Table 1) per pound of body weight per day to maintain body weight. The needs of individual cats will differ from this average according to age, environment, stage of life cycle, and activity level. To calculate how much to feed a cat using Table 1, divide the approximate kilocalories per ounce into the number of kilocalories required by the cat in question. For example, a ten-pound cat requires about 360 kilocalories a day: three and a half ounces of dry; or four and a half ounces of semi-moist; or twelve and a half ounces of canned ration; or ten and a half ounces of canned gourmet, to satisfy its daily caloric needs. Pet foods that are "complete" or "balanced" are formulated so that when caloric needs are satisfied, requirements for other essential nutrients are also met.

The *ingredients list* must contain all items used in the product. The ingredients are listed in decreasing order by weight. Animal protein–containing ingredients should be listed among the first few items, indicating that the product probably contains sufficient animal-source ingredients to supply taurine and essential amino and fatty acids. Canned foods should contain a source of calcium, such as calcium carbonate, sulfate, or chloride, or bone meal, dicalcium phosphate, or ground chicken or fish, which contain ground bone. Toward the bottom of the list, vitamins and trace minerals should be listed, indicating that they have been added.

The third important item on a cat food label is the *statement of nutritional adequacy*. The label should have a statement that the product is complete and balanced for some stage of the cat's life cycle (e.g., growth, maintenance, or all stages). The validation should state that this claim is based on results of animal-feeding trials. Some cat food labels only state that the food meets or exceeds the National Research Countil (NRC) recommendations for minimum amounts of essential nutrients. Feeding a cat a product that has not been test-fed to cats, or carries a claim that it should be used for intermittent or supplemental feeding only, does not guarantee a balanced diet for the cat.

HOMEMADE DIETS

Formulating and compounding a cat food is a difficult, inconvenient, and time-consuming process. Feeding a homemade diet cannot assure the presence or availability of all the nutrients in the right quantities needed by the cat. Commercial, nutritionally balanced products are usually advised unless a veterinarian has recommended a homemade ration and provided a specific recipe that can be accurately compounded at home.

BASIC GUIDELINES FOR FEEDING CATS

Environmental conditions can affect a cat's eating habits. For example, heavily trafficked areas, noise, the presence of other animals, dirty food containers, or nearby litter boxes can deter a cat from eating. A cat owner should be sensitive to a cat's eating behavior, and consider making some adjustments to create optimum feeding conditions for the pet cat.

The proper amount to feed is determined by the caloric content and digestibility of the food and the caloric needs of the individual cat. Basic guidelines on the amount to feed kittens and cats based on *average* caloric content of foods and caloric needs of cats are provided in Table 3. Some pet food manufacturers include feeding guidelines for their cat food. This information is sometimes found on the label, although many cat food labels do not contain feeding directions. Essentially, the proper amount to feed is the amount of food that causes the cat to maintain its optimum body weight. This amount may vary considerably (50 to 100 percent) from the averages contained in feeding guides.

Table scraps and cat treats can be fed from time to time, but should not be given as a steady diet. These foods lack the proper proportion of basic nutrients a cat requires to maintain its health. Treats should not exceed 20 percent of the cat's daily diet. The biggest problem with table scraps and treats is that the cat may come to prefer them. Also, scraps teach the cat to beg and interfere with eating patterns of the family or owner.

Although raw meat is an excellent source of many nutrients, it is not recommended because of the po-

TABLE 3.   **GUIDELINES FOR AMOUNTS TO FEED**

		kcal/lb. body wt.	Dry	Semi-moist	Canned
			(ounces per pound of body weight)		
Kittens:	10 weeks	113	1.1 oz.	1.4 oz.	3.6 oz.
	20 weeks	59	.6	.7	1.8
	30 weeks	45	.45	.6	1.4
	40 weeks	36	.36	.4	1.2
Adult Cats:	Inactive	32	.32	.4	1
	Active	36	.36	.4	1.2
	Pregnant	45	.45	.6	1.4
	Lactating*	56–145	1	1.3	3.3

(Adapted from *Nutrient Requirements of Cats,* National Research Council, 1986.)

* A lactating queen's energy requirements vary according to the number of kittens in the litter and also increase each week of lactation. Amounts given in the above table are for a lactating queen nursing four kittens in week 6 of lactation. The best method for feeding lactating queens and growing kittens is to allow free access to food at all times. This "free-choice" method of feeding allows the queen and kittens to adjust their intake to individual needs. Overeating and obesity are not usually problems in these classes of cats due to the high energy need. On the contrary, an adult cat should be fed the measured amount of food that causes it to maintain optimum body weight.

tential spread of toxoplasmosis. (*See* Chapter 31: Internal Parasites.)

Variety

If a nutritionally complete and balanced food is being fed, there is no need to feed a variety of brands or flavors. A nutritionally complete and balanced cat food, containing several sources of animal protein, is desirable to prevent the cat from becoming addicted to one ingredient. If a complete and balanced food is not being fed, the cat should be converted to one that is complete.

A good method to convert a cat to a new food is to mix the new food with the old, starting at a 1:4 ratio. Increase the amount of new to old food in one-quarter increments (i.e., 1:4, 2:4, 3:4) until the cat is switched to the new food.

Vitamin and Mineral Supplements

A cat food that meets or exceeds the NRC standards has an adequate supply of vitamins and minerals. The use of vitamin and mineral supplements, including brewer's yeast, is unnecessary. As mentioned in Chapter 6: Feline Nutritional Requirements, a critical balance of these nutrients exists and the addition of a supplement without a veterinarian's approval may actually harm the cat.

Food Storage

Unused portions of canned food should be refrigerated to maintain quality and prevent spoilage until the next feeding. *Refrigerated food should be brought to room temperature before feeding.* This will prevent possible digestion problems or food rejection related to temperature differences. Do not heat the food above room temperature. Cats may reject both hot and cold foods. Feedings of canned rations are sometimes divided into two per day; however, one feeding per day is very adequate for most adult, nonreproducing cats. Remember, in the wild, cats may eat only one meal every twenty-four to forty-eight hours.

Unused portions of dry cat food should be stored in a cool, dry location and used within six months after purchasing, since studies show that the potency of several vitamins declines during storage. Store dry cat food in an airtight container to delay further nutrient deterioration, help maintain palatability, and prevent insect and rodent infestation.

FORCE-FEEDING

When sick, a cat may lose its appetite and refuse to eat. This becomes a serious situation if the cat refuses food for more than several days. The veterinarian may recommend force-feeding a cat to prevent further physical deterioration. (*See* "Force-Feeding," Chapter 37: Convalescence—Home Care.)

SPECIAL NUTRITIONAL NEEDS

Throughout a cat's life, there are certain stages that have different nutritional needs. These include pregnancy, lactation, kittenhood, and old age. There are also special nutritional needs associated with certain diseases, such as kidney, liver, heart, and intestinal diseases, lower urinary tract disease (FUS), obesity, and diabetes mellitus. Disease-related nutrition is discussed in the individual chapters dealing with the specific diseases.

Pregnancy, Parturition, and Lactation

Pregnant queens require about 25 percent more energy (i.e., kilocalories) than for normal maintenance. The energy required by lactating queens has been shown to be two to four times more than for normal maintenance. Even at this high level of food intake, lactating queens may lose weight.

Milk production is a function of the suckling stimulus and the physiology of the mammary gland. However, restricting food intake two to three days before weaning the kittens may help to decrease milk production for queens that previously experienced milk-swollen mammary glands.

Kittens

Young kittens (approximately ten weeks old) require at least one and a half times as much protein and three times the number of calories per pound as adult cats. If the kittens are eating a complete and balanced diet, the food intake will provide enough nutrients for proper growth and development of bones, muscles, and other tissues.

Within the first twenty-four to thirty-six hours after birth, the queen's milk contains vital antibodies that provide a certain degree of protection against infectious diseases. (If a kitten is orphaned, *see* "Feeding," Chapter 3: Kittens and Disorders, for recommended feeding procedures.)

By three weeks of age, solid food should be available to the kittens at all times, as they will begin eating solid food at that age. A commercially prepared kitten food can be used. Follow the instructions on the label. If the queen has an inadequate supply of milk, accelerate the weaning process by mixing a milk substitute with the solid food. By the sixth to eighth week, gradually wean the kittens from the queen. A diet for a fully weaned kitten (eight weeks old) should contain 35 percent protein and 17 percent fat in the dry matter and should be fed free-choice to ensure adequate intake of all nutrients.

The Geriatric Cat

The average-life span of the cat is fourteen years. However, proper nutrition can aid in extending the cat's longevity. Old age results in numerous physiological changes that may require changes in the diet. Some of these changes include reduced kidney, heart, and pancreatic function and less physical activity, which reduces caloric need. Commercial diets have been developed that consider these specialized dietary needs. The pet food industry has also taken into account that an older cat's sense of smell is not as acute; therefore, they make the diets highly palatable to stimulate food intake. The liability of these foods is that they can create obesity—a serious medical problem—unless the amount of food offered is carefully controlled. For obesity-prone older cats, a nutritionally complete diet containing less digestible energy (often labeled as "light") is a good option.

COMMON FEEDING PROBLEMS

The following feeding errors are common:

1. *Overfeeding* can lead to the number one dietary disease, obesity. The guidelines in Table 3 help determine how much a cat should be fed initially,

but always feed the amount of food that maintains optimum body weight. (*See* Chapter 8: Diseases of Dietary Origin.)

2. *Feeding dog food to a cat* is a common feeding error, especially if dogs and cats are in the same household. Dog foods are developed for the nutritional needs of dogs, not cats. The nutritional differences between omnivore (dog) and carnivore (cat) diets are profound. Cats, as strict carnivores, require a higher percentage of protein (specifically arginine, taurine), B-complex vitamins, preformed vitamin A, and preformed arachidonic acid (fatty acid). Serious consequences can result if a cat's diet is deficient in these nutrients.

3. *Overdosing with vitamin and mineral supplements* has been known to cause severe medical problems in cats. Imbalances from excess vitamins or minerals can bind other nutrients. Clinically, toxicities of vitamins A and D are more common than deficiencies of these vitamins because of unnecessary vitamin and mineral supplementation to an already balanced diet. A supplement containing magnesium should never be given to a cat, as many cat foods already contain excess magnesium, a factor in causing FUS.

4. *Exclusively feeding all fish, all meat, or all other animal tissues* such as heart, kidney, or liver results in an unbalanced diet and causes related dietary diseases. (*See* Chapter 8: Diseases of Dietary Origin.)

Diseases of Dietary Origin

Diet-induced diseases are caused by a surfeit or a deficit of one or more nutrients. Such diseases are unlikely to occur in cats if they are fed a balanced and complete diet in the proper quantity. (*See* Chapter 6: Feline Nutritional Requirements, and Chapter 7: Feeding Cats.) This chapter provides information on some of the more common diseases related to consumption of an unbalanced diet.

OBESITY

Obesity is the most common diet-induced disease in cats, dogs, and human beings in the United States. When an animal's weight exceeds by 15 percent the optimum weight for its age and sex, it is considered to be obese. Statistics indicate that approximately 12 percent of cats treated by veterinarians are at least 15 percent overweight.

Because the amount of body fat increases with age, middle-aged and older animals have an increased tendency toward obesity. To maintain the optimum weight of a cat prone to obesity, its caloric intake must be carefully controlled.

Signs of Obesity

Obesity in animals is an easily recognized nutritional disorder. The amount of flesh covering the ribs is generally an accurate indicator of an animal's nutritional condition. When an animal is underweight, the ribs are visible if the cat has a short hair coat. At normal weight, the ribs are hidden but can be *palpated* (felt with the fingers) with ease. When an animal is grossly overweight, however, the ribs are difficult, if not impossible, to feel. A more quantitative method to determine the extent of obesity is to have a veterinarian establish an optimum body weight for the individual cat and then weigh the cat monthly to monitor its weight. Generally, a healthy, mature cat weighs approximately eight to ten pounds.

Characteristically in obese cats:

- The abdomen protrudes on either side, or appears pendulous
- The face broadens and appears swollen
- Noticeable bulges are found on either side of the tail head (where the tail joins the body)
- The animal appears to sway from side to side when walking
- Movements appear lethargic
- Respiratory problems may be evident

Many of these signs can also be related to fluid retention due to heart disease. Therefore, an obese cat should be examined by a veterinarian prior to initiating a weight-reduction program.

Obesity negatively affects a cat's health, reducing its life-span. The added weight puts excessive stress on joints, ligaments, and tendons, and can aggravate arthritis. Respiratory problems, such as shortness of breath, occur following exercise because of the excessive amount of body tissue requiring oxygen and the frequent history of inactivity in obese animals. Skin problems can occur more often because obese cats are less able to groom themselves properly. Other medical problems also may be associated with feline obesity; however, few published studies are available in this area.

Causes of Obesity

Obesity results when caloric intake far exceeds energy expenditure over a long period of time. Several other factors can contribute to inordinate weight gain in animals.

Sex hormones (such as estrogen and testosterone) appear to influence body weight. One study showed that castrated male cats ate less food than intact male cats, but they gained more weight. Neutering also may increase the incidence of obesity in male cats, since they have less tendency to roam and to be restless, thus reducing their physical activity.

The nature and quantity of an animal's food have a direct relationship to the development of obesity. Nutritionists have discovered that high-fat diets are conducive to obesity. Fat is higher in caloric density, more digestible, and stores as body fat more effi-

ciently than protein or carbohydrates. Highly palatable diets increase food intake, and thus caloric intake. The cat is frequently characterized as a finicky eater. In reality, most cats are good eaters, but have been made finicky by feeding and management practices. Considering the incidence of feline obesity, a diet of low caloric density and palatability would be of benefit to many cats.

Metabolic disorders, such as *hypothyroidism,* can result in a reduced metabolic rate, slowing the utilization of nutrients. Less than 5 percent of obesity problems in cats, however, can be attributed to such disorders.

Weight Control

The basic principles of weight control are increased physical activity and decreased caloric intake. As a general rule, losing a single pound of fat requires an energy expenditure of 3500 calories, or a consumption of 3500 calories less than maintenance need.

Increase Activity. Getting an obese cat to exercise is difficult for many modern families, but it is not a totally unrealistic expectation. The owner should schedule a regular daily playtime with the cat. Vary the cat's exercise activities to include stretching (e.g., by dangling a toy for the cat to reach for) and vigorous activities (e.g., by dragging a toy across the floor for the cat to chase and leap upon). If the cat has a limited space to roam, provide a carpeted climbing post with stepped platforms. If the cat is trained to a harness, it can be taken on walking excursions. These are just a few of the ways one can increase an obese cat's physical activity to utilize calories.

Decrease Caloric Intake. "Starvation diets" may produce rapid weight loss, but they can also produce very serious abnormalities that may jeopardize the cat's life. *Hepatic lipidosis,* a serious condition of the liver, has been frequently reported in obese cats placed on severely restricted or starvation diets. A judicious, progressive reduction of body weight is a far wiser approach to a feline obesity problem. The caloric intake of overweight cats should be gradually reduced to approximately 20 to 30 percent below the maintenance level in order to produce a slow, steady weight loss. This can be accomplished by reducing the amount fed by 20 to 30 percent; however, this may create stress in the family due to the cat's meowing and pacing. Another alternative is feeding specially formulated diet cat food, available from veterinarians. The feeding instructions, provided by the veterinarian, should be followed carefully.

During weight reduction, high-caloric treats and table scraps should obviously not be fed.

Before an obese cat is started on any weight-reduction diet, a veterinarian should be consulted to make sure no other medical problems exist.

DERMATOSES OF DIETARY ORIGIN

Dry, scaly skin and a thin, dull, brittle hair coat can be the result of a number of different nutritional imbalances. However, if a complete and balanced diet is fed, these problems should not occur.

Protein deficiency causes disturbances in the pigment of the skin and hair coat. Shedding of hair is prolonged. Patchy areas of hair loss may occur on the head, back, abdomen, and legs.

Essential fatty acid deficiency causes a dull, dry, brittle hair coat with progressive hair loss. The skin becomes dry, scaly, and inflamed.

Miliary dermatitis (small skin lesions), dry, scaly skin, and thinning hair may be signs of a *biotin deficiency.*

Cats that have a *deficiency of zinc* in their diets develop a thin, slow-growing hair coat, scaly skin, and ulcerated lips.

If any of these conditions is suspected, the diet should be changed to one of known nutritional adequacy. Supplements should not be added, as they may make the problem worse. If improvement is not seen when a complete and balanced diet is fed, a veterinarian should be consulted, as the cause is probably not related to diet.

THIAMINE DEFICIENCY

Associated neurologic disorders occur when thiamine (vitamin B$_1$) is lacking in the diet. Certain food-processing procedures, and the enzyme *thiaminase,* found in raw fish, can destroy vitamin B$_1$. Fortunately, pet food manufacturers routinely add thiamine and other vitamins to offset processing losses, thus assuring a complete and balanced ration. Cats eating a raw fish diet may suffer a deficiency of thiamine if other

foods are not eaten or the ration is not supplemented in some other way.

The earliest sign of a thiamine deficiency is loss of appetite. Within a few days this progresses to vomiting and a noticeable incoordination of the hind limbs. Neurologic disorders become more pronounced over time and can include circling, dilation of the pupils, convulsions, and tucking of the head into the chest. Treatment by a veterinarian usually consists of an injection of thiamine or B complex vitamins to quickly alleviate signs. If left untreated, affected cats will die. When treated in the later stages of the deficiency, neurologic damage may be irreversible. With the advent and common feeding of complete and balanced cat foods, this condition is extremely rare.

RICKETS AND OSTEOMALACIA

A deficiency in vitamin D causes *rickets* in kittens and *osteomalacia* (bone softening) in mature cats. These diseases are very rare in cats because their vitamin D requirement is minute and most cats have access to sunlight, which causes vitamin D to be formed in the skin.

The first noticeable sign of a deficiency is enlargement of the joints. Kittens show a bowing of the legs and adult cats develop brittle, easily fractured bones. These signs are similar to those of calcium and phosphorus deficiencies and *hyperparathyroidism.* Blood tests are needed to determine the cause of the signs. Treatment involves feeding a complete and balanced diet containing an adequate level of vitamin D. Supplements containing vitamin D are not recommended due to the potentiality of producing vitamin D toxicity, resulting in deposition of calcium in soft tissues.

STEATITIS
(Yellow Fat Disease)

This diet-induced disease can occur in cats fed a diet containing excessive amounts of unsaturated fatty acids. Vitamin E is destroyed during oxidation of those fatty acids. The resulting vitamin E deficiency causes a yellow-pigmented substance to be deposited in the body fat. The pigment produces an intense, painful inflammatory response. Feeding large quantities of red tuna meat is most often implicated in development of steatitis.

The first visible signs of a vitamin E deficiency are a greasy, dull hair coat and flaky skin. As the deficiency progresses, steatitis develops, producing lumpy fat deposits under the skin and especially in the groin. Affected cats develop a noticeable sensitivity to being touched, a reluctance to move, fever, and loss of appetite.

Diagnosis by a veterinarian is usually based on the patient's history and on a surgical biopsy of the fat tissue. Treatment includes feeding a non-tuna diet and vitamin E supplementation. Steatitis can be prevented by feeding cats a complete and balanced commercial cat food not containing red tuna.

NUTRITIONAL SECONDARY HYPERPARATHYROIDISM

This disease is caused by eating a diet deficient in calcium. This type of dietary disorder occurs when cats eat an all–animal tissue diet, such as heart, liver, kidney, or meat. The deficiency of calcium causes calcium to be removed from bone to maintain the blood calcium level and offset the dietary deficit.

The parathyroid glands are stimulated secondarily by the low blood calcium. Kittens are at greater risk because they require a larger amount of calcium for their growth and development.

Reluctance to move, incoordination, and sometimes lameness of the hindlimbs are often the first signs in kittens. Bone fractures readily occur but many may heal unnoticed. *Osteoporosis* (thinning of bone) occurs in mature cats suffering from the disease. The removal of calcium from the bone to supply the missing dietary calcium takes longer in the adult cat than in the kitten due to the lower need and food intake per pound of body weight in the adult. The radiographic tell-tale signs of the demineralization process are bones with thin cortices (outer layers), bone fractures, and alterations in the jaw and teeth (a thinning jawline and exposed tooth roots). Treatment, when possible, consists of providing affected cats with a nutritionally balanced diet, in order to correct the calcium / phosphorus imbalance. Calcium supplements are not recommended because of the difficulty in producing the proper 1:1 to 2:1 calcium-to-phosphorus total dietary ratio using a supplement

with an unbalanced diet. (*See* Chapter 27: Endocrine System and Metabolic Disorders, and Chapter 21: Musculoskeletal System and Disorders.)

CENTRAL RETINAL DEGENERATION

Previously it was believed that this ocular disorder was hereditary in nature. Subsequent studies have shown, however, that *central retinal degeneration* is caused most commonly by a dietary *taurine deficiency*. Cats require taurine in their diet because they are unable to synthesize this essential amino acid.

Blindness occurs as degeneration of the retina progresses. Central retinal degeneration can be prevented by providing a diet containing an adequate quantity of taurine from meat, fish, shellfish, or pure taurine. Most commercial cat foods contain additional amounts of taurine.

VITAMIN A AND D TOXICITIES

Vitamin A and D toxicities occur more frequently than do deficiencies of either vitamin. This is attributed partly to the common belief that kittens require additional quantities of these nutrients for proper growth and development, and the administration of vitamin supplements containing high levels of these vitamins. Contrary to popular belief, excesses of vitamins A and D can overwhelm the body's normal regulatory mechanisms.

Vitamin D. Signs of vitamin D toxicity include weakness, joint pain, and stiffness. A cat with vitamin D toxicity acts much like a cat with vitamin D deficiency. If the condition is not resolved, calcium will be abnormally deposited in various tissues, particularly the kidney, lungs, large blood vessels, and intestinal tract. Once calcification has occurred, other signs indicative of individual organ dysfunction may appear.

Diagnosis of vitamin D toxicity is based on the clinical signs and dietary history that usually includes administration of a vitamin supplement. Treatment consists of removing the source of the excess vitamin D. The veterinarian initially may use cortisone therapy. In cases where extensive calcification of body tissues has occurred, the prognosis is guarded.

Vitamin A. Cervical spondylosis (deformity of neck vertebrae) and deformity of limbs and bones are caused by hypervitaminosis A. It is most often associated with feeding large amounts of liver, cod liver oil, or vitamin A supplements. Dosages approximately one hundred times the recommended daily requirement will induce the disease. (*See* Chapter 21: Musculoskeletal System and Disorders.)

FELINE UROLOGIC SYNDROME (FUS)

FUS includes a wide range of lower urinary tract problems with an equally wide range of causes. Diet has been implicated as one of the causes, especially in the formation of urinary crystals and uroliths (stones). Diets with excessive quantities of magnesium (more than twenty milligrams of magnesium per one hundred kilocalories of metabolizable energy) have been shown to cause the formation of struvite urinary crystals. The ash content of dry and semi-moist cat foods directly correlates with their magnesium content. Hence, the greater the ash content in these foods, the greater is their magnesium content.

Studies show that the pH of urine is affected by food. Dry food fed free-choice causes the urine to be more alkaline for longer periods of time, creating an environment conducive to the formation of urinary crystals and calculi. (*See* Chapter 22: Urinary System and Disorders.)

DILATED CARDIOMYOPATHY DUE TO TAURINE DEFICIENCY

A diet deficient in the essential amino acid taurine has been shown to be a cause of *dilated cardiomyopathy*. However, the incidence of this diet-induced cardiomyopathy should be greatly reduced as most cat foods now contain adequate sources of taurine. (*See* Chapter 20: Circulatory System and Disorders.)

Sex and Reproduction

Cats do not copulate with a rearward presentment on the part of the female, but the male stands erect and the female puts herself underneath him, and, by the way, the female cat is peculiarly lecherous, and wheedles the male on to sexual commerce, and caterwauls during the operation.

—Aristotle, *History of Animals, Book V*

—Oh Auntie, isn't he a beauty! And is he a gentleman or a lady?

—Neither, my dear! I had him fixed. It saves him from so many undesirable associations.

—D. H. Lawrence, "Puss Puss"

Reproductive Physiology

Human beings and some nonhuman primates experience what is known as the *menstrual cycle*. Approximately once a month the female produces a vaginal discharge of blood and tissue—the *menses*—from the nonpregnant uterus, for a period of about five days. Between menstrual periods the ovaries produce an *ovum* or egg, which can be *fertilized* by the male reproductive cell *(sperm)*. Sexual receptivity of the female is not dependent on the stage of the menstrual cycle.

By contrast, most other female mammals—including female cats—experience what is known as the *estrous cycle*. *Estrus* is a recurrent period of varying length,

during which the female ovulates (releases an egg from the ovary), produces a watery secretion from the genital tract, and becomes sexually receptive to the male. Estrus is preceded by several days of *proestrus* and is followed by several days of *metestrus*. It is separated from the next estrus by a quiescent period known as *diestrus* or *interestrus*.

The cat is unusual among mammals in some aspects of its reproductive physiology. Most mammals, including human beings, are *spontaneous ovulators:* at a given stage in the female reproductive cycle, regardless of whether sexual intercourse has occurred, an ovum (egg) is produced by a *follicle* in the ovary. The cat, however, is a *reflex ovulator:* an ovarian follicle will only produce an ovum in response to mating.

Feline reproduction also differs in another way. The cat, like the horse, is *seasonally polyestrous*—that is, the queen experiences estrous cycles during one part of the year (usually February through October in the Northern Hemisphere). During the fall, the cat experiences a sexually inactive period known as *anestrus*.

THE FEMALE

The female feline reproductive system consists of the *vulva* (entrance to the vagina), *clitoris, vagina, cervix* (entrance to the uterus), *uterus,* two *uterine tubes* (or fallopian tubes), and two *ovaries.* The uterus is Y shaped, formed by two *uterine horns* anteriorly and a short body joining the cervix posteriorly. Four (sometimes five) pairs of nipples are found on the lower abdomen and chest wall.

Blood serum levels of *estradiol* (ovarian estrogen) rise during proestrus, from the formation of ovarian follicles (sacs) that are capable of producing eggs (ova). During proestrus, follicle growth and development progress rapidly over a two- to three-day period just prior to the onset of estrus. Estrus usually begins as serum levels of estradiol peak, or during the subsequent rapid decline. Basal (base) estradiol levels of 5 to 20 picograms per milliliter of serum (a picogram, or micromicrogram, is one-trillionth—10^{-12}—of a gram) peak at 40 to 100 pg/ml by or before the onset of estrus. Levels greater than 20 pg/ml are closely associated with the manifestation of sexual behaviors. It is at this time that the queen becomes receptive to the male; she is then considered to be in estrus (in heat).

Ovulation during estrus depends upon the release of sufficient amounts of *luteinizing hormone* (LH) from the *anterior pituitary gland* in the brain. The release of LH is triggered by vaginal-cervical stimulation during *coitus* (sexual intercourse). In actuality, luteinizing hormone-releasing hormone (LH-RH) is first released from the *hypothalamus*—another area of the brain—and subsequently causes release of LH from the anterior pituitary. LH levels in the bloodstream fluctuate episodically, with increases occurring every twenty to thirty minutes, probably due to the episodic release of LH-RH.

One to two days after repeated coitus, the ovarian follicles rupture, sending ova down through the uterine tubes, which is the process known as ovulation. Following ovulation, ova and sperm meet in the uterine tube, where fertilization takes place. Fertilized eggs remain in the uterine tube for about four days before entering the uterus. The *embryos* usually are spaced evenly in both uterine horns. *Implantation* into the wall of the uterus occurs about day 12 or 14 of gestation, with a "band" or *zonary* placenta formed later.

Once an ovarian follicle has ruptured, it forms a glandular mass called a *corpus luteum* (plural, *corpora lutea*), which produces the hormone *progesterone.* If pregnancy occurs, the *placenta* will take over progesterone production by the thirty-fifth to the forty-fifth day.

The estrous cycle and interestral periods are quite variable in length. Proestrus lasts for as many as three days, followed by an estrus of three to twenty days (the average is seven or eight days). Estrus is manifested by a marked change in personality, constant calling, rolling, and rubbing against objects, and exhibition of the crouched mating stance with treading of the hind legs. The interestral period lasts three to fourteen days; it averages nine to thirteen days during the breeding season, but can be as long as thirty days. Thus, the length of an unbred queen's cycle (the interval from onset of one estrus to onset of the next) can range from six to forty days; most cycles last twelve to twenty-two days.

If not mated, most queens will experience nonovulatory estrous cycles throughout a breeding season. This situation results in periods of behavioral estrus (i.e., manifestations of heat) interrupted by periods of sexual nonreceptivity.

THE MALE

The male feline reproductive system consists of the *penis,* two *testes,* the *scrotum,* the *prostate gland,* two *bulbourethral glands,* and the *vas deferens* (a tube that carries the sperm [the male reproductive cells] from the testes to the *urethra* [the channel within the penis through which the urine flows]). The male has four or five pairs of nipples, but they remain nonfunctional.

A protective sheath, the *prepuce,* covers the penis just below the scrotum. The scrotum, a fur-covered sac under the anus, encloses the testes, where sperm are produced. The penis may protrude from the prepuce during licking and grooming or sometimes during stimulating play. The aroma of *pheromones* (odorous secretions) from the queen, and her estrous behavior of persistent vocalization, rolling, rubbing, and extreme affection, ready the male for copulation. An "appeasement" cry from the queen stimulates the tom to mount. During the usually brief *intromission* (insertion of the penis), sperm from the testes, mixed in the vas deferens and pelvic urethra with *seminal fluid* (a clear fluid) from the prostate and bulbourethral glands, is released by the process of ejaculation into the queen's vagina.

Sperm are present in the testes of well-grown toms by twenty-five to thirty-six weeks of age. The average volume of a tomcat's ejaculate is about 0.05 milliliters, containing from millions to hundreds of millions of sperm. Approximately 80 to 90% of the sperm are active and motile in a normal ejaculate. The pH (alkalinity/acidity ratio) of fresh semen is 7.4.

A tom will mark and defend territory. The territory will be staked out by his spraying of a mixture of urine and an anal-gland secretion containing odoriferous lipids (fats), producing the characteristic penetrating "catty" urine odor. Urine spraying may be inhibited by castration of the male or controlled by progesterone therapy in the intact or castrated tom.

THE REPRODUCTIVE LIFE OF THE CAT

In queens, puberty usually occurs between seven and twelve months of age, depending upon their nutritional status, breed, and freedom from disease, and on the season of the year when they are born. A queen may have her first estrus as early as four months of age or some Persians may be as late as twenty-one months of age. Persians tend to mature later than other breeds. If the normal pubertal age and weight of 2.3 to 2.5 kilograms (5.07 to 5.5 pounds) is attained during the anestrous period of October to December, cycling usually begins in January or February. If pubertal weight is attained in early or late summer, then an early pubertal estrus may take place.

Males usually reach puberty at a minimum body weight of 3.5 kilograms (7.72 pounds), which is attainable at nine months of age.

Purebred cats may reach puberty later than nonpurebred cats. Cats that are kept indoors, especially those that are housed without other cats, also may reach puberty at a later age. A British study of several breeds showed that on the average puberty was reached between nine and ten months of age, with considerable breed variation: Himalayans or colorpoints were the latest (average thirteen months), while Burmese were the earliest (average 7.7 months). It was noted also that puberty was affected by age at weaning, season of birth, and natural or artificial increase of daylight length.

The reproductive life of the cat is long, with both

toms and queens known to continue breeding for fourteen years or more. Eight to ten years is common for continuous breeding of a queen. Litter size is reduced with age, but the average queen will produce two litters of two to six kittens (average four per litter). Some queens will produce three litters per year. Siamese cats and Siamese crossbreeds have slightly larger litters (average six kittens). First litters of pubertal breedings are usually small and rearing may be less successful.

The queen is seasonally polyestrous; that is, she is receptive to the male several times within the breeding season. The season in temperate zones usually begins twenty to sixty days after the winter solstice (the shortest day of the year), and it may end any time after the summer solstice (the longest day of the year). In the northern temperate zone, breeding usually begins in January or February and extends through the early part of September. In some cases, it may extend into October or early November. The first cycle usually will occur between January and March, the second from April to early July, and the last during late July through early September. Frequently the first cycles of the year in free-ranging cats have been noted during a January or February thaw. Kittens can be born in any month of the year.

The queen is known as a "long day" breeder, like the mare; that is, she is influenced by the lengthening of daylight. Twelve to fourteen hours per day of continuous artificial light may result in continuous polyestrus, with no anestrous period noted in the fall and winter. Fewer than twelve hours of artificial light per day, in a cat that is not exposed to daylight, may lead to anestrus regardless of the season. Even in breeding colonies with artificial light, some queens will experience a fall anestrus.

Tomcats usually exhibit depressed sexual activity during the fall period.

The *vomeronasal organ* is a blind pouch above the hard palate that communicates with the nasal and oral cavities via the *nasopalatine duct,* which opens behind the incisor teeth. The vomeronasal organ is believed to perceive pheromones, which are chemical odors in urine and glandular secretions; possibly vaginal and vulvar secretions; and residual scent marks in the environment. Both toms and queens produce pheromones, which act as sexual attractants. The production of the tomcat odor released during the spraying of urine for territorial marking is dependent on the presence of androgen (male sex hormones), and is much reduced after castration.

In the estrous female, *valeric acid* is present in vaginal secretions. Tomcats may show an open-mouth *Flehmen* response (exposing the teeth by retracting the upper lip) when sniffing female urine. The odor of valeric acid also induces a restless and lively searching reaction, but without any sexual connotation. Sexually mature queens respond to the odor by exhibiting typical estrous behavior; thus valeric acid also may induce or facilitate estrus in other females.

Catnip leaves contain a chemical substance called *nepetalactone,* which produces a characteristic behavior that simulates the antics of estrous queens. It is an olfactory response mediated by the vomeronasal organ. Catnip is not considered a feline sex pheromone. It is, instead, an hallucinogen that induces pleasurable behavior in cats, independent of sex or the presence of sex organs. Therefore, giving them catnip has no sexual side effects, and they enjoy it. The catnip response appears to be inherited as an *autosomal dominant* trait (i.e., it is not sex-linked; *see* Chapter 13: Genetics).

Cats employ three methods of territorial marking: visual signs produced by scratching; glandular secretions of the head and face; and urine spraying. Tomcats have even been observed to spray the wheels of parked cars, a trait frequently displayed by male dogs.

Mating

When cats mate the result is almost always pregnancy, and then the birth of kittens. Pregnancy is either the result of planned breeding by knowledgeable breeders of purebred cats, or of accidental breeding, where the lives of the mother and kittens will probably be in question. Millions of unwanted cats are destroyed each year because there are not enough suitable homes for them. For this reason, all possible measures should be taken to prevent accidental breeding. (*See* Chapter 15: Birth Control.)

PLANNED MATING

Breeders mate cats as part of an overall plan that includes genetic selection, informed mating procedures, proper medical care, and the placement of kittens in good homes. The goal of such matings is to further the best qualities of two lines of a pure breed by combining them for a desired result in the kittens. The breeders classify the offspring in the following categories: show quality (the most valuable), breeding quality, and pet quality. Planned matings require information, skill, experience, and a good purpose. The information presented here comes strictly from a medical perspective.

Proper Selection

When choosing males and females for mating purposes, many elements should be considered. Both males and females should be examined by a veterinarian before mating. A tomcat selected for stud is usually not mated until he is twelve months of age. Although female cats make excellent mothers and seldom have difficulties (if they are properly cared for), they should not be bred until they are at least ten months old and well developed. If a female is bred before maturity, she may never fully develop physically, since many of the nutrients required for her growth will be passed to the fetal kittens. Furthermore, a female should be examined by a veterinarian before breeding to ensure that she is in good health, mature, and free of external and internal parasites. An examination of the reproductive tract and mammary glands as well as the other body systems is essential. The veterinarian also may recommend a diet and a nutritional supplement for pregnancy.

When a male or a female is selected for breeding, its pedigree and conformation (aesthetic quality) may be important, but must not be the only criteria. Males and females should be selected from parental lines that have a history of normal sexual cycling; do *not* have a history of difficult birthing; have produced good-sized litters, and have reared healthy litters.

These desirable characteristics are genetically based and thus can be inherited. (Chapter 13: Genetics, and Chapter 14: Normal Development and Congenital Birth Defects, offer essential information for the mating selection process.) Pet owners should keep records of all heats, breeding dates, queenings (births), litter sizes, and rearings for providing a breeding history and for making future decisions.

SEXUAL BEHAVIOR

In the queen, sexual behavior is stimulatory; it attracts tomcats. Behavioral maneuvers during proestrus (the period before estrus) are usually subtle—perhaps increased affection (or occasional aggression) and a desire to be petted. Sometimes the cat urinates more frequently than usual. In proestrus or early estrus, a small quantity of a clear, watery vaginal discharge may be present. In one study, 20 percent of cycling queens showed a half- to two-day proestrus in which they demonstrated behavioral characteristics of estrus—attracting toms, rolling in front of them, meowing—but would not allow mounting or copulation.

Estrous behavior of the queen in the absence of a tomcat usually includes persistent vocalization, rolling, rubbing, extreme affection, treading of the hind legs, lordosis (swayback), and tail deviation. A slight forward and lateral set to the ears is common, and an intense facial expression like that seen with aggression or fright. A repeated monotonous howling for as long as three minutes at a time is not unusual and may accompany treading and rolling. This "estrous cry" is given by the queen to indicate that she is in heat and sexually receptive. In the presence of a male, she gives an "appeasement cry" to stimulate him to mount. Restlessness, a general uneasiness, and pacing back and forth may accompany any of these behavioral patterns. A general loss of appetite in both the queen and the tomcat is common during the breeding season. Both males and females accustomed to going outdoors may disappear for days. Fight wounds and ear injuries are frequent at this time.

Copulation

Once the female has shown that she is ready to mate, the waiting, watchful male approaches from the side and grasps the skin of her neck in his teeth. Next he places his forelegs over her shoulders and mounts. He positions himself by straddling her pelvic area and treading along her flanks with his hind legs, sometimes stroking her chest with his forepaws. At this time the queen reflexively positions her perineum (the area between anus and genitalia) by arching her back until her vulva (entrance to the vagina) is almost horizontal, her tail deviating to one side. Once the position is correct, the tom initiates pelvic thrusting with his exposed penis and, on contact and intromission (insertion), ejaculates. The length of time from neck-biting to intromission can vary from thirty seconds to eight minutes. The queen's subsequent coital cry or scream is followed by her quickly rolling or twisting out of the male's grasp and aggressively attacking him if he doesn't move away quickly. She immediately displays a postcoital "after action," consisting of disoriented rolling, stretching, and genital licking, which may last from one to nine minutes.

The coital scream or cry was once thought to be from pain caused by the penile spines, but this reaction can be elicited in queens in or out of estrus, intact or spayed, with any instrument that invades the vaginal and cervical area.

Another mating sequence may occur immediately following the after-action, or the queen may refuse the tom's attempts to remount for a period ranging from several minutes up to five hours.

In one study, the number of copulations with one female ranged from twenty to thirty-six during thirty-six hours of observation. Couplings were more frequent during the first two hours (three to six copulations) than any subsequent two-hour period. The tom stays at some distance to survey and guard his territory. In unplanned matings among free-roaming cats, other toms may challenge him and indeed may even mate with "his" queen. If they are successful, the result can be a litter fathered by two or more different tomcats—an event referred to as *superfecundation*.

The Influence of the Estrous Cycle on Copulation

The average length of estrus in the cat is about five to eight days, with a range of three to twenty days. Periods of ten days or longer are considered prolonged. The duration of estrus is not greatly influenced by mating and induced ovulation, although some believe that estrus may be a day or two shorter in average duration in mated queens. Others have reported the opposite effect, with mated queens in estrus for 8.3 to 8.6 days, and nonmated queens in estrus for an average of 6.2 days.

The duration of proestrus, estrus, and the interestrous periods and cycle interval can be quite variable. Proestrus can really only be characterized early by the presence of a male, or possibly by *vaginal cytology* (see below). A length of zero to three days has been reported for proestrus. The interestrous period will last usually three to fourteen days during the breeding season, but may be as long as thirty days. Thus the length of an unbred queen's cycle can range from seven to forty days, with most cycles being twelve to twenty-two days in length.

Ovulation

Ovulation (release of eggs, or ova) in the queen depends on the release of sufficient amounts of luteinizing hormone (LH) from the anterior pituitary gland in the brain. The queen, as described in the previous chapter, is an induced, or reflex, ovulator; LH is released by vaginal-cervical stimulation during mating. Ovulation usually occurs within twenty-five to thirty hours after mating if sufficient LH has been released. Some investigators have reported the occurrence of ovulation up to fifty hours after mating. Certain queens will not release an ovulatory amount of LH until the second, third, or even fourth day of estrus. The best time to breed queens is on the second or third day of estrus. At least four matings should occur to ensure that the queen releases adequate LH and achieves maximal ovulation.

Induced Ovulation

Some queens may not exhibit typical behavioral signs (except for increased affection) during every heat period, but can be induced to do so if properly handled or when exposed to the tom. Treading, lordosis, and the typical copulatory stance with lateral deviation of the tail can be induced by stroking the flank, back, thigh, or perineum. Rubbing or scratching the back of the neck or shoulder induces treading, but usually not the precoital stance. The ear position and facial expression may be induced by all of these manipulations. Handling and stroking an estrous queen may cause enough neural stimulation to induce ovulation.

Ovulation can be induced in estrous queens by artificially stimulating the vaginal walls or cervix with a lubricated clean thermometer or cotton swab in order to enhance the release of LH. Studies have revealed that sensation from the vagina induces behavioral responses from the queen appropriate to intromission. Ovulation can be triggered by impulses from the vagina or the cervix received during intromission.

Injecting anestrous or estrous queens with luteinizing hormone-releasing hormone (LH-RH) (*see* Chapter 9: Reproductive Physiology) causes LH release and results in ovulation during estrus. Ovulation will also occur in estrous queens within twenty-six or twenty-seven hours of the administration of *human chorionic gonadotrophin* (HCG), which is an LH product produced by the human placenta. Fertilization rates are almost 100 percent if mating occurs within this time. Fertilization rates decline, however, if mating is delayed for more than thirty hours after HCG treatment. Conception can occur fifty-two or more hours after HCG administration, however, indicating that the fertile life of the egg after ovulation is about twenty-four hours.

MATING DIFFICULTIES

Infertility in the Tom

This problem is infrequently seen or reported. Psychological infertility (impotency) may be observed in tomcats undergoing environmental or territorial changes, or in young novice males placed with aggressive, experienced queens. Time and acclimation may result in acceptance and a return of fertility. The chances for a successful mating are improved if the estrous queen is first allowed to visit the tom's location for several days. Not all tomcats will mount any queen, nor will all queens accept any tom.

A tomcat's loss of his canine teeth following trauma (accident) or dental disease may make it difficult or impossible for him to grasp the neck skin of the queen and complete the breeding act. The short jaw and huge ruff of Persian cats can also be handicaps in mating.

A hair ring may form around the base of the *glans penis* (the cap-shaped end of the penis), especially in long-haired cats, or after several matings, resulting in difficult intromission. If the tomcat does not remove this ring during routine cleaning, it can be removed by retracting the prepuce and sliding the hair ring over the penis.

The tortoiseshell male cat is reputed to be sterile, but a few are reported fertile.

Infertility in the Queen

Occasionally a timid queen, low in social standing in a colony of females and matched with an experienced breeding male, will express poor estrous behavior, not allowing the tom to mount and breed. The relative size of the male and female also may influence the success of mating. Females that are too large or too small may make a rapid coital act difficult, resulting in a frustrated and unsuccessful tom. Although the activity of such a male in attempting to breed with a female may be enough to induce ovulation, the absence of intromission and ejaculation will fail to deposit semen for fertilization.

Knowledge regarding infertility in the queen has been enhanced by careful, methodical reproductive examinations and careful record keeping. The use of veterinary diagnostic laboratories to obtain hormone profiles; evaluation of vaginal cytology; provision for good veterinary clinical practices; and client education have greatly furthered success in the diagnosis and treatment of infertility. The veterinary profession as a whole and a number of veterinary colleges and private clinics have made small-animal theriogenology (the study of reproduction) a specialty, as it is for large domestic-animal species.

Some queens do not exhibit noticeable sexual behavior during estrus, causing the receptive period to be overlooked. In such cases, vaginal cytology, performed by the veterinarian, can be of assistance.

Under a microscope, the cells from the lining of the vagina can be seen to change from one stage of the estrous cycle to the next; hence, examination of these cells can determine a queen's current stage in the cycle (*see* Table 1).

Cells for vaginal cytology may be collected with a moistened sterile cotton swab (3-mm or 0.12-inch diameter) or a clean glass eyedropper. The swab or eyedropper is passed into the vagina about 1 to 1.5 centimeters (0.4 to 0.6 inch), by first inserting it into the *vestibule* until resistance is met, and then redirecting it horizontally into the vagina. This ensures that the *clitoris* and *clitoral fossa* (channel) are not entered or irritated. The swab is then rotated several times in the vagina. (As an alternative, about 0.25 ml [0.008 ounce] of sterile physiological *saline* [a salt solution] in an eyedropper can be flushed two or three times into the vagina.) The swab is rolled onto a clean glass microscope slide, which is then immediately fixed in alcohol or air-dried (fluid from the eyedropper can be placed on the glass slide and allowed to dry). The slide is then dipped in a dye solution so that the cells will be stained. Slides should be kept as a reference for changes occurring throughout the estrous cycle.

Smears of vaginal cells should be obtained daily or every other day in order to differentiate the stages of the estrous cycle. In some estrous queens, vaginal swabbing or flushing itself may induce ovulation. If ovulation does not occur during an estrous cycle, the cytology will regress to an anestrous type, and *noncornified epithelial cells* (nonhardened cells of the vaginal lining) will appear.

Red blood cells normally should not be present in the queen's vagina during any stage of the estrous cycle. If they are, the most likely reasons are trauma to the vaginal cavity during sample collection, a genital tract infection, or sampling during early postpartum period.

In early pregnancy or pseudopregnancy (see page 102) there are numerous cells and the reappearance of increasing numbers of intermediate and parabasal cells (lower-level epithelium cells) with a rapid decline in cornified cells. Leukocytes (white blood cells) reappear, with debris and mucus present again. As pregnancy or pseudopregnancy progresses, the smear will resemble that seen in anestrus, with intermediate and parabasal cells predominant and less cells present, although the background may contain a great deal of mucus. Queens that exhibit estrogen surges

---

TABLE 1.　　　**VAGINAL CYTOLOGY SHOWING STAGES OF ESTRUS**

STAGE	CYTOLOGY
Anestrus	Numerous small round epithelial cells (vaginal lining cells) with a *high nuclear to cytoplasmic ratio* (i.e., the cellular nuclei are large) are present. Occasionally *polymorphonuclear leukocytes* (a type of white blood cell) are found. There is an increased amount of cellular debris present.
Proestrus	An increased number of intermediate epithelial cells are present. *Cornified* (hardened) epithelial cells begin to appear more frequently before estrus occurs. There is a decrease in size of the nuclei. There is cellular debris.
Estrus	The smear is dominated by *polyhedral* (many-sided) cornified epithelial cells with curled edges. Because the vaginal fluid is watery, there is less debris than in the other stages of the estrous cycle. Polymorphonuclear leukocytes are absent.
Metestrus	After ovulation, cornified epithelial cells are still present, but the margins are less well defined. Occasionally many bacteria and polymorphonuclear leukocytes are present. During late metestrus, there is an increase in smaller *basophilic* (dark blue staining) epithelial cells.

---

during pregnancy or at the end of gestation may reflect this in their vaginal cytology. If leukocytes are numerous in any smear and show indications of clumping in masses and advanced degeneration or toxicity, or if the smear contains large numbers of bacteria or red blood cells, one could consider an inflammatory process and examine further.

Induction of Estrus (not to be confused with induced ovulation described above). Induction of estrus in a queen can be enhanced by lengthening the daily light cycle to which she is exposed, socializing her with other cycling queens, exposing her to a tom, or administering hormonal therapy.

Various hormonal regimens have successfully induced queens into estrus. An 80 percent efficiency rate has been reported with use of *gonadotropins* (sexual stimulation hormones). This method produces the best results in queens between the ages of one and five years. It consists of an initial dose of *pregnant mare's serum gonadotropin* (PMSG) given intramuscularly. This is then reduced to a lower dosage given on seven consecutive days, depending on the season (lower doses if treatment is given between February and August). When estrous behavior becomes apparent, the dose is further reduced.

A second method, which produces results comparable to those of natural breeding, uses a single injection of PMSG followed in seven days by an injection of smaller amounts of human chorionic gonadotropin (HCG). A third method uses *follicle-stimulating hormone from pituitary extracts* (FSH-P) to induce estrus. FSH-P is administered intramuscularly, daily for five days or until the queen shows signs of estrus. On days one and two of estrus, lower doses of HCG are given intramuscularly to enhance ovulation. The queen should then be bred at least four times on each day of estrus for a period of up to four days.

Estrogens of *estradiol benzoate* or of *estradiol cypionate,* given intramuscularly and repeated in forty-eight hours, will induce false estrus in most queens. Testosterone (male sex hormone), given intramuscularly, has also been reported to induce estrus in queens.

Using gonadotropins to induce estrus in queens may inadvertently lead to the queen's producing waves of ovarian follicles that may contain immature ova, resulting in *cystic follicular degeneration.* Also, excessively long estrous periods lasting two to four weeks may occur following administration of either gonadotropins or sex hormones, unless natural or artificial mating is provided.

The estrous behavior of queens receiving hormonal therapy should be evaluated daily by a handler or by observing the queen's response in the presence of an experienced tom. Studies indicate that queens in which estrus has been induced can produce litters of normal size.

ONSET OF PREGNANCY

Pregnancy in the queen lasts sixty-four to sixty-nine days, with an average of sixty-six days. (Some reports have an average of sixty-three days with a range of fifty-eight to sixty-five days, which is probably based on timing from the last intromission of multiple breedings.) Successful litters have recorded gestation periods of fifty-nine to seventy-one days. Variations also may be due to breed differences, colony differences, litter size, and possibly season of the year. Occasional queens will show estrus during pregnancy, and it is estimated that ten percent of pregnant queens, typically around twenty-one and forty-two days of pregnancy, may show sexual behavior. Possible *superfetation* (a second concurrent pregnancy) can occur at this time. Some queens will be in estrus within seven to ten days following parturition and may conceive if bred at this time, while caring for the litter they just delivered. Most will show lactational anestrus and not return to estrus until fifteen to sixty days (average two to three weeks) postweaning, while queens that have kittens that are removed from them within three days postpartum will return to estrus in six to eight days. Post-abortion estrus can occur within one week.

Following a fertile mating and ovulation twenty-five to thirty hours after sufficient release of LH, ova are fertilized by the ejaculated spermatozoa. Sperm require about one to two hours in the female reproductive tract before they are capable of fertilizing the egg. Ova remain fertile for up to forty-eight hours. Oviduct transport of fertilized ova takes four to five days. Migration of *blastocysts* (the developing embryos) in the uterine horn takes place for six to eight days, with implantation into the wall of the uterus occurring around day 12 to 14.

Corpora lutea form after the ovarian follicles rupture and luteinize within one to three days. Progesterone levels rise over 1 nanogram per milliliter (a nanogram is one billionth, 10^{-9}, of a gram) by day 3 after ovulation, and reach peak levels of 15 to 90 ng/ml by day 15 to 25. Progesterone levels in early pregnancy prior to implantation are not different from pseudopregnant levels, but by day 20, pregnant queens on the average have higher levels. By day 50, placental production of progesterone is adequate to maintain pregnancy and the ovaries' supply is no longer needed.

Levels of prolactin (a pituitary hormone that stimulates lactation) remain low during the first half of pregnancy, increase threefold to fivefold by day 63, and reach peak levels just before parturition. Prolactin levels are elevated in response to suckling during lactation and decline to basal levels two weeks after weaning.

Pseudopregnancy can occur after nonfertile matings, induced ovulation, or occasional "spontaneous" ovulation. Corpora lutea persist for three to seven weeks, with a mean of about forty days, followed by four to ten days of diestrus. Progesterone levels rise over 1 nanogram per milliliter by day 3 after ovulation, and reach peak levels of 14 to 90 ng/ml by day 15 to 25, and thereafter decline. Progesterone levels return to 1 ng/ml within 30 to 50 days, although reports of duration of pseudopregnancy, as the interval from mating to the next estrus, range from 35 to 70 days, with an average being 45 days.

Pregnancy and Parturition

PREGNANCY DIAGNOSIS

Pregnancy should be determined as early as possible following mating. Early diagnosis will ensure proper care of the queen through the gestation period and allow plans to be made for queening and rearing the kittens.

Gestation lasts sixty-four to sixty-nine days (the average is sixty-six days). The most common indication used in determining pregnancy is the change of the queen's nipples from light pink to rosy pink in the second and third weeks following mating. Pregnancy diagnosis is best accomplished, however, by careful abdominal palpation of the uterus between days 17 and 25 when the conceptus (embryo plus accompanying membranes) is round and separated from other conceptuses. After thirty to thirty-five days, the individual elongated fetuses and fetal membranes become difficult to distinguish and pregnancy can resemble an enlarged uterus caused by pseudo-

pregnancy or pyometra (a life-threatening disease of the uterus; *see* Chapter 12: Reproductive Disorders).

The mineralized opaque fetal skeleton will show on abdominal radiographs from the fortieth or forty-fifth day of gestation until term. If done following normal radiographic procedures, this amount of exposure is perfectly safe for the queen and harmless to the kittens. The approximate gestation age can be estimated by the radiographic appearance of mineralized bone in the fetus, since at forty-one days the radius (smaller bone of the lower foreleg) and ulna (larger bone of the lower foreleg) are visible; at forty-three days the tibia (larger bone of the lower hind leg), fibula (smaller bone of the lower hind leg), ilium (upper portion of hip bone), ischium (lower, rear portion of hip bone), and occipital (back part of head) bones can be seen; at fifty-five days the entire skeleton is visible.

TABLE 2.   **REPRODUCTIVE ENDOCRINOLOGY**

HORMONE:	COMMENTS:
Luteinizing Hormone	Released during mating. Ovulating cats have levels of 17 ± 2 ng/ml (nanograms/milliliter; a nanogram is one billionth of a gram), whereas nonovulating cats have high levels of 8 ± 2 ng/ml.
Progesterone	At baseline level (1 ng/ml or lower) during first two or three days of pregnancy but detectable thereafter. The level continues to increase until day 21, when the average level is approximately 30 ng/ml. After day 21 it decreases, to 4–5 ng/ml before parturition. After parturition the hormone level drops to 1 ng/ml or lower. Pseudopregnant queens have a similar increase; however, by day 30 the level begins to decline.
Estradiol	On the day of mating, the level is about 60 pg/ml (picograms/milliliter; a picogram is one trillionth of a gram). During the next five days it decreases rapidly, to 8–12 pg/ml. That level is maintained until parturition, when a slight increase occurs. Pseudopregnant cats follow a similar course, but a more rapid decrease follows mating.
Prolactin	Levels are elevated in the last trimester of pregnancy. The average is 31.2 ± 5.1 ng/ml through the last week of pregnancy; then it increases to 43.5 ± 5.4 ng/ml during the last three days before parturition. About two weeks after weaning, prolactin declines to prelactation levels.

Pregnancy can also be detected by ultrasonography. The amniotic sacs may be visible by day 18 of the pregnancy. By day 26, the fetus and fetal heartbeats are detectable. Fetal development, heart rates, and fetal movement can be followed from day 24 or 25 to parturition. Fetal resorption (disintegration of the fetus within the uterus), fetal death, and mummification can be diagnosed by ultrasonic examination.

A phenomenon known as pseudopregnancy can occur in queens. In fact, a queen can have as many as five pseudopregnancies in a breeding season. Elevated progesterone levels occur in pseudopregnant queens. The pseudopregnancy will terminate within about forty days of its onset as progesterone levels return to prebreeding levels. Ovarian activity is reestablished within seven to ten days after the end of a pseudopregnancy.

A profile of hormone levels measured in the blood can be used to demonstrate the pregnancy cycle. The above table lists the relevant hormones and the various levels they reach at the respective stages.

The progesterone plasma levels in early pregnancy are similar to those seen in pseudopregnancy until implantation takes place at about day 12 to 14. Progesterone plasma levels on day 50 average 13 ng/ml (nanograms per milliliter) in the pregnant queen versus 2 ng/ml in the pseudopregnant one, and on day 62 the average or mean level is 4–5 ng/ml in the pregnant queen versus 1 ng/ml in the pseudopregnant. Elevated progesterone blood levels in pseudopregnancy coincide with the pregnant cat's on her day of implantation and again on about day 28, when the first appearance of regressive luteal (of the corpora lutea that discharged the eggs) changes in the pseudopregnant cat are seen. At this time, blood progesterone levels increase in the pregnant queen, while levels in the pseudopregnant queen decline. At twenty-eight days the progesterone levels in the pregnant queen are also enhanced by an increase in placental progesterone. Corpora lutea of pregnant queens persist and produce progesterone until forty to fifty days into gestation, when placental production of progesterone is adequate to maintain pregnancy. Ovariectomy (removal of ovaries) performed between forty-five and forty-nine days or later will not affect pregnancy and normal kittens will be born at term.

CARE DURING PREGNANCY

The pregnant queen needs a well-balanced diet, with food provided so that, as fetal growth causes increased fetal weight, maternal food intake increases automatically. Overfeeding and excessive weight gain should be avoided. Feeding recommendations of commercial cat food suppliers for pregnant and nursing queens should be followed. Veterinary advice should be sought before supplementation with vitamins, minerals, proteins, or fats.

Nonstrenuous daily exercise to keep good muscle tone is necessary for easy queening. Obesity and poor muscle tone can result in low conception rates and difficult queening.

Medication, vaccination, and worming should be avoided during pregnancy, with treatment being planned and performed prior to breeding if possible. A clean, warm, dry, secluded, comfortable area with a large nesting box should be provided at least ten days before queening, though the queen may not choose to use it. Near term, the enlarged abdomen may cause restricted physical activity. A few days prior to queening, the mammary glands enlarge further and milk is present. The excessive hair in long-haired breeds should be removed from around the teats and vulva prior to queening and the vulvar area, if soiled, should be cleansed.

QUEENING

Rectal temperature falls in the first stage of labor. The queen will search for a warm, dark, secluded place and nest. Mammary gland development is present the last two weeks, and milk secretion can be seen on the last day. The second stage of labor is usually quite rapid; there are a few abdominal strains, similar to those of defecation, before the first kitten is delivered. One or two kittens may be born during this stage of labor. Normal presentation of the fetuses can be either forward or backward as they enter the birth canal. The queen consumes the placenta(s) and cleanses the vulvar area. The queen will clean the kittens vigorously to stimulate breathing and movement. She severs the cord by biting. Placental expulsion, the third stage of labor, follows the fetal delivery quite closely.

The first kitten may be nursed before the delivery of the next. Usually the next kitten is presented in less than an hour. If the queen is disturbed, especially if not confined (or even if confined), labor may cease, kittens may be moved and nursed, and queening may be continued hours, or days, later. Longer intervals between births may be due to superfetation (fertilization from a different ovulatory cycle).

Once the queen's labor has started, she should not be disturbed, except occasionally to check to see that all is well. If she has been having strong contractions for more than two hours, and no kittens have been born, the veterinarian must be called immediately. Mother and unborn kittens weaken rapidly, which lessens their chances of survival, particularly if a cesarean delivery is needed. The queen does not require help in cleaning the kittens or cutting the cords. It is extremely rare for a mother cat not to handle these procedures perfectly. However, she may stop these normal functions if humans interfere. Queens have been known to eat their kittens because of too much human meddling at this stage.

The first litter of a queen with only one or two large kittens may be difficult and assistance may be needed. Healthy queens seldom have difficulty with delivery. Queens that are inbred, have nutritional deficiencies, or have the stress of a disease may have poor uterine contractions ("inertia") and require assistance. Trauma or a nutritional deficiency may result in a pelvic deformity causing difficult delivery. Veterinary assistance for surgical intervention or medication with uterine muscle–stimulating and contracting agents will be needed for difficult births.

Stillborn kittens and placentas are usually eaten by the queen. Cannibalism is seen, but it is more likely in the first queening, especially in highly nervous animals. These queens should not be used for further breeding.

Postpartum hemorrhage, retained fetal membranes, retained dead kittens, and uterine prolapse (inside-out uterus protruding through cervix) are uncommon in the queen. Oxytocin, a uterine-contracting agent, may be used to control hemorrhage. Following uterine prolapse (protrusion of the uterus into vagina or out of the vulva), treatment of shock, or abdominal surgery, removal of the reproductive tract may be needed. Systemic antibiotics may also be indicated. A brown vaginal discharge and enlarged segments of the uterine horns indicate a retained fetus or placenta.

Medical or surgical removal will be needed to correct this condition.

Observe the vulva and surrounding areas of the queen daily for evidence of abnormal discharges. A bloody discharge is usually present for seven to ten days postqueening. Persistent discharges that are odorous or bloody indicate uterine infections or subinvolution (failure to return to normal size) of placental sites in the uterus. The mammary glands should also be examined for evidence of mastitis (inflammation of the mammary gland).

Abnormal vulvar discharges, evidence of fetal resorption or abortions, premature kittens, stillborn or mummified fetuses, or weak kittens with neonatal death call for veterinary attention. Specimens of the vulvar discharge, blood samples, and any fetal or placental tissue or dead kittens should be carefully handled and submitted to the veterinarian or to a veterinary diagnostic laboratory for examination and definitive diagnosis so that meaningful treatment, control, or preventive measures can be instituted. The queen and any remaining kittens should be strictly isolated from other cats, especially pregnant queens, since a contagious agent may be involved.

Feline viral rhinotracheitis, panleukopenia, toxoplasmosis, and bacterial agents can cause the above types of fetal loss. Feline leukemia virus (FeLV) and feline infectious peritonitis (FIP) virus have also been associated with this syndrome.

Diseases that primarily affect other body systems may secondarily affect the pregnant uterus. Any sign of illness should be examined, treated, and recorded by a veterinarian.

Eclampsia (milk fever) is occasionally seen during pregnancy or following birth. It occurs when pregnant or nursing mothers become depleted of calcium. The signs are restlessness, refusal to eat or to allow the kittens to nurse, trembling, and, eventually, convulsions. This condition can be fatal within a few hours, but response to veterinary medical treatment is as dramatically swift as it is life-saving.

Queens with the above postpartum problems may be listless and unable to nurse or care for their kittens. Immediate diagnosis, treatment, and supplemental care for the young are required, or loss of the mother and her kittens may occur. The queen and frequently the kittens need antibiotic and supportive therapy. Antibiotic-sensitivity tests for organisms cultured from vulvar discharges or mastitic milk are important. Whether to separate the mother from her kittens will depend on the severity of the condition, her ability to care for them, and the contagiousness of her infection.

Parturition is accompanied by a decline in progesterone to basal (lowest) levels, but detailed studies are needed to determine if the serum progesterone levels fall to basal levels preceding or following placental expulsion. Estradiol-17B is elevated above the base level of 9 pg/ml (picograms per milliliter) between days 58 and 62 and declines sharply just before parturition. In one study, pregnant queens treated with follicle stimulating hormone (FSH) on days 33–37 and human chorionic gonadotrophin (HCG) on days 38 and 39 developed follicles (average 9.3 follicles/cat), ovulated (average 3.4 corpora lutea/cat), and exhibited behavioral estrus (5 of 7 cats). Estradiol-17B levels gradually increased, but serum progesterone levels remained constant in the treated cats, while in control cats, levels gradually declined as expected. Gestation periods and litter size were not significantly different between treated and control queens.

Prolactin blood levels are elevated during the last third of pregnancy. In the last three days of gestation, levels increase to 43.5 ± 4.5 ng/ml. Suckling stimulus maintains prolactin levels at 40.6 ± 7.2 ng/ml for the first four weeks postpartum, and 27.8 ± 3.1 ng/ml during the last two weeks of lactation. Following weaning, levels decrease to approximately 15 ng/ml, with basal levels of 7.3 ± 0.6 ng/ml maintained after the second week. Pseudopregnancy has no effect on prolactin levels in the queen.

The endocrinology and physiology of parturition in the queen have not been fully studied. A few days before parturition, the queen experiences a decrease in circulating progesterone to slightly above prepregnancy levels and an increase in estradiol-17B levels. Then the estradiol level drops on the day of parturition as circulating prolactin levels increase. The endogenous effects and levels of prostaglandin, relaxin, cortisol, and oxytocin are unknown. Clinically, administration of oxytocin is very effective in causing uterine contractions to end uterine inertia, expel retained kittens or placentas, and initiate milk let-down. Probably endogenous oxytocin is present. The queen will also react to gentle stroking or "feathering" of the vagina during parturition, resulting in uterine contractions.

To determine the sex of the kittens on the day of birth, the anogenital (anus-to-genital) distance is measured with a soft, pliable-plastic millimeter ruler. The distance is shorter in females.

Measuring may not be necessary. Often males and females can be differentiated visually. The male has two dots—like a colon. The female has an exclamation point (anus and vulva).

MATERNAL CARE AND LACTATION

The mother usually remains continuously with her kittens for a period of twenty-four to forty-eight hours. About 2–3 ml (.07 to .10 ounce) of milk is taken by the kittens three times an hour. Kittens double their weight in seven days and open their eyes between ten and fourteen days. They are able to take 4–7 ml (.14 to .24 ounce) of milk at a feeding in the second week. At this time, the queen will leave the nest for several hours. In her absence, the kittens will sleep quietly if

ANOGENITAL DISTANCE OF KITTENS

	Birth	21 Days	42 Days
Males	11 to 16 mm	14 to 21 mm	16 to 23 mm
Females	6 to 9 mm	8 to 13 mm	10 to 15 mm

normal. After feeding, the queen washes each kitten, especially around its head and anal region. She consumes the urine and feces, which are voided in response to grooming. By three weeks of age the kittens have increased their activity to exploring and playing. The queen then teaches the kittens to urinate and defecate away from the nest. Lactation is supplemented by solid food beginning with the third or fourth week; weaning is completed by the seventh or eighth week. (*See* Chapter 3: Kittens and Disorders.)

Reproductive Disorders

It's important to have some knowledge of the normal reproduction cycle and physiology of the cat in order to understand its reproductive diseases and possible infertility problems.

INFERTILITY

A detailed history, general physical examination, and a thorough genital tract examination of the queen are indicated for investigation of an infertility problem. The history should include her fertility and breeding history, her littermates, and maternal and paternal records. Genetic problems are better appreciated if pedigrees are available. The breeding record of males used also should be evaluated.

General health and dietary records should be reviewed. Management practices resulting in psychological or environmental stresses within a cattery may be of significance in some breeding problems. The use of the cat also may be important, particularly if the show ring is involved.

All breeding queens should be blood-tested for feline leukemia virus (FeLV), feline immuno-deficiency virus (FIV), and feline coronavirus (feline infectious peritonitis [FIP]). A complete physical examination, hemogram (blood screen or CBC [complete blood count]), and a urogenital tract examination, including vaginoscopy, vaginal cytology, and palpation, should be performed. Queens with estrous-cycle problems should be followed through these cycles by investigation of sexual behavior, vaginal cytology, and possibly hormone profile testing for progesterone levels. Queens with poor conception or with possible early embryonic or fetal death or abortion problems should be followed throughout breeding and pregnancy with vaginal cytology and culture, blood progesterone levels, pregnancy diagnosis, and, if possible, ultrasonography (ultrasound, for determining fetal viability). Radiographic (X ray) methods for detecting late fetal death or genital-tract abnormalities are available. Laparoscopy (visual inspection of the interior of the abdomen) of the urogenital tract and biopsy of the uterus may be indicated for further diagnosis.

Infertility in the tom rarely occurs; however, when it does, it can be very frustrating to the cat breeder. The microscopic evaluation of semen can provide valuable information on the fertility of the tom's sperm. Semen evaluation includes a sperm count, an estimation of the percentage of motile (spontaneously moving) sperm, and an assessment of sperm morphology (form and structure). Semen for microscopic evaluation can be collected from a tom by using an artificial vagina, by performing electroejaculation under anesthesia, or by flushing the queen's vagina immediately following copulation. The latter of these methods usually results in a poor specimen, although it may still provide valuable information on the motility and morphology of the sperm. Use of the artificial vagina requires training the tom to ejaculate into a small rubber bulb fitted over a test tube. This training may take three or more weeks.

Poor libido and variable testicular degeneration (less functional testes) leading to absence of sperm development have been linked to malnutrition, obesity, hypervitaminosis A (caused by diets containing excessive amounts of liver; *see* Chapter 8: Diseases of Dietary Origin), and hypothyroidism. Proper diagnosis of the condition, and treatment of the cause, usually result in a return to normal fertility with time.

Detailed record keeping, a systematic approach to physical examination, clinical tests and follow-up veterinary visits, and informed owners who are knowledgeable in normal reproductive physiology and common breeding problems are all essential components of a successful breeding program.

ANATOMIC CONGENITAL DEFECTS AND INTERSEXUALITY

Anatomic or congenital defects of the female reproductive system have been reported but are uncommon. Rare cases of *intersexuality* (having characteristics of both sexes present in the same animal) also have been described.

Cystic rete ovarii tubules (meshwork of dilated ovarian tubules) occur in queens of any age. *Uterus unicornis* (uterus having only one uterine horn) has been reported and may be accompanied by absence of a kidney on the affected side. Cysts involving *Gartner's duct* (located parallel to the uterus) or *Bartholin's gland* (along the vulvar lips), the tissues surrounding the ovary and uterus, or the fimbriated (fringed) end of the oviduct, occasionally occur. *Segmental aplasia* (imperfect development of a segment) of the uterus has also been seen.

Congenital testicular hypoplasia (underdevelopment of the testicles) of the tom may be a consequence of fetal or neonatal (newborn) panleukopenia.

Tortoiseshell and tricolored cats are almost always female. If they are male they are usually sterile. The gene for orange coat color in the tortoiseshell is on the X chromosome—the female chromosome. (*See* Chapter 13: Genetics.)

HORMONAL DISTURBANCES

Hormonal disturbances in females, including abnormal expression of estrus (the sexually active period) and anestrus (the sexually inactive period), have been observed. These cases have not been well documented in the form of clinical research studies. The procedures required for proper diagnosis and follow-up are time-consuming and expensive for the owner of an individual pet or breeding cattery. Most of the information that exists originates from basic studies carried out by reproductive physiologists.

Underlying causes of hormonal disturbances in the queen include: prolonged repetitive secretion of estrogens, followed by progesterone, from multiple nonpregnant breeding cycles; cystic follicular degeneration; *corpus luteum* (ovarian follicle after it discharges its ovum or egg) *cysts; granulosa cell* (cells around the ovarian follicles) *tumors.* Some of the disorders which these basic underlying problems can produce include: *cystic endometrial hyperplasia* (exuberant overgrowth of inner lining of the uterus); *hydrometra* (collection of watery fluid within the uterus); *pyometra* (accumulation of pus and bacteria within the uterus); mammary gland *hyperplasia* (overgrowth) and *neoplasia* (cancer); *inguinal* (between abdomen and thigh in the groin) *hernia* (rupture);

possible *alopecia* (absence of hair) on the underside of the body.

In addition, prolonged high levels of estrogen or progesterone have been shown to produce cystic endometrial hyperplasia and *pyometritis* (pus-forming inflammation of the uterus). Therefore, it is a good practice to breed queens at an early age, or to use steroid contraceptives to delay pregnancy but maintain a normal uterus. Once litters have been produced, several nonpregnant cycles should not be permitted because the same disease syndrome may develop. As soon as a queen's producing career has ended, an *ovariohysterectomy* (surgical removal of the uterus and ovaries; or spay) should be performed in order to eliminate the potential threat of pyometritis and ovarian cysts or tumors. Ovarian cysts, commonly observed in cats, occur more frequently in older cats. Functional ovarian cysts may lead to *hyperestrogenism* (excessive secretion of estrogen) or persistently low levels of blood progesterone.

Sex steroid levels, evaluation of sexual behavior, vaginal cytology (microscopic study of vaginal cells), and vaginoscopic (visual inspection of the vagina with a speculum [instrument for viewing body cavities]) and laparoscopic examinations are all useful in the clinical diagnosis of hormonal reproductive disorders in the queen.

The queen is a seasonal breeder and responds to an increase in daylight or artificial light. Pubertal estrus may be seen as soon as four months of age in kittens born early in spring, but in those born in late spring or later it may be delayed for as long as eight months. Continuous anestrus is associated with nutritional imbalance, disease states, *gonadal hypoplasia* (impaired growth of the ovaries or testes), intersexuality, environmental stresses, or insufficient light. Secluded house queens that preferentially select dark areas may never come into estrus. Also, single-housed queens are less likely to show estrus than are socialized queens housed with other cycling queens or with males. *Hypothyroidism* (deficiency of thyroid hormones) is uncommon in cats and is seldom a cause of anestrus. Anestrous queens can be induced to cycle with pregnant mare's serum gonadotrophin or follicle-stimulating hormone therapy. (*See* "Induction of Estrus," Chapter 10: Mating.)

Queens with cystic follicular degeneration often show signs of nymphomania, attracting tomcats but not allowing mating. Many are ill-tempered during this time. The most frequent ovarian cyst in the cat at any age is cystic rete ovarii. These queens do not show nymphomania. Found in queens at any age, these cysts can cause complete destruction of the ovary, resulting in a *cystadenoma* (cystic benign tumor containing glandular structures). Nymphomania should not be misdiagnosed in regularly cycling queens that have not mated or that have received only a single mating with insufficient vaginal stimulation to induce ovulation. Such queens may remain in estrus for ten to twenty days or longer. Queens that have a sterile mating but ovulate will undergo a pseudopregnancy lasting from twenty to forty-five days, and then return to estrus within one to two weeks during the breeding season. These queens will respond to breeding and are usually fertile. (*See* "Onset of Pregnancy," Chapter 10: Mating, and Chapter 11: Pregnancy and Parturition.)

Treatment for queens with cystic follicular degeneration includes attempted luteinization (converting the ovarian follicle into a corpus luteum) of the cyst; induction of ovulation using human chorionic gonadotrophin (HCG); and counteraction of hyperestrogenism with progestins (progesterone). However, progestins may produce endometrial hyperplasia, *endometritis* (inflammation of the inner lining of the uterus), pyometra, or pyometritis. Once a regular cycle has been produced, these animals should be bred. If litters are not desired, ovariohysterectomy is indicated.

Hyperestrogenism and nymphomania can be seen in spayed queens. This is usually due to an ovarian remnant or possibly accessory ovarian tissue between the removed ovary and the attachment of the ovarian ligament to the body wall. A laparoscopic examination or a surgical laparotomy (incision of the abdomen) with identification and removal of the remnant is best accomplished when the cat is showing signs of estrus. At this time the follicles or cysts are present, making the remnant easier to identify. A single injection of HCG may cause ovulation or luteinization with increased blood progesterone levels, but in time the animal will re-cycle. Excised ovarian remnants should be examined microscopically by a pathologist for identification of ovarian structures. Excessive hyperestrogenism in queens can lead to *estrogen toxicity*, bone marrow depression, and resulting deficiency of blood platelets (cells involved in blood clotting), rapid hemorrhagic shock, and death.

Hypoluteoidism (sterility caused by insufficient secretion of progesterone) in queens produces repeated embryo/fetal loss or abortion at the same stage of pregnancy. Other possible diagnoses—infectious diseases, low-grade reproductive tract infections, degenerative endometrial conditions, genetic abnormalities—must be ruled out. Blood progesterone levels taken biweekly are helpful in diagnosing hypoluteoidism. Long-acting progesterone injections, beginning seven to ten days before the expected abortion and terminating seven to ten days before the expected parturition, have been useful in therapy.

In the absence of coitus, the queen usually has no *luteal phase* (period during which the ovarian follicle converts to a corpus luteum and secretes progesterone). Some queens can be stimulated to ovulate by stroking the perineum. If a sterile mating occurs, or if ovulation is artificially induced, corpora lutea are formed and a pseudopregnancy occurs. Very few queens show "overt" pseudopregnancy, however. Occasionally one may see mammary gland engorgement, with the queen allowing young to suckle, or displaying signs of labor or maternal behavior toward inanimate objects. Usually no treatment is necessary. If therapy is indicated, long-acting testosterone or tranquilization may be provided by a veterinarian.

One form of hyperadrenocorticism (overactivity of the adrenal glands) has been seen in cats following prolonged and excessive treatment with *glucocorticosteroids* (a type of steroid), or progestins such as *megestrol acetate* (Ovaban), administered for skin conditions, urine spraying in tomcats, aggressiveness, or prolonged suppression of estrus. This condition is extremely rare.

PATHOLOGY OF THE GENITAL TRACT

Developmental and Acquired Anatomical Conditions

The most common reproductive tract abnormalities of the queen are *uterus unicornis* (lack of one uterine horn) and *segmental aplasia* (lack of development of portions of the tract). One horn (and possibly the ovary on the same side) may be missing, or blind segments of the uterus may be present that become progressively fluid-filled with each estrous cycle. Stenotic (narrowed) or fibrous (thickened) adhe-

sions, or complete closure and scarring of the cervix, may occasionally be diagnosed as a cause of infertility. This usually results when a young queen that has never given birth delivers one or two kittens and in so doing traumatizes the cervix. Diagnosis is made by obtaining a history of infertility and by visual examination of the cervix. The prognosis is poor for further breeding.

Pedunculated endometrial polyps (growths attached by a stem to the lining of the uterus) have been seen in aged queens.

The tom is born with descended testes in the scrotum. *Cryptorchid* (one or both undescended) or *ectopic* (not scrotal, usually between scrotum and body cavity under skin) testes should not be corrected, but instead should be removed when the cat has reached appropriate age, size, and maturity, because these conditions may be inherited.

Neoplasia (Tumors)

OVARIAN TUMORS. *Cystadenomas* are quite common in the ovary of the queen and appear to originate from the rete ovarii. They are multiple, thin-walled cysts containing a clear, watery fluid, and may in time completely replace the true ovarian tissue.

Dysgerminomas are malignant in 10 to 20 percent of cases. These are analogous to the *seminoma* in the testes of the male, and consist of a uniform population of large round or polygonal cells. The dysgerminoma is a highly cellular tumor, containing little connective tissue. It grows quickly, and *necrosis* (cell death) and hemorrhages are frequently present.

Teratomas are rare tumors that contain a mixture of normal and cancerous tissues. They may be solid or cystic, and may contain hair, skin, cartilage, bone, teeth, or muscle. Both malignant and benign teratomas have been reported.

Granulosa cell tumors are usually malignant and will metastasize (spread). These tumors are able to produce steroid hormones—estrogens, testosterone, and progesterone—resulting in either nymphomania, *virilization* (causing male characteristics), or anestrus. Alopecia and prolonged estrus have also been caused by granulosa cell tumors in cats.

MAMMARY TUMORS. Mammary tumors in cats are common compared with other domestic animals, and are seen most often in females (although mammary tumors occur in male cats as well).

Progesterone causes mammary gland *hyperplasia* (overgrowth) in the queen. Hyperplasia can be confused with cancer as well as mastitis (inflammation of the mammary gland), which is caused by bacterial infection of the lactating gland postpartum or during pseudopregnancy.

Feline mammary *hypertrophy* (enlargement), also called *juvenile fibroadenomatous hyperplasia*, may affect a single gland or an entire chain. It is most frequently seen in young, sexually intact females, following an estrus that has resulted in pseudopregnancy or pregnancy, and appears to be progesterone-dependent. Clinically it does not resemble mammary cancer. The enlargement or engorgement is along the entire mammary gland chain. Each gland is round, firm, and larger than normal. Breast tumors are usually solitary small nodules. Feline mammary hypertrophy has been shown to regress following ovariohysterectomy. Spontaneous remission also occurs, usually without recurrence of the disease during subsequent pregnancy or pseudopregnancy. Many affected queens are lethargic and have difficulty walking, owing to the extremely enlarged glands. Ulceration and excoriation (abrasion) of the skin over the enlarged glands is commonly seen, and secondary mastitis may occur. Warm-water soaks and antibiotic therapy are recommended if bacterial mastitis develops.

Malignant mammary tumors comprise between 6 and 11 percent of all feline cancers. They tend to occur in older cats, the mean age at occurrence being 11.5 years. Malignant feline mammary tumors arise most commonly in the anterior glands. In contrast to the situation in the dog, these tumors grow rapidly and are nearly always malignant. Most of them are adenocarcinomas of the *papillary* type. The most common sites of tumor spread are the local lymph nodes and the lung; however, tumor masses also can be found in the liver, adrenal glands, kidney, spleen, and heart. These tumors are frequently lethal.

Nonmalignant ovarian and uterine tumors can be removed successfully by ovariohysterectomy. Mastectomy is indicated for mammary tumors, but it must be kept in mind that recurrence following surgery is common. Vaginal and vulvar tumors are frequently benign and can be surgically removed with relative ease. When the base of the tumor is broad, a *dorsal episiotomy* (incision through the vulva into the va-

gina) may be required in order to obtain adequate surgical exposure.

INFECTIONS OF THE GENITAL TRACT

Vaginitis (inflammation of the vagina) should be suspected when an abnormal vulvar discharge is present. Vaginitis can occur as a single entity or as part of an upper genital tract infection or cancer involving the cervix, uterus, or urinary system. A thorough history, physical examination (utilizing vaginal cytology and culture, and abdominal palpation), and a complete blood count (hemogram or CBC) will assist in determining the extent of the disorder. The abnormal discharge of vaginitis should not be confused with normal vulvar discharge of proestrous-estrous secretions, normal *lochia* (afterbirth discharge), or *subinvolution* (partial return to normal size) of the uterus following delivery. Noninfectious problems, such as vaginal tumors, clitoral hypertrophy, and vulvar or vaginal anatomical abnormalities must be considered in the differential diagnosis.

The entire vagina should be evaluated for inflammation or other abnormalities—tumor, foreign body, anatomic abnormality—using a sterile fiber optics endoscope or small veterinary otoscope head. Smears for cytology should be examined for the type and extent of inflammation and presence of microorganisms. Bacterial culture results should be interpreted, taking into account the number and type of organisms isolated, vaginal cytology results, history of vulvar discharge and infertility, and the extent of vaginitis. Antibiotic sensitivity testing should be performed on any isolated bacteria in order to identify the proper antibiotic to be used. Mild antiseptic douches, such as a tepid 1 percent tamed-iodine (Betadine) solution, are useful in chronic vaginitis. A disposable bovine teat cannula (tube for insertion) or a tomcat urethral catheter also may serve; the vagina can be lavaged with a syringe.

If queens in a cattery are chronically plagued by vulvar discharges and infertility, then culture samples should be obtained from the prepuce or penis of the breeding tom. If an organism is isolated from the sample, then the tom should be segregated from the queens until antibiotic treatment has resolved the problem.

The role of the tomcat in venereal spread of infectious diseases is not well understood. A negative status for toxoplasmosis, feline leukemia, feline immunodeficiency virus, and feline coronavirus would be of importance when obtaining a breeding tom. Appropriate vaccinations should be administered prior to breeding in order to control disease.

CYSTIC ENDOMETRIAL HYPERPLASIA, ENDOMETRITIS, METRITIS, PYOMETRITIS, AND PYOMETRA

Cystic endometrial hyperplasia (overgrowth of normal cells involving glands), endometritis (inflammation of the lining of the uterus), *metritis* (inflammation of the uterus), pyometritis (pus-forming inflammation of the uterus), and pyometra (pus in the uterus) occur commonly in intact female cats, especially those over three years of age. Pyometritis can arise spontaneously, or it can be secondary to a systemic bacterial disease process or to postpartum metritis. *Iatrogenic* (arising as a complication of medical treatment) pyometritis can result from the administration of long-acting progesterone compounds for delaying or suppressing estrus, or from use of estrogens in treating vaginitis. Pyometritis can follow a postcopulation or postinsemination infection, or it can be the final result in the *cystic endometrial hyperplasia-pyometra complex.* This complex affects intact queens. Its frequency of occurrence increases with age, following repeated nonproductive matings, pseudocopulation, and spontaneous ovulation.

Progesterone plays a major role in producing cystic endometrial hyperplasia in the queen. Progesterone greatly increases the susceptibility of the uterus to infection, maintains the functional closure of the cervix, and produces a relaxation of the uterine musculature.

Long-lasting progesterone compounds, used to delay or suppress estrus for as long as two years or more, have produced hyperplasia-pyometra complex in over 10 percent of treated cats. As a result, these products have now been withdrawn from the market and are contraindicated, especially in a female intended to be bred at a later date.

Most cats with cystic endometrial hyperplasia-pyometra complex are older (more than six years of age), are *nulliparous* (having never given birth), and have corpora lutea in their ovaries. There has been speculation regarding this high incidence of corpora lutea in a species that is believed to ovulate only after

the stimulus of coitus. It has been suggested that petting and stroking of a susceptible cat by its owner might be sufficient to induce ovulation. The disease seldom appears during the anestrous season of October through January. The pyometra component often becomes clinically evident between estrous periods or during a pseudopregnancy.

Clinical signs of the cystic endometrial hyperplasia-pyometra complex in the cat are as follows:

In cystic endometrial hyperplasia, no clinical signs of illness are present, because as yet no infection has developed in the uterus. The vulva may be swollen and enlarged, and there may be an excessive mucous discharge that contains no bacteria, no red blood cells, and few or no white blood cells. *Atresia* (functional closure) of the cervix may produce *mucometra* (mucus in the uterus) or *hydrometra* (with one or usually both uterine horns distended by a clear, watery, yellowish-gray, nonodorous fluid).

In cystic hyperplasia associated with endometritis and metritis, clinical signs of illness usually appear during the *metestrous* period (ten to ninety days after estrus). Breeding may or may not have occurred. Signs include an elevated temperature and heart rate, loss of appetite, lethargy, and a rough, dull hair coat. The white blood cell count is often somewhat elevated. Most of these animals will have an odorous discharge from the vulva that persists for several weeks or more. This odorous discharge must be differentiated from one seen in vaginitis or *cystitis* (bladder infection). After a number of weeks, the signs spontaneously regress only to reappear following the next estrous period, often in a more severe form. Chronic endometritis may be associated with stillbirths, abortion, embryonic deaths, small litter size, and infertility.

In pyometra there is a nearly complete closure of the cervix, preventing escape of the odorous exudate (cellular debris) from the uterus, with distention of the uterine horns. The general condition of the cat and its hair coat may be good or poor, depending upon how rapidly the condition develops. Pyometra may develop rapidly (within a week) or may require several months for full expression. The body temperature in acute cases is often elevated; in chronic cases it may be normal; in severe, toxic cases, it may be below normal. Loss of appetite, thirst, dehydration, and occasionally vomiting may occur. The pulse is usually elevated and rapid. The mucous membranes (lips, gums) may be pale and, in some cases, border on the anemic. *Polydipsia* (excessive thirst) and *polyuria* (excessive urination) are commonly seen. In toxic cases, *nephritis* (kidney inflammation) with an elevated *blood urea nitrogen* (BUN) level may be noted. The white blood cell count is often greatly elevated; most of the cells are *neutrophils,* which are important in combating bacteria. A vaginal discharge may be present. It varies in color from yellowish-gray to reddish-brown, and has a characteristically fetid odor. The abdomen in some cases may be distended and pear-shaped; palpation may reveal the distended uterus. Radiographs can be used by the veterinarian to confirm the enlarged uterus.

The course of pyometra is quite variable. Some cases become acute and severe within a week or two and require immediate attention to save the patient's life. In other cases, especially those with an open cervix from which pus is draining, the disease may run a course of a month or more. Usually those cases wherein the cervix remains closed are more toxic than those in which a discharge is present. Cases with *unicornual uterine torsion* (twisting of one uterine horn) have been reported. A *purulent peritonitis* (putrefactive inflammation of the lining of the abdomen) may develop secondary to pyometra. Remissions of the condition may occur.

The treatment for pyometra, metritis, endometritis, and cystic endometrial hyperplasia in the nonbreeding queen is ovariohysterectomy, with supportive therapy consisting of systemic antibiotics and fluids, and blood if necessary. Deep vaginal cultures with analysis of antibiotic sensitivity of the isolated microorganisms are especially important if postsurgical *septicemia* (blood poisoning) and peritonitis are present. The bacterium most frequently isolated from cases of pyometra is *Escherichia coli,* a normal inhabitant of the digestive tract.

Further research in the prevention and treatment of this syndrome in the queen is needed. Attention to hygiene during breeding, queening, and the postpartum period, and routine physical examination of the genital tract, can help decrease the incidence of cystic endometrial hyperplasia-pyometra complex in the cat.

MISCELLANEOUS DISORDERS OF THE GENITAL TRACT

Bite wounds of the scrotum and testes are frequently inflicted during territorial fighting. Fever and scrotal *abscessation* (pus formation) should be treated by a veterinarian. Such injury may necessitate removal of the affected testis in order to save the nonaffected testis.

Endometrial polyps are benign growths found on the lining of the uterus, which project into the uterine cavity. They occur more commonly as a further expression of cystic endometrial hyperplasia. Endometrial polyps may be single or multiple and can be the size of a fetus or larger. Many will have a small stalk (pedicle), by which they are attached to the uterine wall. They are usually cystic. They can *prolapse* (extend out) through the cervix, and may also twist about their stalk. This can lead to a bloody or fetid vulvar discharge. Vaginoscopic examination can reveal the prolapsed polyp, which may resemble a neoplasm. Large endometrial polyps can actually be palpated. Radiographs, following the infusion of radiopaque contrast fluid into the uterus, also can reveal the polyps.

Adenomyosis, or the ingrowth of hyperplastic endometrial glands into the uterine musculature, is also a complication of cystic endometrial hyperplasia. The affected area of the uterus appears as a firm mass and is frequently confused with a tumor.

Torsion of a uterine horn usually is associated with pregnancy, pyometra, endometrial polyps, hydrometra, mucometra, or any other condition that produces an increase in size of a uterine horn. Torsion usually results in shock and sudden death.

Extrauterine pregnancy with or without severe *ascites* (accumulation of fluid within the abdomen) is a frequent finding in the cat. Often it is an incidental finding at the time of surgery or necropsy (autopsy of an animal). The usually mummified fetuses may be found adherent to abdominal organs; some may have been present for years, and are nothing but mineralized masses. Extrauterine pregnancies may occur as a result of the *zygote* (fertilized egg) having been dislodged from the oviduct and dropped into the abdominal cavity, or as a result of uterine rupture. Most such pregnancies are of the latter origin. Some believe that in queens spayed at estrus or soon after, zygotes may be traumatically released by surgery into the peritoneal cavity, where they attach and form a blood supply.

Chronic vaginitis may be secondary to an open pyometra or metritis, but more frequently is secondary to a *dystocia* (difficult birth) or abortion. The vulvar discharge may vary from scanty and intermittent to abundant and continual. Scarring of the cervix or vagina may occur. The prognosis for breeding is poor for any queen with scarring; ovariohysterectomy is advised.

Several infectious disease agents can cause or have been associated with fetal resorption (absorption, dissolution of the cells of the fetus by biochemical means), mummification, abortion, stillbirth, or birth defects. These include feline viral rhinotracheitis virus (feline herpes virus), panleukopenia virus (feline parvovirus), feline leukemia virus (FeLV), *Toxoplasma gondii,* and ureaplasma. Aborted fetuses, stillborns, portions of resorbed fetal material, placentas, and vaginal swabs for culture should be submitted to a diagnostic laboratory for microscopic examination and culture.

Habitual abortion in some queens that occurs constantly at the same stage of gestation may be due to premature regression of corpora lutea, or inability to successfully convert from luteal to placental progestogenic maintenance at day 45 to 50. Suspect queens should be checked for evidence of any infectious disease and should always be confirmed pregnant. Treatment consisting of intramuscular administration of long-acting progesterone has been reported to be successful in some queens. Overdosage of progesterone may lead to masculinization of female kittens and prolonged gestation. The predisposition for premature regression of corpora lutea and the frequent inability to successfully carry fetuses to term may be inherited.

Genetics

For the layman, genetics may seem to be an intimidating subject, but familiarity with the basic principles of genetics is essential for making improvements in any breed. A complete breeding program must include careful selection of breeding stock, which can only be done if the breeder is aware of the genetic nature of the trait of interest. An incomplete understanding of genetics will lead to an ineffectual breeding program, while more certain knowledge will enable the breeder to go a long way in improving a breed.

This chapter discusses patterns of inheritance, the possible goals of breeding programs, and how to choose an effective breeding and selection scheme to improve the characteristic or characteristics of interest. The breeder should be aware that as more traits are included in the selection program, progress for any single trait will automatically be slower.

THE PHYSICAL BASIS OF INHERITANCE

The inheritance of any trait has a clearly defined physical basis, in that the elements of the genetic material can be seen microscopically. The body of a cat is composed of individual cells. Within each cell is a "center of operations," the *nucleus,* which contains the genetic material—the "blueprint"—that specifies the precise structure of the individual animal. Cells that are halted during the division process can be chemically stained to reveal, within the nucleus, the threadlike *chromosomes,* which in mammals are made of DNA *(deoxyribonucleic acid).* It is DNA that carries the genetic information.

All cats have thirty-eight chromosomes per body cell, all contained in the nucleus. When a body cell is observed during its division process, the chromosomes can be seen to duplicate themselves, the duplicates then pulling apart into the two new daughter cells that result from the division. Each new cell retains the same number of chromosomes as the original.

But what happens when reproductive cells, or *gametes* (sperm in the male and ova in the female), are produced? If each had the full number of chromosomes, then fertilization of an egg by a sperm—the joining of two complete cells—would produce an offspring with *twice* as many chromosomes as each parent. This doubling would occur in each generation. In just ten generations the kittens would have over thirty thousand chromosomes! But nature is too careful for that. When we study reproductive tissues, the chromosomes are seen to line up *in pairs,* with one member of each pair going into each reproductive cell. Thus each feline sperm cell or ovum contains nineteen (rather than thirty-eight) chromosomes. When a sperm fertilizes an egg, the resulting progeny cell then acquires 19 + 19 = 38 chromosomes, half from each parent. For breeders, the important conclusion to be drawn from this is that the individual units of inheritance, the *genes,* which are located on the chromosomes, also occur in pairs. This is important in understanding how inheritance operates. The thirty-eight chromosomes (and therefore the genes along them) are in actuality *nineteen pairs,* with *two* genes for any particular trait. More on this later.

Close examination of the nineteen pairs of cat chromosomes shows that shapes differ from pair to pair. In the female, all the pairs of chromosomes consist of two chromosomes that look alike, including the single pair of *sex chromosomes* (all other chromosomes are referred to as *autosomes*). In the male, however, there is one unmatched pair. These are the male's sex chromosomes. The larger sex chromosome (the *X* chromosome) appears physically similar to the female's sex chromosomes and is in the shape of an X. But the smaller sex chromosome, the *Y* chromosome, also named for its shape, is quite different in size and shape. Females have two X chromosomes and are therefore XX with respect to their sex chromosomes. This double-X pattern is what makes them females. Males are XY. An egg from a female can thus *only* contain an X chromosome—that's all the female has. Roughly half of a male's sperm cells will bear an X, half will bear a Y. Hence, it is the male that determines the sex of each kitten: Kittens produced by a Y-

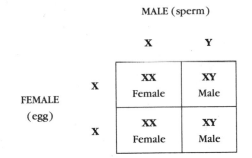

bearing sperm will be males, those produced by an X-bearing sperm will be females.

The above diagram (called a *Punnett square*) can be used with any pair of genes to determine the possible outcomes of a mating. (Here it is used for entire chromosomes—the X and Y sex chromosomes—but it works just as well for an individual gene pair.) The diagram lists the gametes that each of the two parents can contribute (at top and at left), with the squares illustrating the possible progeny-gene combinations that can result from the mating.

MENDELIAN GENETICS

Simple Traits. An Austrian monk and naturalist, Gregor Mendel (1822–84), was the first person to develop a clear understanding of how simple traits are inherited. Remarkably, he achieved this understanding years before the physical basis of inheritance was uncovered. An understanding of the inheritance of sex was achieved later than this, but it makes an excellent first example of genetics in action.

In addition to the genes that determine the sex of the individual, the sex chromosomes of both sexes carry some other genetic information. The Y chromosome has few genes on it other than those involved in sex determination, but the X carries genes for many other traits as well. Such traits are referred to as *sex-linked,* because they are controlled by genes on a sex chromosome.

A celebrated example of sex-linked traits is orange color in cats. This color gene can take two different forms, known as *alleles.* One allele (O) determines orange color, the other allele (o), nonorange color. In this example, nonorange cats will be black, a color actually decided by another gene pair that will appear later. Each X chromosome contains one of the two possible alleles, O or o. (The Y chromosome has no genes for this particular trait.) So for a male cat to be orange, it need have only one O allele, because it has only one X chromosome. However, in this particular case, for a female cat to be orange *both* of her X chromosomes must contain the O allele. Similarly, a male with one o allele is black; a female must have two o alleles to be black. A female with one O allele and one o allele is a tortoiseshell. Male tortoiseshells, which are the result of an error in chromosome separation, have an extra X chromosome—2 X s—and a Y. They are usually sterile. Using a Punnett square, mating a black male (X^oY) with an orange female (X^oX^o) gives the following possibilities:

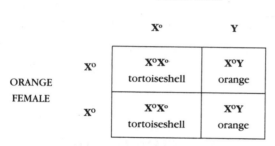

BLACK MALE

		X^o	Y
ORANGE FEMALE	X^o	X^oX^o tortoiseshell	X^oY orange
	X^o	X^oX^o tortoiseshell	X^oY orange

One can readily see that the resulting female kittens will all be tortoiseshell, while the male kittens will all be orange. If the reverse mating had been made—orange male (X^oY) with black female (X^oX^o)—the result would have been tortoiseshell daughters and black sons. When there are different patterns of inheritance for sons and daughters, this is a clue that a trait may be sex-linked.

The outcome of a mating is often more straightforward for genes that are not on the X chromosome, but on the autosomes, which of course represent the majority of genes. In such cases the sexes of the kittens are irrelevant to the genetic outcome, and the parents' sexes are not included in our genetic diagram. Hence, a mating between a longhair with two l alleles and a shorthair with two L alleles gives:

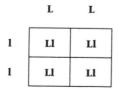

	L	L
l	**Ll**	**Ll**
l	**Ll**	**Ll**

One can readily see that the progeny are all alike, but they are *not* intermediate in hair length. Instead, they are *all shorthairs!* The gene for short hair (L) is thus said to be *dominant,* while the gene for long hair (l) is said to be *recessive.* A dominant gene is capable of expressing its trait *even when carried by only one member of a chromosome pair*—hence, the hair length of the Ll progeny is controlled by the L allele. A recessive gene (such as l) can only be expressed when *both* members of a chromosome pair contain the gene—hence, only ll cats will be longhairs; all other combinations will be shorthairs.

A cat with two identical alleles (either LL or ll, in the case of hair length) is said to be *homozygous* for that particular trait; a cat with dissimilar alleles (Ll) is said to be *heterozygous.* For the shorthair kittens described above, their *phenotype* (i.e., the visible, physical expression of the trait in question, in this case hair length) does not disclose their *genotype* (the genetic makeup of a trait, i.e., whether they are homozygous or heterozygous for the trait), as it did for the tortoiseshell kittens. Judging by appearance alone, a breeder can't tell if those black kittens have two L genes or one L and one l; since L is dominant, the results are the same either way. This is one of the major problems in the genetic evaluation of animals. Often, only a breeding test will disclose which alleles a cat has and can transmit to its offspring.

Gene Interactions. Interactions between different pairs of genes (called *epistasis*) can further confuse prediction of inherited traits. A good example of a two-gene interaction is the dominant white allele (W) and its dominance over the color allele (w), as well as over traits—for example, full color (CC or Cc^b) and Burmese pattern (c^bc^b)—controlled by a separate gene. A heterozygous dominant white cat (in this example, $WwCc^b$—remember, the W allele is dominant to all the others) can produce four different types of gametes: WC, Wc^b, wC, and wc^b—there are two genes involved here, and only one allele from each parental gene pair is present in a normal gamete. The Punnett square for a mating between two such cats is complex, with sixteen squares (4 × 4) representing all the possible outcomes.

Some of the offspring genotypes are repeated in different parts of the square. Because W is the dominant white allele, any kitten with W in its genotype will be white, like the parents. The rest of a white kitten's genotype is irrelevant to its phenotype, because the W allele prevents the expression

MALE (WwCc^b)

		WC	Wc^b	wC	wc^b
	WC	WWCC	WWCc^b	WwCC	WwCc^b
FEMALE	Wc^b	WWCc^b	WWc^{b}c^b	WwCc^b	Wwc^{b}c^b
(WwCc^b)	wC	WwCC	WwCc^b	wwCC	wwCc^b
	wc^b	WwCc^b	Wwc^{b}c^b	wwCc^b	wwc^{b}c^b

of the other alleles. Thus, in this example, there will be twelve white kittens (W in the genotype, i.e., W _ _ _) for every four colored (ww _ _) kittens, that is, a 3:1 ratio. (The blank spaces indicate alleles that do not affect the phenotype under consideration.) Of the four colored (ww _ _) kittens, three will have full color (C in the genotype, i.e., C _) and one will show the Burmese (c^{b}c^b) pattern.

You can next try a similar Punnett square for a mating between two heterozygous black cats carrying the chocolate and Siamese alleles (i.e., BbCc^s). (For a listing of the major alleles of the cat, *see* Table 1 on page 120.) This will provide practice in understanding the inheritance of genes and how genotypes are "decoded" to give phenotypes. The result of the black cat mating should be: nine black kittens (B _C _), three Seal Point Siamese (B_c^{s}c^s), three chocolate (bbC_), and one Chocolate Point Siamese (bbc^{s}c^s). Note in this case that offspring phenotypes arise that would never have been suspected by looking at the parents. This illustrates how difficult it can be to predict the outcome of matings of non-purebred (and therefore more heterozygous) animals.

The example to the right shows a different dominant white (W) male mated to three females.

In general it is difficult to know whether two white cats are *genetically* the same color or not without careful test-matings. The male above is white because of the W allele, while female 3 is white because of a totally different gene, c^a. The gene for full color (C) is carried by the male, but he does not show its effect in his phenotype because the dominant W gene prevents any color expression.

This example illustrates the phenomenon of *multiple alleles at a locus*. (A locus [plural = *loci*] is the position on the chromosome where a specific gene is located.) C, c^b, c^s, and c^a are all alleles (i.e., different forms of the same gene), any one of which may be found at the gene locus on a single chromosome. Matings among cats of all genotypes for this locus have shown that C (full color) is dominant to the other alleles. The c^b (Burmese) and c^s (Siamese) alleles are *codominant*—that is, both are fully expressed in a heterozygous individual—the result being the Tonkinese (c^{b}c^s), intermediate between Siamese and Burmese (this is comparable to the Oo tortoiseshell cat described earlier). The c^a allele ranks next, and at the end of the list is c (pink-eyed true albino), which is recessive to all the other alleles at this locus.

The Colors of Specific Breeds. In general, breeds in which few colors are acceptable in the standard will be more homozygous for those color alleles than will be breeds in which many colors are acceptable. For example, a Siamese cat from a long line of purebred Siamese is almost certainly c^{s}c^s for the gene for color

MALE (WwCC)

FEMALES		WC	wC
1. wwc^{b}c^b Burmese	wc^b	WwCc^b white	wwCc^b full color
2. wwc^{s}c^s Siamese	wc^s	WwCc^s white	wwCc^s full color
3. wwc^{a}c^a Blue-eyed White	wc^a	WwCc^a white	wwCc^a full color

TABLE 1.

MAJOR ALLELES
OF THE CAT

Color

A	agouti (banded hair color)	I	pigment inhibition
a	nonagouti	i	normal pigmentation
		O	sex-linked orange
B	black	o	nonorange
b	chocolate brown		
b¹	red-brown	S	white spotting (incompletely dominant)
C	full color	s	no spotting
c^b	Burmese		
c^s	Siamese	T^a	Abyssinian tabby
c^a	blue-eyed white	T	striped tabby
c	albino (pink eyes)	t^b	blotched tabby
		W	dominant white
D	intense color	w	colored
d	dilute color		

Hair Type

H	normal hair
h	hairless
L	shorthair
l	longhair
R	normal hair
r	Cornish rex
Re	normal hair
re	Devon rex
Wh	wirehair
wh	normal hair

Other

FD	folded ear
fd	normal ear
M	Manx tail
m	normal tail
Pd	polydactyly
pd	normal number of toes

pattern. However, its color points may take many forms, including seal (aaB__), blue (aaB__dd), or chocolate (aabb). Note that the genotype aabb of the chocolate cat can be written with some certainty, because this phenotype depends only on recessive alleles. The genotypes of seal and blue are less certain because the dominant B allele is a determining factor. This is a case where *pedigree* (family) information can be of use. If the Seal Point comes from a line that has never produced any chocolate (bb) kittens, then the breeder can be fairly certain that its genotype probably is BB. A breeding test with cats of the recessive (bb) genotype is the usual method for substantiating such an assumption (*see also* page 122).

Note that in describing a breed's genotype not all of the major alleles are commonly listed if the breed is homozygous for them. For example, the homozygous Seal Point Siamese female's genotype is in actuality aaBBc^sc^sDDiioosswww (refer to Table 1 for descriptions of the other alleles). However, the D, i, o, s, and w alleles are usually not listed because they are homozygous in the breed. Should this line of Siamese cats also produce Blue Points, then the D locus would need to be included because some cats will be Dd (carriers of the blue-point characteristic, but not expressing it because of the dominance of D), or dd (blue-point).

Another way of stating this is to say that alleles are not usually listed *at all* if a breed conforms to what is considered to be its *wild type* (think of the phenotype of the wild cat to picture this). In other words, it is the occasional, naturally occurring *mutation* (genetic change) of wild-type alleles that has formed the basis for development of the different breeds, and it is only these mutated alleles that are listed when describing the genotype of a breed. The agouti (A), black (B), full color (C), intense color (D), normal pigmentation (i), nonorange (o), unspotted (s), striped tabby (T), and colored (w) alleles are all considered to be wild-type alleles. The occasional mutations of these alleles have provided the raw material for artificial selection, which has developed the different breeds. Many, but not all, of the mutants have proved to be recessive in nature.

Returning to the Seal Point Siamese, the usual description of its genotype would simply be aac^sc^s, because these are the only two alleles that differ from the wild type. The B and D loci would be added to the genotype if there were reason to suspect that the Seal Points were not pure-breeding for the intense (D) black (B) color, but were producing also some chocolate (bb) or blue (dd) kittens. (A line that produces some chocolates *and* some blues must also produce some Lilac Points [bbdd].)

Deducing the Genotype. The previous section has provided some ground rules for understanding the genotype of a breed, rather than listing what is known about every breed. Even an "alley cat" of unknown pedigree should not be a complete genetic enigma if the reader has grasped the principles thus far described. Of course, there are many more unanswered questions about an alley cat's genotype than there are about the genotype of a pedigreed feline. Yet even a purebred is capable of occasionally surprising a breeder. Mutations are constantly occurring, most of them never coming to the breeder's attention. Occasionally, however, a mutation occurs that affects an important gene in a particular breed. For example, a Siamese gene might mutate back to a wild-type (C) allele in some of the ova of a Siamese female. If one of these ova should be fertilized by a purebred Siamese male, the kitten produced will be Cc^s. This kitten will not have the Siamese pattern, but instead will have color distributed over all its body. This is the sort of genetic event that can subsequently give rise to accusations of a line's not being purebred, or that an outside male has fertilized some of the queen's ova, and so forth. Breeders should bear this in mind and remember that not all such births signify a breach of ethics.

Following is a useful scheme for deducing the genotype of a cat from its visual phenotypic characteristics:

1. Look at the cat: Does it have unusual features such as a rex coat or extra toes? Does the coat have a particular pattern such as spotting or the Siamese pattern? What color is shown by the colored areas of the coat?
2. Consider the table of major alleles of the cat.
3. If the phenotype results from a recessive genotype, the cat's alleles at that locus are both known. For example, a long-haired cat is ll.
4. If the trait results from a dominant allele, half the genotype is known. For example, a striped tabby is T__ and must also be A__ as only agouti shows stripes (except in the presence of the O allele).
5. Follow some simple rules:
   a) Tabbies must be A__ unless the orange allele is present. In this case, even aa can be striped.
   b) White is "no color" and leaves many questions as a white cat can be white for several different genetic reasons. A white cat is a colored cat with just one locus preventing it from expressing that color. It still passes on color genes to its kittens.
   c) "Silver" or "chinchilla" is believed to be the result of the I__ genotype.
6. Put the pieces together:
   e.g. a short-haired tortoiseshell: aaL__Oo
        a long-haired tortoiseshell: aallOo
        a tortoiseshell Siamese: aac^sc^sL__Oo

a calico shorthair: aaL__OoS__
a blue, short-haired tortoiseshell: aaddL__Oo

Calico is used to describe a tortoiseshell (Oo) with white spotting (S__).

Note: If it is certain that shorthairs are pure-breeding, then the L__ notation can be dropped because all the cats are assumed to be LL wild type.

Thus, even cats of unknown ancestry can be genotypically analyzed to a certain extent. Pedigree and breeding information (data on phenotypes of ancestors and/or the subject's offspring) will permit one to fill in the blanks in at least some parts of the genotype. Purebred cats leave fewer questions in the mind, but remember: Even purebreds can produce some surprises!

Undesired Gene. This term can be used to describe a gene that is not a desirable part of a breed's phenotype (for example, the full color allele in a line of Siamese cats), or one that produces an abnormality. Some abnormalities have formed the basis of distinct breeds—for example, the folded ear of the Scottish Fold breed. Thus a gene that is undesired in one breed may be an essential feature of another. But genes that cause a physical abnormality, such as the Manx tail, may be harmful to an individual's survival if present in the homozygous condition where they have effects higher in the spine also. If such a gene also produces a desirable feature in the breed, then the breeder must accept the fact that the line will have reduced viability because homozygous kittens may not survive to reproduce.

An allele that is *lethal* may display its effect at different stages in the life cycle. For example, an allele may produce an effect that is not apparent at birth but is manifested as the kitten grows older. If as a result of possessing a certain allele a kitten survives for some time but cannot reproduce, then the allele can be considered lethal with respect to its effect on the species, though not necessarily to the individual. At the other end of the spectrum are alleles that produce grossly deformed offspring, dead either at birth or shortly thereafter. Some lethal alleles or genotypes may even kill the fetus *in utero,* so that the breeder's only clue to their existence is the reduced productivity of matings wherein the lethal genotype can be generated.

When kittens are born with an abnormality (a *congenital* abnormality), it cannot always be readily determined that the underlying cause is genetic. It is true that some genes are known to produce abnormalities (for instance, *spina bifida* in kittens homozygous for the Manx allele); congenital abnormalities that show up in highly inbred kittens are prime suspects for being genetic in origin. In noninbred kittens, however, environmental causes must also be considered. Nutritional deficiencies or specific agents such as drugs or microorganisms that influence the development of the fetus can also give rise to congenital abnormalities, which may cause some confusion since they may mimic abnormalities that have a genetic basis. (*See* Chapter 14: Normal Development and Congenital Birth Defects.)

In a breed in which the heterozygous genotype is desired but the homozygous genotype produces a gross abnormality, a breeder has two options: (1) Matings that produce the nonviable kittens can be avoided, in which case a higher percentage of "normal" (but also undesired) kittens will be produced. This will give litters of normal size. (2) If matings that may produce the grossly abnormal kittens are made, the breeder must accept these losses and the fact that such matings will have a lower than normal productivity.

Some alleles have undesirable—but not lethal—effects on individual animals (e.g., *progressive retinal atrophy* [PRA] leading to blindness as a cat ages) and cannot be considered an asset to any breed. A gene such as that producing PRA should certainly be "bred out" of any breed in which it arises.

Breeding Out an Undesired Gene. A recessive allele (h) that causes hairlessness in kittens has a disastrous effect on the individual. A breeding colony will always have some such allele in it, but since this gene is recessive, usually it is only discovered when particular matings—often those between closely related individuals—are made. How, then, can a breeder discover the extent of such a problem and eliminate an unwanted allele from the breeding stock?

First, and most obvious, affected animals (e.g., hh, hairless cats) or their parents (which must be Hh) should be eliminated from the breeding program. The real problem, however, lies in detecting which of the other normal-appearing (H__) cats carry the h allele. *All* offspring from the Hh parents are prime suspects.

If the homozygous recessive type (hh in this example) is not lethal but is able to survive and reproduce, it can be used in test-matings with suspect individuals:

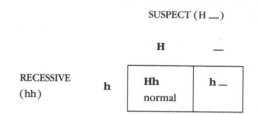

SUSPECT (H __)

		H	__
RECESSIVE (hh)	h	**Hh** normal	h__

If the blank (__) is an h (i.e., if the suspect animal is a carrier), half of the progeny will be expected to be hairless. Of course, it takes only *one* abnormal kitten to prove that the suspect (H__) carries the h allele (i.e., that the suspect is Hh). But how many normal kittens must be produced from such test-matings before the breeder can be reasonably confident that the suspect is HH and thus not a carrier?

If the suspect is a carrier (Hh), the probability of an offspring's receiving an H allele from it is ½. Hence, in the mating of the suspect with the hh test animal:

Chance of 1 Hh kitten $= \frac{1}{2}$
Chance of 2 Hh kittens $= \frac{1}{2} \times \frac{1}{2} = \frac{1}{4}$
Chance of 3 Hh kittens $= \frac{1}{2} \times \frac{1}{2} \times \frac{1}{2} = \frac{1}{8}$
Chance of 4 Hh kittens $= \frac{1}{2} \times \frac{1}{2} \times \frac{1}{2} \times \frac{1}{2} = \frac{1}{16}$, et cetera.

Thus confidence that the suspect is not a carrier increases with each normal kitten produced. The breeder stops when the probabilities drop to an acceptably low level (i.e., less than 1 percent). This will be reached when *seven* successive normal kittens have been produced. (Never forget, however, that just one hh kitten will prove the suspect to be a carrier, and that testing can stop right there.)

If the trait in question prevents the homozygous individual from reproducing, then test-matings must be made with carrier (heterozygous) individuals, i.e., those that have produced affected progeny.

In such cases, greater numbers of offspring must be produced before the carrier status of the suspect can be determined with equal certainty. Only one in four kittens resulting from the mating of two heterozygous individuals will be expected to be homozygous recessive (and therefore affected); the proba-

SUSPECT (H __)

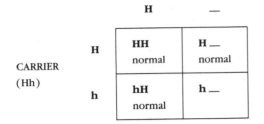

		H	__
CARRIER (Hh)	H	HH normal	H __ normal
	h	hH normal	h __

bility of a kitten's being phenotypically normal is therefore ¾. *Sixteen* successive normal progeny are needed to reach the 1 percent probability level. (Again, test-matings can stop the moment one abnormal kitten is produced.)

Which sex to test? In general, test-matings are performed to test males for undesirable alleles. It is not always practical to expect enough kittens from a single female to adequately test her.

CHARACTERISTICS SHOWING CONTINUOUS VARIATION

The principles of basic Mendelian genetics describe the inheritance of any trait. However, many traits are controlled by a whole spectrum of genes, each of which exerts minute, individually inconsiderable effects on the trait—effects which, acting collectively, can produce a continuous range of phenotypic expression *(continuous variation)*. Traits controlled in such a manner are referred to as *quantitative* traits (as opposed to the *qualitative* traits discussed in the previous sections). Quantitative traits often are influenced by environmental factors, so that the phenotype comes to represent the expression of the genotype as modified by the environment. As you can imagine, continuous variation can significantly magnify the problems of the genetic evaluation of animals.

To understand quantitative traits, consider the case of spotting in a cat's coat pattern. Spots are *qualitatively* controlled by a major allele (S), but the degree of spotting is determined by an unknown number of minor "modifier genes." Thus it is S that determines that a cat will have white spots, while other modifier genes increase or decrease the amount of spotting.

For example, suppose there are only three minor gene pairs (hypothetically, A and a, B and b, C and c) affecting the amount of spotting. If the baseline aabbcc is 10 percent spotted, and each uppercase allele increases the amount of spotting by 10 percent, then animals can vary continuously from 10 percent spotted (aabbcc) to 70 percent spotted (AABBCC). When animals in the entire population are studied, they will be seen to show continuous variation in the amount of spotting, with few animals at the extremes, and most in the middle of the range.

Traits involving such important factors as growth and reproduction are all quantitative traits. Some, such as reproductive traits, have a minor genetic component (called the *heritability*), with a major environmental component (e.g., feeding, health, et cetera). This must invariably influence the breeder in the choice of a breeding program. Selection schemes for such quantitative traits are more difficult to devise than those for qualitative traits, and hence, breeders must understand the genetic basis of the trait of interest in order to evaluate the potential for making genetic progress.

BREEDING PROGRAMS

Inbreeding. Inbreeding is the mating of closely related individuals, often full siblings (brother/sister matings) or parent to offspring. The intention is to produce progeny that are more homozygous, and therefore more uniform, than those produced without inbreeding. However, homozygosity of *detrimental* as well as good alleles will result; thus many inbred lines are lost as a result of a decline in vigor. Sometimes major deleterious alleles are uncovered, but more often a steady loss of vigor and reproductive capability is encountered. Although a good inbred line is very predictable in its breeding performance, close inbreeding is best avoided because of the decline in quality often seen in inbred stocks.

Linebreeding. Linebreeding is a form of moderate inbreeding that attempts to "concentrate" alleles from an outstanding individual without mating close relatives. When the pedigree of kittens in such cases is studied, the same outstanding individual will appear several times in the ancestry of the kittens' parents. Hence, although the percentage of alleles coming from that individual may be quite high, actual inbreeding of the kittens will not be excessive.

Line Crossing (outcrossing). Line crossing is the mating of individuals from different lines in order to extract desirable features from both. Often, linecross or outcross kittens have added vigor. This is due to their enhanced heterozygosity, which results from line differences in alleles at many genetic loci.

Crossbreeding. Crossbreeding is the mating of cats of totally different breeds. Crossbreeds usually are vigorous because of their extensive heterozygosity—a quality referred to as *hybrid vigor* or *heterosis.* Crossbreeding is used in the creation of a new breed or in the introduction of a desired trait into a breed that does not have it. In the latter case, crossbreeding is followed by successive matings back to the pure breed *(grading up),* with stringent selection and culling of breeding stock. First-generation crossbreeds are genetically and phenotypically uniform, but, if mated among themselves, will produce divergent offspring. Hence, if a new breed is being developed, very strong culling of all but the best individuals must be practiced.

· · · · · · · · · · · · · · · · · ·
SELECTION OF INDIVIDUALS FOR BREEDING

Breeders certainly should avoid using in a breeding program any animal that shows or carries an undesirable gene. Beyond this, decisions must be made regarding the best animals to be bred from, with the objective of improving the trait(s) of importance. The more traits a breeder selects for, the slower the genetic progress in any one trait. It is often the case, though, that a breeder wishes to consider a few traits in making selections. How should such selections be made?

Selection intensity has an important role in determining genetic progress. If eight kittens out of every ten that are born are kept for breeding, intensity will be low. If only one in ten is retained, intensity will be high. Genetic progress will be made if the breeder has correctly identified the individual that is *truly superior.*

Traits in which the environment plays a large role in determining phenotype are the most difficult to evaluate. Certainly no one would mistake a cat known to have lost its tail in an accident for a cat carrying the Manx gene. But differentiating among cats with superior conformation—some owing to true genetic superiority, others to being reared under superior environmental conditions—is a constant challenge for the breeder. Briefly put, there are no simple answers.

Selection for several traits can proceed in one of three ways.

The first, *tandem selection,* is a program in which a breeder selects for one trait over several generations, then switches attention to another trait for a period of time. In many cases the first trait will slip backwards once attention to it is dropped. Only for traits that have an underlying positive genetic relationship will advances in one result in progress in the other. Breeders are rarely so fortunate!

In the second procedure, a breeder may decide to establish a "cut-off" point or standard for each trait of interest, breeding only those animals meeting the standard in all traits *(independent culling levels).* This technique maintains selection pressure on all the traits of interest at all times. Its primary drawback is that individuals truly superior in one or more characteristics will not be retained for breeding if they fall short of the standard in only one other trait.

The third procedure is known as the *selection index.* Here, a single "score" or index for each individual is developed, and animals with the highest index values are selected. The selection index depends on three factors for its success. One is the breeder's ability to correctly assess individuals on the traits of importance. If the trait is numbers of kittens produced per queen, for instance, the individual's numerical score is decided objectively. But if the trait is head shape, however, it's much more difficult to assign an objective numerical value. The second factor is the assignment of weights to each trait that reflect the relative importance of each trait to the breeder. If a certain trait is of overwhelming importance, then it's probably best to select on that trait alone and ignore the others. The third factor is the most difficult to assess, the most often ignored, and yet the most crucial to the success of the selection index procedure. This factor is knowledge of the underlying genetics of each trait of interest—the degree to which each trait is heritable (as opposed to being influenced by the environment), and the genetic relationship among the traits. Values for heritabilities and genetic correlations can be assessed reliably only from large-scale breeding programs, and so are usually omitted from the cat breeder's selection index. Nevertheless, such information is the key to a truly effective index.

Summary. The best advice one can offer a breeder who is designing a selection program is to keep it as simple as possible and to concentrate on traits for which reliable information is available. If environment is known to play a major role in the develop- ment of a trait, then comparisons must be made among animals raised and kept under standardized conditions. Otherwise, it will not be possible to distin- guish genetically superior animals from those that are superior for other reasons. Genetic progress can only be made if the genetically superior individuals are identified and used as parents of succeeding genera- tions.

Normal Development and Congenital Birth Defects

It requires nine to ten weeks for a fertilized egg, measuring approximately ½₅₀ inch in length, to develop into a newborn kitten. In addition to the spectacular growth process that occurs during gestation, the developing organism undergoes major transformations that bring about the formation of unique tissues and organs, each in their proper location and with appropriate functions. Knowing how these changes occur in the embryo will help to understand some of the common inherited, induced, and spontaneous *congenital malformations* (birth defects) in cats.

NORMAL FELINE DEVELOPMENT

The development of the kitten can be divided into three phases: *preimplantation,* days 0–12; *embryogenesis,* days 12–24; and *fetal growth,* days 24–term.

Preimplantation

Unlike in dogs, ovulation in cats occurs in response to mating. A queen may accept more than one male during a heat period, which can result in a litter's having several parents.

Fertilization occurs in the uterine tube *(oviduct).* At this stage the female *gamete (ovum* or egg) is encased in an inert sheath called the *zona pellucida,* which itself is surrounded by several hundred ovarian cells (the *corona radiata).* The male gamete (sperm) must penetrate both of these layers in order to contact and fuse with the surface of the ovum.

During the preimplantation stage, the fertilized ovum undergoes cell division, travels down the oviduct, and enters the uterus on about the sixth day of development. There it forms a *blastocyst,* which is a hollow, spherical structure containing about 250 cells, covered by a thin layer of cells specialized to make contact with the wall of the uterus. The cells that will form the *embryo* cluster together at one pole of the blastocyst; most of the remaining cells will contribute to the *placenta,* the tissue that forms the connection between the mother and offspring. At this stage the blastocyst "hatches" from the zona pellucida and floats freely within the uterine cavity.

Embryogenesis

Embryogenesis is the most critical phase of mammalian development. It is during this period that the clustered embryonic cell population becomes totally reorganized into the earliest discernible forms, or *primordia,* of every organ system in the body.

The initial stage of embryogenesis is called *gastrulation.* During this stage the embryonic cells establish three layers of tissues. These tissues begin to undergo programming for specific developmental pathways—in other words, the selective activation of special genes is occurring. Next, the organism enters the *neurula* stage, during which time the primordia of the nervous system, the heart, and the vertebral column are established. This is accomplished by rearrangements in all three cell layers, a process known as *morphogenesis.* Blood vessels also appear during this stage, both within the embryo itself and between the embryo and the immature placenta. These two embryonic stages occur very rapidly, requiring only two to three days in cats and dogs.

The neurula stage is followed by a period of embryonic *organogenesis,* during which the primordia of most of the other organs—including the liver and digestive tract, respiratory system, limbs, sense organs, skull, and urogenital structures—are formed. This stage is completed by about three and a half weeks of gestation in the cat (six weeks in humans), by which time the embryo measures slightly over half an inch in length.

Fetal Growth

Fetal development is characterized by rapid growth. The organ primordia established earlier assume their proper shapes and configurations, nerves develop, and the hormonal and secretory glands of the organism begin to function and control many physiological processes. Cats are born in a very immature condition, and all these processes continue after birth. For example, full development of the visual system is not

EARLY DEVELOPMENTAL STAGES

STAGES	CAT		DOG	HUMAN	
2 Cells	3	days*	4 days*	1.5 days*	
8 Cells	3.5	days	6 days	2.5 days	
Blastocyst	5	days	8 days	4	days
Gastrula	12	days	16 days	14	days
Neurula	13	days	17 days	20	days
4-mm Embryo (⅛ in)	15	days	22 days	28	days
9-mm Embryo (⅜ in)	21	days	25 days	37	days
16-mm Embryo (⅝ in)	24	days	30 days	43	days
Gestation Length	62	days	63 days	266	days

* days following fertilization

accomplished until five to six weeks after birth, while nerve cells in the cerebellum still continue to form and develop for several months.

DEVELOPMENTAL MECHANISMS

Understanding how populations of embryonic cells become transformed from *homogeneous* (uniform) clusters into highly organized, patterned arrays of tissues, each with the correct biochemical characteristics and in the proper location, is a major frontier in biology today. This is by no means simply a matter of scientific curiosity, for locked within the embryo are secrets to mechanisms of tissue repair and organ regeneration, genetic programming, and the control of cell proliferation, which, when unchecked in adult tissues, can result in the formation and spread of tumors.

The problems confronting the embryo can most readily be illustrated by focusing on the developing forelimb. Here, a few hundred embryonic cells must proliferate and form a structure complete with muscles, cartilages, bones, tendons and ligaments, blood vessels, nerves, lymphatic channels, secretory structures, claws, and hair. Moreover, each of these tissues must have a precise shape and relation to all the others, and must constitute a mirror image of the opposite forelimb. Finally, both limbs must grow synchronously and to the same size after birth.

The example of the forelimb illustrates the four basic processes of embryonic development:

GROWTH
MORPHOGENESIS (development of form and shape);
CYTODIFFERENTIATION (the formation of unique cell
  types);
PATTERNING (spatial organization of each tissue).

Although none of these processes is fully understood, developmental biologists have now delineated several of their major characteristics. It appears, for example, that all four processes are interdependent and inseparable. In addition, each process requires that adjacent cells and tissues interact with one another. Sometimes this occurs by direct contact; more often, however, the intercellular dialogue is mediated by chemicals released by the cells. Often the same extracellular molecules have different effects, depending upon the type of receptors for the molecule a target cell has or upon subtle differences in the particular combination of molecules present.

CRITICAL PERIODS

The kinds of interactions described above for limb development occur in every tissue and organ in the kitten embryo. These interactions are extremely sensitive to any sort of chemical or genetic disruption. (Occasionally, these complex spatial and temporal relationships, which must be established for a structure to develop normally, go awry spontaneously, resulting in a congenital malformation.)

The stage during which each organ is most sensitive to disruption is called the critical period of its development. The critical period for most structures occurs in the embryonic stage of development, during the third and fourth weeks of gestation in cats. Reaching the end of the critical period does not guarantee that a particular developing structure is no longer susceptible to disruption; instead, its sensitivity to disruption declines, so that abnormalities, if they occur, are more likely to be very localized in nature.

Disruption of development at earlier stages is usually lethal, resulting either in the immediate death of the embryo or in failure to attach properly to the uterine wall. Statistically, the gastrula stage, which corresponds to the time of initial contact between the embryo and the wall of the uterus, is the time of greatest loss of embryos in all mammals. Up to 70 percent of embryos that die at this stage are found to have severe chromosomal abnormalities.

The final general point to be made about embryonic malformations is that, in many cases, a defect in one system will result in abnormal development of others. As an example, some cardiovascular defects deprive peripheral tissues of a sufficient blood supply for their normal growth. Similarly, a compromise of the nerve supply to any target tissue will result in secondary atrophy of the muscles and immobilization of the joints in that region.

CAUSES OF CONGENITAL MALFORMATIONS

Many malformations, especially those associated with highly inbred breeds of cats, have a heritable basis. This means that the frequency and/or severity of the anomaly is directly affected by the genetic information the developing organism has acquired from its parents. Occasionally this may be due to a single gene alteration or mutation, as in the case of certain enzyme-deficiencies (mucopolysaccharidosis, gangliosidosis, for example).

More often the precise genetic basis for a malformation is less obvious because many genes regulate or are affected by the products of other genes. Some tissues affected in this way include: pigmentation (including defects in vision and hearing in Siamese and Persian cats); the spinal cord and vertebral column (spina bifida [incomplete closure] in the Manx); the limb (polydactylism [added toes]; ectrodactyly [absence of toes]; and hemimelia [absence of all or part of a limb]); and the head (hydrocephalus [enlargement of the head owing to excess fluid in or around the brain]; anencephaly [having no brain]; diprosopus [double-faced deformity]). Genetic alterations may also create situations wherein no single gene product is abnormal, but the collective effect of several genes is inadequate to support the normal development of an organ.

Unless extensive breeding studies are performed, it's usually impossible to define a genetic basis for most congenital malformations. The probability that interactions between families of genes will have a deleterious effect on the developing organism is directly correlated with the amount of inbreeding. *There is no amount of inbreeding that is without risk of increasing the incidence of birth defects.*

Induced congenital defects often are no easier to explain. Any agent that disrupts a normal developmental process is known as a *teratogen*. A teratogen can be a chemical (such as dioxin [a component of Agent Orange], alcohol, heavy metals, complex organic hydrocarbons); a drug (such as aspirin [in rodents only] or griseofulvin [an antifungal medication]); a normal body product delivered at the wrong time or in excess amounts (many steroid hormones); or an infectious agent (the most important being feline panleukopenia virus, which can cross the placenta from mother to offspring and destroy parts of the embryonic brain and sense organs).

In many cases a chemical entering the mother is converted by her into related substances, which can cross the placenta. This is an important feature that makes *comparative teratology* such a difficult scientific area, because each species (and often each individual) has its own unique metabolic processes and rates. The picture is further complicated by the varied structures and transport mechanisms present in the placentas of various mammals. With any suspected teratogen, the time of exposure and dose delivered are critical factors in the outcome.

While a few chemicals and other factors (X rays; *hyperthermia* [abnormally high body temperature]) are known to be teratogenic, there is little direct proof that most chemicals found around the home and yard can cause birth defects. The absence of such proof, however, does not mean that they have been proved harmless. Most chemicals have never been formally tested on companion animals, nor have the possible teratogenic effects of a very low intake of different combinations of normally "safe" chemicals been evaluated.

COMMON CONGENITAL MALFORMATIONS IN CATS

Axial Duplications

Cojoined twins are an anomaly in which two embryos or parts of embryos are attached to one another. In some cases both embryos may be fully formed and attached only at the head, thorax, or abdomen (such twins are often called "Siamese" twins). In other situations only one part will be duplicated—for example, kittens with two faces *(diprosopus),* two heads *(dicephalus),* or two tails have been reported. These anomalies result from duplications that occur between the blastocyst and neurula stages, with those occurring earlier being more complete.

Axial Defects

Malformations of the brain and spinal cord and/or the skeletal tissues surrounding them (vertebral column and skull) are the most common in all domestic animals and humans. Most early defects in nervous system development will cause abnormalities in development of the surrounding skeletal structures, and vice versa.

Spina bifida is a general term that includes all failures of the vertebrae to close normally around the spinal cord. If, as usually occurs, nerves within the spinal cord are abnormal or secondarily compromised by malformed vertebrae, there will be motor and sensory deficits in structures innervated by nerves whose roots exit the spinal cord at or behind the site of the lesion. Taillessness in Manx cats is an example of a condition linked to inherited spina bifida. It is caused by an autosomal (not located on a sex chromosome) dominant gene and shows *incomplete penetrance,* meaning that other genes modify the severity of expression.

Failure of the roof of the skull to form is often correlated with an increased, abnormal expansion of the brain *(exencephaly),* or in severe cases with failure of the brain to form a closed tube *(anencephaly).* In the latter situation, brain tissue secondarily degenerates before birth, leaving an empty crater in the top of the head. These lethal conditions are frequently caused by teratogens, but may occur spontaneously or as a result of genetic factors.

Hydrocephalus is a swelling of the fluid-filled ventricles within the brain that causes an abnormal expansion of the roof of the skull. This condition can result from heritable factors (in Siamese cats), microorganisms, or spontaneous developmental errors.

Cardiovascular Malformations

The heart begins as a simple, straight tube formed on the fourteenth day of development, and in the following two weeks becomes transformed into a four-chambered organ with separate pulmonary and systemic channels. Throughout this period of change, the heart is functional and supplies blood without interruption to all parts of the embryo. This is a remarkable feat of biological engineering.

Not surprisingly, congenital heart defects are common in all animals and represent about 10 percent of diagnosed cardiovascular problems in young animals. Included in this category are failures of the four chambers to become fully separated *(septal defects),* constrictions of a major blood vessel *(aortic* or *pulmonic stenosis),* and abnormal retention of an embryonic blood vessel. The latter includes *patent ductus arteriosus* (PDA), *vascular ring defects,* and *portocaval shunts.*

Patent ductus arteriosus is the most common of the three. In the embryo and fetus there is a vessel, the *ductus arteriosus,* that connects the pulmonary artery directly to the aorta. This permits oxygen-rich blood from the placenta to bypass the nonfunctional lungs and directly enter the systemic circulation. Normally the ductus arteriosus closes within a few days of birth. If it remains open (remains patent), the pulmonary and systemic bloodstreams will mix, causing the heart to work harder and leading to many secondary complications. Patent ductus arteriosus may show an increased frequency in some lines of dogs; no data on heritability are available for cats.

A portocaval shunt is the persistence of an embryonic vein joining the major systemic venous channel of the trunk, the *vena cava,* with *portal veins* carrying blood from the intestines to the liver, where the blood will be filtered and detoxified. If the shunt persists after birth, nonfiltered blood will be allowed to enter the systemic circulation, creating serious metabolic imbalances in the animal.

Both patent ductus arteriosus and portocaval shunts are medically and surgically treatable if they are diagnosed early and are not severe.

Malformations of the Face and Mouth

Cleft palate and *cleft lip* are, according to the published literature, rare in all breeds of cats except the Siamese, in which there is evidence for an inherited predisposition. However, the impression of many veterinarians and cat breeders is that the literature grossly underestimates the incidence of these malformations.

Both conditions result from failure of embryonic facial tissues to grow and fuse together. Either condition reduces the ability of the neonate to suckle, and the animals often choke to death. In humans and some animal breeds, for example Siamese cats, cleft palate sometimes shows a familial pattern and may be accompanied by malformations in other systems. Many unrelated teratogens can cause cleft palate in domesticated species.

Dogs and cats are sometimes bred for particular facial profiles, a potentially disastrous practice. Selecting for any extreme in facial dimension (ratio of length to width and shape of crown) inevitably increases the incidence of craniofacial malformations. Some of these, for example those recently described in Burmese cats, are lethal.

Limb Defects

Malformations involving the absence of some or all structures of the digits or limb are common. *Radial hemimelia* (congenital absence of the *radius,* the long, median bone of the lower forelimb), and *ectrodactyly* and *ectromelia* (absence of the digits and of an entire limb, respectively) are the most frequently seen in this category. *Syndactyly* is a condition in which only a single digit is present. This malformation is debilitating in dogs, cats, and humans, but it is normal in horses.

In most cases of limb reduction the cause is unknown, nor is it understood why forelimbs are more likely to be affected than hindlimbs. The drug Thalidomide causes a reduction in limb structures in humans such that the hands or feet develop close to the shoulder or hip, a condition known as *phocomelia* (seal-shaped limb). Despite many years of intensive study, the precise mechanisms underlying this disastrous teratogenic insult have not been delineated.

Congenital duplication of a limb can include an entire limb *(dimelia)* or only the digits *(polydactyly).* Polydactyly is very common in cats and occurs most frequently on the forepaws. It has been shown to be inherited in an *autosomal dominant* manner; these "double pawed" cats do not usually suffer any ill effects. Occasionally an extra claw becomes ingrown into a pad and causes infection.

Malformations of Visceral Organs

Gastroschisis is a lethal condition in which the kitten is born with the intestines protruding outside of the ventral abdominal wall. It results from a failure of the abdominal wall to form a narrow constriction around the base of the umbilical stalk.

A congenital *diaphragmatic hernia* is an opening in the diaphragm that permits abdominal organs to enter the heart or lung cavities and impinge upon the normal functioning of these organs. This condition, which arises during the early stages of the development of the liver and heart, is unusually common in cats, having been estimated to occur once in every one thousand live births. It occurs as a result of an *autosomal recessive* gene. (*See* Chapter 13: Genetics.)

Malformations of the Visual and Auditory Systems

Congenital abnormalities involving the sense organs are less common in cats than they are in many other species. There have been sporadic reports of *cataracts* (opacity of the lens of the eye) and *dermoid growths* on the cornea or third eyelid, but insufficient data are available to determine whether these defects have a genetic basis. Some congenital cataracts have been linked to viral infection, prenatally or shortly after birth.

Congenital *strabismus* (in which the orientation and thus the focus of the eyes is crossed) is seen frequently in Siamese cats and results in compromise of their capacity for depth perception. The nerve connections between the retina and the brain are also abnormal in these cats; studies of such cases have provided much valuable information on how the visual system develops and operates. This condition is genetic, resulting from the incomplete expression of an albino gene in Siamese. True albinos in other species, including humans, often have similar visual defects.

Another gene, the dominant white gene (W) that suppresses pigment formation in the skin, retina, and iris (*see* Chapter 13: Genetics), may also produce partial or complete deafness. Cats with white coats and blue eyes are especially likely to manifest a hearing problem. At present it is not known how the dominant white gene acts to produce tissue degeneration in the developing ear.

Malformations of the Urogenital System

Malformations of the reproductive and excretory systems are uncommon in domestic cats. There are sporadic reports of *cryptorchidism* (undescended testis) and *hermaphroditism* (presence of male and female sex organs). It is known that in some species cryptorchidism can be inherited, but there is no evidence for this in cats.

Occasionally, congenital absence of one kidney or one *gonad* (ovary or testicle) may be discovered by the veterinarian on routine physical examination of a cat. Such deficits usually do not compromise the health of the animal. Cats with these abnormalities probably should not be used for breeding in the event that a heritable basis exists.

Manx cats often will be born with abnormalities of the *perineal* region (area around the anus and genitals). In the embryo there exists a single cavity (the *cloaca*) that later becomes divided into the rectum and urogenital tract. When the gene that causes tail reduction acts particularly strongly (which inevitably occurs when breeding Manx cats) the cloaca fails to separate into two cavities. Affected animals are *incontinent* (unable to control urination and defecation), and often also have the vertebral and spinal cord anomalies described earlier in this chapter.

MISCELLANEOUS CONGENITAL DEFECT

Seborrhea Oleosa

A *familial seborrhea oleosa* has been recognized in Persian cats. Test breedings and retrospective pedigree analyses suggest that the condition is inherited on an autosomal recessive basis. Both sexes and all coat colors are affected. Kittens are born with varying degrees of greasiness of the skin and hair coat. The hair coat is constantly matted, and the kittens leave greasy deposits on everything they contact. The condition is incurable. Mildly affected cats can be maintained as acceptable pets with frequent bathing. (*See* Chapter 17: Skin and Disorders.)

Birth Control

The control of free-ranging cats in the United States has become an important issue in the last twenty years. One study in a city in Kansas estimated that the cat population increased by 18 percent annually and that 59 percent of the females were spayed. It was calculated that 88 percent should be spayed to maintain a zero population growth. Another perspective is to consider the results of one female cat having a litter of two female and two male kittens, with the same cycle continuing in following generations. In just five generations, or about two years, 324 cats could be born.

The yearly cost to collect, shelter, and destroy abandoned and stray animals exceeds $500 million. Each year there are about 25 million homeless pets, of which 18 million are destroyed because they are never adopted. If current trends continue we can expect the cost, in dollars and pet lives, to continue to spiral upward. However, there is a reasonable solution to the problem—birth control. As a cat owner you are responsible for your cat's sexuality.

FEMALE CATS

Spaying (Ovariohysterectomy)

The surgical removal of the ovaries, oviducts, and uterus is a recommended procedure for all female cats that are six months or older and will not be used in a breeding program. Spaying should be before first heat. The removal of the reproductive organs also eliminates the behaviors associated with an intact female (*see* Chapter 9: Reproductive Physiology, and Chapter 10: Mating), and the risk of reproductive diseases (*see* Chapter 12: Reproductive Disorders). Ovariohysterectomy produces a healthy young cat and eliminates the problem of homeless kittens. For more on the surgical procedure see Chapter 36: Surgery and Postoperative Care.

The spayed cat has a reputation for weight gain, but statistics vary on the frequency of this side effect. Other reported side effects include behavioral changes, decreased physical activity, and decreased vaginal discharge.

If during surgery a small part of the ovaries or

uterus is left in the cat, medical problems can occur. The ovarian tissue will continue to produce hormones, causing the spayed cat to come back into estrus.

If the uterus is not removed or if a portion of it is left, *pyometritis* (inflamed uterus with production of pus) can occur. Pyometritis is a frequent consequence if the drug megestrol acetate or other progestins (progesterone) or estrogens are administered to a spayed cat that still retains a portion of the uterus.

Tubal Ligation

The oviducts (tubes connecting the ovaries to the uterus) are tied off in this surgical procedure. Although it prevents unwanted pregnancies by prohibiting the sperm from reaching the egg, it does not preclude certain reproductive diseases such as pyometritis and tumors from occurring. And since the ovaries are not surgically removed, hormones continue to be produced so that the female cat repeatedly will come into estrus.

Since the surgical risks, recovery period, and operation costs are similar to those of spaying, this procedure is not recommended.

Estrus Control

Estrus control in the queen by means of oral and injectible progestins has been successful in Europe and Australia. These drugs are neither approved nor available in the United States. The progestin *megestrol acetate* has been experimentally and clinically used in the United States to control estrus in cats. It is hypothesized that progestins probably mimic the corpus luteum (a glandular mass that forms in the ovary after the egg is released) and have a negative feedback on gonadotrophic-releasing hormones (hormones affecting the sex organs). Side effects of progestin therapy may include increased appetite, increased body weight, a calming effect, and increased affection. Prolonged and indiscriminate use may produce a Cushingoid syndrome (overactivity of the adrenal glands) or diabetes. Cats with genital tract infections should not be given progesterone or progestins. Indiscriminate use of progestins can lead to cystic endometritis (cystic endometrial lining with accumulation of pus), enlarged mammary glands, and possible mammary gland tumors.

Mibolerone is a synthetic anabolic steroid ap-

proved for controlling estrus in young bitches. It has been used experimentally to prevent estrus in queens. Studies indicate that there were no apparent effects on subsequent estrus, mating, queening, litter size, or developmental defects in kittens. The mechanism of this drug is similar to that of progestin. It suppresses the release of pituitary luteinizing hormone. Side effects include decreased thyroid function, increased serum cholesterol levels, and slight masculinizing in some female cats.

Studies are being done on immunizing cats to prevent estrus. The vaccine would stimulate antibodies against a particular antigen. It is possible to produce antibodies against luteinizing hormone, the zygote (fertilized egg), the zona pellucida (outer layer of the egg), and sperm. However, these techniques are still in the experimental stage and would be an expensive alternative to spaying.

Mismating

Queens that "accidentally" mate can be successfully treated with *estradiol cypionate* (ECP) (an estrogen) administered forty hours after mating. The ova are retarded in transport through the oviduct for at least an additional twenty-four hours, resulting in degeneration in the late proliferative state. Reported side effects from this treatment include endometrial hyperplasia, uterine infections, and blood abnormalities (anemia, thrombocytopenia); also, estrous behavior may persist for seven to ten days following treatment.

Artificial Mating

Because cats are induced ovulators, artificial stimulation of the vaginal-cervical area with an instrument (pseudocopulation) to cause ovulation can sometimes shorten the estrous cycle in the queen. However, she will return to estrus within thirty to fifty days. Cats that have experienced repeated nonproductive matings or pseudocopulation have a higher incidence of cystic endometrial hyperplasia-pyometra complex. This technique is used mostly by cat breeders who want to postpone matings for one or two estrous cycles.

Abortion

Abortion may be induced in cats as late as forty days of gestation with prostaglandin (fatty acids that can stimulate uterine contractions). Induced abortion occurs within eight to twenty-four hours following treatment. Salivation, vomiting, diarrhea, labored breathing, and an increased heart rate may occur shortly after the drug is given. There is a risk of accidental death of the queen within two hours after the injection.

MALE CATS

Neutering (Castration)

This surgical procedure consists of removing the testes, epididymis (a duct connecting the testes to the vas deferens), and parts of the vas deferens (a tube that carries sperm from the testes to the urethra). This procedure has benefits in addition to preventing the impregnation of a female cat. Since the testes produce male hormones, the associated problems of urine spraying, excessive aggression, and the pungent odor of male urine are also eliminated. Some males continue to spray urine even after they have been castrated. This may be more of a behavioral problem than a physiological one. Eventually, most castrated male cats stop spraying.

Castration also results, either immediately or over a period of time, in a decline in fighting and roaming behavior in 80 to 90 percent of male cats. For more on the surgical procedure see Chapter 36: Surgery and Postoperative Care.

Vasectomy

This is a surgical procedure in which the vas deferens is ligated (tied). Although it renders the male cat sterile, it does not eliminate the associated sexual behavior, since male hormones continue to be produced by the testes.

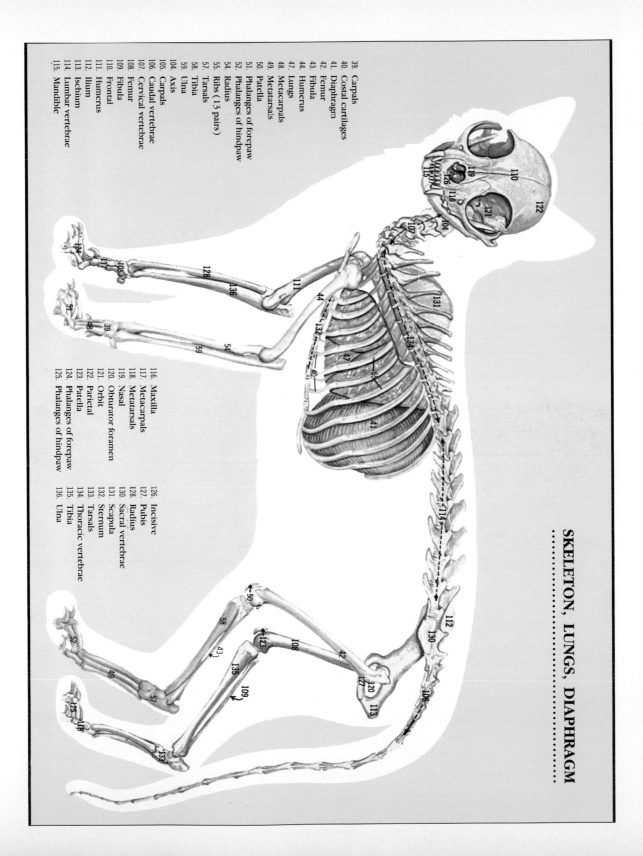

SKELETON, LUNGS, DIAPHRAGM

39. Carpals
40. Costal cartilages
41. Diaphragm
42. Femur
43. Fibula
44. Humerus
47. Lungs
48. Metacarpals
49. Metatarsals
50. Patella
51. Phalanges of forepaw
52. Phalanges of hindpaw
54. Radius
55. Ribs (13 pairs)
57. Tarsals
58. Tibia
59. Ulna
104. Axis
105. Carpals
106. Caudal vertebrae
107. Cervical vertebrae
108. Femur
109. Fibula
110. Frontal
111. Humerus
112. Ilium
113. Ischium
114. Lumbar vertebrae
115. Mandible

116. Maxilla
117. Metacarpals
118. Metatarsals
119. Nasal
120. Obturator foramen
121. Orbit
122. Parietal
123. Patella
124. Phalanges of forepaw
125. Phalanges of hindpaw

126. Incisive
127. Pubis
128. Radius
130. Sacral vertebrae
131. Scapula
132. Sternum
133. Tarsals
134. Thoracic vertebrae
135. Tibia
136. Ulna

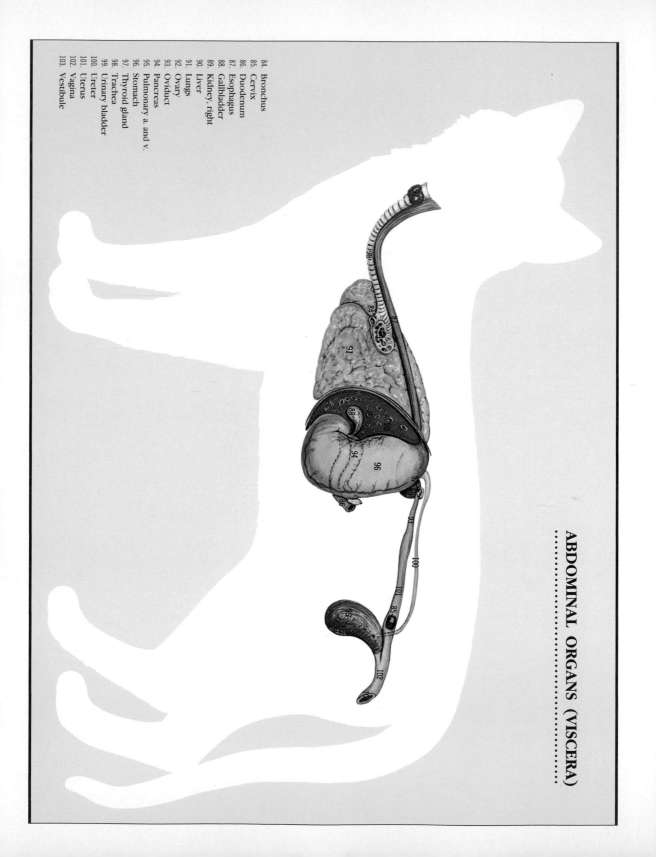

ABDOMINAL ORGANS (VISCERA)

84. Bronchus
85. Cervix
86. Duodenum
87. Esophagus
88. Gallbladder
89. Kidney, right
90. Liver
91. Lungs
92. Ovary
93. Oviduct
94. Pancreas
95. Pulmonary a. and v.
96. Stomach
97. Thyroid gland
98. Trachea
99. Urinary bladder
100. Ureter
101. Uterus
102. Vagina
103. Vestibule

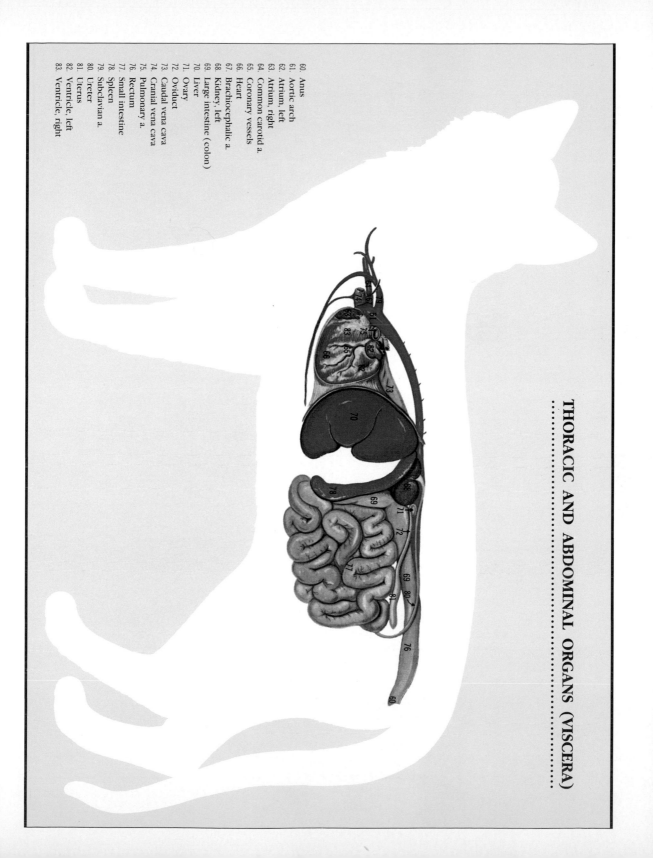

THORACIC AND ABDOMINAL ORGANS (VISCERA)

60. Anus
61. Aortic arch
62. Atrium, left
63. Atrium, right
64. Common carotid a.
65. Coronary vessels
66. Heart
67. Brachiocephalic a.
68. Kidney, left
69. Large intestine (colon)
70. Liver
71. Ovary
72. Oviduct
73. Caudal vena cava
74. Cranial vena cava
75. Pulmonary a.
76. Rectum
77. Small intestine
78. Spleen
79. Subclavian a.
80. Ureter
81. Uterus
82. Ventricle, left
83. Ventricle, right

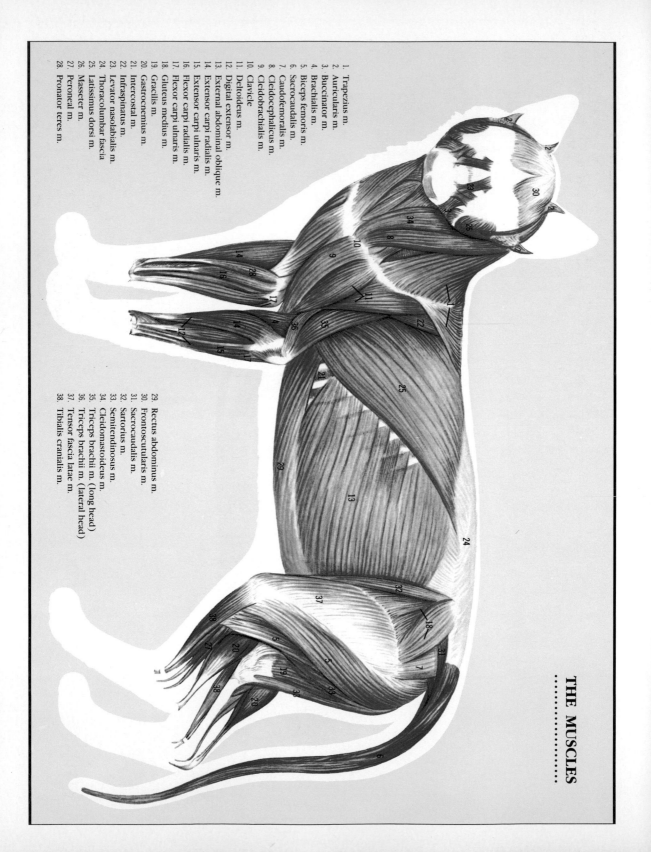

1. Trapezius m.
2. Auricularis m.
3. Buccinator m.
4. Brachialis m.
5. Biceps femoris m.
6. Sacrocaudalis m.
7. Caudofemoralis m.
8. Cleidocephalicus m.
9. Cleidobrachialis m.
10. Clavicle
11. Deltoideus m.
12. Digital extensor m.
13. External abdominal oblique m.
14. Extensor carpi radialis m.
15. Extensor carpi ulnaris m.
16. Flexor carpi radialis m.
17. Flexor carpi ulnaris m.
18. Gluteus medius m.
19. Gracilis m.
20. Gastrocnemius m.
21. Intercostal m.
22. Infraspinatus m.
23. Levator nasolabialis m.
24. Thoracolumbar fascia
25. Latissimus dorsi m.
26. Masseter m.
27. Peroneal m.
28. Pronator teres m.

29. Rectus abdominus m.
30. Frontoscutularis m.
31. Sacrocaudalis m.
32. Sartorius m.
33. Semitendinosus m.
34. Cleidomastoideus m.
35. Triceps brachii m. (long head)
36. Triceps brachii m. (lateral head)
37. Tensor fascia latae m.
38. Tibialis cranialis m.

THE MUSCLES

Anatomy of the Cat

A short-haired black cat always looks longer than any other cat, but this particular one, Babou, nicknamed the Long-cat, really did measure, stretched right out flat, well over a yard. I used to measure him sometimes.

—Colette, "The Long Cat"

Anatomy

A*natomy,* the science of body structure, provides the basic framework for understanding physiology, the science of body function. Anatomical structure represents the sum total of the parts of the individual body systems—the integument (skin), skeleton, musculature, circulatory and immune systems, digestive tract, respiratory tract, urogenital tract, endocrine (hormonal) system, and nervous system. The many and varied components of these systems all interact with each other, to one degree or another, in producing the functioning, living organism.

The purpose of this chapter is to provide a very broad outline of feline anatomy, through a series of anatomical illustrations. The material presented does not represent an exhaustive review of the subject; more detailed descriptions focusing on individual components of the body are available in the other relevant chapters.

THE MUSCLES

Muscles of the Head and Neck. The *frontoscutularis* (30) draws the ears forward, while the *auricularis* muscles (2) draw the ears back. The *levator nasiolabialis* (23) raises the upper lip and dilates the nostrils. The *masseter* (26) is one of the muscles of mastication, helping to close the jaw. The *buccinator* (3) forms part of the cheek, raises the lips, and aids in the movement of food within the mouth. The *cleidomastoideus* (34), part of the *brachiocephalicus* muscle (34, 8, 9, 10; the large expanse of muscle in the chest reaching from the upper forelimbs to the head), acts to flex the neck. The *cleidocephalicus* (8), also part of the *brachiocephalicus,* stretches from the *clavicle* or collarbone (10) to the head and neck, acting to extend the shoulder.

Dorsal Muscles. The capelike *trapezius* (1) raises the head and shoulder. The *latissimus dorsi* (25) is fan-shaped and flexes the shoulder. The thick *thoracolumbar fascia* (24) extends across the back and serves to anchor a number of muscles.

Muscles of the Thorax, Abdomen, and Tail. The *intercostal muscles* (21) connect the ribs to one another. The *external abdominal oblique* (13) is a large superficial muscle that helps form the wall of the abdomen. The *rectus abdominis* (29) borders the ventral abdominal midline. The *sacrocaudalis* (6, 31) acts to manipulate the tail.

Muscles of the Forelimb. The *cleidobrachialis* (9), a branch of the *brachiocephalicus* muscle, helps to extend the shoulder. The *infraspinatus* (22) serves to support the shoulder joint. The *deltoideus* (11), divided into two parts, helps to flex the shoulder. The *brachialis* (4) aids in flexing the elbow, while the *triceps brachii* (35, 36) helps to extend it. The forepaw is under the command of a number of muscles, including the *extensor carpi radialis* (14), *flexor carpi radialis* (16), *extensor carpi ulnaris* (15), *flexor carpi ulnaris* (17), and the *pronator teres* (28). The *digits* (toes) are controlled by *digital flexors* and *extensors* (12).

Muscles of the Hindlimb. The *sartorius* (32) is a straplike muscle that flexes the hip and extends the *stifle* (knee). The *gluteus medius* (18) is a major muscle of the rump. The *caudofemoralis* (7) extends the hip and rotates the thigh inward. The *biceps femoris* (5) flexes the stifle. The *tensor fascia latae* (37) is a triangular muscle that flexes the hip. The *semitendinosus* (33) is the rearmost muscle of the thigh. The *gracilis* (19) helps to draw the thigh inward toward the body. The major calf muscle, the *gastrocnemius* (20), flexes the stifle and helps to extend the foot. The *peroneal* muscles (27) and the *tibialis cranialis* (38) act on the foot.

····················

SKELETON, LUNGS, DIAPHRAGM

Forelimb. The *scapula* (56) is known more familiarly as the shoulder blade. The *clavicle* is part of the forelimb in the cat. It is a small bone imbedded into the muscle. The rest of the forelimb consists of a middle bone, the *humerus* (44), and two lower bones, the *radius* (54) and *ulna* (59). The bones of the forepaw include the *carpals* (39), *metacarpals* (48), and *phalanges* (51).

Hindlimb (pelvic limb). The *pelvis* is composed of three bones: the *ilium* (45), *ischium* (46), and *pubis*

(53). The hindlimb consists of an upper bone, the *femur* (42), which is attached to the pelvis by a ball and socket joint, the kneecap or *patella* (50), and two lower bones, the *tibia* (58) and the *fibula* (43). The bones of the hindpaw include the *tarsals* (57), *metatarsals* (49), and *phalanges* (52).

Trunk. Enclosing the chest cavity *(thorax)* are thirteen pairs of *ribs* (55) with their associated *costal cartilages* (40). The *lungs* (47) are the organs of breathing and respiration, whose expansion and contraction are controlled by a powerful and important muscle, the *diaphragm* (41). The diaphragm physically separates the thorax from the *abdominal cavity.*

Major bones of the feline skull (cranium) include the *frontal* (110), *parietal* (122), *nasal* (119), *incisive* (126), *maxilla* or upper jaw (116), and the lower jaw or *mandible* (115). Within these latter three bones are placed the *teeth.* The *orbit* (121) is the bony cavity within which the eye is situated. The rest of the *axial skeleton* is composed of seven *cervical vertebrae* (107), of which the first is the *atlas* and the second is the *axis* (104); thirteen *thoracic vertebrae* (134), seven *lumbar vertebrae* (114), three *sacral vertebrae* (130), and a variable number (about twenty) of *caudal vertebrae* (106), these latter making up the tail. Through the vertebrae runs the *spinal cord,* the conduit that connects the *brain,* protected within the skull, with the sensory and motor nerves running throughout the body.

The breastbone or *sternum* (132) is composed of eight *sternebrae* and serves to connect the ends of the ribs at the body midline. The *obturator foramen* (120) is an opening on each side of the pelvis through which nerves pass.

····················

THORACIC AND ABDOMINAL ORGANS (VISCERA)

The *heart* (66), the pumping organ that circulates the blood, is composed of four chambers, two *atria* with appendages called *auricles* (62, 63), and two *ventricles* (82, 83). The heart muscle is supplied with oxygen and nutrients by blood from the *coronary vessels* (65). The *pulmonary artery* (75) sends blood from the heart to the lungs for oxygen uptake. The *cranial vena cava,* or *precava* (74), returns blood from the head and upper body to the heart; the *caudal vena cava,* or *postcava* (73), returns blood from the abdomen and lower body. The *aortic arch* (61) is the vessel through which freshly oxygenated blood from the lungs and heart is pumped out into the body. This blood is then passed to the head and upper body by the *brachiocephalic* (67), *common carotid* (64), and *subclavian* (79) arteries, and to the lower body by the *aorta,* the continuation of the aortic arch.

The *liver* (70) is a large, chocolate-colored organ that filters blood from the digestive tract and stores energy, among other functions. The *spleen* (78) is an "immunologic filter" of the blood, containing many important cells of the immune system. The *kidneys* (68) remove toxic waste products of metabolism from the blood, producing *urine,* which travels down the *ureters* (80) on its way out of the body. The *small intestine* (77) and *large intestine* or *colon* (69), form the largest portion of the digestive tract, wherein nutrients are absorbed and solid waste (feces) is generated. Fecal material accumulates in the colon and is excreted via the *rectum* (76) through the *anus* (60).

In the female, eggs *(ova)* are formed in *ovaries* (71), travel down the corresponding *oviduct* (72), and, if fertilized by *spermatozoa* from the male, will implant in the *uterus* (81), initiating a pregnancy.

ABDOMINAL ORGANS (VISCERA)

The *trachea* (98) is a cartilage-containing structure that transports air between the nasal passages and the lungs (91). The air passes through *bronchi* (84) before actually entering the smaller airways within lung tissue. Near the upper end of the trachea is the *thyroid gland* (97), which has an important role in regulating body metabolism. The *pulmonary artery and vein* (95) are the blood conduits for the lungs. The muscular *esophagus* (87) carries food from the oral cavity to the *stomach* (96), where it can be acted upon by digestive enzymes. Also involved in the process of digestion (in addition to the intestines) are the *liver* (90), *gallbladder* (88), and *pancreas* (94). The pancreas is the source of *insulin,* a hormone important in the absorption of nutrients; this hormone is lacking or deficient in animals and humans with *diabetes mellitus.* Food exits the stomach into the *duodenum* (86), which is the upper portion of the small intestine.

Metabolic waste products in the blood are filtered out by the *kidneys* (89), resulting in the production of urine. The urine is transported through the *ureters* (100), collects within the *urinary bladder* (99), and is discharged through the urethra. In the female, the urine is excreted by way of the *vestibule* (103). The *ovaries* (92), *oviducts* (93), *uterus* (101) with *cervix* (85), *vagina* (102), and vulva comprise the female reproductive tract. The male reproductive tract is almost entirely outside the abdominal cavity.

PART VII

The External Cat

The Owl and the Pussy-Cat went to sea
    In a beautiful pea-green boat,
They took some honey, and plenty of money,
    Wrapped up in a five-pound note.
The Owl looked up to the stars above,
    And sang to a small guitar,
"O lovely Pussy! O Pussy, my love,
    What a beautiful Pussy you are,
        You are,
        You are!
    What a beautiful Pussy you are!" . . .
And hand in hand, on the edge of the sand,
    They danced by the light of the moon,
        The moon,
        The moon,
    They danced by the light of the moon.

—Edward Lear, "The Owl And The Pussy-Cat"

Skin and Disorders

FORM AND FUNCTION

Skin is the outer covering of the cat, giving shape, texture, and color to feline form and substance. It performs many functions necessary for the maintenance of life and the prevention of disease. Skin is a waterproof barrier against invasion of the body by harmful microorganisms and disease-causing substances. It retains the body's moisture, thus preventing dehydration and dangerous temperature fluctuations. The skin and its hair coat provide insulation from extremes of heat and cold and are involved in the regulation of the body's temperature. And, to a lesser degree than in the human body, feline skin perspires.

Its sensory surface relays information to the brain concerning aspects of external phenomena, such as atmospheric conditions, the proximity of objects and other organisms, life-threatening temperatures, pain, and wounds, in addition to daily physical sensation.

Skin is the largest organ of the body. In cats it is thinner and more vulnerable to injury than the skin of other animals. Diseases of the skin may appear at any time throughout the life of the cat and may not always begin with an observable skin problem. Some skin disorders are caused by systemic diseases and thus appear as secondary manifestations of those diseases.

Diseases and disorders of feline skin may be caused by bacterial infection, viral infection, fungal infection, traumatic injury, contact with physical or chemical agents, burns, frostbite, nutritional deficiency, emotional stress, parasitism, hormonal imbalance, metabolic dysfunction, allergy, high indoor temperature/ low humidity, self-mutilation, and tumors.

Untreated skin disorders can quickly intensify from the trivial to the serious. Signs such as swellings, growths, hair loss, itching, redness, and various other lesions, require professional veterinary attention.

COMPONENTS OF THE SKIN

Epidermis

The outer layer of skin is the *epidermis*. It contains pigment cells that establish color, helping to screen the body against harmful solar rays. The functions of the epidermis are to protect the body from external conditions, to prevent entrance of harmful material or disease-causing microbes, and to prevent loss of water and salts.

This protection is achieved largely by *keratin,* an insoluble protein material, which is synthesized by special cells within the structure of the epidermis.

The epidermis consists microscopically of five distinct layers. They are the *stratum corneum* (horny outer layer), *stratum lucidum* (clear layer), *stratum granulosum* (granular layer), *stratum spinosum* (spiny layer or prickle cell layer), and the *stratum basale* (basal layer or foundation layer). In haired skin areas the epidermis consists of only four layers, the stratum lucidum layer being absent.

Pigment

There are many color-producing cells in haired skin. *Melanocytes* (clear cells producing the pigment *melanin*) are especially prominent in the epidermis of the lips, footpads, the surface of the nose, prepuce or foreskin of the penis or vaginal folds, scrotum, the top portion of the tail, ears, anus, umbilical skin of the fetus, and in the hair bulbs, which are nipplelike protrusions at the base of each hair (thus the color of the hair coat is produced within each individual hair).

Depending on the color of the coat, the eyelids, nose area, lips, and footpads may be unpigmented, moderately pigmented, or black. Cats with chinchilla or silver coats bear darkly pigmented eyelids.

As red, cream, and tricolored cats mature and age, they develop larger numbers of frecklelike pigmented spots, which begin as pinpoint dots, on the eyelids, lips, nose, and footpads. These may first appear in cats as young as a year of age, coming and going like freckles before becoming permanently established.

Dermis

The *dermis* is the underlying support structure directly beneath the epidermis and provides a second layer of protection from invasion or injury. It is composed of collagen (a protein substance in the white fibers of the skin), elastin (elastic connective tissue), ground substance (connective tissue made from blood elements and other tissue cells), nervous tissue, blood vessels, vessels through which lymph circulates, muscle cells, and other cellular elements. The dermis also supports the hair follicles, sweat glands, and sebaceous glands.

Subcutis

The subcutaneous layer or *subcutis* is found beneath the dermis and is composed of thick bands of collagen fibers and smaller elastin fibers, which interweave and enclose the fatty tissue of the skin.

Hair

Hair consists of long, slender filaments made of lifeless keratin. Each hair consists of a shaft and a root. The root is contained in a sac or follicle. The base of the root is expanded into the *hair bulb,* which sits beneath the dermis and subcutaneous layer.

The exposed part of the hair, the shaft, has three layers: medulla, cortex, and cuticle. The inner *medulla* is composed of a cord containing one to three longitudinal rows of cells that are flattened from top to bottom. The cells are solidly packed near the hair root, but within the remainder of the hair shaft, air spaces and cellular cavities can be found. The *cortex* consists of spindle-shaped cells that are cornified (converted into horny tissue), with their long axis parallel to the hair shaft. These cells contain the melanin pigment that gives the hair its color. The outer *cuticle* is composed of flat, cornified cells arranged like slates on a roof, the free edge of each cell facing the tip of the hair.

Sebaceous Glands

Sebaceous glands are simple saclike structures attached to the hair follicle. They secrete *sebum,* a thick, semifluid substance composed of fat and cellular debris. Sebum is the substance that covers the hair coat with a protective veneer, giving it a lustrous appearance. Two or three sebaceous glands empty into the upper portion of the hair follicles around which they are clustered. Sebaceous glands are larger and more numerous in certain areas of the body: lips, chin, upper eyelids, upper surface of the tail, prepuce or skin fold covering penis or vagina, and scrotum. Sebaceous glands are not found in footpads, and only rarely in other nonhaired areas, where they open directly onto the skin surface. They do not appear to contain nerve structures.

Sweat Glands

There are two types of sweat glands: *apocrine* and *eccrine*. Apocrine sweat glands are found throughout the body as appendages of hair follicles. Saccular and coiled, they are larger in the lips, face, upper surface of the tail, and scrotum. The ducts of the apocrine glands open into the upper portion of the hair follicles around which they are clustered. Apocrine glands are not present in the footpads or other hairless areas. Apocrine glands secrete a milky, scented fluid that may play a role in sexual attraction.

Eccrine sweat glands occur only in the footpads. They are small and extensively coiled and are composed of a single layer of cube-shaped or columnar cells and a single layer of spindle-shaped cells. The ducts of these glands travel through the dermis and epidermis and open directly onto the footpad surface. Eccrine sweat glands appear to promote cooling by the evaporation of their secretions. These secretions are produced in response to elevated body temperature, emotional stress, or excitation.

Arrector Pili Muscles

Arrector pili muscles contain smooth muscle cells and are present in all haired skin areas (however, they are more developed along the back and on the upper surface of the tail). Arrector pili muscles originate in the dermis and are attached to hair follicles; when they contract they cause the hair to stand erect. This action takes place prior to combat with an antagonist or as a response to emotional stress.

Hair Coat

The hair coat consists of three types of hair: primary or guard hairs within the outer coat; awn hairs (intermediate-sized hairs forming part of the primary coat); and secondary hairs (downy hair found in the undercoat). *Guard* hairs are coarse, thick, straight hairs that taper to a fine tip. They insulate the body, protect the skin, and support the sense of touch. *Awn* hairs are thinner but swell just below the hair tip. These hairs also insulate and protect the body. The soft *secondary* hairs of the undercoat are the thinnest hairs in the coat and are evenly crimped or rippled in appearance. They help to regulate the temperature of the body by preventing excessive heat loss. Secondary (or undercoat) hairs are far more numerous than primary or guard hairs.

Specialized tactile hairs called *sinus hairs* are present on the muzzle (whiskers), above the eyes, and on the underside of the lower foreleg. These hairs are thick, stiff, and tapered at the tip.

Average daily hair growth is about 0.29 mm (0.011 inches) for primary guard hairs and about 0.26 mm (0.010 inches) for secondary hairs. Hair replacement in the cat is mosaic in pattern, unaffected by neutering, and primarily responsive to the length of time the cat is exposed to daylight (or artificial light). Outdoor cats in the northeastern United States usually shed noticeably in the spring and fall, while indoor cats often shed noticeably all year long. Sudden shedding of hair may occur following a visit to the veterinarian's examination table or to the show ring, probably because of a loss of telogen hairs (those in the resting stage of the growth cycle) when the arrector pili muscles are activated by fright or other stress. Hair follicle activity is highest in summer and lowest in winter. In summer, about 30 percent of the primary hairs and about 50 percent of the secondary hairs are in the resting phase of the hair cycle. In winter, these percentages increase to about 75 and 90, respectively. This must be kept in mind when attempting to assess the ease of epilation of hairs (pulled out by the roots). Feline hairs are more easily pulled out in winter.

In a typical shorthair cat, the longest primary hairs average about 4.5 cm (1¾ inches) in length. By contrast, the primary hairs in the silky coat of a show cat may exceed 12.5 cm (5 inches) in length. The short-haired type is the fundamental "wild" type and is dominant to the others.

Various mutant hair coat types have occurred, which have been perpetuated as a breed characteristic. The rex mutant is characterized by curly hairs and occurs in two major breeds, the Devon Rex and the Cornish (German) Rex. Cornish Rex cats lack primary hairs, while Devon Rex cats have primary hairs that resemble secondary hairs. Cornish Rex whiskers are often short and curly, while Devon Rex whiskers are often absent or stubbled. In some Devon Rex cats, the coat is completely absent on the chest, belly, and shoulders—a fault many breeders try to eliminate.

The wirehair mutation, seen in the American Wirehair, is characterized by a coat that looks and feels wiry, being coarse, crimped, and springy. All the hairs are curled in an irregular fashion, the awn hairs resembling a shepherd's crook.

Genetically determined hair reduction has occurred from time to time in various parts of the world, producing animals such as the Mexican Hairless cat. However, the only "hairless" breed recognized by the Cat Fancy is the Sphynx (Canadian Hairless). In these cats some thin hairs may persist around the muzzle and on the legs, and transient, fine, secondary hairs may cover the body.

• • • • • • • • • • • • • • • •

DISORDERS OF THE SKIN

Bacterial Skin Diseases

The normal skin of healthy cats is highly resistant to invasion by the wide variety of bacteria to which it is consistently exposed. A small number of pathogenic (disease-causing) bacteria may produce skin infections in the absence of any obvious impairment of the skin's defense system. However, localized disruption of normal skin defenses, as produced by *maceration,* or softening, of the skin (from overexposure to water or topical medications, for example) or physical trauma (from abrasions, cuts, punctures, insect bites, scratching, or rubbing) may predispose to development of overt infection. Treatment with immunosuppressive drugs (such as high doses of glucocorticoids) or the development of immunosuppressive diseases (feline leukemia virus or feline immunodeficiency virus infection, for example) may also predispose patients to skin infections.

ABSCESSES AND CELLULITIS. Abscesses (localized collections of pus) and cellulitis (diffuse inflammation due to infection of soft or connective tissue) are common feline skin disorders. They usually occur secondary to bites and scratches. The bacteria most commonly causing these disease conditions are often found as normal inhabitants of the feline mouth.

An abscess appears as a well-defined, dome-shaped, firm to fluctuant mass in the skin. The redness and heat seen in other types of skin infections are not often seen with abscesses. Abscesses often rupture and drain pus, which may be creamy or watery, white to red-brown in color, and frequently malodorous. The skin over an abscess about to rupture is thin and purple in color. Cellulitis is characterized by poorly-outlined areas of warm, painful, swollen skin tissue, which may ulcerate and become necrotic (dead) tissue.

Abscesses and cellulitis are most commonly seen in intact males of any breed or age, although intact females and neutered members of either sex may be affected. The most frequent locations for abscesses are on the limbs, face, base of the tail, and back, although they may occur anywhere. Signs often appear suddenly and can include pain, swelling, fever, and regional lymph-node enlargement. The lesions are sometimes painful from the time the bite is sustained, while others are painful only while pus is accumulating. Still others are painless throughout the course of abscess development. Anorexia (loss of appetite), fever, and depression may also be seen in affected cats.

The frequency with which a pus-producing infection (abscess or cellulitis) complicates bite wounds in cats makes early preventive treatment of these wounds with antibiotics a legitimate measure. When a cat is presented to the veterinarian within twelve hours of the bite, a single antibiotic injection and local wound treatment can usually prevent the development of bacterial infection. In fully developed abscesses, veterinary therapy would include surgical drainage and removal of dead or diseased tissue, application of drains where indicated, and flushing of the surgical site with antimicrobial solutions until healing is well underway (five to ten days postoperatively). Cellulitis should be treated with hot packs for ten to fifteen minutes three times daily, accompanied by oral or injectable antibiotics until the lesion is brought to a head (production of an abscess) or resolves without pus production.

Castration of intact male cats has been reported to be an effective preventive procedure. Castration results in rapid or gradual decline in fighting and roaming behavior in 80 to 90 percent of the cats treated (about 50 percent stop almost immediately and about 35 percent stop gradually). Some hormone preparations have been effective in modifying aggressive behavior in cats, preventing or reducing the occurrence of fights and subsequent infections. However, these hormones can cause side effects if administered over long periods of time.

FOLLICULITIS AND FURUNCULOSIS. Bacterial folliculitis (inflammation of hair follicles) and furunculosis (boils) are conditions that may be seen as primary bacterial infections or secondary to disorders such as feline acne, ectoparasite infestation (fleas, ticks), and hypersensitivity reactions. The lesions of folliculitis consist of papules (small, solid skin elevations) from which hairs can be seen to emerge and which progress to ring-shaped areas of oozing, ulceration, crusting, and hair loss. Folliculitis can be localized to the chin (secondary to feline acne) or can be present over the head, neck, and back. Hair follicle rupture results in painful nodules and draining tract. Itching, pain, and inflamed lymph nodes can be seen.

Treatment of bacterial folliculitis and furunculosis may include topical and systemic measures. Helpful topical treatments include warm water soaks and shampoo baths with antimicrobial solutions until the lesions are healing (five to seven days). Systemic antibiotic treatment must be guided by laboratory-test and bacterial-culture results.

IMPETIGO. Impetigo (collections of pustules on the skin) has been described in kittens. Because this disease begins on the back or neck and is caused by organisms commonly found in the feline mouth, it seems likely that it is caused by overzealous "mouthing" by the queen as she moves and carries her kittens. The pustules rupture rapidly, leaving behind ringlike erosions and yellowish crusts. The disease is not itchy or painful, and affected kittens are usually healthy otherwise. One or more kittens in a litter may be affected. Treatment with topical wet soaks and systemic antibiotics is curative in seven to ten days.

PARONYCHIA. Paronychia (pus-forming infection of the nail beds) is seen most often in middle-aged and older animals. Paronychia is virtually always secondary to another underlying disease process. Clinical signs include variable degrees of swelling, pain, itching, oozing, redness, hair loss, and crusting of one or more nails. A thick, cheesy, white to yellow material can often be expressed from the nail bed. Nails may be brittle, split, malformed, or shed. The forepaws are most commonly involved. Affected cats may be febrile (feverish) and depressed.

Treatment of paronychia consists of correcting the underlying cause, removal of affected nails where indicated, warm water soaking, and systemic antibiotic therapy. Depending on the underlying cause, paronychia can be a chronic, relapsing, and frequently frustrating disorder to treat.

TUBERCULOSIS. Tuberculosis is a very rare infectious disease of cats in the United States, caused by *Mycobacterium bovis* (cattle form) or, rarely, *Mycobacterium tuberculosis* (human form) or *Mycobacterium avium* (bird form). Transmission occurs by contact with discharges from infected animals or humans (from skin lesions, nasal discharges, and cow's milk) and by feeding cats raw, infected viscera. The development of a specific type of tuberculosis depends on the transmitting organism, the state of health of the host, and how the bacteria are introduced into the skin. Feline infections are frequently without clinical signs and difficult to diagnose by routine laboratory tests, and represent a significant public health hazard. Cats in close association with active cases of bovine or human tuberculosis receive extraordinary exposure and represent a population of animals at high risk. Fortunately, cats are highly resistant to the organism of human tuberculosis, and proven cases of human-to-cat transmission are rare. (*See* Chapter 30: Bacterial Diseases.)

FELINE LEPROSY. Feline leprosy is caused by a nontuberculous *Mycobacterium,* whose identity is still uncertain. The disease is seen in western Canada, Australia, and New Zealand, but is rarely reported in the United States. About 70 percent of affected cats are less than three years of age, and the disease is most often diagnosed in winter. Clinical signs include single or multiple skin lesions and occasional inflamed, swollen lymph nodes. Skin lesions vary from small nodules or abscesses, with or without draining tracts, to extensive nodules 0.5 to 3.5 cm in diameter (⅕ to 1⅖ inches) that frequently ulcerate. Pain, itching, and constitutional signs are usually absent. Skin lesions may occur anywhere, but are most common on the head, neck, and limbs. The therapy of choice is surgical excision, where possible.

ATYPICAL MYCOBACTERIOSIS. Atypical mycobacteriosis is an uncommon disease of cats, caused by various nontuberculous *Mycobacteria* species. Atypical mycobacteriosis is characterized by nodules and plaques (hard patches), draining tracts, and nonhealing ulcers. The belly, groin, and lower back are most often affected. Pain, itching, and constitutional signs are uncommon. The treatment of choice is surgical excision by the veterinarian. However, postsurgical recurrences are common. Treatment with various antimicrobial agents has been unsuccessful. The atypical *Mycobacteria* are usually resistant to the classical antituberculosis drugs. Some cats with atypical mycobacteriosis undergo long-term spontaneous remissions.

RARE BACTERIAL SKIN DISEASES. Other bacterial diseases of cats that can involve the skin include bacterial pseudomycetoma (botryomycosis caused by *Staphylococcus aureus*), actinomycosis, and nocardiosis. However, the incidence of these diseases in cats is very low. Treatment frequently includes surgical excision followed by antibiotic therapy. (*See* Chapter 30: Bacterial Diseases.)

Fungal Skin Diseases

RINGWORM. Ringworm *(dermatophytosis)* is one of the most common skin disorders of the cat. Although young cats are more susceptible, cats of any age can be affected.

Ringworm fungi *(dermatophytes)* invade the most superficial, outer layers of the skin, nails, and hair. Rarely, dermatophytes may produce deep skin infections and even spread to involve other organ systems. The probable source of all ringworm fungi is the soil, although a number of these organisms have given up this mode of existence for a parasitic life on animal or human skin.

When dermatophytes contact the skin, a number of things can happen:

- they may be brushed off mechanically
- they may not be able to establish residence because of an inability to compete with normal skin microorganisms
- they may establish residence on the skin but produce no recognizable lesions
- they may establish residence and cause disease.

Because ringworm fungi usually do not invade living tissue, surviving instead by digesting the keratin in shed skin cells, the only mechanism by which they may cause disease is by the production of toxic or allergenic substances. These substances penetrate the living epidermis into the dermis, where a response to the challenge of toxic or allergenic materials occurs by means of an inflammatory reaction. Thus, ringworm is a type of biological contact dermatitis.

Ringworm appears to be more common in tropical and temperate climates. The major predisposing factors to infection with dermatophytes are thought to include age, skin defects, nutritional status, humidity, immune status of the host, and living conditions. Seasonal variation in the occurrence of ringworm in cats in the United States has been observed. Among the more common ringworm fungi infecting cats are: *Microsporum canis (M. canis), Microsporum gypseum (M. gypseum),* and *Trichophyton mentagrophytes (T. mentagrophytes).* The ringworm fungi are contagious (especially *M. canis*), by both direct and indirect contact, and may pass from animal to animal, animal to human, human to animal, and human to human. Because *M. canis* is so well adapted to the cat, it is not surprising that cats are thought to be the primary source of *M. canis* infections for other animals and humans. Importantly, many cats can carry *M. canis* without showing outward clinical signs of ringworm.

The clinical signs of ringworm are extremely variable: Ringworm in cats may be the skin disorder most *over*diagnosed and *under*diagnosed by both veterinarians and owners. The lesions are often localized, but not always, and are commonly present on the head and limbs. The signs of feline ringworm may include any or all of the following:

- circular areas of hair loss, stubbled hairs, scaling, and crusting, with or without itching ("classical ringworm")
- patchy baldness with or without redness, itching, and scratching
- localized or generalized papular dermatitis, with or without itching and significant hair loss, especially in cases involving *M. canis*
- pigment alterations of hair and/or skin, with or without other signs of skin disease
- large areas of pustular or vesicular (fluid-filled sacs) dermatitis and baldness, with or without itching, especially in cases involving *T. mentagrophytes*
- paronychia (pus-forming nail-bed infection)
- seborrhea sicca (a type of dandruff)
- and other signs of less frequent occurrence.

Veterinary assistance is essential in these cases. Feline ringworm has enormous zoonotic (diseases transmissible from animal to human) implications, and infected cats and their environments should be handled with great care.

Treatment is usually undertaken to prevent further spread of the infection on the patient, to prevent spread to other animals and humans, and to prevent further environmental contamination. To this end, clipping, topical antifungal agents, and appropriate isolation and sanitation procedures are indicated.

Diseased animals should be separated from clinically normal animals and isolated if possible. Exposed, clinically normal animals should also receive topical antifungal therapy. *Because ringworm fungi may persist in the environment for well over one year, environmental surfaces and objects coming in close contact with affected cats should be properly sanitized, disinfected, or destroyed.* Recommended disinfectants include alcohol and diluted household bleach. These procedures and thorough vacuuming (dispose of vacuum bag) are indicated on a weekly basis for at least two weeks beyond clinical recovery.

Feline ringworm may be a self-limiting disease, with spontaneous remission occurring within one to three months. Because of this, oral antifungal therapy is rarely indicated. Cats with persistent, recurrent, or severe ringworm should be treated orally, in addition to the above-mentioned measures. Multiple-cat households or cattery situations may also require oral therapy.

CANDIDIASIS. Candidiasis is an extremely rare yeast infection of the skin and mucous membrane of cats. *Candida* yeasts are considered to be part of the normal microbial population of the intestinal and reproductive tracts. With lowered host resistance caused by prolonged maceration (softening of tissue by soaking), antibiotics, or immunosuppressive drugs, or by inherent or disease-induced immunological defects, serious local or systemic infections may be produced by *Candida*.

Clinical findings include a blister eruption of the skin, nail folds, and external ear, and foul-smelling gray-white mucoid plaques or patches affecting the oral, anal, and vaginal membranes. Correction of predisposing causes is fundamental to successful therapy. Topical application of an antifungal agent may be helpful.

SPOROTRICHOSIS. Sporotrichosis is an uncommon pus-forming disease of cats caused by *Sporothrix schenckii*. This fungus is found in decaying vegetation, sphagnum moss (peat), soil, on rosebushes, and on other environmental substances. The organism is usually introduced into skin tissue by a penetrating wound. Puncture wounds from thorns, wood slivers, bites, and scratches are usually incriminated. Lesions consist of nodules and patches, which are frequently ulcerated, crusted, and draining a brownish-red, oozing material. The lesions often are present on the face, ears, neck, and limbs. Inflamed, swollen lymph nodes are often found.

The treatment of choice by veterinarians for sporotrichosis is sodium iodide. Cats are very sensitive to iodine compounds; signs of toxicity include vomiting, loss of appetite, depression, muscular twitching, hypothermia (low body temperature), cardiovascular collapse, and death. If signs of iodine poisoning appear, treatment must be halted until these signs regress.

Feline sporotrichosis is now recognized as a public health concern for practicing veterinarians, veterinary assistants, veterinary students, and owners who handle cats with skin lesions. All cases of feline sporotrichosis should be considered potentially contagious, especially if open wounds are present.

PHAEOHYPHOMYCOSIS. Phaeohyphomycosis is an uncommon chronic skin infection caused by dark, pigmented fungi. These fungi live in soil and vegetation and gain access to animal tissues by a penetrating wound infection. The vast majority of reported feline cases have involved eight- to ten-year-old males. Lesions consist of nodules and abscesses beneath the skin, which frequently ulcerate and develop draining tracts. They occur most frequently on the face and limbs. Local lymph nodes are usually infected.

The treatment of choice is surgical excision, but recurrences are common. Antifungal antibiotics given orally may be of some benefit.

Parasitic Skin Diseases

See Chapter 19: External Parasites.

Viral Skin Diseases

Viral skin diseases are apparently rare in cats. The following is a brief overview of proven and suspected viral skin diseases in cats. (*See also* Chapter 29: Viral Diseases.)

FELINE LEUKEMIA VIRUS (FeLV). Feline leukemia virus infection has been implicated in a number of feline skin disorders, including chronic or recurrent abscesses and cellulitis, chronic paronychia (nail-bed infection), poor wound healing, seborrhea, and generalized itching. Feline fibrosarcoma (a malignant tumor) in young cats, feline leukemia virus–induced lymphosarcoma (lymph node cancer), liposarcoma (fat cell cancer), melanoma (pigment cell cancer), hemangioma (benign tumor of blood vessels), and multiple cutaneous horns (projections of hard skin) in cats are among the other disorders in this group with skin manifestations. The true relationship in some of these conditions is speculative. Chronic or recurrent abscesses, cellulitis, and nail infections are thought to be caused by the well-known immunosuppressive effects of feline leukemia virus infection.

FELINE HERPESVIRUS INFECTION (Feline Viral Rhinotracheitis [FVR]). Feline herpesvirus infection has been associated with oral and skin ulceration in cats. Skin ulcers are usually superficial and multiple and affect all areas of the skin, including the footpads. In some cases, it is thought that the trauma of shaving the skin or the stress of surgery, or both, may precipitate the development of lesions.

FELINE IMMUNODEFICIENCY VIRUS (FIV). Feline immunodeficiency virus infection causes severe immunosuppression. Because of this, infected cats are predisposed to chronic or recurrent bouts of bacterial infection (abscess, cellulitis, folliculitis), ringworm, and demodicosis (demodectic mange).

FELINE POXVIRUS INFECTION. Feline poxvirus infection is an uncommon disease of cats, which has been described in Great Britain and continental Europe. Lesions include papules, nodules, plaques, crusts, and depressed ulcers. The face, limbs, paws, and lower back are usually affected. Itching, pain, fever, eyelid inflammation, and labored breathing may be seen.

There is no specific therapy for this disease. Spontaneous remission usually occurs within one to two months. Humans are susceptible to infection with a number of animal poxviruses, and transmission of feline poxvirus infection to humans has recently been reported.

PSEUDORABIES. In this rare, rapidly fatal herpesvirus infection of cats, severe itching causes violent scratching and chewing at the skin.

Immunologic Skin Diseases

There are a number of diseases whose origins lie in an inappropriate or exaggerated response of the immune system to foreign substances, which sometimes can result in an attack upon the body's own cells. Some of these diseases are manifested, at least in part, by skin disorders, as described in this section. (*See* Chapter 28: Immune System and Disorders.)

URTICARIA AND ANGIOEDEMA. Urticaria (hives) and angioedema (recurrent wheals or welts) are variably itchy, edematous skin disorders that are rare in cats. Urticaria and angioedema can result from many causes, both immunologic and nonimmunologic. Nonimmunologic factors that may precipitate or intensify urticaria and angioedema include physical forces (pressure, sunlight, heat, exercise), psychological stresses, genetic abnormalities, and various drugs and chemicals (aspirin, narcotics, foods, food additives). Substances reported to cause urticaria and angioedema in cats include certain foods, drugs (penicillin, tetracycline), vaccines (panleukopenia), stinging and biting insects, blood transfusions, plants (nettle), and intestinal parasites.

Urticaria is characterized by an acute onset of localized or generalized wheals (smooth elevated areas), which may be itchy and exhibit serum oozing. Characteristically, wheals are lesions that persist for only a few hours. Angioedema is characterized by localized large, edematous (swollen with fluid) swellings.

Veterinary therapy includes elimination of known causative factors, and symptomatic treatment with adrenaline, glucocorticoids, and antihistamines.

ATOPY. Atopy (inherited allergy or hypersensitivity) is a common, genetically determined, itchy skin disease of cats, in which the cat becomes sensitized to inhaled environmental substances. The clinical signs may be seasonal or nonseasonal in occurrence, depending on the allergenic substance *(allergen)* involved. Skin disorders seen in atopic cats include miliary dermatitis (a minute red rash); eosinophilic granuloma complex; itchy facial skin lesions resulting in hair loss around the lips, nose, ears, and eyes; and symmetrical hypotrichosis (thinning of the hair).

A positive diagnosis of atopy is made by intradermal skin testing (allergy testing). Veterinary therapy includes hyposensitization (allergy shots) or administration of glucocorticoids.

FOOD HYPERSENSITIVITY. Food hypersensitivity is an uncommon, nonseasonal, itchy skin disorder of cats. Unfortunately, information on the specific dietary substances involved in feline food hypersensitivity is meager at best. Many of the skin lesions seen in this disease mimic those of atopy. Surprisingly, signs related to the gastrointestinal tract (vomiting, diarrhea) are seen in fewer than 10 percent of cases.

Diagnosis of food hypersensitivity may be made by feeding a hypoallergenic diet for three weeks and observing if the skin problem improves, then refeeding the normal diet and observing if the skin problem worsens again. Therapy consists of avoidance of offending foods or administration of glucocorticoids (response to the latter is often disappointing). Long-term hypoallergenic diets may be developed by adding single dietary items to the basic hypoallergenic diet and evaluating each item for seven days.

CONTACT HYPERSENSITIVITY. Contact hypersensitivity is probably a rare disease in cats. Substances reported to have caused contact hypersensitivity in cats include plants, topical medications, and home furnishings. The clinical sign is a red rash, which tends to be confined to the hairless or sparsely haired areas of skin. The most likely areas to come into direct contact with the environment are chest and belly, tail, neck, point of the chin, muzzle, and ears. If the allergen is a topical medication or if it is a liquid, aerosol, or powder, then skin reactions may occur in haired areas as well. Reactions to rubber or plastic dishes are confined to the point of contact, the nose and lips. Reactions to collars are usually confined to the neck.

Therapy includes avoidance of the allergen or the administration of glucocorticoids by the veterinarian. Avoidance of the allergen is preferable, but may be impossible depending on its nature or whether it can even be identified. In such instances, glucocorticoids may be very effective.

DRUG ERUPTION. Drug eruption is a rare, variably itchy skin reaction to a drug. Drugs responsible for skin eruptions may be administered orally, topically, by injection, or by inhalation. Any drug may cause an eruption, and there is no specific type of reaction for any one drug. Drug eruption can mimic virtually any skin disease. Reactions to drugs in cats have included:

- a red rash from certain antibiotics and antifungals
- hives, hair loss, and itching from antibiotics
- recurrent swellings from panleukopenia vaccine and certain drugs
- contact hypersensitivity from a number of drugs
- toxic epidermal necrolysis (widespread cell death causing separation of tissues with redness and peeling over the entire body) from certain antibiotics and leukemia virus antiserum.

Diagnosis is based on history, physical examination, and response to withdrawal of the suspected offending drug. Skin reactions usually subside within two to three weeks after administration of the drug is discontinued.

FLEA BITE HYPERSENSITIVITY. Flea bite hypersensitivity is the most common skin hypersensitivity of the cat. (*See* Chapter 19: External Parasites.)

INTESTINAL PARASITE HYPERSENSITIVITY. Intestinal parasite hypersensitivity is a rare disorder of cats. A number of intestinal parasites have been incriminated, including roundworms, tapeworms, and coccidia (a type of protozoan). Clinical signs include a red rash, itchy dandruff, and itching without visible lesions. Therapy includes elimination of the parasites. Most of these cases are in young kittens.

PEMPHIGUS. The *pemphigus complex* is a group of rare autoimmune skin diseases of cats. Autoimmune diseases are disorders within an individual cat wherein the immune system reacts against the body's own cells, resulting in the production of antibodies and "killer" cells that destroy the target tissue. In this situation, the immune system fails to recognize the involved tissue as "self." Autoimmune diseases can be life-threatening without prompt medical attention.

Pemphigus is characterized by production of antibodies against the intercellular cement substance of the skin. Frequently affected areas include the gums, lining of the mouth, nasal region, the facial zone, nails, and surface of the skin.

When the pemphigus antibody attacks its target, it triggers a reaction that culminates in the destruction of cell-to-cell connections. This loss of intercellular cohesion leads to the formation of blisters within the affected skin layer. Feline pemphigus occurs in three forms: *pemphigus vulgaris, pemphigus foliaceus,* and *pemphigus erythematosus.*

Veterinary treatment of feline pemphigus can be difficult, requiring large doses of glucocorticoids, with or without other, more potent drugs. Side effects can be severe, and close physical and laboratory monitoring of the patient is critical. Often, therapy must be maintained for the life of the animal.

SYSTEMIC LUPUS ERYTHEMATOSUS (SLE). Systemic lupus erythematosus is a rare multisystemic autoimmune disorder of cats. The cause of SLE appears to be connected to many factors, such as genetic selection, immunologic disorders, virus infections, and hormonal and ultraviolet light effects. Siamese cats may be especially predisposed to SLE.

The skin lesions of feline SLE are characterized by redness, scaling and crusting, erosions, ulcerations, hair loss, and depigmentation, especially on the face, ears, and paws. Blisters and oral ulcers may also be seen, and paronychia (nail-bed infection) is common. Constitutional signs include loss of appetite, depression, weight loss, and fever.

The prognosis for the affected feline patient is unpredictable and often dependent on the presence of the condition in parts of the body other than the skin. The veterinarian will begin treatment with glucocorticoids until the disease is in remission (a few weeks). Long-term control is achieved with the lowest effective glucocorticoid dosage that will keep the disease in remission. Repeated examinations by the veterinarian are necessary for control of this lifelong disorder and to observe for serious side effects from the medicine.

ERYTHEMA MULTIFORME. Erythema multiforme is an acute eruption of the skin and mucous membranes that is only rarely reported in cats. The cause is not well defined. The disease is believed to be a hypersensitivity reaction associated with various disease states and the administration of certain drugs. Feline erythema multiforme is characterized by a sym-

metrical red rash over the surface of the belly and on the upper part of the legs. The rash enlarges radially and heals centrally, resulting in a ring-shaped or bow-shaped lesion. Scaling, oozing, crusting, erosion, and ulceration are usually not present.

Therapy consists of determining the underlying cause, with symptomatic treatment of the lesions.

TOXIC EPIDERMAL NECROLYSIS. Toxic epidermal necrolysis is a rare, variably painful, blistering, and ulcerative disorder of the skin and mouth. The cause is not well defined. The disease, like erythema multiforme, is believed to be a hypersensitivity reaction associated with various disease states and with the administration of certain drugs, such as antibiotics. Clinical signs include the acute, symmetrical development of widespread blistering, peeling, and ulceration; the lesions are frequently quite painful, resembling a massive sunburn reaction. Constitutional signs include fever, loss of appetite, and depression. Secondary bacterial infection of the lesions may complicate therapy, which is comprised of identification of an underlying cause, and supportive care.

PLASMA CELL PODODERMATITIS. Plasma cell pododermatitis is a rare skin disorder of unknown cause. It begins as a soft, painless swelling of the footpads, which then may progress to ulceration. When ulceration occurs, pain and lameness may be present. The central metacarpal (front) or metatarsal (hind) pads are usually affected, but the digital pads may also be involved. Affected cats may otherwise be healthy. The therapy of choice is not clear. Some cases regress spontaneously, while others occur on a seasonal basis. Glucocorticoids are used to treat the condition but may have little effect on the outcome.

Hormonal and Metabolic Skin Diseases

Many hormones affect the skin and its adjunct parts. This section is limited to hormonal (endocrine) disorders affecting the skin. Clinically, equal symmetrical hair loss on both sides of the body is often the first noticeable sign of a hormonal skin disease. The hair coat is often dull, dry, easily pulled (*epilated*), and fails to regrow following clipping. Matching pigmentary disturbances of the skin may accompany the hair loss. Hormonal skin diseases are not associated with itching and scratching.

HYPERADRENOCORTICISM (Cushing's syndrome). Hyperadrenocorticism in cats is characterized by skin that is thin, abnormally loose, easily bruised or torn, and slow to heal. Symmetrical hair loss on both sides of the body and hyperpigmentation (darkening), common in dogs, are rarely seen in cats with this disease. Hyperadrenocorticism is rare in cats. (*See* Chapter 27: Endocrine System and Metabolic Disorders.)

HYPERTHYROIDISM. Skin lesions attributed to feline hyperthyroidism include excessive shedding, areas of hair loss associated with excessive grooming, and an increased rate of nail growth. (*See* Chapter 27: Endocrine System and Metabolic Disorders.)

DIABETES MELLITUS. Skin lesions associated with feline diabetes mellitus include excessive shedding, symmetrical hair loss, scaly skin (which can be itchy or nonitchy), and skin bumps caused by a reaction to excessive amounts of fat in the blood and tissues. (*See* Chapter 27: Endocrine System and Metabolic Disorders.)

FELINE ENDOCRINE ALOPECIA. Feline endocrine alopecia is an uncommon symmetrical thinning of the hair coat. The cause is unknown. It has been theorized that the disease is the result of a sex hormone deficiency or imbalance, because it is seen in cats neutered at a young age and responds well to sex hormone therapy. Affected cats usually have normal thyroid and adrenal function.

Thinning of the hair begins in the genital and perineal areas. There is a diffuse thinning of the hair, rather than complete baldness, affecting the anogenital region, underside of the tail, inner back surface of the thighs, and abdomen. Hairs in affected areas are easily removed. Itching and scratching are absent. Aside from the dermatological signs, cats with feline endocrine hair loss are normal.

Treatment by the veterinarian consists of combined androgen-estrogen injections. Relapses occur in about 50 percent of cats treated; therefore repeated injections are necessary. Occasional, transient side effects seen with androgen-estrogen therapy are signs of estrus in females and aggression and urine spraying in males. These signs are seen during the first week of therapy. Overdose of either androgen or estrogen can result in severe liver and biliary tract disease.

Thyroid hormone is also effective. After hair regrowth is achieved, maintenance doses are continued on a daily basis. Cats with feline endocrine alopecia are seldom hypothyroid, however; thyroid hormones can "force" varying degrees of hair growth in a number of nonhypothyroid conditions.

TELOGEN DEFLUXION. Telogen defluxion is sudden, massive hair loss that occurs during the resting phase *(telogen)* of the hair growth cycle. It is occasionally seen in cats, especially in the Rex breeds. Systemic illness or stress may cause large numbers of hairs to enter telogen prematurely, resulting in a massive, synchronized shedding of hair. This may occur as a consequence of high fever, anesthesia, estrus, birth and lactation, or any other stressful experience. Physical examination reveals varying degrees of symmetrical hair loss. Hair regrowth is usually noted within four to twelve weeks after loss. No therapy is indicated or effective.

EXCESSIVE SHEDDING. Shedding of hair is a normal event in the life of a cat. Because shedding is greatly influenced by daylight (the *photoperiod*), it tends to be exaggerated in outdoor cats in the spring and fall and may be dramatic enough that the owner believes the cat to be sick. Nonseasonal shedding is seen in indoor cats and in cats that are chronically ill. The shedding of hair by the indoor cat can be frustrating to an owner, but is correctable by establishing a natural photoperiod. Otherwise, the owner is burdened with daily brushing and combing in order to remove shed hairs before they cover rugs, furniture, and clothing, or accumulate as hairballs in the cat's stomach.

The shedding of hair by the chronically ill cat is usually accompanied by skin lesions as well, thin and abnormally wrinkled skin and scaling. Correction of the underlying disorder resolves the skin and hair coat problem.

PREAURICULAR ALOPECIA. Preauricular alopecia is common in normal cats of any breed, sex, or age. Patches of sparsely haired or totally hairless skin are seen bilaterally in the temporal region (in front of the ears). This physiological change can occasionally be mistaken for disease by an owner. Some breeds normally have less hair in this region. The Siamese breed and its crosses are usually very thin-haired from the ear to the eye.

ALOPECIA AREATA. Alopecia areata is a rarely reported disease of the cat. The cause is unknown. It has been reported in association with *hemobartonellosis* (a bacterial infection). Clinically, alopecia areata is characterized by one or more patches of noninflammatory hair loss (no redness, flaking, or crusting), with a predilection for the head and neck. Pigmentary disturbances in the skin may be present. Itching and pain are absent, and affected cats are otherwise healthy. The natural course of feline alopecia areata is unclear. Some cases may undergo spontaneous remission, and some may benefit from injections of glucocorticoids.

Seborrheic Skin Diseases

Seborrheic skin diseases are characterized by local or generalized defects in *keratinization* (production of skin keratin). Altered keratinization results in increased scale or crust formation. This may be accompanied by greasiness, rancid odor, inflammation, and secondary infection. Itching and scratching may also be seen.

SEBORRHEA. Seborrhea is uncommon in the cat. It may be *primary* (cause unknown), or *secondary* to another condition. Secondary seborrhea is by far the more common type in cats.

Seborrhea sicca is characterized by dry skin and hair coat, excessive scaling, variable degrees of hair loss, and itching. This is the most common form of seborrhea seen in cats and is usually secondary to external parasites (especially mites and lice), internal parasites, ringworm, malnutrition, many systemic illnesses, environmental factors such as high temperature and low humidity, and excessive or drying topical medications (shampoos, dips, powders). Affected cats eating balanced diets have been reported to respond to fat supplementation ("fat-responsive dandruff").

Some cats that have not been groomed or that don't do a complete job of grooming themselves will be presented with excessive dead skin on their backs. This is difficult to wash out or even comb out.

Seborrhea oleosa is rare in cats and is characterized by scaling, greasiness, variable degrees of redness and hair loss, and itching. Feline leukemia virus infection, chronic liver disease, and systemic lupus erythematosus (SLE) have been associated with seborrhea oleosa

in cats. In the Rex and Sphynx breeds, greasiness in the skin folds about the claws is common.

Therapy is most appropriately and most effectively directed at the underlying cause. Washing is a useful therapeutic adjunct. For seborrhea sicca, most medicated shampoos are *not* recommended, because they tend to be drying. Nonmedicated, nonirritating hypoallergenic emollient shampoos are preferred. When such shampoos are ineffective, emollient rinses are very effective. For seborrhea oleosa, degreasing shampoos containing benzoyl peroxide or sulfur are indicated. In general, antiseborrheic shampoos are given every three days (suds well, leave on ten to fifteen minutes, rinse well) until the seborrhea is controlled, and then as needed (every one to two weeks). Emollient rinses are applied on a weekly or biweekly basis. *Antiseborrheic agents such as coal tars and phenols (salicylic acid) are toxic to cats. Use only a preparation recommended by a veterinarian.* (See Chapter 14: Normal Development and Congenital Birth Defects.)

TAIL GLAND HYPERPLASIA (stud tail). Stud tail is an uncommon skin disease of cats. The disorder is most common in sexually active purebred male cats, especially Persians, Siamese, and Rex. The term "stud tail" is a misnomer, however, as the condition may occur in castrated males and in intact and spayed females. The *supracaudal organ* (preen gland) of the cat comprises a group of modified sebaceous glands found along the top of the tail. Stud tail is caused by hyperactivity of these glands.

The condition is characterized by an accumulation of blackheads and yellow to black, waxy debris on the skin and hairs of the tail base. Rarely, secondary bacterial folliculitis (inflammation of hair follicles) and furunculosis (boils), pain, and itching will be present as a result of the condition. Often bite wounds occur in the area of the gland, resulting in abscess formation. These lesions should not be confused with or diagnosed as stud tail.

Satisfactory control of the disease can be achieved with degreasing antiseborrheic shampoos, used as needed.

FELINE ACNE. Feline acne is a fairly common skin disease of cats. The cause is unclear; however, feline acne is *not* analogous to human acne. The most common theory as to the cause of feline acne is the cat's failure to adequately clean its chin. The disease is characterized by blackhead formation on the chin and lower lip. Occasionally, secondary bacterial folliculitis and furunculosis will complicate acne, resulting in variable degrees of redness, swelling, pain, and itching. Enlargement of local lymph nodes may be seen.

In some cats with chin acne, changing where they sleep and the bedding they sleep on will facilitate recovery. These lesions are more insidious in cats that rest their chins on hard surfaces or on dirt. Softer, cleaner materials for them to sleep on may be beneficial.

Therapy is usually not required for the blackhead stage of feline acne. Veterinary treatment of the infected stage requires gentle clipping and cleansing with benzoyl peroxide or surgical soaps, manual evacuation of blackheads, warm water soaks, and antibiotics.

Recurrences of feline acne are the rule. If a cat continues to progress to the infected stage, or if the owner desires a clean-chinned cat, maintenance topical therapy with benzoyl peroxide shampoo and the application of benzoyl peroxide gel must be administered every two to seven days, for the life of the cat.

Nutritional Skin Diseases

See Chapter 8: Diseases of Dietary Origin.

Physiochemical Skin Diseases

PRIMARY IRRITANT CONTACT DERMATITIS. This contact dermatitis is uncommon in cats. Primary irritant contact dermatitis requires no prior sensitization. The most common causes are found in flea collars, various topical insecticides, kerosene, turpentine, paint, tars, phenols (coal tars, carbolic acid, et cetera), cresols (disinfectants, antiseptics), various soaps, various oils and greases, highly chlorinated water, iodine compounds, quaternary ammonium compounds, naphthols, fertilizers, acids, salt, benzoyl peroxide, and other topical medications.

Clinical signs include, variably, a red rash, blisters, or death of skin cells in the relatively smooth and bare "contact" areas of the skin (abdomen, thighs, "armpit" areas), perineal area, footpads, ears, chin, and under the tail. Itching and pain may be present. Contact dermatitis does not involve haired skin unless the irritating substance is in liquid (shampoo, dip) or aerosol form. Primary irritant contact in the outer ear can occur when ear mite remedies are administered.

Therapy involves avoidance of the irritant substance, removal of residual irritant with large quantities of water (with or without a gentle detergent, such as baby shampoo), and topical or systemic glucocorticoid administration.

Exposure to road tars, asphalt, and paint deserves special comment. These substances can cause severe irritation and dermatitis. In addition, systemic intoxication can occur if significant amounts of these substances are ingested through the fastidious cat's attempts to clean itself. If the material has dried, affected areas can be clipped; otherwise, they should be soaked with vegetable oil and wiped off, and the cat bathed in a gentle detergent shampoo (baby shampoo or a mild dishwashing liquid). Paint removers or organic solvents should *never* be used, because they are irritating and may produce signs of toxicity. Recently, repeated applications of a mixture of equal parts of mineral oil and acetone have been recommended for tar and asphalt removal. Treatment must be given in a well-ventilated area, and body temperature must be maintained with warm water soaks, as needed.

Flea collar dermatitis is another special case. Clinical signs include variable degrees of dermatitis underneath the collar. Rarely, cats become systemically ill and even die. Therapy consists of removing the collar and symptomatic care. Useful preventive measures include insuring proper fit and frequent observation of the status of the fit. Many cats cannot wear any type of flea collar without experiencing skin lesions.

Cats are exquisitely sensitive to *quaternary ammonium* compounds. Signs of toxicity include excessive salivation, eye and nasal discharges, labored breathing, tongue ulceration, dehydration, and skin and skeletal muscle lesions.

BURNS. Most burns are the result of accidental contact with hot water, cooking oils, tar, or other boiling liquids, chewing on electric cords, or, in rare instances, direct contact with fire. Such injuries are seen in varying degrees of severity and most often occur on the back and down the sides in a "dribbling" pattern. Burn injury may at first seem minor but later produce serious damage to the skin. Serious burns may be hidden by the hair coat. Burned feet and tails may be seen in cats that walk on kitchen stoves and harsh chemicals. Depending on the severity of the injury, affected skin may be red, oozing, and very painful, or necrotic (dead), and thus relatively painless. (*See* Chapter 39: Procedures for Life-Threatening Emergencies.)

FROSTBITE. Frostbite is occasionally seen in outdoor cats during the winter in the colder regions of the United States. The tips of the ears and occasionally the paws and tip of the tail are affected. Clinical signs include scaling and hair loss in mild cases, and necrosis (death of tissue) and shedding of dead tissue in severe cases. (*See* Chapter 39: Procedures for Life-Threatening Emergencies.)

HAIR MATS. Matting of hair is common in longhair cats, especially behind the ears, on the abdomen, and on the back of the hind legs. Matting is more common in obese or sick cats that do not groom themselves well. If the cat is willing, small mats can be moistened with liquid soap, slit with a knife and teased apart with a comb, and combed out. If the mats are extensive, clipping may be required. Prevention of matting requires daily combing and brushing.

SKIN FOLD DERMATITIS. Skin fold dermatitis *(intertrigo)* is rare in cats. It arises in persistent folds of skin that accumulate secretions, maintain moisture, warmth, and microorganism proliferation, and produce constant skin-to-skin friction and maceration (softening from moisture). Obese cats develop skin fold dermatitis in the armpits, groin, and intermammary area. Persian cats with excessively flattened faces and skin folds may develop facial fold dermatitis. "Rumpy" Manx cats may also develop dermatitis in the caudal (tail) depression or dimple. Therapy consists of topical cleansing, weight reduction, surgical removal of the skin folds where feasible, and preventive measures (daily cleansing and light application of nontoxic powders to absorb moisture and reduce chafing).

TEMPERATURE-DEPENDENT MELANOTRICHIA AND LEUKOTRICHIA. Many practitioners have noticed that the hair on the abdomen of a Siamese cat (or Burmese, or Birman) shaved for surgery grows back darker *(melanotrichia),* that hair grows back lighter *(leukotrichia)* in the area of a previous abscess, and that the coats of these breeds of cats are

darker in colder climates. Kittens of these breeds are born white and develop adult "points" under the influence of external temperature. It is believed that the ability of certain parts of the coat to form pigment is inherited. Coat color in these breeds is affected by external temperature and physiological factors that determine heat production and loss. These phenomena appear to be associated with a temperature-dependent enzyme involved in production of the skin pigment melanin.

The coat color changes associated with various external and internal influences on heat loss and production are temporary. The coat usually returns to its normal appearance following the next hair cycle, if the temperature influences are remedied.

PERIOCULAR LEUKOTRICHIA. This condition is characterized by a patchy or complete lightening of the hairs of the mask in a halolike appearance around both eyes ("goggles"). It is occasionally seen in Siamese cats, and is more common in females. Commonly recognized predisposing factors include pregnancy, illness (especially upper respiratory disease), and dietary deficiency. Periocular leukotrichia can also be seen in rapidly growing kittens. The condition is transient and usually resolves within the next couple of hair cycles.

SOLAR DERMATITIS (actinic dermatitis). Solar or actinic dermatitis (inflammation of skin induced by sunlight) is a common disorder in areas of the world with warm, sunny climates. The disease occurs in white cats (especially those with blue eyes), and in cats with white ears and faces. Because of the lack of melanin (skin and hair pigment) and protective hair, these cats suffer essentially from repeated sunburn.

Initially, clinical signs consist of mild redness of the ear margins and occasionally the eyelids, nose, and lips. As the dermatitis becomes more severe, hair loss, scaling, crusting, and itching develop, along with curling of the ear margin. These lesions exacerbate during the summer and regress during the winter. However, the dermatitis becomes progressively worse each summer, until actinic keratoses (more severe sunburn lesions), persistent ulceration, and squamous cell carcinoma (cancer of surface epithelium) develop.

Therapy in the early, noncancerous stage includes keeping the cat out of the sun when ultraviolet rays are most damaging (10 A.M. to 4 P.M.), application of topical sunscreens, and topical or systemic glucocorticoids. Topical sunscreens containing para amino benzoic acid (PABA) and a high sun-protective factor (SPF) should be rubbed in one hour before and at the time of sun exposure, and every three to four hours thereafter, while sun exposure is ongoing.

When areas of persistent ulceration have developed, surgery is indicated. Amputation of both ear flaps (pinnae) is the surgical therapy of choice in severe cases.

CHLORINATED NAPHTHALENE POISONING. Chlorinated naphthalene poisoning has been recognized in cats. The condition is associated with exposure to wood preservatives. Skin lesions seen include bilateral hair loss and scaling and crusting on the face.

SNAKEBITES. *See* Chapter 39: Procedures for Life-Threatening Emergencies.

Inherited Skin Diseases

CUTANEOUS ASTHENIA. Cutaneous asthenia is a group of rare inherited disorders of collagen metabolism. It is also known as Ehlers-Danlos syndrome, dermatosparaxis, "rubber kitten" syndrome, "torn skin," and hereditary fragility and hyperextensibility of the skin. Fragile, stretchy skin is a prime feature of this group of connective tissue disorders.

Cats usually present at an early age with histories of fragile, frequently torn skin. The entire skin is fragile or extremely stretchy, or both. The skin is often thin and velvety in texture ("chicken skin"), and crisscrossed with thin white scars. Fighting, clipping, puncture of a vein, and normal scratching often result in extensive, gaping skin tears ("fish mouth" wounds).

Therapy includes avoidance of trauma. Wounds often hold sutures poorly. Declawing all four feet is usually necessary, as even normal scratching will produce severe skin tears. *Affected cats and their relatives should not be used for breeding.*

HYPOTRICHOSIS. Hypotrichosis (thin hair coat) is occasionally seen in cats. All cases presumably arise through genetic mutation. Some of these mutations have achieved breed status: Cornish and Devon Rexes, Sphynx, and Mexican Hairless. Hypotrichosis

has also been reported in the Siamese breed. In *Siamese hypotrichosis,* affected cats appear normal at birth, but become hairless by ten to fourteen days of age. Some hair regrowth is seen by eight to ten weeks of age, but total hair loss returns by six months of age. A few down hairs may remain and fluctuate seasonally.

In the Sphynx cat, there is little or no hair except for a few short facial hairs and whiskers. The skin often feels oily and has a rancid odor. Gray-black fat deposits collect in the nail folds.

There is no specific therapy for this disease. Affected cats and their relatives should not be used for breeding.

CHEDIAK-HIGASHI SYNDROME. Chediak-Higashi syndrome has been reported in Persian cats with yellow eyes and blue-smoke hair. It is characterized by partial *oculocutaneous albinism* (absence of pigmentation in the irises, retinas, and skin), a bleeding tendency, an increased susceptibility to infection. There is no treatment.

Skin Diseases of Unknown or Multiple Origin

MILIARY DERMATITIS (miliary eczema, "scabby cat disease"). Feline miliary dermatitis is not a single disease, but rather a disease complex. The most common causes of this disorder are flea bite hypersensitivity, inhalant allergy *(atopy)*, food hypersensitivity, bacterial folliculitis (infection of hair follicles), ringworm, cheyletiellosis (mites), and otodectic mange (ear mites). It is characterized by a red and crusty rash that occurs most commonly over the back and tail base. Some degree of itching is invariable and is not necessarily related to the number or type of lesions. Enlargement of local lymph nodes may also be seen. Treatment is most accurately and efficiently rendered when a specific cause has been determined. The reader is referred to the specific diseases within this chapter for therapeutic details.

PSYCHOGENIC ALOPECIA AND DERMATITIS. Psychological stress-related hair loss and skin inflammation are uncommon disorders in the cat. These diseases are self-induced, in that they are a response to a source of pain or irritation or result from a behavioral aberration. They are associated with excessive licking, scratching, or chewing of the hair coat. Organic diseases that may trigger these disorders include anal sac disease, tapeworm infestation, external parasitism, hypersensitivity skin disease, feline urologic syndrome, musculoskeletal disease, neurologic disease, and foreign bodies. In some instances, however, no organic disease can be found. In such cases, one can usually document a change in the cat's lifestyle that preceded the skin problem, such as a change of environment, addition or loss of another family pet, addition or loss of people in the household, unusual confinement, et cetera. Whether organically or psychologically triggered, the disease is perpetuated as a bad habit. Psychogenic skin disease is seen most commonly in the Siamese, Burmese, Himalayan, and Abyssinian breeds.

Psychogenic dermatitis is usually characterized by a single scratching lesion located on an extremity, the abdomen, or the flank. Psychogenic alopecia is characterized by single or multiple areas of hair loss, especially as a "stripe" down the back, or in a symmetrical pattern mimicking feline endocrine alopecia. Careful inspection will reveal that the underlying skin appears normal and that the hairs are stubbled and *not* easily removed by pulling. In the Siamese, hair regrowth in affected areas is much darker in color than normal.

Psychogenic dermatitis is usually managed with short-term glucocorticoid therapy and long-term behavior-modifying drugs. Treatment should be terminated every two months initially to see if the habit has been broken.

Psychogenic alopecia poses a different therapeutic problem. Although behavior-modifying drugs can be used, they are not without possible side effects, which include objectionable personality traits. Many owners, when informed that their pet does not have a serious disease, will choose to live with an alopecic cat rather than give it drugs that may cause undesirable behavior.

EOSINOPHILIC GRANULOMA COMPLEX. A frequently observed disorder, eosinophilic granuloma complex is a group of related lesions commonly found on the skin, lips, and in the mouth. The cause of these lesions is not clear, nor is the relationship between the different forms of the complex well understood. Although clinically distinct, the different lesions appear to be related in that they can all be seen simultaneously or sequentially in the same cat.

In addition, they are all often seen in cats with flea bite hypersensitivity, inhalant allergy (atopy), and food hypersensitivity. Clustering of cases has been reported, suggesting a hereditary or transmissible factor in rare instances; in most cases, the complex does not appear to be contagious.

Clinically, the eosinophilic granuloma complex can be divided into three different lesions.

The *indolent ulcer* (also known as *eosinophilic ulcer* or *rodent ulcer*) is seen in cats of all breeds and ages, and three times as often in females as in males. These lesions are well defined, ulcerated, red-brown, thickened glistening areas that are usually not itchy or painful. Eighty percent of them occur on the upper lip. These lip lesions appear to be *precancerous* and can possibly undergo transformation into squamous cell carcinoma (skin cancer) or fibrosarcoma (connective tissue cancer).

The *eosinophilic plaque* is seen in cats of any breed, age, or sex. The lesion is a well defined, raised, fire-red, ulcerated, oozing area of hair loss that is intensely itchy. Eosinophilic plaques may occur anywhere on the skin or in the mouth; 80 percent of them occur on the abdomen and thighs.

The eosinophilic granuloma *(linear granuloma)* is seen in all breeds, and twice as frequently in females as in males. Although cats of any age may be affected, many lesions occur in cats less than a year of age. The lesions appear in relatively straight lines and are clearly defined, raised, firm, yellow to yellowish-pink areas of hair loss. They may occur anywhere on the skin, but occur most commonly on the hindlimbs. Mouth lesions resemble the skin lesions, but are always present in the form of nodules. Eosinophilic granuloma is the most common cause of "fat-chinned" cats (enlargement of chin, often waxing and waning, the so-called "chin-edema") and "pouting" cats (swollen, protruding lower lip). Eosinophilic granulomas may also affect the footpads.

The therapy of choice for eosinophilic granuloma complex is early, aggressive use of glucocorticoids. In some cats, lesions do not recur, while in others, long-term maintenance therapy is required to prevent relapses. Surgical excision, cryotherapy (freezing), or radiation therapy may be effective in selected solitary, unresponsive lesions. Cats with underlying flea bite hypersensitivity, inhalant allergy, or food hypersensitivity respond dramatically to flea control, hyposensitization, or feeding of a hypoallergenic diet, respectively.

TUMORS, CYSTS, KERATOSES, AND NEVI

Tumors (Neoplasms)

The skin is the second most common site of cancer in cats, after lymphoma. *Feline skin tumors are usually malignant;* thus, early surgical removal and biopsy examination are usually recommended. Siamese cats are at a significantly *lower* risk for skin tumors than are other breeds. There is a marked increase in the incidence of skin tumors in cats greater than five years of age. White cats have an increased risk for squamous cell carcinoma. Therapeutic regimens include surgical excision, cryosurgery (removal by surgical freezing), radiation therapy, chemotherapy, immunotherapy, and various combinations of these therapies.

BASAL CELL AND SQUAMOUS CELL TUMORS. These are the two most common skin tumors of the cat.

Basal Cell Tumor. This benign lesion occurs in older cats. The tumor is usually single, firm, well-circumscribed, rounded, frequently ulcerated, and attached to the overlying skin. It often is heavily pigmented, and thus must be differentiated from *melanoma.* Metastasis (spread of the tumor to other sites) is extremely rare. Treatment consists of surgical excision or radiation therapy. Basal cell tumors only rarely recur.

Squamous Cell Carcinoma. This malignant tumor of the superficial epithelium also occurs primarily in older cats. Excessive exposure to sunlight, presence of nonpigmented skin and a sparse hair coat, and possibly genetic factors are thought to predispose to its development. Squamous cell carcinoma is seen most commonly in white cats and cats with white spotting, especially those with blue eyes. The tumor is usually single, poorly outlined, ulcerated, cauliflowerlike or craterlike with irregular, hardened borders, and is attached to the underlying tissue. It is most commonly found on the head, especially on the ears, lips, nose, or eyelids. Multiple carcinomas of the paws may mimic paronychia (inflammation of the nail beds).

Squamous cell carcinoma is highly invasive locally, but metastasizes (spreads to other organs) more slowly. Spread is usually to the local lymph node, then to the lungs. Treatment includes various combinations of surgical excision and radiation therapy. Wide surgical excision often is curative and represents the therapy of choice. Radiation treatment is also useful, especially where surgical excision is impossible, or postsurgically. Chemotherapy has been disappointing. Hyperthermia (heat treatment) may be an effective treatment for more superficial squamous cell carcinomas.

PAPILLOMA. This is a rare benign tumor of older cats. It is usually solitary, firm, well-defined, cauliflowerlike, and fixed to the overlying skin. Papillomas occur anywhere in the skin, especially on the face, eyelids, and limbs. Therapy consists of surgical excision. Virus-induced papillomas (warts) have *not* been described in cats.

SEBACEOUS GLAND AND SWEAT GLAND TUMORS. Although uncommon in cats, sebaceous gland tumors do occasionally develop in older animals. They occur singly, are fixed to the overlying skin, and usually are benign rather than malignant. When malignant, spread is to the local lymph node, then to the lungs. Early surgical excision of malignant sebaceous gland tumors may be curative, but the prognosis is guarded.

Sweat gland tumors also are uncommon, but may be seen in older cats. They are single masses that are fixed to the overlying skin and usually are malignant. They spread to the local lymph nodes and the lungs. Early surgical excision of these tumors may be curative, but the prognosis is guarded.

FIBROSARCOMA. This malignant growth is the third most common skin tumor of the cat, usually occurring in older animals. The tumor is solitary, variable in size, irregular or nodular in shape, firm or fleshy, frequently ulcerated, and fixed to the overlying skin.

The cause of this particular tumor is unknown; however, fibrosarcomas that are found in *young* cats, and that occur as multiple rather than solitary tumor masses, are caused by the feline sarcoma virus (FeSV). To date, this virus has *not* been associated with solitary fibrosarcomas in aged cats.

Fibrosarcoma is locally invasive. It spreads to the local lymph node and/or to the lungs. Wide surgical excision is the therapy of choice. However, the prognosis is always guarded, because recurrence is common. Radiation therapy, chemotherapy, immunotherapy, cryosurgery, and hyperthermia have all been of little or no benefit.

FIBROMA. This is a benign growth of connective tissue and is uncommon in cats. It is usually solitary, well circumscribed, can be firm or soft, and may be ulcerated. The tumor occurs in aged cats. Therapy consists of surgical removal.

MAST CELL TUMOR. The mast cell tumor is the fourth most common skin tumor of the cat. The mast cell is a connective tissue cell that plays a role in normal inflammatory responses and in allergy. This tumor is especially common in older male cats. It can occur anywhere in the skin, but has a predilection for the head and neck. Mast cell tumors can take a variety of forms; the majority are benign. Some, however, are aggressive, malignant growths that spread to lymph nodes, liver, spleen, and lungs, usually within three to six months.

Therapy of the solitary mast cell tumor consists of surgical excision.

CUTANEOUS LYMPHOSARCOMA. Malignant tumor of lymphocytes is a rare skin disorder of aged cats. Most affected cats are negative for feline leukemia virus (FeLV) infection. Skin lesions include numerous firm, raised, lumpy-bumpy masses often fixed to the overlying skin, which may or may not be showing signs of hair loss; solitary or multiple ulcerated areas; raised, red, frequently ulcerated and itchy patches; or solitary and multiple ill-defined thickenings of the skin. Cutaneous lymphosarcoma in cats is uniformly fatal (usually within a few months), owing to systemic spread of the tumor. Therapy has been disappointing.

MELANOMA. This is a rare tumor of melanin-producing cells in the skin that usually occurs in aged cats. The lesions are frequently solitary, well defined, brown to black in color, and fixed to the overlying skin. Most of these tumors spread to local lymph nodes and to the lungs. Early surgical excision is the therapy of choice, but the prognosis is always guarded to poor.

LIPOMA AND LIPOSARCOMA. These benign (lipoma) and malignant (liposarcoma) tumors of fat cells are uncommon in cats; when they do occur, they are usually seen in older animals. Lipomas are well-defined, firm or flabby, nodular lesions under the skin. Liposarcomas, by contrast, are poorly defined, firm, frequently ulcerated, and locally invasive tumors that are slow to spread to other organs. Therapy includes surgical excision, which is usually curative for both lipomas *and* liposarcomas.

SCHWANNOMA. This tumor of the tissue enveloping nerve fibers is rare in cats; it usually is seen in older animals. The tumor is poorly defined, firm, variable in size, occasionally ulcerated, and fixed to the overlying skin. It is most often malignant. To date all attempted therapies have been of little or no benefit.

HEMANGIOMA AND HEMANGIOSARCOMA. These benign (hemangioma) and malignant (hemangiosarcoma) tumors of blood vessels in the skin are rare in cats; usually they are seen in aged animals. Hemangiomas are solitary, small, well defined, bluish-red in color, and friable (easily crumbled). There is a predilection for the trunk, neck, and limbs. Therapy consists of surgical excision. Hemangiosarcomas usually are solitary, rapidly growing, soft and friable, and commonly occur in the groin or on the hindlimbs behind the knee. Early wide surgical excision is the treatment of choice; recurrence of the tumor is common, however.

SECONDARY SKIN TUMORS. These result from the spread of tumors in other organs to the skin, but have only rarely been reported in cats. Breast cancer, stomach cancer, and lung cancer are among the types of cancer for which cutaneous manifestations have been reported. Therapy of the skin lesions is obviously dependent on the nature of the primary tumor.

Cysts

Cutaneous cysts are classified as *epidermoid* cysts, *dermoid* cysts, *follicular* cysts, and the *dilated pore of Winer*. They are uncommon in the cat. They are usually solitary, well defined, round, firm to fluctuant, bluish in color, fixed to the overlying skin, and filled with a cheesy, greasy, yellowish to brownish-gray material. Ulceration and secondary bacterial infection of cysts may occur. Epidermoid cysts are especially common on the neck and trunk. Dilated pore of Winer is characterized by a cyst with a yellowish, horny, conical structure protruding through a central surface pore, usually on the face. Therapy consists of surgical excision. One should exercise great restraint when tempted to squeeze or otherwise manually evacuate these lesions, because they may rupture into the underlying skin.

Keratoses

Keratoses are firm, elevated, circumscribed areas of excessive keratin production. *Actinic keratoses* are caused by excessive exposure to ultraviolet light (sunlight) and are seen in cats in temperate and tropical climates. They may be single or multiple, appear in lightly haired and lightly pigmented skin, and vary in appearance from ill-defined areas of redness, hyperkeratosis (overgrowth of horny tissue), and crusting, to hardened, crusted, horny patches. Actinic keratoses are most common on the ears and nose. *They are precancerous lesions capable of becoming squamous cell carcinomas.* Therapy includes surgical excision or cryosurgery (removal by surgical freezing); preventing exposure to sunlight is reported to be helpful.

Nevi

A nevus is a well-defined lesion characterized by overgrowth of one or more of the skin's normal cellular constituents. *Organoid nevi* have rarely been described in cats. Either they have been present as long as the owner could remember, or were never noticed at all. Single or multiple, these lesions may be firm or mushy, dome-shaped or pedunculated (stemmed). They occur on the face and head, especially in the temporal region (in front of the ears). Therapy consists of surgical removal.

Sensory Organs and Disorders

Taste, smell, sight, sound, and touch—all these sensations play important roles in a cat's survival, from predation to mating. The sensory organs—mouth, nose, eyes, ears, and skin—are the means by which a cat perceives its environment. When disease affects any of these organs, the ability of the cat to comprehend its surroundings is impaired.

MOUTH

The cat uses its mouth to ingest food, to cleanse the skin and hair coat, and for the various behaviors involved in prey capture. Its *tongue* is long, thin, and facile, with a spiny, abrasive surface. The roof of the mouth is composed of the bony structure of the *hard palate,* which becomes the *soft palate* toward the back. At the back of the oral cavity is the *epiglottis,* an overhanging part of the larynx that prevents food from entering the larynx and windpipe during swallowing.

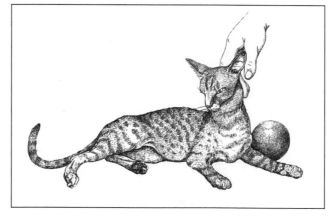

The kitten has twenty-six *deciduous* or "milk" teeth (molars are absent). The adult cat has a total of thirty *teeth:* six upper and six lower *incisors,* two upper and two lower *canines,* six upper and four lower *premolars,* and two upper and two lower *molars.* All adult teeth are in by six months.

Healthy *gums* should be firm to the touch, closely attached to the teeth, and pink in unpigmented areas. (Cats may have black pigment spots on their gums, sometimes in large numbers.) The condition of the gums is a key signal to the cat's health. When the gums (and the mucous membrane around the eyes) are pale, the animal may be bleeding internally or suffering from anemia or a number of other systemic diseases. (*See* "Mouth," Chapter 35: Clinical Signs of Disease.)

Gingivitis (inflammation of the gums) is a frequently encountered—and often frustrating—problem for the cat owner and the veterinarian. It has many causes. Some, such as bad teeth, are easily corrected; others, however, require extensive diagnostic and therapeutic measures to reduce the severity of the problem.

Mild gingivitis is well tolerated by the cat, and only the most observant owner will be aware of its presence. The signs of severe gingivitis are readily apparent and include *ptyalism* (drooling), *halitosis* (bad breath), and pain or difficulty in eating. Examination of the mouth reveals reddened, swollen, and sometimes ulcerated gums, which may be painful or bleed when touched.

Causes of Gingivitis

DENTAL DISEASE. A common and easily treated form of gingivitis results from the accumulation of plaque and tartar. Dental plaque is a layer of proliferating bacteria trapped in the food debris and saliva that coat the tooth. Dental tartar, or *calculus,* develops when plaque mineralizes. Extension of plaque and tartar beneath the gums produces inflammation, with resultant redness, swelling, and, eventually, loosening of the teeth. Professional teeth cleaning and the removal of loose teeth are necessary to restore health to the gums.

Dental cavities can be a significant problem in the cat. Unlike humans, cats most often develop tooth decay just beneath the gum margins, thus producing gingivitis as well as cavities in the tooth surface. Unfortunately, the process of decay is usually so far advanced when the condition is recognized that tooth extraction becomes necessary. Some cats seem particularly prone to the development of cavities and require good oral hygiene measures (to be discussed later) to help prevent tooth loss.

Broken teeth with exposed pulp cavities may develop tooth-root abscesses. Swelling of the gums surrounding the tooth and abscessation of the soft tissues next to the tooth root may result. A swelling or draining tract just under the eye often indicates a tooth root abscess. Tooth extraction and treatment with antibiotics are usually curative. If neglected, the infection may extend to the bones of the jaw. Bone infections *(osteomyelitis)* are difficult to treat and can be dangerous to the cat's overall health.

VIRUSES. Several viruses can cause gingivitis and ulcers in the mouth. Although primarily associated with upper respiratory disease, feline calicivirus can also cause severe oral ulcerations. This virus may persist in the cat's body, causing recurrent gingivitis and upper respiratory disease.

Feline leukemia virus (FeLV) suppresses the body's natural defense mechanisms, rendering the cat susceptible to a number of normally trivial infections, including gingivitis. Gingivitis related to FeLV infection can be especially resistant to treatment.

Medical cure of viral diseases is still not possible. Therefore, treatment generally involves the use of antibiotics to prevent secondary bacterial infections. Some cats require antibiotic treatment indefinitely. These cats have contagious diseases; exposure to other cats should be avoided.

SQUAMOUS CELL CARCINOMA. Squamous cell carcinoma is a malignant tumor that may affect the gums, oral mucous membranes, and underside of the tongue (an important site in old cats). The lesions may resemble ulcers rather than classical "lumps." Difficulty and pain when eating and halitosis are frequent consequences of the tumor. Biopsy is necessary for accurate diagnosis. Surgical removal and/or radiation therapy are the current methods of treatment. Left untreated, squamous cell carcinoma will slowly progress to the point where no treatment is effective.

PEMPHIGUS. Pemphigus is a disorder of the immune system affecting the skin and mucous membranes. Ulceration of the skin, anal and genital mucous membranes, as well of the gums and mouth, may be seen. At one time, most cases of pemphigus were invariably fatal. Now, although the disease is still serious, its effects can often be controlled by the veterinarian using steroids or gold-containing drugs, both of which decrease inflammation. Biopsy and special staining techniques are used to diagnose pemphigus. (*See* Chapter 17: Skin and Disorders.)

EOSINOPHILIC GRANULOMA COMPLEX. The eosinophilic granuloma complex (EGC) produces raised and sometimes ulcerated red or orange-colored areas in the skin, gums, and oral cavity. The cause of the disease is unknown, but it does not appear to be contagious. The appearance is so characteristic that diagnosis only occasionally requires biopsy. Veterinary treatment with steroids or progesterone hormones is often effective, but some forms respond poorly. Radiation therapy may be

THE SKULL AND TEETH

THE SKULL

1. Angular process
2. Condyloid process
3. Coronoid process
4. External auditory meatus
5. Frontal
6. Lacrimal
7. Malar
8. Mandible
9. Mastoid process
10. Maxilla
11. Nasal
12. Orbit
13. Occipital condyle
14. Parietal
15. Premaxilla
16. Ramus
17. Sagittal crest
18. Squamosal
19. Supraorbital process
20. Tympanic bulla
21. Zygomatic arch

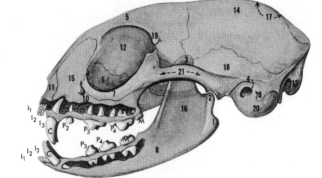

SINUSES AND SKULL CAVITIES

1. Cerebral cavity
2. Frontal sinuses
3. Occipital cavity
4. Turbinates
5. Tympanic bulla

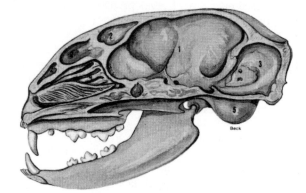

Beck

THE TEETH

DECIDUOUS:

$$2\left(I\frac{3}{3}\ C\frac{1}{1}\ P\frac{3}{2}\right) = 26$$

PERMANENT:

$$2\left(I\frac{3}{3}\ C\frac{1}{1}\ P\frac{3}{2}\ M\frac{1}{1}\right) = 30$$

Normal range for eruption of teeth

		DECIDUOUS	PERMANENT
Incisor	1	2–3 weeks	3½–4 months
	2	2–3 weeks	3½–4 months
	3	3–4 weeks	4–4½ months
Canine		3–4 weeks	5 months
Premolar (upper)	1	none	none
	2	2 months	4½–5 months
	3	2 months	5–6 months
	4	2 months	5–6 months
Premolar (lower)	1	none	none
	2	none	none
	3	4–5 weeks	5–6 months
	4	4–5 weeks	5–6 months
Molar		none	4–5 months

effective in resolving cases resistant to medical treatment, but can only be used when a single lesion is present.

PLASMA CELL GINGIVITIS-PHARYNGITIS. Plasma cell gingivitis is a disease causing an accumulation of plasma cells (the cells that make antibodies) in the gums, oral cavity, and pharynx of the cat. As with EGC, the cause is unknown. Affected areas are glistening and ulcerated, and have an irregular, cobblestonelike surface. The color of this lesion resembles raw beef. The raised, circular, meaty-looking lesion involving the pharynx is especially characteristic. Response to treatment is variable; a number of therapeutic approaches have been investigated, with limited success. Recently, gold-containing drugs have shown promise in treating this condition.

SYSTEMIC DISEASES. Severe kidney disease and diabetes mellitus are sometimes associated with gingivitis and oral ulceration. Cats suffering from these diseases are often obviously ill and require prompt treatment. If the underlying disease can be controlled, the gingivitis usually resolves.

This is not a complete list of the causes of feline gingivitis but it does include those that are most commonly encountered.

Diagnosis and Prevention

Like any disease process, gingivitis is easiest to treat when diagnosed early. A veterinarian can demonstrate how to examine a cat's mouth regularly to discover signs of gingivitis early in its progress. All cats with significant gingival disease should be examined by a veterinarian. If the cause of the problem is not immediately obvious (e.g., bad teeth), diagnostic testing (blood counts, blood chemistry evaluation, FeLV and feline immunodeficiency virus testing, bacterial cultures, biopsies) may be required. Virus isolation cultures for calicivirus are costly but may be valuable to breeders with many affected cats.

Periodic professional teeth cleaning reduces the contribution of dental disease to gingivitis. A cat's teeth can be kept clean by gently rubbing the surface of the teeth with a soft cloth soaked in dilute hydrogen peroxide or salt water. This should be done daily if possible. Toothpastes for humans should *not* be used because the foaming frightens animals and swallowed toothpaste can cause gastrointestinal upsets.

Feeding dry food helps prevent the formation of tartar.

NOSE

Cats have a highly developed sense of smell, which plays a vital role in protection, behavior, appetite, and reproduction. The sense of smell originates with olfactory nerves located in the *turbinates* (rolled structures within the nose that filter, warm, and humidify the inhaled air), septum, and sinuses. These nerves communicate information to the brain for interpretation.

The nose is a major structure of the respiratory system as well as being a sensory organ. A complete description of the structure and function of the nose can be found in Chapter 24: Respiratory System and Disorders. Various diseases that affect the cat's sense of smell, such as sinusitis, rhinitis, and systemic diseases, are covered there.

EYE

The size, color, shape, and design of the eye contribute greatly to the allure of the domestic cat. The lids and the pupils reflect its mood and even play an intrinsic role when it is exerting dominance toward other cats by out-staring a challenger.

The cat's vision evolved as that of a predator. The field of vision is measured by the portion seen by both eyes, the portion that can only be seen by one eye on each side, and the portion unseen behind the head. The cat has a rather large binocular field of 120° directly in front of it, with a relatively small uniocular area of 80° to each side. The posterior blind area accounts for approximately 80°.

In a scientific sense, the cat eye can be more easily explained in structure than in function. The bony structure containing the eyeball is referred to as the *orbit*. When the reference includes the *periosteum* (the tissues covering the bone), it is called the *periorbit*. Periorbital structures include muscle, nerves, blood vessels, and connective tissue. The large, round globe in the center of the orbit is the eyeball. The eyeball is filled with clear *aqueous fluid* in front and *vitreous humor* in back.

Eyeball movement is dependent upon extraocular (outside the eye) muscles and cranial nerves that in-

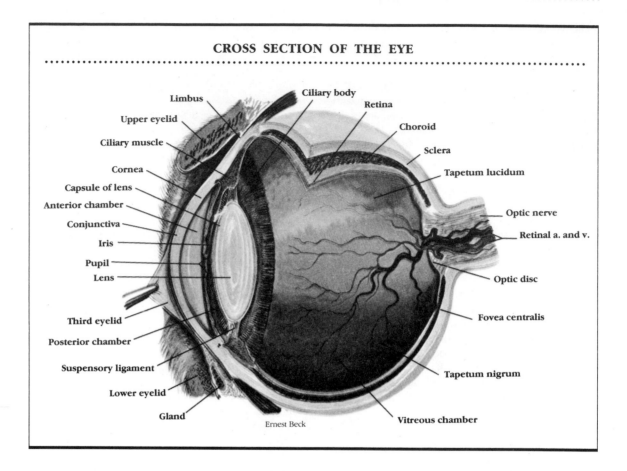

CROSS SECTION OF THE EYE

Limbus
Upper eyelid
Ciliary muscle
Cornea
Capsule of lens
Anterior chamber
Conjunctiva
Iris
Pupil
Lens
Third eyelid
Posterior chamber
Suspensory ligament
Lower eyelid
Gland

Ciliary body
Retina
Choroid
Sclera
Tapetum lucidum
Optic nerve
Retinal a. and v.
Optic disc
Fovea centralis
Tapetum nigrum
Vitreous chamber

Ernest Beck

nervate (stimulate) them. The eye rotates around three axes: the horizontal axis, the vertical axis, and the anterior-posterior axis. The muscles are grouped into three opposing pairs, all of which act together for coordinated movement of both eyes so that both are positioned in the same direction at the same time.

The *lids* and third eyelid (haw) function to protect the eye. The third eyelid is found between the lower lid and the eyeball at the inner corner of the eye near the nose. In its normal position, it is hardly noticeable except when the cat blinks. In some cats, however, it is always partially visible. The third eyelid is usually pale pink but may sometimes be pigmented. Cartilage reinforces its conformation to fit the curvature of the cornea. The base of the cartilage is surrounded by the *lacrimal gland* (tear gland). No specific skeletal muscle is associated with the third eyelid; therefore, passive movements and positional changes in the haws are usually related to eyeball retraction and relaxa-

tion. The return of the haws to normal position is due to the elasticity of the tissue, normal orbital contents, and normal neurological status of the tissues.

If the third eyelids of both eyes are covering a significant portion of the eyeball (prolapsed), it can be a sign that the cat has a gastrointestinal upset or disease. But if the cat shows no other signs of illness and the haws eventually return to their normal position, there may have been an irritant that has dissipated. When the third eyelid covers only one eye, it usually means there is something irritating that eye.

The white, outer layer of the covering of the eyeball is called the *sclera*. The layer beneath the sclera, which contains the blood vessels, is the *uvea*; and the portion of the uvea at the back of the eye is the *choroid*. The lining of the eyelids is the *conjunctiva,* and its continuation over the anterior eyeball is the *bulbar conjunctiva.*

The clear *cornea* is the front of the eye and is the

major refractive surface lens. It reshapes and focuses rays of light on to the retina. Although the cornea is richly supplied with extremely sensitive nerves, blood vessels are considered abnormal in the healthy cornea.

Just behind the cornea is the *anterior chamber*. The cat's anterior chamber is a relatively deep, large space filled with *aqueous fluid*. From the side of the eye, delicate strands of iris tissue can be seen attaching to the inside of the cornea. This structure is referred to as the *pectinate ligament*.

The *iris* provides the color and shape that give the cat eye a character of its own. The color shades vary from brown when the melanin pigment is dense, to orange, to yellow when the pigment is scarce. The yellow-to-green luster of the iris is from *iridocytes* (cells that produce iridescence). The blue to gray color is derived from an iris and retina with very low pigment levels, whereas a truly albino cat, which is very rare, has pink eyes because the total absence of pigment in the iris and retina allow the blood vessels to be seen. Iris color differences have no functional ramification.

At the center of the iris is an opening called the *pupil*. Its size and shape are controlled by the expansion and constriction of the iris around it. The cat pupil is a vertically orientated slit when constricted, which becomes oval to round when it dilates. This type of pupil is characteristic of nocturnal animals who also enjoy lying in the sun. The slit pupil acts as an optical aperture (similar to a camera lens aperture), protective to the lens and retina in bright light while maintaining excellent dorsal and ventral visual acuity or sharpness.

Directly behind the iris is the clear, biconvex *lens*. This structure helps focus images onto the retina, especially for close vision.

The space between the lens and retina contains the clear vitreous. The posterior chamber contains the lens and vitreous humor. The *vitreous* is a clear gel-like material. The vitreous body helps hold the retina in place. Within the *retina* specialized cells called *rods* and *cones* convert light rays into nerve impulses. Other cells relay impulses through the *optic nerve,* at the center of the retina, to the brain's visual center.

When a cat's eyes shine in darkness, the structure responsible for it is a specialized reflective layer beneath the retina, the *tapetum lucidum*. It is positioned mainly in the upper half of the eye so that light below the head is focused on this particularly sensitive area

of the retina. The tapetum is made up of cells with reflecting material that is a crystalline complex of amino acid, mineral, and riboflavin. The tapetal function is to reflect any light not absorbed during its first passage through the retina, back for a second opportunity to be absorbed. Studies have confirmed that responses from the nontapetal retina are less sensitive to light than the tapetal retina. Researchers estimate that a cat's light sensitivity is nearly six times greater than man's, probably mainly due to the tapetal reflection.

The question of the cat's ability to see color has been debated by many. Most observers agree that color has little significance for the cat when used in training. Scientific investigation has ascertained that the retina is endowed with cones that have the ability to analyze some hues of color. How the cat perceives color may never be known.

The *area centralis* of the retina is a highly differentiated area of cone photoreceptors. The ratio of cones to ganglion nerve cells (major nerve-cell transmittors) indicates a more sensitive visual area than the peripheral areas of the retina. It is this area that the cat uses to concentrate on the particle of dust in a ray of sunlight or on a resting fly.

Disorders

EYELID DISORDERS. *Upper Lid Agenesis.* Eyelids can develop abnormally, resulting in defects of the lid. Maldevelopment may affect as much as one-half to two-thirds of the lid. Consequently, facial hair then touches the eyeball, irritating the cornea. The cornea is further aggravated by exposure because of an incomplete blinking ability. The only therapy available is lid reconstruction to remove the irritating hairs and fill the defect.

Lid Ankyloblepharon. The eyelids of newborn kittens normally separate by the fourteenth day. Neonatal conjunctivitis occurs from a bacterial or viral infection while the lids are still fused. Infectious purulent (pus-forming) material causes a bulging of the eyelids. The cornea becomes ulcerated and possibly perforated. One or both eyes may be affected. The bacterium most often isolated is *Staphylococcus* or *Escherichia coli.*

The therapy is to force open the lids to allow for drainage and treatment. This can be done with gentle traction, using a cotton-tip applicator at the inner corner of the eye. If the eye does not open after gentle pressure, the veterinarian will have to cut along the natural lid margin. A culture and microbe-sensitivity test of the exudate (material or pus) retrieved can determine the specific bacteria involved, allowing the appropriate, most effective antibiotic to be used. An oral and topical broad-spectrum antibiotic is suggested until the specific sensitivity is known. Corticosteroid preparations should be avoided. The prognosis is good if the cornea has not perforated.

Entropion. Normally, the lid is in tight contact with the globe (eyeball). Changes in the orbit or globe may cause the lid to lose support so that it folds inwardly, allowing the facial hair to traumatize the cornea and causing it to ulcerate. This is known as entropion. Entropion in cats usually involves the temporal lower lid (its outer portion) and may affect one or both eyes. Blinking, tearing, and ulcerations are usually associated with entropion. Whether an ulcer stimulated the blinking and tearing, resulting in entropion, or the entropion caused the ulcer, is difficult to determine. If the problems are related to the entropion, a surgical correction will halt the damage to the cornea. If the entropion appears to be secondary, therapy can be directed mainly at the corneal ulcer rather than the lid. A contact lens or tissue flap is used as a bandage to protect the cornea for ten to fourteen days. Topical antibiotics are recommended during this healing period.

Blepharitis. Blepharitis is inflammation of the eyelid. It is frequently found in intact males as the result of fighting. Bacterial infections and wound abscesses are common in and around the eye. Veterinary therapy is to establish drainage, flush the abscess with antiseptic or antibiotic, and administer systemic antibiotic as well as a topical ocular antibiotic. Hot compresses aid the absorption of the medication.

Another possible cause of blepharitis may be dermatomycosis (fungal skin infection). The usual agent is *Microsporum canis* (ringworm). Young animals are more frequently involved. Children playing with affected kittens may also develop the infection. As the organism is contagious, the affected animals should be isolated while treated. The organism can persist in a dry environment for one year. Diagnosis is determined from cultures, skin scrapings, and a fluorescence to Wood's light (50 percent of the time ringworm glows in this violet light). Therapy includes clipping all involved hair, using topical antifungal preparations, and oral antifungal medication. (*See* Chapter 17: Skin and Disorders.)

Cat Scabies (Acariasis). Cat scabies is caused by the mite *Notoedres cati*. The skin on the head and neck is usually intensely pruritic (itchy), wrinkled, thick, and crusty. This parasite can survive for only a short time off the host (cat, dog, or man). Skin scrapings demonstrate the mite in most cases. Therapy is to remove the crusty areas and treat with 2.5 percent solution of lime-sulfur, repeated at ten-day intervals for three treatments. Subcutaneous injections of Ivermectin (under the skin) can also be used in two treatments over several weeks. (*See* Chapter 19: External Parasites.)

Atopy (allergy). Atopy of the lids can occasionally be due to food allergies. The typical atopy case has swollen lids with multiple scratches from the itchy sensation. Hair loss is marked. Isolation away from the cat's normal environment and food, with challenge test diets, help define the antigenic cause. (*See* Chapter 17: Skin and Disorders.)

Eyelid Tumors. Eyelid tumors are rare in the cat. Unfortunately, they are usually malignant. The most common tumor is *squamous cell carcinoma* (SCA). It is a cancer of the squamous skin cells that appears as a slow-growing ulcerative tumor on the lid margin. As with other white-haired species, this tumor is prevalent in white cats; the incidences increase with age; metastasis (spread) is late, usually to regional lymph nodes. *Fibromas* are tumors of the connective tissue that are pedunculated (on a stem). Both squamous cell carcinomas and fibromas respond to excision and cryotherapy. Thermotherapy or radiation therapy, as well as immunotherapy, have also been successful. The earlier these tumors are treated, the better the prognosis. (*See* Chapter 33: Cancer.)

CONJUNCTIVAL DISEASES. Complaints of feline conjunctivitis are common. The signs include a discharge from the eye, blinking, and exposed third eyelid. In severe cases, the conjunctiva is swollen and red. The cause is often an infectious agent affecting multiple cats in a household, or there is a history of boarding, grooming, or showing the cat, which indicates the contagious source of the disease. The outdoor cat may develop allergic conjunctivitis from primary plant sources. This type of ocular irritation has a seasonal incidence, but many times bacterial infections prolong or complicate the initial cause.

Viral Conjunctivitis. Viral conjunctivitis often accompanies viral upper respiratory disease. The herpesvirus (cause of rhinotracheitis), calicivirus, and reovirus have been isolated as causative agents. The herpesvirus and calicivirus are the main agents causing upper respiratory infections, which can also cause severe eye infections. It is difficult to make an ocular diagnosis when the only complaint is a watery discharge from one or both eyes without a history of respiratory involvement. The watery eye may be days to weeks in duration with no response to the usual antibiotic therapy. Conjunctival scrapings may be helpful to rule out *Mycoplasma* and *Chlamydia* (microorganisms) within the conjunctiva cells. Cultures are expensive but especially helpful in large cat populations. Once the diagnosis is made, specific therapy, with frequent antiviral preparations, is helpful. Cats with herpesvirus infections usually become carriers, and with stress or corticosteroid therapy develop recurrent clinical signs. The recurrent signs are usually milder and shorter in duration. If the discharge becomes discolored to yellow, orange, or red, and very thick, a secondary bacterial component should be suspected. Antibiotic medications are compatible with antiviral medications; therefore, simultaneous use is advised. (*See* Chapter 24: Respiratory System and Disorders.)

Chlamydia Conjunctivitis. Chlamydia conjunctivitis often begins in one eye and spreads to the other in about one week. The initial discharge is watery, but becomes mucoid (mucuslike) within a few days. As the disease progresses, the discharge becomes more infectious. Chemosis (excessive swelling of the conjunctiva) is characteristic in the acute phase. When chronic, lymphoid follicular hyperplasia of the conjunctiva occurs, it appears as small gray bumps on the conjunctiva surface. Untreated, some cats become carriers with disease lasting months and years. The diagnosis can be determined from conjunctival scrapings that show the microscopic organisms within cells (*See* Chapter 24: Respiratory System and Disorders.).

Therapy includes topical tetracyclines three to four times a day for two weeks. Systemic oxytetracycline three times a day for one week is often beneficial along with topical treatments. Vaccines are available, but difficulty in controlling the disease in catteries and hospitals has been noted because of the short-lived immunity of the vaccine and the presence of the carrier animals.

Mycoplasma Conjunctivitis. Mycoplasma conjunctivitis is caused by the microorganism *Mycoplasma felis*. In many cases this organism occurs with other infectious agents. Initially, the ocular discharge is watery, with marked redness and swelling of the conjunctiva. The third eyelid is usually visible. When the discharge becomes mucoid, a pseudomembrane may develop on the surface of the swollen conjunctiva. The diagnosis can be made from a conjunctival scraping submitted for microscopic cell examination. Topical and/or systemic antibiotics for ten to fourteen days are effective in shortening the disease signs from thirty days to four to five days. *Mycoplasma felis* is sensitive to chloramphenicol, gentamicin, and tetracycline.

Tearing. Lacrimation is an increased production of tears resulting in *epiphora* (an overflow of tears). Other than a lack of tears and epiphora, diseases of the lacrimal system are uncommon in the cat. The ducts of the lacrimal system are very small and can easily become obstructed, resulting in epiphora. The two lacrimal puncta are the small openings to the canaliculi, or ducts, leading to the lacrimal sac. The nasolacrimal duct drains the sac into the nose or mouth. Congenital atresia (absence or blockage) of the puncta or canaliculi occurs, but occlusion (blockage) is usually secondary to inflammation. Facial conformation may contribute to epiphora in extremely short-nosed cats. Tumors of the lid margins or nasal cavity could obstruct the lacrimal flow. Excessive lacrimation is a reflex reaction from ocular irritation. Epiphora must be differentiated from normal lacrimation that has abnormal drainage.

A veterinarian can test the lacrimal system by putting dye in the eye to monitor dye flow into the mouth or nasal cavity. If flow is not demonstrated, irrigation of the system under anesthesia is recommended. Therapy is directed at the cause, which may range from lid abnormalities, conjunctival problems, corneal ulcers, or adhesions, to obstructions.

Keratoconjunctivitis Sicca. Keratoconjunctivitis sicca (KCS) is caused by a lack of tears, the opposite of epiphora. This condition can result from local trauma, extreme inflammation of the conjunctival glands and ducts, denervation (lack of nerve stimulus) of the lacrimal glands, or medication causing glandular dysfunction. Cats with KCS have minimal discharge, chronic conjunctivitis, a lackluster cornea, and squint. If the cause of KCS is denervation, pilocarpine (a drug that stimulates nerve impulses) stimulation can be successful if given topically or orally. Cats find this medication irritating to their eyes and taste buds, but occasionally two drops of 1 percent pilocarpine in their food can be tolerated. The treatment of conjunctival inflammation with an antibiotic ointment is necessary. Tear substitutes or lubricants should also be used. If conjunctival swelling is severe, there is usually a tear deficiency. Corticosteroids may aid in the return of tears by reducing swollen tissues. If the KCS becomes chronic and medical management is unsatisfactory, a parotid duct (salivary gland below the ear) transplant may be considered. Topical cyclosporin (an immunosuppressant drug) in oil has aided the KCS dog population, and it appears to be beneficial to cats with KCS as well.

THIRD EYELID DISORDERS. The third eyelid becomes visible or prolapsed when the globe (eyeball) shrinks in size or changes position, allowing the membrane to move across the eye. It can prolapse for a variety of reasons. Ocular irritation will cause the globe to retract into the orbit, as a means of protection, producing a prolapse. Increased muscle tone, such as with tetanus or poisoning, will cause eye retraction. In decreased orbital tissue mass from dehydration, cachexia (seriously poor health from any cause), and generalized skull muscle atrophy (shrinking or wasting away), the eyeball loses support and becomes situated deeper into the orbit, allowing the third eyelid to become prominent. The eye itself can cause third-lid prolapse as a secondary response to microphthalmos (abnormally small eye), or to posttraumatic or inflammatory eye atrophy with adhesions. Neurogenic causes leading to decreased sympathetic tone (lack of nervous input) will produce a small pupil, lid droopiness, eye retraction, and third eyelid prolapse. This group of signs is known as Horner's syndrome.

An idiopathic (cause unknown) prolapse of both third eyelids is noted in apparently normal cats and may persist for three to six weeks. This type of prolapse frequently responds to one drop of 10 percent phenylephrine (a nerve stimulant) or ½ percent Neosynephrine® twice daily. Probably the biggest percentage of third eyelid prolapses falls into this group of nonocular conditions. These seem to be independent of hydration and weight loss. A disruption in nerve stimulation is present, although no other signs are present. Some veterinarians believe endoparasites can cause these signs. To diagnose the exact cause of third eyelid prolapse requires a thorough ocular and systemic examination. The therapy is directed at the basic cause. Although not particularly aesthetic, the prolapse itself is not usually detrimental to vision and usually resolves with time.

Tumors. Tumors of the third eyelid are rare. They usually include squamous cell carcinomas, hemangiomas (benign masses of blood vessels), hemangiosarcomas (malignant masses of blood vessels), adenomas (benign skin tumors that contain glandular tissue), and adenocarcinomas (malignant skin tumors that contain glandular tissue). Most of these can be successfully treated if they are managed early in their growth; once they have invaded the orbit or eye itself, management is difficult.

"Cherry Eye." Prolapse of the third eyelid that reveals the tear gland at the base has been called "cherry eye." This condition has been thought to be related to inherent factors, most probably skull and orbital conformation. Environmental factors may aggravate the condition. Therapy should be aimed at surgically relocating the gland by attaching it to the front of the globe or periosteum (tissue covering the bone) of the orbital rim. Excising the third eyelid and gland may eventually lead to keratoconjunctivitis sicca.

DISORDERS OF THE CORNEA. *Keratitis* (inflammation of the cornea). The cornea can become less than perfect by its reaction to congenital or acquired lesions. *Superficial keratitis* is often associated with mechanical factors such as traumatic injuries, lid agenesis, entropion, or abscesses. Herpesvirus infection in the young and adult cat is common. *Keratoconjunctivitis sicca* or facial paralysis (lid nerve palsy) leaves the cornea exposed, causing keratitis. Exposure during globe proptosis (bulging) can cause keratitis. Chronic keratitis has the prominent feature of superficial corneal vascularization (formation of blood vessels on the surface of the cornea). The cornea develops varying degrees of opacity due to edema, scarring, cellular infiltrates (abnormal cells within the cornea), and cellular pigmentation. The management of nonulcerative forms (where there is no loss of surface corneal tissue) of superficial keratitis is mainly with topical corticosteroids, but all mechanical causes must be removed prior to their use. The corticosteroids minimize corneal scarring and vascularization. Fluorescein (a dye) staining of the cornea should be negative before corticosteroids are used. Topical antibacterial and/or antivirals should be used if indicated. Atropine (a drug that blocks nerve stimulation to the iris, causing pupil dilation) ointment may be helpful in decreasing ocular pain if ulcerative lesions are present.

Deep keratitis is usually associated with chronic inflammations within the eye. These inflamed eyes often have a small pupil, iris adhesions, and changes in iris color and texture, which means the interior of the eye is undergoing a reactive inflammatory process as well. Veterinary management is directed at those inflammatory signs when present. If corneal ulceration is not present, topical corticosteroids in combination with mydriatics (drugs that dilate the pupil) are recommended. If ulceration is present, topical nonsteroidal anti-inflammatories are recommended with mydriatics. Antiviral medication may be indicated in nonhealing ulcers.

Ulcerative conditions usually heal after neovascularization (new blood-vessel ingrowth). Once the ulcer is epithelialized (covered with epithelium, i.e., surface tissue), topical corticosteroids are recommended to minimize the scarring and persistent vessels. Remember that a normal cornea has no blood vessels. Ulcers that involve only the epithelial layer (the outer layer) will usually heal if given a small amount of protection from a contact lens, which serves the purpose of a bandage. The cat is easily fitted and comfortably wears the lens for seven to ten days. Topical medicated drops do not interfere with the contact lens during this period.

Corneal Sequestrum. Corneal sequestrum is unique to the cat cornea. It has also been called *corneal nigrum, corneal necrosis,* and *mummification.* Characteristically, a black-to-brown plaque forms on the corneal surface. Blinking, squinting, lacrimation, and prolapse of the third eyelid indicate pain. The plaque may continue to increase in size and incite vascularization (development of blood vessels). It does not stain with fluorescein except around the edges, but Rose Bengal stain is positive. A black tearing is commonly noted. The earlier the plaque is surgically removed, the less involved the incision and corrective care. Even though the surgery to remove the sequestrum is relatively successful, there is an occasional recurrence. If it occurs unilaterally, the opposite eye may also develop a sequestrum in the future. Postsurgical topical antibiotic and/or antiviral ointments are indicated for the duration of healing. Bacterial and viral microorganisms may be involved in some sequestral formations.

Complicated Deep Ulcerations. Complicated deep ulcerations, descemetoceles (herniations of the membrane at the back of the cornea), and perforations with iris prolapse (iris protruding through the cornea) are all surgical candidates. The most common cause is claw injury from fighting. Deep ulcerations usually require surgery or gluing with special tissue adhesive. Topical and systemic antibiotics are to be used for two weeks postoperatively.

DISORDERS OF THE ANTERIOR CHAMBER. *Hypopyon* is the accumulation of white blood cells in the anterior chamber of the eye. It appears as either clumps or a fluid line of gray material adherent to the inside of the cornea. The stimulus for this response can be either external (such as a corneal ulceration) or internal (ocular manifestation of systemic disease). Hypopyon is usually sterile. It resorbs when the cause has been resolved. A residual persistent haze on the corneal endothelium (inner corneal layer of cells) is common and of minimal consequence.

Fibrin is the insoluble protein substance of normally clotted blood. Fibrin in the anterior chamber is common after an acute insult such as a perforation from a cat claw. A perforation causes fluid loss before the hole self-seals. Plasma (the fluid portion of blood) from the intraocular blood vessels reinflates the anterior chamber; but since the plasma is rich in fibrin, it organizes into a clot. The condition disappears rapidly as the inflammation resolves. Remnants of fibrin strands are often attached or left floating in the anterior chamber. Occasionally small opaque patches remain attached to the cornea or lens capsule.

Glaucoma is an elevation in the intraocular pressure beyond normal. Aqueous fluid is produced behind the iris in the ciliary body tissue. Even though aqueous fluid is produced in the posterior chamber, it does not intermix with vitreous humor. Their physical properties are much like oil and water. Most theories and proven causes of glaucoma have dealt with outflow obstruction of aqueous fluid. The normal outflow of aqueous is through a meshwork of tissue between the iris and cornea. As the fluid passes through the trabecular meshwork, it drains into the vascular system of the globe. *Secondary glaucoma,* the most common in the cat, is associated with an intraocular disease such as inflammatory adhesions, tumors, and blood or fibrin. The term *absolute glaucoma* is reserved for eyes irreversibly blind from glaucoma.

Glaucoma is an ocular set of signs, not a disease. Therapy must be directed at the disease causing glaucoma, which could be feline ocular lymphoma (cancer of lymphocytes), iris bombé (iris bowed forward by excess fluid trapped between the iris and the lens), anteriorly luxated (dislocated) lens, granulomatous inflammations (collections of reactive tissue), and tumors.

The signs of chronic glaucoma include buphthalmos (enlarged eye), ciliary vascular congestion (red eye), dilated fixed pupil (pupil that does not contract), firm eye (high intraocular pressure), blindness, and corneal haziness from edema (swelling). If the lens is loose in the anterior chamber, it is difficult to document whether the lens luxation started the glaucoma or the glaucoma caused globe distention, which ruptured the lens's fiber support. If the eye is greatly enlarged and the lens is in the anterior chamber, the sight cannot be salvaged. The signs of developing glaucoma are probably more subtle in the cat than in other species, which makes it difficult to catch the disease when it is still possible to regain or preserve some vision.

Once an eye is lost to glaucoma, the remaining eye should be treated preventively with antiglaucoma medication. Carbonic anhydrase inhibitors (drugs that block the enzyme that helps water transfer), beta blockers (drugs that inhibit nerve impulses), and miotics (drugs that contract the pupil) help control the pressure. Secondary glaucoma from inflammations and lymphoma respond to corticosteroid and/or antineoplastic (anticancer) therapy, but the prognosis is poor.

Cats that have gone blind from noninfectious glaucoma often develop greatly enlarged globes that are very disfiguring. A cosmetic removal of the eye contents (evisceration) and volume replacement with a silicone prosthesis has become a popular alternative to eye removal (enucleation). This surgical procedure gives fantastic results in appearance and comfort.

DISORDERS OF THE LENS.

The lens can remain normal throughout life, become sclerotic (hardened), luxate out of its normal position, or become opaque (cataractous).

Nuclear Sclerosis. Of these disorders the most common is sclerosis. Because the lens continues to grow slowly throughout life, the central region becomes compacted and very dense compared to the outer region, which causes the center to become hazy gray with age (nuclear sclerosis). The condition does not interfere appreciably with vision nor does it obstruct an examination of the retina. No therapy is indicated for nuclear sclerosis.

Cataract. A cataract is any opacity of the lens. Cataracts are not as common in the cat as they are in the dog. The most common causes are inflammations, which leave evidence of adhesions; cellular and fibrin debris; direct and indirect trauma, which could injure the lens; and intraocular hemorrhage, which may impair the nutrition of the lens and result in cataracts. Senile cataracts in many cases have no known etiology (origin). Congenital cataracts generally do not progress to blindness. Although they may cause marked visual problems in a kitten, vision improves as the eye and lens grow, because the opacity becomes relatively smaller. Cataract surgery can be performed with relatively good results when the cataract is *not* due to inflammatory causes.

DISORDERS OF THE IRIS.

The cat iris is so visible that anything unusual is of concern. The iris disorders are usually first noted by the owner.

Persistent Pupillary Membranes. These membranes are commonly seen in young cats, but they usually disappear with age. They are nothing more than fine strands of embryonic tissue that bridge the pupil and occasionally attach to the cornea or the lens capsule, causing focal opacities. Persistent pupillary membranes should be differentiated from acquired iris adhesions and inflammatory residues.

Anterior Uveitis. Inflammation of the iris is common in the cat. It is called *iridis, iritis, iridocyclitis,* or *anterior uveitis.* The *uvea* is the middle vascular layer (under the sclera). The front portion of the uvea is the iris. The rear portion is called the *choroid.* The choroid is the blood supply to the retina. Uveitis is frequently bilateral (in both eyes) and often a secondary ocular complication of a systemic disease. The main challenge is the diagnosis, whether the disease is exogenous (from an outside source) or endogenous (from a source in the body) and whether the type of inflammation is granulomatous (collections of reactive tissue usually against fungal or parasitic agents) or nongranulomatous (cells reactive to bacteria or viral agents).

Whatever the classification, the signs are dramatic. Iris coloration changes and the surface becomes hazy and rough. In cats with a blue iris, the coloration becomes darker and duller. The pupil is usually miotic (small), irregular, and immobile due to adhesions. Typically, the inflammation causes the eye to be softer (hypotonic). Photophobia (light hypersensitivity) and blepharospasm (spasm of the eyelid muscle) are common. Decreased vision or blindness may be obvious, especially if the inflammation is bilateral.

The common causes of anterior uveitis are trauma, feline leukemia complex, feline infectious peritonitis, toxoplasmosis, systemic mycotic (fungal) disease, neoplasia (abnormal growth), bacterial infections, toxins, allergies, and lens-protein inflammations.

Most cases of uveitis respond to aggressive anti-inflammatory therapy. If the cause is noninfectious, corticosteroid therapy administered systemically, subconjunctivally, and topically for two weeks will resolve many cases. Topical 1 percent atropine (a drug that blocks nerve stimulation of muscle) is indicated as frequently as necessary to dilate the pupil. Blood samples are used initially for diagnostic evaluation and two weeks later for comparison. If the uveitis is progressive and nonresponsive to anti-inflammatory therapy, additional diagnostic tests are indicated.

If cancer has metastasized (spread) from another site in the body, it is usually difficult to diagnose initially. Inflammation of the iris can spread, causing inflammation of the choroid and retina *(posterior uveitis)*. Active chorioretinal lesions are hazy or lack sharp detail when viewed through an ophthalmoscope. Color changes and pigment clumping are often present.

Vascular pattern alterations seen through the pupil may denote retinal detachment. Lesions with some bulk may represent neoplasms or infections. Therapy should be determined by the concurrent systemic evaluation. When administered, therapy is given systemically as well as topically. Corticosteroids may be contraindicated if infectious or granulomatous causes are suspected.

Iris Color Difference. Iris freckles are common in cats. They are similar to benign nevi (moles) or pigment spots. If they are flat and do not alter the iris surface in either maximum constriction or dilation, they are of little concern, although their size should be monitored. If the spots change and invade iris tissue, the anterior chamber, or the vitreous body, especially displacing lens position, neoplasm should be suspected. Some iris freckles or nodules respond to subconjunctival corticosteroids. Those that do not are usually melanomas (cancers of pigment cells) or adenomas (benign growth of glandular tissue).

Iris Cysts. Iris cysts are black bodies that may be attached or free within the anterior chamber or posterior chamber (vitreous body). With a bright light, these cysts can be easily transilluminated to verify that they are fluid-filled, which differentiates them from iris melanomas. Unless the cysts are extremely large, they are left to do whatever they wish, which is usually roll freely about inside the eye. Visually obstructive cysts can be deflated nonsurgically or by laser therapy.

RETINAL DISEASES. Retinal diseases in cats are varied and complex. They can be indications of systemic diseases such as blood abnormalities ranging from hemorrhages in anemias to hyperviscosity (blood thickening) syndromes. Anemias from haemobartonellosis (*see* Chapter 30: Bacterial Diseases), leukemias, and thrombocytopenias (platelet deficiencies causing poor blood clotting) can manifest as large blot and spot hemorrhages within the retina, behind it, or in front of it. Hyperviscosity syndromes cause vascular distention and effusion (blood escaping into tissues). Lymphoid cancers commonly spread into the retina. Discrete or diffuse gray mottling of the tapetum, retinal detachment, and blood clots are all possible. Definitive diagnosis is usually based on systemic signs and ophthalmoscopic examination of the retina. Rapid recovery may occur with therapy.

Panleukopenia. Panleukopenia can cause a retinal dysplasia (abnormal development) if the virus has infected the kitten between one week prebirth and one week postbirth. The lesions in the tapetum appear as sharply demarcated areas of increased reflectivity and altered color. The nontapetal areas have focal pigment disruption (spotty depigmentation). Cerebellar hypoplasia (underdevelopment of the brain) signs also may be present. Usually no clinical signs are attributed to the eye lesions because the other nervous signs are so outstanding. These cats are very shaky and incoordinated.

Inherited Retinal Degenerations. Inherited retinal degenerations have been reported in the Persian and Abyssinian breeds and various domestic shorthair types. The lesion has a diffuse hyperreflective tapetal appearance with vascular attenuation (thinning of the blood vessels) in the end stages. It is a recessive inherited disease leading to blindness at an early age.

Traumatic Retinal Degeneration. Traumatic retinal degeneration is usually the result of globe proptosis (bulging), especially if the optic nerve and blood vessels are traumatized. Many eyes are saved cosmetically but are blind. Multifocal retinal degeneration (many separate lesions) can be secondary to infections and appear as scars.

Retinal Detachment. Retinal detachment is common in the cat. It can be of variable degrees from various causes. Most detachments are associated with a systemic disease or metabolic problem. Some resolve spontaneously and some resolve when the causative factors are identified and treated. A thorough medical workup is always indicated.

Detachment can be due to feline infectious peritonitis, lymphosarcoma, toxoplasmosis, glomerulonephritis, pyelonephritis, antifreeze toxicosis, trauma, or toxemias (poisonings). Prognosis with therapy is poor, but if the retina becomes detached and disinserted at the periphery, the prognosis is very poor without hope of vision, regardless of therapy.

Nutritional Retinal Degeneration (feline central retinal degeneration). Nutritional retinal degenerations are common in cats. The retinal lesion begins with a focal granularity in the area centralis region. It increases in size to an oval-shaped, hyperreflective region surrounded by a dark margin and can progress to generalized hyperreflectivity, vascular attenuation, and blindness. Retinal lesions in both eyes are symmetrical. In the early stages, no clinical signs are noted. At these stages, the condition can be arrested and blindness prevented if it is diagnosed. The cause of this degeneration is a deficiency in the amino acid taurine. Most well-balanced cat foods are adequate in taurine. Cats fed dog foods or table scraps may become deficient, especially if they are habitually addicted to one type of diet. Fresh dairy products, red meats, fish, and fish oils are high in taurine and serve as good supplemental sources. Taurine can also be given in pill form.

DISORDERS OF THE OPTIC NERVE. The optic nerve of a cat transmits visual impulses to the brain. Radical changes in behavior may indicate problems. Observed changes such as incomplete or complete lack of development of the optic nerve are termed optic nerve hypoplasia and aplasia. Both of these conditions are revealed clinically as blindness, with widely dilated pupils that are unresponsive to light stimulus. These are congenital abnormalities. Optic nerve hypoplasia is difficult to differentiate from acquired optic nerve degeneration, especially in the cat.

Optic Neuritis. Optic neuritis is an acquired abnormality of the optic nerve due to inflammation as it extends into the nerve from adjacent tissues such as the brain, orbit, or retina. Common causes include *Toxoplasma* chorioretinitis (inflammation of the choroid), *Cryptococcus* infection of the retina, orbit, or central nervous tissues, feline infectious peritonitis, neoplasia extensions (metastases) from anywhere in the body, and toxic ingestions. Blindness may or may not be a clinical sign, depending upon where the lesions are located. The optic disc (end portion of the optic nerve) may show abnormal character. Any swelling of the optic disc is considered abnormal in the cat. A diagnostic test giving the greatest amount of information is the cerebrospinal fluid analysis. Specific therapy must be directed at the cause, but symptomatic treatment using anti-inflammatory medication is frequently helpful at reducing the swelling of the optic nerve. If the swelling is not reduced, it can begin to harm the cat's eyesight in a relatively short time.

DISORDERS OF THE GLOBE. The eyeball or globe is generally assessed as being either too big (*buphthalmos*) or too small (*microphthalmos*) or shrunken (*phthisis bulbi*). Microphthalmos is a congenitally small eye, which is common in cats. In eyes that are mildly to moderately small, the structures and function may be relatively normal. Microphthalmos may be part of multiple ocular anomalies such as cataracts, persistent pupillary membranes, retinal dysplasia, and eyelid agenesis. Because the globe is small, entropion and prolapsed third eyelid as well as a small orbit may be present. Phthisis bulbi is an acquired decrease in globe size due to severe intraocular damage. These eyes are blind. The corneas are usually opaque and the globe position deviated (strabismus). Because of the chronic conjunctivitis, entropion, and facial-hair irritation, these globes should be removed (enucleated) to alleviate discomfort and prevent generalized inflammation.

Panophthalmitis. Panophthalmitis is an inflammation of all the ocular tissues, whereas *endophthalmitis* is inflammation inside the globe; both are usually destructive beyond visual salvation. Occasionally, intensive heroic therapy may save the globe but not the vision. Surgical removal of the globe is most frequently recommended for the cat's comfort.

Strabismus (cross-eye). Crossed or esotropic eyes are common in Siamese cats. The degree of globe deviation varies. Occasionally a fine nystagmus (rapid eye movement) is noted. Albino cats and blue-eyed Siamese have a higher number of nerve fibers crossing at the optic chiasm (location where nerves from each eye cross over each other within the optic nerve to the opposite side of the brain). These extra nerve fibers crowd out those fibers needed for binocular vision and normal conjugated (equally coupled) globe position. The globe malposition (cross-eye) is not present at birth. The convergent strabismus condition develops from two to six months of age. It is thought that the strabismus develops as an attempt to compensate for the abnormal retinal transmissions to the brain. These cats certainly compensate, as there appear to be few clinical signs or difficulties with vision.

·····················
EAR

The ear—the organ of hearing and balance—can be divided anatomically into three main components: the *external* ear, which consists of the outer ear itself (known as the *pinna* or *auricle*) and the ear canal; the *middle* ear, which consists of the eardrum *(tympanic membrane)* and the *auditory ossicles* (small bones); and the *inner* ear, which is enclosed within the skull and contains the sensory structures of hearing and balance.

The pinna is a thin, delicate, funnel-shaped structure supported by cartilage *(auricular cartilage)*. It is supplied with a number of muscles and is extremely mobile in cats. The pinna acts to locate and concentrate sound waves, directing them down into the ear canal toward the sensory components of the auditory system. At the terminus of the canal is the eardrum, a translucent membrane that vibrates in response to sound and acts as a connecting wall between the external and middle ear. Within the middle ear are the three auditory ossicles, tiny bones that are responsible for transmitting the vibrations of the eardrum to the inner ear. Also within the middle ear is the origin of the *eustachian tube,* a short canal that communicates with the *nasopharynx* (back of the throat) and acts to equalize pressure within the ear (this is the structure that commonly "pops" in the ear during yawning or a change in altitude). Within the inner ear are the *semicircular canals,* which regulate balance, and the *cochlea,* a curled bone that contains the *organ of Corti,* the actual organ of hearing. Cats are able to capture acoustical signals from the environment far higher than any detectable by the human ear, up to 50 to 60 kilocycles (or *kilohertz*). The upper end of the human auditory range is approximately 20 kilocycles.

Congenital Abnormalities

FOLD-EARS. Inward folding of the tip of the pinna occurs in some individuals and forms the basis for the Scottish Fold breed. Folding is inherited in an *autosomal dominant* manner, that is, only one gene for fold-ear needs to be present for the trait to appear. However, *homozygous* individuals (those having two copies of the gene for folding) are afflicted with a number of serious skeletal abnormalities; *heterozygous* individuals with only one copy of the gene are healthy. Breeding of fold-ears with each other is discouraged because of the probability of producing homozygous offspring.

DEAFNESS IN WHITE CATS. Inherited deafness in white cats is also caused by an autosomal dominant gene. White cats with blue eyes are the most likely to be deaf, those with yellow eyes the least likely.

Acquired Disorders

EAR MITES. Mites *(Otodectes cynotis)* parasitizing the ear canal are a common problem of kittens and adult cats. Kittens frequently acquire an infestation from their mother; in some cases, the number of mites found in the canal can be staggering. Head-shaking, ear-scratching, restless behavior, and presence of brown material in the canal are common signs. Cats also may acquire ear mites from dogs. Neglect of ear mite infestation can have serious, even fatal, consequences. (*See* Chapter 19: External Parasites.)

HEMATOMA. Hematoma, the collection of blood from broken vessels in the space between the auricular cartilage and skin, is a less common problem in cats than in dogs, but no less severe in its physical effects. Fighting, continual shaking of the head, scratching at the ears (as from a mite infestation), or blunt trauma may produce a hematoma. Hematomas may be small and barely noticeable or they may expand and test the limits of elasticity of the overlying skin by producing a taut, balloonlike bulge inside the auricle. A severe hematoma usually permanently damages the conformation of the pinna.

Treatment ranges from aspiration of the bloody contents through a needle and syringe (smaller hematomas) to surgical drainage (larger lesions). In some cases, a soft bandage dressing may be applied post-surgically to prevent swelling and minimize deformity of the pinna.

OTITIS. Inflammation of the middle ear *(otitis media)* or outer ear *(otitis externa)* may be produced by bacteria, fungi, parasites, or foreign bodies. Treatment depends upon the underlying cause. Fortunately, cats, with their upright pinnae and renowned habits of cleanliness, are affected less often and less severely than are their canine counterparts. *Otitis interna* (inflammation of the inner ear) is occasionally seen, presenting with signs of incoordination, loss of balance, or hearing impairment. Purulent infections can lead to fatal meningitis and brain abscess.

Bacterial infections of the outer ear are dealt with by thorough cleansing of the affected ear canal and application of topical antibiotic medication. Foreign bodies—plant awns (bristles, "foxtails"), for example—must be located visually and removed. Ears suffering from fungal infections are cleaned thoroughly and treated with an antifungal medication. *Malassezia,* an especially common yeast, is found in many cases of otitis media in both cats and dogs. Parasite infestations (the mites *Otodectes* and *Notoedres*) are treated with appropriate topical preparations. (*See* Chapter 19: External Parasites.)

Infections of the middle or inner ear are generally more serious and may produce irreversible effects. Rupture of the eardrum and disturbances of hearing and/or balance may occur. Surgery may be required in some cases to remove pockets of pus and to flush affected areas with antibiotics or antifungal medication. The guarded prognosis is dependent upon the identity of the infecting organism and the extent of damage that has been produced to the acoustical structures.

POLYPS. Polyps—small pinkish growths protruding from the surface of a mucous membrane—can occur in cats of any age. In the auditory system, they arise within the middle ear and the external ear canal, often in the vicinity of the eardrum. Chronic ear-mite infestations and perhaps chronic infections may predispose to polyp formation. Treatment, when required, usually consists of surgical excision. A polyp from the middle ear occasionally passes into the nasopharynx, where it may cause gagging.

SQUAMOUS CELL CARCINOMA. Squamous cell carcinoma, a type of skin cancer, occurs often on the pinna of white and white-spotted cats and is associated with excessive exposure to sunlight. (*See* Chapter 17: Skin and Disorders.)

CERUMINOUS GLAND TUMORS. Tumors of *ceruminous glands* (glands that produce the waxy discharge of the ear canal) are seen in middle-aged and older cats. They are dark cystic structures that appear from the margins to the depths of the ear canal. They may even penetrate the eardrum. Ceruminous gland tumors may be benign (adenoma) or malignant (adenocarcinoma). Treatment depends upon the location of the tumor and its extent of growth. Surgical excision may or may not be feasible.

FELINE IDIOPATHIC VESTIBULAR SYNDROME. This is an acute disturbance of balance with a remarkable seasonal predilection (it occurs almost exclusively during the summer months). Mildly affected cats may show nothing more than a slight head-tilt, while severely affected animals will lie down and roll, their sense of balance utterly disrupted. Gradual improvement usually occurs over a period of weeks. Some animals recover completely, while others show residual effects (a head-tilt, for example). The cause is entirely unknown, and there is no treatment that has been proven to be of benefit. Affected cats must be closely cared for and supported until signs of the disease spontaneously diminish.

External Parasites

Parasites are living organisms residing on or within other living organisms. They ingest blood, lymph cells, or tissue from the bodies of their hosts as a source of nutriment. Parasites live at the expense of their hosts, causing considerable injury to their health. Those forms residing within their hosts are *endoparasites,* or internal parasites. Those living on the surface of their hosts are *ectoparasites,* or external parasites. The external parasites of cats include a variety of small to microscopic insects and arachnids: fleas, ticks, flies, lice, larvae, and mites.

Ectoparasitism involves the skin in the form of tissue damage and secondary inflammation causing irritation and pain to the host. Some external parasites, such as fleas, injure their hosts with toxic substances when they draw blood as a food source. External parasites can carry dangerous viruses and bacteria, infecting their hosts. The host may become devoid of energy and vitality, experiencing weakened resistance to infection and disease.

Dermatoses (skin diseases) caused by ectoparasites are the most common skin disorders of cats. They cause suffering through annoyance, irritability, *pruritus* (itching), disfigurement, secondary infections, and *myiasis* (infestation of the body by fly larvae). In addition, ectoparasites may be important in the transmission of viral, protozoal, *helminthic* (parasitic worm), and bacterial diseases.

MITES

Microscopic in size, these troublesome parasites are arthropods (invertebrate organisms with segmented bodies), which resemble insects but belong to the Arachnida, placing them in the same taxonomic class as spiders. Some are barely visible to the naked eye. Although there may be between ten thousand to twenty thousand species of arthropods, only a few belonging to the major subgroups are of direct medical concern for cats.

Notoedric Mange
(caused by the sarcoptid mite, *Notoedres cati*)

Notoedric mange is a rare to uncommon disease of cats, with no apparent age, breed, or sex predilections. The disease is worldwide in geographic distribution. In the United States it appears to be endemic in few areas. *Notoedres cati* is classified as a sarcoptid mite. Females deposit eggs inside the outermost layer of skin (intraepidermal burrows). The life cycle, which is spent entirely on the cat, is completed in about two weeks. The mites are thought to feed on lymph and epidermal cells. Notoedric mange is highly contagious via direct and indirect contact. *Notoedres cati* is quite susceptible to drying and cannot live for more than a few days off the cat.

The first sign of notoedric mange is usually intense, constant pruritus about the head and neck, with scratching and head-shaking. Skin lesions, characterized by erythema (redness), scales, alopecia (hair loss), thick grayish to yellowish crusts, lichenification (thickening of the outer layer of skin), and excoriations (scratches) then appear, especially on the ears and neck. Lesions can also extend to the head, face, paws, and genitalia. A "mousy" odor is often noted. Rarely, notoedric mange occurs as a fulminating dermatitis (sudden and intense skin inflammation) in litters of kittens, with the abdomen, perineum, and limbs most severely affected. In severe, untreated cases, death may result from secondary bacterial infection, interference with eating, loss of appetite, emaciation, and toxemia (blood poisoning). Regional lymphadenopathy (swollen lymph nodes) is usually pronounced.

Veterinary therapy includes isolation; gentle clipping and cleansing of affected areas to remove hair and thick crusts; and total-body parasiticidal dips. Injected glucocorticoids (a type of steroid) and antibiotics may be used to control severe itching and secondary infection (respectively) where appropriate. In-contact cats and dogs should be considered infested, isolated from the symptomatic cat, and dipped twice. As the mite does not persist for long off the host, a single thorough cleaning (vacuum, dispose of bag, and wash) of the environment suffices.

Notoedres cati can also produce skin lesions in humans. Lesions consist of vesicles (blisters), erythematous papules (red bumps), wheals (swollen skin irritations), or crusts and excoriations over pet-contact areas, especially the arms, legs, chest, and abdomen. Itching is severe. If the source of mites is eliminated, the dermatitis in humans resolves without specific treatment within two to six weeks. (See "Eye" in Chapter 18: Sensory Organs and Disorders.)

Sarcoptic Mange
(caused by the sarcoptid mite *Sarcoptes scabiei*)

Dermatitis due to *Sarcoptes scabiei* is extremely rare in cats. Clinical signs resemble those described for notoedric mange. *Sarcoptes scabiei* mites are larger (200 to 400 μ) than *Notoedres cati* and have a terminal anus (rather than dorsal). Because cats are not known to have their own specific variety of *Sarcoptes scabiei*, infections are presumably derived from other species, especially dogs and humans. Morphological studies have emphasized mite variability and the consequent difficulty in distinguishing among mites from different species. Details of clinical signs and veterinary therapy are as described for notoedric mange.

Otodectic Mange
(caused by the psoroptid mite *Otodectes cynotis*)

Otodectic mange is the most common cause of otitis externa (inflammation of the external ear canal) and an occasional cause of skin disease in cats. Skin lesions vary from partial hair loss to redness, scaling, and crusted itching dermatitis. Lesions are most commonly seen on the head, neck, rump, or paws. In one study of feline miliary dermatitis, *Otodectes cynotis* caused four of the 133 cases (3 percent). In addition, *Otodectes cynotis* has been rarely reported to cause skin lesions in humans, which were characterized by itching, blisters, erythematous papules (red bumps), wheals (swollen skin irritations), crusts, and excoriations on the arms and torso. When the source of mites is eliminated, the human dermatosis regresses without specific treatment within three weeks. (See "Ear" in Chapter 18: Sensory Organs and Disorders.)

Lynxacariasis
(caused by the mite *Lynxacarus radovskyi*, or cat fur mite)

Lynxacariasis is an uncommon cause of skin disease in cats. The mite *Lynxacarus radovskyi* attaches to hair shafts. It is thought to spend its entire life cycle on the host and to feed at the base of the hairs. This large mite (2 millimeters long [.078 inch]) can be confused with lice.

Clinically, there are no apparent age, breed, or sex predilections. In affected cats the entire hair coat is dull, easily epilated (removed by roots), and speckled. The skin may be normal, scaly, or reddish in appearance.

Diagnosis is based on history, physical examination, and skin scrapings or acetate tape impressions. Treatment consists of weekly parasiticidal dips or powders for three to four weeks.

Demodicosis, or Demodectic Mange, Follicular Mange
(caused by mites of the genus *Demodex*)

Two species of demodicids have been associated with demodicosis, a rare skin disease in cats. The life cycle of these mites is incompletely known, but is assumed to resemble that of other demodicids, wherein: (1) the entire life cycle (twenty to thirty-five days) is spent on the host; (2) the mites are normal residents of cat skin; (3) the disease is not contagious; and (4) factors that suppress immunity may predispose the cat to develop clinical demodicosis. Generalized feline demodicosis has been seen in association with feline leukemia virus infection, feline immunodeficiency virus infection, diabetes mellitus, and chronic respiratory disease with lymphopenia (decreased lymphocytes in the blood).

Clinically, there are no apparent breed or sex predilections, but demodicosis is most commonly seen in young cats. Localized demodicosis is characterized by single or multiple areas of poorly- to well-circumscribed areas of alopecia with or without erythema, follicular plugging, scaling, crusting, papulopustular dermatitis (inflamed, pus-filled skin elevations), and pruritus. The head, ears, and neck are most commonly affected. Generalized demodicosis may be characterized by the above lesions over a large part of the body or, more commonly, by a symmetrical *hypotrichosis* (thinning of hair) or alopecia over the trunk. *Demodex* mites may also cause a ceruminous otitis externa (waxy secretion and inflammation of the ear canal) in cats.

Treatment for localized demodicosis includes topical keratolytic (to cause peeling of outer layer of skin) and antibacterial agents, or a topical mite-killing agent. The topicals are applied once a day until skin scrapings are negative (three to four weeks). Many cases spontaneously regress without therapy. Demodectic otitis externa (ear mites) is treated with a mite-killing agent and mineral oil twice weekly for four weeks.

Generalized demodicosis has been successfully treated by veterinarians with weekly parasiticidal dips or shampoos until skin scrapings are negative (three to four weeks). Spontaneous remission of generalized demodicosis in cases with no detected underlying disease has been reported after a course of several months.

Cheyletiellosis, or "Walking Dandruff"
(caused by the mites *Cheyletiella blakei, Cheyletiella parasitivorax* and *Cheyletiella yasguri*)

Cheyletiellosis is an uncommon dermatosis of cats. Three *Cheyletiella* mites are known to infest cats: *Cheyletiella blakei* (most common), *Cheyletiella parasitivorax* (common on rabbits), and *Cheyletiella yasguri* (common on dogs). These mites do not burrow, but live in skin surface keratin. They move about fairly rapidly, but periodically attach firmly to the epidermis, pierce the skin with their *chelicerae* (head pincers), and become engorged with tissue fluids. The life cycle is thought to be completed on the host in about thirty-five days. Larvae, nymphs, and adult males usually die within forty-eight hours after leaving the host. Adult female mites may live off the host for ten days. *Cheyletiella* mites have been seen crawling in and out of the nostrils of cats, thus adding a new twist to the epidemiology and therapy of this disorder. Transmission occurs via direct and indirect contact. *Cheyletiella* mites have been found on fleas, flies, and lice, and it is conceivable that these larger ectoparasites may play a transport role in the spread of *Cheyletiella* from animal to animal.

Clinically, there are no apparent age, breed, or sex predilections. Clinical signs of feline cheyletiellosis are variable, and may include dorsally distributed seborrhea sicca (dry, scaly dermatitis), with or without itching; miliary dermatitis (red rash); pruritus with minimal or no lesions; and an asymptomatic carrier state.

Therapy includes isolation and weekly application of parasiticidal dips, powders, or shampoos until two weeks beyond clinical cure. In-contact dogs and cats should be considered infested and treated accordingly. Environmental treatment is important in cheyletiellosis and should include spraying or fogging as described for fleas. Recurrent cheyletiellosis in animals that go outdoors should prompt one to suspect a wild animal source (rabbits, squirrels).

Skin lesions produced by *Cheyletiella* mites in humans have been frequently reported. Human involvement has been reported to occur in 20 to 80 percent of the feline cases. The lesions of cheyletiellosis in humans begin as single or grouped erythematous macules (red spots), which rapidly evolve into papules (skin elevations). Lesions frequently become vesicular (blisterlike) or pustular (filled with pus). Old lesions often develop central necrosis (cell death). Itching is intense. Humans suffering from *Cheyletiella* should see their physicians. The arms, legs, and torso are commonly affected. If the source of mites is eliminated, the human dermatosis resolves without specific treatment within three weeks.

Trombiculidiasis
(caused by harvest mites or "chiggers," *Trombicula*)

Trombiculidiasis is a rare dermatosis of cats. Trombiculid adults and nymphs are free-living and feed on invertebrate hosts or plants. The larvae normally feed (suck tissue fluids) on small rodents, but may also attack cats. Trombiculid larvae measure 0.2 to 0.4 millimeters in length (.007 to .015 inch) and vary in color from red, to orange, to yellow. Trombiculid larvae are usually active in summer and fall, especially in forested and swampy areas, and drop off the host after feeding for seven to ten days.

Trombiculidiasis occurs in late summer and fall. Cats contact the active larvae in forests, grasslands, and fields. There are no apparent age, breed, or sex predilections. Skin lesions consist of papules, pustules, crusts, and excoriations on the head, ears, or paws. Itching is usually intense. Careful inspection may reveal the small larvae in the center of some of the lesions.

Therapy includes a single topical application of a parasiticide; systemic glucocorticoids for severe pruritus; and avoidance of infested environment.

Dermanyssiasis
(caused by the poultry mite, *Dermanyssus gallinae*)

Dermanyssiasis is a rarely reported dermatosis of cats. The poultry mite, *Dermanyssus gallinae,* lives in cracks and crevices in the walls of poultry houses or in bird nests. Adult mites suck blood and are 0.6 to 0.1 millimeters in length (.004 to .023 inch). Lesions consist of papules, crusts, and excoriations on the face and limbs. Itching is intense.

Diagnosis is based on history, physical examination, and demonstration of mites in skin scrapings or in the environment. Therapy consists of parasiticidal dips and eliminating or treating infested premises with miticidal sprays.

TICKS

Ticks are rarely found on cats. They display no apparent age, breed, or sex predilections when they are. In some areas, ticks can always be found, but they tend to be more of a problem in warm, humid climates. *Argasid* ("soft") ticks of the genus *Argas* lay their eggs in sheltered spots, such as cracks in poles, under boxes or stones, and in crevices in walls. Larvae and nymphs suck blood and lymph and drop off the host to become adults. *Ixodid* ("hard") ticks of the genus *Ixodes* lay their eggs in sheltered areas, such as wall crevices, cracks in wood near the ground, and under stones and clods of soil. *Larvae* ("seed ticks") climb onto grass and shrubbery and wait for a suitable host to pass by. (*See* Chapter 30: Bacterial Diseases, and Appendix A: Zoonotic Diseases for information on Lyme disease.) According to the number of hosts required during their life cycle, ticks can be classified into three groups: one-host ticks, two-host ticks, and three-host ticks. Each species of tick is adapted to certain ranges of temperature and moisture. In general, ticks are not terribly host-specific. Local reactions to tick bites are variable, depending on the properties of the tick in question, and on the host-parasite relationship.

Ticks and tick-related dermatoses are seen in spring and summer. Cats bearing ticks usually show little or no evidence of irritation and are most often presented to the veterinarian because the owner noticed a "growth" on the skin. Ticks are usually found on the head, ears, neck, and paws of cats. Rarely, nodules or necrotizing (cell-killing) ulcers may result when tick mouthparts are left in the skin.

Diagnosis is based on history and physical examination. Specific identification of the ticks is of value in determining the control measures required. A few ticks may be removed with a mosquito forceps or

EXTERNAL PARASITES

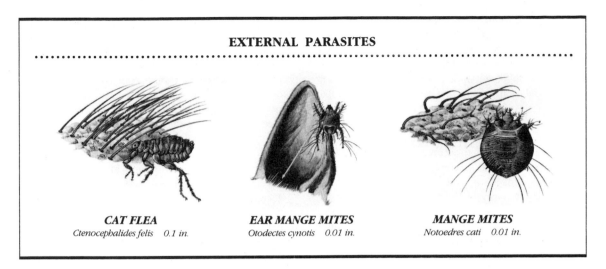

CAT FLEA
Ctenocephalides felis   0.1 in.

EAR MANGE MITES
Otodectes cynotis   0.01 in.

MANGE MITES
Notoedres cati   0.01 in.

large tweezers. The ticks's *capitulum* (head) is grasped as close to the cat's skin as possible, and gentle, firm retraction in the nature of a straight pull-out is used. Severe infestations are treated as described for fleas.

LICE

Pediculosis or Louse Infestation, Pedicular Disease
(caused by *Felicola subrostratus,* the chewing louse of cats)

Pediculosis is an uncommon infestation of cats. Lice are highly host-specific parasites bound to a specific environment and rarely survive longer than seven days off the host. *Felicola subrostratus,* the chewing louse of the cat, feeds on exfoliated epithelium (sloughed-off skin surface) and cutaneous debris. *Trichodectes canis,* a chewing louse of dogs, has been reported to affect kittens rarely. Transmission is by direct and indirect contact. Adult lice (3 to 4 millimeters or .12 to .15 inch in length) stick to hairs by a clear adhesive secretion. Louse populations are much larger (and thus, clinical signs are most obvious) in winter. Pediculosis is often associated with neglect, debilitation, or poor sanitary conditions (overcrowding, filth, and so forth).

Pediculosis has no apparent age, breed, or sex predilections. Clinical signs are variable and include dorsally distributed seborrhea sicca (dry, scaly dermatitis), with or without itching; miliary dermati-

tis; pruritus without lesions; and asymptomatic carriage.

Louse eggs (nits) are readily distinguished from *Cheyletiella* eggs (*see* "Cheyletiellosis," page 179) because the eggs are more oval and are attached to hairs at only one end of the egg (rather than along the entire length of one side).

Therapy includes the weekly topical administration of dips, powders, or shampoos for four to five weeks. Because lice do not live for long off the host, a single thorough cleansing (vacuum, wash, dispose) of the environment suffices.

FLEAS

Fleas are by far the most common ectoparasite of cats. Fleas are not host-specific and cats are occasionally parasitized by fleas from a number of sources. In the United States, the flea most commonly found on cats is *Ctenocephalides felis,* followed by *Ctenocephalides canis,* followed by *Pulex irritans* and *Echidnophaga gallinacea.* Fleas are small (2 to 4 millimeters or .08 to .15 inch in length), brown to black, wingless insects with laterally compressed bodies. Adult fleas are powerful jumpers.

Fleas develop by complete metamorphosis. The eggs, which are ovoid, white, and 1 to 2 millimeters in length (.04 to .08 inch), are laid on the premises in cracks of buildings or on damp ground, as well as in carpeting, behind wall paneling, and in air ducts. Those eggs laid on the host soon fall off. The female flea lays three to eighteen eggs at one time, but with frequent blood meals and frequent copulation, she may lay several hundred over her life span of one year. Adult fleas separated from the host live for two months or longer. Fleas lay more eggs when the environmental temperature reaches the range of 65°F to 80°F and when the relative humidity is high (75 to 85 percent). After an incubation of two to twelve days, the eggs hatch into larvae—active white-bristled worms with chewing mouthparts. They ingest fecal casts (which are black, comma-shaped, and 1 to 2 millimeters long) from adult fleas. Larvae grow and molt twice over a period of nine to two hundred days. The third molt produces an opaque white larva that becomes quiescent and spins a loose, whitish-gray cocoon, inside which it pupates for seven days to one year. The adult flea breaks out of the cocoon and looks for a host on which to feed. In general, fleas are particularly devastating in warmer climates (for example, in the southern United States) and do not survive at elevations over five thousand feet.

Echidnophaga gallinacea fleas (poultry stick-tight fleas) lay their eggs under the host's skin, resulting in local irritation. Poultry and poultry houses are the sources of infestation.

Hypersensitivity to flea salivary antigens plays a critical role in dermatoses seen in flea-infested cats. It is very likely that skin lesions resulting from flea bites occur only in sensitized individuals. Results of intradermal skin testing in cats with flea-bite hypersensitivity suggest that they develop primarily an immediate hypersensitivity reaction.

Cats with simple flea infestation may harbor an incredible number of fleas, yet show few or no clinical signs. There are no age, breed, or sex predilections. Blood loss anemia can be produced in kittens and debilitated adults.

Cats with flea-bite hypersensitivity show varying degrees of pruritic (itchy), erythematous (reddish), papulocrustous (crusty bumpy) dermatitis. The dorsal lumbosacral (lower back) area, thighs, ventral abdomen, head, and neck are most commonly affected. In some cats the cranial or caudal (head or tail) aspects of the body are almost exclusively affected, while in other cats the dermatosis is generalized. A few cats show only intense itching and traumatic alopecia. In a study of 133 cats with miliary dermatitis, seventy-three cases (54.9 percent) were due to flea-bite hypersensitivity; 80.8 percent of the cats with flea-bite hypersensitivity developed clinical signs at three years

of age or older; no breed or sex predilections for flea-bite hypersensitivity were found; 12.3 percent of the cats with flea-bite hypersensitivity had pronounced peripheral lymphadenopathy (enlarged lymph nodes); and 5.5 percent of the cats had recurrent eosinophilic granuloma complex (a disorder of the skin) lesions that paralleled the activity of their flea-bite hypersensitivity. In general, feline flea-bite hypersensitivity is a seasonal disorder in the United States (April to November), except where household infestation has been established and in the southeastern United States where it may be seen year round.

Diagnosis is based on history, physical examination, intradermal skin testing, and response to flea control. Finding fleas, flea eggs, or "flea dirt" (fecal casts) supports the diagnosis. However, it must be emphasized that the presence or absence of these findings neither confirms nor negates the diagnosis in any given animal. Clearly, many cats can have flea infestations that are not contributing to any dermatosis they may have. Likewise, it may be impossible to identify fleas and their products in cats that have been recently bathed or dipped.

Effective control of flea infestations requires the simultaneous treatment of all in-contact cats and dogs, and of the indoor and outdoor environments. Flea control is much easier in animals that are kept exclusively indoors. Flea control on the animals involves the use of various topical parasiticides, which may be selected according to the owner's capabilities and preferences, and according to any idiosyncrasies of the patient. The cat's susceptibility to insecticide toxicity must always be remembered. In general, chlorinated hydrocarbons and most organophosphates are contraindicated. Even carbamates can be toxic in individual cats and in kittens. Most insecticidal products cannot be used on kittens less than two to three months of age. In such cases, light applications of pyrethrin or pyrethroid sprays or shampoos are preferred.

Most shampoos are, in general, ineffective for flea control. They lack residual activity. The often routine shampooing of cats prior to application of parasiticidal dips is not necessary and may be contraindicated, in that it removes skin surface lipid film (a fatlike substance) in which the dips may be soluble.

Powders (pyrethrin and carbamate) are effective, especially for shorthair cats, and should be applied two or three times weekly. Powders tend to be drying and may produce a dull, dry coat and varying degrees of sebborrhea sicca. They may also be irritating to the oral and respiratory mucosa of some cats and humans.

Sprays are effective and should be applied daily or as needed. Pressurized sprays may cause a significant "startle" reaction in the patient, and alcohol-containing sprays can be irritating to the skin. The frequent application of some pyrethrin products to cats can cause toxicity. Pump-action sprays, and those that do not contain alcohol, tend to be better tolerated.

Dips are effective, especially in longhair cats, and are applied weekly. Many cats resent getting wet, and dips can be quite drying. The drying effect can be countered, if needed, by adding one capful of Alpha Keri bath oil, or a similar emollient, per gallon of dipping solution. No feline toxicities have been seen with the approved commercial d-limonene (citrus oil) dips, but neither has there been any appreciable efficacy against fleas.

Flea collars (including the ultrasonic type), oral thiamine (vitamin B$_1$), oral brewer's yeast, oral garlic, and oral sulphur are rarely beneficial in the control of fleas on cats.

The cumulative toxic effects of insecticides are often overlooked. Insecticides from the same class should never be used in different forms on the same animal. For example, organophosphate dips should not be used on a cat wearing an organophosphate flea collar. This principle also applies to insecticides used on the premises. Using carbamate powder on the cat and organophosphate sprays or foggers in the cat's environment may result in toxicity. Cats with flea-bite hypersensitivity may require the occasional or chronic use of systemic glucocorticoids (a type of steroid) to control their dermatitis. Hyposensitization with aqueous whole flea extract has not been very effective. The procedure is time-consuming, expensive, and effective in fewer than 10 percent of cases.

Indoor flea control is most successfully achieved by a multiphasic approach that combines the use of insecticides with premise clean-up. Because flea eggs and pupae are very resistant to insecticides, thorough house-cleaning should be performed first. Thorough vacuuming (with napthalene crystals or crushed mothballs or dichlorvos-impregnated resin strips in the vacuum bag) is very helpful. Second, because the mist of foggers does not penetrate unexposed areas, all cracks, baseboards, closets, and areas beneath furniture should be sprayed with a nonstaining residual insecticide. Thirdly, fogging with a combined adulticide-larvicide product should be done twice at a two-week interval, and then bimonthly or as needed throughout the flea season.

Outdoor flea control is also best accomplished by a multiphasic approach. The outdoor flea-control program should be performed at the same time as the indoor treatments. Sanitary upkeep of these areas includes mowing, raking, and removal of organic debris. There are many insecticidal sprays and dusts available for outdoor use. These are generally applied once or twice monthly during flea season.

Flea bites in hypersensitive humans produce a variety of skin lesions. The typical lesion is an urticarial papule (hives). A tiny hemorrhagic punctum (small blood-spot) is often present in the center of the urticarial lesion, and vesicles (blisters) may surmount the papular lesions. Widespread lesions are common in children. In adults, lesions are fewer in number and characteristically occur in groups of three. Lesions favor exposed extremities and are severely pruritic.

....

FLIES

Myiasis

Myiasis is an uncommon dermatosis of cats and is caused by the larvae of various blowflies and fleshflies. Adult blowflies lay clusters of light yellow eggs in wounds, soiled hair, or carcasses, being attracted by the odor of decomposing matter. Larvae hatch from eggs in eight to seventy-two hours and reach full size in two to nineteen days. Full-grown larvae are grayish-white or pale yellow in color and "hairy" or "smooth." Larvae pupate in the ground, in dry parts of a carcass, or even in the hair of live animals. Larvae produce proteolytic (protein-splitting) enzymes and damage the skin. Myiasis is a seasonal, warm-weather disease, and is most commonly seen in debilitated cats, especially those with neglected wounds, matted hair coats, and feces- or urine-soiled hair coats and skin.

Myiasis has no apparent age, breed, or sex predilections. It most commonly involves the skin around the anus, genitals, eyes, and on the dorsal midline (over the backbone). Lesions are characterized by multiple "punched-out" ulcers that coalesce to produce large ulcers with scalloped edges. Large sections of skin may become undermined and may be seen to "crawl" with the large numbers of maggots. A nauseating odor is usually striking. Heavy flystrikes may cause death by toxicosis.

Therapy includes correcting predisposing causes; gentle clipping and cleansing; removal of larvae by flushing and manual means; and supportive and symptomatic care. Pyrethrin shampoos or sprays (non-alcoholic) may be used to kill the larvae.

Cuterebriasis

Cuterebriasis is an occasional seasonal disorder of cats, most commonly affecting kittens and young cats during the summer months. Adult *Cuterebra* fly species lay eggs in the soil or on plants near the entrances of rabbit and rodent burrows. Larvae may then penetrate the skin of their normal hosts, or of an occasional cat, and develop in subcutaneous cysts. Larvae usually remain in these cats for about one month, then leave to pupate on the ground.

Skin lesions of feline cuterebriasis consist of firm subcutaneous nodules, which become fluctuant (fluid-filled) and develop fistulae (central breathing holes), through which a blood-tinged discharge exudes and the brownish, spiny larva can be seen moving. These lesions usually occur in the neck or lower jaw areas, and are usually single and asymptomatic, but may occasionally be multiple or result in abscesses. Larvae may also parasitize the cranial cavity, nostrils, spinal column, or scrotum.

Diagnosis is based on history and physical examination. Occasionally, the larvae will have dropped out before the cat is seen, and the clinician will be presented with a slowly-healing wound or abscess with a tell-tale circular hole.

Veterinary therapy consists of removing the larva (about 2 to 3 centimeters long, or ¾ to over 1 inch) and symptomatic wound care. The larva is gently extracted with a forceps, enlarging the breathing hole if necessary. Care should be taken not to rupture the larva *in situ* (in the wound), because an anaphylactic reaction (exaggerated allergic reaction) may occur.

The Internal Cat

Tyger! Tyger! burning bright
In the forests of the night,
What immortal hand or eye
Could frame thy fearful symmetry?...

When the stars threw down their spears,
And water'd heaven with their tears,
Did He smile His work to see?
Did He who made the lamb make thee?

—William Blake, "The Tyger"

Circulatory System and Disorders

The circulatory system includes the heart, blood vessels (arteries, arterioles, venules, veins, capillaries), blood, and spleen. This system is responsible for transporting oxygen and nutrients to all body organs; transporting carbon dioxide and metabolic wastes to the excretory organs (e.g., lungs, kidneys); transporting hormones and enzymes throughout the body; regulating the body's temperature; and fighting infectious diseases. Also included in this discussion is the lymphatic system, an interconnecting network of vessels and specialized structures called lymph nodes, which is responsible for removing fluid from tissue spaces and returning it to the bloodstream.

The *endocardium* is a thin, serous membrane (a lining tissue which emits a watery secretion) that lines the internal cavities of the heart, while the *epicardium* covers the outer surface. The *myocardium* is the muscular layer of the heart. The *pericardium* is a serous membrane that encapsulates the heart. The pericardium prevents rapid changes in heart size, prevents excessive mobility of the heart, and protects the heart against the spread of infections within the chest cavity.

The heart has four chambers: left and right *atria* (upper chambers) and right and left *ventricles* (lower chambers). Between the heart chambers and main blood vessels are valves that control blood flow, maintaining one-directional flow. Within the ventricles are *chordae tendineae* (tendinous strings) that connect the *papillary muscles* (conical muscular projections on the ventricle walls) of the ventricles to the *valve leaflets* (cusp of the heart valve). The chordae tendineae and papillary muscles function to properly open and close the valves. The *septum,* a muscular wall, separates the two sides of the heart.

CIRCULATORY SYSTEM

Heart

The heart of a mature cat is about the size of a small plum. The heart wall is composed of various layers.

The right atrium receives deoxygenated blood from the *cranial* and *caudal venae cavae* (large, primary veins). The blood then flows through the *tricuspid valve* and enters the right ventricle. The right ventricle contracts, pumping blood through the *pulmonic* (pertaining to the lungs) *valve* into the *pulmonary artery,* which enters the lungs. The blood exchanges the carbon dioxide, which is a waste product from metabolism, for oxygen. The carbon dioxide is exhaled via the respiratory system. The oxygenated blood travels through the pulmonary veins and enters the left atrium. The blood then flows through the *mitral valve* into the left ventricle. When the left ventricle contracts, it expels the blood through the *aortic valve* into the *aorta.* The blood then travels through smaller and smaller arteries into arterioles, finally reaching the capillaries to exchange oxygen for carbon dioxide with the body's cells. The blood then returns to the heart through a series of venules (very small veins) and veins into the cranial and caudal venae cavae, back to the right atrium.

The contraction and relaxation of the heart is controlled by electrical impulses. Sodium and calcium ions, which are atoms that lose or gain electrons, cause positive or negative charges and influence the conductivity of electrical impulses within the cells (i.e., repolarization and depolarization). The *sinoatrial* (SA) *node,* located between the cranial vena cava and right atrium, is the heart's natural pacemaker. The SA node generates the initial electrical impulse, which is then transmitted to the *atrioventricular node* (located between the right and left atria). After a brief delay, the signal is sent to the *bundle of His* (small band of heart muscle fibers that propagate the atrial contraction rhythm to the ventricles), the bundle branches, and finally to the *Purkinje fibers,* which are modified muscles in the heart tissue that transmit impulses. The electrical impulses generated by the SA node can be affected by the central nervous system; by concentrations of metabolites (products of metabolism), electrolytes (substances capable of ionizing), and hormones; and by certain drugs. The voltage produced by the cardiac muscle cells during depolarization and repolarization can be analyzed by veterinarians with the use of an electrocardiogram (ECG).

A cat's heart normally beats from 120 to 240 times per minute. Strenuous exercise, stress, excitement, or fever will accelerate the number of times the heart contracts to keep up with the body's demand for oxygenated blood.

The pulse is a reflection of the heartbeat. The procedure used to take a cat's pulse is simple; however, a cat's pulse may be more difficult to locate than a human pulse because it is weaker. First, locate the *femoral artery* (on the inside of the hind leg). Carefully press with your fingers along the inside thigh until you feel a pulsating sensation. Once you locate the throb of the femoral artery, count the number of times you feel the pulsations within one minute (or take a reading for fifteen seconds and multiply by four to get the number of heartbeats per minute). Also, the pulse can be taken by feeling the heartbeat through the rib cage.

Another indicator of a healthy, or unhealthy, circulatory system is the color of the gums or tongue. A bluish-gray color (cyanosis) is indicative of insufficient oxygen in the blood, which may be related to heart-lung problems.

Blood

The average mature cat has about 65 ml (2.2 ounces) of blood per kilogram (2.2 pounds) of body weight. Red blood cells, white blood cells, platelets, and plasma are the "ingredients" of blood. Each component plays an integral part in the body's well-being and health.

ERYTHROCYTES (red blood cells). These yellowish, concave, disk-shaped blood cells contain *hemoglobin* (an iron-containing compound protein), which gives them their red color. They are produced, along with their hemoglobin, in the bone marrow. Oxygen inhaled by the lungs binds to the hemoglobin for transportation to the body's cells. The erythrocytes also transport food—which the digestive system has reduced to molecular forms of carbohydrates, fats, and proteins—to the cells, and metabolic waste products (urea, carbon dioxide) for excretion via the liver, kidneys, and lungs.

LEUKOCYTES (white blood cells). Leukocytes come in many forms, but all are responsible for defending the body against disease-causing agents such as bacteria, viruses, and parasites. Most leukocytes are produced in the bone marrow. The types and functions of the various white blood cells are:

Neutrophils. Neutrophils *phagocytize* (surround

and digest) bacteria and other foreign particles. Usually they are destroyed in the process.

Eosinophils. These white blood cells function to detoxify, especially to contain allergic reactions and to suppress parasitic infections. In comparison to neutrophils, their phagocytic abilities are limited. They are not as effective in destroying bacteria.

Basophils. These white blood cells, together with mast cells (connective tissue cells), contain *histamine* and *serotonin,* chemicals that affect dilation of the blood vessels, contraction of the smooth muscles, gastric (stomach) secretions, the heart rate, and *heparin,* an anticoagulant. Histamines also promote hypersensitivity reactions. The number of basophils in the blood seems to be regulated by the pituitary, adrenal, and thyroid glands.

Monocytes. Monocytes are larger in size than other white blood cells. They can rapidly engulf and destroy bacteria, and are capable of destroying fungi and protozoa. Monocytes contain *lysozyme* and other bactericidal substances that aid in destroying pathogens.

Lymphocytes. These unique white blood cells are distributed in the lymph nodes, spleen, tonsils, thymus gland, bone marrow, and blood. Unlike the other white blood cells, they recirculate. The T-cell lymphocytes function in cell-mediated immune responses (immune responses activated by the aid of the cell), which include delayed hypersensitivity, graft rejection, and acquired resistance to infectious organisms. The B-cell lymphocytes synthesize and secrete antibodies, which are functionally manifested by immediate hypersensitivity reactions and by antibody-mediated protection against infectious organisms.

PLATELETS. Platelets assist in the clotting mechanism. Platelets are formed by the breakup or fragmentation of megakaryocytes, which are large cells that are produced in the bone marrow.

PLASMA. This liquid composes 60 to 70 percent of the blood. Proteins, minerals, and sugars make up the plasma, in which the other blood components are suspended. The proteins in the plasma help in blood clotting and in fighting disease.

Blood Vessels

The blood vessels provide a transportation network throughout the body for blood. The arteries are muscular vessels that maintain pressure, thus assisting in the circulation of oxygenated blood through the body. Arterioles are smaller arteries. The capillaries are very small vessels that connect the arteries and veins, thereby forming a complete network for blood flow. The venules (small veins) and veins carry deoxygenated blood to the pulmonary vena cava to return to the heart for recirculation.

Spleen

The spleen, located in the abdomen, has a connective tissue capsule and internal fibromuscular bands (trabeculae) that support it. These trabeculae enable the spleen to contract, thus making blood volume changes possible.

The spleen filters and removes old, damaged blood cells and platelets from the bloodstream and acts as a reservoir for extra red blood cells.

If the spleen is removed, most of its functions will be performed by other blood-forming tissues, which are primarily lymph nodes and bone marrow.

Lymphatic System

The lymphatic system is composed of a highly specialized interconnecting network of lymphatic vessels that transport lymph from all body tissues back to the heart through the venous side of the circulatory system. Lymph is a clear admixture of excess tissue fluid, proteins, solutes, and large molecular particles. Lymph travels from the peripheral perivascular (around a vessel) spaces to regional lymph nodes and through lymphatic vessels back into the venous side of the circulatory system. Lymph nodes are specialized collections of cells, which act as filters for the lymph, removing foreign particles that are then subjected to destruction by the immune system. The lymphatic and immune systems are of great importance in protecting the body against invasion by microbial agents, cancer, and autoimmune (self-attacking) diseases.

DISORDERS AND DISEASES

Heart

Heart disease may be well advanced before the problem is noticed, due partially to the sedentary life style adopted by indoor cats. Early recognition of the typical signs of heart disease can help. Kittens with congenital heart defects grow slowly, are less active, have labored breathing, are in generally poor condition, and have a throbbing heartbeat.

If the left side of the heart is affected, the common signs include *dyspnea* (labored breathing) and noisy breathing. However, if the right side is affected, the cat may have a potbellied appearance due to fluid accumulation.

Shunts, which are bypasses of the normal route of the blood, and faulty valves cause heart murmurs. The murmur is the sound created when blood rushes through an opening that is either smaller or larger than normal.

Congenital Heart Diseases

These are diseases that are present at the time of birth. The incidence of congenital heart disease is low, occurring only in 1 to 2 percent of kittens born. Generally, the Siamese breed seems to be afflicted with a heritable predisposition to several of the congenital heart diseases.

ENDOCARDIAL FIBROELASTOSIS (EFE). This defect most commonly occurs in the Siamese and Burmese breeds. It is characterized by an enlarged left ventricle wall and the conversion of the endocardium into a thick fibroelastic membrane. Sometimes the leaflets of the aortic valve are irregular in size and thickened.

Kittens with EFE will have difficulty in breathing, sometimes breathing with their mouths open. These signs are first noticeable between the ages of three weeks and four months. Sudden death with no apparent signs can occur. Treatment is rarely successful.

ATRIOVENTRICULAR (AV) VALVE MALFORMATIONS. Defects of the mitral and tricuspid valves occur more commonly in the cat than in most species of animals. Cats may have valves that are unusually thick or misshapen, or valves that are improperly attached to the heart wall. Each of these defects renders the valve incompetent of performing its function. The signs indicate the side of the heart that is affected.

Treatment includes medicating with diuretics (agents that promote urination) to reduce the work of the heart, and perhaps digitalis to strengthen the heart muscle. In many cases, the kitten is presented to the veterinarian too late for treatment.

PATENT DUCTUS ARTERIOSUS (PDA). The ductus arteriosus is a vessel that connects the pulmonary trunk and aorta in the fetus, allowing oxygenated blood to bypass the fetus's nonfunctional lungs. PDA is a persistent opening of this fetal connection after birth. Normally the fetal ductus will anatomically close within three days after birth. If PDA is present, signs can occur from one month to five years of age.

The veterinarian's diagnosis is made by hearing a murmur, seeing changes in the electrocardiograph, and interpreting results from contrast radiography of the heart.

Treatment consists of surgical ligation (closing) of the PDA. A normal life can be expected if the surgery is performed early and if the vessel does not reopen. Without surgery, the prognosis is very poor.

SEPTAL DEFECTS. Septal defects are openings that occur in the septum. Ventricular septal defects are openings between the right and left ventricles that allow inappropriate blood flow from the left to the right ventricle (shunt). This is one of the more common congenital defects occurring in the cat. Also, atrial septal defects can occur. These are openings between the right and left atria.

Frequently, no unusual signs indicating illness are observed. However, if signs are present, usually they take the form of respiratory complaints, such as labored breathing or coughing.

The tests used by a veterinarian to detect septal defects include radiography of the lungs and heart, echocardiography (ultrasonic test), and cardiac catheterization with selective angiography (a form of radiography that utilizes a radiopaque dye to visualize the blood vessels and changes of the heart).

Medical treatment consists of diuretics and digitalis (an agent that increases the strength of the heartbeat while decreasing the rate). Prognosis is poor if the shunt is sizable, since surgery to remedy the problem is not currently feasible in the cat.

AORTIC AND PULMONIC STENOSIS. Stenosis is a narrowing at or near the valve. *Aortic stenosis* (constriction of the aortic valve) limits blood flow from the left ventricle. The left ventricle must work harder to provide the necessary blood circulation required by the body, which causes increases in size of the heart muscle (hypertrophy). Signs are the same as for left-sided heart failure: labored and noisy breathing.

Pulmonic stenosis, which affects the pulmonic valve, has the same effect on the right ventricle. Hence, signs are indicative of right-side heart failure: a potbellied appearance when fluid fills the abdomen.

Surgery is the only method used to treat stenosis. Because it requires specialized equipment, it is not readily available.

TETRALOGY (four concurrent defects) OF FALLOT. This is a multiple cardiac defect, which includes pulmonic stenosis; dextroposition of the aorta so that it overrides the interventricular septum and receives venous as well as arterial blood; right ventricular hypertrophy; and ventricular septal defect. Blood shunts from the right to the left ventricle, bypassing the lungs.

Signs of the disorder typically include weakness, cyanotic (bluish) appearance of skin, exercise intolerance, and poor growth and weight gain. Diagnostic procedures performed by a veterinarian may include electrocardiography, echocardiography, and radiography. Treatment may be medical (i.e., drug therapy) or surgical. However, the surgical procedure is complex and requires sophisticated equipment. Prognosis is guarded.

PERSISTENT RIGHT AORTIC ARCH. This congenital defect is a rare deformity in the cat. During fetal development, the aorta is constructed from the right fourth embryonic arch rather than from the left. The result is that the aorta forms to the right of the trachea and esophagus. Because the pulmonary veins develop normally (over the left side of the trachea and esophagus), the esophagus becomes constricted between the major blood vessels. Vomiting results from this strangulation. Surgery will remedy the problem.

Acquired Heart Diseases

These heart diseases are not present at the time of birth, but can develop during the cat's lifetime. They can be of primary or secondary origin.

ARRHYTHMIAS (variations from normal heartbeat). Changes in cardiac electrical impulses disturb the natural rhythm of the heart, thereby causing a variety of arrhythmias. Oxygen deficiency to the heart muscle, acid-base imbalances, electrolyte imbalances, drugs, toxins, and heart disease can cause arrhythmias.

Alterations in serum potassium (potassium levels in the blood) are responsible for a majority of cardiac irregularities that occur with electrolyte imbalances. Imbalances in calcium, sodium, hydrogen, and magnesium can cause critical changes in cardiac conductivity.

Atrial and ventricular premature beats occur when there is an early electrical discharge that does not originate with the SA node (the natural pacemaker). They are frequently observed in cats that have *hypokalemia* (a low level of serum potassium). Hypokalemia can occur from chronic bouts of severe vomiting or diarrhea, or excessive urinary loss due to kidney disease, diuretics, or insulin (in diabetic cats). Treatment by the veterinarian is based on correcting the underlying cause of hypokalemia (e.g., gastrointestinal problems, kidney disease), and administering potassium supplements.

Atrial and/or ventricular fibrillation occurs when the heart sends erratic electrical impulses, preventing complete contraction of the heart muscle. Atrial fibrillation is unusual in the cat, probably because of the small heart size. However, when it occurs, it is usually associated with hypertrophic cardiomyopathy (enlarged heart muscle).

Bradycardia (a slower than normal heart rate) most commonly occurs in cats with urethral obstruction (blockage of the urinary tract). The obstruction causes an electrolyte imbalance (excessive serum potassium) and metabolic acidosis, which slows the heart rate. Severe bradycardia and conduction disturbance in this setting must be treated as an emergency, for death will soon occur.

Tachycardia (a faster than normal heart rate) can be caused by *hyperthyroidism* (excessive functional activity of the thyroid gland), certain congenital defects, and *bacterial endocarditis* (inflammation of the lining of the heart). Tachycardia may also be associated with fear, stress, anemia, or fever.

Usually, decreased cardiac output is associated with arrhythmias, causing reduced blood flow to the brain, spleen, and kidneys. Antiarrhythmic drugs are helpful in treating arrhythmias, but treatment is best focused on correcting the underlying cause of the arrhythmia.

ACQUIRED VALVULAR HEART DISEASES. These are disorders in which one or more of the valves is affected by a primary pathologic process. They can be caused by degenerative processes, systemic bacterial infections, and chronic dental infections. Diseases affecting the valves cause the valves' edges to thicken and shrink (contract) so they do not close completely (leaky valve), and this results in regurgitation of blood. Congestive heart failure can result.

Although bacterial endocarditis occurs infrequently in the cat, when it does occur the left valves are usually affected. Typical signs of infection include fever, lethargy, and loss of appetite.

Broad-spectrum antibiotics are administered to treat infections. However, if heart damage occurs from the infection, your veterinarian may prescribe cardiac drugs or diuretics to assist in cardiac function. The prognosis is fair if bacterial endocarditis is treated early.

MYOCARDIAL DISEASES:

Cardiomyopathy. Cardiomyopathies are primary diseases that affect the heart muscle. The ultimate result is an inability of the heart to compensate for stress, and heart failure may occur. Inheritance, viral infections, autoimmune mechanisms, biochemical disorders, and diet deficiencies (e.g., insufficient taurine) are factors that may contribute to the development of cardiomyopathies.

Cardiomyopathies are subdivided into hypertrophic, dilated, and restrictive. However, an increasing number of cats is being recognized with cardiac disease that cannot be classified into just these three categories. Middle-aged male cats and certain breeds seem more predisposed to cardiomyopathies. Generally, the observed signs of labored breathing, lameness or paralysis, lethargy, and *ascites* (accumulation of fluid in the abdomen) are a result of cardiac arrhythmias, congestive heart failure, or blood clots. In advanced stages collapse may occur. This occurs when a partial or complete temporary suspension of respiration or circulation results from obstructed arterial blood flow.

Hypertrophic Cardiomyopathy (HCM). HCM is the most common form of acquired heart disease in the cat, and it predominately affects young to middle-aged male cats. It is the enlargement of the left ventricular wall, papillary muscles, and septum, which limits the size of the left ventricular chamber. This type of enlargement prevents the heart from expanding (to receive blood) adequately, thus decreasing cardiac output. The incidence of blood clots is somewhat greater than in other forms of cardiomyopathy. The

dynamics of this clotting directly relate to the restricted ventricular filling, which allows the blood to remain for a longer period of time in the left atrium, thereby having a greater chance of forming blood clots.

Signs indicative of HCM include labored and noisy breathing, lethargy, loss of appetite, and possible lameness or paralysis of the hind legs due to arterial blood clots.

Prognosis is fair if arrhythmias and clots can be controlled medically. Treatment by the veterinarian consists of dosages of negative inotropes (substances that affect the force of muscle contractions), diuretics, and carefully controlled doses of aspirin.

Dilated Cardiomyopathy (DCM). DCM occurs primarily in middle-aged to older cats. Also, there is an increased incidence of DCM in Siamese, Abyssinian, and Burmese breeds.

DCM is the enlargement of all the heart's chambers. This enlargement of the ventricles and atria stretches the heart muscle cells, thereby creating thinner, weaker heart walls.

Studies have proven that a deficiency of taurine (an essential amino acid) in the diet can cause DCM. Cat food manufacturers have added additional sources of taurine to cat food to meet the new recommended taurine level.

Treatment by the veterinarian consists of taurine, positive inotropes to strengthen the heart muscle, and diuretics to remove excess body fluid. Usually, if treatment is given in a timely fashion, the cats recover. The incidence of this disease has declined greatly since taurine has been added to cat food.

Congestive heart failure (CHF) commonly results as the disease progresses, especially if it is untreated or unmanageable. CHF is characterized by lethargy and weakness due to reduced cardiac output. If the right ventricle or both ventricles have compromised function, fluid accumulates in the thorax (pleural fluid) and minimally in the abdomen (ascites). Cardiogenic shock or a fatal arrhythmia can cause sudden death in CHF.

Restrictive Cardiomyopathy (endocardial fibrosis). Restrictive cardiomyopathy is not common in the cat. In this disease, fibrous tissue covers the heart muscle, causing rigidity of the heart. This impedes the ability of the heart to expand and contract. Older cats are predominantly affected.

Diuretics and digitalis are used in treatment. Also,

a low-salt diet may be of benefit. The long-term prognosis is guarded.

DIAGNOSIS OF CARDIOMYOPATHIES. Diagnostic tests that may be performed by a veterinarian include electrocardiogram, radiography, serum chemistries, and hemogram (includes blood counts, packed cell volume, percent of hemoglobin). These tests do not necessarily help in differentiating between the various types of cardiomyopathies; however, they can provide vital information on the function of other organs. This information is important in determining appropriate methods of treatment.

Sophisticated tests that can be performed at progressive small-animal clinics or at veterinary college clinics are echocardiography and angiocardiography. These tests can differentiate between the various types of cardiomyopathy.

DRUGS USED IN TREATMENT. Treatment is directed at reducing the workload on the heart and improving oxygenation of blood. Therapy regimen varies according to the type and severity of the cardiomyopathy. Also, a low-sodium diet can be beneficial to the patient by preventing fluid retention. Some of the drugs used by the veterinarian follow:

Furosemide is a diuretic that is prescribed for feline patients experiencing pulmonary edema (lungs filling up with fluid). Diuretics act primarily by blocking reabsorption of sodium.

Digitalis increases the strength of contractions by the heart and reduces the heart rate. Therefore, this drug is used to control atrial tachyarrhythmias (rapid, irregular heart rhythm) and improve cardiac performance. The veterinarian must maintain close supervision of dosage since toxicity can easily occur. An acute onset of vomiting, loss of appetite, and diarrhea are signs of toxicity.

Vasodilators (e.g., nitroglycerin, hydralazine, and captopril) influence the blood vessels, usually by decreasing peripheral vascular resistance (restricted blood circulation in the extremities). This effect is particularly important in counteracting the vasoconstriction that occurs in heart failure. Vasodilators help in preventing the onset of pulmonary edema by reducing pulmonary venous pressure.

Propranolol improves the filling of the ventricles by prolonging the atrioventricular conduction time. When combined with Digoxin, it will decrease the ventricular rate in atrial fibrillation. Propranolol should not be used in cats with asthma, bradycardia, and some types of heart failure.

Dobutamine (i.e., Dobutex) is used for acute heart failure and is given intravenously by the veterinarian.

SECONDARY MYOCARDIAL DISEASES:

Infectious myocarditis is an inflammation of the heart muscle caused by direct invasion of an infectious agent, such as a bacterium, fungus, virus, or protozoan. Treatment consists of diuretics and antithrombic drugs (anticoagulants).

KIDNEY DISEASE. When the kidneys are diseased they cannot perform their functions adequately. This dysfunction affects the cardiovascular system. Kidneys produce *erythropoietin,* a hormone that stimulates red blood cell production. Kidney disease decreases the production of erythropoietin, resulting in anemia. Anemia stimulates the circulatory system to increase circulation. (For information on anemia, *see* "Blood," page 195.)

When the kidneys are unable to remove wastes, a toxic buildup of urea occurs. The toxins stimulate bouts of vomiting and diarrhea, causing a loss of potassium. This loss is further aggravated when additional potassium is lost in the urine. The resulting hypokalemia causes atrial and ventricular premature beats.

Finally, *hypertension* (abnormally high blood pressure) occurs because the kidneys are unable to excrete adequate amounts of sodium. The retained sodium causes fluid retention by the body and circulatory congestion. Chronic hypertension causes hypertrophy of the heart because the heart must work harder to perform its job when counteracting the effects of hypertension.

Treatment consists of diuretics to assist in fluid removal, propranolol, and a vasodilator such as hydralazine.

HYPERKINETIC CIRCULATORY DISORDERS. These are cardiovascular diseases that cause increased cardiac output in the presence of congestive heart failure. Cardiac output is based on heart rate and blood volume from contraction of the left ventricle. The causes include hyperthyroidism, severe chronic anemia, and arteriovenous fistula.

Hyperthyroidism. Hyperthyroid cats secrete excessive amounts of the hormone thyroxine. Thyroxine directly increases the body's metabolic rate and heart rate. Because of the increased metabolic rate and oxygen consumption caused by hyperthyroidism, more heat is produced, resulting in the expansion of blood vessels (vasodilation). Hence, blood flow through the blood vessels increases. As a result, the blood volume handled by the heart is increased and hyperthyroidism increases the heart rate. Because of increased heart rate and the demand to meet the increased peripheral-tissue oxygen need, cardiac work is increased. Over a period of time hypertrophy of the heart occurs.

Approximately 50 percent of hyperthyroid cats have increased heart size as detected by ECG, radiographically, or echocardiographically. (*See* Chapter 27: Endocrine System and Metabolic Disorders.)

Anemia. Severe chronic anemia stimulates an increase in circulation to compensate for the reduction of oxygen-carrying red blood cells by increasing blood circulation. This is accomplished by increasing the heart rate and increasing the diameter of blood vessels (vasodilation).

Treatment is directed at correcting the underlying cause.

Arteriovenous Fistula. Arteriovenous fistula is an abnormal, direct junction between an artery and vein in the absence of a capillary. Congenital defects—and on rare occasions, penetrating wounds—can cause AV fistulas. Cardiac output is increased if the shunt is large, due to blood volume overload. The occurrence of AV fistulas in cats is low.

Treatment is to surgically close all arteriovenous communications. If congestive heart failure existed before surgery, drugs are administered to control the problem.

PERICARDIAL DISEASE. Cats rarely suffer from this malady. However, feline infectious peritonitis (FIP) and congestive heart failure are the most common causes for acquired pericardial disease. The primary manifestation of this disease is *cardiac tamponade* (compression of the heart due to the filling of the pericardium with fluid). This constricts the heart and decreases its ability to expand and contract. Echocardiography is a conclusive diagnostic procedure.

Treatment is based on establishing and then treating the cause. Initially, a *pericardiocentesis* (removal of pericardial fluid via needle aspiration by a veterinarian) is done to relieve the pressure. The removed fluid can be analyzed to help determine the cause of the fluid infiltration into the pericardium. Drugs that may be used include antibiotics, steroids, and diuretics. Surgery may be necessary to alleviate constrictive pericarditis. If FIP is the cause, the prognosis is poor.

HEARTWORM DISEASE. Fortunately, the cat is not the preferred host of the parasite, *Dirofilaria*. However, this disease does occur in cats. (*See* Chapter 31: Internal Parasites.)

Blood Vessels

Various problems can plague blood vessels, such as a blockage caused by a blood clot, or increased pressure from hypertension.

ARTERIAL THROMBOEMBOLISM. The artery becomes blocked by a blood clot (embolus) that breaks free from the site of formation. Causes include cardiomyopathy, congenital heart disease, bacterial endocarditis, trauma to the heart (e.g., heart surgery, cardiac catheterization, penetrating chest injuries), or injury to the aorta or peripheral arteries.

Signs of arterial thromboembolism relate to the area(s) that is obstructed. For example, if the occlusion (blockage) is in the femoral artery, the cat may become lame or paralyzed in that leg as the blood supply is reduced to the tissues; or, if it affects circulation to the brain, the signs are of neurologic origin, such as head tilt, incoordination, and sudden death.

Tests that aid in diagnosis include electrocardiography, angiography, and serum chemistries. Treatment will be based on location of the occlusion and on the cause, but may include anticoagulant and vasodilator drug therapy or platelet suppressants. Follow-up visits are important for monitoring the cat's progress on treatment.

ARTERITIS (vasculitis). This is an inflammation within the wall of an artery, which may be caused secondarily by infectious agents such as feline infectious peritonitis, bacterial endocarditis, heartworms, Rocky Mountain spotted fever, arthritis, or drugs.

The signs depend on the severity of the lesions on the arterial walls and the distribution. Usually, the early signs include lethargy, decreased appetite, weight loss, increased thirst and urination, lameness, and pain. More advanced signs include peripheral neurologic involvement, progressive kidney insufficiency, vomiting, diarrhea, abdominal pain, sudden blindness, and skin ulcerations.

Because the disease is multisystemic, the list is extensive for the diagnostic tests that a veterinarian may perform to determine the primary cause. Treatment is based on the underlying cause.

Blood

Blood, the fluid that circulates through the heart, arteries, capillaries, and veins carries nutrients and oxygen to the body cells and removes waste products of metabolism such as carbon dioxide. Blood consists of a pale yellow liquid (plasma) that contains microscopic formed elements: erythrocytes (red cells), leukocytes (white cells), and thrombocytes (platelets). The red cells and many white cells originate in the bone marrow, while the small white cells (lymphocytes) originate in lymphatic tissues (lymph nodes, thymus gland). The red cells get their color from oxygen-carrying pigment, hemoglobin.

Abnormalities affecting numbers or types of blood elements may be caused by disorders in the blood-forming tissues themselves, by a multitude of disorders elsewhere in the body, or less often in the cat, by deficiencies of nutrients required for blood formation.

DISORDERS OF ERYTHROCYTES (red blood cells). *Anemia.* Anemia is a decrease below normal in the number of red cells. It may be caused by blood loss, as by gastrointestinal bleeding, or by blood-sucking external or internal parasites (e.g., fleas, hookworms). The red cells themselves may be destroyed (hemolysis) by blood parasites (e.g., *Haemobartonella* or *Cytauxzoon*), by drugs or chemicals (e.g., Tylenol, naphthalene mothballs), or by immune processes (*see* Chapter 28: Immune System and Disorders). Finally, the most important cause of anemia in domestic cats is inadequate production of red cells by the bone marrow. The most important depressive influence on the cat's marrow is the feline leukemia virus (FeLV), which also may inhibit production of white cells and platelets. In addition to FeLV, certain drugs may depress marrow function, for example, pyrimethamine, used to treat toxoplasmosis, or chloramphenicol, an antibiotic that is very valuable but potentially toxic in large doses. Inadequate red cell production due to dietary deficiencies is uncommon in cats. Cats get ample iron in food and by swallowing

soil particles when grooming themselves. Deficiencies such as those of vitamin B_{12} and folic acid are of rare natural occurence.

In *blood-loss* and *red-cell destruction anemias,* blood transfusions can be lifesaving until the cause of the anemia can be treated or eliminated. Unhappily, inadequate red cell production due to FeLV cannot be reversed with any measures currently available, and therefore, FeLV-induced anemia has a very poor prognosis, although the lives of affected cats can be prolonged in some cases by blood transfusion and symptomatic treatment for secondary illnesses.

In an FeLV-negative cat whose marrow has been damaged by a toxin or drug, a blood transfusion buys time until the marrow may recover on its own. Sometimes the marrow responds to stimulation with steroids or anabolic hormones. If it does not, a transfusion of marrow from a donor cat may be successful.

Polycythemia. Polycythemia is an increase in the total red cell mass of the blood caused by overactive production of red cells by the marrow. A physiologic compensatory polycythemia can occur in response to a lack of oxygen in the tissues (e.g., in lung or cardiovascular diseases). A relative polycythemia occurs when plasma volume is decreased and the red cells become more concentrated, as in dehydration. True polycythemia is a myeloproliferative disorder of unknown cause in which not only red cells but also white cells and platelets are increased in number. True polycythemia is fairly common in humans but very rare in cats. Good, long-term control is achieved in humans by periodic blood studies and removal of blood as needed to maintain the hematocrit (percentage of red cells in whole blood) at about 45 percent. When platelet numbers increase to a level that poses a danger of forming clots, with a threat of thromboses and embolisms, the patient is treated with a marrow-suppressive drug. In occasional cases, true polycythemia ultimately develops into leukemia.

Blood Parasites. Haemobartonella felis, Babesia, and *Cytauxzoon felis* are parasites that destroy the erythrocytes. This destruction results in anemia. (*See* Chapter 30: Bacterial Diseases, and Chapter 31: Internal Parasites.)

DISORDERS OF LEUKOCYTES (white blood cells). *Septicemia* (blood poisoning). The white cells are an important body defense against threats of many kinds, especially injury and infection. They rally rapidly to the site of a bite wound or foreign object where they engulf infectious organisms, products of degeneration, and other particulate matter. When the challenge is localized, the response may be localized, but in systemic infection, especially if bacteria and their toxins are present in the bloodstream (septicemia), the total number of leukocytes may increase rapidly and spectacularly, with young cellular forms appearing in considerable numbers. In overwhelming cases of septicemia, however, the total of white blood cells may fall below normal—a grave sign. Although leukocytes often fight off infection on their own, serious or persistent infections require antibiotic treatment. Often an antibiotic is chosen on the basis of a veterinarian's experience, but a culture (of pus, tissue, or blood) and an antibiotic-sensitivity test may be necessary.

In certain uncommon feline disorders, abnormal structures may be observed microscopically in white blood cells.

Chediak-Higashi Syndrome. This inherited autosomal (non-sex-linked) recessive trait has been reported in Persians. The normal Blue Smoke Persian has copper-colored irises. Affected Blue Smoke Persians have yellow-green irises with an unusual basket-weave pattern. Microscopically, there are characteristic round, eosinophilic inclusions (granules) occurring in neutrophils, lymphocytes, and eosinophils. These inclusions have not been associated with an increased susceptibility to infections in affected cats. However, a bleeding tendency has been described. Persian cats with this syndrome are not reported to have severe or progressive clinical disease.

Pelger-Huet Disorder. This disorder has been reported to occur in cats. It is characterized by the failure of the nucleus of the granulocyte (a white blood cell) to segment (divide), which may result in impaired granulocyte function.

Mucopolysaccharidoses. This group of inherited disorders in the cat is characterized by inclusions (granules) in neutrophils and lymphocytes. The basis of these disorders is an enzyme deficiency.

Leukemia. Leukemia is a form of myeloproliferative disease or cancer that causes a transformation (malignancy) of the white blood cells (leukocytes). The abnormal leukocytes reproduced in the bone marrow in excess numbers choke off red blood cell production and are incapable of providing protection against pathogens invading the body. Feline leukemia virus (FeLV) is the most common cause of leukemia in the cat. (*See* Chapter 29: Viral Diseases, and Chapter 33: Cancer.)

MYELOPROLIFERATIVE DISORDERS. These disorders may involve any one of the cell types of the bone marrow. The form they usually take is leukemia, which is characterized according to the proliferating cell involved: granulocytic or myelogenous (neutrophilic series), eosinophilic, or basophilic. Proliferations of red cells (erythremic myelosis) and of platelet precursors (megakaryocytic leukemia) also occur, as do leukemias involving cells not of bone marrow origin (lymphocytes, monocytes, plasma cells, and mast cells). The feline leukemia virus is the cause of most of these leukemias. (*See* Chapter 29: Viral Diseases.)

Signs may include weakness, pale mucous membranes, fever, enlarged lymph nodes, liver, and spleen, as well as bleeding tendency and increased bleeding. Diagnostic tests, performed by a veterinarian, include a complete blood count (CBC), FeLV test, and examination of bone marrow removed through a needle. There are no effective treatments for myeloproliferative disorders in the cat.

The prognosis for all forms of myeloproliferative disease is poor. Unlike lymphosarcoma (lymphoma), which is sometimes treatable, these are not localized tumors but systemic disorders; chemotherapy or irradiation, to be successful, would have to destroy the bone marrow. Research is in progress to develop a procedure in cats for bone marrow transplants by destroying the diseased tissue and then replacing it with healthy bone marrow (as is done in human leukemia).

DISORDERS OF PLATELETS (thrombocytes). *Platelets,* disc-shaped, non-nucleated blood elements from precursor cells *(megakaryocytes)* in the bone marrow, are necessary for proper blood clotting. Therefore, any platelet disorder will affect the clotting time of the blood.

Thrombocytopenia. Premature destruction of platelets or their decreased production causes a decrease in the number of platelets circulating in the blood. The most obvious indications of thrombocytopenia are capillary bleeding, such as from the gums or nose, and purplish areas on the skin. Anemia may also be present.

Diagnostic tests used in differential diagnosis may include platelet count, prothrombin time (coagulation rate), complete blood count (CBC), examination of bone marrow aspirate, and various immunologic tests (e.g., antinuclear antibody [ANA], rheumatoid factor), and Coombs' test. (*See* Appendix C: Diagnostic Tests.)

Initial treatment is to control any associated bleeding. Blood transfusions may be necessary during this stage. Drugs used may include corticosteroids or other immunosuppressive drugs to stimulate platelet production. Surgical removal of the spleen (splenectomy) may be helpful in treatment, since the spleen is the major site of platelet destruction and antiplatelet antibody production.

Follow-up visits are important for monitoring the cat's progress in treatment. Relapses can occur suddenly, triggered by live-virus vaccines, infections, estrus, or pregnancy.

Immune-mediated destruction (caused by an antigen-antibody reaction against host tissue) occurs less frequently in cats than dogs. However, when it does occur the underlying causes can be autoimmune diseases such as systemic lupus erythematosus, tumors, or infectious agents. (*See* Chapter 28: Immune System and Disorders.)

Nonimmunologic destruction or injury of platelets can occur from modified live-virus vaccines, vascular diseases, certain drugs, and certain infectious agents such as Rocky Mountain spotted fever.

Decreased production of platelets can be caused by bone marrow suppression, feline leukemia virus, chemical toxins, immune-mediated diseases, or radiation. Of the diagnostic tests, the bone marrow examination is the most definitive for this disorder.

Thrombocytosis. This disorder is an abnormal increase in the platelets circulating in the bloodstream. Thrombocytosis can be caused by myeloproliferative disorders, rheumatoid arthritis, cirrhosis of the liver, osteomyelitis, malignant tumors, or release of platelets from the spleen.

Signs and diagnostic tests are the same as for thrombocytopenia; however, the test results are the opposite. Treatment is directed at the primary cause.

MISCELLANEOUS DISORDERS OF COAGULATION. Cats rarely have disorders of the blood-clotting mechanism. However, congenital defects causing deficiencies of clotting factors VIII and XII have been reported in the cat. In these cases, a normal clot fails to form and bleeding at a wound site will recur (hemophilia). This condition is treated most effectively by whole-blood or plasma transfusions.

The liver requires vitamin K to produce essential clotting factors (VII, IX, X, and prothrombin). Rodenticides containing coumarin or indanedione compounds destroy vitamin K. If enough vitamin K is destroyed, hemorrhaging can result. Outdoor cats are more susceptible to rodenticide poisioning, since they have a greater opportunity to prey on poisoned rodents or track through poisons. Treatment consists of doses of vitamin K_1 for several days to counter the effect of the rodenticide.

Disseminated intravascular coagulation (DIC) is a secondary complication to a wide variety of other disorders. In DIC, the coagulation factors are activated by the primary disease, thus causing the formation of small clots that block arterioles. The body responds by producing a chemical called plasminogen, which dissolves the clot. However, an anticoagulant is formed from the dissolving process. The ultimate result is hemorrhage. Treatment for DIC is based on correcting the underlying cause.

Lymphatic System

The spleen (a flat, oblong organ in the anterior abdomen), lymph nodes throughout the body, and nests of lymphoid tissue in many organs, together with a network of vessels, constitute the lymphatic system. (*See* Chapter 28: Immune System and Disorders.) This system is important in trapping harmful agents and in forming antibodies. Because the spleen and lymph nodes represent a filtering system, they may become enlarged in infectious diseases, and they are sites of spread from malignant tumors.

TUMORS. The most common tumor of the lymphatic system is lymphosarcoma caused by the feline leukemia virus. (*See* Chapter 29: Viral Diseases.) In the abdomen the spleen and lymph nodes may occasionally be the site of a malignant tumor of blood vessels (hemangiosarcoma). It appears that this tumor does not spread as extensively in cats as it does in dogs.

TRAUMA. Injuries involving the abdomen (e.g., car accidents) may rupture the spleen. Minor cracks heal by themselves; severe hemorrhage is a life-threatening emergency requiring removal of the spleen.

CHYLOTHORAX. Chyle (milky-looking intestinal lymph) is carried by a major lymphatic vessel (the thoracic duct) that empties into the vena cava (large vein) in the chest.

Traumatic rupture or, much more often, obstruction of the thoracic duct due to a variety of causes (heart disease, infectious disease, parasitism, diaphragmatic hernia, tumor), leads to accumulation of chyle in the chest cavity. Expansion of the lungs is increasingly limited, so that the cat breathes with ever more difficulty and may die unless the fluid is drained promptly. It is essential to distinguish chyle from other effusions. Diagnosis is dependent on the history, clinical signs, gross and microscopic examination of chest fluid, and radiography (X rays). Treatment is decided upon once the underlying cause of the disorder has been determined. Specific treatment for the condition includes drainage of fluid from the chest, dietary fat restriction, and cage rest. Patients unresponsive to therapy may require exploratory surgery to identify and repair the underlying cause.

Musculoskeletal System and Disorders

THE MUSCULOSKELETAL SYSTEM

The musculoskeletal system comprises the structural elements that give shape and support to the body and allow for movement of its component parts.

The *skeleton* is the bony frame upon which the soft tissues depend for support. Like muscle, it is composed of living tissue. This tissue is supplied with blood vessels, lymphatic vessels, and nerves. Minerals—calcium, magnesium, phosphorus, fluoride —provide the rigidity characteristic of bone; their deposition in the skeleton represents an important reservoir of these substances for the body. The *bone marrow* is the soft center

of the bones and contains blood-forming elements of the blood vascular system—precursor cells of the red and white blood cells. The *periosteum* is the thin and sensitive outer sheath of the bones, a specialized layer of connective tissue that is an important source of growing bone. *Cartilage* is another type of specialized connective tissue that is important in bone growth

and in the formation of *joints,* where it is referred to as *articular cartilage.* Joints are complex structures that consist of articular cartilage, *ligaments* (strengthening bands of fibrous tissue, for stabilizing joint structure), and a highly effective lubricating substance, *synovial fluid,* which facilitates virtually frictionless movement of one cartilage surface against another.

It is frequently convenient to divide the skeleton into two major parts: the *appendicular skeleton,* composed of the limb bones and pelvis; and the *axial skeleton,* consisting of the vertebrae, skull, ribs, and sternum.

Muscle tissue is composed of bundles of muscle fibers, each of which consists of many *myofibrils* (slender, threadlike tissue) protected by a delicate cell membrane, the *sarcolemma.* Around the sarcolemma are wound layers of connective tissue, which ultimately are continuous with the *tendons* (fibrous cords) that connect muscles to bone, or with the *fasciae* (sheets of fibrous tissue), which sheathe and define the muscles. As with bone, muscles are supplied with blood vessels, lymphatics, and nerves.

There are several different types of muscle. *Skeletal muscle* is under voluntary control of the cat's will and composes most of the muscles of movement attached to the skeleton. *Smooth muscle* is not under voluntary control; this type of muscle services the major internal organs and the blood vessels and is responsible for the normal muscular functioning of these structures. *Cardiac muscle* is a specialized muscle tissue found in the heart. Contractions of cardiac muscle occur without conscious control and are responsible for maintenance of the heartbeat for the general circulation of the blood.

MUSCULOSKELETAL DISORDERS

In general, disorders of the musculoskeletal system—with the notable exception of those caused by traumatic injury—are relatively uncommon in cats. Those that do occur are associated with a variety of underlying problems: congenital, metabolic, infectious, inflammatory, or neoplastic. In some cases, the diagnosis may be readily apparent to both the owner and the veterinarian; in other cases, a clinical and laboratory work-up may be required in order to uncover the cause of illness.

Maxillofacial compression (shortening of the lower and upper jaw) is seen in a number of breeds, including the Burmese, Persian, Himalayan, and Angora. This trait has been exaggerated by purposely inbreeding lines of cats showing these accentuated *brachycephalic* (flat-faced) characteristics. The result is that many of these animals are born with attendant problems such as cleft palate or develop abnormalities of tooth eruption or suffer from chronic upper respiratory or ocular disease. An extreme example of this is seen in the "new look" strain of Burmese cats, in which nearly a quarter of the kittens born to "new look" parents are affected with a lethal birth defect. The principal features of this defect involve *exencephaly* (the brain bulging through the skull), involuted eyelids secondary to ocular degeneration, absence of nasal tissue, and presence of four whisker pads. The defect is inherited in an autosomal dominant fashion. For other congenital causes, *see* Chapter 14: Normal Development and Congenital Birth Defects.

Metabolic Diseases

Metabolic diseases involve imbalances in the normal physiological processes of the body. A number of these disorders are dietary in origin, caused by a deficiency or an excess of a certain nutrient, mineral, or vitamin. Others are secondary to an underlying problem, such as kidney failure or cancer. Some metabolic diseases produce serious physical effects that cannot be easily corrected. The diagnosis frequently relies upon clinical and laboratory procedures to identify or confirm the nature of the imbalance.

Hypervitaminosis A. Vitamin A *(retinol)* is a fat-soluble vitamin important in the growth and differentiation of cells. It is present in many foodstuffs, including butter, cheese, egg yolk, liver and fish liver oils, tomatoes, and carrots. Vitamin A normally is stored in liver tissue; excessive consumption of this organ meat is the principal cause of hypervitaminosis A in cats.

Signs of toxicity usually develop after a cat has been fed an exclusive diet of liver, or has been heavily supplemented with vitamin A for a prolonged period of time (months to years). The clinical manifestations are quite characteristic. *Deforming cervical spondylosis,* in which some of the cervical (neck) vertebrae fuse together, results in an inability of the cat to flex its neck. Bony outgrowths *(exostoses)* of the vertebrae, interfering with normal vertebral movement, can often be felt with the fingers. Such deformities, in some cases, can result in damage to associated nerves or nerve roots. Depending upon the severity of the toxicity, similar bony fusions may be found in the elbows and in other limb joints. *Such skeletal changes are irreversible,* unless a dietary alteration is made very early in their development. Other clinical signs secondary to *ankylosis* (immobility of a joint) and impaired movement include poor quality of the hair coat (from lack of grooming), weight loss (from difficulty in eating), constipation, and pain along the neck and back when touched *(cutaneous hyperesthesia).* In cases diagnosed early, replacement of liver with a balanced diet (or cessation of vitamin A supplementation) may allow for regression of signs. Cats with irreversible disease can be made more comfortable with low doses of anti-inflammatory agents. Food and water dishes should be placed a few inches off the floor so that affected cats will be better able to eat and drink. The prognosis is guarded to poor.

Nutritional Secondary Hyperparathyroidism. Calcium is the most abundant mineral in the body and one of the most important. Together with phosphorus, magnesium, and fluoride, it forms the hard structural substance of the bones and teeth. It is essential for the maintenance of cell membranes and for the functioning of molecular transport systems across those membranes. Calcium is required for the normal functioning of the nerves and muscles (including heart muscle) and for blood clotting. It is also an important constituent of many enzymatic reactions. Because of the many important roles calcium plays in the maintenance of life, its circulating levels in the blood and in cellular compartments are very strictly regulated. When this regulation is uncoupled—as by a dietary imbalance—the consequences can be severe.

Nutritional secondary hyperparathyroidism is essentially a calcium deficiency induced in cats by an overzealous consumption of meat. Meat, as a rule, is high in phosphorus but low in calcium content. In nature, cats that catch prey consume more than just the calcium-deficient muscle tissue; bones and other components of the prey feast prevent any potential calcium deficit. Feeding an all-meat diet without adequate calcium supplementation (milk, commercial cat food) predisposes pet cats to the development of a calcium deficiency.

Chronic ingestion of a high-phosphate (oxidized phosphorus)/low-calcium diet, because of certain physiological factors, induces a decrease in the level of circulating calcium. The *parathyroid glands,* adjacent to the thyroid, detect this change and secrete *parathyroid hormone* (PTH) which, among its other activities, helps to extract calcium from its "storage bins" in the skeleton. In this way the parathyroids attempt to restore a normal phosphate/calcium balance and to make calcium available for the vital physiological functions for which it is required. The end result is a thinning and a weakening of the basic bone structure, which can be quite striking when viewed on an X ray of the skeleton. As more and more calcium is removed, the bones become very brittle and susceptible to fractures. Nutritional secondary hyperparathyroidism is most often seen in kittens (whose growing bodies have a special need for minerals) that are confined indoors and fed an all-meat diet. Such cats have no access to calcium supplementation.

Affected kittens show a reluctance to move and may resist being handled. Weakness or limping suggests the presence of fractures. In severe cases, bony deformities develop, such as bowing of the legs, curvature

of the spine, and vertebral compression of the spinal cord or nerve roots. Nerve damage can produce abnormalities such as *ataxia* (incoordination) and partial or complete paralysis of affected muscles. Pelvic fractures can narrow the pelvic canal, resulting in obstruction of the digestive tract and obstipation. Either pelvic fractures or spinal cord compression can produce paralysis of the bladder with subsequent retention of urine.

Animals showing severe bony deformities usually cannot be saved. If the disease is diagnosed at an earlier stage, however, significant improvement can be obtained by calcium supplementation and institution of a balanced diet. Cage confinement for several weeks is required to allow small fractures to heal and to prevent development of new fractures during the recovery process. The prognosis for these types of cases is good.

Older cats that remain indoors and have for some reason been switched to an all-meat diet also may develop nutritional secondary hyperparathyroidism. The signs usually are less severe than those in kittens because active growth of the bones has ceased. Over a period of time, however, progressive demineralization of the skeleton develops and, as with kittens, results in brittleness of the bones and readiness to fracture. Curvatures of the back and pelvic collapse, with resultant effects on the digestive or urogenital system, may be seen. Prognosis and treatment depend upon the severity of the malformations and the length of time the disease has been present.

Renal secondary hyperparathyroidism also results in a calcium-deficient state. In these cases, however, impairment of kidney function, rather than dietary idiosyncrasy, is the root of the problem. The kidneys may be malfunctioning because of chronic disease or a congenital abnormality. The prognosis is guarded, depending upon the underlying cause.

Primary hyperparathyroidism, in which a functional abnormality of the parathyroids causes an elevated output of parathyroid hormone (PTH) with resultant calcium depletion from the skeleton, is extremely rare in cats. It may be produced by a benign parathyroid gland tumor (an *adenoma*). In such cases, surgical removal of the tumor is indicated. Postoperative calcium supplementation usually will be required for a variable period of time. The prognosis is guarded, especially in animals with severe demineralization.

Hypokalemic Polymyopathy. Depletion of potassium from the body, perhaps by chronic loss from malfunctioning kidneys combined with feeding of a low-potassium diet, can produce clinical signs of muscle disease in cats. The loss of potassium induces degenerative changes in muscle tissue that are responsible for the clinical signs. These include generalized muscle weakness, muscle pain, stiffened posture, reluctance to move, and an inability to raise the head because of neck muscle weakness. Signs can be reversed by proper potassium supplementation.

Infectious/Inflammatory Diseases

Osteoarthritis. Degenerative changes in the articular cartilage (thin layer of cartilage on the joint surfaces) can result in *osteoarthritis* (also known as *degenerative joint disease*), manifested chiefly by lameness. The development of this type of arthritis in cats is believed to be similar to the development of chronic arthritis in humans. (Osteoarthritis should *not* be confused with *rheumatoid arthritis* in humans, a disease with an immunologic basis.) Osteoarthritis is a chronic disease of aging, but can also occur as a result of traumatic injury to bone, cartilage, or ligaments (witness the postcareer arthritic problems experienced by many professional athletes, particularly football players). The lameness associated with uncomplicated osteoarthritis typically is exacerbated by cold, damp weather conditions, and by exercise. *Infectious arthritis,* resulting from infection (usually bacterial) in one or more joints, can produce osteoarthritic changes of fairly acute onset.

Diagnosis of osteoarthritis in cats is made by a combination of the history, physical and radiographic (X-ray) findings, and examination of joint fluid. Treatment is based on the underlying cause. Infectious arthritis requires identification of the causative agent and appropriate antibiotic therapy. Judicious administration of anti-inflammatory agents is indicated for most noninfectious cases. Severely affected joints may require surgical fixation *(arthrodesis)* to produce fusion of the joint surfaces (effectively "locking" the joint in place, so that movement—and the pain associated with movement—are eliminated).

Chronic Progressive Polyarthritis (CPP). This is a specific disease of adult cats, usually males, in which chronic inflammatory changes leading to arthritis occur in joints and tendon sheaths of the lower limbs (*carpus* and *tarsus* regions). The cause is unknown, but may be related to one or more viral infections. One form of CPP is similar to a disease of human

beings known as *rheumatoid arthritis.* (Rheumatoid arthritis is a chronic, progressive, ulcerative arthritis that is believed to have an immunologic basis; i.e., antibodies and cells of the immune system appear to be involved in producing the underlying inflammatory response that leads to the destructive arthritic lesions.) Diagnosis of CPP is based on the history, clinical signs, radiography, and joint-fluid examination. Treatment involves anti-inflammatory drug therapy.

Systemic lupus erythematosus (SLE) is a noninfectious inflammatory disease that, like rheumatoid arthritis, appears to have an immunologic basis. It can produce a wide variety of clinical signs involving a number of organ systems, including the skin, and can affect the joints with resultant clinical lameness. Diagnosis is based on the history, clinical signs, examination of joint fluid, and specialized immunodiagnostic tests such as the LE (Leukocyte-Erythrocyte) cell test which detects blood-cells that contain ingested nuclei, and the antinuclear antibody (ANA) test which detects antibodies directed against cell nuclei. Treatment relies on anti-inflammatory drug therapy. The prognosis, in general, is poor.

Osteomyelitis. Deep bone infections *(osteomyelitis)* caused by pus-producing bacteria (or other microorganisms) are most often seen secondary to injury (open fractures, extension from a tissue infection) or orthopedic surgery. With bone injury, contamination of a fracture site occurs before *reduction* (setting) of the fracture can be accomplished. Osteomyelitis resulting from contamination during surgery, although relatively uncommon, must always be considered as a possible consequence of orthopedic procedures. The diagnosis of osteomyelitis is usually made in a fairly straightforward fashion—history, presence of pain and draining purulent tracts, and lameness. Appropriate antibiotic therapy is indicated. It should be kept in mind that osteomyelitis may be a difficult problem to treat and that prolonged antibiotic administration may be necessary. The disease may be chronic or episodic (i.e., subject to periodic recurrence). Occasionally a deep bite by another cat that reaches the bone of the tail or limb and is not treated with an antibiotic results in a chronic osteomyelitis.

Hypertrophic Osteopathy (HO). This uncommon syndrome is characterized by a slowly progressive thickening and proliferation of the surfaces of the long bones and digits. HO is observed secondary to chronic lesions, such as cancer, involving chest structures (especially the lungs). It is believed to be due to lesion-induced changes in blood flow to the affected bones. Clinical signs include lameness, reluctance to move, and swelling of the lower limbs. Diagnosis is based on the history, physical findings, and X rays. The prognosis is dependent upon the nature of the underlying cause; with cancer, the prognosis is poor. With treatable chest lesions, the disease usually resolves along with the primary problem.

Neoplastic Diseases

Tumors of the skeletal structure and musculature are occasionally seen in cats, although the frequency of their occurrence is much lower than it is in dogs. Nevertheless, consideration must be given to *neoplasia* (cancer) in the differential diagnosis of musculoskeletal disease in the cat. Unfortunately, most of the tumors are malignant, and prospects for treatment and recovery may be less than optimal. Osteogenic sarcoma, osteochondroma, and chondrosarcoma are the bone tumors that occur most frequently in cats.

Osteogenic Sarcoma. A destructive tumor of bone, osteogenic sarcoma (also known as *osteosarcoma*) is malignant and hence capable of spreading from the site of its development—a process known as *metastasis.* In cats, osteogenic sarcoma arises most commonly in the hindlimbs or skull. Clinical signs at the tumor site can include local pain and swelling, deformity, and lameness. There may be lymph node enlargement. Osteogenic sarcoma grows less rapidly and spreads less readily in cats than in dogs. Spread usually occurs to the lungs, where metastatic tumors can be identified by chest X ray. The syndrome of hypertrophic osteopathy can be produced by these lung lesions.

Diagnosis of osteogenic sarcoma is made by X ray and biopsy (microscopic examination of sample) examination. Surgical amputation of the affected limb, perhaps combined with chemotherapy, may be indicated. However, if the tumor has spread to the lungs the prognosis is poor.

Osteoma. This is an uncommon, benign tumor that arises most often in the skull. Osteomas are usually single, dense, and slow-growing. Surgical excision may or may not be feasible, depending upon the tumor's exact location and the extent of damage to surrounding structures.

Osteochondroma. This curious benign neoplasm may occur as a solitary mass or as many dispersed tumor masses *(multiple cartilaginous exostoses).* In many species, osteochondromas are inherited; in the cat, these tumors occur in adults and are believed to be caused by feline leukemia virus (FeLV). Clinical signs are related to bony enlargements virtually anywhere in the skeleton. These growths can progress and produce considerable deformity, pain, and interference with movement. Facial tumors may interfere with breathing or chewing. Tumors of the scapula (shoulder blade) can result in atrophy of the associated limb. Tumors arising inside the skull can produce severe neurologic changes, such as arching of the back, blindness, and stupor. Diagnosis is made by radiography and biopsy, along with the history and physical findings. The prognosis is poor.

Osteochondromas frequently are very far advanced by the time veterinary attention is sought, and it may be impossible to remove them. The sheer number of tumor nodules may make surgery a useless endeavor. In addition, most of these cats are FeLV-positive.

Chondrosarcoma. Chondrosarcoma is a malignant tumor of cartilage-producing cells and is uncommon in cats. This form of cancer grows more slowly than does osteogenic sarcoma, and there is less tendency to spread. Clinical signs may resemble those of osteogenic sarcoma. Therapy depends upon the extent of tumor invasion of local tissue and whether or not spread has occurred.

Multiple Myeloma. Multiple myeloma is a malignant tumor of *plasma cells* (white blood cells that produce antibodies) arising from the bone marrow. Usually generalized in man, the tumor in the cat is almost always single. The signs of the disease are many and varied, but can include local swelling, pain, lameness, and fractures at the tumor site. Neoplastic plasma cells may make sizable quantities of characteristic globulins (a class of proteins) that can be detected in the blood. Multiple myelomas grow through and destroy normal bone tissue—the underlying cause for the more common clinical signs. Typical sites for myelomas to arise include the long bones, pelvis, skull, and vertebrae. Diagnosis is made by X ray and by microscopic examination of tumor material. Sometimes the cancerous plasma cells can be recognized in blood smears. Treatment relies primarily upon chemotherapy. The prognosis is guarded.

Tumors of muscle tissue—*rhabdomyomas* (benign) and *rhabdomyosarcomas* (malignant)—are extremely rare in cats and are usually treated by wide surgical excision if the location permits.

Traumatic Injuries

Physical trauma can exert a number of deleterious effects on the musculoskeletal system, many of which require immediate veterinary attention. These effects are the result of powerful physical forces acting upon anatomic structures until the weakest or most vulnerable of the structures gives way. An unexpected leap or fall, aggressive action by human beings or other animals, and encounters with moving vehicles are among the more common causes of traumatic injury in domestic cats.

Injury to the musculoskeletal system can be divided loosely into four broad categories.

A *bruise* (or *contusion*) is an insult of a superficial nature, which results in damage to muscle or bone without disruption of the overlying skin. Such an injury may go unnoticed by an owner and in most cases will heal without complications.

A *sprain* is an injury to a joint involving damage to one or more ligaments (fibrous bands) supporting the joint. Complete disruption of a ligament does not occur (there is no disruption of the joint itself). The joint may be swollen and painful, but in most cases will not require medical attention. Such an injury may or may not be noticed by an owner.

A *luxation* (or *dislocation*) is a major disruption of the supporting structures of a joint. A partial separation of joint surfaces is also known as a *subluxation*.

A *fracture* is the breaking of a bone. Fractures can be *simple* or *compound*. In a simple (or *closed*) fracture, the injury occurs without disruption of the overlying skin. In a compound (or *open*) fracture, bone breaks through the overlying skin, creating a communication between the fracture and the external environment. Obviously, compound fractures are more susceptible to infection by microbial organisms than are simple fractures.

Cats are lightweight animals possessed of an extraordinarily resilient body structure that can absorb bone-shaking impacts with astonishing ease. For the most part, bruises and sprains in cats are of minor medical concern. Luxations and fractures, however, require immediate veterinary attention. (*See* Chapter 38: First Aid.)

Before *reduction* (setting) of a fracture is undertaken, the veterinarian must perform a complete physical examination of the patient so that other, less obvious injuries may be identified. For example, cats experiencing trauma to the forelimbs may have concurrent injuries to the *thorax* (chest) or skull. Injuries to the hindlimbs may be attended by fractures of one or more bones of the pelvis, rupture of the urinary bladder or *urethra* (the tube connecting the bladder and the external urinary orifice), or internal bleeding resulting from trauma to the liver, spleen, or other organs. Radiographs (X rays) may be taken not only to evaluate the primary fracture site but to assess damage to other bones and possibly soft structures. In brief, the patient must be stabilized and a full inventory of its injuries compiled before reparative orthopedic therapy is undertaken.

Fractures of the Femur. Fractures of the thigh bone or *femur* are quite common in cats. Simple fractures of the femur that do not involve hip or knee joints can be repaired by placing an *intramedullary pin* (a stainless-steel rod) down through the center of the bone from end to end. With good alignment of the fractured segments, such fractures heal rapidly. If the femur is fractured into many pieces, a metal *bone plate* may be required in order to realign the fragments and hold them in place. The bone plate is girded to the several fragments by small screws and can be custom-contoured to "mold" to the shape of the underlying bone. Bone plates usually provide a quicker return to function for the patient, but this advantage is offset by the plates' expense and the requirement of specialized equipment for their implantation.

Fractures of other long bones also are usually repaired by some form of pinning or plating. Fractures of the metacarpal and metatarsal bones, if serious, may require reduction with pins or plates but can usually be stabilized with a splint. A fractured toe sometimes has to be removed because of poor healing.

Fractures and Separation of Tail Vertebrae. An automobile injury to the hind end of a cat, in addition to causing pelvic fractures, may separate the first tail vertebrae from the sacrum. The tail dangles limply, and the cat cannot move it. A frequent and grave complication with this injury (even if there is only a contusion to the area) is paralysis of the urinary bladder so that the cat cannot empty it. If an owner is willing to express the urine from the bladder by manual compression several times a day, the cat's ability to empty its bladder may gradually return (over days or weeks). The paralyzed tail should not be removed until and unless there is good evidence that the cat will be able to empty its bladder. Some cats, in time, regain control of their tails.

A fracture or vertebral separation toward the tip of the tail usually requires amputation but sometimes heals with splinting.

Fractures of the Jaws. A common fracture in cats that have been hit by cars or fallen from heights involves the lower jaw, most often at the midline of the chin where the two halves of the mandible are joined. This fracture is easily reduced or stabilized by wiring around the canine teeth or by pinning.

A front-to-back fracture of the hard palate, often accompanying a midline fracture of the mandible, may require side-to-side wiring to prevent development of a permanent opening through which liquids lapped by the cat will get into the nasal passages.

Other fractures of the jaws may need wiring or plating at the fracture site but can often be stabilized by wiring the upper and lower jaws together or by applying a wire-reinforced tape muzzle around both jaws. Despite the limitation of motion, the cat manages to lap liquid food.

Fractures of the Pelvis. Pelvic fractures also are of fairly common occurrence in cats. Because of their light weight and relatively great muscular strength, many cats compensate quite well for minor fractures of pelvic bones. Within a few weeks of injury, a fine meshwork of new bone, called a *callus,* begins growing across the fracture site, helping to stabilize the fracture. In the case of minor fractures, callus forma-

tion will be followed by hard bone formation and eventual return to normal function. In more severe cases, however, such nonsurgical reduction of a fracture ("letting nature take its course") may be harmful. (As a general rule, major fractures of any bony structure, if left alone, can result in serious consequences.) If an unattended fracture involves a pelvic joint structure (the hip joint), it may predispose to the development of arthritis and a permanent limp. Deformation of the shape of the pelvis by traumatic injury may produce other unpleasant effects as well, such as constriction of the intestinal tract (caused by narrowing of the pelvic canal) with resultant chronic constipation or even complete intestinal obstruction. Fractures may also impinge upon nerves and produce severe pain and neurologic abnormalities in the hindlimbs. Hence, any cat suspected of sustaining physical trauma to the pelvis (or to any other body structure) should be presented for evaluation to a veterinarian, to preclude the development of serious secondary complications. Bone plating or pinning may be required to bring pelvic fragments into satisfactory alignment.

Fractures of Vertebrae. Fracture or dislocation of a vertebra may damage the spinal cord, perhaps causing paralysis of the hindlimbs. Where the injury is serious, as when a cat has been struck by a car, the animal may have to be destroyed at once. Occasionally recovery is possible by bone plating or by pinning the spines of the vertebrae.

Urinary System and Disorders

URINARY SYSTEM

The urinary system removes metabolic wastes from the body and regulates the chemical and water components of the blood. Two *kidneys,* two *ureters* (tubes that connect the *kidneys* to the bladder), the *urinary bladder* (a sac made of muscle and membranous tissue that holds urine and discharges it through the urethra), and the *urethra* (a tube from the bladder to the exterior of the body) are the functioning components of the system.

Waste by-products are produced from the metabolism of nutrients. These wastes —primarily the nitrogenous compounds *urea* and *creatinine* —must be removed from the body before levels become toxic to the cat.

The *kidneys,* located behind the rib cage on either side of the spine, contain a unique filtration system that is designed to remove the wastes from the blood. The waste-laden blood enters the kidneys through the *renal arteries* and through smaller and smaller arterial vessels, until it reaches one of the approximately two hundred thousand nephrons in the kidneys. Each *nephron* is comprised of a glomerulus (a tiny web of blood vessels), a proximal tubule, the loop of Henle, and a distal tubule, which drains into a collecting duct. The *glomerulus* separates the fluid and cellular components of blood. The resulting filtrate is further modified in the *proximal tubule,* which provides for the reabsorption of usable compounds such as glucose, amino acids, sodium, and potassium. The usable compounds are then recycled back to the body via the *renal vein.* The *loop of Henle* concentrates the resulting urine. The control of electrolytes and water is accomplished in the *distal tubule* and *collecting duct,* after which the urine drains into the *renal pelvis.* Then the urine empties into the ureters. The urine is stored in the urinary bladder until it is excreted. When the urinary bladder contracts, the urine flows through the urethra to the outside. In males, urine is voided through the penis, and in females, urine is voided between the folds of the vulva. In male cats, the terminal part of the urethra is disastrously constricted by the rigid surrounding tissue of the penis; it is here that urethral "plugs" and tiny sandlike stones lodge and cause potentially fatal blockage.

The kidneys also aid in the production of *erythropoietin,* a hormone that stimulates the production of red blood cells, and produces *renin,* an enzyme which controls blood pressure.

DISEASES OF THE URINARY SYSTEM

Diseases of the urinary system can be categorized into those of the lower tract (ureters, bladder, and urethra) and the upper tract (kidneys).

Lower Urinary Tract Diseases

Lower urinary tract diseases are those that affect the ureters, urinary bladder, and urethra. A cat that displays signs such as straining at the litter box, bloody urine, urinating in inappropriate places, vomiting, loss of appetite, and a uremic odor to the breath should be seen by a veterinarian immediately.

FELINE UROLOGIC SYNDROME (FUS). Feline urologic syndrome is a term for a wide range of problems associated with the lower urinary tract of both male and female cats: inflammation of the urinary bladder and urethra, the formation of urinary stones, and obstruction of the urethra (usually the male's) by tiny stones and plugs. A number of factors seem to be responsible for the syndrome. Therefore, it is not unusual if treatments and methods of prevention vary. It has been reported that up to 10 percent of the feline population may be afflicted with FUS. The consequences of FUS can be fatal if urethral obstruction occurs, especially in the male cat.

Urolithiasis. Urolithiasis refers to the formation of stones in the urinary tract and also to the disorders they cause. The cat's highly concentrated urine favors stone formation when certain substances are present to excess, sometimes as a result of dietary imbalance (e.g., excessive magnesium, forming magnesium ammonium phosphate [struvite] crystals), occasionally as a result of other acquired or congenital disorders. Urolith formation has two developmental phases: initiation and growth.

Uroliths are hardened solids composed of polycrys-

talline (of many crystals) concretions that typically contain 90 percent organic or inorganic crystals and less than 10 percent organic matrix (mucoprotein base, ground substance). Cross sections of uroliths frequently reveal a distinct center with laminations (layers) formed from the center outward, corresponding to the initiation of the urolith at the center and the laminations as the evidence of growth. Uroliths are usually named according to their chemical composition, such as calcium oxalate, calcium phosphate, magnesium ammonium phosphate, ammonium urate, uric acid, or cystine. They may also be named according to their organ location, such as *nephroliths* (*nephros* is the Greek word for kidney), *ureteroliths* (stones in the ureter), *cystoliths* (stones in the urinary bladder), and *urethroliths* (stones in the urethra), or urethral plugs.

A minority of uroliths observed in male and female cats occur in the urinary bladder. Frequently, however, uroliths formed in the bladder pass through, or obstruct, the urethra of the male cat. Nephroliths are less common than cystoliths in cats; ureteroliths have been rarely encountered. Chemical analysis of several hundred naturally occurring uroliths from cats revealed that the great majority were composed primarily of magnesium ammonium phosphate, which is often called *struvite.*

In gross appearance (appearance to the naked eye) and consistency, the feline urolith is unquestionably different from the feline urethral plug of the male cat. The urethral plug is a soft, pastelike, compressible mass composed of varying proportions of crystals and matrix. The urolith has a rocklike consistency and assumes a variety of shapes. Many uroliths of cats are shaped like tiny wafers or discs. By contrast, a urethral plug resembles a maggot about 2 to 3 millimeters (.08 to .12 inch) in diameter. If an obstruction is not relieved, the plug is lengthened as material continues to build up within the urethra.

The formation of uroliths in cats requires a sufficiently high concentration of urolith-forming minerals in the urine, a favorable urine pH (acid-base ratio) for their crystallization to occur, and adequate time in the urinary tract. Urinary tract infection usually is not an important factor in their formation. Congenital and acquired anatomical abnormalities in the lower urinary tract predispose the system to stone formation as well as inflammation and infection.

Many researchers have reported convincing data concerning experimental production of magnesium phosphate and magnesium ammonium phosphate uroliths in cats eating *calculogenic* diets (i.e., high in minerals ["ash"]). Consumption, absorption, and excretion of comparatively high quantities of dietary magnesium appeared to have been important, although other factors also may have played a role. Many of the calculogenic diets used in these studies contained more magnesium than that found in many commercially prepared cat foods. Nonetheless, it does appear that the composition of diets may play a prominent role in the formation of uroliths in cats, particularly the magnesium ammonium phosphate uroliths. Further studies that vary the mineral content, caloric density of the food, percentage of water, and the methods of food consumption by cats are being evaluated by researchers at several institutions. Many significant questions remain to be answered as to the relationship of diet to urolith formation.

Bacterial Cystitis. Cystitis is an inflammation of the urinary bladder, which may be secondary to urolithiasis. Signs of cystitis are frequent trips to the litter box, straining, and often bloody urine. The bladder is usually empty and tightly contracted to walnut size. A bacterial infection of the urinary bladder can result in the infection progressing up the ureters to the kidneys. Therefore, expeditious diagnosis and treatment with appropriate antibiotics are recommended. It is puzzling and frustrating that it is commonly impossible to culture bacteria in cases of urinary tract disease in cats.

Urethral Obstruction. Much controversy exists as to what triggers the formation of urethral plugs. It may well be a combination of factors: abundance of stone-forming minerals from the diet and high concentration and decreased acidity of the urine. Cornell research suggests that some feline viruses may also be involved.

Recent radiographic studies of urethras and urinary bladders of obstructed male cats admitted to the University of Minnesota Veterinary Teaching Hospital have shed new light on this complex syndrome. The studies revealed that urethral obstruction of male cats also may be associated with disease of the prostate gland and tumors or masses that compress the urethra. The investigators conducting the studies have speculated that special secretory glands found only in the postprostatic urethra (the portion of urethra after the prostate gland) produce at least a part of the mucous matrix that contributes to the urethral plugs of obstructed cats. The glands' secretory activity may be enhanced by infections, diets, or inflammatory disorders.

Urethral obstruction in the male ("blocked cat") is a life-threatening emergency for which owners must be alert. The cat keeps licking at its penis and going to its litter box but produces no urine or only a few drops (which may be bloody). Sometimes urinary "sand" is present on the tip of the penis or surrounding fur. Experienced owners may be able to palpate the tense, overfull urinary bladder like a large lemon in the posterior abdomen. *The cat must be taken to a veterinarian at once; a delay of only a few hours can mean death from uremic poisoning.* The owner must not make the common mistake of assuming that the cat is constipated and waste precious time plying the cat with laxatives.

If the veterinarian cannot relieve the obstruction by pressure on the bladder or gentle manipulation of the penis, he or she will try to pass a catheter through the urethra into the bladder, with the aid of a tranquilizer, sedative, or light anesthesia. If that fails, urine must be withdrawn from the overdistended bladder by suction with a needle directly through the abdominal and bladder walls.

If the urethral blockage is very solid and does not yield to attempts at flushing or if a cat suffers repeated episodes of obstruction, the last resort is surgery to provide a new urethral opening (urethrostomy) that bypasses the constricted penile portion of the urethra. Although some urethrostomies fail because of recurrent bladder infection or poor function of the artificial opening, the operation enables many cats that would have died or been euthanatized to live in complete or reasonable comfort. (*See* Chapter 36: Surgery and Postoperative Care.)

Treatment. The type of lower urinary tract disease will determine the treatment prescribed for a cat. Treatment may include one or a combination of the following: diet, antibiotics, or urine acidification. Feeding a low-magnesium diet (less than 20 milligrams of magnesium per one hundred calories) is advisable for cats that are predisposed to urolithiasis or urethral obstruction. For all cats, encouraging exercise and frequent urination, preventing obesity, avoiding extreme confinement, keeping the litter box clean and easily available, and always having fresh water readily available will assist in preventing FUS.

HYPOSPADIAS. Hypospadias is an extremely rare congenital defect resulting when the urethral opening is on the underside of the penis or on the perineum. A chronic, recurrent cystitis occurs with this defect because the surface bacteria can easily migrate into the urinary tract. Reconstructive surgery of the urethra provides an effective treatment.

Upper Urinary Tract Diseases

Kidney disease can be congenital or acquired and can be further classified as to what part of the nephron is affected. When the kidneys malfunction, wastes begin to accumulate in the blood. Excessive accumulation of wastes is toxic to the animal. If the proper balances of electrolytes, minerals, and water are not maintained, additional complications can occur with other organs.

Since the kidneys filter the blood, other diseases and infections can indirectly damage the kidneys, such as uterine infection, diabetes, feline leukemia virus infection, hypertension, feline infectious peritonitis, and severe periodontal disease or tooth infection. Also, ingesting certain toxic materials, such as antifreeze or poisonous plants, can injure the kidneys.

One or more of the following signs may be indicative of a kidney problem.

1. Increased thirst or water consumption with increased urine volume
2. Decreased thirst with little or no urination
3. Decreased appetite
4. Intermittent vomiting or diarrhea
5. Noticeable coat changes (dullness, excessive shedding, breakage of hairs)
6. Weight loss
7. Lethargy
8. Mouth sores
9. Halitosis
10. Discolored tongue
11. Pronounced back pain (a cat assumes a hunched position)
12. Bloody urine

CONGENITAL KIDNEY DEFECTS. Congenital defects result from abnormal development and maturation of the kidneys. *Renal hypoplasia* is the term used when one or both kidneys have a reduced number of functioning nephrons. Kittens may develop normally until one or two years old, when signs begin to appear, such as frequent vomiting, decreased appetite, and decreased urine output. Although there is no cure, treatment consisting of reducing or flushing the body system of the accumulated waste by dietary management and fluids may prolong the cat's life.

Renal aplasia refers to the lack of development of one or both kidneys. Often a kitten will survive with only one kidney, if it develops and functions properly. If both kidneys are absent, the kitten will die at birth or immediately after.

In a cat born with *polycystic kidneys,* multiple cysts replacing normal tissue eventually cause kidney failure.

ACQUIRED KIDNEY DISEASE. The risk of acquired kidney disease is greater for middle-aged or older cats (generally seven years or older). Pyelonephritis, interstitial nephritis, glomerulonephritis, amyloidosis, and hydronephrosis are different types of acquired kidney disease. These diseases can usually be further classified as *chronic* (long-term) or *acute* (short-term).

Acute kidney disease and failure are most often due to urethral obstruction in the male cat. Other frequent causes are rupture of a urinary organ from trauma and ingestion of toxins such as ethylene glycol (antifreeze).

Pyelonephritis is the medical term for a kidney infection. Usually the infection is the result of *cystitis* (bladder infection), which migrates up to the kidney. However, it can also be secondary to a severe infection located elsewhere, such as periodontal disease or pyometra (uterine infection). The kidneys continue to function normally until over 70 percent of the kidney is affected, at which time signs become more noticeable (lethargy, weight loss, sometimes fever). Treatment may be effective if given in the early stages. If the damage has progressed too far, kidney failure will result.

Glomerulonephritis is an inflammatory disease that results from damage to the glomeruli by an antigen-antibody reaction. (*See* Chapter 28: Immune System and Disorders.) Glomerulonephritis may be associated with diseases affecting other body systems, such as systemic lupus erythematosus, endocarditis, pyometra, heartworm disease, viral infections, feline leukemia virus infection, feline infectious peritonitis, or may have no identifiable cause (idiopathic). Subcutaneous and abdominal accumulation of fluid are characteristic signs.

The disease is usually progressive, and the long-term prognosis is guarded, although some cases of spontaneous remission have occurred. Currently, treatment is directed toward the underlying cause and the kidney failure present.

Hydronephrosis occurs when an obstruction prevents normal urine outflow. The retention of urine causes abnormal enlargement of the affected kidneys. Potential causes include urinary stones, tumors, congenital defects, and trauma. Hydronephrosis of one kidney is not life-threatening. Death will occur from kidney failure if both kidneys are affected.

Amyloidosis occurs when an insoluble protein substance (amyloid) is deposited in the kidneys. This is an uncommon disorder in cats, except for the familial amyloidosis in Abyssinians in which the kidney medulla is mainly affected.. In these cats, the disease is usually progressive with little response to treatment. The cause is unknown. Kidney failure eventually results as medullary fibrosis and tubular damage increase. The severity and progression vary; cats may live up to twelve to fourteen years. However, most affected cats die by five years of age. Two drugs (dimethyl sulfoxide and colchicine) have been used experimentally in treating amyloidosis, but the effectiveness of these drugs has not been established.

Interstitial nephritis is usually of unknown cause but may sometimes be the last stage of other different kidney diseases. The damaged kidney tissue has been replaced by nonfunctional scar tissue. The kidneys are greatly reduced in size, with an irregular surface. Treatment is directed toward preserving as much kidney function as possible.

CHRONIC KIDNEY FAILURE. Chronic kidney failure occurs when about 70 percent of functional kidney tissue has been destroyed. There are many possible causes, including glomerulonephritis, interstitial nephritis, congenital renal diseases, kidney infections, feline leukemia virus infection, feline infectious peritonitis, hypertension, amyloidosis, and toxic chemicals. Sometimes it is not possible to determine the underlying cause of kidney failure.

Cats with chronic kidney failure may have decreased appetite, lethargy, vomiting, foul mouth odor, increased water intake and urine output, joint pain, and a tendency to bleed easily.

The objective of treatment is to control the progression of the disease. There often is no cure. Initial treatment may include fluid therapy to restore hydra-

tion, electrolyte balance, and acid-base balance in the patient. A diet low in protein and phosphorus will slow the progression of the disease. These special diets are less palatable, and a cat may refuse to eat the food. However, adding poultry fat or clam juice, or warming the food may entice a finicky cat to eat.

KIDNEY STONES. Kidney stones are rare in cats; however, when they do occur, they can be very painful. Kidney stones are mineral deposits that accumulate and form into "stones." If kidney function is impaired by kidney stones, surgery may be needed to remove the stone(s) or affected kidney. However, if the stones are small and not adversely affecting the kidneys, medication may slowly dissolve them.

KIDNEY TUMORS. Kidney tumors are rare in cats, except for the very common lymphosarcoma associated with the feline sarcoma virus (FeSV). (*See* Chapter 33: Cancer.)

KIDNEY SUBCAPSULAR CYSTS. A subcapsular cyst develops when the capsule (covering membrane) of the kidney is separated from the kidney and distended by fluid accumulating under the capsule. However, subcapsular cysts are rare in cats. If, in elderly cats with chronic interstitial nephritis, both kidneys are involved, then no treatment is possible. In cats of any age traumatic injury can give rise to a cyst usually involving only one kidney. Such a cyst may be handled surgically by drainage and removal of the cyst wall.

DIAGNOSIS. If a cat demonstrates any signs of kidney problems (*see* "Upper Urinary Tract Diseases," page 209), a veterinarian will take blood and urine samples for testing. When kidney disease is suspected, the blood levels of *urea nitrogen* (BUN) and creatinine are checked. A marked elevation in these two levels indicates that the kidneys are not adequately filtering wastes from the blood. A creatinine clearance test (quantitative test that measures the kidneys' ability to remove endogenous creatinine) can provide useful information on glomerular filtration rate. Other blood constituents that may be measured to evaluate the kidneys' regulatory functioning include potassium, calcium, phosphorus, glucose, total protein, and albumin. A complete blood count will provide information on any inflammation or infection that might be present. A complete urinalysis provides additional information on the extent of kidney damage or establishes if an infection is present in the urinary tract.

Significant changes in the size, shape, or position of the kidneys can be seen with radiographs (X rays). Sometimes mineralization of the kidneys indicates chronic inflammation or a mineral imbalance. Also, kidney stones may be detected.

An intravenous pyelogram (IVP) procedure consists of injecting a harmless dye, which can be seen radiographically. During the procedure, several radiographs are taken to provide information about the entire course of the urinary tract.

Ultrasound studies of the kidneys are also being used to diagnose kidney disease. This noninvasive technique is currently available at larger animal hospitals and veterinary school clinics.

The removal of a small piece of kidney tissue for microscopic evaluation (biopsy) can provide insight as to which kidney disease is present. However, it is of little value in assessing kidney function.

Test results can differentiate between kidney failure and kidney dysfunction. Kidney dysfunction does not necessarily imply kidney failure, but simply impaired function. In cases where only one kidney is damaged (congenital malformation, trauma, or infection), the other kidney, if healthy, will adequately compensate in most cases. Kidney failure of a type that cannot be reversed by treatment ends in death.

TREATMENT. Treatment is determined by the type of kidney disease and the amount of damage done to the kidneys. Surgery may be indicated in the case of unilateral hydronephrosis, whereas antibiotics may be administered for pyelonephritis. In addition, the veterinarian administers fluids to correct electrolyte (mineral) imbalances and combat dehydration.

When kidney dysfunction progresses to the extent that retained protein waste products and electrolyte disturbances are evident, dietary changes are recommended. The diet should be low in protein and phosphorus and high in nonprotein calories (carbohydrates and fat). The metabolism of carbohydrates and fats yields products excreted via nonkidney routes. Commercial foods are available that are formulated to meet these special dietary requirements. Also, a veterinarian can suggest a homemade diet that will meet the same nutritional needs.

When kidney failure rapidly develops, it may be possible to restore the kidney to adequate function, provided the cat can be supported with fluid therapy. Supportive care may require *peritoneal dialysis*. This procedure uses the abdominal cavity as the exchange reservoir for large-volume fluid flushes, which remove the metabolic wastes. It is a *temporary* life-saving maneuver. Presently, kidney transplants are not feasible in veterinary medicine.

Nervous System and Disorders

THE NERVOUS SYSTEM

The nervous system is divided into two very complex, interconnected masses of circuitry: the *central nervous system* (CNS), which consists of the *brain* and *spinal cord,* and the *peripheral nervous system* (PNS), which consists of the *cranial, spinal,* and *peripheral* nerves.

Each nerve or *neuron,* whether within the CNS or the PNS, is composed of a *cell body* (containing the *nucleus* and surrounding *cytoplasm*), short, branching processes called *dendrites,* and an extended fingerlike process known as an *axon*. Dendrites act as receptors for the neuron, picking up both inhibitory and excitatory signals from interconnecting nerve cells. The axon is the transmitter of the neuron; it sends electrical impulses out from the nerve cell body to other nerves or to organs that the neuron affects. The site at which one neuron connects with another is known as a *synapse*. Transmission of a signal across the synapse involves the movement of chemical *neurotransmitters*

from the terminal portion of the axon to receptors on the recipient neuron.

Many functions of the nervous system are under voluntary, conscious control; many are not. An example of conscious control is the movement of an arm or leg. *Motor* nerve impulses from the brain, in response to a conscious command, travel via the spinal cord and peripheral nerves to the appropriate muscle groups to produce the desired muscle action. An example of involuntary, or unconscious control, is the regulation of *motility* (movement) within the wall of the digestive tract, which, although influenced by conscious states, is performed for the most part in the absence of controlled supervision by conscious processes. A similar control mechanism is involved in regulation of the beating of the heart.

The neurons responsible for these largely unconscious "housekeeping" functions of the body are referred to collectively as the *autonomic nervous system.* These nerves, which include elements of both the CNS and the ANS, control not only the muscular contractions within the viscera (internal organs) and blood vessels, but also the secretory activities of many glands. Within the autonomic nervous system, two separate functioning (and often antagonistic) entities are recognized. One, the *parasympathetic nervous system,* whose neurons originate in the brain and lower portion of the spinal cord, is in control when conditions are normal. The other, the *sympathetic nervous system,* whose neurons originate at all levels of the spinal cord, takes over when the body is under stress by increasing the heart rate, dilating the pupils, and increasing blood supply to the muscles.

The *hypothalamus* is a critical portion of the brain concerned with operation of much of the autonomic nervous system, production of certain hormones that are subsequently stored in the pituitary gland, and regulation of body temperature, sleep cycles, and food and water intake. The *thalamus* is a portion of the brain that serves as a conduit for sensory information coming from the rest of the body and for nerve impulses concerned with balance and coordination arising from the cerebellum.

The brain is the ultimate control center of the body, coordinating all other systems through the spinal cord and the complex network of peripheral nerves. It is surrounded by three protective layers of tissue known as the *meninges.* The brain proper is composed of the *cerebrum,* the *cerebellum,* and the *brain stem.* The cerebrum is divided into four lobes, each with very particular functions. The *frontal lobe* is concerned with intelligence, behavior, and fine motor skills; the *parietal lobe* processes and interprets sensory perceptions (e.g., smell, taste); the *occipital lobe* is devoted to vision; and the *temporal lobe* is concerned with complex behaviors and hearing. The cerebellum is responsible for the coordination of movement, while the brain stem houses many of the twelve *cranial nerves,* which control facial muscles and certain specialized functions of the head (sight, hearing, smell). The brain stem also acts as a nerve conduit, connecting the brain to the spinal cord.

The spinal cord, also covered by the meninges and further protected by encasement within the vertebral column, is the major thoroughfare for the transmission of motor nerve impulses from the brain to the peripheral nerves, and of *sensory* nerve impulses ascending from the peripheral nerves to the brain. The spinal cord also is capable of simple *reflexes,* in which

certain sensory and motor neurons, interconnecting within the cord, carry out their activities in the absence of control from higher brain centers. (A common example is the *patellar reflex,* in which a sharp blow applied just below the kneecap results in a forward jerk of the lower leg.)

NEUROLOGIC DISORDERS

Fortunately for cat owners and their charges, disorders of the nervous system occur relatively rarely in cats (less than 1 percent of the feline population). The most common causes are injury from vehicular accidents and falls from great heights. Drug toxicities, poisonings, feline ischemic encephalopathy, peripheral vestibular dysfunction, tumors, nutritional deficiencies, and congenital defects are also contributing causes of nervous system disease in felines.

The brain and spinal cord are unique tissues, and this very uniqueness can make neurologic dysfunction difficult to treat. Moreover, the capacity for regeneration and repair in the CNS is limited; consequently, many animals (and human beings) experiencing neurologic injury are left permanently incapacitated.

The diagnosis of neurologic disease is based primarily on the patient's history and on a complete physical and neurologic examination. The neurologic examination is designed to identify the location of the disease within the nervous system. The examination is divided into five areas of interest: *mental attitude and behavior,* in which functioning of the higher brain centers is evaluated; *gait,* which tests for strength and coordination of the limbs; *postural reactions,* which test for more subtle deficits in limb function; *spinal nerves,* in which muscle tone, skin sensation, and spinal reflexes (such as the patellar reflex) are evaluated; and *cranial nerves,* in which visual, auditory, and other nerve functions involving the head are examined.

Trauma

Head injuries occur in approximately 40 percent of cats injured by automobiles. Although the brain is well protected within the skull and bathed in *cerebrospinal fluid,* which helps to cushion shocking blows to the head, major traumatic injuries nevertheless can inflict considerable damage on the brain and produce neurologic complications. If the brain is bruised (a *contusion*), a cat will appear dazed but remain conscious. With a *concussion* (a violent shock to the brain), however, a cat loses consciousness momentarily or for a longer period of time.

Signs of brain injury appear rapidly, usually within twenty-four hours of trauma. The signs will vary according to the degree of damaging pressure that has been applied to the delicate brain tissue and other injured areas:

Mild: Pupil size, ocular movements, and respiration are normal; slight weakness is observed in the cat's movement and gait.

Moderate: The cat is semiconscious; pupil size and ocular movements may be abnormal; there is generalized weakness, sometimes spasticity; breathing is irregular.

Severe: The cat is *comatose* (unconscious); irregular breathing (gasping) is noted; the heart rate slows; abnormal pupils and an absence of ocular movement are noted.

Trauma to the central nervous system may be a life-threatening situation requiring immediate examination of the patient by a veterinarian. Corticosteroids, antibiotics, and anticonvulsant drugs are commonly used to treat brain contusions and concussions. Severe head injuries are more difficult to treat and require immediate emergency attention and medication to alleviate post-traumatic swelling of brain tissue. Various neurologic problems, such as behavioral changes, may occur as a result of severe brain damage.

Congenital Disorders

Congenital disorders of the CNS are uncommon in cats. *Hydrocephalus,* which is quite common in certain breeds of dog, is rarely encountered in the cat. It occurs when the normal flow of cerebrospinal fluid in and around the brain is obstructed, causing fluid buildup and subsequent pressure-related damage to brain and spinal-cord tissue. This problem usually occurs during fetal development. The severity can only be determined as the kitten matures. There is to date no widely effective treatment.

Manx cats, a tailless breed, are predisposed to *spina bifida,* a malformation of the *lumbosacral* (lower back) vertebrae, with associated changes in the spinal cord. Related problems include poor control of urination and defecation *(incontinence)* and impaired ability to move the hindlimbs. There is no effective treatment for this condition.

Veterinarians at Cornell University have recognized that *griseofulvin,* a medication for the treatment of ringworm, can produce birth defects in kittens when given to pregnant queens. These defects have included cleft palate, spina bifida, hydrocephalus, shortened tails and hindlimbs, and absence of the lower jaw, among others. (It must be kept in mind that the administration of *any* drug to pregnant animals should be viewed with extreme caution.)

Panleukopenia virus (infectious feline enteritis virus or feline distemper virus) can infect the brain of unborn kittens. Infected kittens are born with an underdeveloped cerebellum, which is manifested by a stiff, swaying gait, wide-based stance, and bobbing head, becoming grossly apparent as the kittens begin to ambulate. These signs become increasingly noticeable but do not progress in severity. Some animals can compensate reasonably well for their defect, but the cerebellar damage is permanent. This disease can be prevented quite easily by vaccination of the queen. (*See* Chapter 29: Viral Diseases.)

Lysosomal storage diseases, such as *gangliosidosis,* occur in all species and constitute an important group of metabolic disorders. The basis of these disorders is an enzyme deficiency. Cellular degeneration occurs because the animal stores in various tissues substances that cannot be broken down into simpler compounds because of the deficiency (or absence) of the proper enzyme. Signs often reflect central nervous system involvement because affected neurons cannot be replaced. Cerebellar involvement is common. Lysosomal storage disorders are inherited, with signs first becoming apparent at about one to three months of age. (*See* Chapter 27: Endocrine System and Metabolic Disorders.)

Portosystemic shunts are vascular abnormalities that prevent normal blood flow to the liver. These congenital abnormalities produce neurologic disturbances due to the lack of normal detoxifying activity by the liver. Clinical signs include excess salivation, lethargy or depression, and seizures.

Infectious Diseases

Infections of the central nervous system involve a spectrum of disease-producing microorganisms.

Cryptococcosis is caused by a yeast, *Cryptococcus neoformans.* It can produce disseminated *meningo-encephalomyelitis,* a widespread inflammation of the brain, spinal cord, and meninges. Signs can include depression, incoordination, paralysis, and seizures. The infection may also involve the eye or the upper respiratory tract and nasal passages. In many cases, signs referable to infection of the latter structures predominate and neurologic disturbances are absent. The exact mode of transmission of the agent is uncertain, but it may be inhaled or perhaps inoculated through small breaks in the skin. Treatment is of no avail once signs of neurologic disease are apparent. Prognosis is poor. (*See also* Chapter 32: Fungal Diseases.)

Feline infectious peritonitis (FIP), a coronaviral disease, can produce an inflammation of the meninges, brain, and spinal cord. Although predominantly affecting tissues of the chest and abdominal cavities, FIP can also involve the nervous system, usually with a fatal outcome. Neurologic signs can include *posterior paresis* (partial paralysis of the hindlimbs), tremors, head-tilt, behavioral changes, and seizures. There is no effective curative treatment for FIP at present. (*See* Chapter 29: Viral Diseases.)

Rabies is a viral disease that is inevitably fatal once the clinical signs are manifest, and may produce neurologic signs in the cat (as well as in many other animal species and in human beings). Rabies in cats can assume the "furious" form of the disease, similar to that often seen in dogs. Rabid cats are extremely dangerous animals for human attendants and owners because of their viciousness and quickness of action (rabies is transmitted by the bite of an affected animal, which introduces rabies virus–laden saliva into the wound). Death follows within ten days of the onset of clinical signs. Rabies in cats can be prevented by vaccination. (*See* Chapter 29: Viral Diseases, and Appendix A: Zoonotic Diseases.)

Parasitic Diseases

Toxoplasmosis is caused by a tiny crescent-shaped protozoan organism, *Toxoplasma gondii,* which infects a wide range of animal species. Cats, domestic and wild, are the *definitive host* (host wherein the adult or sexually mature stage of the parasite is produced) and represent the primary reservoir of infection throughout the world. Domestic cats are by far the most important species in transmission of this parasite to other animals and to human beings. Sometimes infected cats develop *Toxoplasma gondii*–induced disease (toxoplasmosis), which is often pneumatic in nature, though it also may involve inflammation of the brain and spinal cord. Injury to the central nervous system can be severe, and such cases are generally considered untreatable. (*See* Chapter 31: Internal Parasites.)

Larvae of the fly *Cuterebra* occasionally gain access to the brain in cats. Apparently the larvae burrow in from the hind part of the head, because the signs sometimes are related to hind brain (lower half of the brain) injury. The condition is considered uncommon. Aberrant heartworms *(Dirofilaria immitis)* may also reach the brain, with fatal consequences. (*See* Chapter 19: External Parasites.)

Nutritional Disorders

Central nervous system injury associated with nutritional disease is rare in cats. Thiamine (vitamin B_1) deficiency may produce a degenerative disease of the brain in cats and in other species. Usually this occurs when cats are fed a diet rich in fish containing a thiamine-destroying enzyme (e.g., herring, carp, and many others). Commercial cat foods generally provide adequate quantities of thiamine, and this condition is now infrequently encountered. Affected cats may be incoordinated and seizures may occur. Handling an affected cat will often induce it to tuck its head down and roll itself up into a ball. Prompt supplementation with thiamine may cure this disorder in its early stages. (*See* Chapter 8: Diseases of Dietary Origin.)

Degenerative Diseases

Degenerative disorders of the nervous system are occasionally encountered in older cats. The degeneration of supportive tissue of the spine may cause *intervertebral discs* (the cartilaginous structures between the vertebrae) to shift out of place, putting pressure on the spinal cord and resulting secondarily in inflammation. In severe cases, paralysis may be produced. Fortunately, intervertebral disc prolapse is not common in the cat. Degenerative spinal cord disease *(myelopathy)* has also been observed.

Tumors

Meningioma is the most common neurologic tumor in cats. It arises from the meninges. Although benign and well circumscribed, its continued expansion does damage by compression of brain tissue. Depression, circling, and seizures are some of the neurologic signs that may be produced by this tumor. Important behavioral signs may be loss of litter-box training, failure to recognize house and family, and restless wandering and howling. Radiographs of the skull may show the tumor, due to the associated calcification that can occur within it. CT scans are more helpful in diagnosis. Surgical removal, if possible, is the recommended treatment.

Lymphosarcoma, which is caused by the *feline leukemia virus,* is another important neurologic tumor in cats. It is a malignant tumor derived from lymphoid cells (specialized cells of the immune system), and may arise in many different areas of the body. Within the nervous system, lymphosarcoma may be diffusely invasive, but usually occurs as a solitary lesion pressing upon the spinal cord. Clinical signs usually consist of posterior paresis (paralysis). The prognosis for cats with neurologic disease caused by lymphosarcoma is grave.

Miscellaneous

Feline ischemic encephalopathy is a syndrome in the cat somewhat akin to stroke *(apoplexy)* in man. Onset of the disease is acute and is the result of sudden deprivation of the blood supply to a portion of the brain. Usually observed in mature cats, it is characterized by depression, circling, incoordination, or seizures. These acute signs often resolve in a few days, leaving a permanent deficit that may be behavioral, visual, or related to some other neurologic function. The cause of this disorder is unknown.

Epilepsy is a recurrent seizure disorder. Seizures occur as the result of a variety of causes, including infection, stroke, tumors, trauma, and toxicities. *Hypoglycemia* (low blood sugar), liver disease, and kidney failure also can produce seizures.

Feline hyperesthesia syndrome is a very important clinical, treatable, neural disorder. It is also known as rolling-skin syndrome, neurodermatitis, neuritis, psychomotor epilepsy, and pruritic dermatosis of Siamese cats.

The signs usually develop between the age of one and four years. Most cats exhibit moderate signs of ripping of the skin of the dorsum of the back, biting or licking at the tail, flank, or pelvis, hallucinations, glassy eyes with widely dilated pupils, frantic meowing, swishing of the tail, running crazily around the house and attacking objects, including the owner, without provocation. The cats may even have generalized seizures. Signs may last seconds to several minutes with no apparent pattern as to when they occur. Treatment is most successful using anticonvulsant drugs.

The most common type of seizure is the *grand mal.* Before the onset of a seizure, a cat will become restless and may show excessive affection. During the seizure itself, the cat usually collapses onto its side, showing spasmodic leg movements and chewing or twitching contractions of the facial muscles. Urination, defecation, vomiting, and pupillary eye changes may occur. After the seizure the cat may exhibit confusion and fatigue.

Most seizures in cats presented to the Small Animal Clinic at Cornell University have been traced to organic disease. Therefore, epileptic cats should be carefully screened for thiamine deficiency, hypoglycemia, infectious diseases, and tumors. Epileptic cats are treated over the long term with anticonvulsant drugs to control the seizures (there is no "cure"). Relatively little information is available on prognosis and long-term therapy in cats with nonprogressive seizure disorders.

Peripheral vestibular dysfunction (PVD) is very common in the cat, resulting from diseases that interfere with cranial nerve VIII (the *vestibulocochlear nerve*). The disease is typified by loss of balance (i.e., falling, rolling, stumbling), head-tilt, disorientation, and rapid eye movements. The onset usually is sudden, with the earliest signs being vomiting and apparent nausea. There are numerous causes for PVD, including congenital disorders, fracture of the bony *labyrinth* (a structure of the ear), tumors of the middle or inner ear, and chronic middle/inner ear infections *(otitis media-interna).* The course of treatment is based on the nature of the underlying cause.

Horner's syndrome occurs when neurons of the nervous system are disrupted by (usually traumatic) injury to the upper spinal cord, by tearing of the nerves themselves, or by middle-ear inflammation. Thus, Horner's syndrome is not a specific disease but a sign of neurologic disorder. The "classical" signs of Horner's syndrome include constriction of the pupil, protrusion of the third eyelid, sinking in of the eyeball, and drooping of the upper eyelid. Treatment depends on the underlying cause of the disorder and on the extent of damage that has been incurred. The prognosis is guarded. (*See* Chapter 18: Sensory Organs and Disorders.)

Respiratory System and Disorders

The function of the respiratory system is comparable to that of a fireplace bellows: Both are designed to provide oxygen to maintain combustion. In the case of living organisms, the combustion is the metabolism of nutrients—their conversion into energy. The oxygen combines with nutrients during metabolism; then the waste product, carbon dioxide, is expelled during exhalation.

The respiratory system consists of the *upper respiratory tract* (nose, sinuses, pharynx, and larynx) and the *lower respiratory tract* (trachea, bronchi, and lungs).

The interior of the nose (the nasal cavity)

is enclosed by bone and cartilage and is divided in half by a vertical plate called the *nasal septum,* composed of bone and cartilage with a mucous membrane cover. Within the nasal cavity there are numerous rolled structures called *conchae* and *turbinates.* These structures provide a greater surface area to aid in filtering, warming, and humidifying the

inhaled air before it enters the lungs. The sense of smell originates with olfactory nerves located in the turbinates, septum, and sinuses. Cats have a highly developed sense of smell, which plays a vital role in protection, behavior, and appetite. The entire nasal cavity is lined with a layer of cells with hairlike projections, the *ciliated epithelium.* The epithelium is supplied with numerous blood vessels and nerves. Throughout the nasal cavity there are *serous glands* (producing clear liquid) and *mucous glands* (producing mucus) that form secretions to maintain moisture levels within the nasal cavity.

The *sinuses* are spaces containing air, in the bones of the face. In the cat, the frontal sinuses, those above the eyes, are most fully developed. There are small sinuses in the adjoining bones.

The *pharynx* extends from the back of the nasal cavity to the larynx. The *soft palate* (posterior continuation of the hard palate) divides the pharynx into *dorsal* (upper or *nasopharynx*) and *ventral* (lower or *oropharynx*) parts.

The *larynx* (voice box, Adam's apple) at the back of the pharynx is the entrance to the trachea. The larynx is made up of a group of nine cartilages, which serve variously as a sphincter to control the opening to the trachea and to produce vocal sound. The larynx contains the "true" vocal cords, with which cats meow, cry, and growl, and also the "false" vocal cords with which they purr. Changes in the voice and purr of cats can be important clues to disease conditions.

The *trachea* is the tube made of cartilage known as the windpipe. It passes down the neck just below the *esophagus* (the tube from the oropharynx to the stomach) and conducts air down the neck from the larynx.

Inhaled air passes through the nose, pharynx, and larynx into the trachea, which divides at its lower end into two main airway passages (the *bronchi*), leading to the right and left lungs. The bronchi branch into smaller passageways *(bronchioles)*. Each bronchiole terminates in a small air sac (an *alveolus*). Small blood vessels *(capillaries)* surround each alveolus. It is within the alveoli that inhaled oxygen passes through cell membranes into the capillaries, where it attaches to the hemoglobin pigment of the red blood cells. Simultaneously, the carbon dioxide produced by metabolism within the body cells and transported via the blood to the alveoli is expelled back into the atmosphere during exhalation.

Each time air is inhaled, a complex series of mechanisms is set into motion. A vacuum is formed within the chest cavity to draw the air into the lungs. This is accomplished by the interaction of the muscles of the rib cage *(intercostal muscles)* and the muscle that separates the abdominal and chest cavities *(diaphragm)*. The intercostal muscles and the diaphragm expand the rib cage, creating negative pressure in the chest cavity that "pulls" the lungs open. Conversely, positive pressure in the chest is required to expel air from the lungs. A thin, delicate membrane called the *pleura* surrounds the lungs *(visceral pleura)* and lines the inside of the chest cavity *(parietal pleura)*. The pleurae provide a friction-free environment in which the lungs, chest muscles, and heart may interact.

The nose is also the respiratory system's first defense against harmful particles that are inhaled, such as dust, pollen, and microbes. The larger inhaled particles first become trapped in the mucous secretions of the nasal cavity. The ciliated epithelium moves the particles to the pharynx where the secretions are swallowed and eliminated by the digestive tract. The particles (especially pollen and dust) may also stimulate the nerve centers and cause sneezing. The smaller particles trigger a protective reaction within the trachea and bronchi. The body's immune system sends defense cells *(macrophages)* through the blood vessels to the irritated site to engulf the foreign particles. This triggers an increase in glandular secretions, contraction of bronchial muscles, and dilation of blood vessels. The macrophages migrate by *ameboid action* (resembling an ameba in movement, the cell extends cytoplasm and then follows) up the terminal bronchioles with the ingested particles and become embedded in the mucous layer. A coughing reflex then expels the foreign particles from the respiratory system, either by expectoration or swallowing.

RESPIRATORY DISEASES AND DISORDERS

Diseases affecting the respiratory system can be complex in nature and sometimes frustrating to treat. In addition, diagnosis may be difficult because signs of sneezing, coughing, and nasal discharge are characteristic of several respiratory diseases.

Infectious Respiratory Diseases
(Upper and Lower Respiratory Tracts)

Originally, all infectious feline respiratory diseases were thought to be "pneumonitis" caused by *Chlamydia psittaci*. Extensive research in several countries has shown that *Chlamydia psittaci* is not the main cause of infectious respiratory disease of cats but that in fact there are numerous agents that produce clinical diseases that may be difficult to distinguish from one another. *Feline viral rhinotracheitis* and *feline calicivirus infection* are approximately equal in incidence and account for the majority of feline respiratory diseases. It is important to realize that multiple infection can occur in the same cat; thus, an agent that normally does not produce clinical disease will exacerbate an infection caused by another agent of respiratory disease.

Feline Viral Rhinotracheitis (FVR, "rhino," feline herpes). Feline viral rhinotracheitis is an acute respiratory disease of cats caused by a herpesvirus (feline herpesvirus-1), a DNA (deoxyribonucleic acid) virus that is quite labile (chemically unstable), being sensitive to acid, heat, and most disinfectants. (*See* Chapter 29: Viral Diseases.) FVR virus will survive only eighteen to twenty-four hours at room temperature. There is only one FVR virus; all isolates of FVR virus that have been studied belong to a single serotype (a taxonomic subdivision).

Feline Calicivirus (FCV). Feline calicivirus infection is an acute respiratory infection of cats caused by one of a number of strains of calicivirus. This virus is an RNA (ribonucleic acid) virus similar to human cold viruses. (*See* Chapter 29: Viral Diseases.) The calicivirus is more resistant than the herpesvirus, surviving for one or two weeks at room temperature.

Feline Chlamydiosis (pneumonitis). This acute respiratory disease is caused by the psittacoid agent (a microorganism first seen in birds), *Chlamydia psittaci (Miyagawanella felis, Bedsonia felis)*. It is labile, being sensitive to heat, ether, acids, and broad-spectrum antibiotics.

Reovirus Infection. The feline reovirus is similar to reoviruses of many other species. The prefix "reo" stands for "Respiratory Enteric Orphan," indicating that this virus replicates in the respiratory and enteric tracts of various animals, often without producing disease. The virus is a resistant RNA virus, and more than one serotype may exist.

Chronic Upper Respiratory Infection. Chronic, mild upper respiratory infection has become a relatively common problem, especially in catteries. While some of these infections are due to herpesvirus or calicivirus, the cause of many of the outbreaks remains unknown. Some of these chronic infections may be part of the feline immunodeficiency syndrome caused by the feline immunodeficiency virus (FIV).

Feline Infectious Peritonitis (FIP). FIP is a severe, usually fatal, generalized disease of cats caused by a coronavirus. In the initial infection, virus may enter through and replicate in the respiratory system. While FIP and feline leukemia are not normally included in the respiratory disease complex, one should be aware that these viruses may affect the respiratory system. (*See* Chapter 29: Viral Diseases.)

Mycoplasma Infection. Mycoplasma can frequently be isolated from cats with respiratory disease and probably play an important role as secondary invaders. These are labile organisms and may be susceptible to antibiotics.

Bacteria. Numerous bacteria may be involved as secondary invaders in respiratory diseases. The role of bacteria in feline respiratory disease has not been fully determined, but *Bordetella* appears to cause severe bronchopneumonia (lung inflammation that begins in bronchioles) as a concurrent infection with some of the above viruses. It is not known whether or not this bacterium, or any of the numerous other bacteria that are common secondary invaders, can produce respiratory disease without initial infection by a virus.

SPREAD OF DISEASE. The route of viral infection is either oral or intranasal. The acute disease develops after an incubation period of from one to several days after infection, depending upon the severity of exposure and the virus involved. The clinical disease lasts from one to several days or may linger for weeks in some cases, again depending upon the severity of the infection and the virus involved.

Infected cats will discharge virus or other agents in the saliva, the nasal and ocular (eye) discharges, the feces (of cats with calicivirus and reovirus infections), and the urine (of cats with calicivirus infections). Infection of susceptible cats occurs by direct contact, by contact with cages, food dishes, water dishes, or litter pans that have been contaminated with virus or other agents, and by aerosol exposure (moisture droplets drifting in the air) from infected cats. These viruses may be transmitted several feet by aerosol droplets. Hands, clothing, or shoes of persons handling and caring for infected cats frequently become contaminated and can serve as a vehicle for transmitting these respiratory disease–producing agents to susceptible cats.

An important aspect of the spread of the respiratory diseases of cats is the presence of a carrier state. After recovery from FVR, cats will continue to shed herpesvirus intermittently from the oropharynx (back of the mouth) for many months. Cats infected with calicivirus have been shown to shed virus continuously from the throat, and occasionally in the feces, for long periods of time. Mother cats that had FVR or FCV as kittens may pass the virus to their young. Severe stress or another viral or bacterial infection may cause those animals carrying virus to become infectious to other cats.

METHOD OF DISEASE PRODUCTION. Oral, ocular, or intranasal (within the nose) infection results in a local infection of the epithelium (lining) of these regions, which then spreads to involve the remainder of upper respiratory epithelial cells; the infection may even spread to the lungs. The infection generally remains superficial but may spread through the blood (viremia) to produce a generalized infection. Feline viral rhinotracheitis (FVR) generally does not produce a viremia; but in certain instances viremia may occur, and infection of the osteoblasts (bone-forming cells) may result. Viremia in pregnant cats may result in infection of the fetuses and abortion.

Although the clinical disease in feline calicivirus infections is often milder than in FVR, the spread of virus is generally greater. Infection occurs not only in the respiratory mucosa (mucous membrane) but may also occur in the intestine. Severe pneumonia may occur in calicivirus infection, and ulcerations of the tongue and/or the hard palate are common.

In any respiratory viral infection, the disease may be complicated by secondary bacterial or other viral infections.

DIAGNOSIS. Feline respiratory disease is easily diagnosed, but the exact cause is extremely difficult to determine clinically. The diagnosis is made by the veterinarian on the basis of clinical signs and can be confirmed by special laboratory tests.

Clinical Signs. Several of the agents involved in the feline respiratory disease complex can produce signs that are essentially identical in any given case.

Sneezing and coughing are the first clinical signs observed, especially in FVR, and are followed by the eyes developing a sensitivity to light, becoming red and swollen, and producing a watery discharge. Frequently, only one eye is involved initially, but involvement of the second eye occurs in a few hours. The eye discharge usually becomes thicker and contains pus. Infection of the nose frequently causes a runny nose, and subsequently, in one or two days, a thick nasal discharge which may dry and form crusts. These crusts block the nostrils and force the cat to breathe through the mouth. Excess salivation may occur, especially if tongue ulcers are developing. The animal is usually depressed and may stop eating. There may be a fever, especially early in the infection.

There are some generalities that may help in determining the agent involved. FVR usually is a severe infection, especially in young kittens. Ulcers of the eye may develop, followed only rarely by a severe infection of the entire eye and total blindness. Severe sneezing is usually indicative of FVR.

Calicivirus infections generally are milder than FVR.

If pneumonia develops, however, the mortality may be high (30 percent), especially in young kittens in colonies or catteries. Ulcers of the tongue and palate generally can be attributed to calicivirus, and pneumonia is most likely due to calicivirus.

Reovirus infection is mild, with signs usually restricted to a mild eye and nose infection.

Chronic upper respiratory infection usually presents as intermittent mild ocular and/or nasal watery discharge, which persists for months to years.

Laboratory Tests. Diagnosis can be confirmed by viral isolation in the laboratory. Pharyngeal (throat), ocular, or nasal swabs may be submitted by the veterinarian to a laboratory where the swabs are placed in cell cultures for viral isolation. In most cases, the pharyngeal swab produces the best chance of viral isolation.

TREATMENT. Treatment for feline respiratory disease is, for the most part, symptomatic. Broad-spectrum antibiotics are indicated to prevent secondary bacterial infections. In pneumonitis, broad-spectrum antibiotics are specifically indicated, since this agent is susceptible to antibiotics. With chronic upper respiratory infection, broad-spectrum antibiotics usually result in transient improvement but not a cure. Eye ointments containing antibiotics are indicated for relief of the conjunctivitis (eye inflammation). The routine use of ointments containing corticosteroids (steroids), however, is contraindicated unless there is specific need. In human herpes infection, there is definite evidence that corticosteroids may lead to the development of ulcerative keratitis (inflammation with ulcers of the cornea), and there is some indication that a similar problem may exist when corticosteroids are used with FVR.

With severe infections, fluids are indicated to overcome dehydration. Oxygen therapy (placing the cat in a controlled atmosphere with increased concentration of oxygen) is also indicated if the animal is severely distressed from lack of respiratory function. Systemic vitamin injections may be indicated, because the cat is not eating. Some clinicians have indicated that vitamin C is valuable, while others dispute the value of vitamin C in treatment of respiratory disease. A controlled study showed that large doses of injectable ascorbic acid had no beneficial effects on preventing or reducing the severity of FVR.

Good nursing care is extremely important in treating respiratory diseases of the cat. It is important to clean the dry, crusted material from the nose in order to allow drainage of the nasal passages. Vaporization (using a humidifier) may be helpful in decreasing the swelling in the membranes and removing the nasal discharges. Baby foods are beneficial; cats tend to eat baby foods before regular cat food because they are more palatable.

There are some specific products that may be beneficial in treatment of herpes infection in the cat. There are specific antiviral compounds that are beneficial in treatment of ocular herpesvirus infection. There are other antiviral agents being developed that may, in time, prove beneficial.

PREVENTION. Prevention of feline respiratory disease depends upon identification and restriction of the source of virus (infected cats); reduction of the concentration of virus in the environment; and immunization of cats by vaccination.

Since the major source of infection is direct contact of susceptible and infected cats, any means of reducing or preventing direct contact between these cats will greatly reduce the chance of infection. The use of isolation or quarantine areas to house new cats, cats that are on the show circuit, or cats that have been sent away for mating, is widely recognized. These cats should be isolated for a period of at least two weeks and observed for signs of illness. Even with this precaution, these animals may be chronic carriers of infection and may introduce infection when they enter the cattery or household.

Because these viruses are also transmitted by aerosol, it is very important to have proper air-flow conditions within catteries. The humidity should be kept at a reasonably low level, and the ventilation should be good, with ten air changes per hour within the room. Infected cats or cats that are starting to sneeze or cough should be immediately isolated in a distant corner of the room, in a separate room or, preferably, in a distinct isolation ward.

Many queens are carriers of virus and transfer this virus to the kittens after the kittens have lost the temporary protection acquired from their mother's colostrum. It may be beneficial to wean kittens at a relatively early age (four to five weeks) when the kittens still have some protection from passive maternally derived antibodies. These kittens can be removed and raised away from the adults and thus break the line of transmission.

One should be constantly aware of the methods to prevent indirect spread of infectious agents. Dishes and other utensils that cats may come in contact with should be disinfected between uses. It is preferable to use disposable dishes. Persons handling or caring for infected cats should wash their hands between cats. If rubber gloves are worn, these can be disinfected and washed between cats. The weak link in any control measure is usually the people involved.

Household bleach (sodium hypochlorite, Clorox, diluted 1:32 or four ounces per gallon of water) is excellent for disinfection of food and water dishes, litter pans, cages, and floors. (*See* Chapter 37: Convalescence—Home Care.)

The most effective way of preventing infection is immunization with vaccines. Extensive research in recent years has resulted in the development and marketing of several vaccines to protect cats against FVR and FCV. These, in addition to the pneumonitis vaccine, provide considerable protection against the most important respiratory diseases.

Numerous respiratory vaccines are available in a variety of combinations. Many are also combined with panleukopenia (enteritis, "distemper") vaccine and some also include rabies vaccine. The three basic types of respiratory vaccines are (1) modified-live virus (MLV or attenuated) vaccines for injection; (2) inactivated or "killed" vaccines for injection; and (3) MLV vaccines for intranasal administration.

These vaccines provide reasonably good protection against severe infection by respiratory viruses. Vaccinated cats may still become infected, but they usually do not show any signs of illness. Virus may replicate in small amounts in the superficial cells of the upper respiratory tract, which are protected from the antibodies of the bloodstream. An occasional vaccinated cat (approximately 10 percent) may have a watery eye for one or two days after exposure to FVR virus, and some cats may sneeze a few times. These adverse reactions are mild compared to the severe disease normally seen with FVR.

Kittens should be vaccinated against FVR and FCV (and chlamydia, if it is a problem in the area) at eight to ten weeks of age and again three to four weeks later. These vaccinations can be given at the same time as those for panleukopenia. If problems with infection in younger kittens are encountered in a cattery, kittens should receive their first FVR/FCV vaccine at four to five weeks of age and their second vaccine at eight to nine weeks of age.

All cats should receive annual booster vaccinations

for FVR and FCV. Pregnant cats should not be vaccinated with the MLV vaccines; rather, breeding queens should be vaccinated at least one month prior to breeding.

There is, as yet, no need for a vaccine for the remaining agents in the respiratory disease complex. The reovirus has not been shown to be a significant cause of disease in the cat. The information presently available indicates that mycoplasma and bacteria are secondary invaders and, as such, do not warrant the development of vaccines. (*See* Appendix B: Vaccinations.)

Noninfectious Respiratory Diseases

SINUSITIS. Inflammation of the nasal sinuses usually develops subsequent to direct injury, allergy, cancer, or ascending (moving up into the sinuses) fungal, viral, or bacterial infections. Cats with sinusitis have intermittent bouts of sneezing, with evidence of a milky-white or thick, yellowish nasal discharge. Sometimes the discharge is streaked with blood. The cat's appetite remains normal, since its sense of smell is unaffected.

Radiographs (X rays) are required to confirm a diagnosis of sinusitis. Treatment is based on identifying the underlying cause. For example, antibiotics will be employed for a bacterial infection, or antihistamines for an allergy. However, if medical therapy is unsuccessful, surgery to drain and flush the sinus may be the only alternative.

FUNGAL RHINITIS. *Cryptococcosis neoformans* is the most common cause of fungal rhinitis (inflammation of the nasal cavity) in the cat. (However, *Blastomyces* and *Sporothrix* have also been reported to cause fungal rhinitis on rare occasions.) Signs include sneezing with a thick nasal discharge. Usually the discharge is from only one nostril, unless the condition is chronic. (*See* Chapter 32: Fungal Diseases.)

NASOPHARYNGEAL POLYPS. Polyps are benign, pendulous growths associated with chronic inflammation. Noisy breathing, nasal discharge, and occasional sneezing are common signs. Head shaking may also be observed, particularly if the polyps have caused chronic inflammation of the middle ear (otitis media). Sometimes cats will also have a voice change or have difficulty in swallowing. The cause is questionable, but feline calicivirus has been isolated in some cases. Treatment consists of surgical removal of the polyps.

NASAL CAVITY TUMORS. Cancer of the nasal cavity is uncommon in cats. Tumor types that have been reported include adenocarcinoma, squamous cell carcinoma, fibrosarcoma, and lymphosarcoma. Facial deformity may occur as the tumor mass increases in size. Diagnosis and treatment are based on identification of the tumor type and its extent of spread.

NASAL TRAUMA. Injury to the nose, such as a blow to the head, will cause a nosebleed (epistaxis) along with the sneezing of blood. Treatment is based on severity of the trauma. If the bleeding is persistent or severe, a blood transfusion may be necessary. Obstruction from swollen, inflamed tissues or bone fragments can result from severe nasal trauma. Usually the obstruction will resolve when the swelling subsides.

REVERSE SNEEZE. (This condition occurs more commonly in the dog than the cat.) The condition is characterized by the rapid inhalation of air, which may sound like snorting or gagging. The cause can be a foreign material lodged in the pharynx, nasal polyps, or a nasal tumor. Treatment is based on the cause.

BRACHYCEPHALIC AIRWAY SYNDROME. Short-nosed cat breeds (such as Persians and Himalayans) are predisposed to this syndrome. Their typically short skulls cause distortion of the nasal passages and pharynx and, thus, a narrowing of the airway. Affected cats must expend more energy to inhale air. This subsequently leads to thickening of the mucous membranes and elongation of the soft palate, eventually causing breathing problems. Noisy, raspy breathing usually occurs following increased physical activity, stress, or excessive heat stress. Treatment may entail surgery. A tracheostomy (permanent surgical opening in the trachea) will relieve a collapsed or dysfunctioning larynx. Small triangular snips of tissue can be removed to increase the width of the nasal openings.

LARYNGITIS. Inflammation of the mucous membranes of the larynx is usually associated with an upper respiratory tract disease or a tumor. Treatment is based on the identification of the cause.

BRONCHIAL ASTHMA. Bronchial asthma is a correctible airway obstruction caused by a hyperreactive immunologic and/or neurologic response to certain stimuli. Constriction of the bronchi, excessive mucus production, and cellular debris within the bronchioles cause the obstruction. Reports indicate that this condition is more common in the Siamese breed, and that stress seems to exacerbate an attack. Furthermore, the basic anatomy of the cat's respiratory system may actually make it more susceptible to asthmatic attacks than other animal species. These anatomical differences include an increased number of seromucous bronchial glands, especially in older cats, and a thick bronchial wall capable of increasing the constriction on the bronchi. Cat litter dust, feather pillows, cigarette smoke, aerosols, and disinfectants containing quaternary ammonium compounds have been implicated as irritants precipitating an asthmatic attack. If inhaled foreign particles cannot be eliminated, an inflammatory or allergic reaction results.

A chronic, convulsive cough with raspy or wheezy breathing between attacks is typical of asthma. The affected cat appears more comfortable in a sitting or sternal position when it lies down (lying upright, not on its side). Diagnosis is based on medical history, signs, and selected diagnostic tests (e.g., radiographs, tracheal wash). Sometimes a veterinarian will perform additional tests to rule out other conditions, such as parasitism (parasitic infection).

Drugs that enhance the dilation of the bronchioles and bronchi (e.g., corticosteroids, epinephrine, aminophylline) are effective in treating asthma. However, *these medications can only control asthma and are not a cure.* Therefore, asthma requires a commitment to long-term treatment.

ASPIRATION PNEUMONIA. The expression "it went down the wrong tube" describes the cause of aspiration pneumonia. During the process of swallowing mucous secretions, food, or fluids, the possibility exists that the material may accidentally be rerouted down the trachea rather than the esophagus. In a normal healthy animal, the coughing reflex will quickly expel the material before it can do any harm in the lungs. However, certain conditions can predispose a cat to aspiration pneumonia. These can include seizures, unconsciousness, force-feeding, esophageal disorders, mechanical obstructions, and persistent vomiting. Treatment is based on the nature and quantity of the aspirated material.

PULMONARY EDEMA (EXCESS FLUID IN THE LUNGS). Pulmonary edema is not a disease in itself but rather the manifestation of other disease processes. Diseases that can precipitate pulmonary edema include heart failure, asthma, pneumonia, lung tumors, and kidney disease, as well as poisons and thoracic trauma (chest injury). These conditions can act in one or more of the following ways to cause pulmonary edema. They may (1) increase the permeability between the capillaries and alveoli; (2) obstruct the lymphatic drainage of the lungs; and (3) alter pressures within the capillaries and lung tissues. The lymphatic system (the network of vessels that transport clear body fluids) helps to protect against edema by draining off the excess fluid by increasing the diameter of the lymph vessels. However, if the lymphatic system cannot remove the excess fluid, then the connective tissue and alveoli fill with fluid. The signs of pulmonary edema—labored and rapid breathing, wheezing, and open-mouth breathing— are consistent with respiratory distress.

Diagnosis is based on patient history, signs, and thoracic radiographs. Veterinary treatment focuses on eliminating the fluid to increase ventilation. The use of diuretics removes excess fluids, and bronchodilator drugs improve ventilation.

THORACIC TRAUMA. Injuries to the chest wall caused by either a blunt blow (e.g., a fall from great height) or penetration of a sharp object can result in *pneumothorax* (air in the chest cavity). Blunt blows can cause a tear in the thin visceral pleura, allowing air inhaled into the lungs to leak into the chest cavity. Since the pleural space is occupied with air, the lungs have less available space for expansion during inhalation. This can be a life-threatening emergency.

Signs include fast but shallow respirations which progress to slow, labored, abdominal breathing, even while the cat is resting. If severe respiratory distress occurs, the mouth and tongue will turn a bluish-gray color *(cyanosis)*. As a first-step life-saving action to remove air, the veterinarian may perform a *thoracentesis* by aspiration of the accumulated air or fluid from the chest. External wounds are surgically closed.

PLEURAL EFFUSIONS. Any accumulation of liquid in the chest cavity is referred to broadly as an effusion until its exact nature is known. A tear in a blood vessel may result in *hemothorax*. *Chylothorax* is occasionally due to a traumatic tear in the major duct that carries chyle (fat-laden lymph from the intestine) to the thoracic vena cava. More often in the cat it is caused by tumor, infection, or parasitism that interferes with lymphatic circulation in the chest.

A "watery," pale yellow, relatively clear fluid is associated with circulatory disturbances, as in heart and liver disease, and especially with lymphosarcoma of the thorax.

Inflammatory effusions are present in the "wet" form of viral *feline infectious peritonitis* and in *pyothorax*. Fever is common with both. In the former, a characteristic "syrupy," amber fluid contains much protein and moderate numbers of inflammatory cells. In the latter, there is a pus-containing fluid with a variable, usually mixed, bacterial population. The source of the infection in pyothorax may be somewhere in the mouth or respiratory tract, or a distant bite abscess may be responsible. Often no source of infection is evident.

Drainage (aspiration) of fluid is temporarily lifesaving and is essential for diagnostic purposes, but the long-term outlook for most disorders causing pleural effusions is poor.

Digestive System and Disorders

The digestive system has a unique and difficult role. It must break down food into nutrients and take these into the body, while at the same time serving as a barrier to the hordes of bacteria and other potentially disease-producing agents that are accidentally swallowed. Considering the complexity and difficulty of its tasks, it is not surprising that the digestive system is afflicted by a large number of diseases. Digestive upsets are among the most common health problems in cats.

Despite this, the digestive tract of most cats functions well year-in and year-out, with only minor upsets. Although there are a great number of diseases discussed in this chapter, many are rare or easily prevented.

mouth and ending at the anus. Thought of in this way, it becomes apparent that the *lumen* (interior) of the digestive tract is actually "outside" the animal proper. Nutrients must cross the lining of the intestine before they are truly "inside" and available to the cat. The function of the digestive tract is to break down food into components small enough to be transported across the lining and into the bloodstream, which then distributes them throughout the body. Maintenance, growth, repair, and reproduction depend on an adequate supply of these nutrients.

The Upper Gastrointestinal Tract

The digestive tract begins in the mouth. Here, the teeth tear and crush food into smaller bits. This provides much more surface area for the digestive enzymes to work on. The cat has four major pairs of salivary glands. Saliva is produced in these glands and by smaller glands in and around the oral cavity (mouth). Saliva is composed of two different secretions. The serous (watery) secretion contains the enzyme ptyalin, which helps in the digestion of

FORM AND FUNCTION

All higher animals, including the cat, are essentially tubular. That is, the digestive tract can be thought of as a tube running through the body, beginning at the starch. The mucous (jellylike) secretion lubricates the food for easier swallowing.

There are only two major problems associated with salivary glands in the cat, and both are rare. The first is *neoplasia of the salivary gland*. These tumors are usually very aggressive. The second condition is the *salivary mucocele* or *cyst*, which forms when the salivary gland or duct is injured, causing the saliva to collect in the tissues and to develop a saclike cyst.

SWALLOWING. The act of swallowing transfers the food from the oral cavity into the *esophagus* (the muscular tube extending from the mouth to the stomach) and on into the stomach. Swallowing seems a deceptively simple, virtually "unconscious" act. It is, however, an extremely complex and coordinated set of muscular actions. First, the food must be moved to the back of the mouth. Then, the opening to the *trachea* (windpipe) must be closed, while the entrance to the esophagus is opened. Next, the tongue moves backward like a piston, pushing the food into the esophagus. Finally, a ring of contraction forms behind the food and, moving like a wave, propels the food down into the stomach. (The food doesn't just fall down by gravity, which is why astronauts can swallow even when weightless.)

Any disease that interferes with this complex, coordinated sequence of events can have serious consequences, because the path of air entering the lungs and the path of food entering the digestive tract actually cross in the *pharynx* (back of the mouth). If the first phase of swallowing is not perfectly coordinated, water or food can enter the lungs, resulting in severe, potentially fatal aspiration pneumonia. (*See* Chapter 24. Respiratory System and Disorders.)

The movement of food from the esophagus into the stomach is also complex. Normally, the opening between the esophagus and stomach is kept tightly closed to prevent the strong stomach acid from splashing up and damaging the lining of the esophagus (a condition known as *gastric reflux,* or *reflux esophagitis,* which is fairly common and quite distressing in humans). During a swallow, the opening into the stomach must relax momentarily to allow the food to pass. If this does not happen at just the right moment, the food piles up in the lower end of the esophagus. The esophagus becomes progressively larger, a condition known as *megaesophagus.*

Megaesophagus. The cause of megaesophagus is not known for certain. It is believed to result from a congenital defect of the innervation (nerve supply) of the esophagus and stomach that interferes with their proper coordination. The disorder appears to be inherited. The classic signs of the condition are that a young cat fails to grow properly and is plagued by regurgitation. *Regurgitation* differs from vomiting in that it is a passive process; sometime after eating (a few minutes to an hour or more) the cat opens its mouth and the food just falls out, without any of the strong abdominal contractions associated with vomiting. Regurgitated food is completely undigested, lacks the odor of stomach acid, and frequently retains the tubular shape of the esophagus. The distinction between vomiting and regurgitation is important because they have very different causes and treatments.

If the swallowing mechanism is functioning properly, food passes into the stomach, where it is mixed with strong acid and powerful protein-digesting enzymes produced by the stomach lining. The stomach itself is a powerful muscular organ that repeatedly contracts to mix the food and enzymes. After a time, the distal (far) end of the stomach, called the *pylorus,* opens, and a portion of the food is propelled into the first part of the small intestine, called the *duodenum.* Again, there must be precise coordination of the stomach contractions and the opening of the pylorus. Incoordination, or failure of the pylorus to open sufficiently, results in delayed gastric emptying, which can be a cause of chronic vomiting. Swallowed foreign objects, (balls, thimbles, foil or plastic wrap, et cetera) can also interfere with gastric emptying and cause cats to vomit off and on for prolonged periods.

The Small Intestine

Within the duodenum, food is mixed with bile produced by the liver and with pancreatic juice from the pancreas. The bile contains bile salts that play an important role in the digestion and absorption of fats. Fat absorption is vital because fats are the most concentrated source of energy in the food, and because vitamins A, E, D, and K are fat-soluble. Diseases that interfere with fat absorption usually result in severe weight loss and can also lead to deficiencies of these vitamins.

The pancreatic juice neutralizes the stomach acid and contains an assortment of powerful enzymes that break down complex proteins, fats, and carbohydrates into their building blocks, which can then be transported across the intestinal lining and into the bloodstream for distribution. A deficiency of pancreatic enzymes results in severe maldigestion, poor growth due to a lack of nutrients, and weight loss despite a ravenous appetite. This condition, known as *exocrine pancreatic insufficiency,* is fairly common in dogs but quite rare in cats. It can be controlled to a certain extent by pretreating the food with enzyme preparations.

The processes of digestion and absorption continue as the food moves into the main portion of the small intestine, the *jejunum.* This long narrow tube undergoes constant rhythmic contractions. These are of two types: *segmental contractions,* which act principally to mix the food, enzymes, and bile; and *propulsive movements,* which are rings of contractions that move toward the anus, pushing the intestinal contents along.

As the principal function of the intestinal tract is the absorption of nutrients from foodstuffs, evolution has resulted in a number of modifications that enhance this process. First, the intestinal tract is very long (the cat's intestine is eight to ten times longer than its body). This provides a large surface area across which absorption can occur and increases the amount of time available for the process. A second adaptation is that the interior of the intestine is lined with millions of minuscule (almost microscopic) fingerlike projections called *villi.* They greatly increase the surface area available for absorption.

The Large Intestine

From the small intestine, food moves into the large intestine. A substantial amount of the water is reabsorbed here, as well as certain nutrients. The large intestine supports great concentrations of bacteria, as many as 100 billion per gram of feces. These bacteria continue to break down the remaining food, producing a number of vitamins in the process. The bacteria in the large intestine are not harmful and serve a number of important functions, not the least of which is protection against disease. Because they occupy virtually all of the available environments (niches), the normal bacteria tend to exclude disease-producing bacteria *(pathogens).* A disadvantage of some antibiotics is that they destroy the normal intestinal bacteria, making the cat more susceptible to pathogenic bacteria or fungi.

The large intestine also acts as a storage area for fecal material until voluntary defecation. Like swallowing, defecation is a complicated act involving coordinated muscular action. Cats may lose control of their bowel movements (fecal incontinence) for a number of reasons, including diarrhea, automobile injuries to the pelvis, or diseases that affect the nerves supplying the rectum or anus. At the opposite extreme is excessive retention leading to constipation.

DISEASES OF THE DIGESTIVE TRACT

Many different kinds of insult can result in malfunction of the digestive tract. These include pathogenic bacteria, viruses, protozoa, and parasites, as well as mechanical obstructions, tumors, and inherited defects. Some are preventable, others are not. Most can be treated successfully. It is helpful to differentiate those diseases that appear suddenly from those that come on more slowly and last for a long time. Because many different diseases can produce similar clinical signs, a veterinarian will need to make the final determination of the specific cause. Careful and accurate observations by the owner are vital to prompt diagnosis and timely therapy, however.

Important Observations

- When did the problem begin?
- Was it sudden in onset or gradual? (Some diseases can be excluded from consideration on this question alone.)
- What was the problem like when it started and has it changed over time?
- Does the cat defecate more frequently, about the same number of times as usual, or less than usual? (Diseases of the large bowel tend to increase the number of times the cat defecates, while diseases of the small bowel tend to increase the volume more than the number. Obstruction and other lesions of the colon may lead to constipation and reduced defecation.)
- Is there anything abnormal about the feces? For example, is there visible blood, excessive mucus, worms, or abnormal coloring?
- Does the cat seem to show pain or excessive straining when it defecates?
- Does the cat show evidence of overall illness (fever, depression, prostration) or is the problem confined to the digestive tract? (As noted below, some problems are "just" digestive, others are

"whole-cat" diseases with digestive signs. The latter have quite different treatments and implications for recovery; therefore, careful observation is important.)

- Is the cat strictly an indoor cat, or can it run free? (Important in terms of possible exposures.)
- Could the cat possibly have gotten into something potentially toxic? (Check house plants.)

History plays a critical role in diagnosing a cat's illness. Accuracy and honesty from the owner are the fastest means of obtaining an accurate picture of the cat's digestive history and problem.

Diseases That Begin at Birth

A few of the diseases that affect the digestive tract begin at birth. These include various malformations.

Proper function of the digestive tract requires a continuous passage from the mouth to the anus. Sometimes, for reasons not completely understood, there are conditions in which a segment of the intestinal tract is extremely narrow *(intestinal stenosis)* or fails to form *(aplasia)*. This is most likely to occur in the distal part of the large bowel, a condition known as *atresia coli*. A similar condition is *imperforate anus,* in which there is no connection between the rectum and the outside. In either case, there is no way for the fecal material to pass out of the body; it simply backs up in the large bowel. Surprisingly, animals can live for quite a long time without defecating. Affected kittens may appear completely normal for the first few days or weeks of life. They soon begin to fall behind their littermates and become potbellied from the accumulated fecal material. The key finding, though one that is easily missed, is that these kittens never defecate. By the time the disease is discovered, the large bowel is usually stretched beyond repair.

Intestinal Diseases That Start Suddenly

Many different conditions can result in an acute onset of vomiting and diarrhea. These include mechanical obstructions, bacterial and viral diseases, and intoxications (poisonings). All acute conditions, especially if severe or accompanied by constitutional signs (depression, fever, prostration, et cetera), require veterinary attention. This is especially true in kittens; because of their small body mass, they can dehydrate in a matter of hours. Severe dehydration is fatal.

FIRST AID. First aid for vomiting and diarrhea includes taking away all food (eating often makes the problem worse) and limiting access to water. Otherwise, the cat may get into a vicious circle of drinking and vomiting, which only makes the dehydration worse. If you can't get veterinary care right away but are worried about dehydration, provide the cat with several ice cubes to lick. This should slow the rate of water intake sufficiently to avoid inducing vomiting.

Another word of caution: Do not give milk to kittens with diarrhea. The ability to digest milk is one of the first functions lost as a result of many kinds of intestinal disease; feeding milk products under these conditions can worsen the diarrhea. Sick cats should be provided with a warm, quiet place near the litter box, and the litter should be changed frequently.

OBSTRUCTIONS. Anything that blocks the free passage of ingesta through the intestinal tract can result in vomiting and diarrhea. The closer the obstruction is to the beginning of the intestinal tract, and the more complete it is, the more sudden and severe the disease. Complete obstruction of the pylorus or duodenum causes a sudden onset of intractable vomiting. The more the cat tries to eat or drink, the more it will vomit. Such cases are medical emergencies; the cat's condition can deteriorate very rapidly. Such obstructions are most likely to result from inadvertently swallowed foreign objects (such as a small rubber ball or a baby bottle nipple).

Obstructions further along the digestive tract, particularly if they are not complete (so that some ingesta can pass around or through them), often have a chronic course spanning several days or even weeks. The signs may increase and decrease repeatedly. Such partial obstructions can result from a swallowed object; an abnormal kink or twist; or from a tumor or swelling in the intestine or in an adjacent organ that presses on the bowel and partially occludes (closes) it. One section of the bowel can even "telescope" into another, a condition known as *intussusception,* which sometimes occurs as a secondary complication of severe bowel irritation *(enteritis).*

Hairballs are often blamed for partially obstructing the bowel and causing episodes of vomiting in cats. They are probably overdiagnosed, but since they are readily cured, it is best to rule them out first by treating the cat with laxatives (either a commercial preparation for cats or petroleum jelly).

Intestinal obstruction can be diagnosed by radiography (X rays). Because the intestines and many kinds of obstruction are approximately the same density as other abdominal contents, they may not show up clearly on X rays, and positive contrast radiography may be necessary to diagnose the problem. In this procedure, the cat is given a solution of barium sulfate (by mouth, if an upper intestinal tract obstruction is suspected, or by enema, if lower bowel disease is suspected). Barium is very dense and stops most of the X rays. It shows up clearly on radiographs of the abdomen. By taking radiographs at various times after the cat has been given the barium mixture, one can follow the progress (or lack of progress) of the barium through the intestine. Obstructions, constrictions, or foreign objects are often clearly outlined.

The most infamous, and easily preventable, intestinal obstruction in cats is so-called "string enteritis." This happens when a cat or kitten finds a string or thread and needle left within its reach. If, in the course of its play, the cat swallows the thread (frequently with the needle still attached), the end often gets caught around the base of the tongue while the rest passes into the stomach and intestine. The result is an acute onset of severe vomiting and diarrhea, rapid dehydration, and depression, which result from the intestine "bunching up" in its attempt to pass the string and needle.

The key to the diagnosis is to look underneath the cat's tongue for the tell-tale loop of thread or string. The obvious temptation is to try to pull the thread back up. *Do not pull on the string.* As you pull, the thread will straighten out and cut like a knife into the curving walls of the intestinal tract, producing fatal lacerations. *See the veterinarian.* She or he will determine whether surgery is needed or whether the loop can simply be cut, allowing the string to pass through the intestinal tract naturally.

STRANGULATED HERNIA. Another potential cause of intestinal obstruction is a strangulated hernia. A hernia is the unnatural protrusion of an organ or tissue through a body opening. The opening can be natural, for example, the inguinal ring (through which the spermatic cord passes), or unnatural, like a tear in the diaphragm or abdominal muscles. If the opening is large enough, loops of bowel can pass through and become strangulated (closed or blocked). This is rare, but when it happens, it is a surgical emergency. The signs are those of acute bowel obstruction plus evidence of a hernia, or a history of previous abdominal trauma.

The most common hernia in cats is an *umbilical hernia,* most often seen as a small bulge at the navel. Most umbilical hernias are small, contain mostly fat, and are more disfiguring than dangerous. If the opening is larger than the end of a finger (press gently on the bulge and palpate its borders), then there is a risk of bowel entrapment, and the hernia should be surgically repaired.

The other fairly common "natural" hernia is an *inguinal hernia.* It appears as a bulge where the inside of the thigh joins the abdominal wall. An inguinal hernia can contain fat, loops of bowel, one horn of the pregnant uterus, or even the urinary bladder, and should be examined by a professional.

Veterinary literature suggests there is an element of heredity in the development of umbilical and inguinal hernias, although the exact means of inheritance is not known. It is difficult to give advice on breeding affected animals. As a general rule, a small hernia in a cat with no previous family history of the problem is not a sufficient reason to exclude it from the breeding program. Cats with large congenital hernias or those with affected siblings or parents should not be bred.

Traumatic hernias are all too common in cats. They result most often from cats being hit by cars, or bitten by dogs, but they can be part of the "high-rise syndrome," a fall from a high window. (*See* Chapter 39: Procedures for Life-Threatening Emergencies.) The most common defect is a tear in the abdominal muscles, but a rip in the diaphragm can occur, allowing loops of small intestine to slide into the chest. If this happens, the most obvious sign is likely to be difficulty in breathing, rather than gastrointestinal disease.

Often loops of bowel and/or parts of other organs can slide freely in and out of the various types of hernias; tipping the cat upside down or very gently pressing on the hernia may "reduce" it. But there is always a danger that the bowel will get trapped in the hernia in such a way that its blood supply will be partially or completely cut off. When this happens, that loop of bowel begins to die, and bacteria and toxins are released into the abdominal cavity. Without emergency treatment, the cat rapidly lapses into shock and dies.

For this reason, all hernias should be examined by a veterinarian. If they are large enough to cause problems or be potential sites of strangulation, they should be repaired surgically. Most hernias can be successfully corrected, especially if the animal is otherwise healthy. If a piece of bowel or other organ becomes trapped and the animal is dangerously ill, then the chances for successful repair and recovery are greatly reduced.

VIRAL ENTERITIS. A number of viruses can cause acute inflammation of the intestine *(enteritis)* with its attendant vomiting and diarrhea. (*See* Chapter 29: Viral Diseases.) The most serious cause of enteritis in cats is *feline panleukopenia virus.* This is an extremely small, hardy virus that occurs throughout the world. Before vaccination became common, virtually every cat became infected in the first year or two of life. Many died. Excellent vaccines are now available, and owners of vaccinated cats need not fear the disease.

Feline panleukopenia affects cells throughout the body, but its effects are most pronounced on the digestive tract and blood cells. The number of white blood cells of all types is drastically reduced by infection, which explains the disease's scientific name, panleukopenia (pan = all, leuko = white, penia = decreased number of cells). The disease is also called feline distemper, although this is confusing since it is in no way related to canine distemper.

The disease produced by feline panleukopenia virus reflects its peculiar life history. The virus can replicate only in rapidly dividing cells. Two of the most important populations of rapidly dividing cells are found in the bone marrow and in the intestine (both the white cells and the intestinal lining are constantly being replaced throughout life). Death of the cells in the bone marrow leads to the panleukopenia; death of the cells in the intestine leads to loss of intestinal lining and potentially fatal vomiting and diarrhea.

All cats should be vaccinated against panleukopenia. Kittens should be vaccinated at eight to ten weeks of age and again at twelve to fourteen weeks. Annual boosters are then recommended. The vaccines are highly effective and long-lasting; although the disease continues to occur among stray and feral cats, it is virtually unknown in vaccinated animals.

Recently, a panleukopenialike enteritis syndrome has been recognized in adult, well-vaccinated cats. Veterinary scientists were at first perplexed, but now know that this syndrome is one of the many devastating effects of *feline leukemia virus* (FeLV) infection. It is believed that the vaccines available against FeLV should also prevent this enteric disease.

Another group of viruses capable of causing diarrhea in cats is the *feline enteric coronavirus* group. These are discussed in more detail in the section on *feline infectious peritonitis,* because of their close and confusing relationship to the infectious peritonitis virus. (*See* Chapter 29: Viral Diseases.) They are widespread, although relatively infrequent causes of diarrhea and vomiting. There is no vaccine available. Even natural infection does not appear to confer lasting immunity, so that hope for effective prevention is dim. Fortunately, the clinical signs are generally mild and recovery is usually prompt.

Rotaviruses have recently come to the attention of medical scientists. In man, they are among the most common causes of infant diarrhea. Feline rotavirus was first isolated by researchers at the Cornell Feline Health Center in 1981. Antibodies indicative of infection are found in most adult cats, indicating that infection is common. As with feline coronavirus, most cases appear to be mild or inapparent. This may not be true in very young cats, and fatal cases have been recorded in kittens. Tests are available to detect rotaviruses in fecal specimens from infected cats, but there is no vaccine as yet.

Several other viruses, including one called an *astrovirus* (first reported by the Cornell Feline Health Center) appear able to cause diarrhea and vomiting in cats, although more research is needed to define their importance and distribution.

There are no specific antiviral drugs available to treat these diseases because viruses actually take over control of cells within the cat's body and subvert them to the production of more viruses instead of products needed by the cat. Because the viruses are being produced by the cat's own tissues, it is difficult to find compounds that harm the virus without also harming the cat. Virtually all antiviral compounds discovered to date are much too toxic for routine use.

The goal of therapy for viral diseases, then, is to support the cat until its own defense mechanisms can overcome and eliminate the virus. Supportive care consists of fasting (to rest the gut) and either subcutaneous (under the skin) or intravenous fluids to prevent or correct dehydration and electrolyte derangements that can result from severe vomiting and diarrhea. Drugs may also be used to control the vomiting and diarrhea if they are especially severe. The use of such drugs in mild cases has now generally fallen into disfavor, and several have been shown to do more harm than good.

It is generally agreed that antibiotics are inappropriate unless there is a clear indication that secondary bacteria have entered the bloodstream or that the cat's immune system is depressed (as in panleukopenia). In the past, antibiotics were overused in both human and veterinary medicine. Health care providers felt that although they might not do any good, they couldn't do any harm. Current wisdom is that antibiotics can do harm by fostering resistant bacteria and by upsetting the normal intestinal flora. Good veterinarians avoid the overuse of antibiotics.

BACTERIAL ENTERITIS. Cats appear to be relatively resistant to bacterial enteritis. Two diseases, *salmonellosis* and *campylobacteriosis,* are of concern, however, because of their *zoonotic* potential; that is, both can be transmitted to humans. Both diseases and their health hazards are discussed in detail in Chapter 30: Bacterial Diseases. The point to note here is: Always use caution and scrupulous hygiene when handling a cat with diarrhea, cleaning up accidents, or emptying the litter pan from such an infected cat. Only a few of the diseases of cats are transmissible to humans, but the possibility always exists. Teach children to avoid contact with cat feces and to wash their hands after playing with the cat, especially after it uses its litter pan. (*See* Appendix A: Zoonotic Diseases.)

In general, intestinal bacterial diseases are self-limiting. That is, the cat will recover on its own following supportive therapy (fasting and fluids followed by a bland diet). In the case of salmonellosis, antibiotics are usually unnecessary. They may also be counterproductive, favoring development of a chronic carrier state (allowing a low-level constant infection). In the case of campylobacteriosis, specific antibiotics have been shown to hasten recovery and to shorten the period of infectivity. These are areas of active research; consult your veterinarian.

DIETARY DIARRHEA. Not all acute diarrheas are infectious or even serious. Intestinal upset can be produced by a sudden abrupt diet change, or "dietary indiscretion," such as when the cat finds a bowl of whipping cream left unattended on the kitchen counter. Such diarrheas are typically mild and self-limiting, and are unaccompanied by other signs of constitutional illness. As a general rule, changes in diet should be introduced gradually, slowly substituting one food for the other.

INTOXICATIONS (Poisonings). Cats, in general, have good sense about avoiding toxins. Even so, there are a number of intoxications to which they fall prey, many of which begin as acute bouts of vomiting and diarrhea. Two of these—acetaminophen and aspirin intoxication—are a direct result of humans incorrectly treating their cats, and two others—ethylene glycol and phenol intoxication—are attributable to human carelessness. All four are readily preventable.

Aspirin is so safe and so widely used by humans that it is tempting to assume that it is also safe for pets. *But aspirin is not a safe medication for cats.* Cats metabolize aspirin much more slowly than people. If the dose is not carefully regulated, they can easily be given a fatal overdose. A single five-grain aspirin tablet can produce signs of toxicity, and if given repeatedly, can result in death (one five-grain tablet for a five-pound cat is the equivalent of thirty tablets for an average human).

Signs of *aspirin toxicity* include depression or hyperexcitability, loss of balance, vomiting, and diarrhea. Treatment for acute toxicity includes fluids, diuretics, and bicarbonate to help the kidneys excrete the drug. Aspirin can be used effectively in cats, but only if the dose is appropriate and carefully monitored. It should never be given without consulting a veterinarian.

Many owners, aware of the dangers of aspirin toxicity, assume that *acetaminophen* (e.g., Tylenol) would be a safe substitute. Again, even a single tablet can be toxic. The principal effect is on the blood, but liver damage can lead to gastrointestinal signs.

Cats are uniquely susceptible to *phenols* (distilled coal tar and water). Intoxication can follow the application of phenolized skin preparations or coal-tar products such as certain shampoos and disinfectants. A toxic dose can be ingested as the cat grooms itself. Lysol (which derives its disinfectant action and characteristic odor from phenol) should not be used to disinfect litter pans, bowls, or bedding.

Signs of toxicity include salivation, vomiting, and sometimes diarrhea. There may be involuntary muscle twitching and loss of balance. Treatment includes bathing the cat to remove any phenolic compounds still on its coat, administering intestinal protectants (Pepto-Bismol), and providing good general nursing care.

Ethylene glycol is the active ingredient in antifreeze. It apparently tastes good, as both dogs and cats will readily lap up antifreeze that has been spilled or left about after the radiator fluid has been changed. The body's attempts to break down the compound lead to the formation of crystals that clog the kidneys, resulting in acute renal failure. The clinical signs resemble drunkenness for approximately twelve hours after ingestion. Later, as the kidney damage becomes increasingly severe, affected cats will experience vomiting and diarrhea, depression, central nervous signs, and finally lapse into a fatal coma. If caught quickly, the renal damage can be halted by large doses of intravenous alcohol and other measures. Safe storage and disposal of antifreeze will prevent this fatal condition.

Another common source of intoxication for cats is the misuse of insecticides in an effort to control fleas. *Only products approved for cats should be used on cats.* Cats are more sensitive to many pesticides than are dogs; certain products safe for dogs can be fatal to cats. Never apply a product intended for household or yard use to a pet. The results could be tragic. Depending on the specific product involved, the signs of intoxication vary, but typically include apprehension, excessive salivation, and digestive system and nervous system disorders. First aid includes calling the veterinarian and the National Animal Poison Information Network (217–333–3611) and bathing the animal to remove as much residual toxin as possible.

There are many other potential environmental toxins to which a cat could fall prey, including insecticides, rodenticides, fertilizers, and certain house plants, to name only a few. The list grows longer each year. Many, but not all, of these poisons can produce the sudden appearance of gastrointestinal signs. If you suspect your cat has been poisoned, note carefully the circumstances (for example, pesticide spraying by a neighbor), call the veterinarian, collect some of the suspect material if possible, and check with the National Animal Poison Information Network. (*See* Chapter 39: Procedures for Life-Threatening Emergencies.)

Chronic Intestinal Disease

Cats, like people, are prone to a number of diseases that produce intermittent vomiting and/or diarrhea lasting for weeks or even years. Such conditions are distressing to both the owner and pet and can be severely debilitating. They also can be very difficult to diagnose, so that the owner's role as observer becomes even more important when the disease is chronic. Do not rely on memory. Make detailed notes or daily charts. This is especially important when different therapies are being tried. The only way to know for certain which treatment helps the cat most is to have good records of such details as weight gain or loss, number of bowel movements daily, character of the stool, and the frequency or severity of vomiting. This information can be extremely useful to the veterinarian treating a cat with a chronic intestinal disease.

PARASITES. While a number of parasites can be important causes of disease in kittens, many adult cats can harbor most intestinal parasites with little or no problem. (*See* Chapter 31: Internal Parasites.) An important exception to this rule is *giardiasis,* which is an intestinal infection by the one-celled parasite of the species *Giardia.* Cats with giardiasis often have stools that vary from soft to normal. They tend to be unthrifty (are unable to make proper use of nutrients) and have trouble gaining or maintaining their weight. The biggest problem with giardiasis is making the diagnosis. Giardia organisms are very small and hard to recognize in fecal specimens. The methods usually employed for identifying parasites in feces distort giardia beyond recognition, so special solutions and techniques must be used. Worse, the organisms seem to be passed intermittently, so that repeated examinations may be needed to nail down the diagnosis.

The stomach worm *Ollulanus tricuspis* also is a potential cause of chronic gastrointestinal disease in adult cats. Although many cats harbor this parasite without any clinical signs, it can be a cause of chronic vomiting. Diagnosis depends on demonstrating larvae in the vomitus; they cannot be detected by fecal examination. Levamisole has been reported as a treatment, but efficacy and safety studies are incomplete. There is no other known treatment at the present time.

KIDNEY OR LIVER FAILURE. A healthy gastrointestinal system both contributes to, and depends on, the health of the entire body. Digestive upsets can result from disease in other organs, especially in the kidney or liver.

Renal disease is common in older cats. With age and accumulated damage from disease, the capacity of the kidneys to clear waste products declines. When the kidneys can no longer keep up with the rate at which waste products are produced, wastes begin to accumulate in the bloodstream, causing adverse effects in many organs, especially the gastrointestinal tract. Cats with failing kidneys have poor appetites, lose weight, are pale, and suffer periodic vomiting and diarrhea. Oral ulcers and fetid breath are common. It is impossible to reverse chronic renal failure, but the cat can be made more comfortable and its life extended by treatment. (*See* Chapter 22: Urinary System and Disorders.)

Liver failure is much less common than kidney failure, but no less serious. Among its many functions, the liver also serves as a blood filtering and cleansing device. Liver disease, which can itself have many causes (*see* Chapter 26: Liver, Pancreas, and Disorders), also leads to an accumulation of toxic waste products in the bloodstream. The most noticeable of these is *bilirubin,* the yellow breakdown product of recycled hemoglobin (the oxygen-carrying element of red blood cells). The accumulation of bilirubin gives cats (and people) the characteristic yellow discoloration known as jaundice, most noticeable in the whites of the eyes.

The signs of liver disease are those of generalized illness—depression, lethargy, loss of appetite, increased thirst and urination, occasional vomiting, and diarrhea. Detailed biochemical tests are required to firmly establish that the liver is indeed responsible. Treatment depends on the nature of the liver disorder, its severity, and its chronicity. In general, the liver shows remarkable ability to regenerate itself. Complete recovery, particularly from acute conditions, is possible.

FELINE IMMUNODEFICIENCY VIRUS (FIV).

Feline Immunodeficiency Virus (FIV), formerly called Feline T-lymphotropic lentivirus (FTLV), is a newly discovered virus that is closely related to the human AIDS virus. The FIV virus causes severe depression of the immune response and results in a host of secondary infections and complications. Among these are chronic diarrhea, weight loss, infections of the gums and teeth, conjunctivitis, and respiratory infections.

The secondary infections can be treated and the cat made more comfortable, but the virus infection itself is incurable. A rapid in-office test has been developed to help identify infected cats and limit spread of the virus, but no vaccine is yet available. (*See* Chapter 29: Viral Diseases.)

CANCERS.

A tumor or neoplasm (literally meaning "new growth") can arise in almost any tissue, including the tissues of the intestinal tract, when the mechanisms that regulate cell replication are disrupted. Normally, the growth of cells and tissues in the body is under very tight control. Many tissues, like those of the bone marrow, skin, and intestinal lining, continue to multiply throughout life. But the number and kinds of cells are always kept in balance with the body's needs. Cancer results when something upsets the mechanisms that regulate cell multiplication and replacement. That "something" can be a virus, a toxin, radiation, or perhaps the aging process itself. The result is the same, however: one cell or a group of cells begins to divide and grow out of control, without regard for the needs of the body or surrounding tissues.

In the intestinal tract, this can have a number of untoward consequences. The tumor, because of its sheer size, may cause a partial intestinal blockage, producing intermittent vomiting and diarrhea that gradually worsen as the tumor grows. In the case of *alimentary lymphosarcoma,* the tumor cells may infiltrate the intestinal wall where they interfere with the absorption of nutrients, producing chronic diarrhea and severe weight loss. Exploratory surgery, with the removal of a small piece of bowel for biopsy, is usually required to accurately diagnose intestinal cancer. If the tumor has not spread too widely, it may be possible to remove the section of affected bowel. Certain cancers also respond well to chemotherapy and/or radiation.

EOSINOPHILIC ENTERITIS.

A similar but apparently non-neoplastic disorder is eosinophilic enteritis. As in alimentary lymphosarcoma, the bowel wall is invaded by abnormal numbers of white blood cells, in this instance a particular type known as eosinophils. Why this happens is unclear, although eosinophilic enteritis is often part of a generalized overpopulation and invasion of eosinophils known as the *hypereosinophilic syndrome.* Cats with eosinophilic enteritis have long-standing problems of vomiting, diarrhea with occasional blood, and weight loss. Some cases respond to corticosteroid (steroid) therapy.

CHRONIC INFLAMMATORY BOWEL DISEASE.

One of the most devastating human diseases is Crohn's disease, a chronic inflammation of the bowel of unknown origin, which leads to abdominal pain, diarrhea, and bleeding into the stool. Cats suffer a similar disorder, whose cause also remains unknown (hence, "idiopathic"). The signs of the disease are frequent attempts to defecate that result in only a small amount of stool each time, blood-streaked or blood-tinged feces, and obvious pain or straining at stool. The diagnosis depends on the history, physical examination, and colonoscopy (instrument examination of the colon) under general anesthesia. A colonoscope is an instrument that can be inserted in the rectum to allow the veterinarian to inspect the rectal and colonic mucosa (lining). Ulcerations, polyps, tumors, and other lesions of the large bowel can be readily detected. Small tissue samples can also be collected for microscopic examination (biopsy).

Several drugs are available to ameliorate the effect of chronic bowel inflammation. The most effective is usually Azulfidine, a compound used in humans with similar disorders. Some cats appear to be cured; the drug may be stopped after several weeks without a return of the signs of the disease. But many cats get only incomplete relief and must be maintained on this or other drugs for life.

Diseases Causing Constipation

Most of the diseases discussed thus far have been those involving diarrhea and excessively fluid or frequent stools. But cats are also plagued by the opposite problem, constipation: difficulty defecating and hard, dry stools. As with diarrhea, there are many possible causes. While constipation is less likely to be life-threatening, it should not be ignored because, untreated, it can lead to more serious or permanent disorders.

CLINICAL SIGNS. The clinical signs of constipation are well known: crouching and straining for prolonged periods with either no feces being passed or only a small amount of hard, dark, dry stool. Cats with constipation may also have poor appetites, lose weight, and lack energy or enthusiasm. Diarrhea and constipation can coexist. Long-standing constipation can so irritate the lining of the colon that it is stimulated to excrete fluid. The feces already in the colon may be so hard and dry, however, that they are virtually impervious to liquid and remain unsoftened by the additional secretions. When this happens, the cat

will continue to strain at stool, passing dark watery fluid and sometimes small hard fecal balls.

CAUSES OF CONSTIPATION. As noted earlier, defecation is actually a complex, highly coordinated muscular act. Any interference with the correct timing of the various actions (relaxing the anal sphincter, colonic contraction, abdominal press, et cetera) can lead to constipation. Dietary composition, psychological factors, and certain disease processes can also lead to fecal retention.

NEUROLOGIC CAUSES OF CONSTIPATION. Diseases that affect the nerves supplying the colon and anus can result in constipation. The two most important of these are dysautonomia and idiopathic megacolon.

Feline dysautonomia (also known as Key-Gaskell syndrome, for the two researchers who first described it) was unknown before 1982. For a number of years, the disease was believed to occur only in Europe, but recently cases have been discovered in the United States as well. Little is known about the disease, except that it in some way disturbs the autonomic (subconscious) nervous system. The signs are quite apparent: widely dilated pupils that do not respond to light, due to denervation (loss of nerve stimulation) to the iris; dry mouth and eyes due to denervation of the salivary and tear glands; constipation due to the loss of sympathetic innervation of the colon; and, often, vomiting and regurgitation with the development of megaesophagus due to disturbance of coordinated swallowing. Fortunately, the disease is still very rare, since there is neither a means of prevention nor cure.

Idiopathic megacolon, as its name implies, is a massive enlargement of the colon without apparent cause. The primary defect is believed to be improper innervation (poor nerve supply) of the colon and rectum that results in ineffective contractions and the inability to empty the bowel. Lumbosacral spondylosis in older cats may trap spinal nerves involved in colon motility and defecation. As a result, feces pile up in the colon, which gradually enlarges. A harmful cycle is established, since the dilated bowel is even less effective at expelling feces. Depending on the severity of the disease, cats with this condition may manage fairly well on laxatives and occasional enemas. More serious cases will require partial surgical removal of the colon, a difficult piece of surgery with many complications, but one which can restore normal or nearly normal bowel function to some affected cats.

PAINFUL DEFECATION. Cats can become constipated simply because defecation hurts. An infected or impacted anal sac or perianal bite abscess could make moving the bowels painful. In order to minimize the frequency of this pain, the cat holds its stool as long as possible. This, too, initiates a harmful cycle; the longer the stool is retained, the harder and drier it becomes and the more difficult and painful to pass. This leads to more retention, more drying, more constipation, and so forth. The solution is to resolve the primary condition as soon as possible. Until then, the cat should be fed bran or other bulk-forming agents and given laxatives as necessary to produce a softer and less painful stool.

PSYCHOLOGICAL CAUSES. Just as physical pain can lead to constipation, so can psychological upsets. Cats may refuse to defecate in a litter pan that has not been cleaned or has a radically different kind of litter, especially a strongly scented one. A change in the family (a move to a new environment, or a new baby who competes for attention) can upset the cat's normal bowel habits. Cats often register their feelings about such changes by inappropriate defecation and house-soiling (*see* Chapter 5: Misbehavior), but they also may refuse to defecate, leading to constipation. In the case of litter pans, it's best to keep the pan clean and to introduce new litter gradually by substituting increasing proportions of the new litter mixed with the old familiar brand. If your cat has a history of constipation, it may be wise to anticipate major upsets by adding bran or other bulk-forming agents to the cat's diet.

MEDICATIONS. A side effect of a number of medications, including preanesthetics, diuretics, antihistamines, and even barium, is constipation. Tell the veterinarian if the cat is, or has been, receiving medication for any reason. Fortunately, drug-induced constipation is seldom severe and usually responds well to mild laxatives and/or changing the dose or type of medication.

OBSTRUCTION. Obstructions to the flow of intestinal contents in the upper gastrointestinal tract lead to vomiting and diarrhea; obstructions of the colon or rectum can lead to constipation. Causes include frac-

tured pelvis (for example, following a car accident), which narrows the pelvic opening, impeding the passage of feces. This cause may be complicated by pain, making the cat unwilling to try to defecate. Tumors of the colon itself or adjacent structures can have the same effect.

Perhaps the most easily cured cause of constipation has the serious-sounding designation of *pseudocoprostasis* (literally, false fecal impaction). Pseudocoprostasis is seen when hair around the anus (usually in longhair breeds) becomes soiled and matted across the anus, preventing the cat from passing stool. The condition may appear quite serious, with the animal straining and crying in distress. The solution is simply to clean or clip away the matted material. Hence, it is important to check the hind end of any otherwise healthy longhair cat who develops a sudden onset of painful constipation.

ENDOCRINE CAUSES. Several different *endocrinopathies* (hormone disturbances) can lead to constipation, including diseases of the thyroid or parathyroid glands. The constipation problem will resolve once the underlying condition is recognized and treated. Severe, generalized debility from a serious illness or disease in another organ can also lead to constipation. Cats with other serious health problems should be fed diets that promote soft bowel movements in order to avoid this unnecessary and stressful complication.

TREATMENT FOR CONSTIPATION. The treatment for constipation in cats is the same as in people: high-bulk diets, laxatives, and occasionally suppositories or enemas. A word of caution here: *Never use a commercially prepared liquid enema on a cat.* Many of these enemas contain high concentrations of phosphate, concentrations that can prove lethal for cats.

Giving a cat an enema is a job best left to professionals. Repeated enemas over the course of several days, together with mechanical removal of extremely hard feces, or colonic massage through the abdominal wall, may be necessary in severe cases. In cats with mild constipation, one or two pediatric suppositories may be used instead of an enema. *Bisacodyl* or *DDS* (dioctyl sodium sulfosuccinate) suppositories are more effective than glycerin suppositories.

After the original impaction has been cleared, the stool should be kept soft through the use of bulk-forming laxatives. These are natural or synthetic cellulose products or derivatives that are nondigestible, nonabsorbable, and hydrophilic (water-attracting). They add bulk to the stool and help keep it moist. Many commercial products are available, but, in general, bran is just as effective and much less expensive. It can be mixed with canned or moistened food as part of an ongoing constipation-prevention program.

Unlike laxative medications, which, if overused, can lead to dependency, bran is a natural product that can be used indefinitely with no known side effects. The usual recommendation is for one to two tablespoons per four hundred grams (fourteen ounces) of canned food. Check with your veterinarian for specific recommendations.

Liver, Pancreas, and Disorders

The exocrine glands discharge secretions through ducts, as compared with endocrine glands, which secrete hormones directly into the circulatory system. The major organs discussed in this chapter are the liver and the pancreas. Other exocrine glands, such as the salivary glands or sweat glands, can be found listed in Chapter 25: Digestive System and Disorders, or in Chapter 17: Skin and Disorders, respectively.

THE LIVER

The liver is one of the largest organs in the body. It is divided into a number of discrete sections, or *lobes,* each of which is composed of thousands of minute structural and functional units *(lobules).*

Among the major functions of the liver are assistance in the digestion of food; storage of energy (sugar) in the form known as *glycogen;* release of energy by breakdown of glycogen; synthesis of certain proteins and fats; storage of certain vitamins; produc-

tion of blood-clotting factors; the manufacture of *bile,* important in the absorption of fats; and the manufacture of certain hormones.

The blood supply to the liver is composed of oxygenated blood from the *hepatic artery* and deoxygenated blood from the *portal vein* (coming from the digestive tract). Branches of these two vessels, together with a *bile ductule,* make up the *portal triads* at the periphery of each liver lobule. Blood moves from the periphery of the lobule (from the portal triad) toward the *hepatic vein,* from which it exits the liver on its return to the heart.

A major anatomical feature of the feline liver, distinct from that of the canine, is the joining of one of the *pancreatic ducts* (coming from the *pancreas*) to the *common bile duct* (originating in the liver) before attachment to the small intestine. Normally, digestive enzymes and bile flow through these passageways and are deposited within the uppermost portion of the small intestine, the *duodenum.* Because of this anatomical arrangement in the cat, occasional backward flow of enzyme- and bile-enriched juices from the intestine may produce inflammation in the liver or pancreas.

A unique and important feature of feline liver physiology is a deficiency in the enzyme *glucuronyl transferase*. This enzyme is required for a process known as *glucuronic acid conjugation*. Most waste substances excreted by the liver are excreted in a water-soluble form. This is done so that, once waste products are released from the liver cells, they cannot passively diffuse back across the fat-soluble cell membranes. They are "trapped" in the extracellular spaces and excreted. Glucuronic acid conjugation is the major pathway (process) by which fat-soluble compounds are transformed into water-soluble compounds. The cat's natural deficiency of this metabolic pathway explains the special feline sensitivity to certain drugs, such as aspirin, which, as a result, are only slowly and inefficiently excreted.

Another significant feature is the inability of cats to make *arginine*. This amino acid is involved in the conversion of *ammonia* (a waste product of protein metabolism) in the blood to *urea* for excretion through the kidneys. When arginine is not provided in sufficient amounts in the diet, muscle tissue is broken down to release the trapped arginine within it. Malnourished cats thus may be especially susceptible to increases in the level of ammonia in the blood, with resultant signs of neurologic dysfunction.

Diagnosis of Liver Disease

CLINICAL SIGNS. Cats with liver disease often are not presented to a veterinarian until late in the course of their illness. Cats are experts at hiding the fact that they are ill, causing liver dysfunction to go unnoticed until significant liver damage has occurred. Many of the clinical signs associated with liver disease may also be seen in other disease states, so diagnosis usually requires laboratory testing. Among the clinical signs evident in liver disease are inappetence, vomiting, diarrhea, fever, weight loss, dehydration, seizures, and, occasionally, increased water consumption *(polydipsia)* and increased urination *(polyuria)*. *Hepatomegaly* (enlargement of the liver) and *jaundice* (deposition of yellow bile pigment in the skin and mucous membranes) may be observed on physical examination. Inflammatory diseases of the eyes *(chorioretinitis, anterior uveitis; see* Chapter 18: Sensory Organs and Disorders) can be seen with systemic diseases that can affect the liver, such as *feline infectious peritonitis* (FIP) *(see* Chapter 29: Viral Diseases) and *toxoplasmosis* *(see* Chapter 31: Internal Parasites).

HEMATOLOGY. A *nonregenerative anemia*—an anemia in which no regeneration of red blood cells in the bone marrow is evident—is often seen in cats with liver disorders. The white blood cell count may be normal, or it may be elevated as a result of stress, liver cell death, or infection. Deficiencies in the blood-clotting mechanism may also occur in severe liver disease.

LIVER ENZYMES. *Alanine aminotransferase* (ALT) is an enzyme found within liver cells. The normal blood level of this enzyme increases when damage to liver cells—whether the result of inflammation, cell death, oxygen deprivation, fatty infiltration, or bile duct blockage—has occurred. Persistent elevation of ALT levels suggests ongoing liver cell injury. *Aspartate aminotransferase* (AST) is a liver cell enzyme that is also found in muscle cells and red blood cells. Because of its wider distribution in the body, elevations in AST levels are not as specific for liver cell injury as are elevations in ALT. Another enzyme, *serum alkaline phosphatase* (SAP), is produced in many tissues but is of greatest importance in the liver and bone. *Gamma glutamyl transferase* (GGT) is more specific for liver disease than either AST or SAP and is especially useful for diagnosis of *cirrhosis* (degeneration of normal tissue) and bile duct obstruction.

ALBUMIN. Albumin is a major protein component of the blood plasma and is important in maintenance of fluid pressure balance within the blood and tissues. Albumin is manufactured by the liver, and its production can be maintained until severe liver failure (80 percent loss of functional liver mass) has occurred. Decreased levels of albumin in the blood attributable to liver dysfunction thus are not seen until end-stage disease is at hand.

AMMONIA. Ammonia is a toxic by-product of protein metabolism that is detoxified to urea within the liver. Normally, maintenance of proper blood ammonia levels is dependent on functional liver mass, normal portal blood circulation, and sufficient dietary protein intake. Elevation of blood ammonia levels after fasting or during *ammonia tolerance testing* indicates an abnormality in any of these three areas. Severely elevated blood ammonia levels often produce signs of neurologic dysfunction.

BILIRUBIN. Bilirubin is a breakdown product of red blood cells. Unconjugated water-soluble bilirubin is transported in the blood to the liver, where it is taken up and conjugated (joined with glucuronic acid) to form water-soluble *bilirubin glucuronide.* This conjugated form of bilirubin may then be stored in liver cells or passed out into the bile. In the small intestine, bilirubin is degraded to *urobilinogen,* the majority of which is excreted in the feces. A small amount is retained and eliminated in the urine or recirculated through the liver. The detection of urobilinogen in the urine thus indicates that the *entero-hepatic circulation*—the movement of material between the digestive tract and the liver—is intact. However, the presence of even trace amounts of bilirubin in feline urine is considered abnormal and an indication of disease involving the liver, bile ducts, or excessive destruction of red blood cells. Jaundice usually develops when bilirubin levels in blood serum rise above 1.5–2.0 milligrams per one hundred milliliters.

LIVER FUNCTION TESTS. Although a number of these procedures (detection of elevated levels of liver enzymes, blood ammonia, or bilirubin) are useful in the diagnosis of liver disease, they are only secondary indicators of the status of liver function, i.e., they do not measure liver function directly. Liver function tests (indocyanine green and sulfobromophthalein clearance, ammonia tolerance, and bile acid levels) have been designed to demonstrate and quantify the extent of the liver's functional capacity in health and disease. Liver function tests are necessary to confirm a decrease in functional liver mass and thus justify more invasive diagnostic techniques such as percutaneous needle biopsy or exploratory surgery.

LIVER BIOPSY. In most cases a liver biopsy is necessary to establish a specific diagnosis so that appropriate therapy may be applied. One of three major techniques may be used: (1) *percutaneous needle biopsy,* in which a sample of liver tissue is retrieved by passing a biopsy needle through the skin, guided either by feel or by ultrasonic monitoring; (2) *laparoscopy,* in which a biopsy needle is guided by sighting through a narrow flexible tube inserted into the abdomen; and (3) *exploratory surgery,* to directly retrieve liver tissue.

The risks inherent in each technique need to be weighed against the potential benefits of the information gained. When biliary obstruction outside the liver is suspected, exploratory surgery is the technique of choice.

A blood clotting profile must be obtained before biopsy of the liver because of the frequent association of clotting abnormalities with liver disease. Even if normal clotting values are obtained, a supply of fresh whole blood should be available for transfusion during biopsy.

SEROLOGIC TESTING (study of antigen-antibody reactions). Serologic testing for *feline leukemia virus* (FeLV), *feline infectious peritonitis* (FIP), and toxoplasmosis should also be included in the diagnostic work-up because of the association of these entities with some feline liver disorders.

Liver Diseases

HEPATIC LIPIDOSIS. Hepatic lipidosis is a common liver disease of cats, in which fats *(triglycerides)* accumulate within the liver cells. Hepatic lipidosis often presents as a secondary manifestation of an underlying primary abnormality, such as obesity, diabetes mellitus, or toxemia (spread of bacteria in the blood). Cases wherein an underlying abnormality cannot be identified are diagnosed as idiopathic (cause unknown). The most common clinical signs of hepatic lipidosis include weight loss, inappetence, dehydration, enlargement of the liver, and jaundice. Hepatic encephalopathy (neurologic abnormalities secondary to liver failure) and bleeding disorders have also been reported. Serum levels of certain liver enzymes (ALT, SAP) may be markedly elevated. A definitive diagnosis is based on microscopic examination of liver biopsy tissue. Initial therapy includes restoration of fluid and electrolyte balance to correct dehydration. The most important aspect of therapy is reinstitution of proper protein and caloric intake. This may be accomplished by intravenous feeding, forced oral feeding, or administration of appetite stimulants.

CHOLANGIOHEPATITIS COMPLEX. The term *cholangiohepatitis* is used to describe a number of related inflammatory disorders of the liver and biliary tract. These disorders are categorized into at least three forms, according to the predominant inflammatory cell type identified within liver biopsy samples. Although little is known about this complex of diseases, it is believed by some that each of the three forms represents a different stage in the progression of a single disease entity. Clinical signs seen are nonspecific and can include intermittent inappetence, fever, lethargy, vomiting, soft stools, and jaundice. Biochemical testing usually reveals marked increases in serum bilirubin and ALT, with moderate increases in SAP and GGT. Definitive diagnosis rests on microscopic examination and bacterial culture of liver biopsy tissue.

Three to five weeks of specific antibiotic therapy may be indicated for the *suppurative* (pus-forming) form of the disease, in which the *neutrophil* is the primary inflammatory cell infiltrating the liver lesions. The *nonsuppurative* form, in which *lymphocytes* and *plasma cells* predominate, requires immunosuppressive drug therapy with steroids. The aim of therapy is to control the disease; a complete cure is rarely obtained. The *biliary cirrhosis* form, in which bile duct tissue is replaced by tough connective tissue, is believed to be the final stage in the progression of the disease. It is not observed very often because cats with cholangiohepatitis rarely survive long enough for it to develop. At this stage, serum GGT may be the only liver enzyme that is elevated; the others may have all been depleted by the chronic inflammatory disease process. The prognosis is very poor. Medical management at the final stage is primarily supportive and aims to maintain adequate hydration and nutrition. Ideally, the nutrient requirements should be provided by a primarily carbohydrate diet in which the minimum protein requirement is supplied by protein of high biologic value (severe protein restriction is *not* recommended, however). A multiple-vitamin supplement should also be included.

ACUTE HEPATIC NECROSIS. Acute hepatic necrosis (liver cell death) may be caused by infectious diseases, toxins from microbial or other sources, or oxygen deprivation *(hypoxia)* secondary to anemia, shock, or congestive heart failure. Serum ALT and AST levels are markedly increased, while normal or moderately increased levels of SAT and GGT are seen. During the two to three weeks following the liver insult, serum enzyme levels will gradually decline to normal. Cats with acute hepatic necrosis may also have elevated bilirubin levels or blood clotting abnormalities. Initial treatment should involve removal or binding of the toxic material (if such is suspected), using saline enemas or activated charcoal passed by stomach tube. Supportive care should include antibiotics, fluid therapy, B-complex vitamins, and potassium and glucose supplementation. Dietary considerations are similar to those outlined for hepatic lipidosis.

EXTRAHEPATIC BILE DUCT OBSTRUCTION. Obstruction of the bile duct external to the liver proper may be caused by inflammation, cancer, or a *stricture* (narrowing) within the duct or its associated organs (pancreas, duodenum). Less often, gallstones *(choleliths)* or migration of parasitic worms may produce obstruction. The presenting clinical signs can include inappetence, weight loss, fever, intermittent vomiting, and jaundice. Biochemical testing usually reveals markedly elevated serum bilirubin and liver enzyme levels. If complete biliary obstruction exists, urine urobilinogen decreases to undetectable levels, feces become *acholic* (lightly colored, because of the absence of bile in the intestine), and bleeding tendencies develop. Radiographic (X-ray) evaluation of the abdomen or chest may occasionally be helpful in identifying cancers. *Ultrasonography* (ultrasound) can be used to determine if obstruction is present and may sometimes be able to elucidate a cause, e.g., gallstones or obstructive masses. Surgical intervention and correction ultimately are necessary in the majority of cases.

PORTOSYSTEMIC VASCULAR ANOMALIES. Cats with congenital abnormalities in the blood vasculature system of the liver may present with signs of encephalopathy (disease of the brain causing seizures, head-pressing, incoordination, coma), poor growth rate, inappetence, weight loss, drooling, depression, vomiting, and diarrhea. Biochemical parameters may be normal or may show only minor alterations. The most remarkable abnormality demonstrable is impaired liver function, as measured by bile acid values or other liver function assays. Ultrasonography or *mesenteric angiography* (injection of dye into the vasculature) is necessary to confirm a diagnosis. Surgical correction of the anomalous vessel(s) is the recommended therapy, but is not a guarantee of recovery of normal function. The prognosis is always guarded.

THE PANCREAS

The pancreas is located near the liver. It is classified in the endocrine system as well as the exocrine system because the pancreas contains the ductless glands the *islets of Langerhans,* small clusters of hormone-producing cells that secrete insulin. The pancreas itself produces pancreatic fluid, containing digestive enzymes, which passes through the pancreatic ducts into the intestines.

Pancreatic fluid contains *pancreatic amylase,* which changes starch into maltose; *lipase* and *phospholipase A,* which break down fats into fatty acids and glycerol; and the proteolytic enzymes *trypsin, chymotrypsin,* and *elastase,* which break down proteins to peptides. The proteolytic enzymes are stored by the pancreas in inactive forms called proenzymes. When they are secreted into the duodenum, *enterokinase* is released by duodenal mucosa and activates trypsin. Then trypsin activates all the other proleolytic enzymes. The simplified nutrients then enter the bloodstream to be delivered to the cells.

Diseases of the Pancreas

ACUTE PANCREATITIS. Acute pancreatitis is uncommon, but can occur in obese cats that get little exercise and may have eaten a meal with high fat intake. Steroid administration and a decrease in the blood supply to the pancreas each may play a role in the production of acute pancreatitis. When pancreatic cell damage takes place, pancreatic enzymes are released and begin breaking down the fat in other adjacent tissues, resulting in bleeding, shock, endotoxemia (bacterial toxins in the bloodstream), and possibly death.

Clinical diagnosis is based on intuition and specu-lation. A cat that has had an episode of vomiting, fever, and anorexia, which responds to supportive care in forty-eight to seventy-two hours, may indeed have had acute pancreatitis. Many cases are not diagnosed until after the cat's death, when a necropsy (autopsy of an animal) is performed.

TRAUMATIC PANCREATITIS. This is usually caused by an accident such as being hit by an automobile, or falling from a height, as in high-rise syndrome. (*See* Chapter 39: Procedures for Life-Threatening Emergencies.) The trauma or injury to the pancreas allows leakage of the enzymes into the surrounding tissues and abdomen, resulting in the same clinical picture as in acute pancreatitis.

CHRONIC PANCREATITIS. Chronic pancreatitis usually results from recurrent bouts of acute pancreatitis. It is usually subclinical (symptomless), found at necropsy in older cats. Chronic pancreatitis may lead to diabetes mellitus and exocrine pancreatic insufficiency, but the typical signs of maldigestion are extremely rare in cats. Pancreatic insufficiency results from a decrease or near absence of the digestive enzymes necessary to break down fats, carbohydrates, and proteins, causing malnutrition.

PANCREATIC NEOPLASIA. Primary neoplasias, or tumors of the pancreas, are uncommon. When diagnosed they are usually adenomas, adenocarcinomas, or islet cell tumors. Secondary neoplasia occurs more commonly as lymphosarcoma associated with feline leukemia.

NODULAR HYPERPLASIA. This is a common finding in old cats, at necropsy. It appears as lumps or thickenings in the tissue of the pancreas. It is not a malignancy and probably has little clinical significance.

Endocrine System and Metabolic Disorders

Endocrine glands lack ducts for the secretion of their hormones; instead their hormones are emptied directly into the bloodstream. Hormones can be classified into two categories: the *protein* or *polypeptide* type, which tends to have an immediate effect on the animal's body; and the *steroid* type, which is made of fatty substances and tends to have a longer-lasting effect. The cat's endocrine system includes the following glands: thyroids, parathyroids, adrenals, pancreas, gonads (testes and ovaries), and pituitary.

The *thyroid glands* are located bilaterally adjacent to the larynx (upper part of the trachea [windpipe]). They secrete two major hormones, *thyroxine* (T_4) and *tri-iodothyronine* (T_3). These hormones help regulate the overall metabolism of the body. Adherent to the thyroid glands are the *parathyroid glands.* These four small glands, divided into pairs, produce *parathyroid hormone* (PTH), which

controls the metabolism of calcium and phosphorus in the body.

Adjacent to each kidney are the *adrenal glands.* The outer region of the adrenal gland, the *cortex,* produces the steroids referred to as *corticosteroids: cortisol* and *corticosterone,* which elevate blood sugar, increase fat and protein breakdown, and are active in many other body processes; and *aldosterone,* which controls sodium, chloride, and potassium balance through the *renin-angiotensin system* (an enzyme system that controls blood pressure by stimulating contraction of blood vessels). Some corticosteroids are also called *glucocorticoids,* because they affect the metabolism of carbohydrate, fat, and protein; others are known as *mineralocorticoids,* because they affect the regulation of electrolyte and water balance. Some corticoids (corticosteroids) such as corticosterone, actually possess both properties.

The inner part of the adrenal gland is the *medulla*. It produces *epinephrine* (adrenaline), which elevates blood glucose and increases blood pressure and cardiac output.

The *pancreas* serves as both an endocrine and exocrine gland. (*See* Chapter 26: Liver, Pancreas, and Disorders, for information on the pancreas's exocrine function.) The pancreas secretes many hormones, but the most important is *insulin,* produced by the islet cells of Langerhans. Insulin regulates the metabolism of glucose (blood sugar) and other fuel molecules in the body.

The *gonads* produce steroid hormones, which influence reproduction and fertility in both males and females. In the male, the testicles produce *testosterone;* in the female, the ovaries produce *progesterone* and *estrogen.*

The *pituitary gland* is located at the base of the brain. Just as the brain is the "nerve center" for the nervous system, so is the pituitary gland the control center for the other endocrine glands. The pituitary gland secretes four major hormones that control and regulate different endocrine glands: *adrenocorticotropic hormone* (ACTH) controls the adrenal cortex; *thyroid stimulating hormone* (TSH) stimulates the thyroid glands to make T_4 and T_3; *follicle-stimulating hormone* (FSH) stimulates growth of the ovarian follicles in females and sperm production in males; and *luteinizing hormone* (LH) stimulates the male testicles to secrete testosterone and stimulates the female ovaries to produce estrogen and progesterone. The pituitary gland also produces *growth hormone* (GH), which stimulates growth. Should the pituitary gland malfunction, other endocrine glands under its control may also malfunction. (Fortunately, cats only rarely develop problems associated with the pituitary gland.)

Synthetic Corticosteroids

The synthetic corticosteroids used by veterinarians in the treatment of a wide range of animal diseases are quite similar to the naturally occurring hormones. The synthetic product *cortisone,* for example, actually is made in small amounts by the adrenal cortex; it is believed to be a precursor of cortisol. Thus synthetic cortisone administered by injection is used by the adrenals to make cortisol. Corticosteroids, both natural and synthetic, have an anti-inflammatory effect that is beneficial in inflammatory conditions such as arthritis and certain skin diseases.

DISORDERS

Problems begin to occur when there is an overproduction (hyper-) or underproduction (hypo-) of hormones. Certain endocrine disorders, such as hyperthyroidism, more commonly occur in cats; whereas other disorders, such as Cushing's syndrome or Addison's disease, are very rare.

Hyperthyroidism

Hyperthyroidism is the overproduction of *thyroxine* (T_4) and *tri-iodothyronine* (T_3). This endocrine disorder more commonly occurs in middle-aged to older cats. It is not yet known whether feline hyperthyroidism is the result of a primary thyroid disorder or whether an external factor such as nutrition or environment may be stimulating the thyroid glands to produce an excessive amount of thyroid hormones.

Classic signs of hyperthyroidism include weight loss, increased appetite, hyperactivity, restlessness, increased fluid intake and urination, vomiting, diarrhea, and muscle weakness. Often the hair coat looks unkempt and dull. The heartbeat feels strong and rapid. Heart problems related to hyperthyroidism subside once the hyperthyroid state is corrected. A middle-aged or older cat displaying those signs should be taken to a veterinarian for examination. (*See* Chapter 20: Circulatory System and Disorders.)

Because the signs can be suggestive of other diseases, a veterinarian will probably suggest a complete blood count, routine serum biochemical tests, and serum thyroid hormone concentrations to aid in a definitive diagnosis. During the physical examination, the veterinarian will also feel the neck region to determine if the thyroid glands are enlarged, indicating hyperthyroidism. Either one or both glands may be affected. In approximately 90 percent of cats diagnosed as being hyperthyroid, both thyroid glands are diseased.

There are three basic forms of treatment available: surgery, antithyroid drugs, and radioactive iodine therapy. Each form of treatment has its advantages and disadvantages. The treatment chosen by a veterinarian will be based on several factors, including the cat's age and the presence of associated heart disease or other medical problems.

Surgery. Surgical removal of the enlarged thyroid gland(s)—*thyroidectomy*—is a curative treatment. However, hyperthyroid cats are increased anesthetic and surgical risks, usually due to their advanced age and the effect the disease has had on the cat's heart and metabolism. Also, postoperative complications can occur. The most common problem is a calcium imbalance known as *hypocalcemia.* This occurs when the parathyroid glands are inadvertently injured or removed during surgery. However, if only one parathyroid gland remains, it can compensate and maintain the proper calcium-phosphorus balance. If hypocalcemia does develop, it usually occurs within the first three days after surgery. Signs of hypocalcemia include weakness, muscle tremors, tetany (muscle spasms), and convulsions. Hypocalcemia can be remedied by administering calcium supplements.

When both thyroid glands are removed, a thyroid supplement is given daily, with a blood test scheduled about every six months to monitor dosage levels. If only one thyroid gland is removed, the remaining gland usually can maintain the proper hormone balance without additional treatment.

Antithyroid Drugs. Antithyroid drugs only alleviate the signs of hyperthyroidism. If doses are missed, the signs will recur. The most commonly used drugs are *propylthiouracil* (PTU) and *methimazole* (MMI). Both drugs act by inhibiting the synthesis of hormones by the thyroid glands.

Adverse reactions can occur with these drugs. Loss of appetite, vomiting, and lethargy appear to occur more frequently with PTU than with MMI. In most cats, these mild reactions are transient and disappear in a few days. However, if gastrointestinal signs continue, contact the veterinarian. Other problems usually associated with PTU are skin rashes, facial swelling, and itching.

Another regimen of treatment can include dosages of iodide (a form of iodine) and propranolol (a drug that decreases the heart rate and output). Complete blood counts and platelet counts will probably be scheduled on a regular basis by the veterinarian to monitor the cat's treatment.

Radioactive Iodine Therapy. Radioactive iodine is an effective treatment because it selectively destroys functioning thyroid tissue. Ideally, it is the best form of treatment. However, it is difficult to find a facility that can treat a cat with radioactive iodine, because its usage is strictly regulated by the government. For example, after treatment, cats must be quarantined for five to thirty days while their secretions and excretions containing radioactivity are collected and disposed of according to regulations.

Hypothyroidism

Hypothyroidism rarely occurs in cats. The decreased hormone secretion is related to a loss of functioning thyroid tissue. Cats afflicted with this disorder continue to gain weight even when fed reduced amounts of food. Other noticeable signs include a dull hair coat (sometimes with associated hair loss) and scaly inflexible skin. Also, because their metabolism is slow due to the hormone deficiency, hypothyroid cats appear sluggish and their body temperature is lower than normal. Diagnosis is based on blood tests. Treatment of hypothyroid cats consists of administering a thyroid hormone substitute. Frequent follow-up visits to the veterinarian may be necessary to establish the correct dosage. Once hypothyroidism has been diagnosed, treatment is required for the life of the cat.

Hyperparathyroidism

The parathyroid glands are sensitive to the balance of calcium and phosphorus in the blood. If there is an excess of phosphorus or a deficit of calcium, the parathyroid glands will overproduce the parathyroid hormone. This overproduction causes calcium to be removed from the bones to reestablish the proper calcium-to-phosphorus ratio in the blood.

Excessive phosphorus in the blood can be caused by kidney disease or feeding your cat a diet limited to organ meats (e.g., heart, kidney). A calcium deficit commonly occurs in kittens due to the rapid growth of bones during the formative months.

A tumor of the parathyroid glands can cause an overproduction of the hormone that is totally unrelated to the calcium/phosphorus ratio in the blood. However, such tumors rarely occur in cats.

Signs of hyperparathyroidism include lameness, paralysis, incoordination, and bone fractures. A cat diagnosed as hyperparathyroid will probably receive dietary supplements of calcium and phosphorus, and possibly vitamin D to aid in metabolism of calcium and phosphorus. If the hyperparathyroidism is severe, restriction to a cage may be necessary to allow time for bones to rebuild and to prevent possible fractures.

Hypoparathyroidism

This disease most commonly occurs secondary to removing the thyroid glands (thyroidectomy) to treat hyperthyroidism. Because the attached parathyroids are small, they may be accidentally removed during surgery. Signs of hypoparathyroidism directly relate to the decrease of calcium in the blood. These include loss of appetite, weakness, prolapse of the third eyelid (noticeable protrusion of the membrane of the inner corner of the eye), and muscle tremors. If these signs occur, immediately contact a veterinarian. Treatment consists of prescribed dosages of calcium and vitamin D.

Hyperadrenocorticism
(Cushing's Syndrome)

This rare disorder is characterized by excessive production of cortisone by the adrenal glands. In 90 percent of the feline cases of hyperadrenocorticism, the cause is related to overstimulation by the pituitary gland. In the remaining 10 percent of the cases, tumors (adenoma) of the pituitary gland and the adrenal glands cause them to secrete excess cortisone.

A cat afflicted with Cushing's syndrome may exhibit a poor hair coat and hair loss, weakness, enlarged abdomen, increased thirst and urination, and increased appetite. If the syndrome is pituitary-dependent, the signs include bilaterally symmetric body-hair loss, thin skin, and recurrent infections. However, if the disorder is caused by an adrenal tumor, the skin will be thin and scaly, but with no hair loss.

A veterinarian will perform various blood tests to determine the underlying cause of the hyperadrenocorticism, since treatment is based on the cause. If the cause is determined to be tumor-related, then surgery is recommended to remove the affected adrenal gland.

Medical therapy can be instituted. However, there are associated side effects (lethargy, vomiting, weakness, loss of appetite, and diarrhea) reported with the medication used.

Hypoadrenocorticism
(Addison's Disease)

Addison's disease is caused by atrophy or destruction of the adrenal cortex. This destruction may be caused by an immune-mediated disease or may be secondary to infectious diseases, tumors, obstructed blood flow to the tissue, or the drug (mitotane) used to treat hyperadrenocorticism. Lethargy, loss of appetite and weight, weakness, dehydration, and low body temperature are associated with Addison's disease.

There has been only one reported case of a cat with *primary* hypoadrenocorticism. However, secondary adrenocortical insufficiency has been documented in cats given glucocorticoids or progestogens (forms of the female hormone progesterone) such as megestrol acetate. These particular medications inhibit ACTH release and synthesis by the pituitary gland, which regulates the adrenal glands.

Diabetes Mellitus

The common form of diabetes that occurs in the cat is *diabetes mellitus*. *Diabetes insipidus* has been reported in the cat but appears to be extremely rare. Diabetes mellitus is caused by the inability of the body to utilize sugar in the blood because inadequate amounts of insulin are produced by the pancreas. The sugar is excreted in the urine, causing increased volume of urination and increased thirst, which are the first early signs of this disease. If the disease is neglected, it progresses to produce signs such as lethargy, increased appetite, weight loss, rear leg weakness, diarrhea, and vomiting, followed by loss of appetite.

Diabetes mellitus is a recognized disease entity in middle-aged and older cats (rarely younger than eight years), affecting both males and females. Physically, most affected cats will be overweight in the early stages of the disease, while in those cases where treatment has been delayed, they will become emaciated and show muscle wasting. Other physical findings include thinning or loss of hair coat. Signs compatible with chronic infections, such as chronic bladder disease, and continuing sore and inflamed tongue and gums can also occur.

A veterinarian's diagnosis of diabetes is based on clinical signs, physical examination, laboratory tests, and the persistent presence of abnormal amounts of blood sugar and sugar in the urine. Diagnosis is not based on a single elevated blood sugar test because stressed cats can have temporary sugar levels that are abnormally high. With diabetes, urinalysis results will always reveal sugar in the urine, and in more advanced cases, toxic ketone bodies will be found. *Ketones* are a by-product of the body's digestion of its own tissues to produce energy when sugar cannot be metabolized to be used. Presence of ketones is not a favorable sign.

The cat is usually hospitalized from four to ten days, during which time the diagnosis will be confirmed and treatment started to stabilize the patient's body systems. A management routine for treatment is then established to fit the needs of the cat.

Home treatment of diabetes is not easy for many owners. The owner must be willing to continue giving treatment for the rest of the cat's life. Home care of the diabetic cat requires strict adherence to a predetermined time schedule with close attention to detail, vigilant observation, and no excuses.

The treatment schedule varies for each individual case; however, it usually consists of several basic procedures:

1. Hypodermic injections of insulin are given once or twice daily, depending on the type of insulin prescribed, since they differ in their peak action times and duration of activity. The objective is to have the highest blood sugar levels coincide with the peak level of insulin in the blood. This is done by coordinating the kind of diet and times of feeding with the type and schedule of insulin given. Strict adherence to the same daily schedule is vital to successful treatment.

2. A diabetic cat can be accurately regulated if blood glucose values are determined at the peak of insulin action. Test strips are available that require only one drop of blood to test sugar levels. The veterinarian performs this test in the hospital as part of the routine to stabilize the cat. However, it would be useful for the owner to learn to perform the test at home.

3. A regulated amount of canned cat food is fed at the time of injection. The largest amount should be given either six hours or twelve hours after the injection, depending on the type of insulin prescribed. Again, times and amounts are critical to success.

4. Ideally, urine sugar should be checked just prior to the next dose of insulin. Increases or decreases in dosage can be made accordingly by the veterinarian. Many times it is difficult to obtain urine samples from cats. If a cat uses a litter pan, plastic wrap can be placed over the litter. A drop of urine can then be salvaged for glucose determination. When urine glucose determination is not possible, the dose of insulin should be based on the previous day's dose and clinical signs.

5. Periodic reexaminations by the veterinarian are important, especially if diabetic regulation is a problem. Concurrent disease (chronic renal disease, hyperthyroidism) or decreases in injectable insulin requirements may be identified. Some cats can be temporarily diabetic, and if insulin therapy is continued despite the decreased need, fatal hypoglycemia (low blood sugar) may result.

Successful home treatment of the diabetic cat requires considerable owner education by the attending veterinarian about the specifics of the cat's case. Written instructions for each procedure are necessary and must be supplemented with sufficient demonstrations and practice for cat owners to become confident to do what is required of them.

Consistency is essential. Once the home treatment schedule and routine have been adjusted properly, everything should remain basically the same. There must be no change in time schedules, dosages, diet, exercise, or testing procedures except by consultation with the veterinarian. A periodic recheck would be indicated before a change is made.

As is the case with many diseases, the outlook is better in diabetes if treatment is started early. The cat can lead a normal life with proper treatment if no other disease or tumors of the pancreas causing diabetes are present. Long-standing cases where irreparable damage may have occurred do not have as optimistic a prognosis.

Hypoglycemia

This malady is caused by an excess of insulin. It usually results from an overdosage of insulin to the diabetic cat and is easily treated with sugar or syrup given orally. It should be treated only upon the direction of the veterinarian. However, hypoglycemia can also be caused by a tumor in the pancreas, though such tumors rarely occur in cats.

Signs of hypoglycemia include mild weakness and mental confusion, which will progress to incoordination, severe mental confusion, epileptic-type seizures, and, finally, loss of consciousness.

Infertility

Infertility in both the male and female cat often is directly related to deficiencies in the reproductive hormones. (*See* Chapter 12: Reproductive Disorders.)

Dwarfism and Acromegaly
(Giantism)

Dwarfism and acromegaly rarely occur in cats. Dwarfism is caused by a deficiency of growth hormone (GH) in a young cat. Acromegaly occurs when there is an excess of GH. The excessive production of GH in cats is usually the direct result of a pituitary-gland tumor affecting GH-producing cells.

Diabetes Insipidus

This disorder is caused by a deficit of the pituitary's antidiuretic (urine-concentrating) hormone or by the kidneys' inability to respond to the hormone. Signs are extreme thirst, elimination of vast quantities of urine, and gradual wasting. Cases occur occasionally in cats as a result of head injury or pituitary tumors.

Immune System and Disorders

I t is impossible to overstate the importance of immunologic processes to the health and well-being of higher living organisms. From the earthworm burrowing deep within the soil, to the gray tabby sprawled before the winter fire, to the thinking, creating human being—within all, intricate cellular and biochemical mechanisms are constantly at work to prevent colonization by foreign invaders. Without these protective immune responses, higher organisms would exist at the mercy of a perilous environment populated by microbes and parasites intent on assaulting the body and producing disease. Moreover, disease conditions arising within the host, such as certain tumors, would also have free rein were it not for the complex interplay of cells and molecules collectively referred to as the *immune system*.

Despite decades of investigation and an accumulation of data sufficient to choke the vaults of several libraries, many immunologic secrets remain undisclosed. For technical reasons that are well beyond the scope of this discussion, the immune system—its components and their functions—has proven an inordinately elusive target for scientific inquiry. What will be discussed here, in relation to cats, are the more well-accepted aspects of the anatomy and physiology of the immune system, with brief descriptions of some feline diseases whose origins lie within the immune system itself. (Readers with a deeper interest in this topic are referred to any of the several excellent texts now available in veterinary or human immunology. It should be noted that the following discussion, in general, is readily applicable to the human immune system as well.)

ANATOMY AND PHYSIOLOGY OF THE IMMUNE SYSTEM

Cells and molecules—some cells so nondescript in appearance that their origins and functions for many years went unrecognized; molecules, some of which occur in significant quantities in the blood, others in vanishingly small amounts—of such cells and molecules are the squadrons of the body's immunologic defense system composed. As was discussed in Chapter 20: Circulatory System and Disorders, the immune system is intimately connected with two other systems of the body—the blood circulatory system and the lymphatic system. The blood circulatory system is responsible chiefly for transporting oxygen and other substances to the tissues and removing metabolic waste. Among the materials transported are some important constituents of the immune system: *antibodies,* specialized proteins capable of interacting with molecules and cells foreign to the body; *lymphocytes* and *monocytes,* cells capable of responding to the presence of foreign material; and *lymphokines,* "messenger" molecules by which cells of the immune system signal and instruct one another and, in some cases, direct other activities occurring in body tissues. Among the more important lymphokines are *gamma-interferon* and the *interleukins.* In addition, the spleen acts as an important immunologic "filter" that traps and destroys foreign material, as well as host cellular debris (dead or dying red blood cells, for example) that circulates through the bloodstream.

The lymphatic system is composed of a highly specialized interconnecting network of vessels that transport a fluid called *lymph* from body tissues back into the circulatory system. Lymph is a clear admixture of excess tissue fluid, proteins, solutes (substances dissolved in a solvent), and other components. Within the lymph circulate certain lymphocytes, moving regularly from the lymphatic system to the circulatory system and back again. *Lymph nodes* are specialized organs within the lymphatic system that act as filters for removing foreign particles, which are then subjected to destruction by the immune system. The lymph nodes' immunologic filtering of lymph can be considered analogous to the spleen's immunologic filtering of the blood.

The end effect of all this incessant filtering and circulating is the creation of a highly desirable system of surveillance, wherein the cells and molecules of the immune system are continually "scanning" the blood and lymph for signs of foreign invaders, abnormal cellular material (cancer cells, for example), and host cellular debris, all of which are targets for immunologic removal.

The tissues or organs of the immune system can be divided into two principal groups: *primary lymphoid organs* and *secondary lymphoid organs.* Primary lymphoid organs are those in which the production and development of lymphocytes is regulated. In mammals, primary lymphoid organs consist of the *bone marrow,* the *mucosal-associated lymphoid tissue* (MALT—lymphoid tissue associated with the digestive, respiratory, and urogenital tracts), and the *thymus,* an organ in the chest that regulates the maturation of specialized lymphocytes called *T cells.* Secondary lymphoid organs are those in which foreign substances (*antigens,* materials capable of being recognized by the immune system) are trapped and destroyed by immune system cells. These organs consist of the lymph nodes, spleen, and portions of the bone marrow and MALT.

Antigens—which can be bacteria, fungi, viruses, parasites, toxins, or altered body cells—are engulfed and processed by specialized white blood cells known as *macrophages.* These cells can be found in great quantities in secondary lymphoid organs. Once an antigen has been engulfed, the macrophages begin signaling local lymphocytes, which have sensed the presence of the antigen, to mount an immune response against it. A subgroup of T cells known as *helper T cells* assists other lymphocytes, known as *B cells,* to produce antibody against the antigen. (The cells that actually make the antibody are end-stage B cells known as *plasma cells.*) The mounting of an antibody response to an antigen is referred to as a *humoral immune response.* Helper T cells also assist in the maturation of another line of T cells referred to as *cytotoxic T cells.* Cytotoxic T cells are responsible for tracking down and destroying altered or infected body cells (for example, a body cell infected by a virus, or a tumor cell with altered surface molecules that the body interprets as being "foreign"). Also important in destroying such cells are macrophages themselves, which not only aid in initiating an immune response but also inactivate many antigens. (Other white blood cells known as *neutrophils* can engulf and destroy foreign material, especially bacteria, but they do not "direct" the activities of lymphocytes quite the way macrophages can.) A population of specialized lymphocytes known as *natural killer cells* also is important in destroying tumor cells and virus-infected cells. The mounting of a cytotoxic T cell/macrophage/natural killer cell response to an antigen is referred to as a *cellular* or *cell-mediated immune response.*

The net effect of these two interconnected immune responses is to attack the inciting antigen from several different angles, in order to enhance the probability of its successful immunologic destruction. Such a multipronged "fail-safe" attack is also desirable because of the varied nature of the different antigens with which the body can be confronted. Not all immune mechanisms perform as efficiently against different types of antigens (a virus versus a parasite, for example); hence, the greater the number of immune mechanisms mobilized, the greater the chance that the invader will be repulsed. In some cases, certain antigens can preferentially stimulate immune mechanisms that are especially effective against them.

Antibodies, known also as *immunoglobulins,* are important mediators of a number of immune responses. Several different types or *classes* of immunoglobulins exist. The most common type, *immunoglobulin G* (IgG), is found in the blood and tissue fluids and in humans is capable of crossing the mother's placenta into the fetal circulation (this does not happen to as great an extent in cats). A second type, *IgM,* is a much larger molecule than IgG and is found almost exclusively in the blood. IgM is the first immunoglobulin type to be produced in the blood following the initial exposure to an antigen. A third type, *IgA,* is the major immunoglobulin found in the secretions bathing the surfaces of the body's mucous membranes. Such surfaces are frequent sites of contact between antigens and the immune system; IgA thus plays an important role in patrolling these surfaces and preventing antigens from gaining access to the body. (This IgA-mediated surface-monitoring system is also known as the *secretory immune system.*) A fourth immunoglobulin type, *IgE,* exists in vanishingly small quantities in the blood, but is also present on the surface of cells known as *mast cells.* These cells and IgE (along with another cell type known as the *eosinophil*) are important in protecting the body against invasion by certain parasites. Unfortunately, mast cells and IgE are also responsible for the development of certain *allergies.* The last immunoglobulin type, *IgD,* is found on the surface of certain lymphocytes, where it apparently functions as a *receptor* or sensor for the detection of antigen.

Antibodies in and of themselves do nothing more than attach to antigens; they do not destroy them. Instead, attachment of antibody to an antigen sets into motion mechanisms responsible for the antigen's removal. In the case of IgG and IgM, the presence of these antibodies adhering to the surface of an antigen is a signal to cells of the immune system—macrophages, neutrophils, eosinophils, and certain lymphocytes—that an antigen is present and needs to be removed, by being either engulfed or directly destroyed. In addition, complexes of antigen and antibody attract components of a specialized series of blood proteins known as the *complement system,* whose major role is to disrupt the surface structure of microbes and altered body cells.

The immune system overall is said to possess two vital characteristics: *specificity* and *memory.* At the risk of repeating a previous point, it is impossible to overstate the importance of these two attributes. Specificity refers to the ability of individual components of the immune system—immunoglobulins and lymphocytes—to respond to individual antigens. Each antibody molecule recognizes one and only one type of antigen; the same is true for each individual lymphocyte. When a particular antigen appears, those lymphocytes capable of responding to it are preferentially stimulated, and those antibody molecules capable of binding to it are bound, so that humoral (pertaining to body fluids) and cell-mediated immune responses to that antigen are produced. In this way the energies of the immune system are directed toward the inciting antigen. Memory refers to the fact that exposure of lymphocytes to an antigen results in the production of a population of *memory lymphocytes,* which continue to circulate once the antigen has been removed. Should that antigen ever again attempt to invade the body, memory lymphocytes will quickly trigger a massive immunologic assault that will repulse the invader. It is for this latter reason that, in many diseases, a single, symptomless exposure to the disease agent, or a single bout with the disease, will produce a solid and long-lasting immunity.

DISORDERS OF THE IMMUNE SYSTEM

In certain instances, mechanisms of the immune response may go awry, so that harmful effects deriving from the response become more serious than those produced by the inciting antigen itself. In such cases it is the inappropriate response on the part of the immune system that leads to disease. This section will discuss briefly some of the consequences of an improperly functioning immune response. Some of the topics are covered in greater detail in other chapters in this book.

Allergy and Anaphylaxis

True allergies are the result of an inappropriate response on the part of IgE and mast cells to relatively innocuous antigens, e.g., house-dust mites, pollen, dander. In human beings, allergies frequently are manifested by signs of respiratory disease (reddening and tearing of the eyes, scratchiness of the throat, sneezing) or skin lesions. In cats, skin lesions seem to predominate as common manifestations of allergy. Many of the sensitizing antigens (or *allergens*) appear to be inhaled. Occasionally, food hypersensitivities also may be manifested by skin lesions. Treatment of such problems relies on accurate identification of the underlying cause of the allergy, followed by avoidance of the allergen, dietary modification, or possibly therapeutic intervention by the veterinarian. (For a full discussion of allergy-related skin diseases in the cat, *see* Chapter 17: Skin and Disorders.)

Anaphylaxis represents an extreme example of an IgE/mast cell–mediated response. In cases of anaphylaxis, contact with a sensitizing substance results in a massive *degranulation* (release of granules) of IgE-coated mast cells lying beneath mucosal surfaces. The granules released from these cells are possessed of an armory of noxious compounds, including *histamine, serotonin,* and *leukotrienes.* These substances can produce a range of deleterious effects, such as constriction of airways and blood vessels within the lungs and contraction of smooth muscle within the digestive tract and bladder. The release of histamine also causes an itchiness about the face and head of a cat undergoing anaphylaxis. The changes within the lungs—constriction of breathing passages and reduced outflow of blood—result in *dyspnea* (difficulty breathing). An affected cat also will salivate profusely, urinate, become incoordinated, may attempt to vomit, and ultimately collapse. Anaphylaxis is a life-threatening situation that arises abruptly (within minutes) following contact with the inciting allergen. The treatment of choice is *epinephrine* (adrenaline), which must be administered immediately. Natural causes of anaphylactic reactions in cats are relatively few in number; some "non-natural" causes include protein components of vaccines and certain medications (such as penicillin). It must be kept in mind that what is going on here is an inappropriate overreaction of an idiosyncratic nature—obviously, not all substances induce anaphylaxis in cats, and neither are all cats sensitized to the extent that anaphylaxis can occur.

Autoimmune Hemolytic Anemia

Autoimmune hemolytic anemia (AIHA) is a disease condition in which antibodies attach to the host's red blood cells, resulting in immunologic destruction of the cells and thereby in anemia. In most cases this destruction occurs in an organ such as the spleen, without spillover of red cell pigment *(hemoglobin)* into the blood (i.e., there is no jaundice). The cause or causes of AIHA are unknown, but the disease is often associated with other problems occurring simultaneously in the same animal, e.g., blood *platelet* (clotting cell) disorders or feline leukemia virus infection. It is thought that many cases of AIHA are the result of exposure to drugs or viruses that bind to the surface of red blood cells, allowing for the attachment of specific antibody, with subsequent removal of the antigen/antibody-coated cells by macrophages in the spleen.

The onset of the disease can be sudden or gradual. Cats with acute-onset AIHA may be presented to the veterinarian in a collapsed state, with a rapid heart rate, pale mucous membranes, and a low red blood cell count. With a more gradual onset of anemia, the patient is allowed progressively to compensate, so that the disease signs may be much less severe.

Amelioration of AIHA is dependent upon the use of *corticosteroids* (such as prednisone) to suppress the immune-mediated disease phenomena. In some cases, treatment may be required for a prolonged period (months to years) to avoid recurrence; in others, medication may be slowly withdrawn after a short period. Because the cause is frequently unidentified, it is difficult to provide more specific therapeutic recommendations. The prognosis is usually guarded.

Pemphigus

Pemphigus is an immunologically mediated skin disease with a number of related manifestations. It is discussed fully in Chapter 17: Skin and Disorders.

Systemic Lupus Erythematosus

Systemic lupus erythematosus (SLE) is a rare, multisystemic disorder of unknown cause, characterized by a general derangement of the inhibitory controls on certain key immune response mechanisms. In this disease, a variety of immune mechanisms begin to attack basic structural components of the body—some as basic as the *deoxyribonucleic acid* (DNA) within the nucleus of cells. *Autoantibodies* directed against host-cell components attach to cells in the blood, kidneys, skin, and elsewhere, producing an immunologic assault upon the host.

Signs that can be seen in affected cats include kidney failure with loss of protein into the urine, AIHA, *thrombocytopenia* (drop in blood platelet count), arthritis, and skin lesions involving the face and borders of the mucous membranes. In most species the diagnosis is made on the basis of the history, clinical signs, and results of certain laboratory tests, including the *LE cell test* (detection of cells in the blood that contain ingested cell nuclei) and the *antinuclear antibody* (ANA) test (detection of antibodies directed against cell nuclei). Because of the rarity with which SLE is seen in cats, there is relatively little information available on the diagnostic significance of these laboratory tests in feline cases. Treatment, as with AIHA, frequently involves the use of immunosuppressive medications such as corticosteroids. The prognosis is always guarded.

Polyarteritis Nodosa

Polyarteritis nodosa is a rare systemic disorder of cats in which immune-mediated damage to arteries and arterioles occurs. The vascular damage is probably due to deposition of antigen/antibody complexes in blood-vessel walls (unlike SLE, there is no association with autoantibody formation). The cause is unknown. Clinical signs in cats can include fever, malaise, weight loss, joint pains, and mouth lesions. The diagnosis is difficult to make, and there is no recognized treatment.

Lymphosarcoma

The most common tumor of the immune system of cats is lymphosarcoma, a malignant tumor of lymphocytes. Feline lymphosarcoma is caused by feline leukemia virus. For fuller discussions, *see* Chapter 29: Viral Diseases, and Chapter 33: Cancer.

Multiple Myeloma

Multiple myeloma is a malignant tumor of plasma cells (the cells that make antibody). For a discussion of this disease, *see* Chapter 21: Musculoskeletal System and Disorders.

Myeloproliferative Disorders

These are a series of primary blood disorders involving abnormal production of cells within the bone marrow. Most cases in cats are believed to be caused by feline leukemia virus. For a full discussion, *see* Chapter 29: Viral Diseases.

Immunodeficiency Syndromes

Important immunodeficiency syndromes have been reported in a number of species. Such syndromes often represent inherited conditions that are present at birth but do not become manifest until maternally derived immunity has declined. The most well known of these disorders is the combined immunodeficiency (CID) syndrome seen in Arabian foals. In Persian cats and white tigers, *Chediak-Higashi syndrome,* a disorder of blood cells, has been reported. (*See* Chapter 20: Circulatory System and Disorders.)

Most immunodeficiency syndromes of cats are associated with specific viral infections—feline leukemia virus and feline immunodeficiency virus. For further information on these two infections, *see* Chapter 29: Viral Diseases.

Viral Diseases

A *virus,* in the words of one eminent scientist, can be thought of as "a piece of bad news wrapped in protein." Unlike bacteria and fungi, viruses are not living organisms; rather, they consist in essence of a length of *nucleic acid*—their genetic material—that is surrounded and protected by a protein coat. (Some viruses have in addition to this coat a soft outer *envelope,* which confers some special properties.) The genetic material of viruses is composed of one or the other of two types of nucleic acid, either *ribonucleic acid* (RNA) or *deoxyribonucleic acid* (DNA).

Viruses carry out no independent metabolism: They do not respire, they do not process nutrients, they do not generate waste products, and they rely on living cells of the host for their reproduction. A virus outside a cell is an inert bit of particulate matter; once inside, however, the virus seizes command of the cell's biosynthetic machinery, converting the cell into a "high-tech" factory for the production of new virus particles.

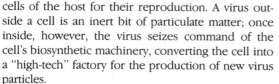

Many viruses eventually kill their host cells, resulting in disease and provoking an assault by the immune response of the host. Sometimes this response may go awry, so that the harmful effects of the immune response are actually more serious than those of the virus disease itself. Other viruses provoke little, if any, reaction, and some can remain dormant or latent in the host for years. The vast majority of all virus infections appear to be asymptomatic in nature—that is, the infections are so mild and the host response so effective that clinical signs of disease never develop.

Very few virus diseases are responsive to specific antiviral therapy. Instead, the secondary effects of a virus infection are addressed in an effort to protect the host against secondary bacterial or fungal infection while the immune response to the virus is developing. Most successful attacks against viral invasion are carried out by the body itself. The most effective therapy for viral diseases is prevention, i.e., vaccination. Most antibiotics and antifungals have no effect on viruses, while clinically useful drugs with specific antiviral activity are still relatively few in number and restricted almost exclusively to some very specific virus infections.

FELINE VIRAL DISEASES

Feline Panleukopenia Virus (FPV)

Feline panleukopenia (feline infectious enteritis, feline "distemper," feline ataxia or incoordination) is a highly contagious viral disease of cats characterized by its sudden onset, fever, inappetence (loss of appetite), dehydration, depression, vomiting, decreased numbers of circulating white blood cells (leukopenia), and often a high mortality rate. Intrauterine (within the uterus) infection may result in abortions, stillbirths, early neonatal deaths, and cerebellar hypoplasia (underdevelopment of the cerebellum) manifested by incoordination (ataxia) in kittens beginning at two to three weeks of age. All members of the cat family (Felidae) are susceptible to infection with feline panleukopenia virus, as are raccoons, coatimundis and ringtails, in the family Procyonidae. Many excellent vaccines are available to protect cats against panleukopenia. In unvaccinated populations, however, panleukopenia remains the most severe and destructive disease of cats.

THE CAUSE. Feline panleukopenia virus is a very small and very stable virus classified in the parvovirus group. The genetic material of the virus is composed of a single strand of DNA. The virus is highly resistant to most disinfectants—ether, chloroform, acid, alcohol, and heat (56°C or 132.8°F for thirty minutes)— but is susceptible to Clorox bleach. Replication (reproduction) of the virus in the host occurs in cells that are themselves actively reproducing.

OCCURRENCE AND TRANSMISSION. Although it can affect cats of all ages, feline panleukopenia is primarily a disease of kittens. The characteristics of the disease may vary considerably from population to population and from outbreak to outbreak. In susceptible populations, the disease may affect nearly 100 percent of individuals; in other populations, only a few animals may be affected. Panleukopenia rarely occurs in populations in which vaccination is routinely practiced.

There is a seasonality to the occurrence of panleukopenia that usually coincides with the production of new populations of susceptible kittens. This seasonal effect may vary according to geographic location. In the northeastern United States, most cases of panleukopenia are seen during the summer and early fall. However, outbreaks of panleukopenia may occur at any time of the year.

Transmission of FPV occurs most commonly by direct contact with infected cats or their excretions. During the early stages of the infection, virus is shed in feces, urine, saliva, and vomitus. In addition, fleas may transmit FPV from infected to susceptible cats during the acute stage of the disease. The virus may also be spread by contact with contaminated objects, such as food bowls, litter pans, bedding, and cages, or by persons (on hands or clothing, for example).

The remarkable resistance of FPV to environmental conditions requires thorough cleansing and disinfection of premises before the introduction of new cats. Once infection with FPV has occurred on premises, however, infectious virus may persist for months to years. New cats should be vaccinated against panleukopenia at least two weeks before their introduction to infected premises. (See Chapter 37: Convalescence —Home Care.)

PATHOGENESIS. The virus usually enters orally, with infection occurring primarily in the lymphoid tissues of the oropharynx (tonsillar area) and intestine. Within twenty-four hours of infection, virus is present in the blood and in this way is distributed throughout the body. Within two days of infection, nearly every body tissue contains significant amounts of virus. As circulating antibodies appear, the amount of virus present gradually decreases. Small quantities of virus may persist for up to one year in certain tissues, but the strong immune response of the host usually neutralizes the virus as it is shed, so that most persistently infected kittens are not infectious.

The most severely damaged tissues in the infected newborn cat are those undergoing rapid cell division —the thymus and the cerebellum (rear of the brain). Cells of the small intestine, which have a slow turnover rate in neonates (newborns), are not damaged, although virus is present within them. In older kittens, the development of the disease also depends on the reproductive activity of the various tissues within the body. Lymphoid tissues, bone marrow, and the surface cells of the intestine are the most severely affected.

CLINICAL SIGNS. The severity of the clinical signs exhibited can vary tremendously from case to case. Many cats undergo a subclinical infection and do not show signs at all; the only method of diagnosis would be viral isolation or serology (detection of antibody). Others may experience a very mild clinical infection, in which a mildly elevated temperature, slight inappetence, and a borderline drop in the white blood cell count are observed. In the "typical" case of panleukopenia, clinical signs develop suddenly. The animal may have a rectal temperature of 104°F or greater and may be severely depressed and not eating. Vomiting usually occurs, and severe diarrhea may develop in twenty-four to forty-eight hours. If vomiting and diarrhea continue, severe dehydration and electrolyte imbalances occur.

Affected cats often assume a typical "hunched" posture with the head between the forepaws. Sometimes the head will hang over a water bowl or food dish. They often act as though they would like to drink and may even take a lap or two of milk or water, but are unable or reluctant to swallow. The hair coat becomes rough and dull and there is a loss of elasticity of the skin due to the dehydration. The third eyelid (in the corner of the eye, near the nose) often appears. The abdomen is painful and touching it will elicit a pain response. The lymph nodes in the abdomen are enlarged, and the digestive tract contains excessive amounts of gas and liquid. Cats that are not going to survive develop a subnormal temperature, with coma and death following in a few hours.

The mortality rate in an outbreak of panleukopenia may vary from 25 to 75 percent. Acute deaths may occur with kittens showing no warning signs, often causing the owner to suspect poisoning. More commonly, deaths occur within the first five days of illness in uncomplicated cases, or later in cases subsequently complicated by other problems. If a cat survives the first five days of illness, and secondary complications such as bacterial infections or dehydration do not develop, then recovery should follow fairly rapidly. It usually requires several weeks, however, for the animal to regain its lost weight and condition.

Signs in kittens infected *in utero* or just after birth go unnoticed before sudden death, or until the development of ataxia (incoordination) at about two weeks of age when the kittens begin ambulating. The incoordination is exemplified by rolling or tumbling as the cat attempts to walk, by an involuntary twitching of the head, or by swaying of the body. If they are coordinated enough to obtain food, the kittens will survive; however, the ataxia will persist throughout life with little, if any, improvement or compensation as they grow older.

DIAGNOSIS. A presumptive diagnosis of feline panleukopenia can be made by the veterinarian on the basis of the history, the clinical signs, and the presence of leukopenia (decreased number of white cells in the blood). The diagnosis can be confirmed by *necropsy* (autopsy) examination, virus *isolation* (growth of the virus in cells in the laboratory), identification of virus in infected tissues, or by demonstration of an increase in circulating antibodies by testing paired (acute and convalescent) serum samples taken several weeks apart (the increase in antibodies indicates recent infection).

TREATMENT. Panleukopenia normally has a high mortality rate, but with diligent effort and good nursing care this can often be reduced. The main objective is to keep the affected animal alive and in reasonably good health until the natural defenses take over, i.e., the appearance of antibodies and increase in numbers of circulating white blood cells. Antibodies usually appear about three to four days after the first signs of illness; two to three days later, the sharp "rebound" in white blood cells can be expected to occur. Thus, if the patient can be supported for five to seven days after onset of the disease, the chances of recovery usually are good. Veterinary supportive care is aimed at the vomiting, diarrhea, and dehydration, which may dangerously upset fluid and electrolyte balance, and at preventing secondary bacterial infections.

Secondary viral respiratory infections are common complications of panleukopenia. The FPV infection may act to trigger a latent respiratory virus, such as *feline viral rhinotracheitis virus* or *feline calicivirus*. Dual FPV/respiratory virus infections usually produce a more severe illness than if either virus alone had infected an animal.

PREVENTION. There are several excellent vaccines available to immunize cats against panleukopenia. These vaccines are highly effective and produce long-lasting immunity. Because panleukopenia is an entirely preventable disease, one cannot overemphasize the importance of proper immunization.

Immunization should be initiated by the veterinarian when kittens are eight to ten weeks of age. A second vaccination should be given four weeks later. In areas where the prevalence of infection is high, and for maximal protection, a third vaccination may be indicated at sixteen weeks of age. If a kitten is twelve weeks of age or older at the time of initial vaccination with a modified live-virus vaccine, a booster vaccination need not be given until it is at least one year of age. Annual booster vaccinations are recommended for all cats.

Immunity acquired from the queen via colostrum (initial breast milk) must be considered when establishing a routine vaccination program. Interference by maternally acquired (passive) immunity is the most common cause of vaccine failure. There exists a direct correlation between the FPV antibody level of the queen at the time of birth and the duration of passive immunity in the kitten. This passive immunity, if of sufficient strength, will not only protect the kitten against virulent FPV but will also react with vaccine virus and interfere with immunization. Vaccination must be performed after kittens have lost most or all of their maternally derived immunity.

The use of FPV antiserum (clear blood liquid containing antibody) to immunize cats passively is indicated if an unvaccinated animal has been exposed to virus or is likely to be exposed before vaccine-induced immune responses can develop. Antiserum is also indicated for colostrum-deprived or orphaned kittens. The routine use of antiserum in unexposed kittens is *not* recommended, however; instead, kittens should be vaccinated during their first visit to the veterinarian's office, and revaccinated as indicated. (*See* Appendix B: Vaccinations.)

Feline Leukemia Virus (FeLV)

The feline leukemia virus is the causative agent of the most important fatal infectious-disease complex of American domestic cats today. It is an RNA (ribonucleic acid) virus belonging to the family Retroviridae. *Oncogenic* (tumor-causing) *retroviruses* similar to FeLV have been identified in a number of animal species: cattle, domestic fowl, certain nonhuman primates, and rodents. The oncogenic retroviruses are commonly referred to as *RNA tumor viruses,* or *oncornaviruses (oncogenic RNA viruses).*

Other retroviruses, known as *lentiviruses,* can produce noncancerous diseases in cats, sheep, goats, and horses. The feline lentivirus, known as *feline immunodeficiency virus* (FIV), is the cause of an immunodeficiency syndrome similar to that produced in humans by the human immunodeficiency virus HIV, which causes AIDS.

Retroviruses carry with them an enzyme, *reverse transcriptase.* This enzyme is used to produce a DNA copy of the retroviral RNA, which is then inserted into the genetic material of the infected cell. This alien invader, known as a *provirus,* then is reproduced whenever the host cell reproduces and can serve as the blueprint for the production of new retrovirus particles. A cell infected with a retrovirus thus is infected for the length of its lifetime, as are all of its daughter cells. Because a version of their genetic material becomes a part of the total genetic information of the cells they infect, retroviruses are among the most intimate parasites known in nature.

THE CAUSE. Individual particles of FeLV consist of two distinct morphologic (structural) components: a dense inner core or *nucleoid* and an outer envelope containing an immunologically important protein known as *gp70.* This protein is the principal antigen (substance against which an immune response can be mounted) present on the virus surface. *Virus-neutralizing antibody* (VNA) directed against gp70 is an essential component of a successful immunologic response to FeLV, and its presence in the blood is an indication of past FeLV exposure. Most cats with high levels of VNA are resistant to subsequent FeLV infection. Most *persistently viremic* cats (cats, many of which are otherwise healthy, in which FeLV circulates in blood cells for a prolonged period of time, as the result of an ineffective immune response) produce little or no VNA.

A second major antigen of the FeLV particle is the protein *p27,* which is a structural component of the inner viral core. This protein can be found in great abundance in infected blood cells and in soluble form in plasma and serum of viremic cats. The primary importance of p27 lies in its role as the major FeLV antigen detected by the two "FeLV tests"—the IFA (*immunof luorescence assay*) test and the ELISA (*enzyme-linked immunosorbent assay*) test—commonly used in veterinary clinical practice today.

Suppression of normal protective immunologic responses is one of the most important consequences of persistent infection with FeLV. A major cause of this *immunosuppression* appears to be a specific FeLV structural protein, *p15(E)*, which is associated with the viral envelope. The significance of FeLV-induced immunosuppression is especially apparent when considering the array of secondary diseases associated with FeLV. In addition, immunosuppression induced by p15(E)—even by p15(E) from "inactivated" virus —is an important consideration in the design of an effective FeLV vaccine.

In nature, FeLV infections appear to be restricted to members of the cat family, including domestic breeds and certain small exotic cats—sand cats, European wild cats, jungle cats, and possibly leopards.

PATHOGENESIS. After infection of lymphatic tissues surrounding the site of initial virus penetration, a low-grade *transient viremia* (virus in the bloodstream) involving small numbers of infected white blood cells occurs within two weeks of exposure. In this way the virus is transported to other regions of the body, especially systemic lymphatic tissue, intestinal tissue, and bone marrow. These areas contain populations of rapidly dividing cells wherein FeLV replication can be enhanced. Infection of white blood cell and *platelet* (cells involved in blood clotting) precursors in the bone marrow, plus the subsequent release of infected cells into the circulation, result in a second, more profound viremia *(persistent viremia)*. In those cats that resist widespread infection with FeLV, virus containment takes place in the early lymphatic stage of infection, after a transient viremia has occurred. In those animals destined to become persistently viremic, infection proceeds to extensive involvement of the bone marrow, pharynx, esophagus, stomach, bladder, respiratory tract, and salivary glands.

All persistently viremic FeLV cats excrete infectious FeLV and probably do so for the rest of their lives. Consequently, they serve as a source of infection for healthy, uninfected, susceptible cats with which they come into contact. Cats that develop immunity experience an initial transient viremia lasting from one to two days and for as long as eight weeks, during which time they too may shed infectious FeLV.

Excretion of FeLV occurs primarily in salivary secretions, although virus may also be present in respiratory secretions, feces, and urine. The social grooming habits of cats, licking and biting, sneezing, and the urban practice of sharing litter boxes and feeding bowls, probably represent the major modes of spread of FeLV among pet cats. *In utero* transfer of FeLV across the placenta and excretion of FeLV in colostrum and milk are also known to occur, so that kittens may become infected either through an infected queen or by close contact with other persistently viremic cats. Prolonged close contact (days to weeks) between cats is probably required for effective transmission of FeLV. Virus can also be spread in blood transfusions from viremic cats.

A significant percentage of adult cats that are exposed to FeLV develop immunity and do not become persistently viremic. In some of these cats, however, the virus may remain sequestered for a variable period of time somewhere in the body as a *latent infection*. To date the only recognized hazard associated with latent infection is the possibility that some latently infected queens may transmit FeLV to their kittens through the milk. Latently infected cats do not transmit FeLV by any other route and do not seem to be susceptible to developing any of the FeLV-associated diseases. The duration of these latent infections is variable, but most cats appear to become truly FeLV-free within two or three years after their infection first occurred. Unfortunately, there is no readily available test to identify latently infected cats.

In common with a number of other similar viruses, FeLV is extremely labile (chemically unstable) once outside the cat and is rapidly inactivated by alcohol and most common household detergents and disinfectants. The infectivity of virus in saliva left to dry at room temperature has been shown to decline to inconsequential levels within three or four hours.

CLINICAL SIGNS. Persistently viremic FeLV cats are subject to development of a number of diseases that are either directly or indirectly caused by FeLV. Those directly caused by FeLV include lymphosarcoma, a number of myeloproliferative disorders, several types of anemia, the panleukopenialike and thymic atrophy syndromes (shrinking or wasting away of the thymus), at least one form of kidney disease, and certain reproductive disorders. Diseases indirectly caused by FeLV include a myriad of conditions that develop secondary to FeLV-induced immunosuppression. The prognosis for survival of persistently viremic cats is poor; approximately 50 percent will die within six months of infection, while over 80 percent will be dead within three years of infection.

Lymphosarcoma (LSA). Lymphosarcomas are

among the most common malignancies of American domestic cats. (*See* Chapter 33: Cancer.) These tumors consist primarily of solid masses of proliferating *lymphocytes* (a type of white blood cell) and comprise the majority of the malignancies caused by FeLV. Several forms of LSA have been identified; their classification is based most commonly on their anatomic distribution.

The *alimentary form* of LSA is characterized by tumor-cell infiltration of the digestive tract and other organs, e.g., lymph nodes, liver, kidneys, and spleen. Common presenting signs include inappetence, weight loss, vomiting, diarrhea, bloody stool, and jaundice. Occlusion (blockage) of the bowel by the proliferating tumor results in constipation or obstipation (difficult, painful bowel movements or complete blockage).

The *thymic* (of thymus gland in the chest) or *mediastinal* (of area between the lungs) *form* is characterized by the presence of a large tumor mass infiltrating within the chest, with spread to regional lymphatic tissue and sometimes to other structures. Clinical signs are a reflection of pressure effects of the mass and the severe fluid accumulation within the chest that frequently accompanies the tumor. Physical examination may reveal difficult respiration, muffled heart sounds, coughing, difficult swallowing, and incompressibility of the chest wall.

The *multicentric form* of LSA is characterized by primary involvement of many lymphatic tissues of the body, with additional involvement of other structures, such as the liver, bone marrow, kidneys, spleen, and lungs. Presenting signs are variable, depending on the precise anatomic distribution of the tumor, but often include painless swelling of peripheral lymph nodes and enlargement of the spleen, liver, and, often, of the intestinal lymph nodes.

Atypical forms of LSA also occur and consist usually of solitary tumor masses involving primary sites of origin in nonintestinal, nonlymphatic structures. These include the kidneys, central nervous system, eyes, and, rarely, the skin or bones. Presenting signs vary according to the location of the tumor.

Lymphocytic leukemia is characterized by the presence of circulating cancerous lymphocytes in the blood and bone marrow. Lymphocytic leukemia may precede the development of LSA or it may be associated secondarily with LSA. Presenting signs usually consist of nonspecific inappetence, depression, and weight loss. More specific signs that may be seen include anemia, fever, jaundice, and enlargement of the liver, spleen, and lymph nodes.

Myeloproliferative Disorders. These primary bone-marrow disorders are characterized by abnormal proliferation of one or more *hematopoietic* (blood cell–forming) cell lines. Presenting signs often include inappetence, depression, weight loss, relentlessly progressive anemia, fever, jaundice, peripheral lymph node enlargement, and enlargement of the liver and spleen secondary to massive infiltration by abnormally proliferating cells.

Nonregenerative Anemia (NRA). NRA is probably one of the most common manifestations of FeLV infection. This type of anemia, also known as *hypoplastic, aplastic,* or *depression anemia,* is characterized by a severe reduction in the number of red cell precursors in the bone marrow, resulting in failure to produce an adequate number of circulating red cells. Sometimes there may be a *pancytopenia,* in which red cell, white cell, and platelet cell precursors are all affected. NRA may occur alone, or may be associated with LSA or myeloproliferative disease, or may precede the development of an FeLV-induced malignancy. Because many severely ill cats with NRA are euthanatized, the true incidence of subsequent malignancy cannot be accurately determined. Unfortunately, clinical signs are usually not detected until the anemia is well advanced. Common signs include inappetence, depression, weight loss, respiratory difficulty, pallor of the mucous membranes, and increased heart rate. Coinfection with *Haemobartonella felis,* the parasite causing feline infectious anemia, may contribute to the severity of the anemia.

Panleukopenialike Syndrome. As the name implies, this is a syndrome resembling *panleukopenia* (feline "distemper") that has been observed in some FeLV-infected cats known to be properly immunized against panleukopenia. Presenting signs often include inappetence, depression, dehydration, weight loss, fever, vomiting, diarrhea (which may be bloody), and a profound reduction in the number of circulating white blood cells. Anemia may also be present. Although affected cats may respond transiently to supportive therapy, the disease is progressive and always fatal.

Kittens born to persistently viremic queens often develop a syndrome of lethargy, inappetence, wasting, stunted growth, atrophy of the thymus gland and other lymphoid structures, and enhanced susceptibility to infection with other disease-causing agents ("fading kittens"). The degree of thymic atrophy can be severe, amounting to virtual disappearance of the organ in some cases. These kittens do not gain weight and often do not nurse vigorously. Many die from secondary bacterial or viral infections within the first few weeks of life. Those that survive are carriers of FeLV and thus are capable of transmitting the virus to other susceptible cats. The syndrome may also precede the development of an FeLV-induced malignancy.

Glomerulonephritis. This type of kidney disease has been described in cats in association with LSA, lymphocytic leukemia, and granulocytic leukemia (cancer of granulocytes, a type of white blood cell). In addition, glomerular disease in the absence of malignancy has been reported in FeLV-infected cats. In one study, the leading cause of death in an FeLV-infected household of 134 cats over a five-and-a-half-year period was glomerulonephritis.

Queens infected with FeLV may experience one or more reproductive disorders, including fetal resorption (biochemical disintegration of the fetus), abortion, infertility, *endometritis* (inflammation of the uterine lining), and the birth of fading kittens. Abortions characteristically occur late in gestation and are more frequent in high-density, multiple-cat households. It has been reported that nearly 75 percent of FeLV-infected queens will experience abortions or fetal resorptions.

The array of secondary disease entities associated with FeLV-induced immunosuppression represents one of the most important manifestations of FeLV infection. It has been estimated that nearly 50 percent of all cats with severe bacterial infections and infectious anemia and 75 percent of cats with *toxoplasmosis* (a protozoan disease) have an underlying FeLV infection. In addition to these, FeLV-induced immunosuppression has also been associated with chronic mouth and gum infections, poorly healing or recurrent abscesses, deep skin infections, chronic respiratory infections, acute *colitis* (inflammation of the large bowel), severe ear infections, and feline infectious peritonitis. (It should be kept in mind that all of these problems may also be seen in cats *not* infected with FeLV.) FeLV-induced immunosuppression probably contributes also to the development of FeLV-induced malignancies.

DIAGNOSIS OF FeLV INFECTION. Two types of FeLV blood tests are in common use: the *enzyme-*linked immunosorbent assay* (ELISA, or kit test, which can be performed in the veterinarian's office) and the *immunofluorescence assay* (IFA, Hardy test or slide test, which must be sent out to a diagnostic laboratory). Both tests detect the p27 protein of FeLV as it circulates in the bloodstream, either free in the blood (ELISA test) or within infected white blood cells (IFA test). Interpretation of a positive or a negative test depends on which of these two tests has been performed.

FeLV is present in the blood during two different stages of the infection. The ELISA test can detect the primary (transient) viremia stage, before the bone marrow has become infected, when the cat's immune system has an opportunity to ward off the virus. Transiently viremic cats characteristically test ELISA-positive and then revert to negative status within about eight weeks. It is important that a positive FeLV test be repeated in eight to twelve weeks in order to determine whether the viremia is transient or persistent. The ELISA test can also detect the virus in the persistent viremia stage—after the virus, in a certain percentage of cats, invades the bone marrow and establishes a firm and lifelong foothold. ELISA tests are also available to detect FeLV in secretions—saliva and tears. There is some degree of variability in these latter tests, and some positive animals may be missed. At this time saliva/tear tests are probably best reserved for screening purposes and for testing cats that are difficult to bleed.

The IFA test detects circulating virus primarily during the second stage. If the infection progresses to this stage, a "point of no return" is reached. Thus the majority of cats testing positive by the IFA test remain positive for life. These cats, as well as most (70 to 100 percent) of those that are ELISA-positive, are shedding FeLV in the saliva and are infectious to other cats.

Occasional discrepancies between the two FeLV tests have been noted. When such a discrepancy arises, it is important to remember that the two tests detect FeLV in two different "compartments" of the blood (blood fluid versus white blood cells).

If a cat is positive by ELISA and negative by IFA at the same time, it may mean that the virus is at the primary viremia stage. However, some healthy cats may remain ELISA-positive and IFA-negative for a prolonged period of time. These cats are still carrying FeLV but are apparently not shedding it in saliva (and thus will not transmit it to companion cats) and most appear to be resistant to the disease-producing effects of FeLV.

TREATMENT. The therapeutic goals of the veterinarian in treating many of the FeLV-associated diseases are to provide palliative relief from clinical signs and to prolong life. However, therapy should be advocated only if there is the possibility of maintaining a good quality of life for the prospective patient. In addition, ethical questions regarding prolonged treatment of persistently viremic cats shedding an oncogenic (tumor-causing) virus into their environment must also be addressed by both the veterinarian and cat owner.

A variety of chemotherapeutic regimens have been developed for FeLV-induced tumors, and in certain cases these can produce a temporary remission. Cats in remission may continue in a reasonably healthy state for a period of weeks to several months (some longer). However, it must be understood that these are only remissions and, in most cases, not lifelong cures. The drugs that are used are very potent and their effects must be monitored carefully so as not to overdose the patient.

PREVENTION. Elimination of FeLV from an infected household can be achieved by implementation of an FeLV-test-and-removal program using the IFA test. This program has been highly effective in removing FeLV from infected multiple-cat households. In a survey of forty-five households from which 159 FeLV-positive cats were removed, 561 of 564 (99.5 percent) FeLV-negative cats remained negative upon subsequent retesting. Multiple-cat households in which FeLV-test and removal has not been implemented have experienced infection rates over *forty times greater* than those experienced by households in which the program has been successfully introduced.

FeLV-Test-and-Removal. All cats in the household should be tested by IFA, regardless of age or condition. All cats found positive should be removed and the household premises cleaned with a commercial detergent or disinfectant (a solution containing four ounces of household bleach per gallon of water is often recommended, but soap and water will work as well). All litter boxes and food and water bowls should be replaced. Cats that initially tested negative should be retested several times over a period of eight to twelve months, in the event that they were infected just before the first test, prior to the onset of

detectable viremia, or are cycling in their level of detectable viremia. The time period between exposure and viremia is extremely variable, and an infected cat that tested negative initially may be positive when tested again later. During the testing period, no new cats should be allowed to enter the household. If any FeLV-positive cats are found on subsequent testing, then they should be removed and another period of quarantine and testing imposed. All cats in the household should test negative for FeLV on two tests taken at least three months apart for the household to be considered "free" of infectious FeLV.

All new cats entering an FeLV-negative household should be tested prior to entry. Any positive cats should be excluded from entering the household. Cats testing negative should be quarantined in separate quarters for three to five months and retested negative one to two times before being allowed to intermix with the established FeLV-negative household population. New cats should ideally be obtained only from other households or catteries practicing FeLV-test-and-removal.

Routine yearly or twice-yearly testing for FeLV is suggested for cats in catteries due to the variable incubation period of infection. Persistently viremic cats should never be used for breeding purposes, in part because infected queens will transmit the virus to their viable offspring.

If an FeLV-positive cat is removed from a single-cat household, a waiting period (up to thirty days) should be observed before repopulation with one or more FeLV-negative cats. The litter box and feeding dishes should be replaced and the premises thoroughly cleansed.

Certain modifications of the test-and-removal program may be made for households in which both FeLV-negative and FeLV-positive cats are kept. The positive cats in these households should be isolated from contact with all other cats. This will not only prevent the spread of infectious FeLV to susceptible cats, but will also decrease exposure of potentially immunosuppressed, viremic cats to other infectious agents, to which they may have a heightened susceptibility. No new cats should be introduced at any time, and the FeLV-positive cats should not be allowed to breed. Separate litter boxes and feeding dishes should be maintained for positive and negative cats. Cleanliness and personal hygiene should be observed at all times, and it has been suggested that separate clothing be kept for contact with FeLV-positive cats to minimize mechanical transmission of the virus. As we have seen, however, FeLV is relatively labile in the environment, and the degree of virus transmission possible under these circumstances is uncertain, but is probably minimal.

Two vaccines are currently available commercially for prevention of FeLV infection. The decision to vaccinate is made on an individual basis and should be an important point of discussion with the veterinarian. There are complex pros and cons to vaccinating against FeLV; the advice and experience of the veterinarian are essential in helping owners reach a correct decision.

PUBLIC HEALTH SIGNIFICANCE. The public health significance of FeLV, most importantly the question of oncogenic potential for human beings, is still largely unsettled. Surveys designed to determine the prevalence of circulating FeLV and/or antibody to FeLV in human serum have produced conflicting results over the years. However, most recent surveys have failed to find evidence of FeLV infection of human beings, including many with LSA or other malignancies. Until a more complete understanding of the public health implications of FeLV can be obtained, it is prudent to restrict as much as possible human exposure to persistently viremic cats. Neonates (human infants) and immunosuppressed individuals (those on immunosuppressive drug therapy, or AIDS patients, for example) are of special concern in this regard. It must be emphasized, however, that as of this writing there is no conclusive evidence that any human illness (including cancer) has ever been caused by FeLV.

Feline Infectious Peritonitis (FIP)

Feline infectious peritonitis is an important and complex disease of cats caused by a virus belonging to the family Coronaviridae. Coronaviruses are a large and widely distributed group of RNA viruses and are important causes of disease in birds and mammals. Cats are susceptible to infection with several other viruses in this group that appear to be closely related to the *FIP virus* (FIPV). These include *feline enteric coronavirus* (FECV), *canine coronavirus* (CCV), and the swine agent, *transmissible gastroenteritis virus* (TGEV).

THE CAUSE. FIPV possesses a broad spectrum of *virulence* (disease-producing capacity), i.e., some strains of FIPV are avirulent or of low virulence, while others consistently produce FIP. FECV strains, by contrast, typically are of low virulence and produce disturbances of the digestive tract that affect only a minority of infected cats—usually very young kittens. In nature, FIPV infections appear to be restricted to members of the cat family, including domestic breeds as well as certain exotic species: sand cats, caracals, lynx, cougars, cheetahs, jaguars, leopards, and lions.

The routes by which FIPV is spread from cat to cat have not been identified with absolute certainty, but it is most likely that initial infection results from ingestion or inhalation of the virus. Close contact with infected cats or their excreta is usually required for efficient virus transmission. Transmission across the placenta to the developing fetus is suggested by occasional observations of FIP in stillborn kittens, but the frequency with which this occurs is unknown.

In common with many other viruses of this type, FIPV is relatively unstable outside the host and is rapidly inactivated by many common soaps, detergents, and disinfecting agents. Household bleach diluted 1:32 in water or in combination with the disinfectant A-33, to give a final concentration of 1:32 bleach and 1:64 A-33, has been recommended for decontamination purposes.

PATHOGENESIS. Studies performed over the past several years have succeeded in identifying some of the major host-virus interactions of FIPV infection. After infection of white blood cells (*leukocytes*) within lymphoid tissue at or near the site of initial virus penetration, a primary *viremia* (virus in the blood) involving virus and/or virus-infected cells occurs within one week after exposure. In this way virus is transported to other areas of the body, especially to organs such as liver, spleen, and lymph nodes. These structures contain large populations of certain leukocytes, such as *macrophages,* which appear to be primary target cells for FIPV infection. Blood-borne spread of virus also results in infection of circulating white blood cells (*monocytes*) and, importantly, in localization of virus and virus-infected cells within the walls of small blood vessels. A secondary viremia may occur after initial infection of target tissues and result in further spread of virus throughout the body. Deposition of virus, virus-infected white blood cells, and virus-antibody complexes within blood vessel walls produces an intense, destructive inflammatory response (*vasculitis*), which damages vessels and allows for escape of fluid components of blood into intercellular spaces, eventually accumulating as characteristic "FIP fluid" within body cavities.

CLINICAL SIGNS. Though it is possible that "mild" cases of FIP that spontaneously resolve may occasionally occur, this is considered a rarity. Virtually all cats with FIP will die. Fortunately, FIP is a relatively uncommon disease, even in crowded catteries.

Most cases of FIP occur in cats less than three or four years of age. The onset of clinical signs may be sudden (especially in kittens) or it may be slow and insidious, with the severity of signs gradually increasing over a period of weeks. Some of these signs may be quite nonspecific: intermittent inappetence, depression, weight loss, fever. In many cases, affected cats may continue to eat and remain alert and responsive for a considerable period of time; however, fever (which may fluctuate at different times of the day) is a constant finding and usually persists until the last few hours of life.

The two major forms of FIP can be distinguished on the basis of fluid accumulation—the presence of fluid in one or more body cavities in *effusive* ("wet") FIP and its absence in *noneffusive* ("dry") FIP. Effusive FIP is the more fulminant (sudden and severe) form of the disease, with a more rapid onset and shorter clinical course than the noneffusive form.

An accumulation of fluid within the abdominal cavity, with progressive, painless enlargement of the abdomen, is probably the most common clinical manifestation of effusive FIP. Respiratory distress may develop when abdominal fluid accumulation is excessive or, more commonly, when accumulation of fluid occurs within the chest cavity, resulting in compression of the lungs and a release of fluid into airways. Other signs that may be seen include *jaundice* (yellowing of the mucous membranes and skin) and a mild *anemia* (low red blood cell count). This anemia may be exacerbated by coinfection with feline leukemia virus or *Haemobartonella felis* (the organism causing feline infectious anemia). Gastrointestinal, ocular, and neurologic signs may also occur in cases of effusive FIP. The course of effusive FIP is quite variable, but the usual survival time after onset of clinical signs is about two or three months. Some young kittens may survive for no longer than a few days, while some adults may live for six to eight months with active clinical disease.

The onset of noneffusive FIP is often insidious, with clinical signs reflective of involvement of specific organ systems in the FIP inflammatory process. Weight loss, depression, anemia, and fever are almost always present, but fluid accumulation is usually minimal. Clinical signs of kidney failure (such as increased water consumption and urination), liver failure (jaundice, neurologic signs), pancreatic disease (vomiting, diarrhea, voracious appetite, diabetes mellitus), neurologic disease (hindlimb incoordination, loss of balance, tremors, behavioral changes, paralysis, seizures), or ocular disease (inflammation of the eye, retinal disease, blindness) may be seen in various combinations in cats with severe organ impairment. The disease course is usually more chronic than in effusive FIP. Some cats, especially those with primary ocular involvement, may survive for as long as a year or more.

FIPV was once incriminated as a possible cause of reproductive problems in breeding queens—infertility, fetal resorptions (biochemical disintegration of the fetus), abortions, stillbirths, birth of weak "fading" kittens, congenital malformations, and neonatal heart disease (acute congestive cardiomyopathy). There is no conclusive published evidence that the virus plays a role in any of these disease processes. To date the only disease of neonates known to be caused by FIPV is FIP itself.

DIAGNOSIS. The clinical diagnosis of FIP is made by evaluation of the history and presenting signs and the results of supporting laboratory tests. It must be kept in mind that a definitive diagnosis of FIP can only be made by microscopic examination of tissues—either by biopsy or at necropsy (autopsy). Any diagnosis made in the absence of such examination must be considered presumptive; hence, the vast majority of clinical diagnoses of FIP are presumptive in nature. However, when the clinical signs and laboratory data support a presumptive diagnosis of FIP, then such a diagnosis may be made with a very high degree of confidence, especially when the typical effusion fluid is present. Evaluation of effusion fluid remains one of the most useful diagnostic aids for FIP.

Most cats with FIP have moderate to high *titers* (levels) of coronavirus antibody, but this finding must not be overinterpreted. The presence of coronavirus antibody in any cat, healthy or diseased, is indicative of only one thing: previous exposure to FIPV or to one or more closely related viruses (FECV, CCV, TGEV). *The antibody test does not prove that a cat has FIP or has been exposed to FIPV.* In most cases, a positive antibody test, while consistent with a diagnosis of FIP, cannot differentiate a cat that is actively diseased from a healthy carrier of the virus or from a cat that has been infected by one of the other closely related viruses. *A positive antibody test is simply an aid in diagnosis, and nothing more.* It should be given no more weight than any of the other routine laboratory procedures used at arriving at a diagnosis. *It therefore follows that the diagnosis of FIP must never be made simply on the basis of a coronavirus antibody test.*

The natural reservoir of infection appears to be infected cats. The most important source may be clinically healthy carrier cats—those that carry and excrete FIPV but show no ill effects. Studies suggest that *some* healthy, antibody-positive cats may be carriers. The problem that arises is that there is as yet no diagnostic test for identifying these carriers (i.e., there is no test for FIP that is equivalent to the "Hardy test" for feline leukemia virus). *Thus a cat with a positive antibody test is not necessarily a carrier of FIPV.*

TREATMENT. No curative therapy for FIP currently exists; the disease is virtually always fatal once clinical signs have become apparent. Palliative therapy combines high levels of corticosteroids and broad-spectrum antibiotics, in an attempt to slow down the FIP inflammatory disease process and minimize secondary bacterial infections. This therapy serves only to modify the disease course and, in most cases, does not provide a cure.

A number of supposed "treatments" for FIP have been touted in recent years, including experimental medications and megavitamin supplementation. To date there is no published scientific evidence that any of these potions is of benefit to affected cats.

PREVENTION. A safe and effective vaccine for FIP is not available. Experiments thus far reported using FIPV, TGEV, FECV, and CCV preparations have been unsuccessful in conferring uniformly protective immunity. It is not anticipated that a vaccine will be available for some time.

Until a vaccine or a diagnostic test for FIPV carriers is available, control of coronavirus infections must be based on accurate identification and isolation of cats with FIP and on maintenance of coronavirus antibody–negative catteries (when possible). Breeders should be advised to remove cats persistently infected with feline leukemia virus or feline immunodefi-

ciency virus, reduce cattery crowding, and avoid inbreeding their animals. Breeding particular pairs of cats that tend to produce kittens with FIP should be discouraged; alternatively, problem breeding stock may be eliminated from the cattery altogether.

A test-and-removal program for healthy coronavirus antibody-positive cats cannot be recommended on the basis of current knowledge. Because there is no available diagnostic test that can specifically identify carriers of FIPV, there is no medical reason for destroying healthy antibody-positive cats (i.e., a positive antibody test only indicates past exposure; it does not mean necessarily that a cat is still carrying the virus). In addition, a positive antibody test does not identify which coronavirus (FIPV, FECV, CCV, TGEV) was responsible for producing the antibody. *Euthanasia of healthy antibody-positive cats is a medically unjustified procedure.* Instead, control must be exerted at the level of admission. In an antibody-negative feline household, prospective new residents should ideally test negative both before and after a six-week quarantine period prior to entry, and after returning from show or stud. In any antibody-positive household, testing will be of little benefit. The most important procedure one can implement in such a household is the rearing of litters in isolation with individual queens, in order to minimize exposure of the young to other members of the group. A queen that consistently produces kittens that develop FIP, either within the cattery or after placement in a new household, should probably be eliminated from the breeding program.

Feline Immunodeficiency Virus (FIV)

Feline immunodeficiency virus, previously called feline T-lymphotropic lentivirus (FTLV), is a newly recognized feline virus belonging to the family Retroviridae. Although it is related to another retrovirus, feline leukemia virus (FeLV), FIV does not cause cancer and is not classified with FeLV in the *oncornavirus* subfamily of retroviruses. Instead, FIV has been placed in the *lentivirus* subfamily, along with the viruses causing *progressive pneumonia* in sheep, *infectious anemia* in horses, *arthritis-encephalitis* in goats, and *acquired immunodeficiency syndrome* (AIDS) in human beings.

The immunodeficiency syndrome associated with FIV, with its array of secondary infections, anemia, and low white blood cell counts, is indistinguishable from the noncancerous syndromes associated with FeLV infection. Prior to the first identification of FIV in California, cats that presented with what seemed to be an FeLV-associated disease but that repeatedly tested negative for FeLV were nevertheless assumed to be infected with FeLV. Now that a test for FIV is available, it is becoming apparent that at least 15 percent of such FeLV-negative cats are in reality infected with FIV. The prevalence of FIV infection in the general, healthy, United States cat population, however, is estimated to be about 1–3 percent.

THE CAUSE. The genetic material of FIV, like that of other retroviruses, consists of single-stranded RNA. The production of a double-stranded DNA copy of this RNA is an essential step in the replication (reproduction) of FIV within the host. This step requires a special viral enzyme, *reverse transcriptase*, which the virus carries with it when it infects a cell. The double-stranded copy of the viral genetic material then is inserted into the DNA of the host cell, where it may remain in an inactive state for some time before production of new virus particles is initiated.

Antibodies to FIV do not bind to FeLV, nor do antibodies to FeLV bind to FIV, so that the two viruses are *antigenically* unrelated. In addition, FIV is not antigenically related to *human immunodeficiency virus* (HIV), the lentivirus responsible for AIDS.

PATHOGENESIS. Very little is known about the sequence of events following initial infection with the virus. The primary mode of transmission is unknown, but bite wounds represent a likely possibilty, when one considers that free-roaming male cats are most frequently infected with FIV. Casual, nonaggressive contact among cats does not appear to be an efficient means of spread. Transmission from an infected queen to her kittens does occur, but it is uncertain whether this is an *in utero* (during gestation) event or occurs after birth. Sexual contact probably is not a primary means of spread.

Following initial infection, the virus appears to be carried to regional lymph nodes, where it may replicate in a subpopulation of white blood cells known as *T-lymphocytes* or *T cells*. These cells are suspected of being the primary target cells of FIV because culture techniques require the use of feline T-lymphocytes in order to grow the virus in the laboratory. The virus then spreads to lymph nodes throughout the body, resulting in a generalized *lymphadenopathy*

(enlargement of the lymph nodes). This stage of the disease usually passes unnoticed by an owner unless the nodes are greatly enlarged. Some time later—perhaps days but possibly weeks to months—the cat may develop a fever and a drop in the white blood cell count (*leukopenia*). A low red blood cell count (i.e., anemia) also may develop. The cause of these sometimes precipitous declines in blood cell types is unknown, but may be due to a loss of precursor cells in the bone marrow. There then follows a largely enigmatic period (sometimes measured in years) during which the cat appears normal, despite being persistently infected with FIV. Eventually, signs of immunodeficiency begin to develop, compromising the cat's ability to protect itself against infection. Bacteria, viruses, protozoa, and fungi, which can be found in the cat's everyday environment and generally are innocuous to a healthy animal, can cause severe illness in an immunocompromised individual. It is these secondary infections that are responsible for most of the clinical signs associated with FIV infection.

CLINICAL SIGNS. The clinical signs of the immunodeficiency syndrome are diverse in nature because they involve an array of secondary infections. General unthriftiness (failure to thrive) is frequently the only outward sign that a problem exists. Fever of at least 103°F often is present in the later stages and may be much higher at times. A very common presenting complaint is a loss of appetite or evidence of pain while eating, due to infection of the gums (*gingivitis*) and mouth (*stomatitis*). These conditions can lead to inflammation of the tissue around the teeth (*periodontitis*), with eventual loss of the teeth.

Chronic, nonresponsive or recurrent infections of the skin, urinary bladder, and upper respiratory tract are often seen. Persistent diarrhea due to infection of the intestinal tract is also a frequent problem. Abortion of kittens or other reproductive failures have been seen in infected queens. Some infected cats have experienced seizures, *dementia* (mental deterioration), and other neurologic disorders. Slow but progressive weight loss also is common, with severe wasting occurring late in the disease process.

It is suspected that some FIV-infected cats have been infected for several years. A few of these cats have histories of recurrent illnesses with periods of relative health between episodes. In such cases, leukopenia and anemia also appear to cycle, with episodes of low cell counts followed by recovery to nearly normal levels. However, the overall trend seems to be progressive, with cell counts dropping lower during each subsequent episode.

DIAGNOSIS. Diagnosis is based on the history, the clinical signs, and the result of an FIV antibody test. This test is performed at certain commercial and university veterinary diagnostic laboratories and is also available in kit form for use in private veterinary clinics. All positive results should be confirmed by a second test, preferably using a different procedure. A positive FIV antibody test indicates that a cat is infected with FIV (probably for its lifetime) and is capable of transmitting the virus to other susceptible cats. *It should be noted that eight to twelve weeks may elapse after infection before detectable antibody levels appear.*

TREATMENT. Therapy of the secondary infections associated with FIV is based on the clinical signs and the nature of the infectious agent. Use of antimicrobial (antibiotic or antifungal) drugs to control bacterial and fungal infections has been moderately successful, but must be continued for long periods or reinstituted as new infections occur. Supportive care, including intravenous fluids, blood transfusions, and feeding of high-caloric dietary supplements, is frequently required. The use of corticosteroids or other anti-inflammatory drugs may be indicated in some cases to control gingivitis and stomatitis. Anabolic steroids (those that promote growth and tissue repair) may help to combat weight loss and wasting.

It must be kept in mind that these measures are not directed at combating FIV itself. The drug AZT, useful in therapy for AIDS patients, may also be of use against FIV, but the drug is expensive and difficult to obtain, and its side effects are apparently greater in cats than in humans. Drugs designed to enhance or modify the immune system may someday be of benefit in treating FIV infections.

PREVENTION. No vaccine is available to prevent FIV infections. Owners can protect their cats only by preventing them from contacting infected cats. Pets kept indoors and away from free-roaming cats are highly unlikely to contract FIV infection. Catteries and multiple-cat households should test all their cats and isolate or remove any positives. Once FIV-negative status has been achieved, all prospective additions should be tested prior to introduction to the household.

PUBLIC HEALTH SIGNIFICANCE. Although FIV is similar structurally to HIV and causes a disease in cats similar to AIDS in humans, it is a highly species-specific agent. Only cells of feline origin have been found to support FIV replication. There is no cross-reactivity between FIV and any of the other lentiviruses. Initial studies indicate that veterinarians, owners, and researchers who have had close contact with FIV-infected cats show absolutely no evidence themselves of FIV infection. It appears at this time that FIV infections are restricted solely to cats.

Rabies

The specter of rabies has been known throughout Asia and Europe since the days of antiquity. Today rabies can be found on all continents of the world except Australia and Antarctica. It is ordinarily a disease of bats and carnivores, including the domestic dog and cat and many wild species. Despite the availability of excellent human and animal rabies vaccines, rabies remains a special cause of concern among human populations, especially in the developing world.

In the developed nations, canine rabies vaccination programs have all but eliminated cases of rabies among human beings. Animal rabies, however, still occurs with varying frequency. Among domestic species in the United States, cats now surpass dogs in the number of rabies cases reported each year. Although those numbers remain small, they serve as a reminder of the continual presence of this ancient scourge.

THE CAUSE. Rabies is caused by a bullet-shaped virus belonging to the family Rhabdoviridae. Rhabdoviruses are enveloped viruses and hence are relatively easily destroyed by common household soaps and detergents.

OCCURRENCE AND TRANSMISSION. Rabies is maintained in nature by wild and domestic carnivores and by certain other wildlife species. In the United States, skunks play a major role in spreading the disease, especially in the midwestern portion of the country, where they are now the primary reservoirs of infection. Raccoons are important in transmission in the southeastern states and have recently begun to spread the disease to more northern areas of the Atlantic seaboard. Wild foxes are important reservoir hosts in Europe and to a certain extent in North America as well. In the Caribbean and much of the Americas, bats are important reservoirs. In Latin America, vampire bats are particularly notorious for spreading rabies. The only rodent species of any importance in rabies transmission appears to be the woodchuck, in the mid-Atlantic and midwestern United States. Among domestic species, only dogs and cats are important carriers of the infection. In most developing nations today, dogs remain the primary reservoir of the disease and the principal source of human exposure. Rabid animals excrete vast numbers of rabies virus particles in their saliva—a fact that accounts for the primary means of rabies virus transmission, i.e., the bite of an infected animal.

PATHOGENESIS. The incubation period—the time between exposure to rabies virus and the development of signs—is quite variable, ranging from one week to one year. Most of this variability appears to reflect the length of time the rabies virus spends within muscle cells at the site of the bite, prior to gaining access to the nervous system. Once the virus has entered nerve endings, however, it advances relentlessly up the nerve bodies until it reaches the spinal cord and eventually the brain. From there it can spread to other tissues important in transmission of the virus—the salivary glands, respiratory system, and digestive tract. To date, the actual mechanism by which the virus produces locomotor and cerebral derangement, with eventual death of the host, remains unclear.

CLINICAL SIGNS. In general, signs of rabies in cats are similar to those observed in other domestic species, but the signs seen in each individual case may vary widely. Two principal forms of rabies are recognized: an excitatory, or "furious" form, and a paralytic, or "dumb" form. In actuality, most rabid animals exhibit some manifestations of both forms. The paralytic form of rabies always represents the terminal or end stage; however, some animals may die during the convulsive seizures of the furious stage without exhibiting the final stage. Some will show few or no signs of excitement, the clinical picture reflecting instead the effects of paralysis.

During the furious stage, which lasts variably for one to seven days, affected animals become wild and aggressive. *Rabid cats are extremely dangerous animals because of their viciousness and quickness of action.* Rabid animals frequently snap at imaginary objects and may attempt to bite any animals or humans that approach them. If restrained, an animal may chew viciously on metal chains or the bars of its cage. It may break its teeth, lacerate its mouth and gums, and drool a ropy saliva tinged with blood.

Within a short time these signs give way to those of the final or paralytic stage, which lasts only for a day or two. The paralysis usually appears first in the muscles of the head and neck, the most characteristic sign being difficulty in swallowing. Signs of localized paralysis are quickly succeeded by more generalized paralysis, with death following usually within two to four days of onset.

For both animals and humans, rabies is an inevitably fatal disease once clinical signs have appeared (only three human survivors are documented in the medical literature). Therefore, utmost care must be taken if one suspects that a pet has been exposed to the rabies virus.

DIAGNOSIS. A definitive diagnosis of rabies can be made only by laboratory examination of brain material from an affected animal. Considering the grave prognosis for recovery from rabies once clinical signs have appeared, it is imperative that an accurate diagnosis be obtained. *Any wild or domestic mammal that has bitten a human being and is showing signs suggestive of rabies should be humanely destroyed,* and the head submitted to a qualified rabies laboratory for diagnostic testing. In addition, any bat or wild carnivore, *regardless of signs manifested,* that has bitten a human being should be destroyed immediately and the brain examined for the presence of rabies virus (this latter action is necessary because of the variable period of salivary virus-shedding that can occur *before* clinical signs appear). Any *healthy domestic animal* that has bitten a human being should be confined for at least ten days and observed for the development of clinical signs of rabies.

An *unvaccinated domestic animal that has been bitten by or exposed to a known rabid animal* should either be destroyed or placed in quarantine for six months and vaccinated for rabies one month prior to release. A *rabies-vaccinated domestic animal that has been bitten by or exposed to a known rabid animal* should be given a rabies booster immunization immediately and observed by the owner for ninety days.

If signs of rabies appear during the time of observation, the animal should be humanely destroyed and the brain examined to confirm the diagnosis of rabies.

Currently three methods are available for the laboratory diagnosis of rabies: *immunofluorescence microscopy,* the most rapid and accurate method, in which slides of brain tissue are examined for the presence of rabies virus using special antibodies and a fluorescent microscope; *histopathology,* in which sections or smears of brain tissue are examined for the presence of *Negri bodies,* intracellular inclusion bodies seen in many (but not all) cases of rabies; and *mouse inoculation,* which is frequently used to confirm positive results or to investigate further suspected cases that have proven negative by other methods.

TREATMENT. Because of the potential risk of exposing susceptible humans to rabies virus, treatment of animals suspected of having rabies is *strongly discouraged.* Treatment of humans exposed to a rabid animal, however, must be aggressively applied. Treatment of humans consists of thorough flushing and cleansing of the bite wound with soap and water (the importance of this simple step cannot be overemphasized); administration of rabies immune globulin (rabies virus antiserum) to exposed individuals who have never been vaccinated against rabies; and administration of the human diploid-cell rabies vaccine in five doses, given on days 0, 3, 7, 14, and 28 postexposure.

PREVENTION. In the United States and most other countries of the world, effective rabies vaccines are available for use in domestic animals. Mass immunization of dogs has been employed for many years to control the spread of rabies by creating an "immunological barrier" between wildlife reservoirs of rabies and human populations. Several countries, including England, Iceland, Japan, and the Scandinavian nations, have succeeded in eradicating rabies by implementing control programs and very strict quarantine regulations. *It is recommended that all dogs and cats be vaccinated for rabies at three months of age and revaccinated as required by vaccine specifications.* At present, there are no rabies vaccines licensed for use in wild animals. (*See* Appendix A: Zoonotic Diseases, and Appendix B: Vaccinations.)

PUBLIC HEALTH SIGNIFICANCE. The signs and course of rabies in humans are similar to those seen in animals. Both excitatory and paralytic symptoms may be manifested. The incubation period, as in animals, is quite variable—from about two weeks to as long as a year—but on the whole averages between three and six weeks. The course of the disease is short —only a few days—*and the mortality rate is essentially 100 percent.* For the safety of humans and their pets, cat and dog owners should see to it that their animals are routinely vaccinated against this most deadly and uncompromising of viral diseases.

Feline Viral Rhinotracheitis (FVR)

See Chapter 24: Respiratory System and Disorders.

Feline Calicivirus Infection (FCI)

See Chapter 24: Respiratory System and Disorders.

Bacterial Diseases

B acteria are minute, single-celled microbes, whose ancestry can be traced back to the very dawn of life on earth. These minute creatures surround us in our everyday lives yet remain invisible to the unaided human eye. They are complex, metabolizing, self-reproducing, living organisms—in stark contrast to viruses, which are inanimate, subcellular (smaller than cells), chemical entities incapable of reproduction except within living cells. The genetic material of bacteria contains both types of nucleic acid: *ribonucleic acid* (RNA) and *deoxyribonucleic acid* (DNA), whereas a virus contains only one or the other. Many bacteria are free-living inhabitants of the environment, and through their biochemical activities are instrumental in maintaining local and global ecosystems. Other bacteria are found on the skin and mucous membranes of higher organisms. There, they often exist in harmonious balance with their hosts, from whom they derive nourishment and for whom

they often represent a beneficent presence. An example of the latter is the bacterial population of the large intestine, aiding digestive processes and synthesizing certain important vitamins. Occasionally, if given the opportunity, these bacteria may gain access to deeper tissues of the host and produce disease.

However, another extremely heterogeneous group, comprising many different types of bacteria, readily invade and compromise the well-being of the host. They are classified as *pathogens*—microbes able to produce disease. These pathogens are the primary microscopic agents of importance to veterinarians, their clients, and their patients.

Bacterial diseases include a wide range of infections that can occur at different times in the life of a cat. Infection may develop during the neonatal period, for example, when kittens receive their first exposure to bacteria at a time when all of their body's defense mechanisms are not yet fully active. The feline body can also be invaded during adulthood, when certain bacterial infections may be promoted, at least in part, by *immunosuppressive* agents, which depress the immune system. Among such agents are steroid drugs and feline leukemia virus. In essence, three factors often interact to produce infection and disease: the host (cat), the causative agent of disease (in this case, bacteria), and the environment (stress factors, change of diet, parasitism, concurrent disease, et cetera). This chapter on bacterial diseases of cats presents information on the nature of the causative bacteria, clinical signs, diagnosis, treatment, and significance for human health.

Fortunately, many bacteria are sensitive to the action of substances known as antibiotics. Antibiotics act in a number of different ways, either to kill bacteria directly or to inhibit their multiplication. Some antibiotics target essential metabolic reactions of bacteria, while others interfere with the chemical synthesis of important constituents of the bacterial cell wall. Antibiotics in common use in feline medicine today include penicillin, ampicillin, amoxicillin, tetracycline, oxytetracycline, erythromycin, kanamycin, and gentamicin.

Unfortunately, resistance to antibiotics has arisen among many bacterial species. The survival of the resistant species through Darwinian modes of natural selection has been enhanced by the use of antibiotics. A bacterial organism capable of resisting the effects of an antibiotic will have a selective reproductive advantage over the bacterial organism that succumbs to the antibiotic. The resistant organism may actually thrive as a consequence, perhaps to the detriment of the host. Control of antibiotic resistance among bacteria is dependent upon two important elements: the identification of new and unique antimicrobial (antibiotic) substances to overcome resistance; and greater discrimination in the use of available antibiotics to preclude the development of new resistant organisms.

STAPHYLOCOCCAL INFECTIONS

Staphylococci are a diverse group of bacteria causing disease, in many animal species, including the cat. Staphylococci are usually associated with the skin, glands of the skin, and mucous membranes (especially those of the nose, throat, and anus). The major species of staphylococci associated with disease in cats are *Staphylococcus aureus, Staphylococcus simu-*

lans, and *Staphylococcus intermedius.* Some staphylococci are opportunistic agents capable of causing disease when conditions are suitable. Others commonly are associated with infections such as *abscesses* (walled-off, pus-filled lesions).

Staphylococci often cause infections of the skin, eye, nose and throat, urethra, vagina, and gastrointestinal tract. Such local infections are the most common of all bacterial infections. Local infections of the skin often begin with superficial scratches or wounds and usually result in the formation of discrete abscesses. Hair follicles may also become infected, resulting in *folliculitis.* Scratching or trauma can lead to a deeper local infection and the spread of bacteria to surrounding tissues. A *boil* may result when a hair-follicle infection spreads to deeper tissues and produces a firm nodule containing pus. A *carbuncle* is an even deeper skin infection containing many pockets of pus. Of the skin infections described thus far, the carbuncle is the most severe and in some cases can lead to *septicemia* (leakage of bacteria into the bloodstream).

Treatment of simple local infections and small abscesses usually involves hot-packing the lesions and observing the patient for spread of disease and development of additional signs of illness. Deeper infections may require hospitalization so that antibiotic therapy may be instituted and monitored. Often lesions are hot-packed and surgically drained. (*See* Chapter 17: Skin and Disorders.)

Severe baterial infections of the chest cavity called *pyothorax* (accumulation of pus in the chest cavity, is also known as *empyema*) usually require surgical drainage and antibiotic therapy. Outer-ear infections *(otitis externa)* usually respond to topical therapy, cleaning and flushing, and antibiotic treatment. Middle-ear infections *(otitis media)* may require surgical drainage and antibiotic therapy. (*See* Chapter 18: Sensory Organs and Disorders.)

Staphylococci sometimes are involved in infections of the uterus in association with other bacteria, such as *Escherichia coli* and streptococci, in what are termed "mixed" infections. Clinical signs can include presence of a vaginal discharge, loss of appetite, lethargy, vomiting, weight loss, and abdominal distention. Treatment by the veterinarian consists of uterine drainage and antibiotic therapy. The prognosis is generally good but is dependent on the degree of damage sustained by the uterus. (*See* Chapter 12: Reproductive Disorders.)

Staphylococci are also known on occasion to cause

urinary-tract infections in cats (a disease entity distinct from *feline urologic syndrome,* which is of unknown cause). Antibiotic therapy usually is indicated.

STREPTOCOCCAL INFECTIONS

Streptococci are frequently involved in mixed bacterial infections *(see* "Actinomycosis," below, and "Nocardiosis," below). Streptococcus canis has been associated with outbreaks of contagious lymphadenitis (swollen lymph nodes). Affected cats present to the veterinarian with signs of fever, depression, enlarged lymph nodes, inflamed throat, and tissue swelling of the jaw. Ocular infections, limb abscesses, and systemic disease with bacteria in the blood *(septicemia)* may also occur. These outbreaks of streptococcal disease among cats are similar to outbreaks of "strep throat" seen in human beings.

Fortunately, most streptococci are susceptible to penicillin or penicillin-type antibiotics. Streptococcal infections are treated in much the same manner as are staphylococcal infections.

ACTINOMYCOSIS

Actinomycosis is caused by anaerobic (growing in the absence of oxygen) bacteria of the genus *Actinomyces.* These bacteria are common inhabitants of the oral cavity of cats. Trauma and puncture wounds probably allow these normally harmless organisms to gain access to sterile tissues. Traumatized tissue often dies and produces an anaerobic microenvironment suitable for the growth of *Actinomyces.* A few *Actinomyces* species are also capable of growing in the presence of small amounts of oxygen. Inflammation and an influx of inflammatory cells (phagocytic cells from blood and tissue linings that destroy foreign particles) at the site of bacterial penetration result in the formation of an abscess. Draining tracts frequently extend from the abscess to the skin surface. Yellow-colored *sulfur granules* (clumps of bacteria mixed with dead and dying cells) can be seen in the pus draining from these lesions.

It is common for *Actinomyces* to be recovered along with other oral bacteria in mixed bacterial infections. These other bacteria can include *Pasteurella multocida* and the two anaerobes *Bacteroides* and *Fusobacterium.* Trauma to the mouth and bite wounds inflicted by hostile animals are thought to be primary sources of infections. Infection within the oral cavity may extend itself outward to the skin surface or may spread deeply to the bony tissue of the skull *(osteomyelitis).* A breakdown of the defense mechanisms of the respiratory tract (as by concurrent viral infection, for example) may allow extension of an oral infection to the lungs.

The most common form of actinomycosis seen in cats is the skin form, presenting as superficial tissue abscesses with draining tracts extending from the abscesses. Dissemination of the infection to produce systemic disease is rare; when it does occur, lung and bone are frequent sites of extension. Systemic actinomycosis may be accompanied by fever, breathing difficulty, exercise intolerance, and weight loss.

Facial abscesses and draining tracts can originate from an infected tooth root or from bone. The pus coming from the draining tracts varies in color from light red to gray, depending on the number and kinds of other bacteria present. The pus usually contains yellow-colored sulfur granules, as described above.

Actinomycosis must be differentiated from fungal infections and from other bacterial infections. Diagnosis is based on radiography (X rays), cytology (examination of cells in a lesion), and especially on bacterial culture of pus or affected tissue.

Actinomycosis cases presenting as simple bite-wound abscesses in the skin usually require only draining and flushing of the abscess with a disinfectant solution. Antibiotics are not required unless a fever is present. If there is bone involvement (osteomyelitis), surgery is indicated to remove the affected tissue; prolonged antibiotic therapy must then follow to prevent recurrence. With lung involvement, chest drainage must be established surgically to drain off pus. Actinomycosis resulting from tooth root infection requires surgical removal of affected tissue (including the tooth) and treatment with an antibiotic.

NOCARDIOSIS

Nocardiosis is similar in many ways to actinomycosis. *Nocardia* is a soil bacterium encountered through inhalation of dust, by wound contamination, or by ingestion. *Nocardia,* however, is aerobic (only growing in the presence of oxygen), while *Actinomyces* is not. In nocardial infection, there is a greater likelihood of lymph node involvement and systemic spread of disease than in actinomycosis. The draining tracts produced by *Nocardia* contain granules of a much smaller size than the actinomycotic sulfur granules.

Cats with nocardiosis are usually presented to the veterinarian with severe systemic illness—labored respiration, fever, emaciation. Because of the draining tracts in the skin and the debilitating disease picture, actinomycosis, fungal infections, and tuberculosis all must be considered as possibilities when making a diagnosis. The diagnosis is based on the history, physical examination, radiography (X rays), cytology (examination of cells), and bacterial culture, and identification of *Nocardia* in draining pus or in biopsy material.

Depending on the severity of systemic illness, some cats may be successfully treated with long-term antibiotic therapy. In severely ill patients the prognosis must be guarded. Localized lesions can be excised and drained. Lung involvement requires surgical drainage and antibiotic therapy.

SALMONELLOSIS

The salmonellae comprise nearly two thousand different member types of the genus *Salmonella,* bacteria found throughout the environment and in wild and domestic animals. *Salmonella* bacteria are responsible for a spectrum of maladies ranging from uncomplicated intestinal disease and diarrhea to life-threatening systemic illness. Clinical salmonellosis in cats is relatively uncommon and few references to it exist in the scientific literature. Surveys conducted by sampling feces or rectal swabs of "normal," nondiarrheic cats have revealed a *Salmonella* carrier rate ranging from zero up to 14 percent (it is likely that these surveys underestimate the true numbers of infected carrier cats because not all cats carrying the organism shed it at the time they are tested). Stray cats and shelter cats are more likely to be carriers and to be excreting *Salmonella* in feces than are pet cats.

Cats appear to be highly resistant to *Salmonella* infection unless they are stressed or suffering from concurrent illness. The source of the salmonellae is most likely to be either contaminated feed or carrier animals (whether clinically ill or healthy). Contamination can arise from rodent or bird feces, raw or undercooked contaminated meat and table scraps, or commercially prepared foods that are contaminated during processing.

Cats usually acquire salmonellosis by ingestion. Once ingested, the bacteria can cause a spectrum of clinical signs. Salmonellae that survive the acidity of the stomach go on to invade the small intestine and local lymph nodes. From this point the bacteria either are contained by the body's defenses or proceed to invade the bloodstream, from which they reach other tissues such as the liver and spleen. Owing to their fastidious grooming habits, infected cats quickly contaminate their fur and environment with salmonellae. Clinically ill animals often shed large numbers of bacteria in feces and sometimes in saliva.

Clinical signs of salmonellosis in cats are seen after a two- to four-day incubation period and can include fever, poor appetite, diarrhea, vomiting, and abdominal pain. More severely ill cats may be profoundly depressed and lethargic. Diagnosis must be based on the history and physical examination, bacterial cultures of rectal swabs or fresh feces, blood cultures (when indicated), and cytology (for presence of inflammatory cells in feces).

The treatment of salmonellosis is a subject of some controversy. In cases of uncomplicated *Salmonella* enteritis (intestinal inflammation) with diarrhea, but without signs of systemic illness, it is best to treat symptomatically by replacing fluids and electrolytes lost through vomiting and diarrhea. Antibiotic usage is *not* encouraged in such cases because of the risk of producing antibiotic-resistant salmonellae and because the antibiotic may eliminate normal intestinal bacteria that serve to protect the cat from harmful microorganisms. In cases of systemic illness, however, wherein a threat to the life of the patient is perceived, antibiotic therapy should be instituted.

Salmonellosis is of great public health significance because salmonellae can infect not only pets but pet owners as well. Cats—especially if very young, very old, or immunosuppressed—should be regarded with some caution when showing signs of diarrhea, fever, depression, vomiting, and inappetence. Salmonellosis is transmitted by the fecal-oral route; anything that can be done to break that cycle of infection will help to limit spread of the bacteria. Hands should be washed often, especially after handling the ill cat, its toys, food dishes, or other possibly contaminated materials. All litter should be bagged and disposed of promptly and properly. Disinfectants such as diluted chlorine bleach should be used to clean floors and other surfaces where the cat eats and sleeps and where the litter box is kept. Food and water bowls should be cleaned as often as possible. (*See* Chapter 37: Convalescence—Home Care.) Young children, older adults, and individuals on immunosuppressive drug therapy or antibiotics should be kept away from the affected cat, especially for the first few weeks post-infection, until the numbers of salmonellae shed by the cat have declined. The cat's feces should be cultured periodically by the veterinarian to assess the level of excretion of the bacteria. If a recovered animal subsequently shows signs of vomiting and diarrhea, especially after some obvious stress factor (antibiotic treatment, travel, vaccination, diet change, et cetera), the veterinarian should be notified. If anyone in the family becomes ill with diarrhea, severe abdominal pain, and fever, a physician should be consulted as soon as possible. It should be explained to the physician that a pet in the household has been diagnosed as a *Salmonella* carrier. The physician should then contact the attending veterinarian for specific details about the case.

Unfortunately, there are no vaccines available to protect cats against salmonellosis. Because salmonellae are ubiquitous in nature, it is very unlikely that the disease will be eradicated. Most cases of feline salmonellosis can be prevented, however, by maintaining a high level of household hygiene, by not feeding raw or undercooked meat to cats, and by having a cat checked promptly by a veterinarian if any clinical signs suggestive of salmonellosis are observed. A caveat: Cats that hunt are more likely to contact infected prey animals (rodents, birds) than are cats that remain house-bound—an important consideration. (*See* "Salmonellosis" in Appendix A: Zoonotic Diseases.)

CAMPYLOBACTERIOSIS

Campylobacter jejuni (*C. jejuni*) is commonly found in the intestinal tract of many wild and domestic animal species. Many infected animals are asymptomatic carriers, excreting the bacteria in feces. Only rarely has *C. jejuni* been documented as a cause of diarrhea in dogs and cats. In human beings, however, it is recognized as one of the major bacterial causes of diarrhea. Human beings acquire *C. jejuni* in any of several ways: direct contact with a carrier animal; contact with contaminated feces; contact with contami-

nated food, water, or inanimate objects; or contact with human carriers. Major food sources of human infection include poultry, milk, and pork. (*See* Appendix A: Zoonotic Diseases.)

Among cats *C. jejuni* is typically found in young kittens and older cats. The infected older cats most often are strays, or those suffering from concurrent illness, or those in close contact with possible carrier animals (as in kennels or shelters). Cats probably acquire it by ingestion of raw or undercooked poultry or other meat products, ingestion of wild rodents, contact with food or water contaminated with rodent feces, contact with other carrier animals or birds, or from the run-off of contaminated soils.

Clinical signs of campylobacteriosis vary from a mild illness (at most characterized by intermittent or chronic diarrhea) in older cats to the more serious appearance of watery diarrhea, loss of appetite, vomiting, and fever in young kittens. Because of a greater opportunity for exposure, it would appear that stray cats are more likely to exhibit clinical illness than are household pets. Cats that are housed in close physical proximity (in shelters or kennels) with carrier animals are more likely to become infected. Diagnosis of *Campylobacter* infection is based on the history, physical examination, and results of supportive laboratory tests (bacterial culture of fecal or rectal swabs).

Most mild cases of campylobacteriosis in cats are self-limiting and do not require treatment. Others, however, such as those characterized by severe diarrhea and fluid loss, require good nursing care and oral or intravenous replacement of fluids and electrolytes. Animals with a fever and persistent diarrhea may require antibiotic therapy in order to avoid further disease complications.

Cats, as a reservoir of *C. jejuni*, account for only a small proportion of human infections. Young children are at greater risk of disease than are adults. Cat litter should be bagged and properly disposed of, and hands should be washed frequently, particularly if a cat is acutely ill or has just recovered from recent illness.

PLAGUE

Plague is caused by *Yersinia pestis* (*Y. pestis*), the agent of the infamous "Black Death" of fourteenth-century Europe. However, in twentieth-century America it is referred to as *sylvatic* plague, meaning "sylvan" or "of the forest," because it primarily affects wild rodents. In the western United States, *Y. pestis* is enzootic (widespread but producing disease in relatively few animals). An epizootic outbreak of disease (attacking many animals and causing many deaths) can occur when diseased rodents die and their fleas, which carry *Y. pestis,* are forced to seek other animal hosts. Spread of infection is facilitated by the ease with which predators, such as cats, can capture disease-weakened prey. Plague in cats is of special concern because of the potential threat to human health. (*See* Appendix A: Zoonotic Diseases.)

Cats are infected primarily through the bite of rodent fleas or through ingestion of infected rodents. *Y. pestis* does not survive for a lengthy period outside of the mammalian host. Sensitive to the effects of drying, it can, however, persist for a short time in saliva, respiratory secretions. and pus from abscesses.

Plague takes three forms: *bubonic, pneumonic,* and *septicemic.* Bubonic plague, the most common form seen in cats, cannot be differentiated clinically from the common bite-wound abscesses caused by bacteria such as *Pasteurella, Streptococcus,* and *Staphylococcus.* Once a cat has been bitten by an infected rodent-flea, the lymph node draining the region of the bite enlarges and becomes inflamed, forming what is called a *bubo* (hence the name, bubonic). An abscess forms in the bubo that eventually ruptures and discharges thick, creamy pus. Affected cats are depressed, inactive, febrile (feverish), and lose their appetites. Cats are usually bitten by fleas around the head, neck, and eyes, and the affected lymph nodes are those in the jaw and head area.

Occasionally, infected cats may develop a more severe disease course, the septicemic form of plague, involving many organs. There are large quantities of bacteria in the blood with or without initial lymph node involvement.

The pneumonic form of plague is not common in cats. It is caused by the inhalation of *Y. pestis* rather than by a flea bite. While bubonic and septicemic plague are minimally transmissible, the pneumonic form is *readily* transmissible between mammalian hosts.

Any cat from a plague-enzootic area showing signs of lymph node enlargement or an abscess should be suspected of harboring *Y. pestis.* Diagnosis is based on the history, physical examination, and bacterial culture of lymph node aspirates (sample drawn through a needle from a node), pus draining from skin abscesses, or blood.

Plague-suspect cats should be treated for fleas whether or not fleas are present, and strict precautions by the veterinarian should be taken to guard against human exposure and infection. Such precautions include restricting the number of people caring for the cat, isolating the cat in a room by itself, and wearing surgical masks, gowns, and gloves when handling the cat or specimens from the cat. Treatment involves prompt administration of antibiotics to which the plague organisms are susceptible.

In all suspected cat-plague cases, *the state public health department must be notified so that surveillance and control measures may be instituted to prevent an outbreak.* Human beings can become infected with *Y. pestis* through the bite of an infected rodent flea, by direct contact with infected tissues (e.g., as when hunters dress game), or by contact with an infected cat. Transmission from cats to humans has occurred through cat scratches or bites, the bite of rodent fleas carried by an infected cat, or by aerosol from cats with pneumonic plague. Because the mortality rate is considerable in the human disease, diagnosis of feline and human infections must be made rapidly.

TULAREMIA

Francisella tularensis (*F. tularensis*), the cause of tularemia, is enzootic (widespread but producing disease in relatively few animals) in wildlife in North America. *F. tularensis,* like *Yersinia pestis* (the cause of plague), is a zoonotic agent; that is, it can be transmitted to, and produce disease in, human beings. Tularemia in cats appears to be quite rare and is usually associated with large die-offs in infected rodent populations.

Clinical signs in cats with tularemia may include inappetence, vomiting, and sudden weight loss. Prime sources of infection include infected rodents and rabbits. The mucous membranes of the mouth and throat appear to be primary avenues of infection after ingestion of infected meat. Another source of infection is from the bite of an infected tick or deer fly.

Diagnosis is based on recovery of *F. tularensis* from draining ulcers, lymph node abscesses, or other affected tissues. Extreme caution should be exercised when handling cats or specimens from cats suspected of harboring *F. tularensis;* a mask and surgical gloves should be worn on such occasions.

Cats apparently succumb very quickly to tularemia, making rapid diagnosis essential to successful treatment. Recovery from tularemia, like the disease itself, is rare.

PASTEURELLOSIS

Pasteurellosis in cats is caused by *Pasteurella multocida (P. multocida).* As is the case with *Actinomyces, P. multocida* is a common bacterium found on the mucous membranes of the feline oral cavity and upper respiratory tract. It is not usually considered a cause of disease in cats unless it is introduced deeper into body tissues. Because it is a normal inhabitant of the mucous membranes of cats and possesses a number of important *virulence factors* (ability to infect tissues or spread disease), *P. multocida* can produce disease if host defense mechanisms are compromised. In certain cases, infection may extend into the thoracic cavity in the form of *pyothorax* (fluid pus in the chest), abscesses, and pneumonia. Cat bites also spread infection.

Pyothorax usually results from the spread of pneumonia or abscesses into the chest cavity. *P. multocida,* an aerobic bacterium (one requiring oxygen), and anaerobic bacteria (those growing without oxygen) are commonly recovered from the pus. Diagnosis is based on the cytology and culture of aspirated (drawn through a needle) pus, chest radiography (X rays), and hematology. Affected cats are usually presented to the veterinarian with signs of *dyspnea* (difficulty breathing), fever, and fluid in the chest. Treatment consists of drainage of pus from the chest and the administration of appropriate antibiotics, often for a prolonged period.

Cat-bite abscesses. The skin over a bite wound in cats usually heals very quickly, resulting in the formation of an abscess beneath the skin. Bite-wound abscesses are common on the face, head, legs, and back of the cat. Affected cats may have few clinical signs other than swelling over the abscess. Some cats, however, exhibit fever, inappetence, and depression. The site of the bite wound may discharge a foul-smelling pus. The disagreeable odor is produced by anaerobic bacteria, which are often present along with *P. multocida.* Diagnosis is based on the history, physical examination, cytology, and bacterial culture of the abscess material. Although abscesses that drain spontaneously often require little treatment, deeper lesions may necessitate surgical drainage and antibiotic therapy.

MYCOBACTERIAL DISEASES

Mycobacteria are a diverse group of bacteria that are widespread in soil and water. Mycobacterial diseases are characterized by the formation of *granulomas—*chronic inflammatory nodules containing walled-off bacteria. A granuloma is formed when an animal's inflammatory cells (phagocytic cells from blood and tissue linings that destroy foreign particles) engulf mycobacteria but cannot kill them, resulting in an influx of more inflammatory cells. The body attempts to repair the damage caused by this chronic infectious process by walling off the infected area, producing a granuloma. In some cases, the cat's immune response can actually damage the cat more than it damages the bacteria.

Tuberculosis. Most cases of tuberculosis occur in either human beings (in whom the causative agent usually is *Mycobacterium tuberculosis*) or cattle (in which the agent usually is *Mycobacterium bovis*). *Tuberculosis remains a relatively rare disease in North American cats.* When it does occur, it is more likely due to *M. bovis* than *M. tuberculosis.* The decline in tuberculosis in cats has resulted undoubtedly from the decline of tuberculosis in cattle and the advent of milk pasteurization. However, whenever cats have access to unpasteurized milk or uncooked meats, the possibility exists of exposure and infection.

Cats become infected usually by ingestion of mycobacteria present in contaminated food or milk, or by exposure to contaminated objects that have come into contact with infected cattle. After being ingested, the bacteria enter the small intestine and localize in the associated intestinal lymph nodes. Infected cats shed *M. bovis* in their feces and can remain a source of infection on a farm even after infected cattle have been culled from the herd. Occasionally, tuberculosis in cats disseminates from the local lymph nodes, resulting in serious systemic disease.

Clinical signs of tuberculosis localized to the intestinal tract can include vomiting, diarrhea, weight loss, and enlargement of intestinal lymph nodes. If localization has occurred in the upper or lower respiratory tract, cats may exhibit respiratory difficulty (especially after exercise), fever, cough, difficulty swallowing, and tonsillar enlargement. If the disease progresses to involve additional body sites, then persistent fever, weight loss, dehydration, irregular appetite, and enlargement of many lymph nodes throughout the body may be seen. Ocular infections can result from systemic spread of the disease. Often abscesses and draining tracts in the skin occur in the areas around the eyes. Skin tuberculosis also occurs in cats, presenting as small nodules or flat, draining ulcers, in the skin of the head, neck, and legs.

A diagnosis of feline tuberculosis may be an elusive one. Clinical signs, radiography (X rays) of the abdomen and chest, and laboratory examination of needle aspirates or biopsies of lymph nodes, tracheal washes (flushing of material from the trachea and bronchii), abdominal and thoracic effusions (fluid buildup), skin biopsies, or draining tracts in the skin—all may be helpful at one time or another in diagnosing the disease. Examination of stained smears of these body tissues for the presence of mycobacteria should be attempted. Cultures for the recovery and identification of the mycobacteria take many weeks to produce results, but will provide a conclusive diagnosis and are important for determining the source of the infection.

Tuberculosis in cats often is in an advanced stage by the time of diagnosis, and prolonged treatment, which will probably not completely eliminate the mycobacteria from the host, may be required. Considering also that humans in contact with infected cats are at risk of infection, *it is inadvisable to attempt treatment of these animals.* Cats with tuberculosis represent an obvious public health hazard because the causative mycobacteria are shed in the stool, saliva, and from open draining lesions. *Public health authorities should be notified at once if tuberculosis is suspected.*

Feline Leprosy. Feline leprosy is caused by *Mycobacterium lepraemurium.* Exactly how cats acquire this infection is unknown, but it seems likely that a rodent reservoir is involved rather than cat-to-cat transmission. Feline leprosy is usually found in cats less than four years of age. The disease is manifested as a chronic skin infection, with ulcerated nodules or lumps on the head and limbs. The nodules begin as small, movable lumps in the skin that rapidly enlarge. Occasionally, regional lymph node enlargement and systemic spread of disease are seen. Cats with feline leprosy generally are in good health except for the ulcerated skin nodules, which are painless and do not provoke scratching.

Unfortunately, no simple test is presently available that will diagnose feline leprosy. Diagnosis is made by a combination of procedures including physical examination, biopsy of ulcerated nodules, and direct smears of the nodules to look for mycobacteria. Treatment consists of surgical excision of the skin nodules. Unfortunately, recurrence of nodule growth is common. No preventive measures are available.

Controversy exists over the relationship between *M. lepraemurium* and the agent of human leprosy, *Mycobacterium leprae.* Although there is *no known public health risk* associated with feline leprosy, it is deemed advisable for immunosuppressed individuals to avoid prolonged close contact with affected cats. (*See* Chapter 17: Skin and Disorders.)

Environmental Mycobacteria. The so-called "atypical" or "environmental" soil mycobacteria are gaining importance as agents of feline disease. These organisms usually are harmless unless they gain access to the cat's body—by contamination of traumatized skin, puncture wounds, or surgery sites—or if a cat is immunosuppressed. Once the organisms take up residence, nodules, ulcerated areas, draining tracts, and chronic abscesses may result.

Biopsies for both culture and pathology should be obtained for diagnosis. Usually the mycobacteria are resistant to drug treatment and, therefore, surgical excision of skin lesions is attempted; unfortunately, the lesions often recur after surgery. Because uncertainty exists regarding the risk of infection for human beings, care should be taken when handling infected cats and contaminated litter boxes and cages. (*See* Chapter 17: Skin and Disorders.)

CAT-SCRATCH DISEASE

Cat-scratch disease (CSD) is of importance not because of any problems that it causes in cats but because of the problems it causes in human beings. The disease is associated with human beings who come in contact with cats. In most cases, CSD is relatively benign and self-limiting, and until recently it was of unknown cause. In 1983, pathologists using special staining techniques identified a bacterium in the tissues of CSD patients; in 1988, the bacterium was finally recovered and grown in the laboratory. This still unnamed bacterium also produces a CSD-like disease in armadillos.

Human patients usually have had recent contact with a cat or experienced a recent cat scratch, bite, or lick. A small papule (tiny skin nodule) first develops at the site of contact or inoculation. This is followed by painful enlargement of the local lymph nodes, which may last for weeks to months. Usually the enlarged nodes eventually return to normal size, but in a few instances CSD produces a more severe clinical picture, with high fever, skin rash, bone lesions, and possibly seizures. Common symptoms in humans include fatigue, loss of appetite, fever, and headache. Most cases of CSD occur in children. Occasionally, cases are clustered in families, suggesting a common source of infection. The usual sites of primary exposure are the hands and forearms, followed by the legs, neck, and face. Other types of puncture wounds —from porcupine quills, rose thorns, rabbits, and dogs —have also resulted in CSD, suggesting that cats may be nothing more than mechanical transmitters of the causative organism, whose ultimate source in nature remains unknown.

Most human cases of cat-associated CSD have involved a newly acquired kitten or stray, rather than a long-term house pet. The interval between the cat scratch and the development of lesions varies from three to fourteen days. Most cats associated with CSD in humans have been healthy and have not reacted with skin-test material used to aid diagnosis in human patients.

The diagnosis of CSD is based on a history of patient contact with a cat, lymphadenopathy (disease of the lymph nodes), and a positive CSD skin test. The test involves injection of sterilized CSD lesion material into the skin of a patient and observing whether a local reaction occurs; however, it may not be performed by all physicians. Other laboratory tests designed to rule out other causes of disease are usually negative. Characteristic microscopic lesions of CSD can be identified in biopsies of affected lymph nodes. The presence of the suspected causative bacterium in the biopsy material is especially suggestive of CSD.

Because the disease usually is benign and self-limiting, therapy in most cases is not warranted. Sometimes the physician will aspirate pus from the lymph node to alleviate the pressure and pain caused by nodal enlargement. The aspirated pus should be cultured for other causes of disease and should be submitted for microscopic examination. Surgical removal of the swollen lymph node is usually not necessary. Antibiotic therapy has not been shown either to prevent symptoms from developing or to shorten the disease course.

The ultimate source of the CSD organism in nature is unknown. If cats are shown to be common reservoirs of infection, it might be possible to limit spread of the disease by breaking the cycle of transmission from cat to human with a few simple measures:

- prevent cat bites and scratches (especially in young children) by teaching the children to play gently with pets;
- prevent pets from licking a child's chapped hands or any open wounds;
- if cat bites or scratches do occur, be sure that the wound is carefully cleaned and that a topical disinfectant is applied (a physician should be consulted if the wound becomes infected or if any of the symptoms of CSD develop).

HAEMOBARTONELLOSIS (FELINE INFECTIOUS ANEMIA)

The *Rickettsiae* are specialized bacteria that live on or within body cells. Feline infectious anemia (feline haemobartonellosis) is caused by the rickettsial organism *Haemobartonella felis,* which attaches to feline red blood cells. This parasite is thought to be responsible for about 10 percent of all feline anemia cases. Sometimes feline infectious anemia occurs secondarily to an underlying immunosuppressive disease, such as feline leukemia virus infection (and possibly feline immunodeficiency virus infection as well).

The disease is seen most often in young male cats one to three years of age; the risk for males is 2.5 times that for females. Seasonally, feline haemobartonellosis occurs slightly more frequently in the late spring. The precise mode of transmission has not been determined, but it is known that blood from an infected cat must somehow be transferred to a healthy cat to produce the disease. Biting insects, particularly fleas, are considered likely carriers of the parasite. The organism has been found in stillborn kittens and in kittens within three hours of birth, so that *in utero* transmission also appears to occur.

The most common clinical signs are depression, weakness, loss of appetite, and pallor of the mucous membranes. Weight loss, vomiting, and dehydration may also be seen. Signs are somewhat dependent on the rapidity with which the anemia develops. If the anemia develops gradually, a cat may lose a considerable amount of weight, yet remain reasonably bright and alert. If the anemia develops quickly, however, a cat will lose little of its weight, but will be markedly depressed and jaundiced (yellowish discoloration of the mucous membranes). Early during the disease process the rectal temperature will be elevated (104°F–105°F).

Identification of the parasite in stained blood smears is the key to diagnosis. However, owing to the cyclic appearance of the parasite in the bloodstream, several blood samples taken sequentially over a period of days may be needed to locate the parasite on the patient's red blood cells.

Antibiotics are usually effective in treating feline infectious anemia. Oxytetracycline has been the most widely used and seems to be the most efficacious. *Cats must be treated for at least three weeks*—a shorter period of treatment may result in recurrence of disease. In addition, treatment with a glucocorticoid such as prednisolone may be prescribed to treat immune-mediated injury to the red blood cells. During the disease process, the immune system recognizes the parasite-coated red blood cells as "foreign" and attempts to remove them, thus worsening the anemia. In fact, such immune-mediated injury, rather than direct injury by the parasite, represents the major cause of the anemia.

No drug appears to eliminate the parasite from infected cats totally and, consequently, recovered animals remain chronically infected but clinically healthy. With proper therapy, most cats recover from the acute phase to remain inapparent carriers (carriers may suffer one or more additional attacks of the disease at some time in the future or may remain free of the disease for life). A comprehensive flea-control program for both the animal and the environment is prudent, because blood-sucking insects may have a role in the spread of the *Haemobartonella* parasite.

LYME DISEASE

Lyme disease is one of the fastest growing communicable diseases in the country and poses a significant medical and veterinary health threat. Lyme disease is caused by the spirochete *Borrelia burgdorferi*. The disease presents as a wide spectrum of clinical signs associated with the musculoskeletal, cardiac, and nervous systems.

The primary carrier of the Lyme disease organism is the three host deer tick, *Ixodes dammini*. Studies indicate that the major hosts for these ticks are the white-footed mouse for larvae and nymphs, and the white-tailed deer for adults.

Cats become infected from their predation of the mice or they serve as carriers for humans by carrying the immature ticks into the house on their fur. The disease is treatable in cats using the drug tetracycline.

CHLAMYDIOSIS

See "Eye," Chapter 18: Sensory Organs and Disorders, and Chapter 24: Respiratory System and Disorders, for details on infections caused by *Chlamydia*.

C H A P T E R 3 1

Internal Parasites

A parasite is an organism that finds its food source by living in or on another animal, which is referred to as the *host*. This particular relationship benefits the parasite but may harm, or occasionally prove fatal, to the host. Parasites can be one-celled organisms, such as protozoa, or complex organisms, such as insects or worms. This chapter deals with those parasites that thrive inside the body, classified as *protozoa, nematodes, cestodes,* or *trematodes.* For information on external parasites (i.e., fleas, ticks, mites) refer to Chapter 19: External Parasites.

Protozoa

Protozoa are small organisms that are usually composed of a single cell. They

differ from bacteria in that their genetic material is separated from the rest of the cell by a nuclear membrane. They may contain highly specialized structures for movement, feeding, and locomotion. *Flagellated protozoa* are ones with projections for locomotion, called flagella. Also, some have developed life cycles

in which arthropods (ticks) are used to transmit the disease between hosts.

The protozoan of most concern to cat owners is *Toxoplasma gondii,* which is capable of causing human disease when people become part of the life cycle. *Toxoplasma* is related to another group of protozoa that includes *Cryptosporidium, Isospora, Sarcocystis, Cytauxzoon,* and *Babesia.* Sexual stages occur in the life cycle of these parasites, unlike the others that will be discussed. Cysts develop from these sexual stages that are called oocysts. Oocysts undergo a maturation process wherein the cytoplasm of the oocyst divides to produce infective agents called sporozoites. When sporozoites get into a new host, they penetrate a host cell and form a nest of organisms, called a schizont. The schizont eventually ruptures, and the individual organisms from the schizont enter other cells and form more schizonts. Finally sexual stages are again formed. (Thus, a typical cycle can be considered as progressing from sexual stages to oocysts to sporozoites to schizonts to more schizonts to sexual stages.) Usually the sexual stages occur in the intestines of the cat, except in *Cytauxzoon* and *Babesia,* where the fusion of the sexual stages occurs in the intestine of a tick.

Nematodes

Nematodes are superficially earthwormlike creatures that are often called *roundworms.* Those best known to most cat owners are the large roundworm, *Toxocara cati,* and the cat hookworms. Again, as with other parasites, knowledge of the life cycle of these parasites can help in the control of these pests of the cat.

Cestodes

Adult cestodes are commonly called *tapeworms* because some specimens are quite large and ribbonlike or tapelike in appearance. Larval cestodes are sometimes called bladderworms, because the larvae often contain a fluid-filled space. Neither the adult nor the larval tapeworm has a gut or digestive system. Rather, they absorb nutrients from their surroundings through the surfaces of their bodies. Larval tapeworms are found in the tissues or body cavities of their hosts. Cats become infected by eating the animal containing the larval stage. Depending on the species of tapeworm involved, the intermediate host may be either an invertebrate or a vertebrate animal.

Adult tapeworms live in the intestine of their host. At one end of the body of the tapeworm is a structure called a scolex or holdfast. This structure may contain hooks or suckers and is used by the tapeworm to anchor itself to the intestinal mucosa. The other end of a tapeworm's body is usually composed of a series of repeated segments that contain both male and female reproductive organs. Those segments nearest the scolex contain immature reproductive structures, while those further away contain mature organs. The segments that are furthest from the scolex are usually packed with eggs. Eggs may be shed by the terminal segments, or the terminal segments may sometimes detach from the remainder of the body. In the latter case, the detached segments may break down and relese their eggs into the fecal stream, or the segments may pass from the body with the feces or actively migrate out of the anus of the host. Those segments that leave the host intact will often migrate, dispersing eggs into the environment. Usually, an owner becomes aware of a cat's tapeworm infection when the detached segments are seen in the animal's stool or attached to hair around the anus or perineum.

Trematodes

Trematodes are solid-bodied organisms. Their common names are *flukes* or *flatworms.* Usually, both the male and female sexual organs occur in the same animal, but fertilization often occurs between two individual organisms. Eggs produced by the adult fluke pass into the environment, and the stage that hatches from the egg, called a miracidium, will not complete its development unless it enters a gastropod, usually a snail. Within the snail, the miracidium develops and replicates, producing numerous progeny called cercariae. These cercariae leave the snail and then may enter intermediate hosts or encyst on vegetation. The encysted stage is called a metacercaria. The animal that will serve as the host of the adult fluke becomes infected by eating the animal or plant bearing the metacercarial stage. Another means by which animals become infected is by the direct penetration of cercariae through the skin. This last form of transmission is rare but important, because it is the means by which the schistosome, a trematode that infests humans, enters its host. Most cats, because of their predations and carnivorous nature, become infected by ingesting hosts that contain the infective metacercariae. In the United States, there are only a few species of trematodes that infect cats, and their occurrence is relatively rare.

GASTROINTESTINAL PARASITES

Gastrointestinal parasites rob a cat of good nutrition and health. The vomiting, diarrhea, anemia, and dehydration associated with these parasites weaken a cat, making it more susceptible to viral and bacterial infections and diseases. One study estimates that 10 percent of early deaths of kittens are parasite-related.

Protozoa

TOXOPLASMOSIS. *Toxoplasma gondii* is possibly the parasite of greatest concern to cat owners. It is not because this parasite causes severe disease in

INTERNAL PARASITES

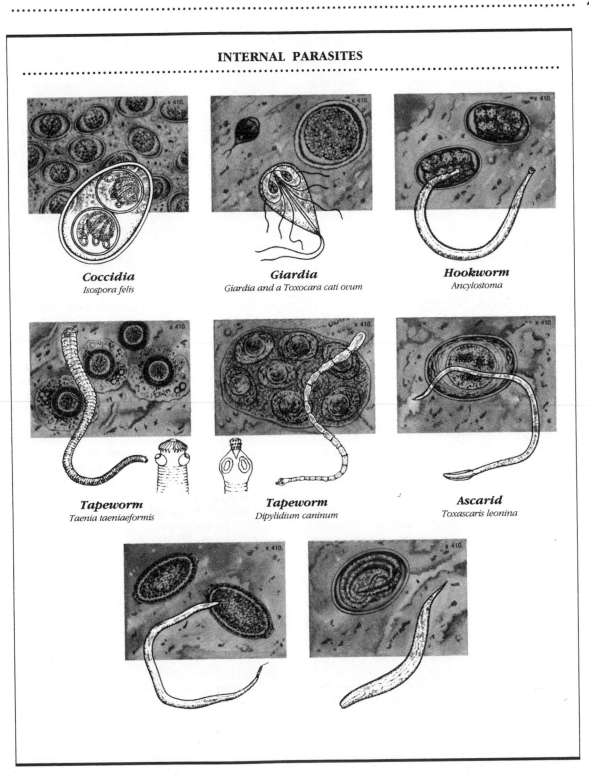

Coccidia
Isospora felis

Giardia
Giardia and a Toxocara cati ovum

Hookworm
Ancylostoma

Tapeworm
Taenia taeniaeformis

Tapeworm
Dipylidium caninum

Ascarid
Toxascaris leonina

cats (which it occasionally does), but rather because of the severe disease that can be caused to the human fetus of a mother that becomes infected during pregnancy. To understand how to prevent this disease in humans and how it can be controlled, it is necessary to become familiar with the many nuances and intricacies of the life cycle of this parasite.

Domestic cats, as well as wild felids, are the only animals that shed the oocysts of this parasite in their feces. These oocysts are small (0.01 mm in diameter [.0004 inch]), and after they are passed in the feces, they require two to three days to develop to the infective stage that contains the infectious sporozoites. If another animal, such as a mouse, sheep, bird, or man, ingests the oocysts, schizonts develop within numerous tissues of the animal, causing acute disease. If the animal survives the acute form of the disease, it goes on to develop a chronic, usually symptomless, disease state, with schizonts being found predominantly in the muscles and the brain.

Cats can become infected by ingesting raw meat containing schizonts or by ingesting the oocyst. Thus the cycle can pass from cat to cat without any cat eating raw meat. Fortunately, whether cats become infected by ingesting raw meat or oocysts, they will only shed oocysts in their feces for one to two weeks. Long-term immunity to the infection is not 100 percent. If cats become infected a second or a third time, some may still shed oocysts, although for a shorter period of time.

A diagnosis of toxoplasmosis in a cat depends on finding the oocyst in the feces of the infected animal. Although anti-*Toxoplasma* antibody levels are often measured in cats, a high level of antibody only means that a cat was infected previously, and, as stated above, these cats can still shed oocysts if they are reinfected. Work is presently under way to develop serological tests (blood serum tests for antibodies and antigens) that could tell if a cat has been recently infected, but even with these tests, it will not be possible to assure owners that their cats will not shed oocysts into the environment. Therefore, at present, the best that can be done is to determine at any one point in time that the cat is not shedding oocysts.

Occasionally in cats the disease spreads to other areas of the body. There has also been one report of transplacental transmission occurring in the cat. In these cases, there may be fever, diarrhea, and perhaps generalized wasting, and the outcome is usually fatal. Diagnosis in these cases has usually been based on postmortem examinations, but in some cases, especially those from zoos or other types of breeding establishments, the diagnosis has been based on a recent rise in the *Toxoplasma* antibody level. This last form of diagnosis is not worthwhile unless antibody levels are checked at consistent periodic intervals.

Healthy, adult humans seldom develop disease due to *Toxoplasma* infection. In fact, it has been estimated that toxoplasmosis exists in its chronic form in approximately half the people in the United States. A previously uninfected adult who acquires an infection usually develops swollen lymph glands. Adults with some type of immunosuppression—e.g., AIDS or immunosuppressive therapy—will sometimes undergo a reversion to an acute form of the disease. When the host's immune system does not function properly, the schizonts continue to rupture and new cells are infected and destroyed. In such cases, toxoplasmosis becomes a life-threatening condition and treatment is difficult.

Toxoplasma gondii exerts its most devastating effects on fetuses. Infection of the fetus occurs if the mother acquires her first toxoplasmosis infection during pregnancy, and there are a number of such instances—two to six cases per one thousand pregnancies in the United States. In cases of fetal infection, the infection may be severely damaging or fatal to the infant. If a woman has a high anti-*Toxoplasma* antibody level at the beginning of pregnancy, there is little to be feared from toxoplasmosis during the pregnancy. It would still be prudent to exercise the control procedures outlined below.

The effects on prenatally infected infants depend on when during pregnancy the child was infected. The most seriously affected are those that become infected during the second or third trimesters of pregnancy. These infants, at birth or soon thereafter, may develop lesions in their retinas, calcified lesions in their brains, or sometimes hydrocephalus (water within the brain's cavity, which causes pressure on the brain with resulting loss of function). Often these lesions may be fatal. In other instances, there may be no signs at birth, although central nervous system damage may appear several years later. It has also been suggested that toxoplasmosis causes abortions in humans, but this has not been proven. Children born to mothers with currently inapparent infections who previously gave birth to a *Toxoplasma*-infected child will not be at risk of infection.

Other forms of toxoplasmosis occur in children

who become infected later in life. These children may have a flulike disease followed by a rash. In some cases, there may be heart disease or pneumonia. A third form of the disease in these children may involve the central nervous system and is usually fatal. Others may develop lesions in the retina of the eye, which may be so severe that the eye will have to be removed. Fortunately, these are all relatively infrequent occurrences.

Control of toxoplasmosis is based on good sanitation practices. Cat feces should be disposed of properly and frequently, and cats should be prevented from defecating in children's play areas. Feces and cat litter boxes should not be used on gardens or in compost. Vulnerable owners, especially those who are pregnant, should avoid cleaning litter boxes. Do not feed raw meat to cats. Similarly, if owners want to avoid infection, they should not ingest raw or under-cooked meat. Cats that hunt may be a source of oocysts.

CRYPTOSPORIDIOSIS. *Cryptosporidium* is a minute parasite (the oocyst is 0.005 mm in diameter [.0002 inch]), whose life cycle takes place entirely within the small intestine of its host. It is spread from host to host by small oocysts containing sporozoites, which are passed in feces. The oocyst protects the enclosed sporozoites from the extremes of the environment until they find a new host to infect. Once in a new host, the sporozoites hatch out of the oocyst and infect an intestinal cell. They go just under the cell membrane of the host cell and form small nests of organisms that protrude into the intestinal lumen (the space within the intestine). Additional nests of organisms occur, until finally the sexual stage is again formed and oocysts are produced, which are passed in the feces. The infections are usually self-limiting and last only one to two weeks. Occasionally, often in immuno-compromised individuals, the infection can persist, as can the associated disease.

Although only a few sporozoites may gain access to a host, the multiplication that occurs within schizonts can produce thousands of organisms from one sporozoite. Although the initial sporozoite only infects and damages one host cell, more cells become affected as schizonts form and rupture. Because the *Cryptosporidium* organisms are so small, they do damage by producing numerous small perforations in the cells that have been infected. As more cells become affected, problems develop with absorption, which results in a yellowish, watery diarrhea. It is fortunate that most infections with *Cryptosporidium* are self-limiting, because there is currently no specific treatment for an infection with this parasite.

There is reason to believe that the species of *Cryptosporidium* in cats can infect people and other animals. Also, when the oocyst is passed in the feces, it already contains sporozoites and is infective to the next host. Thus, a cat with diarrhea caused by *Cryptosporidium* must be considered a source of infection to all other animals and people in the household.

The diagnosis of cryptosporidiosis is made by finding the oocysts in the feces of the infected animal. The small size of this organism makes this difficult, but as more veterinarians have become aware of its significance, the chances of a correct diagnosis have improved over past years.

If a cat is diagnosed as having cryptosporidiosis and has severe diarrhea, it should probably be housed in isolation or at the veterinarian's clinic until the diarrhea passes, or until oocysts are no longer being shed. If the diarrhea persists for more than several weeks, there may be reason to believe that there is a problem with the cat's immune system.

COCCIDIOSIS. *Isospora felis* and *Isospora rivolta* are two species of coccidian protozoa that parasitize the small intestine and the beginning of the large intestine of the domestic cat and its various wild relatives. Their life cycles are very similar to that of *Cryptosporidium,* with two significant differences. Their oocysts are much larger, 0.02 to 0.05 millimeter (.0008 to .002 inch), and the oocysts require several days in the soil for the development of infective sporozoites. It is because the oocysts require development in the external environment that routine fecal removal is safe and can prevent infection or reinfection.

There is very little disease associated with *Isospora* infections. The oocysts are often seen in the feces of young cats, but it does not appear that these parasites cause diarrhea. Occasionally, under crowded housing conditions with poor sanitation, kittens can develop dysentery due to *Isospora,* which can actually be fatal. In these cases, the stools will contain mucus and be bloody. Diagnosis is based on finding the oocysts in the feces, but in such situations, animals may succumb to the disease during the schizont stage of the infection before oocysts have had time to form. If a diagnosis is made, treatment with sulfonamides (sulfa drugs) can be undertaken. It may be one week before there is improvement. Adult cats rarely shed oocysts in their feces and almost never would be suspected of having *Isospora*-induced disease.

SARCOCYSTOSIS. The protozoan *Sarcocystis* differs from *Cryptosporidium* and *Isospora* in that the schizont stages occur in a host other than the cat. All that occurs in the cat is the formation of sexual stages and oocysts containing sporozoites. (The sporozoites are passed in what is called a sporocyst, which can be considered a subcyst within the oocyst. The oocyst wall breaks down before the sporocysts are passed in the feces.) There is almost no disease associated with cats in which the sexual cycle of this parasite occurs. Knowledge of this parasite is mainly of interest because cats serve as a source of infection for other animals.

There are several species of *Sarcocystis* that use the cat as a final host. The schizonts occur in various animals, such as cattle, sheep, swine, rabbits, and mice, that have ingested the sporocysts containing sporozoites, which have been passed in the feces of a cat. These animals often become ill as the schizonts develop in various tissues of their bodies. If the animals survive the initial acute phase of the infection, with the schizonts forming throughout their bodies, they go on to a more chronic condition, wherein schizonts develop within muscle cells. The schizonts developing in the muscle cells can become quite large and appear as white streaks within the muscles of the infected animal. It is these large schizonts that give the parasite its name *Sarcocystis,* which means "muscle cyst." Cats become infected by eating raw meat that contains these large schizonts. Thus, cats can be prevented from spreading this disease by feeding them only cooked meat products.

GIARDIASIS. *Giardia lamblia* is a protozoan parasite about 0.01 millimeter long (.0004 inch) that is found within the small intestine of cats, humans, and other mammals. There are two stages in the life cycle: the trophozoite (feeding) stage and the cyst (environmentally resistant) stage. The stage that lives and feeds in the small intestine is the trophozoite. Each trophozoite has two nuclei, flagella that provide locomotion, and an adhesive disk that attaches to the mucosal surface of the small intestine. The trophozoites reproduce by dividing, but due to some unknown stimuli, they sometimes form a cyst wall instead. The trophozoite within the cyst will undergo a single division,

and thus each mature cyst contains two trophozoites. Because the cyst has no means of motion or adhering to the mucosa, it is carried away by the passing fecal stream and leaves the body with the stool. The cysts in the feces are immediately infective to another host. The cysts can gain access to a new host by direct fecal-oral contamination. Another means is via contaminated water. If the feces are deposited into a large volume of water or carried into this water by rainfall, the cysts that are freed in the highly diluted feces can get into a new host that ingests the contaminated water. The cysts can remain viable in this water for extended periods of time. When a new host is infected, the trophozoites break out of the cyst and set up a new infection. Because the trophozoites can divide, the ingestion of one cyst is capable of producing huge numbers of organisms within the small intestine.

Most animals infected with *Giardia* never develop disease, although they may keep passing cysts for months or years. In the occasional animal, however, massive numbers of trophozoites will develop. The large number of trophozoites will coat the surface of the small intestine and interfere with the absorption of nutrients and fluids by the intestine. This malabsorption leads to severe diarrhea. During the diarrhea, the gut becomes overactive, the cysts do not form, and some trophozoites are swept out in the fecal stream. Usually, however, the diarrhea passes after several days to weeks, and the stools become normal again. Often, though, the diarrhea is recurrent. A yellowish, soft stool, foamy to frothy in appearance, may be another indication of *Giardia*. There will seldom be blood in the stool.

A diagnosis is made by finding the trophozoites or cysts in the feces of the infected animal. Treatment includes administering a *Giardia*-specific drug. Cleaning and disinfecting cages and litter pans with a dilute solution of liquid bleach will destroy organisms that have been shed in the environment and help prevent reinfection. Providing clean water and a high-quality diet are equally important in a treatment regimen.

There is evidence that giardiasis may be transmitted to humans. Therefore proper precautions should be taken to avoid contracting the disease from an infected animal. Following good hygienic principles, such as washing your hands after contact with an infected cat, is recommended.

TRICHOMONIASIS. Trichomonads are flagellated protozoans that live in the large intestine of animals.

They are transmitted from animal to animal by fecal-oral transmission, and there is no cystic stage in the life cycle. It is now believed that *Pentatrichomonas felis,* from the cat, is the same as *Pentatrichomonas hominis,* found in man, and it has been shown to be cross-transmissible from one host to the other. However, cross-transmission is probably not a major source of infection for either man or cats.

Trichomonads are sometimes found in the stool when an animal has diarrhea, and controversy has developed as to whether they are actually causing the diarrhea when no other obvious pathogen is present. The diarrhea in some cats with trichomoniasis has subsided after treatment, implicating the parasite as the cause. However, some believe that the diarrhea would have stopped anyway, continuing the controversy. Diagnosis is made by finding the flagellated protozoans during a fecal examination.

Nematodes

ROUNDWORMS (*Ascarids*). When the terms "rounds" and "roundworms" are used, they are usually referring to *Toxocara cati* and *Toxascaris leonina.* Often both species will occur together in the small intestine of a cat, but *Toxocara cati* is the more commonly encountered of these two species. Ascarids can grow to be three to five inches long.

The life cycle of *Toxocara* includes several methods for infecting its host. The female worms produce eggs that are passed in the feces. It will be several weeks before an infective larva develops within the egg. These eggs are quite resistant to environmental extremes and can persist for years in the soil; therefore, large numbers can build up in contaminated areas. Cats can become infected by ingesting the eggs or by eating rodents containing infective larvae in their tissues. However, the most likely method for a cat to become infected is by the transmammary transmission of larvae from a queen to her kittens. Some of the larvae ingested by adult cats migrate to tissues of the body, where they persist for years. Somehow, the larvae become reactivated by the pregnancy and migrate to the mammary glands, where they are carried to the kittens in the milk. The mother cat may not be shedding eggs in her feces at the time she is passing larvae to her offspring in her milk.

Toxascaris leonina lives in the small intestine of the feline host where the female worm produces eggs. The eggs are not infective when passed in the feces of the cat and require several days or weeks in the soil for the infective-stage larva to develop. After the eggs are infective, cats are usually infected directly, i.e., by the accidental ingestion of infective eggs. If the infective eggs of *Toxascaris leonina* are ingested by a small rodent, the larvae are capable of persisting in the tissues (much like those of *Toxocara canis*), and cats can become infected by eating these infected animals. Infections with *Toxascaris leonina* are usually benign, and the worms can be removed with anthelminthic (deworming) treatment.

The disease produced by *Toxocara* is usually benign. Large numbers of worms are capable of intestinal blockage and perhaps hemorrhage, but the presence of a few worms is usually not life-threatening. Occasionally, adult worms will be found in the vomitus of infected cats, but the worms may not be the cause of the vomiting. Infections can be diagnosed by finding the characteristic eggs in the feces, and treatment is relatively easy. There is currently no assured method of preventing the transmammary passage of the larvae in the milk of the queen.

The control of *Toxocara* infections depends mainly on regular fecal exams, appropriate therapy, and sanitation. Due to the resistance of the eggs to environmental extremes, it is best to prevent the infection from entering an enclosure where it is not desired. However, the soil is likely to be contaminated if infected cats have been using it recently. There are no simple ways to decontaminate soil containing eggs.

There is a disease in humans called *visceral larva migrans* that is most commonly caused by the migration of the larvae of *Toxocara* in the deeper tissues of the body and then can be referred to as larval toxocariasis. (*See* Appendix A: Zoonotic Diseases.) In most instances, the larvae have been identified as the larvae of the dog roundworm, *Toxocara canis,* but on rare occasions they have been the larvae of *Toxocara cati.* The humans, usually children, probably become infected by the accidental ingestion of eggs in contaminated soil. The larvae behave in the children as they would in an infected rodent, i.e., they migrate to various tissues of the body, where they persist as dormant larvae. Although most of the cases in humans are symptomless, heavy infections may produce severe disease requiring treatment. If cats ingest the eggs of the dog roundworm, *Toxocara canis,* the larvae migrate about the body of the cat as they would in a small rodent. The disease produced in an infected cat is similar to that seen in humans with visceral larva migrans.

HOOKWORMS. There are several species of hookworms that infect cats. The species involved are members of two different genera, *Ancylostoma* and *Uncinaria*. The adult hookworms live in the small intestine. These worms are long-lived and are probably capable of living the life span of a cat. The female worms produce eggs that are carried into the environment with the feces. If the temperature and humidity are optimal when the eggs are washed out of a stool into sandy soil, a larval stage develops, hatches, and matures into an infective-stage larva. Cats can become infected by either ingesting these larvae or by larvae penetrating the skin. In cases where a cat becomes infected by mouth, the larvae develop to adults within the mucosa and lumen (space within) of the small intestine. In those cases where larvae penetrate the skin, the larvae migrate through the lungs of the cat before settling down in the small intestine and developing to adult worms.

Kittens can become infected by the passage of larvae in the milk of the queen. Whether larvae enter a cat by ingestion or penetration, they do not all develop to adults in the small intestine. Some of the larvae will enter various tissues of the body and become dormant. The larvae will remain within these tissues for years, but when the queen becomes pregnant, they migrate to the mammary glands and are carried to the kittens in her milk.

In dogs that have been treated for hookworms, it has been noted that often the infection will reappear without any additional exposure of the animal to larvae. It has been shown that dormant larvae are continually becoming reactive and are migrating from the tissues back to the gut, where they continue their development to the adult stage. Similar work has not been done in cats, but it may help explain why some animals seem impossible to treat.

Hookworms cause anemia due to blood loss. The hookworms cause blood to enter the small bowel from the intestinal wall, and the feces becomes black in color and tarry in consistency. In acute infections, such as those that occur in kittens, there will often be very black or even bloody stools, and the animal may die from blood loss. In chronic cases, the blood is lost at a slower rate, and although the animal may show no overt signs of infection, it will be suffering from anemia. The animal should recover quite readily after treatment with a dewormer.

Hookworms can be transmitted to humans. (*See* "Cutaneous Larva Migrans" in Appendix A: Zoonotic Diseases.) The infective-stage larvae on the soil are also capable of penetrating the skin of man and other animals. In humans, these larvae migrate about the skin, causing a small, red, itchy trail. Finally, the larvae either die or enter the deeper tissues of the body and become dormant. The trails left by the larvae in the skin have given this disease the name "creeping eruption." When large numbers of larvae are involved, lung disease may develop, resulting in hospitalization. Another name for this disease is "plumber's itch," so called because in the southern United States plumbers crawling in the sandy soil under raised houses will develop the typical creeping-eruption lesion. In these cases, treatment along with supportive therapy may be undertaken. In small mammals such as mice or rats, the larvae may persist in the tissues, adding a fourth manner in which a cat can become infected: by the ingestion of one of these infected rodents.

OLLULANUS TRICUSPIS. *Ollulanus tricuspis* is a tiny worm, less than a sixteenth of an inch long, which lives in the stomach of cats. The females of this worm give rise to an infective-stage larva, which is passed from cat to cat in vomitus. The condition is only rarely diagnosed in fecal exams because these larvae are not routinely passed in the feces. Although there is usually no significant pathology associated with these worms, they do cause inflammation of the mucosal lining of the stomach that might result in a cat with a history of chronic vomiting. Levamisole, a worming medication, has been recommended for treatment.

PHYSALOPTERA. Various species of *Physaloptera* are commonly found in the stomachs of raccoons, skunks, opossums, and other carnivores. The adult worms are white and about an inch in length. They embed their heads in the lining of the stomach. The female worm lays eggs that already contain larvae when they are passed in the feces. The larvae in the eggs are not infective to another mammalian host until they have undergone a period of required development in the body of a beetle or a cockroach. The next host, such as a cat, becomes infected when it eats one of these insects containing infective larvae.

Infected cats may show an increased propensity for vomiting, and often the diagnosis may be based on the worms found in the vomitus. The worms may also cause gastric bleeding and slightly blackened stools. A diagnosis is made by finding the eggs in the feces. The infection can be treated with worming medication.

THREADWORMS *(Strongyloides).* These very small worms, one-eighth to one-fifth of an inch in length, occur in the intestine of their host. They differ from the other nematodes because there is no parasitic male as part of the life cycle. *Strongyloides stercoralis* is mainly a parasite of the small intestine of the human, which occasionally gets into the dog and rarely into the cat. *Strongyloides tumefaciens* is a rare parasite of the large intestine of the cat.

The parasitic female of *Strongyloides* lives threaded through the lining of the intestine. It lays eggs that develop and hatch within the intestine; the larvae leave the host in the feces. If the conditions are correct when the stool is deposited on the soil, the larvae develop to the infective stage. The infective larvae enter new hosts by penetrating the skin. After entering the host, the larvae migrate through the lungs before entering the intestine. In the intestine, the larvae thread their way into the intestinal wall and develop into the parasitic females. On certain occasions, the larvae deposited on the soil may undergo a single, free-living developmental cycle. In this free-living cycle, adult males and females develop that are dissimilar morphologically (structurally) to those which are parasitic. The free-living females lay eggs that ultimately develop into the same infective larvae. These larvae also infect hosts by penetrating the skin, thus following the usual parasitic cycle.

The disease associated with a *Strongyloides stercoralis* infection is usually minimal. The major sign may be diarrhea. *Strongyloides tumefaciens* produces nodular lesions in the large bowel and, like *Strongyloides stercoralis,* diarrhea. A diagnosis is made by finding the characteristic larva in the feces. There are drugs that have been shown to be successful in the treatment of the threadworms.

Humans are probably the major source of infection for cats with *Strongyloides stercoralis.* Usually, the infection will be a rather rare occurrence. However, if one cat in a household becomes infected, there is a good chance that the others may also be infected from larvae that have developed in the soil.

TRICHINOSIS. *Trichinella spiralis* is a small nematode, less than an eighth of an inch long, which is capable of developing in the small intestines of most mammals. The worm in the intestine causes only minimal disease. The actual disease, *trichinosis,* is caused by the larvae that are found within muscle cells.

The life cycle of *Trichinella spiralis* passes directly from one host to the next by the ingestion of tissues; there are no stages that occur which are external to a host. A cat will become infected by eating meat that contains the larvae of *Trichinella.* In the small intestine of the cat, the larvae that are digested from the meat will thread themselves through the mucosa and rapidly develop into adults. Adults mate within thirty hours of the ingestion of the meat. The females begin to deposit larvae about six days postinfection and continue to produce them until the adults pass from the body of the cat with the feces, four to sixteen weeks later. The larvae that are produced are carried throughout the body by the bloodstream, and those that enter muscle tissue will enter muscle cells. In the muscle cells, the larvae become encapsulated. The larvae can live for years before being ingested by another host. The disease occurs in three phases.

The first phase is a diarrhea that corresponds to the development of the adults in the small intestine. This phase occurs one to several days after the infected meat has been ingested and usually continues for about a week postinfection. This phase also will often be accompanied by fever and nausea.

The second phase of the disease may be the most significant. This is caused by the larvae entering the muscle fibers and results in the loss of their function. The amount of disease seen in this phase is dependent on the number of larvae the animal originally ingested. The more larvae that enter the intestine, the more adults there will be in the intestine, which means more larvae will enter the muscle fibers. If enough muscle fibers are affected, the animal will undergo a loss of muscle function, which may result in stiffness of the limbs and perhaps death.

The third phase is a chronic phase, in which the larvae persist in the muscles. This phase is usually asymptomatic, the larvae usually being an incidental finding at necropsy (autopsy). The chronic form of the infection is not uncommon; surveys in the United States have shown rates of infection in cats from 3 percent to 22 percent.

Only rarely are cats recognized as having infections with *Trichinella spiralis.* Usually, the signs would be too mild to warrant the attention of a veterinarian; there might even be fatal cases that go undiagnosed. Serology (testing for antibodies) for trichinosis is not usually employed in the diagnosis of infections in cats, although serological tests are used in people and swine. Diagnosis will probably continue to be based on the fortuitous finding of adult worms expelled in diarrheic feces of the infected animal.

Cats probably become infected during predation, since rodents harbor a background level of infection. There is also the possibility that they become infected by eating raw or undercooked meat. Smoking, salting, and drying of meat cannot ensure the destruction of any larvae that are present. Similarly, freezing may not kill larvae. Thus, it is best to avoid feeding cats raw meat or meat prepared in any of these fashions.

The treatment of trichinosis is difficult because a diagnosis is not usually made until the larvae have reached the muscle cells. Then the larvae are usually resistant to most drugs. However, recent improvements in chemotherapy have made it possible to treat the disease more successfully.

Cestodes

DIPYLIDIUM CANINUM. This is the most common tapeworm parasite of the cat. The adults can grow to two feet in length in infected animals. Eggs are not usually passed in the feces. Instead, it is more usual to have motile (spontaneously moving) segments expelled with the stool. These segments are about the size and shape of cucumber seeds, and they crawl about the environment after leaving the body of the cat, disseminating masses of eggs. The cat owner is often aware of infections before the attending veterinarian. It is possible that infections may not be diagnosed on the basis of a typical fecal exam because eggs may not be present in the feces.

The ubiquity of *Dipylidium caninum* stems from the life cycle of this parasite. The eggs released by the motile segments are ingested by the small wormlike larvae of the flea that are also developing near areas where the feces have been deposited. In the flea larvae, tapeworm larvae develop that are infective to the cat. Some of the flea larvae die as a result of the infection, but others go on to develop into adult fleas. Cats become infected by ingesting infected fleas while grooming. Cats begin to shed segments containing eggs two to three weeks later, and the cycle continues.

There is little disease seen in infected cats, but the motile segments can be quite disconcerting to owners. Infections can be very difficult to remove, however, because fleas in the environment can serve as reservoirs for future infections of the cat. Although deworming medications can be used to remove adults from a cat's intestine, to remove the tapeworms from the environment it is necessary to control the flea population. Without flea control, cats could be treated monthly with dewormers and still develop infections with new populations of adult worms each month.

Children can become infected with the adults of *Dipylidium caninum* by ingesting infected fleas. Although infections in children are not common, they do occur. Adults, possibly because of age-related immunity, tend not to support infections with this parasite. There is little disease associated with the infection in children or in cats, but again, the motile segments passed in the feces can be quite disconcerting to parents.

HYDATIGERA TAENIAFORMIS. This is probably the second most common tapeworm seen in cats. Again, infections are often diagnosed by the owner because motile segments are passed with the feces of the cat. These segments tend to be square and are capable of migrating some distance after leaving the body of the cat. Also, as with *Dipylidium caninum,* the examination of the feces may not reveal eggs even though the owner is seeing segments on a regular basis.

Cats become infected with this parasite by eating rodents containing the larval stage, which is called a *strobilocercus.* The rodents become infected by the ingestion of the infective eggs passed in the feces. This parasite is seen in cats that have the opportunity to hunt for prey. There is little disease associated with this infection in the cat, and treatments with dewormers will remove the infection. However, to prevent cats from being reinfected, it is necessary to keep them indoors to curb their predatory behavior.

There have been very rare reports of humans infected with the strobilocercus stage of this parasite. In these cases, the people probably became infected by the ingestion of the eggs passed in the feces of the cat. The tapeworm larvae were found in the livers of the infected individuals.

SPIROMETRA MANSONOIDES. This tapeworm is typically seen in cats that hunt in the wild. The natural host is probably the lynx or the bobcat. The adult worm may be about eight inches long, but infections often go unnoticed because segments are not passed in the feces. The characteristic eggs will, however, be recovered by fecal examinations.

The life cycle typically involves two or more hosts other than the cat. When an egg that is passed in the feces lands in fresh water, a free-swimming larval stage hatches, which will continue its development only if ingested by a small aquatic organism, such as the crustacean called *Cyclops*. The cycle ends unless the infected crustacean is eaten by an amphibian, reptile, or small rodent. If the cycle continues, a larval stage called a *sparganum* develops in the tissues of these animals. The cycle is completed when a cat ingests one of the animals containing a sparganum.

There is little pathology associated with the infection of cats with the adults of *Spirometra*. The most significant effect is one on the sensibilities of the owner on occasions when a large number of mature segments are passed in the feces. This can be prevented by having fecal examinations performed to look for eggs in the stools of cats that hunt. When eggs are found, treatment to remove the adult tapeworms can be performed.

On rare occasions, larval stages of *Spirometra* have been found in humans. The infection in humans is named after the larval stage and is called *sparganosis*. Humans presumably become infected by one of three methods: ingestion of infected aquatic organisms in drinking water; the eating of raw or inadequately cooked intermediate hosts, such as frogs; or the rather odd method seen in Southeast Asia, wherein freshly killed frog tissues are applied to eye wounds. In the latter instance, the sparganum leaves the body of the freshly killed frog and migrates into the orbit of the eye to which it has been applied. Although infections in humans do occur, there is no direct transmission of infection from cats to their owners.

DIPHYLOBOTHRIUM LATUM. This large tapeworm is a parasite of humans, dogs, bears, and occasionally cats, which is found principally in the northern United States and in Canada. The adults of this tapeworm can be quite large, reaching lengths of thirty feet or more in humans. The life cycle of this parasite is similar to that of members of the genus *Spirometra*. The first larval stages are found in minute aquatic organisms; the second larval stages are found in freshwater fish. Cats and other animals become infected with the adults of this parasite when they eat raw fish containing the larval stage. Again, there is little pathology seen in infected cats. Infections can be diagnosed by finding eggs in the feces, and the adult worms can be successfully removed with deworming medications.

MESOCESTOIDES. Several species of *Mesocestoides* occur in wild carnivores in the United States. The life cycle is still inadequately known. The first intermediate host has not been identified, but the second intermediate host is a small rodent or similar animal. Cats, like other carnivores, become infected by the ingestion of one of these infected animals.

The adults of this group of worms may be several feet in length and are known to multiply by asexual division within the intestine of infected dogs. This is important when the disease is treated, because unless all portions of the adult tapeworms are removed by the treatment, the worms can recolonize the infected animal.

ECHINOCOCCUS MULTILOCULARIS. This small tapeworm (about one-eighth to one-fourth of an inch in length) is usually found in foxes, coyotes, and other canines. It has been reported from the central portion of the northern United States, Canada, and Alaska. In recent years, it has been expanding its range in the United States, but this may be due to an increased awareness by observers. Similarly, more and more cats are being diagnosed as infected, but this again may be due to increased awareness by diagnosticians. A diagnosis is made by finding eggs in the feces of the host, but currently the eggs of *Echinococcus* cannot be differentiated from those of *Hydatigera*. A cat shedding segments of *Hydatigera* could also be infected with *Echinococcus,* and in areas where both parasites are endemic, there would be no way to be certain which parasite was involved on the basis of a fecal examination.

Echinococcus multilocularis uses small rodents as intermediate hosts. These rodents become infected by the ingestion of the eggs of this parasite, which are passed in the feces of an animal harboring the adult tapeworms. In these rodents, a larval stage develops in the liver that is called a *multilocular hydatid cyst.* The cysts tend to progressively invade the liver of the intermediate host, and up to 90 percent of this organ may become involved. A cat or other host becomes infected by ingesting one of these infected rodents and may develop an infection of a very large number of adult worms from the numerous larval cestodes that are present. The cat will begin to pass eggs in its feces about a month after it has eaten the infected rodent.

There is little disease in cats harboring the adult tapeworms of this species. It is important that they be treated, however, because this parasite can be a significant cause of disease in infected humans. If cats are diagnosed as being infected, they should be hospitalized or confined until fecal examinations show they are no longer shedding eggs into the environment.

Humans that accidentally ingest the eggs of *Echinococcus multilocularis* develop larval tapeworms in a manner similar to that seen in the rodent intermediate hosts. In humans, the cysts progressively invade the liver tissue. This produces a slow-growing liver disease that is quite similar in appearance to a carcinoma of the liver. Also, like a carcinoma, the parasite may metastasize to other organs such as the brain or lungs. The infection can often be fatal. Although rather rare in the United States, cases have been reported, and if the range of this parasite is truly expanding, more cases are to be expected. The disease is serious enough to warrant attention, and cats may serve as a possible source of infection for man. Regular fecal exams in endemic areas should allow cats with predatory habits to be kept free of infections.

Trematodes

CRYPTOCOTYLE LINGUA AND SPECIES OF *APOPHALLUS*. These flukes, which are one-fourth of an inch or less in length, live in the small intestine of their hosts. Cats become infected by ingesting raw fish containing the metacercarial (resting or maturing) stage of the parasite. The natural hosts are wild, fish-eating mammals and birds. There is apparently no serious pathology associated with these parasites. Reports of infections with these parasites are rare, so little is known about their treatment.

ALARIA AMERICANA. This is a small trematode, which lives within the small intestine of its host. Cats become infected by eating frogs and small rodents that contain the metacercarial stage. The natural hosts of this parasite are the raccoon and other wild carnivores. Cats can probably support large numbers of flukes withut showing any signs. Reports of this infection have been rare, and there has been little work done on treating these infections.

BLOOD PARASITES

Certain parasites (*Cytauxzoon* and *Babesia*) live within the blood cells. Because these parasites destroy the red blood cells, anemia occurs. Biting and blood-sucking insects (i.e., ticks, fleas) have been implicated as the vectors for blood parasites as well as intestinal parasites.

CYTAUXZOONOSIS. *Cytauxzoon felis* is a parasite of the bloodstream. The life cycle of *Cytauxzoon* can be summarized as follows. Sporozoites in the salivary glands of the tick are injected into an animal along with the saliva during a bite. Nests of living organisms then develop within the cells lining the smaller blood vessels. Later, these nests occur in red blood cells, and finally sexual stages are found in the red blood cells. When a tick feeds, it ingests sexual stages from the animal and mating occurs in the gut of the tick. Then, within the tick, an oocystlike structure develops that contains sporozoites, which will eventually migrate to the salivary glands. When the infected tick bites another animal, the infection is passed along.

In the United States, it appears that wild felids, such as bobcats, are the usual hosts for *Cytauxzoon*. In these animals, it appears that the disease is without signs. However, when domestic cats become infected, the disease has a rapidly fatal course. Observed signs have included loss of appetite, labored breathing, lethargy, dehydration, depression, pale mucous membranes, and a high fever. Cats usually succumb to the disease within a week after signs appear.

At this writing, the disease is rare; it has been reported only from the southern United States, and there is no successful treatment regimen.

BABESIOSIS. *Babesiosis* is a disease of cats, found outside of the United States, which is similar to cytauxzoonosis. *Babesia* organisms live in blood cells and are transmitted from cat to cat by ticks. In Africa, Asia, and South America, species of *Babesia* have been found that use wild and domestic cats as a primary host. Animals infected with one of these feline species of *Babesia* may develop anemia, weakness, dehydration, and lethargy. Fortunately, a species of *Babesia* specific for cats has never been found in North America.

On the islands that lie along the southern coast of New England, there is another species of *Babesia, Babesia microti,* which is a parasite of small wild rodents. The disease is transmitted from rodent to rodent by the bite of an infected tick. Occasionally, people have also been bitten by infected ticks and become infected with this parasite and have developed a malarialike disease. Cats have never been found infected with this parasite.

TRYPANOSOMA CRUZI. Trypanosomes are protozoans that inhabit the bloodstream. One species, *Trypanosoma cruzi,* infects cats in South and Central America, but has not been reported from cats in the United States. This parasite is present in wild animals, such as opossums and raccoons, throughout the southern and southeastern United States, with rare cases of infection occurring in humans and dogs. The number of cases of infection in humans and domestic animals in the United States has probably remained low because the triatomid bugs that transmit this disease have not become used to living in human dwellings, as they have in South and Central America. In the United States, the triatomid bugs that are present prefer to live in the wild.

There are two forms of disease caused by *Trypanosoma cruzi.* The acute form is a possibly fatal disease in which numerous organisms can be found in the blood of the infected animal. A second form of the disease, the chronic form, is caused by a form of this parasite that is found in muscle cells, especially muscles of the heart. In the chronic disease, there is destruction of the heart muscles with the obvious consequence of cardiac problems. There is treatment for the animal during the acute form of the disease, but once the damage is done to the muscle cells, little can be done to restore the muscle's function.

RESPIRATORY PARASITES

LUNGWORMS. *Aelurostrongylus abstrusus* is a nematode that lives in the lungs of infected cats. The adult nematodes are threaded through the lung tissue, and the female worm lays eggs that develop and hatch in the lung. The resulting larvae move up the trachea and enter the digestive tract via the esopha-

gus. These larvae do not take up residence in the gut, but are passed to the external environment in the cat's stools. Unless the larvae that are passed in the feces are eaten by a snail or a slug, they will never develop to the stage infective to the cat. However, if they are eaten by a snail, the larvae will migrate to the snail's body tissues and undergo the development that is required to become infective. If a small rodent eats the infected snail or slug, the larvae will encyst in the tissues of the rodent. A cat becomes infected by eating a snail or a small rodent that has infective larvae in its tissues. The cat will begin to shed larvae in its feces about a month and a half after eating the infected snail or rodent.

The disease produced by *Aelurostrongylus abstrusus* is usually a very mild respiratory distress, which is often unnoticed. In severe cases, the respiratory signs will become more pronounced, and the cat's breathing could become compromised enough to cause death. The disease is diagnosed by finding the larval stage in the feces. Infected cats are easily treated with worming medications.

LUNG FLUKE. *Paragonimus kellicotti* is a stout-bodied fluke, about one-fourth of an inch in length, which lives within cysts in the lungs of its host. Usually there are two or more flukes in each cyst. The natural hosts of this parasite are mink and other wild carnivores, and it has been reported throughout the central and eastern United States and Canada. Infections, however, are sporadic among cats because the cat must ingest an infected intermediate host, a crayfish, to become infected. The stages in the crayfish then migrate to the lungs of the cat, where they develop to adult flukes. About six weeks after a cat ingests an infected crayfish, it will begin to shed eggs of *Paragonimus kellicotti* in its feces.

Light infections with *Paragonimus kellicotti* will be asymptomatic. When large numbers of flukes are present, there will be signs of pulmonary disease. A diagnosis is made by finding the eggs in the feces. Treatment can remove these parasites from the cat's lungs.

HEART PARASITES

HEARTWORM. *Dirofilaria immitis* is a nematode mainly considered to be a parasite of the dog. However, cats do become infected and may develop disease. The adults of this parasite are five- to ten-inch-long, thin, white worms, which live in the heart of their host. The cat is not a good host because usually the parasite's life cycle is not completed.

Cats, unlike dogs, rarely have *microfilariae* (a small larval stage) in the blood for extended periods of time; in the dog a microfilaremia may persist for years. Without microfilariae it is difficult to determine if an animal is infected. When present in the blood, they are relatively easy to identify. If they are not present, the diagnostician must rely on clinical signs, serologic tests (for antigens or antibodies), radiographic or ultrasonic findings, or electrocardiograms. For this reason the disease is less commonly diagnosed in the cat.

The disease in cats is similar to that seen in dogs. There is a thickening and folding of the internal walls of the heart, which might lead to obstruction of the blood vessels. Dead worms are carried to the lungs by the bloodstream, where they cause problems with breathing; in some instances, these can be life-threatening situations. Often, however, the disease in cats will go unnoticed until the animal is necropsied for some other reason.

Cats can be protected from infection by preventing their being bitten by mosquitos. There is preventative medication approved for dogs that is sometimes used for cats living in areas of high prevalence, such as the southeastern United States. The use of such medications should be left to the discretion of the local veterinarian. If cats do become infected, they can be treated. However, treatment for heartworms is a serious undertaking. It will often require the hospitalization of the animal for observation, because once the worms are killed, they will be carried to the lungs. After treatment, there is a short period of time when the animals must be watched very closely for pulmonary disease. These signs can be kept under sufficient control to protect the life of the cat if the animal is hospitalized.

LIVER PARASITES

LIVER FLUKES. *Platynosomum concinnum* is a thin fluke, about a quarter-inch long, which lives in the bile ducts of its cat host. The infection is mainly restricted to the southern United States, Hawaii, Puerto Rico, and other tropical areas. Cats become infected by ingesting a lizard containing a larval stage.

The prevalence of infection may be quite high among cats in southern Florida and the tropics, where, in some instances, up to 75 percent of the examined animals have been found infected.

Usually, the infections remain asymptomatic, but if large numbers of worms are present, a destruction of the liver due to blocked bile ducts can develop. Diseased cats may show signs of lethargy and loss of appetite or perhaps vomiting and abdominal distension. A diagnosis is made by finding the eggs that are carried from the bile ducts to the intestine, which are then passed in the feces. Treatment is possible and quite efficient in removing these parasites.

Four liver flukes, *Amphimerus pseudofelineus, Metorchis albidus, Metorchis conjunctus,* and *Parametorchis complexus,* have on rare occasions been reported from cats in the United States. Cats acquire their infections by eating raw, freshwater fishes containing metacercariae; the natural hosts are various wild, fish-eating mammals. These parasites are capable of causing hepatitis in their hosts, but the rarity of their occurrence has allowed very little work to be done on the treatment of these infections.

MISCELLANEOUS

CAPILLARIDS. There are four capillarid nematodes that affect cats. Until recently, they have all been considered members of the genus *Capillaria,* but it appears that there may be some validity in using different names. The four species in the cat are: *Eucoleus aerophilus,* which is found in the mucosa of the trachea and bronchi; *Aonchotheca putorii,* which is found in the mucosa of the stomach and small intestine; *Pearsonema plica,* which is found in the mucosa of the urinary bladder; and *Capillaria hepatica,* which is found in the liver.

The life cycles of the parasites are direct. The eggs of *Eucoleus aerophilus* and *Aonchotheca putorii* leave the host in the feces of the infected animal. The eggs of *Pearsonema plica* are found in the urine of the infected cat, and in the case of *Capillaria hepatica,* the animal must die to release the eggs into the environment so they may enter the soil where they embryonate. Earthworms may serve as hosts to larvae, but they are probably not a major source of infection for cats. Cats probably become infected by the ingestion of eggs either during grooming or by eating soil-contaminated foodstuffs.

The disease seen depends on the species of worm involved. *Eucoleus aerophilus* parasitizes the airways of the lung, and the signs that are seen are related to the involvement of this organ. Although infections are usually symptomless, there may be a harsh, dry, nonproductive cough. *Pearsonema plica* of the urinary bladder also is usually asymptomatic, but again, in some cats there is an inflammation of the bladder wall that will respond to treatment. *Aonchotheca putorii* is apparently asymptomatic, as is *Capillaria hepatica.* Treatments have been described for the species occurring in the lungs, stomach, and urinary bladder that are effective. *Capillaria hepatica* of the liver is usually diagnosed as an incidental finding at necropsy, but drugs have been used in humans that are also effective in cats.

VISCERAL AND CUTANEOUS LEISHMANIASIS. The genus *Leishmania* is composed of a group of flagellated protozoans, which are transmitted from host to host by the bites of very small mosquitolike flies called phlebotomines. The disease caused in the animal that is bitten is partially dependent on the species of *Leishmania* involved. With some species, the organs affected by the parasite are liver and spleen, while with other species, the lesions may be restricted to the skin. Hence, the first-mentioned form is termed *visceral leishmaniasis* and the second form is *cutaneous leishmaniasis.*

Both cutaneous and visceral leishmaniasis are rare in the United States. Visceral disease has been seen in cats that have been brought back to the United States from South America or areas surrounding the Mediterranean Sea. The cutaneous form of the disease has been seen in rare instances in cats in the south-central United States. Treatment of both forms of the disease is possible, although sometimes difficult.

EURYTREMA PROCYONIS. Eurytrema procyonis is a parasite of the ducts of the pancreas, and the raccoon is probably the common host of this parasite. Cats probably become infected by eating grasshoppers containing the larval stage. Infected cats will show signs of inflammatory pancreatic disease, which include intermittent vomiting and weight loss. The disease is relatively rare in the United States, and little work has been done on its treatment.

Fungal Diseases

The term *fungus* includes yeasts and molds, which live primarily in the environment, where they degrade dead organic material enzymatically (use enzymes to accelerate chemical reactions). Among the more common, recognizable fungi are mushrooms, bread molds, and baker's yeast. Fungi are of great importance ecologically because their digestive processes *(decomposition)* help to release nutrients trapped in organic debris back into the biosphere.

A yeast is a unicellular, budding fungus, forming bud-shaped spores. A mold is a filamentous (threadlike) fungus. Some disease-producing fungi, such as those causing the systemic mycoses and sporotrichosis, are *dimorphic,* which means they are capable of existing in two different forms. They are molds at cooler atmospheric temperatures and yeasts at warmer temperatures within the body of a host.

Some fungi, if given the opportunity, can produce disease in animals and in human beings. Often, fungal disease results because of some underlying defect in the immunological defenses of the host, e.g., inherited absence of immune system components, or acquired defects produced by immunosuppressive virus infection or administration of immunosuppressive medications. In other cases, such as ringworm, infection occurs commonly in the normal host, but usually is transient in duration—once the immune system has been alerted, the fungus is gradually eliminated. Fungal diseases in the latter category can be managed fairly easily; those in the former category may be resistant to treatment and life-threatening to the host. (*See* Chapter 17: Skin and Disorders.)

Ringworm (Dermatophytosis)

Ringworm is the most common fungal disease of cats. The highly contagious ringworm fungi *(dermatophytes)* invade the most superficial outer layers of the skin, nails, and hair, subsisting on *keratin* (protein of hard tissues) from shed skin cells. Although ringworm is often a self-limiting disease, with spontaneous remission occurring within one to three months of onset, treatment of some cases can be long and costly. (*See* Chapter 17: Skin and Disorders.)

Cryptococcosis

Cryptococcus neoformans is a yeast infection with a predilection for the central nervous system in most species. *Cryptococcus* is surrounded by a large capsule, which is in part responsible for the organism's ability to produce disease. It is found in bird droppings, particularly those of pigeons, and less commonly in the soil. Most cases result from inhalation of the organism.

In cats, cryptococcosis presents most often as a respiratory illness, characterized by sneezing, snuffling, raspy breathing, and production of a thick nasal discharge. It may also present as a hard, nodular skin swelling on the head, most often over the bridge of the nose. Neurologic abnormalities and eye disease may result.

Diagnosis is based on identification of the organism by India ink stain, in smears of nasal discharge, skin lesions, or cerebrospinal fluid. Samples should also be sent out to a laboratory for culture in order to confirm the diagnosis.

Response to treatment in cats with generalized disease is usually poor. Surgery (when appropriate) and administration of antifungal drugs are the current mainstays of therapy. Cats with cryptococcosis may have an underlying immune defect, such as infection with feline leukemia virus or feline immunodeficiency virus, making treatment a difficult endeavor.

Aspergillosis

Aspergillus comprises a large group of fungi that are often found in the air, soil, and in animal feeds. They are opportunistic invaders with a predilection for producing respiratory tract disease. Some species resident in moldy feed produce *aflatoxins* (poisons that can cause serious illness if ingested).

In cats aspergillosis presents most often with signs of respiratory or digestive tract involvement, often secondary to panleukopenia virus infection. Chronic sinusitis, pneumonia, and inflammation of the esophagus have been described, although diagnosis is sometimes impossible before death. Surgery and an-

tifungal medications have been used to treat the disease. The prognosis is variable, depending upon the immune competence of the cat and on the location and extent of the infection.

The Systemic Mycoses: Blastomycosis, Histoplasmosis, Coccidioidomycosis

The systemic mycoses are a group of rare fungal diseases in which inhalation (usually) of the causative organism is followed by widespread dissemination of the fungus to internal organs. These fungi, including the three to be discussed here, *Blastomyces, Histoplasma,* and *Coccidioides,* each exploit specialized environmental habitats and their distribution is geographically restricted. In the vast majority of cases, exposure to these organisms results in the production of immunity in the host, rather than disease. In a small percentage of infections, however, the fungi are not checked by the immune response, proceeding instead to engineer a serious (often fatal) illness. It appears that inherited or acquired defects of the immune response of the host often underlie susceptibility to these fungal disease agents.

An important feature of the fungi causing systemic mycoses is their dimorphic nature. In the environment they exist as filamentous fungi (molds). However, upon inhalation or inoculation of the filamentous form, they convert into a yeast form that grows in the tissues of the host. One significant consequence is that, in general, affected animals or human beings are not directly contagious to others. Rather, it is the filamentous environmental form of these organisms that is infectious, and thus dangerous.

Blastomycosis is caused by *Blastomyces dermatitidis,* a presumed soil fungus that is found in the mid-Atlantic, north-central, and Ohio/Mississippi river valley areas. Blastomycosis is extremely rare in cats. Following inhalation or inoculation, the organism can produce respiratory disease, skin lesions, ocular disease, or central nervous system abnormalities. Presumptive diagnosis is made by identification of thick-walled, budding *Blastomyces* yeast forms in biopsy or lesion material. Definitive diagnosis is made by culture and identification of the organism. Treatment consists of systemic antifungal medication. The prognosis is guarded except in the case of superficial skin infections, which may respond well to therapy.

Histoplasmosis is caused by *Histoplasma capsula-*

tum, a soil fungus found in the midwestern and eastern states. The organism is particularly fond of bird and bat droppings, wherein it can be found in large quantities. *Histoplasma* is especially common in soil on which chickens are raised. Histoplasmosis is very rare in cats. Following inhalation, respiratory disease (coughing, nasal discharge, difficult breathing) results most commonly. Diarrhea and neurologic abnormalities may also occur. Presumptive diagnosis is made by identification of the small, intracellular *Histoplasma* yeast forms in biopsy or lesion material. Definitive diagnosis is made by culture and identification of the organism. Treatment consists of systemic antifungal medication. The prognosis, unfortunately, is poor.

Coccidioidomycosis, the most severe of the systemic mycoses, is caused by *Coccidioides immitis,* which resides in soil of the dry cactus country of the southwestern United States. The organism is aided in its spread through the soil by burrowing rodents. Wind and dust storms whipping up the dry soil can spread the filamentous fungal forms over great distances. The disease is uncommon in cats. Skin, bone, and eye lesions have been observed most often. Presumptive diagnosis is made by identification of the large *spherule* form (parasitic stage wherein endospores develop) of the organism in biopsy or lesion material. Definitive diagnosis requires culture of the organism in the laboratory. Treatment consists of systemic antifungal medication. The prognosis is guarded except in the case of superficial skin infections, which may respond to therapy.

Candidiasis

Candidiasis is an extremely rare yeast infection of the skin and mucous membranes. *Candida* yeasts are considered to be part of the normal microbial population of the intestinal and reproductive tracts. With lowered host resistance caused by prolonged maceration (softening of tissue by soaking) of skin, antibiotic therapy, or immunosuppressive drug medication, serious local or systemic infections may be produced. (*See* Chapter 17: Skin and Disorders.)

Sporotrichosis

Sporotrichosis is an uncommon pus-forming disease caused by *Sporothrix schenckii.* This fungus is found in decaying vegetation, on rosebushes, sphagnum moss, wood splinters, and other environmental sources. Infection usually occurs by implantation following a penetrating wound. (*See* Chapter 17: Skin and Disorders.)

Phaeohyphomycosis

Phaeohyphomycosis is an uncommon chronic skin infection caused by dark, pigmented fungi. These fungi live in soil and vegetation and gain access to tissues usually by means of a penetrating wound. (*See* Chapter 17: Skin and Disorders.)

Phycomycosis (Mucormycosis, Zygomycosis)

Phycomycosis is a general term describing disease caused by a number of specific fungi, especially *Rhizopus, Absidia,* and *Mucor.* These are classical molds —*Rhizopus* frequently coats the surface of old, moist bread—and only occasionally do they produce disease in animals, usually as opportunists (invading if host defenses are compromised).

Phycomycosis is rare in cats. Skin and intestinal disease have been observed most often. Certain predisposing factors, such as prolonged antibiotic therapy, feline leukemia virus infection, and diabetes mellitus, are probably necessary for permitting these fungi to grow within the host. Treatment method and prognosis are dependent upon the nature and extent of the disease process produced.

Mycetoma

Mycetoma is a general term for fungus-induced, tumorlike skin lesions found most commonly on the extremities. The causative fungi are found within the lesions in the form of granules (small, beadlike masses). Mycetomas are rare in cats, but when they do occur, they are localized most often to the extremities or head. Treatment method and prognosis are dependent upon the nature and extent of the lesions.

Protothecosis

Protothecosis is a rare disease caused by a colorless alga, *Prototheca.* (By convention, *Prototheca* is usually included in discussions of fungal diseases.) Algae, such as seaweed, are among the most important of plants, because they are responsible for producing most of the oxygen present in the atmosphere. *Pro-* *totheca* lesions have been reported on the extremities and head of cats. Because some of these lesions are highly invasive, surgical removal is sometimes not possible.

Cancer

Neoplasia is the uncontrolled, progressive proliferation of cells under conditions that normally should be restrictive of cell growth. The accumulating cell mass, referred to as a *neoplasm* or *tumor,* is composed of abnormal cells that have become unresponsive to normal regulatory signals. This unresponsiveness may be due to genetic damage induced by physical or chemical agents, to usurpation of the genetic machinery by a virus, or to unknown causes. In many cases, a genetic predisposition exists that may advance the likelihood of tumor development. In other words, an individual's genetic make-up may in part determine the outcome of an encounter between that individual's cells and an *oncogenic* (tumor-inducing) stimulus.

Tumors may be classified broadly into two groups, *benign* and *malignant.* In general, benign tumors proliferate slowly, do not invade neighboring tissue or spread to other regions of the body, and often are amenable to curative surgical excision. Malignant tumors, on the other hand, grow more rapidly, are highly invasive and *metastasize* (spread to other areas of the body) readily, and are much less amenable to curative surgical excision.

Malignant tumors are subdivided further into two general types, *carcinomas* and *sarcomas,* depending upon their tissue of origin. Carcinomas originate within *epithelial tissue* cells (those lining the internal and external surfaces of the body), while sarcomas arise from *connective tissue* cells (those cells within an organ or structure that bind it together and support it). Malignant tumors, also known as *cancers,* are more likely to result in death of the host because of their potential for uncontrolled spread and are a more dangerous type of neoplasm than most benign tumors.

In this chapter, general principles of *oncogenesis* (tumor causation) and diagnosis and treatment of tumors will be discussed. Further information regarding specific tumor types can be found in other chapters covering specific organ systems or infectious disease agents.

Causes of Neoplasia

Most tumors that arise in human beings and animals are of unknown cause. This situation exists not because of a lack of medical investigation; research into the origins of neoplasia has been intensively pursued for decades, especially since the discovery of tumor viruses and cancer-causing chemicals. The fact that the cause of most neoplasms remains undiscovered is a consequence of the innate complexity of neoplastic disease processes, the frequently prolonged incubation period between exposure to a *carcinogen* (tumor-inducing agent) and actual tumor development, and the probably frequent involvement of more than a single factor in the development of many neoplasms (i.e., neoplasia in many cases is a multistep process). Nevertheless, despite these formidable obstacles, a number of carcinogens have been identified; among them are agents causing tumors in domestic cats.

PHYSICAL AGENTS. The most important physical agent known to cause tumors in humans and animals is *radiation*. Implicated sources include *ultraviolet* radiation (sunlight) and *ionizing* radiation (X rays and radioactive isotopes of the elements radon, strontium, and cesium). Excessive exposure to sunlight is associated with the development of squamous cell carcinoma of the ears in white cats. (*See* Chapter 17: Skin and Disorders.)

CHEMICAL AGENTS. Many chemical agents, including asbestos, cigarette smoke, arsenic, and vinyl chloride, are recognized carcinogens in human beings. To date, however, relatively few chemicals have been proved to be carcinogenic for cats.

VIRUSES. In cats the *feline leukemia virus* (FeLV) is the recognized cause of several types of cancers, including *lymphosarcoma* (cancer of lymphoid tissue) and *myeloproliferative disorders* (bone marrow cancers.) (*See* Chapter 29: Viral Diseases.) In addition, a mutant form of FeLV known as the *feline sarcoma virus* (FeSV) causes *multiple fibrosarcomas* (cancers of connective tissue) in young cats and is responsible

also for some cases of *malignant melanoma* (cancer of pigmented skin cells).

OTHER DETERMINANTS OF NEOPLASIA. A number of other factors, exclusive of defined carcinogens, also influence the complex interplay of events leading to the development of neoplasia. Included among these are variables such as age and diet. Some tumors arise more commonly in older animals, while others develop more often in younger animals. Such variation is probably related to differences in the origins of different types of tumors and the inherent susceptibility of animals to neoplasia at different stages of the life cycle. In cats, for example, newborn and very young kittens are more susceptible to infection and tumor development mediated by FeLV than are adolescent and adult animals. Duration of exposure to an oncogenic agent is also of importance, as is seen with sunlight-induced squamous cell carcinoma on the ears of white cats.

There is increasing evidence that diet may also be an important contributing factor in the development of neoplasia. Although dietary constituents themselves may not necessarily cause cancer, there may be secondary effects modified by diet that influence cancer progression, e.g., the recent indications that foods such as bran, which decrease transit time through the digestive tract, may be of help in preventing cancer of the colon whereas soft foods that remain in the tract for longer periods of time increase the likelihood of colon cancer.

Mechanisms of Tumor Induction

The precise biochemical mechanisms by which normal, healthy cells are transformed into abnormal cells unresponsive to cellular control mechanisms are not yet clear. However, studies in recent years using oncogenic *retroviruses* (viruses of the family Retroviridae) from a number of animal species have begun to raise the curtain of darkness, yielding dim but hopeful glimpses of the complex molecular machinery responsible for the production of tumors. The following is a discussion of some of the events involved in some retrovirus-induced neoplasms.

It has been known for some time that the incubation period may be quite prolonged for some retroviruses, such as FeLV, but may be quite short for others, such as FeSV. The vast majority of retroviruses with short incubation periods are *replication-defec-*

tive; i.e., they cannot reproduce themselves within host cells unless those cells are co-infected with a "helper" virus that provides the replication-defective viruses with materials they lack. Most of the defective retroviruses that have been closely examined share at least one common feature: the possession of genes coding for the production of a protein unnecessary for replication, but essential for tumor development. These genes, generally referred to as *v-onc* genes, appear to be closely related to normal genes (*c-onc* genes) found in the cells that the virus has infected. It appears that genetic exchange *(recombination)* between a nondefective retrovirus (such as FeLV) and the host cell's genetic material (the c-onc) is responsible for the production of defective retroviruses containing v-onc genes (i.e., the FeLV has mutated to form FeSV, owing to the acquisition of an onc gene. In the process, genes essential for viral replication are lost, so that the resulting mutant virus is defective).

The functions of c-onc genes are not totally clear, but it is believed that most of them are intimately involved in normal cellular growth processes and in the control of cellular *differentiation* (the process by which cells "mature" into fully functioning units). Acquisition of c-onc genes by retroviruses during recombination (which probably occurs as an error during the normal viral replication cycle) confers on the new, defective retroviruses the ability to disrupt normal cellular proliferation and differentiation—a recognized characteristic of the disorders referred to as neoplasia. Tumors induced by defective retroviruses have short incubation periods because the causative viruses carry onc genes with them and thus can initiate the cascade of events leading to neoplasia soon after they infect a cell.

The mechanisms by which nondefective retroviruses with prolonged incubation periods induce neoplasia are less clear, but it may be that the *location* in the host-cell chromosome at which these retroviruses insert their *proviral DNA* (a copy of their own genetic material, which they insert into the chromosome of the infected cell; *see* Chapter 29: Viral Diseases) is critical. Thus insertion of proviral DNA near a c-onc gene may inappropriately activate that gene in some way, leading to neoplastic transformation of the cell. This may explain the lengthy incubation periods, since it may require months to years of random proviral insertions in many cells before activation of a critical c-onc gene occurs.

It now appears that some chemical carcinogens

also act by turning on or modifying c-onc genes. Moreover, inherited genetic abnormalities in these genes or their regulatory components may result in the production of certain tumors. There is also evidence for the existence of *anti-oncogenes*—genes whose presence *represses* neoplasia and in whose absence (e.g., by a hereditary abnormality) certain specific kinds of tumors may develop. In the case of multistep cancers, other as yet undefined factors may be required for neoplasia to be fully expressed in an individual cell.

Diagnosis of Neoplasia

Definitive diagnosis of neoplasia relies on the identification of tumor cells by microscopic examination. Although the history, clinical signs, and results of radiografhic (X-ray) studies may strongly suggest a diagnosis of tumor, only microscopic evaluation of the actual cells themselves—by biopsy or *necropsy* (autopsy)—will confirm the diagnosis.

Complete physical and biochemical evaluation of the patient, together with identification of the tumor type and the extent of tumor spread, allows the clinician to clinically *stage* the tumor, i.e., to determine the present state of progression of the neoplasm. This is critical not only for determining the *prognosis* (outlook for improvement) of the case, but also for developing an appropriate strategy for therapy. Clinical staging of tumors also allows for comparison of the efficacy of different methods of treatment. By identifying stages of development of individual tumor types, clinicians are able to compare treatment of patients in equivalent stages of tumor progression, and thus determine the true efficacy of a given therapy.

The clinical manifestations of neoplasia are seen in many forms. Superficial tumors may arise as classical "lumps" within tissue without involvement of the overlying skin, or they may break through to the outside, leaving an eroded or ulcerated skin surface. Deeper tumors may produce no outward physical abnormalities; instead, functional aberrations of affected organs (the lungs or liver, for example) may give rise to clinical signs that are noted by an owner. The effects of a tumor frequently are due to a "crowding out" of normal cells by the tumor cells. The destruction of normal cellular architecture that results soon produces a disruption of normal function with the development of corresponding clinical signs.

Tumor cells, unresponsive to normal growth-inhibitory signals, literally invade and replace normal tissues of the body. In many cases, large masses of neoplastic cells are tolerated by the immune system and not recognized as being abnormal. This failure of the immune system to halt the spreading menace may be due to the fact that many tumor cells, having arisen from normal body cells, are not recognized by the immune system as "foreign," and hence are not destroyed. There also may exist "blocking factors" that cover up sites on the tumor cells, which might otherwise act as targets for the immune response.

With many neoplasms, the tumor cells themselves are readily accessible to the veterinarian. Samples of tumors located in skin or the underlying tissue can be obtained by *fine-needle aspiration* (insertion of a needle into the tumor itself and withdrawal of cells into a syringe) or by impression smears on surface tumors, and then examined under a microscope. Similarly, certain tumors of the liver, kidney, and lung may be amenable to biopsy by passing a special biopsy needle or other instrument through the body wall. Swollen lymph nodes may be seen in many tumor cases; fine-needle aspiration of these nodes often will reveal the presence of tumor cells interspersed among the normal nodal cells. Tumors of the bone marrow (myeloproliferative disorders, leukemias) may be identified by aspiration of bone marrow tissue and sometimes by the presence of tumor cells circulating in the bloodstream (in which case the abnormal cells may be observed on routine blood examination procedures, such as a *complete blood count* [CBC]). Some tumors of the bladder shed tumor cells in the urine, which then can be identified by normal urinalysis procedures.

A thorough physical examination of the patient and evaluation of the appropriate diagnostic test results are essential for reaching a definitive diagnosis of neoplasia in cats. Full cooperation of the owner with the veterinarian is then required to decide upon an appropriate course of therapy, if the tumor is amenable to treatment. Therapy should be advocated only if there is a possibility of maintaining a good quality of life for the patient. The prognosis for neoplasia in cats in many cases is quite good, especially if the tumor is discovered early and is not extensively invasive in nature. The longer the duration of tumor progression, the less likely is the chance that the tumor can be successfully removed. Highly malignant tumors, such as cancer of the mammary glands in cats, offer a poor prognosis, even with the sophisticated diagnostic

and therapeutic measures available to veterinarians today.

Lymphosarcoma and the myeloproliferative disorders are known to be caused by feline leukemia virus (FeLV). (*See* Chapter 29: Viral Diseases.) In many cases, a diagnosis of either of these two malignancies relies on determination of the FeLV status of the patient, i.e., whether the cat is persistently infected with FeLV. It must be kept in mind, however, that final diagnosis of the tumor type (as is the case for other neoplasms) must rest on microscopic examination of the tumor cells themselves.

Treatment of Neoplasia

A number of treatment modalities are available for tumors occurring in domestic animals. Among these are the more established therapies of surgery, chemotherapy, and radiation therapy. Among the newer available methods of treatment are cryosurgery, hyperthermia, phototherapy, and immunotherapy. Some of these treatment methods are readily available in private veterinary clinics, some in a handful of highly specialized facilities, and others only at university or other research centers. In some cases, the attending veterinarian may refer a patient for specialized therapy at a university veterinary teaching hospital because of the unavailability of the necessary equipment or expertise in the private sector.

SURGERY. Surgery remains the most successful treatment modality for neoplasia in veterinary medicine today. It is the most effective treatment for solid cancers and is a cornerstone of many combination-treatment protocols. In many cases, surgical removal of a tumor may be curative in itself. Well-delineated malignant tumors that have not spread widely, as well as most benign tumors, often are amenable to surgical excision. Many solid tumors that cannot be surgically removed, or at least partially reduced in size, are untreatable by most of the other available treatment methods.

The growth characteristics and extent of spread (if spread has occurred) of a tumor must be determined for a reasonable prognosis to be made. In many cases of localized neoplasia, diagnosis of the tumor type and surgical excision of the tumor itself are a combined procedure, i.e., the tumor is removed and a sample of it is submitted for biopsy evaluation. In other cases, an *aspiration smear* of cells taken from the mass is obtained before surgery and examined microscopically. Certain types of cancer, for example, lymphosarcoma and mast cell neoplasia (a connective-tissue tumor), may be identified quite easily using this technique. Knowledge of the tumor type, and subsequent evaluation of the tumor's extent of spread by physical examination and radiologic diagnosis, will help in deciding whether surgery is a reasonable therapeutic option.

With malignant neoplasms, the most important prognostic indicator is the extent of spread. Many malignant tumors have a predilection for spreading to certain distant sites, such as the liver or lungs. Often, removal of such a tumor is performed by first excising the primary tumor mass and then applying one or more other methods of therapy, e.g., radiation or chemotherapy. The intent is to prevent local recurrence of the tumor at the surgical site and to reduce in size and eventually eliminate metastatic lesions in other organs. Use of surgery prior to other modes of therapy is advantageous in that it greatly reduces the tumor load and thereby increases chances for a cure.

Owners must also be aware of the limitations of surgical intervention in their pets' diseases. Some tumors, for example, feline fibrosarcoma, a connective-tissue cancer, and mammary carcinoma, are notorious for their resistance to complete excision and their frequently rapid recurrence after surgery. Certain bone tumors (osteogenic sarcoma, fibrosarcoma) may require radical surgical excision (amputation of a limb) in order to assure a reasonable chance of patient survival.

Taken together, these considerations underscore a common theme of modern cancer treatment, i.e., that no one treatment method can be considered complete in itself. Modern cancer therapy involves instead a combination of approaches, implemented either sequentially or simultaneously, which together may be effective in controlling and even eliminating an individual tumor. Combination therapy is no stranger to the medical armamentarium: after all, the same principle has been applied to the treatment of other diseases, such as tuberculosis, for many years. Thus, owners must be aware that treatment of their pets' neoplastic diseases may involve a variety of techniques, all of which have the common aim of halting the disease process. Unfortunately, no one "magic bullet" for cancer yet exists.

CHEMOTHERAPY. Tumors that are not amenable to complete surgical removal must be approached by some other means. One of the most common and established methods is chemotherapy. In general, chemotherapy is the most effective treatment available for metastatic tumors—those that have spread beyond the site of the primary tumor. Surgery to remove the primary tumor thus may be accompanied by chemotherapy (and/or another treatment method) aimed at destroying the metastatic lesions.

Chemotherapy involves the administration of *cytotoxic* (cell-poisoning) drugs by the veterinarian that act to destroy tumor cells. Many such anticancer drugs have side effects because their actions are not directed specifically toward the tumor. Many of them are effective against rapidly dividing cells, which make up a significant proportion of the cells of many tumors, but have secondary effects on normal rapidly dividing cell populations, such as those in the bone marrow or digestive tract. The severity of some side effects seen in humans undergoing cancer chemotherapy may make continued treatment intolerable. Side effects seen in veterinary patients, however, are usually much less severe and more readily manageable. In fact, many anticancer drugs commonly used in veterinary medicine are tolerated surprisingly well by patients. Nevertheless, patients undergoing chemotherapy must be carefully monitored during the course of therapy. Common parameters that the veterinarian will follow include clinical appearance of the patient and status of tumor regression, complete blood count (looking for dangerous decreases in red and white blood cells and platelets, which may result from toxic effects of the anticancer drugs on the patient's bone marrow), and tests that monitor functioning of the liver and kidneys.

Some of the more common anticancer agents used in veterinary chemotherapy today are delineated below. Many of these drugs are particularly useful against *hemolymphatic* tumors (tumors of blood and lymphatic cells).

Alkylating Agents. These substances act by breaking and cross-linking DNA and thereby interfering with cell division. Examples include chlorambucil (Leukeran), cyclophosphamide (Cytoxan), and melphalan (Alkeran).

Antimetabolites. These substances are structurally similar to normal molecules required for DNA synthesis, but functionally disruptive once incorporated into the DNA. Examples include cytosine arabinoside (Cytosar) and methotrexate (MTX).

Vinca Alkaloids. These are natural products of plants that bind to *microtubules* within the cytoplasm of cells and inhibit cell division. Examples include vinblastine (Velban) and vincristine (Oncovin).

Glucocorticoid Hormones. These substances act—by mechanisms that are still not fully understood—by inhibiting cell division and also by directly destroying tumor cells. Examples include prednisone, prednisolone, and dexamethasone (Azium).

Antitumor Antibiotics. These antibiotics are produced by fungi and apparently exert their anticancer effect by binding to DNA and interfering with cell division. Examples include bleomycin (Blenoxane) and doxorubicin (Adriamycin).

Other Agents. These include L-asparaginase, a bacterial enzyme that kills cancer cells by depleting their supply of the amino acid L-asparagine, and hydroxyurea, which interferes with the metabolism of RNA, a nucleic acid important in normal cell functioning.

The technique of choice in chemotherapy is the selection of several drugs for use in combination. This allows the clinician to attack the tumor with drugs that act in different ways, thus decreasing the chance that resistance will arise. Unfortunately, development of resistance by tumor cells is one of the more common complications of chemotherapy.

Chemotherapy itself may be only one of two or three treatment methods used in treating a cancer patient. The goal always is to attack the cancer from several different angles in order to kill as many abnormal cells as possible and minimize the chances of developing resistance.

RADIATION THERAPY. Radiation therapy (radiotherapy) is the "paradoxical" therapy within the anticancer arsenal, in that radiation is known not only to cause cancer but to help cure it as well. The exact mechanism by which radiation kills cells is not known, but the apparent result is damage to the cellular DNA and interference with cell division. Cell types with a low rate of division, such as nerve and muscle cells, are relatively resistant to the effects of ionizing radiation—hence, they are referred to as being *radioresistant.* Tumors involving these cell types thus would not be expected to be responsive to radiation therapy.

Tissues containing populations of rapidly dividing cells—the bone marrow, skin, and digestive tract, for example—are considered to be more *radiosensitive.* Tumors involving these tissues thus would be expected to respond to radiation therapy. The disadvantage of this radiosensitivity is that sensitive tissues uninvolved in the disease process may suffer excessive damage during treatment—especially the skin, which, of course, is quite exposed in most radiotherapy procedures useful in domestic animals. Despite popular opinion to the contrary, tumor cells are not necessarily more radiosensitive than their normal cell counterparts.

Radiation therapy is one of the most widely used therapies for neoplasia in human beings, and there are many benefits in this treatment modality for veterinary patients as well. The principal advantage of radiation therapy is its ability to reach tumor masses difficult to remove surgically because of size or anatomic location. Radiation therapy is also useful in combination with chemotherapy because it can greatly reduce the size of the target tumor-cell population.

CRYOSURGERY. Cryosurgery is a technique whereby local application of intense cold (freezing) is used to damage and destroy neoplastic tissue, with the goal also of preserving normal tissue adjacent to the tumor site. Because cryosurgery must be applied locally to an affected site, tumors amenable to cryosurgical techniques must be relatively accessible (tumors involving the skin and mucous membranes, for example) to avoid freezing as many normal cells as possible. The advantages of this type of procedure include minimal damage to surrounding tissue, absence of systemic side effects, ready visual access to and control of the procedure, and effectiveness in the face of failure of other more conventional treatment methods. This last statement is especially important, because cryosurgery at this time must be considered as an adjunct or ancillary procedure, not intended to replace other tested curative techniques, such as local surgical excision.

During cryosurgery, a *cryogen* (substance that produces cold), such as liquid nitrogen, is applied directly to the tumor itself. Within the tumor, and within a small area just outside the tumor, an area of freezing ($-50°C$ to $-60°C$) develops, known as an *ice ball.* Temperature probes are inserted into the ice ball to determine the extent of cooling and the margins of the ice ball itself, that is, the size of the tissue area that has been frozen. Among the tumors most amenable to cryosurgery include those involving the skin, oral cavity, ears, and eyelids.

Disadvantages of the cryosurgical technique are sloughing of dead tissue during the first several weeks after the procedure, length of time for healing of lesions, and postoperative scarring. However, cryosurgery is an extremely useful procedure and should be considered among the treatment options whenever removal of a surface-oriented tumor is considered.

Anesthesia is required to restrain movement and control pain during the cryosurgical process. The level of anesthesia required depends primarily on the location of the tissue to be frozen. Local anesthesia of the tumor site, combined with mild tranquilization of the patient, may be all that is required in many cases.

HYPERTHERMIA. Hyperthermia, or heat therapy, is in many ways the opposite of cryosurgery, in that it relies on the local application of heat to destroy neoplastic cells, either by direct cytotoxic effects or by damage to the local *microvasculature* (small blood vessels) supplying the tumor. As with cryosurgery, most tumors amenable to treatment by hyperthermia are in relatively accessible locations. Difficulties arise when trying to standardize heating (41°C to 43°C) of tumor lesions while at the same time minimizing the deleterious effects of heat on the normal surrounding tissue. These difficulties are concentrated in two primary areas: the design of effective applicator probes for applying heat, and temperature changes mediated by blood circulation within the target site. Because of nonuniform heating, the killing effectiveness of hyperthermia will vary at different sites within the target area itself. As with cryosurgery, implant thermometers are needed in order to monitor temperature fluctuations within the target tissue.

Despite much investigation over the past decade, hyperthermia remains a relatively ineffective method of treatment when used alone. Often, however, significant benefits may be achieved when hyperthermia is used in conjunction with another treatment method, such as radiation therapy or chemotherapy.

Whole-body hyperthermia, a procedure in which the core body temperature of the patient is raised, is a systemic procedure that has recently been investigated in several treatment trials in veterinary medicine. Its greatest potential may be the treatment of deep metastases that are relatively inaccessible to local application of heating. To date, this treatment method remains investigational and appears, like local hyperthermia, to represent an ancillary treatment to be used in conjunction with other therapies.

PHOTOTHERAPY. Phototherapy (also known as *photodynamic therapy)* involves the use of a special compound, *hematoporphyrin derivative* (HpD), in combination with light, for the treatment of solid tumors. Phototherapy is based on the observation that HpD preferentially accumulates or is retained within cancer tissue to a greater extent than in normal tissue. Following accumulation, exposure of the tumor site to red light of a specified wavelength causes the accumulated HpD within the tumor to react with oxygen to produce *singlet oxygen,* a highly toxic substance damaging to cells. From this it is clear that the tumor cells, with their higher levels of HpD, will be more severely affected than normal cells in the vicinity. Herein lies the specificity of phototherapy for tumor tissue, strongly contrasting with the broader killing effects of radiation, chemotherapy, cryosurgery, and hyperthermia. The most effective light delivery system consists of a laser or series of lasers producing a continuous beam of red light delivered to the site by glass–fiber optic technology.

Application of phototherapy in veterinary medicine remains investigational and limited to a small number of private practitioners and research institutions. However, promising results in dogs and cats have been reported. Side effects appear to be minimal.

IMMUNOTHERAPY. Immunotherapy involves a "boosting" of immune responses in order to assist in the destruction of tumor tissue. Like several other newer methods of therapy, immunotherapy appears to be relatively ineffective when used as the sole method of treatment. In combination with other methods, however, such as surgery, chemotherapy, or radiation therapy—all of which are used to reduce dramatically the size of the tumor mass—significant benefits may be achieved in many cases. Tumors amenable to immunotherapeutic techniques usually are small and localized in nature.

A variety of substances with immune-boosting capabilities *(immunopotentiators)* have been investigated over the past eighty years. Among the more *non*specific of these immunopotentiators are:

- *Biological products* such as *bacillus Calmette-Guerin* (BCG) (a live bacterial preparation useful in immunization against tuberculosis) and *Corynebacterium parvum* (a killed bacterial product), both of which nonspecifically enhance immune responses to many microbial agents and also to many tumor cell types
- *Chemical or synthetic products* such as *levamisole* and *thymosin* (which help restore normal function to a number of important cells of the immune system).

More specific therapy involves the use of substances related to the target tumor cells themselves: e.g., tumor cell vaccines containing viable, modified, or killed tumor cells, or important fragments from the cells.

Other, newer immunotherapeutic approaches include:

- *Interferons* (natural substances that can inhibit virus replication and also the growth of tumor cells)

- Other important *lymphokines* (immune-regulatory substances) such as *interleukin-2*
- *Extracorporeal immunosorption* (also known as *plasmapheresis*) in which "blocking factors" interfering with the immune response to tumors are removed from the patient's bloodstream
- *Monoclonal antibody therapy,* in which highly purified antibodies specific for a given tumor are chemically linked to a toxic compound and injected into the patient. The antibodies then "home" to the tumor target and deliver their toxic cargo with pinpoint accuracy.

Immunization Against Neoplasia

Several vaccines are available for the prevention of certain virus-induced tumors in animals. These tumors include lymphomas and leukemias in cats caused by feline leukemia virus; papillomas (warts) in cattle caused by bovine papillomaviruses; and lymphoma (Marek's disease) in poultry caused by Marek's disease virus, a herpesvirus. Unfortunately, these represent only a small fraction of the tumors that arise in domestic animals.

Geriatrics

There was an old man from Peru
Who dreamed he was eating his shoe.
He woke in a fright
In the middle of the night
And found it was perfectly true.

—Anonymous

So, we'll go no more a-roving
So late into the night,
Though the heart be still as loving,
And the moon be still as bright.

—George Gordon Noel,
Lord Byron,
"So, we'll go no more a-roving"

Aging Cats and Disorders

Cats, like people, experience old age in their own individual ways. Advances in veterinary medicine and health care have helped to extend the cat's normal life span. It is not unusual for cats to live twenty years and longer, although the average life span is between ten and fourteen years. A cat's longevity depends on good health care through all stages of life.

Aging is a natural process. It develops with a gradual decline in the metabolism rate, which causes decreased drug tolerance, inability to regulate body temperature, decreased caloric needs, and decreased immunity to diseases. Progressive degeneration of organs that secrete hormones (thyroid glands, adrenal glands, pancreas, and pituitary gland) result in associated diseases such as hypothyroidism or hyperthyroidism, hypo- or hyperadrenocorticism, and diabetes mellitus. The abilities to taste, smell, see, and hear also diminish with age.

Physical and behavioral signs may reflect these bodily changes. Physical signs may include a cloudy appearance of the eyes; thinning hair coat; decreased

tolerance of the cold; flabby skin; prominent spine and hips; joint stiffness or lameness; graying of the muzzle; atrophy of the muscles; and hearing loss. Behaviorally, the older cat is less tolerant of environmental changes; sleeps more and is less active; and seems more irritable.

After eight or nine years of age, a cat becomes more susceptible to the diseases associated with old age—chronic kidney disease, dental disease, tumors, and liver disease. The importance of the veterinarian's yearly checkup increases because the earlier a disease is diagnosed, the better the cat's chance of recovery or longevity. Keeping vaccinations current helps to protect against panleukopenia, respiratory diseases, feline leukemia, and rabies.

SPECIAL CARE FOR THE ELDERLY CAT

Feeding

In general, commercial cat foods (labeled "100 percent complete" or "meets NRC requirements for maintenance") should be the staple food. Small amounts of cheese, eggs, cooked fish, and other high-quality protein foods may be added as flavoring agents if the cat is reluctant to eat. Food with a strong aroma may entice the older, more finicky cat to eat. A change in diet may be necessary if the cat has developed diabetes, heart disease, or kidney disease, which require special dietary treatment.

The veterinarian may also recommend vitamin and mineral supplements, appetite stimulants, and hormones according to the individual cat's needs. However, if the cat is voluntarily eating a balanced diet, supplements will not be necessary, and could even be counterproductive by destroying the nutritive balance of the diet.

Because older cats are less active and have a reduced metabolism rate, many tend to become overweight. The quantity of food must be adjusted to meet their decreasing activity level. The National Research Council (NRC) recommends feeding the older cat only thirty-two calories per pound of body weight on a daily basis.

Progressive weight loss also can be a very serious problem in older cats; it may signal kidney failure, presence of a tumor, diabetes mellitus, liver disease, or other conditions. It is important to monitor a cat's weight every three months and keep a record of any changes.

Exercise

An older cat is less agile as arthritis develops and muscles begin to atrophy. Accordingly, the cat will limit its physical activity. However, engaging a cat in

moderate play can promote muscle tone and suppleness, increase blood circulation, and improve gastrointestinal motility (spontaneous movement). During exercise, a pet owner must be alert for signs that might indicate heart disease, particularly labored breathing or rapid tiring.

It may be necessary to relocate food dishes and litter boxes for cats who are severely restricted by arthritis and muscle atrophy.

Grooming

Daily grooming offers a good opportunity to examine the cat for unusual lumps, skin lesions, or external parasites. Unusual lumps or lesions should be examined by a veterinarian for appropriate treatment. (For control of external parasites, refer to Chapter 19: External Parasites.)

Daily brushing or combing removes loose and dead hairs before they can be ingested by the cat during self-grooming and form hairballs. Hairballs cause more problems for an older cat since the gastrointestinal tract is less motile and impactions occur more frequently. Brushing also stimulates blood circulation and sebaceous gland secretions in the skin, creating healthier skin and hair coat.

Older cats may not use scratching posts as frequently to remove the outer sheaths of their claws. Therefore, nails should be checked weekly and trimmed if necessary.

Daily removal of plaque is a prime factor in preventing and controlling dental disease. There is documented evidence that daily cleaning reduces tartar formation by 95 percent, or 76 percent for weekly cleanings. If a cat has never had its teeth professionally cleaned or there is a buildup of tartar, professional dental cleaning by a veterinarian is essential.

Home dentistry consists of gently rubbing your cat's teeth and gums with a piece of gauze soaked in a dilute solution of hydrogen peroxide, or 2 percent potassium permanganate, both of which can be purchased at a drugstore; or the veterinarian can provide a 0.2 percent chlorhexidine solution sold as Nolvasan or a feline toothpaste. (Do not use human toothpastes —they cause excessive salivation and if swallowed may result in gastrointestinal upsets.) Gently rub the teeth and make sure to include the gums. If the cat's teeth are cleaned at a regularly scheduled time, it becomes a habit that is more easily performed by both participants. Eventually a soft-bristle, child-sized

toothbrush can be substituted with some cats. However, others may never tolerate the brush.

Reducing Environmental Stress

Older cats are usually less adaptable to changes in their environment. Therefore, special attention should be given if the cat must be boarded during vacation time. Sometimes having a familiar object(s) prevents the cat from becoming too emotionally distraught in a strange environment. A better alternative, if possible, is to have the older cat cared for by neighbors, friends, or relatives in its own home.

Other stressful experiences for the older cat include the introduction of a new pet or moving to a new home. In both cases, the cat's territory is drastically changed or altered, thereby causing emotional stress. Such stress can be alleviated, somewhat, by giving the cat more affection and attention.

DISEASES OF OLDER CATS

In addition to a decreasingly effective immune system, which leaves older cats more susceptible to certain diseases, there are other diseases caused by tissue degeneration which are more prevalent in the older cat.

Kidney Failure

Chronic interstitial nephritis (destruction of tissue within the kidney), marked by a shriveling and scarring of the kidneys, is the most common cause of chronic kidney damage and death in the older cat.

Weight loss, increased urination, increased thirst, poor appetite, bad breath, mouth ulcers, and occasional vomiting are indicative of kidney disease. However, these signs typically do not occur until about 70 percent of the kidney's functions are lost. They are related to the buildup of toxic wastes in the blood that are normally removed by the kidneys. If unchecked, the condition will prove fatal.

The effects of kidney failure can be diminished, although not cured, through medication and a special low-protein diet, which produces fewer waste products for the kidneys to clear. Special dietary foods can be obtained through a veterinarian or, with the veterinarian's assistance, a diet may be formulated that will meet the disabled cat's specific requirements. As always, but even more so in the case of kidney disease, clean, fresh water should be available at all times.

Tumors

A cat's chances of developing cancer increase with old age. An accumulation of carcinogens (cancer-causing products) in the body, or an impaired immune system have been implicated, at least in part, in this increased incidence of cancer in older cats.

Feline leukemia is the most threatening and common form of cancer in cats. It is contagious among cats and considered nearly 100 percent fatal. Disease manifestations are varied, but may include anemia, fever, poor appetite, weight loss, vomiting, diarrhea or constipation, depression, and labored breathing. Tumors associated with feline leukemia commonly occur in the lymph nodes (lymphosarcomas), kidneys, and intestines of older cats. Lymphosarcomas may or may not be apparent to the touch, and often can be revealed by blood tests, radiographs, and tissue samples. Because there is no cure, and a painful end is inevitable, many veterinarians recommend humane euthanasia for cats suffering with leukemia. (*See* Chapter 29: Viral Diseases.)

Meningioma is the most common tumor of the central nervous system of cats. At least 66 percent of the affected cats are older than ten years of age. The tumor arises from the meninges (membranous tissue covering the brain). The tumor is usually benign; however, neurological problems (seizures, paralysis, personality changes) may become evident when the tumor begins to compress the underlying brain tissue.

Ceruminous gland tumors originate from the ceruminous glands that produce wax in the external ear. Signs associated with these tumors include head shaking, ear scratching, and a discharge from the ear. These tumors may be benign or malignant.

Intact queens or females spayed late in life are more prone to the development of *mammary tumors*. Unfortunately, approximately 85 percent of these tumors are malignant, with early metastasis to lymph nodes, liver, and lungs. These flat, hard nodular cancers are easily hidden by fur until they are far advanced. The best precaution against breast cancer in the cat is spaying *before the first heat*.

Radiation therapy, chemotherapy, or surgical removal can be effective on some tumors, though the risks of associated trauma are greater for the aged cat.

Digestive System

The digestive tract remains relatively free of the ravages of old age and is usually the last system to show signs of deterioration. It is thought that the rapid cell turnover in the gastrointestinal tract provides a degree of protection against the degenerative effects of aging.

Constipation is one of the more common problems of older cats. Occasional feeding of milk can help produce a softer stool. Bulk-forming agents such as wheat bran or a mild laxative can minimize hairballs that would otherwise accumulate in the stomach or intestine; occasionally, hairball obstruction may require surgical removal. Regular use of hairball medications and feeding of moist, bulky foods can help control constipation. Neither laxatives nor hairball medications should be used more than once a week unless recommended by a veterinarian, because they can interfere with absorption of vitamins and minerals.

Diarrhea is not as common as constipation. If it persists in spite of medication and dietary changes, it may be a sign of disease and requires a veterinary examination.

Oral Problems

Cats are not prone to tooth decay in the visible parts of the tooth. Cavities in the roots, just under the gums, are very common, especially in cases of chronic mouth infections (stomatitis). They are susceptible to tartar buildup and resultant oral diseases such as gingivitis (inflammation of the gums) and stomatitis. These problems are more prevalent in cats fed primarily soft diets and human foods. Signs of oral problems are bad breath, excessive salivation, brownish-yellow tartar deposits, and difficulty in eating or refusal to eat. In advanced cases of gingivitis, the gums are red, swollen, and very painful, tooth sockets ooze pus, and teeth become loose and fall out. Veterinary examination is necessary. (*See* Chapter 18: Sensory Organs and Disorders.)

Skin Problems

Because the older cat has a depressed immune system, skin irritations and wounds are slower to heal. Also, nutritional deficiencies can occur in older cats which can influence the health of the skin and hair coat.

Musculoskeletal

The older cat experiences chronic degeneration of muscles, joints, and vertebral discs. Arthritis is common with typical signs such as lameness and stiffness. Currently, there is no way to prevent or cure this disease. However, there are medicines that can alleviate the pain and discomfort of inflamed joints.

Bones become more brittle as changes occur in metabolism and in the absorption of calcium and phosphorus by the digestive system, thereby making the older cat more susceptible to bone fractures.

Hyperthyroidism

This disease predominately affects older cats (ten years of age and more) and is one of the most common feline endocrine disorders. Hyperactivity, sudden weight loss, increased appetite and stool volume, increased fluid intake, and increased urination are typical signs. Fortunately, the disease is treatable. (*See* Chapter 27: Endocrine System and Metabolic Disorders.)

Heart and Circulatory Disorders

Some cats born with heart defects may show no signs until later in life, when there is increased demand on the heart and circulatory system. Heart disease in cats usually occurs in middle age (six to eight years).

The most commonly acquired heart disease is cardiomyopathy, or failure of the heart muscle. Only hyperthyroidism and chronic kidney disease are more common than hypertrophic (enlarged) cardiomyopathy in older cats. (*See* Chapter 20: Circulatory System and Disorders.)

Unfortunately, some of the signs of heart disease (lack of energy and appetite, decreased activity, long rest periods) can be easily confused with the normal signs of old age and overlooked until the disease is too far advanced for treatment. Other signs to watch for are a cat that often lies flat on its breastbone and is reluctant to move from this position, panting (due to fluid accumulation in the chest and resultant breathing difficulty), and, in severe cases, a bluish-gray tongue (due to inadequate oxygen supply).

Anemia is a frequent malady of older cats that can be caused by a multitude of different chronic diseases or parasite infestation. Anemia is easily detected and treated by a veterinarian.

Diabetes Mellitus

Degeneration of the islet of Langerhans cells of the pancreas, resulting in decreased insulin production, causes diabetes mellitus. The disease is characterized by an unquenchable thirst, ravenous appetite, and increased urination. Fortunately, the disease can be controlled by dietary alteration and/or by administering daily dosages of insulin, which aids in the metabolism of carbohydrates. (*See* Chapter 27: Endocrine System and Metabolic Disorders.)

Liver Disease

The liver of the older cat is susceptible to tissue degeneration and scarring (cirrhosis). The functioning liver tissue is replaced by scar tissue. Signs indicative of liver disease include vomiting, lethargy, anorexia, neurologic dysfunction, and watery diarrhea. There is no cure for cirrhosis, but dietary management as prescribed by a veterinarian can slow the rapid degeneration.

Brain Atrophy

The gradual degeneration of brain tissue (encephalomalacia) can occur in older cats. There is no treatment available for this disease. Incoordination, confusion, and lethargy are common signs.

BEREAVEMENT

A pet's life span under the best circumstances is a fraction of its human caretaker's. An average cat lives ten to fourteen years. A fifteen- to eighteen-year-old cat is considered ancient. There are even a few fortunate cats and their humans who spend twenty years together. But the sadness of losing a pet and the ensuing grief is inevitable. It is an experience that may occur several times in a lifetime.

The human/companion-animal relationship has become the subject of great interest, considerable discussion, and investigation by those in the field of mental health. Psychologists, psychotherapists, and animal behaviorists recognize its importance.

In 1969, Dr. Elisabeth Kubler-Ross, in her groundbreaking work *On Death and Dying,* offered five classic stages of the dying experience: denial and isolation, anger, bargaining, depression, and acceptance. Since then, others writing on bereavement have defined similar stages for those who mourn or grieve the death of a loved one. In recent times, some psychologists, therapists, and mental health workers have focused their attention on helping patients cope with their overwhelming grief after suffering the death of a pet. Several excellent books on the subject have been written and many animal clinics have a bereavement counselor on staff or maintain a referral list.

A major difference between human loss and pet loss is the support system available to the respective mourners. When a human dies, the bereaved survivor turns to family, friends, and neighbors for sympathy, kindness, understanding, and help. When a pet dies, the owner's family or social group may not be sensitive to that person's grief. Those who do not share their lives with a pet are often unable to understand the closeness of a relationship between a human and an animal or the emotional stress involved when death brings it to an end. The veterinarian and his or her staff may be the only source of sympathy the grieving pet owner has. Pet-loss therapy and counseling are, therefore, a positive medical option when trying to cope with overwhelming feelings of grief.

The death of a pet has special implications for children and the elderly. A much cherished cat may represent special memories for an older person that are connected with departed loved ones or a happier time of life. Older pet owners living alone face special problems when a companion animal passes away. The idea of acquiring another pet seems unthinkable, despite the fact that it could be of great benefit. Resistance to another pet is based on the fear of not outliving it and worrying about its survival. Coping with a kitten that is bursting with energy is also likely to make an older person apprehensive about starting over with a new pet. The answer could lie with the acquisition of a mature cat, one that understands life in a human setting, including the use of a litter pan and scratch post. Another type of pet altogether is a viable option. There is much pleasure to be had with goldfish or caged birds, which are less demanding and easier to care for. Although a new animal cannot replace one that has held a special place in the heart and mind, it can be of great benefit. Studies have shown that pets can help people live longer, healthier lives.

Children also experience grief when a family pet dies. How parents relate to their child's feelings can have a lasting influence. The need for support and acknowledgment of the death and the emotions it produces are vital for mental health and well-being. Provoking discussion and the free expression of feelings on any and all aspects of the pet's life and death can only create a greater understanding of death and the value of life. Allowing a child to go through the mourning process helps to create the psychological defenses necessary for future losses of greater magnitude. If questions are raised by a grieving child, try to answer them truthfully and without contrivance. Parental support helps children sort out facts from fiction, thus neutralizing many fears associated with death. When a pet dies, a child may experience the loss as much as any adult. After a respectful interval of time, a new pet may be the right prescription for such a child.

EUTHANASIA

All too often the owner must face the dilemma of euthanasia. When a pet is medically evaluated by a veterinarian, it is the owner's responsibility to determine whether or not to provide treatment. Euthanasia may relieve or stress the cat's owner, depending on the circumstances. In many cases, the cat is critically ill with no chance for recovery. Euthanasia may be suggested as a compassionate alternative to a lingering death encumbered with pain and suffering. The burden of the decision can be overwhelming and fraught with feelings of desperation, denial, anger, and guilt. What is needed at that time is a rational basis for a decision. Some diseases are treatable, even cancer, offering a measure of life extension. In such instances, euthanasia is not the only alternative. Other conditions, such as renal failure, congestive heart failure, or some forms of metabolic disease, may offer no hope at all. Euthanasia then becomes the only "humane" consideration.

Pets offer companionship, emotional intimacy, and feelings of well-being to their human caretakers. Hopefully, humans create happy, pleasurable lives for their pets. When well-being turns to suffering, alternatives should be considered.

As long as an ailing animal is enjoying life without pain, there is justification for its continued presence. The quality of life, not life that is merely existence, can help the owner determine a cat's reason for living.

Unlike humans, animals have no concept of death. There cannot be apprehension, traumatic fear or panic when the inevitable occurs. There is simply unending, peaceful sleep.

The Sick Cat

I don't know as there is anything of continental or international interest to communicate about those cats. They had no history. They did not distinguish themselves in any way. They died early—on account of being overweighted with their names, it was thought,—Sour Mash, Apollinaris, Zoroaster, Blatherskite,—names given them, not in an unfriendly spirit, but merely to practise the children in large and difficult styles of pronunciation. It was a very happy idea —I mean, for the children.

—Mark Twain, from a letter to *Saint Nicholas* magazine

Clinical Signs of Disease

RECOGNIZING DISEASE

Cats are solitary creatures, which makes it difficult for even the most concerned owner to detect signs of illness. Feline health care is increasingly important now that cats are the nation's number one pet.

The American Veterinary Medical Association Council on Public Relations recently reported these findings. In addition to the cat's stoic demeanor, the Council found that:

• There is critical need for improved feline health care in the United States. Many cat owners are unaware of the necessity for regular veterinary care and are unable to recognize signs of illness in their cats themselves.

• Barely 59.5 percent of cat owners currently take their cats to veterinarians, compared with 77.6 percent of dog owners. The average dog visits the veterinarian 1.5 times per year, while the average cat does so only 0.79 times, because many cat owners do not perceive the need for regular feline health check-ups.

These authoritative findings underscore the responsibility of the cat owner. To determine when professional help is needed, the owner must know the cat thoroughly.

NORMALS

The most useful cues to possible problems in a healthy cat are deviations from what are considered the "normals." People know themselves well enough to recognize changes in their bodies and do something about them if they so choose. Cats, however, do not have that freedom to choose sophisticated therapy over the self-help they are capable of. Sometimes they drink more when thirsty; they do not eat if sick; they are listless when injured; and so forth. Beyond that, the good judgment of the owner is needed to provide even adequate health care.

One must be alert to changes in the normals for a

particular cat. To know what is normal, the cat must be observed from the time it is a healthy kitten. Written notes on the cat's usual behavior and activities are helpful, since an owner's memory may fail. The topics discussed here can provide a framework for a chart. Such data increases one's knowledge and serves as important baseline information for the veterinarian in case of illness. Questions can be answered more easily, supplying necessary clues to the diagnosis and treatment. A reliable written record of a cat's life-style allows the veterinarian to know almost as much about the animal as its owner, so he or she can recognize possible problems and alleviate them.

In general, a normal, healthy cat is alert, curious about its environment and all that it encounters, and has a good appetite but rarely overeats unless food is always available. A healthy cat's eyes are bright and clear; the coat is clean and well-groomed (cats are very conscious of hygiene); the stools are well-formed; and the urine is blood-free, a clear amber color, and not overly frequent. The cat sleeps soundly and frequently, napping often in the daytime as well as at night, changing positions almost imperceptibly. In addition to any daytime activity, it can also be active in the middle of the night when feeling "kittenish." Depending on its individual personality, it will seek and dispense affection on various schedules and be aloof other times. Persistent seclusion for more than twenty-four hours is a sign of possible problems and warrants investigation.

In judging its health status, each cat must be regarded as an individual, different and independent, to determine when human intervention is needed.

There is a secondary benefit to studying a healthy cat. In addition to observing it and noting its various habits and behavior, the owner needs to handle and examine the cat almost daily to know what normal is. Gently done, this human contact appears to be petting, a sign of affection, which is pleasing. This conditioning makes the cat a more tractable patient for the professional to treat when that need arises, especially in the initial visits.

LEADING FELINE HEALTH CONCERNS

The Morris Animal Foundation conducts an animal health survey every few years to learn what animal owners feel are the leading health concerns for their pets and what are the leading causes of death.

For cat owners, *feline leukemia* (FeLV) was the leading health concern; feline urinary syndrome (FUS) was next, including cystitis and bladder blockage. Concern for feline infectious peritonitis (FIP) was followed by kidney disease, then the nonfatal problems of fleas and nutrition.

The leading cause of death was feline leukemia virus (FeLV). Next was kidney failure, with cancer third. Old age was fourth in line, followed by feline infectious peritonitis (FIP) and heart failure.

Familiarity with the signs of these major diseases enables the owner to recognize early indicators that might suggest further examination is necessary. The absence of these signs offers the owner peace of mind.

SIGNS

A routine for observation can be developed using a knowledge of the more important diseases and what is normal for a particular cat.

Behavior

A cat is, by nature, a solitary animal with a desire to take care of its problems itself and can compensate quite well for minor discomforts. It may just want to be left alone for a while. This is normal unless it lasts more than twenty-four hours, at which time human intervention is warranted. Changes in habits, personality, and behavior, subtle as they may seem, should alert the owner just as the appearance of swelling, blood, or an impaired leg would.

Pain

Pain as a sign is often difficult to discern. The cat may just want to be left alone and not handled, or may stay inside. More severe pain will often cause panting. A normally placid animal may growl if approached and even scratch or bite in self-defense. Hiding can also indicate pain or some medical problem. Visible signs of pain are reason enough to seek immediate medical help instead of waiting the customary twenty-four hours.

General Signs

After changes in attitude, behavior, or personality have been seen as an initial sign, attention should be given to any physical changes from what has been determined to be normal for that particular cat. Attitude changes may not be apparent at first; therefore, physical signs are important.

All the human senses should be used, not just sight. Hearing, touch, and smell are equally important to gather data. A "sixth" sense, to know that something is amiss without tangible evidence, can be developed over a period of time. This is when a written checklist of physical findings proves invaluable.

Physical Signs

Look for:

- Changes in appetite, bowel movements, water drinking (too little/too much), urinating (excessive/straining), vomiting.
- Distentions, swellings, changes in the appearance of the hair coat, skeletal distortions, bilateral sym-

metry (are the left and right the same?). Start at the tip of the nose; examine the top, bottom, and both sides of the body, to the end of the tail.

- Changes in activity, gait, balance, sight, hearing, touch response, awareness, head position.
- Bleeding from external wounds, abscesses, tumors, fractures. Hidden internal bleeding is indicated by a pale color of the gums and the mucous membrane lining of the eye.
- Distressed breathing indicates an emergency requiring immediate professional care. Coughing or sneezing with no other signs does not represent an emergency situation. Collapse warrants immediate professional attention.
- Fever (over 102.2°F) can be caused by external factors: hot environmental temperature, excessive activity, frightened agitation; or internal factors: infection, abscesses, systemic bacterial or viral diseases, unknown causes.

OWNER'S EXAMINATION

All this suggested attention to detail is not intended to make the cat owner a veterinary diagnostician. It is a guide to know when corrective measures are necessary and when to seek veterinary help.

Finding bad odor, blood, pus, discharge, or breaks in the skin in any anatomical area should be considered abnormal and will not be listed repeatedly in the chart. The following is a guide for routine anatomical examination, area by area.

AREA OR SYSTEM	LOOK FOR:	AREA OR SYSTEM	LOOK FOR:
Head	Bright Eyes Twitching Hair Loss Distortion of Features Swellings Lumps Redness Pimples on Chin Position of Head	Mouth	Pale or Blue Gums or Tongue Salivation (excessive) Growths Ulcers Misaligned Teeth Difficulty Swallowing or Eating Swelling Halitosis Open-mouth Breathing
Nose	Paleness Lumps Sneezing (persistent) Nasal Discharge	Eyes	Drooping Eyelid Excessive Tears Redness of White of Eye (bloodshot) Swelling of Lids Cloudy Surface Pupils: Constantly Wide, or of Different Size

AREA OR SYSTEM	LOOK FOR:	AREA OR SYSTEM	LOOK FOR:
Eyes	Rapid, Rhythmic Eye Movement Yellow Color to White of Eye Discomfort (persistent pawing)	Urinary	Excessive Thirst and Urination Futile Straining Not Using Litter Pan (except spraying by uncastrated male)
Ears	Crusts or Infection Swelling of Flaps Peppery Dirt inside Ear Scratching at Ears	Tail and Tail Head	Paralysis (dragging) Loss of Feeling Tender Swelling
Neck	Stiffness Awkward Position Pain on Movement	Legs	Abnormal Position Lack of Use Limping Pain
Chest	Hard Lumps Tender Swellings Crackling Paperlike Feel under Skin	Skin	Hair Loss Hair Matting Hair Dull and Dry
Lungs	Coughing Panting Rapid Breathing (closed mouth) at Rest Shallow Breathing Noisy Breathing (except purring) Distressed Breathing (panicky)		Crusts Scabs Wounds Pain Itching Yellow Color
Abdomen	Painless Lumps, Particularly in Females Enlargement and Swelling Discoloration (bluish-purple) Discomfort and Tenderness Severe Pain with Extreme Restlessness Protrusion or Bleeding from Rectum	Actions	Feverish Feels Cold Not Eating Excessive Eating Weakness Lack of Alertness Confusion Circling or Falling Convulsions Weight Loss or Obesity Change in Behavior
Digestion	Not Eating Vomiting (except occasional hairball) Diarrhea Straining on Stool Change in Character of Stool Not Using Litter Pan Weight Loss Obesity		
Genital	Persistant Estrus in Unspayed Female Fetid Vaginal Discharge Abortion Difficult Queening Lumpy or Swollen Breasts		

INDEX OF COMMON SIGNS

The listing of common signs and the possible condition or illness causing them is not intended to be all-inclusive or all-exclusive. This information was selectively taken from a computerized database called *Consultant,* developed at Cornell by Maurice E. White, D.V.M., for computer-assisted diagnosis and information management of all possible feline diseases, including diseases from all parts of the world.

Signs were selected that might commonly be encountered in an everyday relationship with a cat. They are divided into *General* or *Systemic,* meaning signs that affect the entire body of the cat, and *Area* or *Anatomical,* meaning signs that affect only one specific part of the cat's body.

Many are generalized signs of various diseases or pathological conditions, requiring further differentiation by a veterinarian for specific diagnosis. Thus *this listing is to be used merely as an aid* in narrowing down the possible causes responsible for that sign in each particular case and providing the owner with guidelines to determine when to seek veterinary care. When a choice is to be made regarding when to call the veterinarian, always err on the "too soon" rather than on the "too late." This will allow the veterinarian to use his/her time judgment, especially regarding after-hours emergency calls.

COMMON SIGNS

These lists will give some indication of what may be causing a clinical sign. Most of them are serious and indicate a need for prompt veterinary attention.

SIGNS, GENERAL OR SYSTEMIC	POSSIBLE ILLNESS, CAUSE, OR CONDITION	SIGNS, GENERAL OR SYSTEMIC	POSSIBLE ILLNESS, CAUSE, OR CONDITION
Abnormal Behavior, Personality	Aggression Feline Infectious Peritonitis Head Trauma Hyperthyroidism Insecticide Poisoning Uremia Urine Spraying and Fighting	Convulsions	Brain Trauma Encephalitis Heat Stroke Hypoglycemia (Low Blood Sugar) Hypocalcemia Kidney Failure Liver Failure Poisoning
Abortion (Uninduced)	Early Embryonic Death, Resorption Feline Infectious Peritonitis Habitual Feline Abortion	Depression	Anemia Dehydration Feline Infectious Peritonitis Feline Urological Syndrome Fever Kidney Failure Malnutrition Miscellaneous Disorders
Circling (as a Specific Behavior Change)	Brain Trauma Chemical Poisons Inner Ear Infections Vestibular Syndrome		
Constipation	Debilitating Diseases Dehydration Feline Infectious Peritonitis Fractures of the Pelvis Intestinal Neoplasia Intestinal Obstruction Megacolon	Diarrhea	Colitis Food Sensitivity Intestinal Parasites Organophosphate Toxicity

SIGNS, GENERAL OR SYSTEMIC	POSSIBLE ILLNESS, CAUSE, OR CONDITION	SIGNS, GENERAL OR SYSTEMIC	POSSIBLE ILLNESS, CAUSE, OR CONDITION
Emaciation	Feline Infectious Peritonitis Kidney Failure Liver Failure Malnutrition	Lameness	Abscess Arthritis Hyperparathyroidism Strains/Sprains Miscellaneous Injuries
Falling, Incoordination	Brain Trauma Chemical Poisoning Ear Infections, Severe Generalized Trauma Pelvis Fracture Spinal Trauma Vestibular Syndrome	Loss of Appetite (Anorexia)	Abscess/Fever Anemia Dehydration Intestinal Obstruction Injury/Trauma Tumors
Fever	Bacterial Infections Excitement Heat Stroke Tumors Viral Infections of Unknown Origins	Overweight Abnormality	Aggressive and Dominant Behavior Diabetes Mellitus Excessive Eating (Polyphagia) Hyperadrenocorticism
General Paralysis	Drug Overdose Chemical Poisoning Injury Malnutrition Shock Spinal Trauma	Skin, Painful	Abscesses Allergic Dermatitis Burns Flea Allergy Dermatitis Miscellaneous Injuries
		Skin Itching	Allergic Dermatitis Flea Infestations Food Allergy
Hemorrhage	Hit by Automobile Fight Wounds Injury to the Tongue Nasal Tumors Miscellaneous Injuries	Thirst, Excessive (Polydipsia)	Chronic Kidney Failure Diabetes Mellitus Glomerulonephritis Hyperthyroidism Pyometra
Hypothermia (Low Body Temperature)	Anemia Antifreeze Toxicity Cold Stress (Exposure to Cold Temperatures) Kidney Failure Shock Brain Trauma	Underweight or Chronic Weight Loss	Diarrhea Feline Infectious Peritonitis Hyperthyroidism Kidney Failure Liver Failure Malnutrition Persistent Fever Severe Stomatitis
Jaundice	Bile Duct Obstruction Blood Destruction Diseases or Conditions Gall Bladder Inflammation Liver Disease	Urine, Excessive Amounts (Polyuria)	Chronic Kidney Failure Cystitis Diabetes Mellitus Glomerulonephritis Pyometra

SIGNS, GENERAL OR SYSTEMIC	POSSIBLE ILLNESS, CAUSE, OR CONDITION	SIGNS, GENERAL OR SYSTEMIC	POSSIBLE ILLNESS, CAUSE, OR CONDITION
Vomiting	Esophageal Foreign Body Food Sensitivity Gastric or Intestinal Foreign Body Hairballs Inflammation of Stomach and Intestines Intestinal Obstruction Overeating	Breathing, Abnormal	Allergic Bronchitis Chest Trauma Feline Infectious Peritonitis (Fluid in Chest) Feline Rhinotracheitis Head Trauma Thoracic Fluid Effusions Thoracic Tumors, Associated with Feline Leukemia
Weakness	Anemia Bacterial Infections Dehydration Fever Leukemia Trauma Viral Infections	Breath—Foul Odor	Abscess in Mouth Inflammation of Mouth Kidney Failure (Uremia) Oral Foreign Bodies Periodontal Disease Tooth Abscess or Decay Tumors in Mouth, Pharynx, or Tongue
Abdominal Pain	Abscess Chronic Bladder Infection Chronic Intestinal Infection Fight Wounds Intestinal Obstruction Trauma	Coughing	Allergic Bronchitis Foreign Bodies in Trachea or Bronchus Parasites in Lungs Pulmonary Edema Pulmonary Neoplasia Tonsillitis
Abdominal Swelling	Abdominal Tumors Bladder Distention Feline Infectious Peritonitis Overeating (Obesity) Pregnancy Severe Constipation	Deafness	Congenital Deafness Especially Blue-Eyed White Cats Ear Canal Polyps and Tumors Ear Infections Ear Mites, Severe and Chronic Senile (Old Age) Deafness
Blindness	Degeneration of Retina in Old Age Feline Infectious Peritonitis Feline Leukemia Head Trauma Senile Cataracts Taurine Deficiency Vitamin A Deficiency Wounds to the Eye	Ear Discharge	Abscesses from Fight Wounds Ear Canal Polyps and Tumors Ear Infections Ear Mites Wounds and Lacerations
		Hair, Dull	Feline Allergy Dermatitis Lack of Grooming by Cat Malnutrition Metabolic Disorders Neglect by Owner Parasitism

SIGNS, GENERAL OR SYSTEMIC	POSSIBLE ILLNESS, CAUSE, OR CONDITION	SIGNS, GENERAL OR SYSTEMIC	POSSIBLE ILLNESS, CAUSE, OR CONDITION
Hair, Loss (Alopecia)	Abscesses from Fight Wounds Flea Allergy Dermatitis Endocrine Alopecia Lick Granulomas or Lesions Psychogenic Alopecia	Mouth—Swelling	Abscess or Infection Fractures of Mandible or Maxilla Inflammation of the Mouth Oral Foreign Body Trauma to Tongue Tumors of Mouth, Pharynx, and Tongue
Hair, Matted	Chronic Disease Failure to Groom Failure to Shed Undercoat Feline Infectious Peritonitis Metabolic Disorders Neglected Longhair Cats	Mouth, Pale Mucous Membranes	Anemia from Blood Loss Anemia from Chronic Infection or Neoplasia Blood Parasites Feline Leukemia Flea Infestation, Heavy Shock Trauma
Head Tilt	Brain Tumor Ear Infections Ear Mites Trauma to the Head Vestibular Syndrome Wounds to the Pinna and Ear	Mouth, Red Mucous Membrane	Chemical Irritants Gingivitis (Periodontal Disease) Hyperthyroidism Inflammation of the Mouth Oral Foreign Body or Abscess
Head Swelling	Abscesses from Fight Wounds Bee Stings Subcutaneous Air from Skull Fractures or Wounds Tight Collars Trauma and Hemorrhage from Injuries	Mouth, Tongue Swelling	Chemical Irritant Foreign Body in the Tongue Injury or Trauma to Tongue Tumor of Tongue or Mouth
Jaw, Paralysis	Abscesses Facial Nerve Damage Foreign Body in the Tongue Fractured Mandible Trauma	Neck Pain	Abscess from Wounds Fracture of Vertebra Foreign Body (i.e., Needle or Splinter in Neck) Injury or Trauma Reaction to Injection Given in Neck
Mouth, Excessive Salivation, Frothing at the Mouth	Chemical Irritants Ingested Foreign Body in Mouth or Tongue Inflammation of the Mouth Periodontal Disease Reactions to Noxious Substance	Nose Bleeding	Excessive Sneezing Injury to Nose (Head Trauma) Nasal Tumors Sinus Injury Warfarin Poisoning

SIGNS, GENERAL OR SYSTEMIC	POSSIBLE ILLNESS, CAUSE, OR CONDITION	SIGNS, GENERAL OR SYSTEMIC	POSSIBLE ILLNESS, CAUSE, OR CONDITION
Paralysis, Leg (Front or Rear)	Abscess Blood Clot in Vessels to Rear Legs Fight Wounds Fracture of Bones in the Legs Injury to the Leg Nerve Damage from Trauma Spinal Injury or Tumors	Sneezing	Allergic Rhinitis Chronic Sinusitis Nasal Foreign Body Nasal Tumors Upper Respiratory Infection
Skin Emphysema (Subcutaneous Air)	Chest Injury with Lung Penetration Chest Compression from Being Hit by Automobile Fractured Ribs Perforated Trachea from Wounds Skull Fracture with Sinus Damage	Swallowing, Difficult	Fight Wound Abscess of Neck or Head Foreign Body or Tumor in Mouth or Esophagus Fracture of Mandible, Maxilla, or Hyoid Swallowed Irritants Tonsillitis Viral Infection Such as Rhinotracheitis or Calici
Skin Pimples and Pustules	Ant Bites Bite Wounds from Kittens Chin Acne Impetigo in Kittens Pyoderma		

Surgery and Postoperative Care

SURGERY

Surgery has saved the lives of many cats and has greatly improved the quality of life for hundreds of thousands of others. Thus, there should be no apprehension in the minds of owners when surgery is suggested by a veterinarian as a way to solve a cat health problem that cannot be solved in any other way. There are many such cases where the owner will be thankful and most appreciative that the expertise of feline surgery has progressed so their beloved pet can be saved and returned to a happy life.

Surgical neutering allows many cats to be accepted in thousands of homes where the mating and estrous

cycles would be otherwise too offensive and malodorous, in addition to resulting in unwanted litters of kittens. At the other end of the surgical spectrum, a heart pacemaker has been successfully implanted in a cat to correct its cardiac arrythmia. Many other such sophisticated surgical procedures are routinely in use in many private practices, though some are available only at teaching veterinary institutions.

The purpose of this chapter is not to detail every step in some common surgical procedures that a pet cat may need; rather, the intent is to help allay apprehension, familiarize the owner with modern surgical principles, and show that all surgery is not a crisis situation but a safe means to alleviate some health problems.

Advances in science and technology have been adapted to benefit the cat. Some, such as those in virology, have even originated with the cat. However, the medical community, veterinary and human, acknowledges and teaches that there is no surgery without risk. In the past the greatest risk was anesthesia. This is no longer the case. It may help the owner to think of anesthesia as one step beyond restful sleep. Prospective surgery can be faced with the assurance that all aspects of medical science will be available to produce a favorable result.

When contemplating surgery for a cat, weighing all the advantages and disadvantages helps to organize the choices into groups or categories.

Surgery can be considered for:

1. The removal of a natural organ or tissue, such as ovaries or testes, for a preventive purpose. The benefits derived must be considered in the decision to excise or not.
2. The removal of diseased tissue, unwanted new growth (tumors), or altered anatomical structures that interfere with normal function.
3. The correction of faults in the anatomical structures caused by trauma, accident, or other outside influence, such as fractures, abscesses, lacerations, ruptured internal organs, hernias, or intestinal foreign bodies.
4. The correction of physiological dysfunction, as in urinary stoppage, heart disease, thyroid disease, adrenal disease.
5. A modification of anatomical structures necessary to return the body as close as possible to normal function and good health.

Kinds of Surgery

Surgery is divided into several groups:

1. *Elective surgery* is that in which the owner and veterinarian have a choice not necessarily based on the health of the animal. Elective surgery would be: spaying the female to eliminate estrus and re-production; or castrating the male to eliminate spraying, offensive urine odor, and fighting; or de-clawing to prevent destructive behavior. Benefit versus risk must be weighed.
2. *Necessary surgery* is that which needs to be done for the benefit of the cat's welfare, health, and good life, but without urgency and within a reasonable period of time. Fractures, lacerations, abscesses, bladder stones, uterine infections, and other disorders that are not immediately life-threatening are included in this group.
3. *Emergency surgery* is that which needs to be done immediately to save a cat's life. Massive bleeding (internal and external), compromised breathing, wounds permitting protrusion of internal organs, large tears in skin with displacement of tissue, and severe head injuries are conditions that present a threat to life and produce extreme pain, requiring immediate attention and surgery.

Surgical Steps

Preparation for surgery is as important as the anesthesia, the recovery period, or even the surgery itself. Fortunately, elective and necessary surgery provide sufficient time to evaluate the patient regarding the risks involved. There is time to decide whether to operate or not. Current techniques, such as X rays, blood and other fluid tests, or various diagnostic procedures, reduce risk to a minimum. Also, there is time to properly prepare the patient by withholding food and water, giving preoperative medications, and stabilizing conditions for successful surgery.

In emergency surgery, the same procedures are followed but within the time available to save life. Abbreviated methods are used to keep the patient alive for surgery.

Many times X rays are necessary to give the surgeon essential information that he cannot learn by seeing or feeling. Where and what bones are fractured? What internal organs are involved or enlarged? And so on.

Complete blood counts (CBC) may determine the need for transfusions, presence or degree of infection involved, and, combined with blood chemistries, can give an indication of the health status of the whole animal.

Urine analysis will not only determine the status of the urinary system, but can also point out other systems that need either stabilizing before surgery, or monitoring and further evaluation.

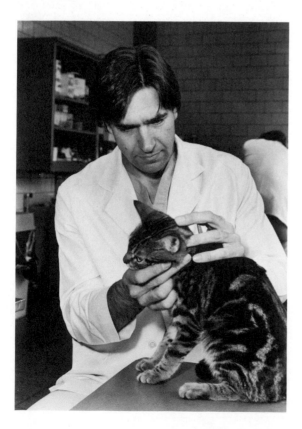

Quite often these preoperative tests are necessary to decide what kind of anesthesia and medications will be safest for that particular patient.

The owner must withhold food overnight (eight hours or more) before taking the cat for surgery, and allow no water for several hours. This is necessary to prevent vomiting during the procedures or recovery and subsequent inhaling of food or liquid to cause suffocation or inhalation pneumonia.

Evaluation of the patient for an elective procedure in a young, vigorous, and healthy-appearing cat can often be limited to a complete physical examination and determination of vaccination status. Obviously, mature or aged cats with complicated medical problems may need complete diagnostic work-ups, which may take a day or two before decisions can be made.

When emergency surgery is required to save the life of the patient, the time spent in evaluation must necessarily be shortened but yet thorough enough to maintain all vital functions such as blood circulation, breathing, prevention of shock, et cetera, until surgery can be performed.

Anesthesia

Anesthesia involves the use of drugs and various agents (anesthetics) for the purposes of blocking the sensations of touch, pressure, or pain. Because the cat cannot be taught to hold still and because of his innate nature to resent being held, general anesthesia is most often used, although occasionally in simple procedures tranquilizers or sedatives with local anesthetics can be effective. There is a great variety of general anesthetics: injection for short-term procedures; inhalation for longer ones; or a combination of both that will avoid pain, safely keep the animal still, relax the muscles, and erase the memory of what happened so the animal is not left with the memory of trauma or, perhaps, a fear of people. Safety and uneventful recovery are the prime factors in choice of anesthetics.

Efforts begun in the 1970s to develop a new dissociative anesthetic culminated in 1987, when approval was granted for a new product known as Telazol[R]. Drug studies have shown this new injectable drug to be a safe anesthetic for cats, with a wide margin of safety. Varying doses, depending on the animal's condition and the type of surgery to be performed, have been used in a wide range of diagnostic and surgical procedures.

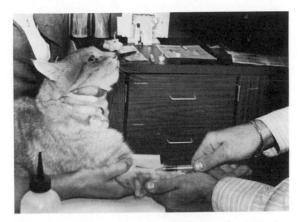

Before anesthesia for a surgical procedure is started, preinduction procedures are carried out. Sedatives and tranquilizers can be given by injection to relax the cat so it will be tractable and easily handled for the rest of the surgical preparation. These preanesthetics will also reduce the amount of general anesthetic needed during surgery, again with the objective of increased safety. Anticholinergic drugs, such as atropine, are given to decrease salivation, to slow intestinal activity, and to prevent reflex abnormal slowing of the heart rate when certain internal organs are manipulated during surgery.

Simple procedures such as catheterizations and applying casts may be done with just the preanesthetic medications. Supplementing with local anesthetics will allow the patient to tolerate suturing of minor wounds, opening abscesses, and simple operations where pain is minimal and of very short duration.

When indicated, intravenous catheters are placed for intravenous (IV) medication or anesthetics and vital sign–monitoring equipment positioned during this preinduction period. If possible, the hair is clipped from a large area around the surgical site before the general anesthetic is started to shorten the time it is used.

The surgery to be performed and the evaluation of the patient dictate the kind of general anesthetic to be used. Intravenous general anesthetics are available with a great variety of characteristics, which are best suited for specific circumstances. Some are ultrashort-acting barbiturates, some with differing recovery time and qualities. Others have differing effects on various organs and physiological systems.

The same is true of the inhalation gas anesthetics that are commonly used. Some gas anesthetics should be avoided in the presence of liver disease; others should not be used on patients with cardiac disease or compromised circulation. Thus, planning the kind of anesthetic for each individual is very important to the success of the surgery.

Gas anesthesia is administered by a "closed" system. A plastic tube (endotracheal tube) is inserted into the trachea after the cat is anesthetized with the intravenous drug used in the preinduction period. The tube is connected to an anesthesia machine, which administers oxygen and the gaseous anesthetic of choice.

Monitoring

The inhalant gas anesthetic gradually replaces the intravenous one as that wears off. This transition is carefully monitored by checking vital signs with observation and monitoring equipment. The monitoring continues throughout the anesthesia stage and early recovery period.

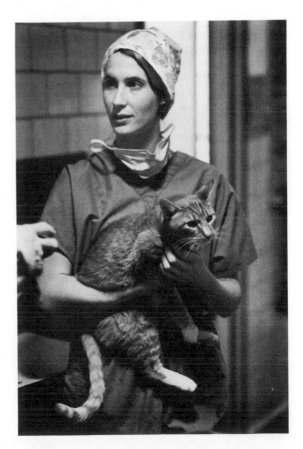

Pulse rate and strength, respirations, and mucous membrane color are important evaluations that are made during any surgery. Some cases require that blood pressure, urine output, central nervous system or reflex reaction depression, and other physiological functions be included in the monitoring.

Besides making the depth of anesthesia easy to regulate, the routine use of the anesthesia machine has other advantages for the patient. The cat can be allowed to breathe independently by its own stimulation or it can be controlled by the anesthetist. Forced respiration—manual or with the mechanical respirator—is necessary during diaphragmatic hernia repair and other open-chest surgery. It is also life-saving if breathing should stop or be excessively depressed.

The use of narcotic drugs and narcotic antagonist drugs (drugs that work in opposition to the narcotic on the nervous system) is helpful in alleviating excessive pain during or following surgery. Narcotics are particularly suited because their effects can be quickly reversed by a specific antagonist if the need arises.

Surgical Preparation

After the evaluation is completed, catheters in place for intravenous fluids, and anesthesia started, the surgical site is shaved and cleaned. The area involved is meticulously scrubbed with soap, sterile water, and antiseptics to insure a sterile field for surgery. To avoid contamination, sterile drapes cover the patient, the table, and instrument trays. The surgeon and assistant wear sterile caps, gowns, masks and gloves, just as in human surgery. The operating room is used only for surgery to keep it as clean as possible. It is equipped with special operating lights, anesthesia machines, and vital-sign monitors. Care is taken to maintain the patient's normal temperature with supplemental heat by placing the cat on a pad that circulates warm water. A metal table can dissipate body heat very quickly.

Recovery

After the surgery is completed, the incision and stitches, if used, are protected by sealing it with an antiseptic spray bandage, since cats do not care for regular bandages and make efforts to remove them. Regular bandages and casts are only applied when the type of surgery requires their use, and then special shields or collars are needed to keep them in place and protected.

The anesthesia is discontinued and the intravenous catheters removed if fluids are no longer necessary. The patient is taken to a warm, quiet, and protected recovery cage for observation until fully conscious and able to navigate without injuring itself. This may take just a few minutes or hours, depending on the kind of anesthesia, the patient's general condition, the extent of surgery, or other factors involved.

A specially constructed incubator is used when recovery is prolonged or with critically ill patients. It has a thermostatically regulated heat source (circulating water pad), oxygen inlet and equipment to continue intravenous therapy and monitor urine output or other vital functions when intensive care is required.

Hospitalization

The length of time a cat spends in the hospital after surgery varies according to the particular circumstances. Many simple, uncomplicated cases may go home as soon as the patient is conscious. Some routine major surgeries where a body cavity has been opened, such as a spay, might be ready the next day. More complex life-saving operations will require much longer monitoring and hospital treatment to allow proper healing and return of normal function. Orthopedic surgery also requires close observation for longer periods of time.

The patient's status at the time of surgery, regardless of the length or complexity of the procedure, influences the length of stay in the hospital. Age is taken into consideration, as well as the effect of the problem on the general condition of the patient at the time of examination, its temperament for confinement, and its prior health history. The potential for complications arising at home coupled with the owner's ability to give proper convalescent care are additional considerations.

POSTOPERATIVE CARE

This vital part of successful recovery is owner-dependent. Convalescent time at home to completion of healing is affected by the same factors that determined hospital stay (i.e., age, status, physical condition, kind of surgery). Over 75 percent of soft-tissue healing occurs by the fourteenth day, while bone fractures require four to eight weeks or longer to produce a good union and return of function.

Specific instructions for each individual case must be followed, but some general surgical after-care procedures are consistent:

1. Rest and confinement are necessary until recovery is complete.

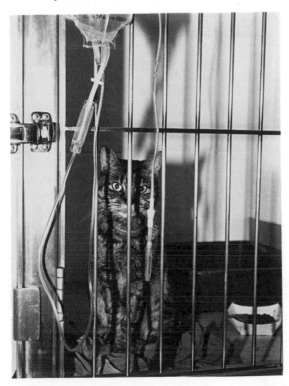

2. Empathy mistakenly can lead to giving extra treats or overfeeding. In the absence of special diet instructions, the previous normal feeding routine should be followed.
3. Extra vigilance is necessary until recovery is complete. The incision and sutures should be checked daily for swelling, discharge, and irritation.
4. Follow-up appointments are an extremely important part of surgery and should be kept as scheduled.
5. If any uncertainty arises, a call for advice is easy to make and welcomed by the veterinarian, will avert problems and will ease the owner's mind.

COMMON ELECTIVE SURGERY

Castration

This most common elective surgery of the male cat is universally accepted by knowledgeable owners to stop objectionable behavior in order to have an acceptable household pet.

The surgery removes the testes, the source of sperm, as a birth control measure. It eliminates production of the hormones that cause an uncastrated male to roam; to be markedly aggressive toward other cats, leading to persistent fighting; and to spray malodorous urine for marking territory outside and even in the house.

This surgery is for the convenience of the owner and should be done at seven to ten months of age, when sexual development is about complete but the undesirable habits have not been established. Usually it is one-day surgery, with little home care required. Confinement indoors for a few days will provide him rest and the owner the opportunity to watch for excessive licking of the scrotum or swelling. Sometimes shredded paper towel or newspaper are substituted for earthen or commercial litter in the pan to help keep the scrotal area clean until healed.

The operation itself is brief, with short-term anesthesia normally used. The scrotum is shaved and surgically scrubbed for sterility. A single incision is made in the scrotum or over each testicle, depending on the surgeon's preferred technique. The spermatic cord is divided between the spermatic duct and the blood vessels, which become two natural sutures that are used as self-ties to prevent bleeding from the vessels. Some prefer to clamp and tie the cord with man-made suture material. No stitches are placed in the scrotum.

Occasionally a conscience-stricken owner will ask about merely doing a vasectomy as a method of birth control. The veterinarian must explain that the male cat will be sterile but the remaining testicles will continue producing male hormones, which cause the undesirable habits that the surgery of castration is usually intended to correct.

Ovariohysterectomy
(Spaying)

This procedure is done as a population control measure and for the convenience of the owner to eliminate the annoying actions of a female cat "in heat" or estrus, which can occur repeatedly, intermittently, or sometimes continuously, until the cat is mated or artificially stimulated to ovulate. The increasing amount of daylight in the spring influences the onset of heat, which continues until daylight decreases in September or October. Twelve to fourteen hours per day of continuous artificial light may cause continuous polyestrus with no anestrus period noted in the fall and winter. (*See* Chapter 9: Reproductive Physiology.)

If the female is an outdoor cat, she will attract uncastrated males that will fight, destroy gardens and other property, and be a nuisance. Indoors, the cat in heat will seek constant attention and affection, vocalizing almost continuously, rolling on the floor or rubbing against people's legs. She becomes nervous and easily agitated.

There are several valuable health applications involved in spaying. Removing the uterus eliminates the possibility of a severe uterine infection known as pyometra, which is frequently seen in the unspayed cat. This disease is very debilitating and can be fatal if unnoticed and untreated. (*See* Chapter 12: Reproductive Disorders.) Spaying a cat before its first heat may help to reduce the incidence of mammary cancer in the cat, although it does not totally eliminate the possibility. Mammary cancer in the cat is much less common than in the dog; however, when a mammary tumor does appear in a cat, it is much more likely to be malignant. Also, certain skin disorders can be avoided by ovariohysterectomy.

It is best performed at approximately six months of age. Unlike castration, this procedure is considered major surgery because the abdomen is invaded, and therefore requires a hospital stay of twenty-four hours or more, depending on the practice of the veterinarian.

An inhalation general anesthesia of a long duration is used. A large area of abdomen is shaved, scrubbed, and prepared for sterile surgery. The abdomen is incised and opened, the ovaries and uterus located and withdrawn outside, blood vessels closed with sutures placed beyond the ovaries and at the uterine stump that will be left. Both ovaries, uterine horns, and the body of the uterus are removed. Care is taken to remove all ovarian tissue because even a very small amount can produce signs of estrus. The muscles and abdominal wall are stitched closed with material that will remain and be absorbed after healing. Skin closure can be done with the same material. However, many surgeons prefer to use nonabsorbable sutures, which are removed in ten days to two weeks.

Home care is not complicated. The patient's activity should be limited until the skin sutures are removed, in order to avoid strain on the healing muscle and skin. If the cat licks the incision excessively, or if there is swelling, or the skin opens near it, the veterinarian should be called. Most cats ignore satisfactory surgery and pay very little attention to trouble-free incisions.

Occasionally owners ask if tying the fallopian tubes, the method recognized from human experience, would be a simpler substitute. Veterinarians are universally opposed to this procedure and rarely agree to use it. It will prevent unwanted pregnancy but it will not eliminate the other reasons for complete removal of the ovaries and reproductive tract. Without ovariohysterectomy, the estrous cycles will continue, and the reproductive organs will continue to be subject to life-threatening tumors, infections, and other diseases of this system. Also, abdominal pregnancy outside the uterus would remain a possibility; however, there are no statistics available to prove or disprove this consideration.

Declawing

The humane implications of this procedure are the subject of much emotional discussion and debate. Declawing is elective surgery that is not necessary for health reasons. The only benefit derived is to the owner, by preventing destruction of household furnishings and property if a particular cat cannot be trained to stop ruinous scratching. (Perhaps an oblique benefit to such a cat might be justified in that declawing will save him his home if all else fails.)

Rather than to advise, we will attempt to present what is known and to describe the surgery, leaving the pondering and decision-making to the owner.

General anesthesia is used to avoid pain. There is no evidence of post-operative discomfort beyond that of any other surgery. A tourniquet is placed and the feet are scrubbed surgically without clipping the hair (except in longhair cats), and then they are soaked in antiseptic. The nail is *not* pulled; instead, the end bone of the digit holding the claw is amputated at the joint, leaving a smooth surface covered with skin, which is usually sutured with absorbable material. The feet are bandaged and several days of hospitalization are required.

After the bandages are removed, the cat is sent home with instructions for indoor confinement for a week to avoid digging in the dirt. Shredded paper may be substituted for litter in the pan.

Psychological effects of declawing have not been demonstrated or reliably discounted. Routinely, the hind feet are not declawed; thus cats can still hunt with success, climb small-diameter trees, and defend themselves.

Perineal Urethrostomy

This surgery cannot be classified as elective. In fact, it is often necessary surgery and sometimes emergency surgery. It is included here because of the high incidence of feline urinary syndrome (FUS), resulting in the very common performance of perineal urethrostomies. Both male and female cats are plagued with the formation within the bladder of small crystals composed primarily of struvite crystals with less than 1 percent of calcium phosphate and less than 1 percent of calcium oxalate. These crystals usually form in the presence of bacterial infection, but may be the by-product of a virus residing in the bladder wall or a metabolic abnormality in the cat.

Female cats rarely suffer from obstruction of the urethra as a result of crystal formation. This is because the diameter of the female urethra is large enough to allow expulsion of most of these small crystals. But the male cat's urethra at the level of the penis becomes much narrower than that of the female, and it is in this area that urethral obstruction occurs. Urine backs up within the bladder as a result of urethral obstruction, and eventually kidney function is im-

paired. The resulting accumulation of various waste products within the cat's bloodstream can cause death.

The surgical answer to the male cat's dilemma is to remove the penis and its small-diameter urethra and make a new opening for the remaining portion of the urethra below the anus. The remaining portion of the male urethra is similar in diameter to that of the female and crystals can be passed more easily. It is important to note that the urethrostomy does not alter the production of crystals; it only changes the route of their expulsion.

Longer hospitalization is required than with the other common surgeries described. The preceding decline in the general condition of the patient that is caused by FUS, and the longer healing process involved in this more complicated surgery, dictate closer monitoring of the entire animal and the operative site. Sometimes a catheter is left in place for a period of time or until the sutures are removed.

Post-operative home care requires close attention from the owner, with important specific instructions from the veterinarian to be followed pertaining to each individual case. Rest and confinement are needed. Again, shredded paper is substituted for litter in the pan.

Convalescence— Home Care

The skill of the owner in giving home care and the extent to which he or she is willing to give treatment are prime factors in the success of any medical treatment program. Hospitalization can be avoided in some cases, or shortened in others, if the owner develops more than the usual layman's expertise. The information in this section, "The Sick Cat," and in Part XI, "Medical Emergencies," provides an excellent basis for learning how to care for a convalescing cat. Home care will lessen the cat's anxiety caused by separation, and also result in lower medical costs.

While many cats do well in hospital situations, the unique nature of the cat and its great attachment to its habitat mean that sick cats usually do better at home. Hospitalization is best kept to a minimum.

Early study is advisable because the owner's knowledge can often be the first help that is given in an emergency. Also, cat owners should purchase items to include in a separate medicine kit or cabinet exclusively for pet use before the need arises.

Good home care for a convalescing cat will be made easier and more effective if a few general principles are followed:

1. The procedure should be thought out and planned in advance according to instructions that have been given by the veterinarian.
2. Appropriate equipment, supplies, and drugs need to be available and ready for use. One room should be prepared where the cat can be confined, so it cannot hide in some undiscovered corner of the house.
3. Adequate assistance should be available.
4. A sense of calmness should prevail, along with a confident attitude that all will be accomplished.
5. Nursing care should be performed after the patient's quiet period rather than after eating, activity, or playtime.

6. The patient's temperature should be taken first if it is part of the prescribed care, before the cat becomes excited and elevates the temperature.

7. Written records should be kept, with the date and time of each entry. Notes should be kept on: *incision,* in which the owner should look for discharge, swelling, exceptional redness, pain, odor (unless expected); *bandages/casts,* to observe whether there is dryness, swelling, odor, cleanliness, excessive cold or warmth, mutilation, comfort, and function capability; and *physical signs,* such as unusual appetite, eliminations, drinking, or activity.

Taking a Cat's Temperature

A cat's temperature is important information to have before a veterinarian is called and taking it may be part of the prescribed home treatment and convalescence. Taking the temperature reading of a cat may seem a formidable task to the uninitiated, but if done calmly, gently, and with confidence, it can become routine. Use a human rectal thermometer (never a thin-walled oral one). Shake it down to at least 96°F and lubricate it with K-Y Jelly or petroleum gel. An electronic digital type is easier to read.

A second person can hold the cat gently on a counter, allowing it to grasp the edge with its front paws, which decreases the opportunity for injury as well as giving the animal a sense of security. The assistant can hold the cat's head comfortably with one hand and the front legs at the elbows (never the feet) with the other. A soft voice in calm conversation with the cat is soothing.

If there is no assistant, stand the cat on a counter and, holding the tail upright with one hand and gently gripping the cat's body with that elbow, insert the thermometer with the other hand.

If the cat resists, it may be necessary to roll-wrap it in a towel. Use a towel large enough to cover all four feet and wrap completely around the cat more than once. Leave the head and the anus exposed.

Place the thermometer with slow, gentle but steady pressure against the anus. At first there will be firm resistance from the rectal muscles, which will relax with continued gentle pressure. Patience and time are necesssary in this maneuver. Insert about one inch and leave for one to two minutes if a glass rectal thermometer is used.

If it is not possible to get a rectal temperature, a less accurate estimate can be taken by holding the thermometer in the armpit (under foreleg) or in the groin between the hind legs, which are held together for two or three minutes. Absolute disaster will result if the thermometer is placed between the lips and teeth or anywhere in the mouth. Cats bite down on anything placed in their mouths, including a finger. The response is a defense mechanism to destroy a possible threat.

A normal temperature in the cat should range between 100.4°F and 102.5°F, with 105°F being a danger sign. Temperatures over 108°F can be immediately life-threatening if caused by heat stroke or heat exhaustion (which requires cooling in a cold-water bath). The cat is not as susceptible to brain damage as the human from extremely high fevers from other causes.

The thermometer should be wiped clean before reading, and the results recorded on paper, not left to memory. With the glass thermometer it is customary to report temperatures to the closest tenth of a degree.

RESTRAINT. *Minimal restraint.* The best restraint is the least restriction. Always begin with petting and gentle holding. Just enough restraint to accomplish the objective should be used, since cats resent forceful efforts. Force will cause panic, as will rough, sudden movements and loud angry voices and noises. The cat's environment should be calm and peaceful.

Simple distraction, by holding the cat up with gentle shaking or petting, can be sufficient restraint for giving injections or other simple procedures.

Two-person restraint. An assistant can restrain a cat by stretching it out on a table or bench with the scruff of the neck in one hand and the hind legs (above the hocks, never the feet) in the other. Holding firmly, the assistant can pull the hind legs back. When possible the cat can be allowed to grasp the edge of the table with its front paws to stabilize itself.

One-person restraint. When there is only one person, the area of examination must be determined first. Stand the cat on a counter and grasp the area or limb with one hand, while gently gripping the cat's body with that elbow as described above, for taking the cat's temperature.

In all attempts keep the claws pointing down toward the table, remain calm and firm, and try to work quickly. Restraint with one person is often difficult. It may be necessary to use roll-wrapping or a cat bag.

Roll-wrapping. If the cat is extremely agitated, roll-wrapping is the best solution. Use a towel that is large enough to envelop all four paws and wrap around the cat more than once. Leaving the area of examination exposed, completely wrap the towel around the animal firmly but gently. Many animals relax and calm down once they are incapacitated.

Cat bags. These are made of canvas with hooks, snaps, or zippers. The cat is placed in the open bag, which is then zipped and closed around the cat.

Force-Feeding

Smell is important to a cat's eating habits. A cat that can smell the food is more inclined to eat, so it helps to clean a clogged nose of any nasal discharge by gently using warm water and soft cotton until the nose is clear. Addition of pungent fish foods will sometimes stir a finicky appetite. If not, high-calorie nutrient pastes are available that can be force-fed as is or mixed with other food and liquids to make a mixture that may be easier to administer.

The cat's head is held from the top with thumb and finger on the side ridges of the face that are just below the eyes. The head is tipped up, the mouth partially opened with a finger, and a strip of paste squeezed into the mouth or placed on the roof of the mouth. With the head held tipped, the cat will make licking motions and usually begin swallowing. If the head is turned loose, the cat is apt to shake its head and expel the paste. The paste can be pressed against the teeth as well.

When liquid foods are administered, the head is held in the same manner. A plastic syringe (without needle) or a small kitchen basting syringe is used. The tip of the syringe is inserted into a pouch formed where the upper and lower lips meet, between the side of the cheek and the teeth. The liquid must be administered slowly and patiently, allowing adequate time for swallowing. Stroking the throat will sometimes stimulate swallowing. Once swallowing has started, continue squeezing liquid slowly into the pouch until the patient decides it's time to rest. Allow sufficient rest time, using constant praising and stroking to regain the cat's confidence, and repeat the process.

Water is administered in the same way. Flavoring the water with just a little of the cat's favorite treat might make it more acceptable. Some cats are not frequent water drinkers.

If force-feeding must be done alone, wrapping the cat in a towel, leaving just the head out, is almost mandatory. Force-feeding requires assistance, time, and great patience, but it is essential for recovery if the patient will not eat on its own.

Administering Medicines

Medicating a cat is a difficult task. The personality of the cat is the most important matter to remember when giving medications. A cat is an independent animal, unwilling to accept things that are done for it or to it. Mentally establishing an aura of confidence, calmness, kindness, patience, and persistence will make the chore bearable and successful to both the cat and owner. The cat bag is often an important aid.

EXTERNAL (SKIN) MEDICINES. Cleanliness is a fetish with cats. A cat's constant desire to lick itself

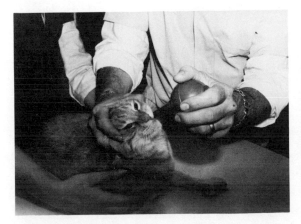

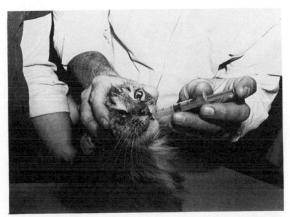

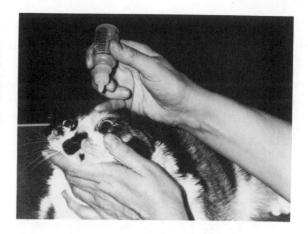

clean requires patience and time with skin medications. Ointments or liquids should be rubbed in thoroughly. Hold the cat and play with it for ten or fifteen minutes until the medication can be absorbed or dries. Some medicines may be sufficiently bitter to prevent licking. Discuss this with the veterinarian.

Medicated baths are to be carefully given following prescribed directions. As in any bathing, the ear canals are plugged with cotton and a drop or two of mineral oil placed in each eye for protection from bath solutions or soap. Care should be exercised to avoid getting the bath solutions into the mouth, and, if so instructed, the cat may have to be held and dried to avoid licking. Always remember to remove the cotton plugs from the ears.

INJECTIONS. Some conditions such as diabetes require hypodermic injections. Ask the veterinarian for a demonstration before attempting to give an injection. There are many variables with the different injectables (i.e., storage, shaking the vial, warming, disinfectants to use, injection locations). To cover them in the text would be impractical and could lead to errors if misinterpreted.

ORAL MEDICATIONS. *Pastes.* There are several medications available in paste form, such as vitamin-mineral mixtures, hairball treatments, and nutritional/caloric supplements. Since they are made for oral use in cats, the manufacturers have taken pains to make them palatable, so they are usually accepted by the cat. If they are not, see and follow the same instructions as for Tablets/Capsules, below.

Liquids. Palatability is an important consideration in

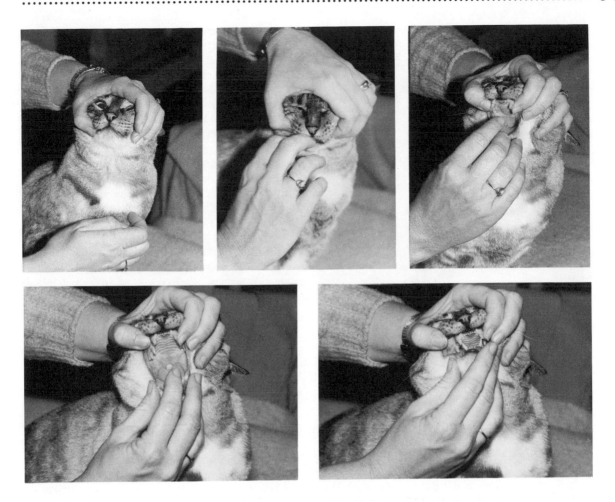

the preparation of liquid medication to be given orally to cats. Mix particularly distasteful liquids in small amounts with one of the pastes described above or the cat's favorite treat on a trial basis (if the label indicates that the medicine is compatible with what is used). Strong fish tastes are worth trying.

The proper dose then should be mixed and given as prescribed at the proper time. Do *not* mix the entire dose in the regular meal. The cat may decide not to eat, may roam for a time, or just may not appreciate having its food tampered with. This will upset the dosage schedule, greatly reducing the efficacy of treatment.

Tablets/Capsules. Medication for cats is put up in tablet or capsule form because it may work best or might only be effective in this form. For example, one medication might have a protective coating to avoid

being destroyed by stomach acids before it reaches the intestines. Granules and powders may be put in capsules to avoid extremely bitter and unsavory tastes. One should always ask for approval from the veterinarian before the tablet or capsule is crushed and combined with something else.

A little butter may help in swallowing, as long as the tablet does not become too slippery to handle. Hold the cat's head from the top with thumb and finger on the side ridges of the face that are just below the eyes; tip the head up. Hold the pill between the thumb and forefinger of the other hand, using the third finger to gently prop open the mouth. Drop the pill as far back in the throat as possible on the midline. Continue to hold the head back and stroke the throat until swallowing occurs. After the pill is dropped, a quick short poke with the forefinger, the

eraser end of a pencil, or a cotton-tipped applicator may move the pill over the base of the tongue. This maneuver must be done quickly but with great caution so as not to damage the cat's throat or become bitten. Ask for a demonstration before attempting this technique.

Remember to give sincere praise, attention, and even a little treat when the pill is swallowed. This show of empathy will prepare the cat for the next encounter.

Disinfection

This topic rightfully deserves a place in convalescence and home care management. It is especially important in multiple-cat households to help reduce infectious diseases within the feline population.

Disinfectants, antiseptics, and sanitizers are used to reduce or eliminate disease-causing microbial organisms.

The effectiveness of these preparations against several common feline viruses (feline herpesvirus I, which causes rhinotracheitis, feline calicivirus, and fe-line panleukopenia virus) has been investigated at the Cornell Feline Health Center, as a component part of the Antiviral Substances Program of the Infectious Disease Branch of the National Institutes of Health.

The antiviral activities of thirty-five commonly used products were evaluated. Of the products tested, sodium hypochlorite appeared to be the best overall antiviral product for routine disinfection or decontamination of cages, floors, and food dishes in animal facilities. It is effective, inexpensive, and readily available. The most common form is ordinary household bleach (house-brand chlorine bleach or Clorox, 5.6 percent sodium hypochlorite, at a recommended dilution of 1:32 in water—one cup Clorox to two gallons of water).

To increase detergent activity, Clorox can be combined with several products without loss of its antiviral activity. Caution is advised with these combinations because no attempt was made to critically evaluate potential biohazard effects from long-term exposure to such combinations. For example, sodium hypochlorite mixed with ammonia compounds releases ammonia gas, which is toxic in excessive quantities; therefore, any space being disinfected with a combination of Clorox and any ammonium compound should be well ventilated to prevent humans and animals from inhaling strong concentrations of ammonia gas.

However, Clorox has been used routinely in combination with A-33 (Airkem), a quaternary ammonium detergent (a class of chemical compounds) with a pleasant odor, for several months in the animal facilities and clinic wards (1:32 Clorox and 1:64 A-33) with no apparent ill effects.

The occurrence of fatal hemorrhagic diarrhea in dogs, caused by canine parvovirus, is an excellent example of the need for effective antiviral disinfectants to decontaminate wards and adoption shelters. The use of effective decontamination measures in adoption shelters and pet shops will greatly reduce the occurrence of viral diseases in dogs and cats passing through these facilities.

Decontamination will eliminate or decrease the quantity of virus exposure and increase the average length of time between entry of the animal and infection. In most cases, this will allow sufficient time for immunization to provide solid protection.

Medical Emergencies

A little cat played on a silver flute.
And a big cat sat and listened;
The little cat's strains gave the big cat pains,
And a tear on his eyelids glistened.

—Arthur Macy, "The Boston Cats"

First Aid

The actions taken immediately after a cat has had an accident or suffered from a sudden illness can save its life. Some illness may have been present for some time but is discovered at the sudden onset of signs that constitute an emergency.

Cats of course cannot explain verbally what happened to them or what they feel, but certain life signs reveal vital information to help determine a course of action. Is the cat breathing? Is its heart beating? Is it bleeding? Is its temperature normal? Is it behaving abnormally?

Cats in pain are frightened and will often try to run away and hide. To administer help the person must forcibly restrain the animal with blankets or bags to avoid being bitten or scratched. Speaking to the cat, using its name, and handling it with a firm but gentle grip will often calm a panicked cat enough to allow treatment.

An understanding of the normal structures and functions of a cat's body is needed for comparison when attempting to determine what is wrong with a cat that is in pain or unconscious.

The key objectives of first aid are:

1. To preserve life
2. To alleviate suffering
3. To promote recovery
4. To prevent aggravation of the injury or illness until veterinary assistance can be obtained.

CHECK FOR NORMAL VITAL SIGNS

It is essential to know the normal temperature, pulse, and breathing rate of your cat in order to accurately judge the severity of illness or injury. Cats vary, as people do, but these are general guidelines:

Temperature	100.4°F–102.5°F
Pulse	160–240 per minute
Respirations	20–30 per minute

WHAT TO DO IN THE EVENT OF AN EMERGENCY

1. *Remove the cause* of the injury if possible.

2. *Clear airways* so the cat can breathe. Remove any collar or harness from the cat's body. Clear the nose and throat of any foreign material, blood, or fluids. Place the animal in the position that makes breathing as easy as possible.

3. *Give artificial respiration* (*see* Artificial Respiration, page 346) if the patient is not breathing.

4. *Treat cardiac arrest with CPR* immediately (*see* CPR, page 347). Often a sharp blow on the side of the chest, just behind the shoulder, will suffice. Continue CPR until the cat's heart is pumping on its own and the cat is breathing.

5. *Stop or control bleeding* as soon as possible. Use pressure bandages, pressure points, or tourniquets as needed.

6. *Cover any wounds* with clean, dry dressings.

7. *Keep the patient warm* with blankets, box, or in a warm car, et cetera.

8. *Do not move* or manipulate the patient unnecessarily. An injured animal will usually assume the least painful position, with the injured part uppermost. When it is necessary to move the patient, support and protect the injured area to prevent further damage and pain. Use blankets, rugs, and boards or boxes to support an animal being transported.

9. *Treat for shock.* If the cat is unconscious, place its head slightly lower than the rest of its body to treat shock and to prevent the patient from inhaling fluids or materials in the mouth. *Do not give anything by mouth,* not even water or medicines. If the cat is conscious and not seriously injured, give small amounts of drinking water.

10. *Promptly transport the cat to a veterinary facility* for professional care.

11. If possible, *have someone phone the veterinary hospital or surgery,* while you are on the way, to alert the staff of your need for emergency care. The person who calls should give a brief description of the injuries, so the hospital personnel can make preparations for your arrival.

12. *Don't speed on the way!* A patient that won't survive a few minutes probably can't be saved, and the rough ride to the hospital may aggravate injuries. Risking an additional accident—to yourself or your pet—is not justified by any emergency.

For a reference point, you should determine these rates for your cat when it is healthy and keep a record in your first-aid kit. Excitement or exercise will increase the normal rates, as in humans, so your most valid measurements will be obtained when the cat is at rest. A good time to measure normal pulse and respiration is when you and your pet are relaxing together in the course of a normal day.

To find the pulse, press your first two fingers against the inside of the upper hind leg, where the large femoral artery is found. Count the pulse for at least sixty seconds. You can also see or feel the heartbeat on the chest wall directly behind the cat's "elbow." In an emergency situation, the heartbeat or pulse should be taken and reported to the veterinarian. An extremely fast pulse indicates a state of shock. A weak pulse indicates a dire situation, which should receive immediate veterinary attention.

To determine the breathing rate or respiration, watch the cat's chest movement. Count either inhalations or exhalations (not both) for one minute. Rapid breathing can indicate shock or lack of oxygen. Labored breathing may be a clue that there is an obstruction. Shallow breathing is a sign of weakness or chest pain. Irregular breathing is a very serious sign, calling for an immediate veterinary examination. Among the many problems it could indicate are fractured ribs and punctured or collapsed lung.

Unless your cat is unusually docile, you will need a helper to hold it while you take its temperature. (*See* Chapter 37: Convalescence—Home Care.)

CREATE A FIRST-AID KIT

The following list does not include common household items, which are assumed to be already in the house, such as scissors, pliers, blankets, soap, bicarbonate of soda, and mineral oil. Towels or large cloths or blankets should be available to restrain the cat if it is hysterical. The numbers in parentheses in the list indicate quantity.

CONTENTS FOR A CAT FIRST-AID KIT

MATERIALS AND EQUIPMENT

Gauze bandages, 1″ and 2″ rolls (1 each)
Gauze dressing pads, 3″ x 3″ (8)
Adhesive tape, 1″ roll (1)
Roll of cotton wool (1)
Triangular bandage (1)
Rectal thermometer (1)
Cotton balls (6)
Tweezers (1)

MEDICATIONS

3% hydrogen peroxide (2oz.)
Milk of magnesia tablets, 5 gm (10)
Activated charcoal tablets (20)
Kaolin mixture (2 oz.)
Antibacterial ointment
　For eye, ⅛ oz. tube (1)
　For skin, ⅛ oz. tube (1)

Always replace materials and medications after they have been used.

HOW TO RESTRAIN AN INJURED CAT

Injured cats often do not recognize their owners, whom they normally trust. Nor do they understand the concern and help that people are trying to give them. Cats in pain are afraid and do not understand the source of that pain. Their natural instincts are to escape and hide; if they cannot, they will strike out at anyone who approaches to avoid a repetition of the incident that caused the pain.

Veterinarians can use medicine, tranquilizers, sedatives, and anesthetics to alleviate the suffering of a cat. First aid is the process necessary to get the cat to the veterinarian.

In general, the cat is a very independent creature. Its personality necessitates forcible restraint, or confinement to an area where it thinks it is free but is not. An injured cat may wound anyone offering medical assistance by biting, or by scratching with any of its four feet. It is almost impossible to muzzle a cat, so one must avoid the mouth area. Restraint of the feet is important.

To humanely "disarm" the cat's claws, secure the two front legs together, just above the feet, by winding adhesive tape around them two or three times. Then fasten the rear legs together in a similar manner. Hold the head firmly. The cat can now be examined and treated carefully and effectively.

Actually, the cat is usually a bluffer and will respond well to confident but firm handling. It is also forgetful and forgiving. If a cat becomes angry at forced treatment, release it. Soon it will once again be docile and approachable.

Picking Up or Carrying a Cat

1. Reassure the cat. Talk to it quietly, gently stroke its head and ears, and run your hand down its back.
2. With your hand over the cat's head and your elbow over its tail move your hand under its chest (sternum) and lift, with the cat's lower body resting on your forearm and snuggled against your body. The other hand can either grasp the scruff of the cat's neck or cradle its chin.

PRINCIPLES OF RESTRAINT

1. Approach the patient with a firm but kind and quiet manner. Use its name if you know it and allow the animal to sniff the back of your closed fist.
2. Do nothing to further injure the patient.
3. Restrain the patient in a way that will not allow it to injure itself.
4. Protect yourself from injury that may be inflicted upon you by the patient.
5. Place the cat in a situation different from its usual secure environment (on the top of a table instead of on the floor, for example). The newness will create uncertainty but not pain, and the patient will be more cooperative and easier to treat.

3. Transport a cat in a basket, cat carrier, or cloth bag, such as a pillowcase or burlap bag, tied closed. The cat cannot see out and will feel snug and secure. If the head is to be examined, or oral medication is to be given, loosen the bag and expose only the head; this effectively restrains the rest of the patient in the bag.

Restraining Unruly or Aggressive Cats

1. In most instances an unruly or biting cat can be controlled with a folded blanket or thick towel. Drop the blanket over the cat in its box or cage and pick up the animal inside the blanket. With the cat rolled in the blanket and only a foot or the head protruding, you can apply medication or bandages without danger to either the patient or the handler.
2. Use thick leather or canvas work gloves when handling an aggressive cat. When cats scratch and bite, the wounds are severe. They will almost always attack the face or hands. Place obstreperous patients in a strong bag or cat box and take them to the veterinarian, where drugs can be used for restraint. This is safer, wiser, and more humane.

WHAT TO DO ABOUT CHOKING

Warning: Choking is one of the signs of rabies. If a strange cat appears to be choking but has no obvious

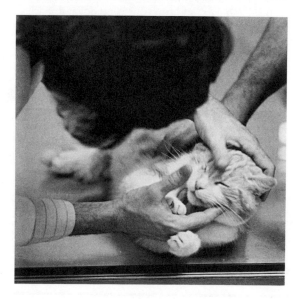

injury, rabies is a possibility. The same is true of any cat that has not been vaccinated. *If you do not know the cat, stay away from it and call the nearest animal control center.*

If the cat is one you know and you believe that an object, such as a bone, might be in its throat and obstructing the cat's breathing, reach in with your fingers or tweezers and try to remove it. If the blockage is further down, lay the cat on its side, place the heel of your hand just behind the last rib, angling slightly upward, and push firmly, but not so firmly as to break the ribs. Four quick thrusts should dislodge the obstruction; if not, try again. If unsuccessful, take the cat to a veterinarian.

COPING WITH BREATHING DIFFICULTIES

Any foreign object in the nasal passages, throat, trachea, or bronchi can physically prevent the flow of air into the lungs. Penetrating chest wounds can result in collapsed lungs. Any tearing of the diaphragm, which normally acts to expand the lungs, will also interfere with effective breathing.

Look for these signs to determine if the cat is in respiratory distress:

1. Mucous membranes (gums and lining of the eyelids) may be pale or blue in color (cyanotic), indicating poor circulation or inadequate oxygenation of the blood.
2. Labored respiration may occur: gasping, open-mouthed breathing, or slow, shallow breathing. A cat in sudden respiratory distress, as from choking, may paw at its face.
3. The cat may be unconscious, with dilated pupils.

If the respiratory problem is caused by something other than simple obstruction, you must resort to artificial respiration.

Artificial Respiration

Remove the cat's collar, open the mouth, and pull the tongue forward so that it does not block the throat. Pull the head and neck forward, then put your hands on the ribs, push down suddenly, and release. This drives the stale air out of the lungs, and an elastic

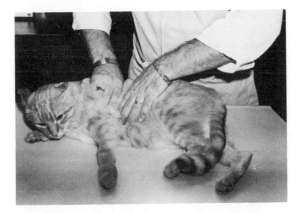

recoil mechanism will allow them to fill once more. Repeat about once every five seconds.

If the chest cavity has been punctured, the elastic recoil mechanism will not be working, and you will have to actually blow air into the lungs. Hold the cat's mouth and lips closed, put your mouth over its nose, and blow firmly into the nostrils for about three seconds. Watch the chest carefully. Blowing too hard can cause lung damage. After a two-second rest, repeat. Keep this up for thirty minutes or more, or until the animal has begun breathing on its own, or has been pronounced dead by a veterinarian. The cat's progress can be monitored by checking the color of its gums. If it begins to fight the procedure, breathing is improving.

WHEN BREATHING AND HEARTBEAT STOP

Cardiopulmonary Resuscitation (CPR)

CPR is an important lifesaving technique that has become widely accepted for humans through classes offered by the Red Cross and other groups. These same techniques may "breathe" life back into a seemingly lifeless pet.

CPR provides short-term, artificial breathing and heart contractions for an unconscious animal whose breathing and heartbeat have stopped. CPR sustains the animal until it can perform these functions again on its own. An animal can suffer respiratory and heart failure from a traumatic experience, such as being hit by a car, ingesting a toxic material, or from shock.

An animal is considered unconscious if it is unre-sponsive to stimuli, such as pinching and shaking. *Do not perform CPR on an animal that has a heartbeat. Do not perform artificial breathing on an animal that is already breathing unless the breathing is very shallow. These techniques could injure the animal if it is breathing normally or has a heartbeat.*

Breathing can be determined visually as the chest rises and falls during inhalation and exhalation. Feel the heartbeat by placing your fingers on the left side of the chest wall, above the point of the elbow. Visual signs of an absence of heartbeat include fully dilated eyes and cool, grayish-blue gums. Feel the heartbeat on a healthy cat to become familiar with the sensation.

Artificial Breathing. If the animal is not breathing but has a heartbeat, then only artificial breathing is needed. (*See* "Artificial Respiration," page 346.)

Heart Contractions. If there is no heartbeat or respiration, cardiopulmonary arrest has occurred and CPR must be administered. It consists of compressing the heart while administering artificial breathing. Both therapies are applied, one immediately following the other. A rhythm must develop between continual heart compressions and artificial breathing technique.

1. With your free hand place the thumb on the cat's chest at the point of the elbow and your fingers on the opposite side of the chest cavity for compression.
2. Squeeze gently, but firmly, at a rate of one compression per second.
3. After five cardiac compressions, follow with artificial breathing without breaking the rhythm of the cardiac compressions. (*See* "Artificial Respiration," page 346.)

Another variation is to place the animal on its right side on a firm surface. Place one hand under the body and the other hand above it, so the entire upper chest area is enclosed. Use both hands to compress. Compress the chest five times, then move one hand to the nose and mouth and administer respiration once; then repeat.

Continue CPR for a few minutes, while observing the animal for signs of life, such as spontaneous respiratory efforts or a heartbeat. If breathing and heart rate are not restored, continue CPR up to fifteen minutes. After fifteen minutes, revival is unlikely. If at all possible, have someone drive you to the veterinarian while you continue giving CPR.

Caution: Severe cardiopulmonary complications may result if you attempt CPR on a conscious, breathing animal.

HOW TO CONTROL BLEEDING

Injuries to the soft tissue include cuts, lacerations, abrasions, and abscesses. To control bleeding, first try the direct-pressure technique. Place a clean, preferably sterile, gauze pad directly over the wound and apply firm, even pressure. If blood soaks through the gauze, *do not remove it,* or you may disrupt any clot that has begun to form. Just place another pad on top and continue to apply pressure. If a limb is injured, it may help to elevate it, but do this with care to avoid causing further damage to possible fractures.

If direct pressure does not stop the bleeding, try indirect pressure on the arteries supplying the area. The useful pressure points on a cat are inside the upper surface of the forelimb and hindlimb and at the underside of the base of the tail. Very firm pressure to these areas will reduce the amount of bleeding from those respective extremities.

If neither type of manual pressure controls the bleeding from a leg or tail wound, you may apply a tourniquet as a *last resort.* Avoid this step unless absolutely necessary, for gangrene (death and decay of tissue) may result if a tourniquet is left on too long. *Never apply a tourniquet around the neck.* The procedure for applying a tourniquet is:

1. Use a one-inch-wide gauze bandage roll; wrap twice around the limb or tail, between the wound and the body, about two inches from the wound. Do not use a narrower bandage or a string. It will cut into the underlying skin.
2. Tie a half hitch (one tie of the line) in the bandage, put a pencil or stick on top, and tie a square knot above.
3. Twist slowly until the bleeding slows to a trickle. Fasten the stick in place by tying or taping gently. The tourniquet should be released briefly every ten to fifteen minutes.
4. Cover the wound lightly with sterile gauze.

Once a tourniquet is in place, take the cat to a veterinarian without delay. If the tourniquet must remain in place over fifteen minutes, release it for one minute for every fifteen minutes it is in place, then retighten. Watch for shock. (*See* "Shock," page 350.)

Closed or internal wounds are harder to detect and therefore harder to treat. They may appear as contusions (bruises) or hematomas (swollen areas filled with blood). Internal wounds may be suspected if the cat is bleeding from the mouth or anus, vomits or defecates blood, or is in a coma or state of shock with no signs of external injury. Emergency treatment consists of keeping an airway open, treating for shock, immobilizing fractures, and seeing a veterinarian as soon as possible.

SOFT-TISSUE INJURIES

Less serious wounds can be treated as follows: Wash hands thoroughly and restrain the cat. First smear a bit of ointment or petroleum jelly *around* the wound area, so the hair will stick together and not fall into the wound as you clip the fur away with scissors. Next, clean the wound carefully, first with water and then with an antiseptic. Wet a cotton swab or gauze pad and clean the wound by washing gently from the center of the injured area, working outward. When the cotton swab becomes soiled, throw it away and use a fresh one to prevent contaminating the antiseptic with dirt from the wound.

Safe antiseptics for cats include hydrogen peroxide, alcohol, Bactine, dilute Betadine, and iodine. After cleaning, blot away any excess water gently with a sterile gauze pad and apply a suitable antibiotic, such as nitrofurazone, iodine, Merthiolate[R], or Bacitracin[R]. Cover the ointment with a sterile gauze pad and bandage. Be sure the dressing is taped carefully in place so the cat cannot easily reach the loose ends and untie it. Keep the bandage clean and dry, changing it every other day so that you can monitor the healing process. See a veterinarian if you suspect the wound is deep enough to require suturing (stitches). The sooner the veterinarian sees the wound, the better the chances for a surgical closure.

Abscesses

Wounds, especially bite or puncture wounds, are very prone to infection and formation of abscesses. Often, the first evidence that a cat has been in a fight is the hard, hot, painful swelling of an abscess appearing

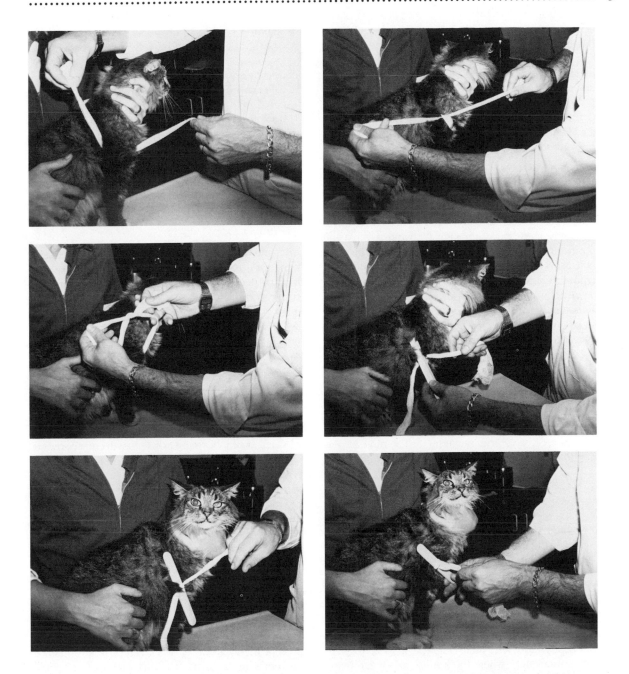

some time after the fact; the initial bite may have caused a small undetected hole.

Clip the fur around an abscess and clean the skin as described above. "Hot-pack" the area with a clean towel soaked in a solution made from a pint of hot water with two teaspoons of salt added. The water should be as warm as possible without being uncomfortable. Hold the compress on for ten to fifteen minutes as often as possible, the ideal being every two hours. Reheat the solution each time. The abscess may open, and pus should drain from the area within a day or two. When it does, rinse the wound with the salt solution, apply an antibiotic, and bandage the area loosely so as not to prevent drainage. It is wise to take any cat with an abscess to the veterinarian, particularly if the procedure described above has not resulted in drainage. The infection may have to be opened surgically and drained, and systemic antibiotics may be prescribed.

Deep Puncture Wounds

Deep puncture wounds to the chest are extremely hazardous. The great danger is that air or blood will enter the chest cavity through the wound, replacing the normal vacuum with a positive pressure that will collapse the lungs and cause the cat to suffocate within minutes. Try to cover this type of wound with an airtight seal, such as plastic or gauze. *Do not try to remove the penetrating object* (such as a garden stake), *or you may allow more air to enter.* Leave the object in place and treat for shock until you can get the cat to your veterinarian. Prompt attention is mandatory.

Eyes

Eyes are very delicate organs. Any injury to them should receive veterinary attention. The most important things you can do are:

1. Stop any bleeding. Use direct pressure with a gauze pad placed over the eye.
2. Keep the surface of the eye moist with contact lens solution, olive oil, or water.
3. Cover the eye lightly with sterile gauze.
4. Take the cat immediately to the veterinarian.

SHOCK

Shock is often difficult to recognize because it may not appear until after an accident, as much as eight to ten hours later, when the cat is no longer being watched closely. In shock, the volume of circulating blood is decreased or the blood vessels collapse, and the heart loses much of its ability to pump blood. This decreases the oxygen supply to the tissues. The body tries to compensate by speeding up the blood flow, increasing the oxygen flow to the blood, and reducing

or shutting off blood flow to nonvital organs. The signs of shock, listed below, reflect these changes:

1. Decrease in or loss of consciousness
2. Pale mucous membranes (gums, rims of the eyes, et cetera)
3. Body feels cold to touch
4. Feeble and rapid pulse (greater than 240 per minute)
5. Shallow and labored, but rapid breathing (greater than 40 per minute)
6. Inability to stand (sometimes, but not always)
7. Involuntary passage of urine and/or feces (not always)

Prompt supportive therapy must begin immediately if the cat is to recover from this collapse of the circulatory system. First stop the bleeding and give artificial respiration if breathing has stopped. Provide a warm, quiet environment and use cardiopulmonary resuscitation if needed. (*See* "Cardiopulmonary Resuscitation," page 347.) Make sure the cat is positioned on its side, with head lower than the rest of the body, so that gravity can assist blood flow to the brain. If the heart seems to be working on its own, massage the leg and trunk muscles to encourage blood return from these areas.

A cat in shock will frequently be thirsty, but giving it water could be dangerous. In severe shock, the digestive tract will not efficiently absorb water. A semiconscious cat may accidentally inhale rather than swallow water. The most effective way of increasing blood volume is by intravenous transfusion, which must be administered by a veterinarian.

INJURIES TO BONES

Fractures and dislocations usually are not life-threatening, unless they cause severe bleeding, interfere with breathing (as broken ribs may do), or crush a vital part of the spinal cord or brain. However, prompt immobilization of a fracture is important to prevent a simple break from turning into a compound fracture (one that breaks through the skin) or complicated fracture (one that may damage internal organs). A severe fracture also may cause shock; and complications of infection can lead to blood poisoning.

Recognizing a broken bone can be difficult. A cat with a broken leg will show pain and inability to use

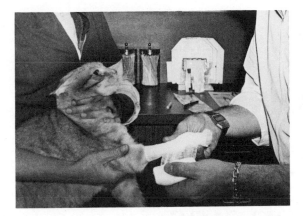 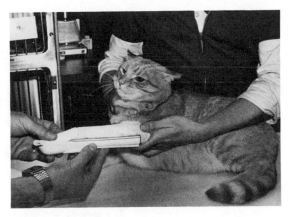

the leg. There may be swelling around the fracture site, or the cat might hold its leg at an unusual angle or show an unusual range of motion in the middle of a leg rather than at a joint. A sensation called "crepitus," a suggestion of grating or scraping, can be felt when the leg is moved gently. With spinal injuries, the cat will often be unable to use its legs. It is crucial to avoid aggravating the damage with movement or manipulation. If a break is suspected, do not try to verify it by physical manipulation. Immobilize the affected area, if possible, and quickly, gently, transport the cat to a veterinarian.

The most direct method of immobilizing a fractured leg is to apply a splint. Almost any long, stiff object can be used in an emergency. A simple cylinder of newspaper or a towel wrapped around the leg may suffice. When using sticks, there must be two, one on the inside and one on the outside of the leg.

Any hard object used should be padded so that it does not chafe the leg. *A splint will only be effective if it extends past and immobilizes the joints above and below the injury.* Tape the support in place, taking care not to make it so tight that it cuts off the circulation.

Fractures of the vertebral column and skull are serious, but these areas cannot be splinted. Place the cat in a padded box to avoid any unnecessary movement of the cat's body and head and take it to a veterinarian promptly.

Additional care is needed to prevent bacteria from entering the wound of a compound fracture. *Do not push the broken edges of bone back together*. Just cover the injury with a sterile cloth and apply the splint as previously described. Your veterinarian will do a more thorough cleanup and setting of the fracture site once the cat's condition has stabilized.

Procedures for Life-Threatening Emergencies

The best time to read this chapter is before an emergency arises. The first step to take when a cat is involved in a life-threatening situation is to dial the veterinarian's office, home, answering service, or an emergency clinic. Get help calmly and quickly.

PLANT POISONING

Japanese yew, mountain laurel, lily of the valley, philodendron, dieffenbachia —what do all of these ornamental plants have in common? Though all are beautiful, they all are potentially toxic when ingested, and cats are particularly susceptible. Fortunately, poisoning of cats by plants is relatively uncommon. Most outdoor cats have enough activity to keep them occupied, but bored house cats are somewhat more likely to chew on available plants. When plant poisoning does occur, it may be a life-threatening emergency, requiring quick action if the cat is to survive.

The list of plants potentially dangerous to cats is long. Some of the more common plants, the signs of poisoning, and suggested treatment are summarized in the Reference Guide (pages 354–56). In addition to the specific treatments given, a few general principles should be remembered. First and foremost, get the poisonous material out of the cat. Take the plant away if the cat is caught in the act. In most cases, try to induce vomiting to get the offending plant material out of the stomach.

Some easy ways to induce vomiting are:

1. Give ¼ teaspoon of syrup of ipecac once; or,
2. Give 1 teaspoon of a 1:1 mix of hydrogen peroxide and water (repeat a few times at twenty-minute intervals if needed).

If the source of poison is unknown, take the cat and *a sample of the vomitus* to the veterinarian immediately.

Do not induce vomiting in these cases:

- Plants that cause throat irritation, such as Dumb Cane (dieffenbachia) or philodendron, will burn just as much coming back up as they did going down, so it is safer to leave them in the stomach.
- Two hours after eating, most of the poison has probably entered the intestines or passed into the bloodstream, so making the animal vomit at that point does not help.
- If the cat is unconscious or semiconscious, chances are very good that it will inhale the vomit and suffocate.

Once the cat has vomited, try to inactivate any poison that may be left in its system. A crushed activated-charcoal tablet fed to the cat will *adsorb* (bind) to the toxins, so they can pass out of the body before being absorbed in the intestinal tract. This can be repeated several times at thirty-minute intervals. Do not confuse activated charcoal tablets (purchased from the drugstore) with charcoal dog biscuits marketed for mouth odor or charcoal briquets for a barbecue. Do not give activated charcoal in addition to syrup of ipecac, even if the cat has vomited; the two bind together and inactivate each other. Induce the conscious cat to drink as much lukewarm milk or water as possible. This will help dilute the toxins in the gastrointestinal tract. Milk has a soothing, coating effect on the intestines. If necessary, feed liquids carefully with an eyedropper.

Evaluate the cat's general appearance. Is it slipping into shock? Is it having trouble breathing? Keep the animal comfortable and warm. Give artificial respiration if necessary. (*See* Chapter 38: First Aid, pages 346–47.)

In all cases an immediate visit to the veterinarian is necessary to determine the severity of the poisoning or the presence of secondary complications or to administer specific antidotes.

Prevention. Undoubtedly the best treatment for plant poisoning is prevention. Keep poisonous plants hanging out of a cat's reach, or in a separate room that is off limits to animals. In the warm months, outdoor plants can carry chemical poisons. Highly toxic herbicides and organophosphate pesticides on grass clippings can be deadly. (*See* "Chemical Poisoning," below).

CHEMICAL POISONING

Fortunately, chemical poisoning is not a common occurrence among cats, possibly because of their finicky eating habits which often prevent them from ingesting substances that are harmful to them. However, two other qualities get them into trouble with poisonous agents. Cats are curious and fastidious animals. Curiosity can lead them into situations that are better left alone, such as walking across a wet, freshly disinfected or waxed floor to look out the window, or scampering across a lawn that has recently been sprayed with weed killer to chase a leaf. Fastidiousness can cause them to lick off the disinfectant, wax, or weed killer, no matter how unpleasant the taste. This indirect ingestion can be responsible for chemical poisoning.

Cats also can be indirectly affected either by catching and eating rats or mice that have eaten poisoned bait or by walking through tracking powders that then are ingested during grooming. Most of the rodenticides marketed today use anticoagulant chemicals rather than the more hazardous compounds of strychnine or fluoracetate. Cats are relatively resistant to anticoagulant rodenticides and would have to ingest large amounts. Anticoagulants must be eaten in sufficient amounts over an extended period of time to kill even a rodent. However, it can take as long as five days before signs are apparent. If any signs occur, call the veterinarian.

Tracking powders are more commonly used by professional exterminators. The tracking powders are more of a direct threat to cats, especially if the powders are placed in an area that is frequented by cats. The powders adhere to the feet and fur of both rodents and cats, and the poisons are then involuntarily ingested when the animal grooms itself. If you observe your cat ingesting rodenticide tracking powders, follow the instructions for inducing vomiting outlined below. Then the cat should be bathed to remove any residual poison on its body.

Sadly, cats may be inadvertently poisoned by owners who administer medications without first checking with their veterinarians. Severe reactions can be caused by giving an over-the-counter drug to a cat that is also receiving a prescription drug obtained from the veterinarian.

Inhalation accounts for another method of chemical poisoning. This usually occurs when a cat is unable to escape and has no choice but to breathe automobile exhaust fumes, sprayed pesticides, smoke, gas escaping from a heater or stove, or other toxic fumes.

REFERENCE GUIDE: FIRST AID FOR PLANT POISONING

TYPE OF ILLNESS	COMMON PLANTS	PLANT TOXINS	TREATMENT
A. UPPER GASTROINTESTINAL			
1. Oral and esophageal irritation; ulcers, swelling, and irritation in mouth and throat; excessive salivation. Swelling in throat may sometimes interfere with breathing.	Dieffenbachia Philodendron Caladium Skunk cabbage Jack-in-the-pulpit	Oxalate crystals and/or histamines	*DO NOT* induce vomiting. Give milk or water to wash out the animal's mouth and throat; an eyedropper is good for this, but make sure that you don't force liquid down the trachea. Usually this type of poisoning is not fatal, but if the animal seems to be having difficulty in breathing, take it to the veterinarian.
B. LOWER GASTROINTESTINAL			
2. Gastric irritation: violent vomiting and nausea immediately after eating the plant. May see central nervous system excitement followed by depression, coma, or death in severe cases.	Amaryllis Daffodil Tulip Wisteria Note: especially bulbs of all the above	Gastric irritants: possibly alkaloids	Induce vomiting. Give activated charcoal to adsorb (bind) the rest of the toxins. Give lots of water with an eyedropper, then give 1–3 tbsp. of milk to coat the intestines. Take the cat to the veterinarian.
3. Intestinal irritation: nausea and vomiting, abdominal pain, and diarrhea immediately after eating.	English ivy Alfalfa Beech Daphne Iris	Saponic glycosides Coumarin glycosides	Same as above. Induce vomiting, give activated charcoal and lots of water, then milk.
4. Nausea, vomiting, abdominal pain, and diarrhea immediately after eating.	Bird of paradise Box Crown of thorns English ivy Euonymus Honeysuckle	Other gastrointestinal irritants	Same as above. Induce vomiting, give activated charcoal and lots of water, then milk.
5. Vomiting, bloody diarrhea, abdominal pain after a latent period of up to 18–24 hours after eating. May see depression, fever, low blood pressure, coma or convulsions, even death.	Castor bean Precatory bean (rosary pea) Black locust	Toxalbumins	Induce vomiting. Give lots of fluid by mouth to help overcome dehydration. Get cat to the veterinarian as soon as possible; these plants are EXTREMELY toxic, and only one bean or pea may be fatal.

TYPE OF ILLNESS	COMMON PLANTS	PLANT TOXINS	TREATMENT
6. Vomiting, abdominal pain, bloody diarrhea, dry mouth, all after a latent period of 18–24 hours after plant was eaten. May proceed to nervous system stimulation followed by depression, i.e., trembling, salivation, and paralysis. May lead to cardiac arrest.	Nightshades Jerusalem cherry Potato (green parts and eyes)	Solanine glycosides	Induce vomiting if possible, but exercise caution: The gastrointestinal tract may already have suffered extensive damage that vomiting would exacerbate. Get the cat to your veterinarian promptly so that he or she can provide the necessary supportive therapy.

C. CARDIOVASCULAR

TYPE OF ILLNESS	COMMON PLANTS	PLANT TOXINS	TREATMENT
7. Slow, irregular heartbeat; intense vomiting, abdominal pain also seen a few hours after ingestion. Signs may progress to include excitement, followed by coma and death.	Foxglove Lily of the valley Oleander Monkshood Larkspur	Digitalis glycosides Alkaloids	Get the cat to the veterinarian at once. The digitalis glycosides have a severe depressant effect on the heart. *This is a life-threatening emergency.*
8. Labored breathing, collapse. May suffer muscle tics, terminal convulsions, and death.	Cherry pits Peach pits Apricot pits Almond pits Apple seeds Hydrangea	Cyanogenetic glycosides	Take the cat to the veterinarian *immediately*. Cyanide poisoning interferes with the ability of the blood to release oxygen into the tissues, so the cat effectively suffocates while its blood is full of oxygen. Your veterinarian will have the necessary chemical antidotes for this poison.

D. NERVOUS SYSTEM

TYPE OF ILLNESS	COMMON PLANTS	PLANT TOXINS	TREATMENT
9. Trembling, pupil dilation, heartbeat irregularities. Sudden death may occur with no prior signs. The signs will vary with the amount eaten. If only a small amount is ingested, you may see nausea, vomiting, and abdominal pain along with mild neurologic signs.	Yews, e.g., Japanese yew English yew Western yew American yew	Taxine (alkaloid)	Induce vomiting and get the cat to the veterinarian *immediately*. Yew is so poisonous that the most common finding is sudden death. Owners often do not even realize that the yew had been nibbled.
10. Rapid heartbeat, salivation, shaking, twitching, staggering, then difficult breathing and collapse within a few minutes to hours of eating plant.	Indian tobacco Golden chain Mescal bean Poison hemlock Tobacco	Nicotinic stimulants	Get the cat to the veterinarian *immediately*. Specific chemical injections are required to counteract the effects of nicotine poisoning.

TYPE OF ILLNESS	COMMON PLANTS	PLANT TOXINS	TREATMENT
11. Staggering, convulsions, salivation, vomiting, abdominal pain.	Rhubarb (leaves, upper stem)	Soluble oxalates	Induce vomiting, then take the cat to a veterinarian. The oxalates are absorbed into the bloodstream, interfering with body calcium (leading to convulsions) and may be deposited as crystals in the kidneys, causing extensive damage there.
12. Thirst, dry mucous membranes, dilated pupils, gastrointestinal upset, fast, weak heart, delirium, convulsions, coma, death.	Belladonna Henbane Jimsonweed Jessamine Datura	Atropinelike agents	Get the cat to the veterinarian *immediately*. Chemical antidotes and supportive care that only a veterinarian can provide are necessary to save the animal's life.
13. Alterations in behavior, violent convulsions and tremors.	Periwinkle Chinaberry Coriaria Moonseed Water hemlock Marijuana Morning glory	Other assorted neuroactive compounds	Induce vomiting and get the cat to the veterinarian. Specific antidotes and supportive care (oxygen, fluid therapy, tranquilizers) may be necessary.

Signs of Poisoning

Reactions to chemical poisoning are varied, depending on the kind of substance, the amount ingested or inhaled, and the previous condition of the cat. At one extreme, a cat may show intense excitement or convulsions; at the other extreme, there may be lethargy, even coma. Danger signs include excessive drooling, difficulty in breathing or swallowing, muscle spasms, trembling, vomiting, and diarrhea. A cat with carbon monoxide poisoning may have telltale bright red lips and tongue and will appear weak and dizzy. Obviously, any strange odor on the breath or body bears investigation, and a spilled container of chemicals or medicine may point to a toxic encounter.

A given amount of a toxic substance will generally have the strongest effect on kittens, old cats, and weak or sick cats. Every poison does not have a specific antidote, but certain emergency procedures can be successful if administered quickly.

The signs associated with anticoagulant poisoning include weakness, easy bruising of the skin, pale mucous membranes, difficulty in breathing, nosebleeds, and blood in vomitus and stools. However, it can take as long as five days before these signs are apparent. If you observe any of the aforementioned signs, schedule an appointment with a veterinarian. If possible, take samples of any bloody stools or vomit for analysis. The veterinarian may perform certain blood tests to determine the extent of the poisoning.

First Aid for Ingested Poisons

If a cat has been poisoned, someone must call immediately to alert the veterinarian that an emergency case is coming, while first-aid procedures are begun. Tell the veterinarian what type of poison is involved (if you know it), the cat's signs, what first-aid measures are being performed, and when the cat will arrive. *Note:* If the cat is convulsing or is unconscious, first aid is inadequate. Wrap the animal in a blanket and rush to the veterinarian without delay for expert attention.

In most cases, if the cat is conscious and is not

convulsing, induce vomiting. *Note: Do not* induce vomiting if the cat has swallowed an acid, an alkali, or kerosene. *See* the special section on these agents that follows.

The goal when inducing vomiting is to remove poison from the stomach before it can pass to the intestines and be absorbed into the bloodstream. Open the cat's mouth without tipping its head way back and pour in *one* of the following:

1. ¼ teaspoon of syrup of ipecac
2. 1 to 2 teaspoons of hydrogen peroxide
3. 1 tablespoon of dry mustard mixed in a cup of water. Give 1-teaspoonful doses.

Repeat or alternate these measures every five or ten minutes until the cat vomits. Save the vomit and especially the chemical container, if available. Bring these to the veterinarian to help identify the poison and choose specific treatment. To save time, one person may drive while another attempts to induce vomiting.

If there is no way to see a veterinarian, try to determine if there is a specific antidote to the poison— something that will neutralize or detoxify the poison that has already entered the bloodstream. Check the label on the container, if available, or call the nearest Poison Control Center, if the poison is known. *Note:* Some specific antidotes must be injected.

If no specific antidote is available, give water or milk, force-feeding if necessary, to dilute the poison already in the cat's system. If activated charcoal (the kind purchased in a pharmacy, not charcoal briquets) is available, mix several teaspoons into the liquid. The charcoal will adsorb (bind to) poison in the intestine, so that it is passed out of the body without entering the bloodstream. *Do not* use the charcoal if the cat has been given syrup of ipecac, for they will bind together and inactivate each other. Try coating the intestines to slow absorption. Feed the cat one to three tablespoons of vegetable oil or egg whites.

If the cat is severely depressed, try reviving it with one to five tablespoons of strong tea or coffee, but *never give liquids to an unconscious cat.* It may become necessary to give artificial respiration. (*See* Chapter 38: First Aid.) While traveling to the veterinary hospital, keep the cat warm and lower its head to allow liquids to drain out of the mouth.

Signs of warfarin (anticoagulant rodent poison) poisoning develop over a period of four to five days. These include depression, fever, skin discoloration, labored breathing, and prostration. The treatment consists of a blood transfusion and doses of vitamin K. Do not attempt to diagnose this condition and initiate vitamin therapy on your own. Chances of the cat's full recovery are very good if the condition is treated early.

Acids, Alkalis, and Kerosene

Acids, drain cleaners (alkalis), and kerosene will burn the mouth and throat both going down and coming up. Do not compound damage to the body by inducing vomiting. Instead, give the following general antidotes:

For acids: give antacids, e.g., baking soda solution or a single dose of one teaspoon milk of magnesia per five pounds of body weight.

For alkalis: give one to five teaspoons of a mixture of vinegar (or lemon juice) diluted with an equal part of water.

Acids, alkalis, and kerosene can be diluted in the system, and the intestines can be coated by giving oral doses of milk, vegetable oil, or egg whites.

First Aid for Inhaled Poisons

The first remedy for a cat that has inhaled deadly fumes is fresh air. Put the cat outside in the open air, regardless of the weather. Artificial respiration may be required. (*See* Chapter 38: First Aid.) A veterinarian will be able to administer oxygen and respiratory stimulants, if needed. Recovery generally occurs within a few hours, although temporary blindness or deafness has been known to occur, then disappear spontaneously within a matter of days or weeks.

Prevention

Keep toxic substances out of a pet's reach. If the label says "Keep out of the reach of children," then keep it out of the reach of cats, too.

Never give your cat medication that has not been approved by a veterinarian. If the cat is on a prescription drug, ask the veterinarian about possible toxic reactions before administering *any* additional medicines.

Keep the cat in the house until lawns that are freshly sprayed with insecticide or fertilizer have

---

COMMON HOUSEHOLD POISONS

Acetaminophen (Tylenol)	Drain Cleaner	Lye	Rat Poison
Antifreeze, Coolants	Dye	Matches	Rubbing Alcohol
Aspirin	Fungicides	Metal Polish	Shoe Polish
Bleach	Furniture Polish	Mineral Spirits	Sleeping Pills
Boric Acid	Gasoline	Mothballs	Snail or Slug Bait
Brake Fluid	Hair Coloring	Nail Polish and Remover	Soaps and Detergents
Carbon Monoxide	Herbicides	Paint	Suntan Lotion
Carburetor Cleaner	Insecticides	Paint Remover	Tar
Cleaning Fluid	Kerosene	Permanent Wave Lotion	Turpentine
Deodorants, Deodorizers	Laxatives	Phenol	Windshield Washer Fluid
Diet Pills	Lead	Photographic Developers	Wood Preservatives
Disinfectants			

---

dried. However, rain will dilute the poison sufficiently to remove danger, allowing the animal to go out afterwards. Some pesticides are toxic to humans and animals. No one should remain in the vicinity where they are being sprayed.

Open the garage door when warming a car engine. Animals could be napping or even trapped inside. Noxious fumes can be deadly for both animals and humans. Maintain good ventilation in any area when working with chemicals that give off fumes, and be certain stoves and furnaces have no gas leaks. Common sense goes a long way toward keeping a cat sound and healthy.

HEAT STROKE

What is moderately hot for a human being can be deadly for a cat. Unfortunately, cats are intolerant of high environmental temperatures that their owners easily withstand. Human body temperature is reduced by releasing sweat at the surface of the skin. A cat's only defenses against high temperatures are rapid breathing and licking its fur. If a cat is exposed to a situation where the air is warmer than its internal temperature (anything over 102.2°F), heat stroke (hyperthermia) is inevitable. Feline deathtraps are poorly ventilated cars parked in the sun, restriction to concrete runs without shade, or confinement to cat carriers in hot weather. Short-nosed cats (such as Persians), asthmatic cats, and overweight cats are especially susceptible to heat stroke.

On a hot summer day, a cat may be on the verge of heat stroke if it suddenly begins rapid breathing, panting, salivating, or vomiting. These signs should be considered a serious warning.

Treatment

A mild case of heat stroke can be treated by immersing the cat in cool water or wrapping it in cool, wet towels to reduce its body temperature. However, if the cat shows signs of weakness or overheating, it should be taken to a veterinarian for treatment. It may be given oxygen to prevent brain damage, fluid therapy to correct dehydration, various treatments to reduce the body temperature below 103°F, and other supportive care. In severe cases, blood may flow from the cat's nostrils. This may be indicative of *disseminated intravascular coagulopathy* (DIC), a bleeding disorder precipitated by prolonged, excess body heat. If the cat reaches this stage, response to therapy is poor.

Prevention

Always provide adequate ventilation for a cat when traveling in a car. When parking a vehicle, locate it in a heavily shaded area and keep the windows open; but preferably do not leave cats, or any animal, in a parked vehicle. Always provide plenty of fresh drinking water. Long-haired cats with matted coats will dissipate body heat better if they are clipped for the summer months.

Humans tolerate heat better than cats. If the weather is hot for humans, it is worse for cats.

BURNS AND FROSTBITE

There are many causes of burns: contact with flame or direct heat, flying cinders and sparks, steam, hot liquids, spattered cooking oil, hot tar, and caustic chemicals.

Burns are classified as either major or minor, superficial or deep. Major burns cover more than 5 percent of the body surface. A superficial burn affects only the surface skin. A deep burn damages or destroys the deeper layers of skin and possibly the underlying tissues. A deep burn may destroy the hair follicles, so that scar tissue will form and the fur will be permanently gone.

Secondary effects of burns can be destructive, even fatal. These include shock, infection because of exposure of the wound to bacterial invasion, and toxemia from the absorption of poisons produced by the damaged cells or bacteria.

Intensive, prolonged care is necessary for a cat that has been deeply burned. Recovery from deep burns is possible, with proper therapy, if 15 percent or less of the body surface is affected.

Thermal Burns

Thermal burns are injuries caused by contact with flames, hot objects, or hot liquids. Chemical or electric burns are classified separately. Household accidents are the most common causes of thermal burns, a large portion of which occur in the kitchen. A cat may be spattered by hot grease from a frying pan or scalded by boiling water, or the footpads may be burned by walking across a hot stove. These accidents are often the result of carelessness by the owner and could be avoided if dangerous items were kept out of the pet's reach.

When the skin is burned, the small blood vessels dilate, allowing fluid to escape and accumulate in the surrounding tissues, causing localized swelling. Some fluid comes to the surface, making the burned area moist and red. If the burns are massive and the protective layer of skin is completely absent, the rapid loss of fluid may cause severe shock.

When a cat has been scalded by hot liquid or steam, the hair and skin are still in place. In this instance, the size of the burn can be determined by the red appearance and by the fact that it will feel hot to the touch. Fluid released by the blood vessels after a scalding may mat the hair over the wound, hiding the damage. This can give harmful bacteria time to multiply. An infection and accumulation of pus may be hidden for some time. Later, the cat shows signs of illness.

An injured cat characteristically becomes very defensive and may resist attempts to help it, because of fear and pain. An owner must be prepared to restrain the cat in order to treat the burn. One's priorities should be to relieve pain, prevent or treat shock, prevent infection, and stimulate healing.

Treatment of Superficial Burns. To relieve the pain of a superficial burn, apply ice packs or immerse the affected area in cold water. Dry gently. If possible, remove the hair from around the wound to minimize chances of infection.

Do not apply butter or any oil-based ointment; these may intensify the burning sensation. Also, *do not* apply human medications; these may be toxic if licked by the cat.

Instead, apply a thin film of an antibiotic such as a topical ophthalmic (eye) ointment or one of the following home remedies: some "jelly" from the inside of the leaf of an aloe vera ("burn") plant; or a wet dressing of Burrow's solution made with water and Domebro tablets or powder, available at most pharmacies. Either of these home remedies will reduce pain and inflammation when applied repeatedly to keep the injured area moist.

Cover the area with a clean dressing, held in place with a bandage. Take the cat to a veterinarian for further examination and treatment if the burn is serious. Otherwise, check the bandage daily. If the burn becomes infected or doesn't begin to heal within several days, it is time to see the veterinarian.

Treatment of Deep Burns. Extensive or deep burns need immediate veterinary attention. Call ahead to make sure a veterinarian will be ready and able to treat the cat as soon as it arrives; this will save precious time.

Meanwhile, soak a clean cloth in cold water and apply it very gently to the burned area. Keep the patient warm and monitor for signs of shock as you transport it to the veterinarian. Protect the wet dressing with thick, clean, dry bandages or towels and keep the cat calm during the journey.

In cases of severe burns, the victim loses a great

amount of fluid. The veterinarian may choose to establish an intravenous route of fluid therapy to counteract this loss.

If for some reason it is impossible to obtain immediate veterinary treatment, clean the visible debris or foreign matter out of the wound with simple contact-lens solution or a sterile salt solution. This can be made by adding one teaspoon of salt to one pint of boiled water and allowing it to become lukewarm. Sterile distilled water can take the place of the boiled water. If the injury is dirty or greasy, first cleanse it gently with soap and warm water, then with the saline solution.

Electrical Burns

Electrical burns are perhaps the most dangerous kind and are often fatal. They are usually caused by chewing through a plugged-in appliance cord, lightning, or coming into contact with an improperly insulated appliance. Electrical burns most often happen at the corners of the mouth or on the tip of the tongue, appearing as red, sometimes blistered flesh, which is painful to the touch for the cat. The burn itself is not nearly as life-threatening as the electric shock that accompanies it. Cats may be jolted into cardiac arrest and death.

A slower developing, equally treacherous complication is *pulmonary edema*. It is a build-up of excessive fluid in the lungs, which can appear an hour after the electric shock occurs, and, if untreated, can be fatal. Any animal that has suffered an electrical burn should be taken directly to the veterinarian, even if there are no apparent complications. An electrical burn is a life-threatening emergency. Brain or nerve damage is a strong possibility, and, in most cases, the cat does not survive without immediate veterinary attention.

Do not attempt to treat the actual burn at home. The other complications are far more serious, so the cat should be seen by a veterinarian as soon as possible.

The first priority is to treat the animal for shock. It is highly possible that the cat will need cardiopulmonary resuscitation. (*See* "Cardiopulmonary Resuscitation," Chapter 38: First Aid.) Have another person alert the veterinarian that the cat is on its way.

Signs of shock may include respiratory distress, a pale or blue color to the lips, gums, and lining of the eyelids, stiffness in the limbs, a glassy stare, and perhaps total collapse. As the cat goes into shock, its temperature drops rapidly. It is imperative to keep the cat warm, using a heating pad, hot-water bottle, or warm blanket.

Prevention. Decrease the possibility of electrical shocks by unplugging all appliances that are not in use. Young animals (up to about eighteen months of age) can be expected to gnaw on electrical cords and other items. Especially during these early months, they should not be left unattended near potential sources of electric shock.

Chemical Burns

There are two general types of chemicals that cause burns: acids (e.g., turpentine, toilet bowl cleaners) and alkalis (e.g., lye, drain cleaners, caustic soda). A strange odor may be one of the first telltale signs that a cat has come in contact with one of these agents. Either kind of chemical will cause painful redness of the skin and may even eat away the skin if left on for an extended period of time. The cat may further injure itself by licking at the noxious substance. It is important to wash the chemical from the skin quickly, soothe and protect the injury, and obtain veterinary care.

Wear rubber gloves to cleanse the corrosive substance from the animal. Wash away acids with an alkaline solution, consisting of one teaspoon bicarbonate of soda dissolved in one pint of warm water. Wash away alkalis with an acidic solution, consisting of equal parts of vinegar and warm water. These opposing types of solutions will neutralize the chemical causing the burn. If the nature of the chemical is unknown, wash the area with plain water.

Check the chemical container, if available, to see if a specific antidote is listed, and if so, apply it to the burned area. If this is not possible, apply one of the home remedies mentioned for thermal burns (*see* page 359) to soothe pain.

When the cat's face and eyes are burned, restrain its body in a thick blanket, if possible. A second person may be necessary to help with treatment. Hold the eyelids open and gently flush them with copious amounts of lukewarm water. A bulb syringe will help guide the water directly into the eyes. Eyes are extremely fragile and must be treated as quickly and gently as possible. As soon as the caustic substance has been removed, take the cat to a veterinary hospital.

Frostbite

Frostbite and freezing cause tissue damage similar to burns. They occur when an animal is exposed for a long period to extreme cold and high winds. Circulation becomes impaired in the extremities (ears, tail, feet) and ice crystals form in the tissues, causing major damage. The affected area may first turn very pale, then, after thawing, become red and scaly. Frostbite causes severe pain; therefore, handle an affected cat with extreme care.

First, move the cat to a warm place. Use moist, warm packs or a warm blow-dryer to bring the temperature of the affected area rapidly back to normal. Do not use excessive heat and *do not rub the frozen areas. This may cause further damage or loss of tissue.* Apply an antiseptic such as eye ointment to the affected area. Call a veterinarian; he or she may prescribe oral antibiotics to prevent or fight infection, and sedatives for pain.

It may take five to ten days before new tissue can be seen replacing the dead, frozen tissue. If healing is not evident, there is a danger of gangrene, and some amputation may be necessary.

In the case of serious freezing, the entire body temperature will be dangerously low and the cat may be comatose and near death. Quickly reverse this decline by immersing the cat in *warm,* not hot, water (102°F–105°F, 39°C–41°C). Dry very gently and thoroughly with a warm blow-dryer, then wrap the cat snugly for warmth. Treat signs of shock and take the animal quickly to a veterinarian. If you are snowbound and cannot get out, try to feed the conscious cat frequent small amounts of warm broth or other warm liquid.

Frostbite and freezing can be prevented by keeping the cat indoors in times of extreme cold or by ensuring access to a sheltered dry area in a barn, garage, or porch. Once affected, animals are more prone to frostbite in the future, so recovered animals should be carefully protected during future cold weather.

INSECT STINGS

Insect stings, particularly those of wasps and bees, are a hazard. Cats are fascinated by movement and will jump and snap at wasps or bees, often getting stung in the process. Resultant swelling can be severe and dangerous, especially in the mouth or throat. Swelling within the mouth or throat, or pressure caused by swelling on the neck, can block the air passages and threaten suffocation. Swelling of mucous membranes in the mouth leads to excessive salivation and difficulty in eating. Ice packs will help to reduce swelling, but persistent swelling indicates a systemic, possibly allergic reaction, which should be treated *immediately* by a veterinarian.

For a simple bee sting, the first course of action is to remove the stinger. If it is a wasp or bee sting in the mouth, wash the mouth with a mixture of one teaspoon baking soda to one pint of water. If the sting is on the skin, gently swab the painful area with rubbing alcohol. Immediately apply a paste of baking soda and water to help relieve the itching. Use this treatment for all types of insect bites that cause a mild, local reaction.

Ticks are prevalent in wooded areas in the summer. These parasites fasten onto the cat's body, embed their heads into the skin and suck blood, eventually swelling up to resemble a coffee bean. To remove a tick, cover it with an alcohol-soaked piece of cotton; never try to burn it with a match or cigarette. After a few minutes it should begin to back out of the cat's skin. Lift it off with tweezers, taking care to keep the head intact. Fragments of the head which remain in the skin can cause infection. Place the tick in a jar of alcohol to kill it, then flush it down the toilet. Swab the affected area of skin with alcohol and let it dry.

DROWNING

This is a seldom reported cause of accidental death in cats. Most cases occur in young animals that fall into a water bowl, a deep pool of rainwater, backyard swimming pools, streams, or rivers. If they cannot find the steps, as in a pool, or otherwise cannot climb to safety until rescued, then they will drown. Rescue and first-aid measures should be tried and are aimed at getting the water out of, and air back into, the lungs. Holding the cat up by the hind legs will get rid of most of the water. Begin CPR by gentle chest compression and mouth-to-mouth resuscitation. If the water is cold, then warming the cat in warm water or with blankets

may help; then take the cat to the veterinarian as fast and safely as possible.

HIGH-RISE SYNDROME

Cats fall from heights so frequently in big cities, especially in warm climates, that a new feline trauma syndrome has been identified: High-rise Syndrome (HRS). There is an increase in cases seen during the summer and fall. In air-conditioned buildings, incidents of HRS have been related to a window or screen being left open or an air-conditioning unit being replaced or cleaned. Most owners doubt, at first, that their pets have actually fallen. Instead, they report that the cat has run out an open door into the street where it was the victim of a traffic accident. In cases where owners have seen their pets fall, some report that the cat was sleeping in the sun one minute, and then rolled off the railing, or fell as it leaped for a bird and missed.

Cats can fall from great heights and survive. Some of the stories recorded at the Henry Bergh Memorial Hospital of the ASPCA in New York City reveal that cats have survived falls from as high as eighteen stories onto such surfaces as concrete, asphalt, dirt, and car roofs. One cat fell twenty stories onto shrubbery; another fell twenty-eight stories onto an awning. These are not exaggerations. It is quite possible that other cats, elsewhere, have survived longer, higher, more spectacular falls.

Cats have an efficient balancing mechanism and usually fall in an upright position with their legs extended and head down, landing on their feet. A triad of injuries has been observed that are symptomatic of the manner in which cats fall and land.

The three main injuries are epistaxis (bleeding from the nose), a split in the hard palate (the roof of the mouth), and pneumothorax (air in the chest, outside the lungs). When a cat hits the ground, its legs break the fall, but the lower jaw impacts on the upper jaw, splitting the hard palate, with resultant bleeding from the nose. Broken canine teeth also result from the chin hitting the ground, and the lower jaw may be fractured, too. The force of impact on the legs can cause fractures of one or both rear legs or of smaller bones in the front legs. The chest often hits the ground, forcing free air out of the lungs and into the chest, which makes breathing difficult.

Since HRS has been recognized and its major associated injuries have been identified, cats that suffer long falls have an increased chance of survival, because veterinarians know what problems to look for and how to treat them. The first step should be a quick, nonstressful physical exam with primary emphasis on diagnosing and treating pneumothorax. If such a condition is found, the veterinarian can place a tube into the chest to remove the trapped air and allow the lungs to expand more fully. The tube can be left in place so air can be drawn off periodically if needed. This traumatic pneumothorax usually re-

solves itself in time, as the cat stabilizes and heals the tears in its lung tissues. Once the cat is breathing more easily, a more detailed exam can be given to evaluate any fractures. These are repaired in a routine manner. It is important for veterinarians to check the hard palate in HRS cases, because fractures in this region may go undetected. Once found, they can generally be repaired without complications.

High-rise Syndrome is an urban problem, one that is more difficult to prevent than it would seem. One must be cautious when leaving an animal on a patio or near an open window. Providing a short, protective barrier along outside railings or ledges, or screens wedged in front of child window guards, might prevent a fall. There is no more effective preventive measure than closed windows and doors.

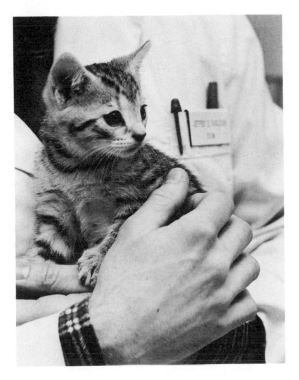

Zoonotic Diseases: From Cats to Humans

S
ociety is reevaluating the role of pets. This is evident from the increasing prevalence of signs excluding animals from public places and by public outcry over the aesthetics and health aspects of animal excrement in parks and streets. New concerns about pet involvement in human disease have arisen from well-publicized findings that cats are a definitive host for the parasite causing toxoplasmosis. Concerns have also risen from unproven assertions such as feline leukemia virus is involved in human cancer, or that the ownership of small dogs is related to the development of multiple sclerosis. There is a significant portion of the population that does not enjoy the companionship of dogs and cats and may be all too ready to implicate them as the cause of real or imagined human ills.

A review of current knowledge of pet-associated human diseases will provide a basis for scientifically acceptable pet management. Some generalizations are appropriate to introduce the topic.

People contract most infectious diseases from other people. However, they can acquire some diseases from pets and sometimes these have tragic outcomes. There are over two hundred zoonoses (animal diseases transmissible to man). Of these, only a few are associated with pets. The magnitude of the problem is largely unappreciated because only the tip of the zoonotic-disease iceberg is visible, and because most pet-borne zoonoses are "dead-end" situations with little subsequent person-to-person transmission. In addition, many pet-borne diseases have nondescript and subtle signs that make an accurate diagnosis difficult. Unless animal association is obvious, the case is unusually severe, or a unique clustering of cases results in an investigation, pet-associated diseases are usually underreported.

VIRAL DISEASES

Rabies

Rabies is probably the most feared of the zoonotic diseases, in spite of the low number of human cases reported in the United States over the past several years.

Although rabies is prevalent in the wildlife population of the country (foxes, skunks, raccoons, and bats are the primary wildlife reservoirs in the United States), man is at a greater risk of acquiring rabies from pet animals because of his closer association with them.

When a rabid animal bites a victim, rabies virus is introduced into the wound. It first grows locally in the muscle cells at the site, and after a variable period of time invades the peripheral nerve(s) supplying the area. The virus travels along the nerve until it reaches the central nervous system, where its presence causes the clinical signs associated with rabies. From the central nervous system, the virus next extends to certain peripheral tissues, such as the salivary glands, where it is shed in the saliva and can introduce the disease into a new host.

In most animals, rabies is characterized by behavioral changes (agitation, restlessness, excitability progressing to aggression) and unexplained paralysis. Sometimes only paralysis is seen.

Cats are highly susceptible to rabies and about 75 percent of rabid cats show a pronounced furious phase before progressive paralysis sets in. This makes them particularly dangerous transmitters of rabies, as their attacks may be exceptionally vicious, inflicting deep puncture wounds.

In 1981, for the first time, rabid cats in the United States outnumbered rabid dogs, by approximately 30 percent. Investigation of sixty-four rabid cats in Iowa in 1981 revealed that none had a history of rabies vaccination. Only dogs are required by many state and county health codes to be vaccinated. This is an unfortunate state of affairs, since cats, especially young males during their nighttime prowling activities, are frequently exposed to rabid wildlife (especially skunks and bats). Reports of documented animal rabies more than doubled in the United States in the three years between 1978 and 1981. Vaccination of pets and livestock is the most effective control measure in preventing disease and subsequent human exposure.

There are a number of effective rabies vaccines available for use in cats. Care must be exercised to use *only* a product that is *licensed* for use in cats, as rabies has actually been produced by vaccinating cats with modified live-virus vaccines intended for use in dogs. Kittens should be vaccinated at three months of age and revaccinated one year later at fifteen months, after which they should receive annual or triennial boosters. (*See* "Rabies," Chapter 29: Viral Diseases.)

Cowpox in Man

Cowpox in man, which is a mild skin eruption, has been reported recently from Holland and the United Kingdom as an infection apparently acquired from domestic cats, among other sources. The cowpox virus, or a closely related virus, probably circulates in a rodent reservoir such as wood mice and voles. In cats, the original lesion is often observed around a bite, which suggests that the cat could acquire the infection from an animal source while hunting. Cowpox is not known to exist in the United States.

BACTERIAL DISEASES

Animal Bites

Animal bites are the most common pet-associated human-health problem in the United States. Approximately one of every 170 people in the country is bitten each year. Children are the most frequent victims because of their small size and their greater tendency to engage in bite-provoking activity. While rarely fatal, animal bites are painful and expensive. (The Maryland State Department of Health and Hygiene reports an average cost to the victim of $150 per bite.)

Pasteurella wound infection is a frequent consequence of bite wounds. Caused by a bacterium that is normally found in the mouths of cats and dogs, the infection causes swelling, inflammation, and intense pain within a few hours after the bite. (*See* "Pasteurellosis," Chapter 30: Bacterial Diseases.)

Dysgonic fermenter-2 (DF-2) is a recently recognized bacterium that has been isolated in 8 to 10 percent of cat mouths. It is an organism of low virulence, usually causing illness only in people with impaired defense mechanisms against infection, such as those whose spleens have been removed.

Other diseases, less common, but still occasionally associated with bites, include tetanus, staphylococcal infection, tularemia (a plaguelike disease), erysipeloid (a skin infection), and bubonic plague.

Campylobacter Enteritis

It has only been within the last few years that the bacterial organism *Campylobacter jejuni* has been recognized as an important cause of enteric (small-intestinal) disease in humans. Patients have symptoms of fever, headache, abdominal pain, and other body aches, followed by severe diarrhea, which becomes watery and often bloody. The illness is reported to last from a few days to three weeks.

Information is still emerging on the sources of infection for man. Domestic poultry have been shown to be carriers of the organism, and recent work has implicated contact with infected household pets as another source of infection for man. Isolation rates of *Campylobacter jejuni* from domestic cats have varied from 2 to 45 percent depending on the age and location of the population studied. Most isolations have been made from kittens, and disease in man has been reported after contact with kittens with diarrhea. However, a case in a young woman was recently reported in which her infection was acquired from an apparently healthy adult cat. When the patient changed brands of cat litter, the cat ceased to use its litter pan and began soiling the floor. The patient evidently became infected while cleaning up after her pet. When a cat uses a litter pan, humans have reduced exposure to the feces, and to some extent, the litter has a drying effect on the organism, which also reduces the chances of human exposure. Since litter boxes are commonly used for cats, infected animals are an unlikely source of infection for man, but it is obvious from this case that the potential is there. (*See* "Campylobacteriosis," Chapter 30: Bacterial Diseases.)

Cat-Scratch Fever

This disease of humans, associated with the scratch of a cat, has been convincingly shown to be caused by a bacterial agent. Within one to two weeks of a cat scratch, a primary inoculation lesion develops at the site of the injury. Seven to twenty days following the injury, the local lymph node(s) swell, become painful, and may abscess. Many patients have mild fever, loss of appetite, generalized pains, and other systemic signs. The enlargement of the lymph nodes may last from a few weeks to several months and may be confused with other diseases such as infectious

mononucleosis or lymphosarcoma. Most patients recover with no complications. Over 99 percent of cat-scratch fever cases report contact with cats. Some students of the disease believe that cats are only mechanical transmitters of cat-scratch fever and are not themselves infected. Now that a causative agent has been isolated, it should be possible to determine the mechanism whereby man becomes infected. (*See* "Cat-Scratch Disease," Chapter 30: Bacterial Diseases.)

Chlamydiosis

Feline chlamydiosis causes sneezing, and nasal and ocular discharges in infected kittens or cats. Direct contact with these infected animals has been shown to cause conjunctivitis (inflammation of the tissues around the eye) in humans. (*See* "Feline Chlamydiosis," Chapter 24: Respiratory System and Disorders.)

Lyme Disease

Lyme disease is a serious health hazard for humans and their pets, as well as for many wild and domestic animals. It has been reported in over forty states. This tick-borne disease is rarely fatal but causes serious medical harm when it is not diagnosed and treated in its early stage. House cats that are allowed to roam freely outdoors can be exposed to infected ticks and inadvertently carry them home to humans.

Lyme disease was first identified in 1975 in Lyme, Connecticut, hence its name. The condition is produced by a bacterium, the spirochete *Borrelia burgdorferi* that is carried by the tiny deer tick *(Ixodes dammini)* in the northeastern and central United States. In addition to the deer tick the California black-legged tick *(Ixodes pacificus)* has also been identified as a carrier in the western United States but to a lesser degree. The lone star tick *(Amblyomma americanum)* has been identified as an additional carrier in New Jersey and farther south. The rapid spread of Lyme disease is attributed to migrating birds which may be transporting the infected ticks.

Symptoms of the disease are varied and extensive. Three stages are usual in humans, often beginning with a red rash around the skin where the tick was attached. The rash appears as a large circle swollen in the center. Other symptoms may include weakness, fatigue, headaches, chills, fever, pains in the joints, and stiff neck.

When left untreated the symptoms may disappear only to recur several months later in a second stage with greater intensity plus dizziness, irregular heartbeat, and painful discomfort throughout the musculoskeletal system. The third stage may appear months or even years after the initial episode with possible skin ailments, paralysis, disorders of the nervous system, eye and ear problems, breast tumors, stomach disorders, cardiac symptoms, and most notably, arthritis of the large joints.

The white-footed mouse serves as a repository for the bacterium *B. burgdorferi,* which is asymptomatic in the mouse. A tick in its larval stage five days after hatching attaches itself to the mouse. The tick ingests the bacteria as it drinks the mouse's blood. In the second year of the infected tick's existence it seeks another blood meal from any available animal including deer, rodents, birds, dogs, cats, or humans. It will stay attached for three to ten days to satisfy its needs before dropping off. The *B. burgdorferi* spirochetes are thus transmitted to the tick's host, which could be an animal or a human. However, the host is not invaded by the spirochetes instantly. Infection may not occur for hours after the tick has attached itself to the host.

Treatment for Lyme disease consists of antibiotic therapy, reported to be more effective in the first stage of the disease. Early detection and prevention are the most important factors for dealing with this wide-spreading disease. Avoid tick-infested areas. Stay alert for tick bites. Consult a doctor and follow all medical instructions when early symptoms appear following a possible tick bite.

Rocky Mountain Spotted Fever

Rocky Mountain Spotted Fever is an infectious disease caused by the microorganism *Rickettsia rickettsii.* It is transmitted to humans and other vertebrates by the wood tick, *Dermacentor andersoni,* the dog tick, *Dermacentor variabilis,* the lone star tick, *Amblyomma americanum,* and the rabbit tick, *Haemaphysalis leporispalustris.* Although cats occasionally transmit ticks, they do not contract the disease. It was first reported in the Rocky Mountain states, hence its name. Cases have been reported throughout the United States, Canada, Mexico, and Central and South America.

The first symptoms occur several days following the bite of an infected tick. They begin with chills, fever, muscle pain, weakness, and headache. Three to five days later a spotted rash appears on parts of the hands and feet, progressing to the back, and eventually to the entire body. The spots may bleed, causing profuse reddish eruptions. Antibiotic treatment is effective. Untreated cases may be fatal.

Salmonellosis

Salmonellosis is an intestinal disease caused by the bacterial organisms of the *Salmonella* family. The most common route of infection is oral ingestion of contaminated water or foodstuffs. Birds and rodents serve as important sources of exposure. A recent outbreak in the northeastern United States occurred in cats that had either eaten sick birds or had been around bird feeders, after which they developed "songbird fever." The affected cats were depressed, off their feed, and had high fevers, with vomiting and diarrhea (often bloody) reported in some cases. Salmonellosis can spread to humans and is of public health significance. The organisms may be shed orally, conjunctivally, and in the feces. (*See* "Salmonellosis," Chapter 30: Bacterial Diseases.)

Plague

We usually think of plague in association with epidemics of "black death" in residents of medieval cities, but the disease also exists in the wild rodent population in the western United States, where sporadic cases of bubonic plague in man are associated with exposure to rabbits and rodents, or their fleas. Cats also can acquire plague under natural circumstances through contact with infected rodents or their fleas and have transmitted the disease to man on a number of occasions. Infected cats appear acutely ill, manifesting signs such as a loss of appetite, lethargy, and fever, and frequently a draining abscess or lymph node; a pneumonia may also be present. Cats can be involved in spreading the disease to man in a number of ways. They may mechanically transport infected rodent fleas into their owner's home or, additionally, may carry infected rodents from the wild to human residences. If the cat itself becomes infected, it can infect man by direct contact. Case reports would indicate that man can acquire the disease either following a bite wound from an infected cat or from nonbite contact with cats having plague pneumonia. Both humans and cats respond to treatment with broad-spectrum antibiotics if initiated early in the course of the disease. While it is not a disease of national importance, owners and veterinarians should keep plague in mind when handling cats from areas where the disease exists in rodents. *Any case of plague must be reported to the public health department.* (*See* "Plague," Chapter 30: Bacterial Diseases.)

Q Fever

Q fever (Q for query) is a zoonosis caused by the rickettsial (a specialized bacteria) *Coxiella burnetti,* which is endemic in many parts of the world. Cattle, sheep, and goats are the primary animal reservoirs of infection. In Nova Scotia, Q fever is endemic in rural areas, where it causes up to 20 percent of community-acquired pneumonia, requiring hospitalization. The infection is associated with exposure to products of feline parturition (giving birth). The mechanism of human exposure is inhalation of the organisms, which may then cause pneumonia.

FUNGAL DISEASES

Ringworm

Ringworm is a superficial infection of the keratinized areas of the body (hair, skin, and nails) caused by several varieties of fungi. The two most important species affecting the dog and cat are *Trichophyton mentagrophytes* and *Microsporum canis.* Both species can infect man. *Microsporum canis* is very well adapted to cats, and in approximately 90 percent of infected animals, no evident lesions can be seen. When lesions do occur, they are most often on the face and claws.

The disease is transmitted to man by direct contact with infected animals or indirectly by spores in the hair and scales shed from such animals. Ringworm acquired from cats commonly infects the scalp or the body. On the scalp it begins with a papule (small bump), the hair becomes brittle, and the infection spreads in a wider circle, leaving scaly bald patches. On the body there are similar lesions, with a tendency to form rings with reddish borders.

Since infected cats are so frequently without any clinical signs, this can be a difficult disease to avoid. Cats that appear to be healthy can be examined with an ultraviolet light, which gives a brilliant greenish-blue fluorescence from hairs infected with *Microsporum.* (*See* "Ringworm," Chapter 17: Skin and Disorders.)

PARASITES

The human reactions to shared external parasites are listed in Chapter 19: External Parasites.

Toxoplasmosis

Almost all carnivorous species can become infected wtih *Toxoplasma gondii* by eating raw meat containing infective forms of this protozoan organism. Cats are unusual in that they are the only animals in which the organism can complete its complex life cycle and be excreted in the feces. Depending on environmental conditions, the form of the organism shed in the feces becomes infective in the soil in one to four days and is a potential source of infection for carnivores, noncarnivores, and man.

In the cat, signs of *Toxoplasma* infection vary from being inapparent to such clinical manifestations as weight loss, fever, diarrhea, pneumonia, encephalitis, and ocular disease. The infection may be fatal in young kittens. Older cats usually survive.

In man, *Toxoplasma* infection is usually inapparent. Sometimes primary infection is associated with fever, lethargy, and lymph node enlargement. Infection of the eye, with subsequent loss of sight, may occur. The most severe consequence of human toxoplasmosis is fetal infection, acquired transplacentally (through the placenta) when a pregnant woman undergoes primary infection. Following transplacental infection, babies can be normal and healthy at birth. Sometimes, however, fetal death or abortion occurs. In addition, children can be born at term with ocular disorders, mental retardation, cleft palate, or neurological defects, or they may not show any signs of illness until the second or third decade of life.

Discovery that the cat is the natural host of toxoplasmosis aroused concern about cats as a hazard to human health. For a time controversial and confusing recommendations were forthcoming, but further research has put the hazard of cats as an immediate source of *Toxoplasma* infection for man in a much less alarming perspective. In controlling transmission of toxoplasmosis to man, the first concern should be the most probable source of the infection, which is ingestion of incompletely cooked meat. The second concern would be hand-washing after handling raw meat. Cat feces cannot be totally disregarded as a hazard, however. If they contain *Toxoplasma* oocysts and have incubated under appropriate conditions for one to four days, they can be infective for man and remain so for more than a year. Areas known to be contaminated with cat feces should be avoided. Sandboxes should be covered when not in use. Pregnant women must be particularly cautious; they should not clean litter pans or sandboxes, and they should wear gloves while gardening. Since the *Toxoplasma* oocysts require one to four days to become infective after being shed in the feces, daily emptying of litter pans and proper disposal of their contents is an excellent control measure. (*See* "Toxoplasmosis," Chapter 31: Internal Parasites.)

Cutaneous Larva Migrans

Eggs of several species of hookworms affecting dogs and cats are passed in the feces of these animals; under favorable environmental conditions (wet, sandy soils and warm temperatures), they develop into infectious larvae, which can penetrate the skin of people in contact with the contaminated soil. The larva produces a local papule (small bump) at its entry site and later migrates through the skin, producing tunnels over which vesicles (blisters) form at the surface. The tissue reaction to this migration causes intense itching in the patient and frequent secondary bacterial infection due to scratching.

The larvae can remain alive and travel in the skin for up to several months. Healing is spontaneous, but can be hastened by administration of an anthelmintic (agent destructive to worms).

Frequent worming of dogs and cats and banning them from areas where children play with sand are useful control measures. (*See* "Hookworms," Chapter 31: Internal Parasites.)

Visceral Larva Migrans

Eggs of the dog roundworm (*Toxocara canis),* and less frequently the cat roundworm (*Toxocara cati),* reach the soil in the feces of infected animals. After an appropriate incubation period, they become infective for both animals and humans and remain so for a prolonged period. Children may ingest the eggs while eating soil or playing in feces-soiled areas. In humans, the eggs may be rejected or hatch in the intestine and migrate to various parts of the body (liver, lung, muscle, eye, or central nervous system) via the lymphatic vessels. Depending on the site of migration, the symptoms range from pneumonitis (inflammation of the lungs), swollen liver with abdominal pain, muscle and joint aches, cough, rashes, to skin nodules. Convulsions may occur, and if larvae reach the eye, visual deficiencies may result.

It is crucial to keep children from areas likely to be contaminated with animal feces. Worming of puppies and kittens also contributes to the control of visceral larva migrans. (*See* "Roundworms (Ascarids)," Chapter 31: Internal Parasites.)

Tapeworms

Dipylidium caninum is spread to humans by ingestion of fleas containing a developmental stage of the tapeworm. (*See "Dipylidium caninum,"* Chapter 31: Internal Parasites.)

• • • • • • • • • • • • • • • • • •

To summarize the subject of disease transmission from pets to man, people are more likely to contract transmissible diseases from one another than they are from their pets. Nevertheless, there are some diseases that are transmitted directly or indirectly by pets. This transmission is usually complex and generally requires close contact between susceptible people and animals or their excretions. Such contact often involves lack of common sense and gross violations of sound hygienic practice. Thus it is most common to see pet-borne zoonoses in children.

Responsible pet owners can participate in controlling zoonotic diseases by vaccinating their pets for rabies, limiting excessive contact of infants and pregnant women with pets, seeing to it that pet feces and urine are handled in a hygienic manner, and supporting efforts to avoid the unrestricted presence of pets in parks, swimming areas, beaches, sandboxes, and gardens.

Vaccinations

T he incidence of many infectious diseases in cats has been reduced greatly through the use of vaccines. While no vaccine is 100 percent effective, the proper use of vaccines will allow kittens the best opportunity to grow up as healthy, robust cats. Vaccination is not a trivial medical procedure. Rather, it is a simple procedure that initiates a complicated biological process, resulting in the immunization or protection of the cat against the infectious agent or agents involved. There are many factors that must be taken into consideration before vaccination occurs, and many more considerations about the complications that occasionally occur after vaccination. Because of these numerous considerations, some of which can be life-threatening, vaccination of cats should be done only by a veterinarian or under the supervision of a veterinarian.

Vaccination versus Immunization

The terms "vaccination" and "immunization" are often used interchangeably; however, they are not synonymous. Vaccination refers to the process of giving the vaccine. Immunization refers to the process whereby the immune system recognizes the various foreign proteins or antigens present in the vaccine and produces antibodies and/or other aspects of the immune response against those antigens. This immune response provides protection for the cat against the infectious agent in question. The aim is that in all cases "vaccination" will result in "immunization," but in reality, no vaccine or vaccination is 100 percent effective. Therefore, a small percentage of cats vaccinated against a particular disease will not be immunized against that disease.

Nature of the Vaccine

Several types of vaccines are available for vaccination of cats. First, *inactivated vaccines* are ones in which the infectious agent involved in the vaccine has been treated in some way (usually by chemicals), so that it no longer can infect and replicate within the host. These vaccines are considered to be safe and to require longer to produce an immune response; they tend to produce a shorter period of immunity.

A second type of vaccine is comprised of the *modified live-virus* (MLV) *vaccines* (also referred to as "attenuated" vaccines), which contain viruses that have been altered by various techniques, so that they no longer produce clinical disease. Viruses in these vaccines can replicate within the host and stimulate a rapid and excellent immune response. In some cases, vaccine virus may be shed from the vaccinated cat to infect other cats that may come in contact with the vaccinated cat. MLV vaccines should not be administered to pregnant cats.

A third type of vaccine is *subunit vaccine*. In this type of vaccine, a portion of the infectious agent is separated from the rest of the agent and serves to stimulate the immune system of the cat to develop antibodies against the whole virus or agent. Because there is no living virus or agent present, subunit vaccines are considered to be safe.

Genetically engineered vaccines comprise a fourth type of vaccine. While none of these are licensed at the time of this writing, there are a number of researchers working on genetically engineered vaccines, especially recombinant (involving genetic exchange) vaccines. The future should see a number of unique recombinant vaccines for various infectious diseases of the cat.

Route of Vaccination

The route by which the vaccine is administered may affect the speed and degree of protection provided. In all cases, vaccines should only be administered according to the directions from the manufacturer or the veterinarian. *Feline panleukopenia* (FP) vaccine can be given *intramuscularly* (IM) or *subcutaneously* (SC) with equal effect. Certain MLV-FP vaccines can also be given by the *intranasal* (IN) route, but they will not result in immunization if administered orally.

The modified live-virus respiratory vaccines appear to be slightly more effective by the IM route, but they can be given SC. Vaccines licensed for IM or SC vaccination must not be given by the IN route.

The IN respiratory vaccines are administered by allowing the cat to inhale drops of vaccine into the nostrils. One or two drops are also placed in each eye (conjunctival sac). These vaccines produce rapid local, as well as systemic, immunity. Owners should be aware that vaccinated cats may sneeze and develop mild ocular and/or nasal discharge four to seven days after IN vaccination. Occasionally, ulcers may develop on the tongue following vaccination. Vaccinated cats shed vaccine viruses for long periods after IN vaccination.

Most rabies vaccines must be given by the IM route.

Precautions for Vaccination

While vaccination may appear to be a simple, innocuous procedure, there are several potential adverse effects and several precautions concerning vaccination of cats that must be kept in mind. Because of these, it is recommended that vaccines be administered only by licensed veterinarians, or by licensed animal health technicians or animal owners under the supervision of a licensed veterinarian. While severe reactions to vaccination are not common, life-threatening reactions on occasion do occur. A trained professional must be available to administer life-saving medications if such a reaction does occur.

The value of a vaccine is only as good as the quality maintained during production. Therefore, only vaccines obtained from reputable companies where adequate quality control is maintained should be used.

The following are specific precautions or possible adverse effects that might be encountered when vaccinating cats.

Production of Disease from Vaccine. If the vaccine virus is not modified sufficiently, clinical disease can result following vaccination. Examples are mild respiratory disease after intranasal vaccination, or clinical rabies following vaccination with a living vaccine not licensed for use in the cat. Improperly prepared vaccines may contain virulent virus. The stress of vaccination may trigger a latent infection into a clinical disease.

Effect on Fetus. Developing fetuses are much more susceptible to damage by vaccine viruses than are kittens or adult cats. Fetal death, abortions, resorptions, or congenital birth defects can be the result of vaccination of a pregnant cat with certain vaccines.

Allergic Reactions. Occasionally severe and even fatal allergic reactions can occur after vaccination. With appropriate knowledge and medication, these reactions can be counteracted.

Infection. Improperly handled equipment and vaccines can become contaminated with bacteria, resulting in abscess formation and/or generalized bacterial infections.

Nerve Injury. An improperly placed injection can result in injury to a peripheral nerve with resulting lameness or paralysis.

Failure of Vaccine to Immunize. The use of vaccines that have lost their immunizing ability, the vaccination of kittens that still have maternally derived immunity, and the vaccination of immunocompromised cats are examples that may result in vaccine failure. Exposure to virulent virus later will result in severe clinical disease.

Age of the Cat

The most frequent cause of vaccine failure with feline panleukopenia (FP) vaccines is interference caused by maternally derived immunity. Nature has devised a marvelous method of providing temporary protection to young animals by passing immunity in the form of specific antibodies from the mother to the newborn through the first milk, or colostrum. Thus, kittens born to immune queens are solidly protected for a few weeks, but these kittens eventually become susceptible after the passive immunity wanes. The level and duration of passive immunity following nursing are determined by the antibody titer (concentration of antibody in serum) of the queen at parturition. Although the majority of kittens can be immunized successfully at eight to ten weeks of age, occasional kittens may not be susceptible to vaccination until twelve weeks of age. Therefore, if FP vaccines are given at ages less than twelve weeks, they should be repeated at three- to four-week intervals until the cat is at least twelve weeks old.

The same principles of colostral transfer, antibody half-life, and vaccine virus neutralization apply to the respiratory viruses, feline viral rhinotracheitis (FVR), and feline calicivirus (FCV). There will be interference with respiratory vaccines if the maternally derived titers are high enough. Generally, the FVR and FVC antibody titers are much lower than the FP titer, and therefore the duration of interference (and passive protection) is much shorter. This protection generally does not last longer than five to six weeks for FVR and seven to eight weeks for FCV. By eight to ten weeks of age, the vast majority of cats can be successfully vaccinated against FVR and FCV.

....

VACCINES

Feline Panleukopenia (FP) Vaccines

There are many excellent vaccines available for immunization of cats against panleukopenia (feline "distemper," feline infectious enteritis). If these are used correctly and at the proper age, cats should be completely protected against this very severe viral infection.

Several slightly different programs for the immunization of cats against panleukopenia have been recommended over the years. Most veterinarians recommend that kittens should be vaccinated starting at eight, nine, or ten weeks of age, and the vaccination should be repeated three to four weeks later when the kittens are at least twelve weeks old (*see* Table 1).

If there is any question about exposure to feline panleukopenia virus prior to eight weeks of age, kittens can be vaccinated as early as four weeks of age. Vaccination is then repeated at four-week intervals until the kitten is at least twelve weeks old.

Feline Viral Rhinotracheitis (FVR) Vaccines

FVR vaccines are produced in combination with FP and feline calicivirus (FCV) vaccines, as a triple FP-FVR-FCV vaccine, or as a four-way vaccine with feline chlamydial vaccine. The FVR vaccines produce significant protection following vaccination and, as such, should be part of the routine vaccination program, as outlined in Table 1. As a result of local viral replication, vaccinated cats develop a rapid anamnestic response (rapid reappearance of antibody) when exposed to virulent virus. Some of these exposed vaccinated cats may sneeze, and an occasional one may have watery eyes for one to two days, but severe systemic disease does not occur in properly immunized cats as it does in unvaccinated, susceptible cats.

TABLE 1. **FELINE VACCINE RECOMMENDATIONS**

DISEASE	TYPE OF VACCINE	AGE AT FIRST VACCINATION (weeks)	AGE AT SECOND VACCINATION (weeks)	REVAC-CINATION	ROUTE OF ADMINIS-TRATION
Feline panleukopenia (FP)	(1) Inactivated	8–10	12–14	Annual	SC or IM
	(2) MLV	8–10	12–14	Annual	SC or IM
	(3) MLV-IN	8–10	12–14	Annual	IN
Feline viral rhino-tracheitis (FVR)	(1) Inactivated	8–10	12–14	Annual	SC or IM
	(2) MLV	8–10	12–14	Annual	SC or IM
	(3) MLV-IN	8–10	12–14	Annual	IN
Feline calicivirus (FCV)	(1) Inactivated	8–10	12–14	Annual	SC or IM
	(2) MLV	8–10	12–14	Annual	SC or IM
	(3) MLV-IN	8–10	12–14	Annual	IN
Chlamydiosis	(1) Live Attenuated	8–10	12–14	Annual	SC or IM
Rabies	(1) Inactivated	12	64	Triennial	IM
Feline leukemia virus (FeLV)	(1) Inactivated	9	12*	Annual	SC or IM

MLV = modified live-virus
IM = intramuscular
IN = intranasal
SC = subcutaneous

* A third vaccination may be required at twenty-four weeks of age.

Feline Calicivirus (FCV) Vaccine

The same parameters (i.e., route of vaccination, an-amnestic response when challenged, and good clinical protection against virulent-virus exposure, but not protection against local viral replication) apply to FCV vaccines as to feline viral rhinotracheitis (FVR) vaccines. These vaccines are produced in combination with FVR vaccine and recommendations are the same as for FVR (*see* Table 1).

Feline Chlamydial Vaccine

Feline chlamydiosis (feline pneumonitis, FPn) is a mild to severe, chronic, respiratory and ocular disease caused by *Chlamydia psittaci*. Vaccines currently available produce significant protection following a single vaccination. As with other respiratory vaccines, complete protection is not afforded, but clinical signs, if they do occur, are restricted to a very short course and are mild and local. Chronic disease (characteristic of natural infection in susceptible cats) usually does not occur in vaccinated cats.

The chlamydial vaccines are available in combination with other vaccines. The vaccines now are produced from infected cell cultures instead of eggs, thus eliminating some of the side effects occasionally seen when egg-origin vaccines were used.

A chlamydial vaccine should be part of the routine vaccination program for cats. The age at which to vaccinate is not critical, since there appears to be little interference with maternally derived antibody by the time kittens are old enough to be vaccinated. The first vaccination is usually given at eight to ten weeks of age, with a second vaccination three to four weeks later. Annual revaccinations are recommended (*see* Table 1).

Rabies Vaccines

Cats should be routinely vaccinated for rabies in any area where rabies in wildlife (skunks, raccoons, foxes, bats) is endemic. There is a high correlation between skunk rabies and cat rabies. Skunk rabies is endemic throughout the central United States, from Canada to Mexico. Raccoon rabies is endemic along the East Coast, from Florida to Pennsylvania, and it is rapidly moving northward. Some states have legislation requiring rabies vaccination and licensure of cats.

Only inactivated rabies vaccines specifically licensed for use in cats should be used. Cats vaccinated with an MLV vaccine intended for dogs have actually developed rabies. Cats should be vaccinated after twelve weeks of age, then revaccinated one year later. Booster vaccinations are given every three years, or according to state regulations.

Feline Leukemia Virus (FeLV)

Vaccines are now available to protect cats against feline leukemia. While these vaccines are not 100 percent effective, they do provide a useful aid in reducing the incidence of feline leukemia virus infection in cats. The vaccines are only effective in healthy, FeLV-negative cats. Immunization requires a series of two or three vaccinations, followed by a yearly booster.

While FeLV vaccines are safe for most cats, allergic reactions can occur in a small percentage of cats shortly after vaccination. These reactions include local pain or discomfort at the site of vaccination. A few vaccinated cats have developed transient fever and malaise anywhere from a few minutes to a few hours after vaccination.

Feline Infectious Peritonitis (FIP)

There is a great need for an effective and safe vaccine for feline infectious peritonitis. Experimental vaccines are under study, but at the time of this writing, there are no FIP vaccines licensed for use in cats.

Diagnostic Tests

Often, identifying the ailment affecting a cat is not an easy task. For the veterinarian, the cat's history and clinical signs may suggest several diagnoses. Today's sophisticated diagnostic tests can help establish an accurate diagnosis. Accurate identification of the underlying disease problem is crucial for selecting an appropriate treatment. Although the initial cost for diagnostic testing may seem high, it more than pays for itself in the long run by reducing the cost of treatment and hospitalization.

Bacteriology and Mycology

Many diseases are caused by bacteria (*see* Chapter 30: Bacterial Diseases) or fungi (*see* Chapter 32: Fungal Diseases). *Bacterial and fungal cultures* and *antibiotic sensitivity tests* are particularly useful in diagnosis of an infection and in prescribing the appropriate treatment.

Bacterial Cultures. Scrapings from skin, swabs from lesions or mucous membranes, tracheal wash samples, and samples of blood, urine, or tissue all may be used for the isolation of bacteria in culture. A sample that has been collected from any of these sources and kept either in a bacterial transport media or sterile container is inoculated onto an appropriate medium, such as *agar* (a gel extracted from algae) and allowed to incubate at appropriate growth temperatures in an incubator. If any growth occurs, the bacterium is identified by a variety of tests, including (1) viewing stained organisms microscopically; (2) growth in differential media; and (3) specific immunological reactions of organisms with reference antisera (serums that react only with specific organisms).

Antibiotic Sensitivity Tests. Once a bacterium has been identified, a sensitivity test is performed to determine which antibiotic is most effective against it. This is important because bacteria can become resistant to an antibiotic to which they were once suscep-tible. In the interim, a veterinarian may prescribe a broad-spectrum antibiotic to initiate treatment. With the results of the sensitivity test, a more specific drug may be prescribed, one that has a more effective activity on the bacterium.

Sensitivity testing requires culturing the bacteria as described above. However, for this test, small paper filter discs impregnated with different antibiotics are placed on the agar culture plate, which has been streaked with freshly isolated organisms. After the culture has been incubated for eight to twenty-four hours, it is examined for bacterial growth. Control areas of the culture plate, and areas around the paper discs containing antibiotics to which the organism is resistant, will show uniform bacterial growth. If there has been no growth around a particular paper disc, the antibiotic in that disc is considered to be effective against the cultured bacterium. The minimum inhibitory concentration (MIC) method gives more precise information on each antibiotic dosage used. MIC is used in veterinary diagnostic laboratories.

Fungal Cultures. The same general techniques are used to diagnose fungal infections, except that special growth media and temperature conditions must be provided. In addition, the incubation period may require several weeks. Sensitivity tests are not routinely performed, however.

Virology/Immunology

Unlike a bacterium or fungus, a virus is inert outside a living cell; only inside a cell can it reproduce itself. Viruses can be recovered from affected animals, but virus growth in culture is a much more complex procedure than the growing of bacteria, requiring specialized equipment not available at all veterinary diagnostic laboratories. It is also time-consuming and expensive. Other techniques, such as direct identification of viruses in tissue cells or blood cells, are used more often.

Serology is the laboratory study of antigens and antibodies in serum (the clear portion of the blood, minus *fibrinogen,* a clotting factor). When bacteria, viruses, or toxins invade the body, specific antibodies are produced which are capable of attaching to each specific microbe or toxin. The concentration or quantity of antibody present in a serum is commonly expressed as a *titer*. The titer is determined by diluting the serum out until the specific antibody activity being tested for is lost. Usually the highest dilution of serum showing appreciable antibody activity is referred to as the titer. A positive or high-serum antibody titer against a specific virus indicates that the cat being tested has had previous exposure to that virus, either by natural infection or by vaccination. For example, a serum antibody titer of 1:5,000 against feline panleukopenia virus indicates either previous infection with the virus or previous vaccination with a panleukopenia virus vaccine.

The *enzyme-linked immunosorbent assay* (ELISA) is an enzyme immunoassay that can be used to detect either antibody or antigen, depending on how the test is set up. Enzyme immunoassays rely on enzyme-induced color changes in small plastic test wells for measurement of antigen or antibody levels. Commercial test kits that provide either a positive or negative result have been developed, which make it possible to perform this type of test at the veterinarian's clinic rather than at a diagnostic laboratory. The ELISA test can be used as an aid in diagnosing feline leukemia virus infection, feline immunodeficiency virus infection, toxoplasmosis, heartworm, and feline coronavirus infection. The coronavirus antibody test can identify coronavirus antibody, but it cannot distinguish which coronavirus: feline infectious peritonitis, feline enteric coronavirus; canine coronavirus, or transmissible gastroenteritis virus. There is now a rapid in-office kit to test for feline immunodeficiency virus. *KELA* is a kinetics-based ELISA, wherein the speed of the reaction (the kinetics) of antibody with antigen is measured, and from this a titer is calculated by computer.

The *immunofluorescence assay* (IFA) (fluorescent antibody test) uses a fluorescent-labeled antibody in a reaction that detects antigen present on or within cells. The test may be set up to measure either antigen or antibody, and an ultraviolet-light microscope is required to see the reaction. This is one of the most widely used tests in diagnostic laboratories. (The Hardy test or slide test for feline leukemia virus is an immunofluorescence assay.)

Virus neutralization (VN) measures the effect of serum antibody against "live" virus. The procedure consists of combining diluted serum and virus, allowing them to interact, and then adding them to cell cultures. After incubating for a period of time, the culture is viewed microscopically for the presence or absence of viral effects on the cells. If viral effects are greatly diminished or are absent, it indicates that specific antiviral antibody is present in the test serum.

Parasitology

Diagnostic tests are often performed to determine the presence of internal parasites. The easiest way to determine the presence of internal parasites is by a *fecal examination.* A small sample of fresh feces is collected, liquefied with a saturated salt or sugar solution, and centrifuged (spun to separate the heavier particulates). When a small amount of the sample is placed on a slide and viewed under a microscope, the ova (eggs) or larvae (immature forms) of various parasites are visible and can be identified.

Heartworm microfilariae in the blood can be detected by one of several specific enzyme immunoassays, or by the *Knott's test* (a technique for staining the microfilariae in a blood sample).

External parasites can be identified by removing the parasite directly (in the case of those parasites readily visible to the naked eye) or by scraping affected skin areas. The scrapings are viewed microscopically to check for the presence of parasites too small to be seen with the unaided eye.

Hematology

Hematology tests analyze blood in a variety of ways. The most common test is the *hemogram,* which involves a series of tests including a *complete blood count* (the number of red and white blood cells per unit volume of blood), *hemoglobin* (the percent of oxygen-carrying pigment in red blood cells), *packed cell volume* (volume of cells in relation to the fluid volume of blood), and a *blood smear* (a thin layer of blood smeared on a slide, stained, and viewed under the microscope to identify the maturity and type of blood cells present and any abnormalities of the cells).

Coagulation tests provide important information on the factors that affect the blood's ability to clot. These tests may include prothrombin time, platelet count, clot retraction, fibrinogen, coagulation time, and thromboplastin time. All of these tests are important in attempting to diagnose life-threatening bleeding disorders.

The *Coombs' test* is actually an immunologic procedure for the detection of antibody on red blood cells. Results are given as positive or negative. A positive result means that red blood cells from the patient have clumped together in the small plastic test wells, because they (the cells) are coated with antibody—an abnormal condition. The Coombs' test is used to diagnose *autoimmune diseases,* such as autoimmune hemolytic anemia and systemic lupus erythematosus. These diseases develop when the immune system attacks the body's own cells. The LE cell test (*leukocyte-erythrocyte*) combines serum from patients with systemic lupus erythematosus with normal leukocytes causing the leukocytes to engulf the erythrocytes.

Clinical Chemistry

Blood is a connective tissue whose liquid component (plasma) "bathes" the cells of all tissues. Serum (plasma without clotting factor) can be very useful in diagnosis of metabolic diseases in which abnormal levels of blood constituents are found. Some of the tests can be performed quickly in the veterinarian's office, such as blood glucose (sugar), to test for diabetes mellitus, or blood urea nitrogen (BUN), to determine if the kidneys are removing the urea nitrogen and converting it into urine. The more sophisticated tests for electrolytes, enzymes, and minerals are usually sent to diagnostic laboratories for analysis.

Most diagnostic laboratories have automated clinical chemistry systems, which allow many specific tests to be run on a small quantity of serum. In addition to blood glucose and BUN, tests available include creatinine, phosphorus, calcium, cholesterol, total protein, albumin/globulin ratio, sodium, potassium, and chloride. By comparing the results of these assays with normal values, the veterinary clinician can detect abnormalities indicative of specific organ dysfunction.

Endocrinology

Several tests are available for measuring hormone levels in the blood. Increases or decreases in hormone levels are indicative or even diagnostic of certain metabolic diseases. Such tests may be required periodically to monitor the effectiveness of a given treatment. Sophisticated equipment is needed to perform some of these tests, although rapid in-office diagnostic kits are now available for a limited number of them.

Following are some of the assays that may be performed at larger veterinary hospitals, at veterinary colleges, or at commercial diagnostic laboratories.

TEST	FUNCTION OF	DIAGNOSTIC OF
ACTH response	Adrenal glands	Cushing's syndrome, Addison's disease
Cortisol	Adrenal glands	Cushing's syndrome, Addison's disease
T_3, T_4	Thyroid glands	Hyper- or Hypothyroidism
TSH	Thyroid glands	Hyper- or Hypothyroidism
HCG	Gonads	Some reproductive problems

Cytology and Histopathology

Cytology is the microscopic evaluation of cells obtained by scraping a tissue surface (e.g., mucous membrane), washing (e.g., tracheal wash), needle aspiration (e.g., from bone marrow or lymph node), or aspiration of fluids (e.g., cerebrospinal fluid or urine). Histopathology is the study of tissue changes that occur during or accompany a disease. Diagnosis is based on the microscopic appearance of the cells as seen in stained smears, or by specific immunological reactions (as in the immunofluorescence test).

A *biopsy* is a small sample of tissue used for microscopic examination or culture. Biopsies can be obtained by needle aspiration or by direct surgical removal. Inflammation, cancer, and specific infectious agents often can be identified by this procedure.

Urinalysis

Urinalysis is a series of physical and chemical tests that aid in diagnosis of urinary tract disorders. A sample of urine is examined for its physical properties (clarity, color, and specific gravity); tested biochemically for pH, protein, glucose, bilirubin, and ketones; and examined microscopically for the presence of blood cells, crystals, casts (solid, tubular deposits), and bacteria. Urinalysis is also helpful in detecting diseases affecting other systems, for instance, glucose in the urine can indicate diabetes mellitus.

Electrocardiography

This procedure records the electrical activity of the heart muscle during contraction and relaxation. Abnormal tracings seen on the graph paper readout aid the veterinarian in diagnosing heart disease.

Echocardiography

This ultrasound technique is used to provide remarkably precise visual images of the exterior and interior of the beating heart. Echocardiography often is a valuable substitute for more invasive techniques such as *catheterization* (passage of a small tube through a vessel into the heart) and angiography (X ray of the coronary arteries after a dye has been injected).

Radiography

A number of tests use radiographs (X rays), from the simple images produced on X-ray film to more complex procedures requiring a contrast medium to view internal organs more precisely. Such procedures include intravenous pyelography (IVP) for evaluating the kidney and angiography for evaluating the heart. These more sophisticated radiographic tests often are available only at veterinary teaching hospitals located at university veterinary colleges.

Glossary

....

ABDOMINAL PALPATION. Examination by hand and fingers of the surface of the abdomen, in order to detect abnormalities within the abdominal cavity.

ABSCESSATION. Pus formation within a closed cavity.

ABSCESSES. Walled-off, pus-filled lesions.

ACARIASIS. Mite infestation.

ACHOLIC FECES. Lightly colored feces due to the absence of bile in the intestine.

ACQUIRED IMMUNODEFICIENCY SYNDROME. AIDS in human beings; infection with the human immunodeficiency virus can result in AIDS.

ACTINOMYCES. Bacterium common in the mouth of cats, other animals, and humans.

ACUTE HEPATIC NECROSIS. Liver cell death.

ACUTE. Short-term; of short duration; short and relatively severe.

AD LIBITUM. Free-choice, at will.

ADDISON'S DISEASE. Hypoadrenocorticism; i.e., insufficient secretion by the adrenal cortex.

ADENOCARCINOMA. Malignant tumor of glandular tissue.

ADENOMA. Benign tumor of glandular tissue.

ADIPSIA. Absence of thirst.

ADRENAL GLANDS. Endocrine glands located adjacent to the kidneys.

ADRENALINE. Epinephrine, a hormone secreted by the adrenal glands.

ADRENOCORTICOTROPIC HORMONE (ACTH). A hormone produced by the pituitary gland, which controls the cortex of the adrenal gland.

ADSORB. To bind to a surface.

AEROBIC. Growing in the presence of oxygen.

AEROSOL EXPOSURE. Exposure to an infectious agent via moisture droplets drifting in the air.

AFLATOXINS. Poisons (mold toxins) that can cause serious liver injury if ingested.

AGAR. A gel extracted from algae.

AGENESIS. Congenital absence of an organ.

ALANINE AMINOTRANSFERASE (ALT). An enzyme found within liver cells.

ALBUMIN. A major protein component of blood plasma.

ALDOSTERONE. A hormone secreted by the adrenal cortex, which regulates sodium, chloride, and potassium balance.

....

ALKALI. Any one of a group of compounds that forms soap when mixed with fat.

ALKALOID. One of a group of substances found in plants; usually bitter; e.g., atropine, caffeine, morphine, nicotine, quinine, strychnine.

ALLELE. Different form of a given gene.

ALLERGEN. Substance that can produce an allergic reaction.

ALOPECIA. Absence or loss of hair.

ALOPECIA AREATA. An inflammatory disease resulting in patchy loss of hair.

ALVEOLUS. One of many small air sacs that comprise the innermost structure of the lungs.

AMEBOID ACTION. Action resembling an ameba in movement; with reference to cellular movement wherein the cell extends its cytoplasm and then follows it.

AMELIA. Congenital absence of a limb.

AMINO ACIDS. Nitrogen-containing molecules; the chief structural components of protein.

AMMONIA. A waste product of protein metabolism.

ANABOLISM. The body's conversion of simple substances to complex compounds.

ANAEROBIC. Growing in the absence of oxygen.

ANAMNESTIC RESPONSE. Rapid reappearance of antibody.

ANAPHYLACTIC REACTION. Exaggerated allergic reaction.

ANATOMY. The study of the structure of the body.

ANDROGEN. Any male sex hormone.

ANEMIA. Low red blood cell count, reduced hemoglobin, or reduced volume of packed red cells.

ANENCEPHALY. Congenital absence of the brain.

ANESTRUS. The sexually inactive period in a seasonally polyestrous cycle, usually during the fall or winter months.

ANGIOEDEMA. Recurrent wheals or welts on the skin, caused by capillary abnormalities.

ANGIOGRAPHY. Radiograph of blood vessels after being injected with a contrast medium.

ANTHELMINTIC. Dewormer; medication for intestinal parasites.

ANKYLOSIS. The immobility and consolidation of a joint secondary to injury, infection, or nutritional disorder.

ANORECTIC. Having no appetite.

ANOREXIA. Loss of appetite.

ANTEMORTEM. Before death.

ANTERIOR CHAMBER. A large space filled with aqueous fluid at the front of the eye, between the cornea and lens.

ANTIBIOTICS. Chemical substances, such as penicillin or streptomycin produced by various microorganisms, which when diluted are able to kill or inhibit growth in other microorganisms.

ANTIBODY. Specialized proteins produced by the immune system in reaction to the presence of a foreign substance (bacteria, viruses, toxins) in the body, which are capable of binding to the specific antigen on that substance; immunoglobulin.

ANTIFUNGAL. Chemical substances such as griseofulvin, produced by microorganisms or by other means, used in the treatment of fungus infections.

ANTIGEN. A substance capable of inducing a specific immune response in a body by binding to a specific antibody; can be a property of bacteria, viruses, tissue cells, or foreign proteins.

ANTI-ONCOGENES. Genes whose presence represses cancer, and in whose absence, by an hereditary abnormality, certain specific kinds of tumors may develop.

ANTIMICROBIAL. An antibiotic or antifungal drug.

ANTINEOPLASTIC. Anticancer.

ANTISERUM. Clear blood liquid containing antibody, taken from an animal that has been injected or infected with the antigen.

AORTIC STENOSIS. The constriction of the aortic orifice or of the aorta.

APLASIA. Imperfect development of a tissue or organ.

APNEA. Cessation of breathing.

APOCRINE GLAND. Special type of gland, such as a sweat gland attached to a hair follicle.

AQUEOUS FLUID. Fluid produced by the ciliary process and filling the anterior chamber of the eye.

ARACHIDONIC ACID. Essential fatty acid found in animal fat.

ARMAMENTARIUM. In medicine: collection of medical equipment, techniques, and medicines.

ARRHYTHMIA. Variation from normal heartbeat.

ARTERITIS. Inflammation of an artery.

ARTHROPOD. An invertebrate organism with a segmented body; examples include insects and crustaceans.

ASCARIDS. Roundworms, usually *Toxocara cati;* in humans, the disease is called visceral larva migrans.

ASCARIASIS. Infection by roundworms.

ASCENDING. Moving up.

ASCITES. The accumulation of serous fluid within the abdominal cavity.

ASCORBIC ACID. Vitamin C.

ASPARTATE AMINOTRANSFERASE (AST). A liver cell enzyme that is also found in muscle cells and red blood cells.

ASPIRATED. Inhaled into the lungs or withdrawn by a syringe.

ASPIRATION SMEAR. The procedure by which a preparation is drawn through a needle and then smeared onto a glass microscope slide for examination.

ATAXIA. Incoordination.

ATOPY. Inherited allergy.

ATRESIA. Congenital absence or blockage of an orifice or tubular organ.

ATRESIA ANI. Absence of anal opening.

ATRIUM (plural: ATRIA). One of two upper chambers of the heart.

ATROPHY. Shrinking or wasting of a tissue or organ.

ATROPINE. A drug that blocks nerve impulses, for example, to the iris, causing dilation of the pupil.

AURICLE. External ear, pinna; the term *auricle* also refers to a small blind sac or ear-shaped pouch attached to an atrium of the heart.

AUTOIMMUNE RESPONSE. Immune response directed against the body's own tissues.

AUTONOMIC NERVOUS SYSTEM. Subconscious nervous system.

AUTOSOMAL. Referring to the paired body chromosomes, not to a sex chromosome.

AUTOSOME. An ordinary paired chromosome without any sexual characteristic.

AXON. The single fingerlike extension from a nerve cell.

AWN HAIRS. Intermediate-sized hairs forming part of the primary coat.

BACILLUS CALMETTE-GUERIN (BCG). A live bacterial preparation of the tuberculosis organism, useful in nonspecifically stimulating the immune system, and in vaccination of humans against tuberculosis.

BACTERIAL ENDOCARDITIS. Inflammation of the lining of the heart, caused by bacteria.

BACTERIAL FOLLICULITIS. Inflammation of hair follicles, caused by bacteria.

BASAL. Base, lowest.

BASOPHIL. A specialized white blood cell.

BASOPHILIC. Dark blue staining.

BENIGN. Non-cancerous; a tumor that is not cancerous (i.e., will not spread); harmless.

BETA BLOCKER. A drug that inhibits certain nerve impulses.

BILATERALLY. On both sides.

BILIARY CIRRHOSIS. A disease of the liver characterized by destruction of the normal architecture, which is replaced essentially by scar tissue.

BILIRUBIN. A yellow breakdown product of recycled hemoglobin from red blood cells.

BINOCULAR VISION. Focusing both eyes on a single object.

BIOPSY. The procedure by which a small sample of tissue is obtained for microscopic examination or culture.

BLASTOCYST. An early stage of the developing embryo.

BLEOMYCIN. An antibiotic.

BLEPHAROSPASM. Spasm of the eyelid muscle, causing closure.

BLOOD. A fluid that circulates through the blood vessels, carrying oxygen and nutrients to body cells.

BLOOD PLASMA. The liquid component of blood (as opposed to blood cells).

BLOOD SMEAR. A thin layer of blood smeared on a slide, stained, and viewed under the microscope to identify the maturity and type of blood cells present and any abnormalities of the cells.

BLOOD UREA NITROGEN (BUN). Nitrogenous waste products in the blood.

BLOOD VESSELS. Arteries, arterioles, venules, veins, capillaries; the conduits for the transport of blood throughout the body.

BOIL. Hair-follicle infection that has spread to deeper tissues, producing a firm nodule containing pus.

BONE MARROW. The soft tissue within bones; contains blood-forming elements—precursor cells of the red and white blood cells.

BRACHYCEPHALIC. Flat-faced; having a short, wide head.

BRADYCARDIA. Slowing of the heart rate.

BRONCHI. The larger air passages leading from the trachea and branching within the lungs.

BRONCHIOLES. Smaller branches of air passages leading from the bronchi to the alveoli (small air sacs in the lungs).

BRONCHOPNEUMONIA. Lung inflammation that begins in bronchioles.

BULBOURETHRAL GLAND. Gland located on the male urethra that produces seminal fluid which, when mixed with sperm, forms the ejaculate.

BUPHTHALMOS. Enlargement of the eye.

CACHEXIA. Seriously poor health and malnutrition from any cause.

CALCULUS (plural: CALCULI). Dental tartar; urinary stone.

CALCULOGENIC. Stone-forming.

CALICIVIRUS. *See* Feline Calicivirus.

CALORIE. Unit defined as the amount of heat needed to raise the temperature of one gram of water one degree Celsius (centigrade). However, the larger *kilocalorie* is usually referred to as *calorie* in the nonscientific community.

CAMPYLOBACTER JEJUNI. A bacterium commonly found in the intestines of animals.

CANCER. General term for a malignant tumor.

CANNULA. A tube used for insertion.

CAPITULUM. Head.

CARBONIC ANHYDRASE INHIBITOR. A drug that blocks the enzyme that helps turn carbonic acid into carbon dioxide and water.

CARBUNCLE. A deep skin infection containing many pockets of pus.

CARCINOGEN. A cancer-causing substance.

CARCINOMA. A cancer of epithelial cells.

CARDIAC TAMPONADE. Acute compression of the heart due to filling of the pericardial sac with fluid.

CARDIOMYOPATHY. Disease of the heart muscle, which may become weakened, thickened, or thinned and stretched.

CARDIOPULMONARY RESUSCITATION (CPR). First-aid technique to revive a patient who has no heartbeat or respiration.

CARTILAGE. A connective tissue important in bone growth and formation of joints.

CASTRATION. The surgical removal of the testes.

CASTS. Solid, tubular deposits in urine.

CATABOLISM. The body's breakdown of complex molecules, such as protein and fat, to simpler compounds.

CATARACT. Lens opacity in the eye.

CAUDAL. To the rear of; toward the tail.

CELLULAR DIFFERENTIATION. A process by which cells "mature" into fully functioning units.

CELLULITIS. Diffuse inflammation resulting from infection of deep connective tissue.

CENTRAL NERVOUS SYSTEM (CNS). The brain and spinal cord.

CENTRIFUGE. To spin in order to separate out the heavier particulates in a fluid.

CEREBELLAR HYPOPLASIA. Underdevelopment of the cerebellum, manifested by incoordination.

CEREBELLUM. Portion of the brain concerned with motor function, balance, and coordination.

CEREBRUM. Portion of the brain concerned with conscious thought, perceptions, and skills.

CERUMINOUS GLANDS. Glands that produce the waxy coating of the ear canal.

CERVICAL SPONDYLOSIS. Degenerative and proliferative disease of the neck vertebrae.

CERVIX. Entrance to the uterus.

CESTODES. Tapeworms; a class of internal parasites characterized by production of segments.

CHEMICAL OXIDATION. Production of energy by the combination of a substance with oxygen.

CHEMOSIS. Excessive swelling of the conjunctiva (membrane covering the inner surface of the eyelids and the exposed surface of the eyeball).

CHEYLETIELLOSIS. Infestation with the mites *Cheyletiella blakei, Cheyletiella parasitivorax,* or *Cheyletiella yasguri.*

CHLAMYDIOSIS. A bacterial infection caused in cats by the genus *Chlamydia psittaci.*

CHLORAMPHENICOL. An antibiotic; toxicity can cause depression, diarrhea, anorexia, severe weight loss, or anemia.

CHOLINE. A B vitamin important in proper function of the nervous system and in fat metabolism in the liver.

CHOROID. Coat within the back of the eye containing pigment and blood vessels.

CHORIORETINITIS. Inflammation of the choroid.

CHRONIC. Long-term; of lengthy duration; persisting over a long period.

CHRONIC CARRIER STATE. Situation in which an animal or human maintains (carries) an infection by a disease agent for a prolonged period of time.

CHRONIC INTERSTITIAL NEPHRITIS. Destruction of tissue within the kidney, marked by a reduction in size and by scarring of the kidneys.

CHYLE. Intestinal lymph; milky-looking, fat-containing fluid taken up by the intestine during digestion of food, and passing by the thoracic duct into the venous circulation.

CHYLOTHORAX. Accumulation of chyle in the chest cavity.

CILIARY VASCULAR CONGESTION. "Red eye," a condition involving blood vessel congestion within the eye.

CIRRHOSIS. Liver disease characterized by replacement of functioning tissue by scar tissue.

CO-FACTOR. A required constituent for enzymes involved in protein metabolism.

COITUS. Sexual intercourse.

COLITIS. Inflammation of the large bowel (colon).

COLLAGEN. Protein constituent of connective tissue.

COLOSTRUM. Milk produced during the first day or two after birth that is high in protein and antibodies; "first milk."

COMATOSE. Unconscious and unable to be aroused.

COMPLETE BLOOD COUNT (CBC). Number of red and white blood cells per unit of blood volume, the proportions of the different white cells, and the amount of hemoglobin.

COMPOUND FRACTURE. Fracture that breaks through the skin; open fracture.

CONCEPTUS. Embryo or fetus plus accompanying membranes.

CONCUSSION. Violent shock to the brain.

CONGENITAL MALFORMATIONS. Birth defects.

CONGENITAL TESTICULAR HYPOPLASIA. Underdevelopment of the testicles.

CONJUNCTIVA. Membrane lining the eyelids and covering the white surface of the eyeball (sclera).

CONJUNCTIVITIS. Inflammation of the conjunctiva.

CONNECTIVE TISSUE. Tissue that binds together and is the support of various structures of the body.

CONTAGIOUS STREPTOCOCCAL LYMPHADENITIS. Strangles; an inflammatory disease involving lymph nodes infected with streptococci.

CONTINUOUS POLYESTRUS. Reproductive cycles with no anestrous period noted in the fall and winter.

CONTRALATERAL. Opposite side.

CONTUSIONS. Bruises.

COOMBS' TEST. An immunologic procedure for the detection of antibody on red blood cells.

CORNEA. The thick transparent outer coat at the front of the eyeball.

CORNIFIED. Hardened.

CORONAVIRUS. A group of viruses including one that causes feline infectious peritonitis in cats.

CORPUS LUTEUM. Ovarian follicle after discharge of the ovum or egg.

CORTEX. Outer region of the adrenal gland, brain, or kidney.

CORTICOID. Corticosteroid.

CORTICOSTEROIDS. Steroid hormones, cortisol and corticosterone, produced by the cortex of the adrenal gland; corticosteroids elevate blood sugar, increase fat and protein breakdown, and have an anti-inflammatory effect on conditions such as arthritis and dermatitis.

CORTICOSTERONE. A corticosteroid hormone.

CORTISOL. A corticosteroid hormone.

CORTISONE. A corticosteroid found in small amounts in the adrenal cortex; synthetic cortisone is administered by injection, to be used by the adrenal glands to produce cortisol.

CRANIAL. Toward the head.

CRANIOSCHISIS. Failure of the roof of the skull to form.

CREPITUS. Sensation or sound of grating or scraping when fragments of fractured bone rub together.

CRYOSURGERY. A procedure by which a local application of intense cold (freezing) is used to damage and destroy cancerous tissue.

CRYOGEN. The substance that produces extreme cold during cryosurgery.

CRYPTORCHID. Having a condition wherein one, or both, of the testes is undescended or ectopic (under the skin in the groin or in the abdominal cavity).

CUSHING'S SYNDROME. Hyperadrenocorticism; overactivity of the adrenal glands.

CUTANEOUS HORNS. Projections of hardened skin.

CUTANEOUS HYPERESTHESIA. Hypersensitivity of the skin.

CUTEREBRIASIS. Penetration of *Cuterebra* fly larva beneath the skin.

CYANOCOBALAMIN. Vitamin B_{12}.

CYANOSIS. Bluish discoloration of the skin from lack of blood oxygen.

CYCLOSPORIN. An immunosuppressive drug important in organ transplantation.

CYSTADENOMA. A benign tumor of cystic and glandular structures.

CYSTIC ENDOMETRIAL HYPERPLASIA. Exuberant overgrowth of uterine lining with formation of cysts.

CYSTIC RETE OVARII TUBULES. Meshwork of dilated ovarian tubules.

CYSTITIS. Inflammation of urinary bladder.

CYSTOLITH. A bladder stone (as in the urinary bladder or the gall bladder).

CYTODIFFERENTIATION. Formation of unique cell types.

CYTOKINES. Messenger molecules by which cells of the immune system signal and instruct one another; interleukin and gamma-interferon are examples.

CYTOLOGY. The microscopic examination of cells obtained by scraping, aspiration, or biopsy.

CYTOPLASM. The fluid and substances within a cell that surround the nucleus.

CYTOTOXIC. Toxic to cells; e.g., cytotoxic drugs to destroy tumor cells.

DEFINITIVE HOST. Host in which the adult or sexually mature stage of a parasite is produced.

DEMENTIA. Mental deterioration.

DENDRITES. Short branching extensions from a nerve cell.

DEOXYRIBONUCLEIC ACID (DNA). A nucleic acid; genetic material.

DERMATOMYCOSIS. Fungal skin infection.

DERMATOPHYTOSIS. Ringworm.

DERMATOSIS. Any skin disease, especially one of noninflammatory origin.

DERMIS. Support structure beneath the epidermis or outer layer of skin.

DESCEMETOCELE. Herniation of membrane at the back of the cornea.

DEXTROSE. Blood sugar; glucose.

DIABETES MELLITUS. Diabetes; disease involving insufficient insulin production by the islets of Langerhans in the pancreas.

DIAPHRAGM. The large muscle used for breathing which separates the abdominal and chest cavities.

DICEPHALUS. Congenital malformation involving development of two heads.

DIESTRUS. Interestrus; the quiescent period between one estrous period and the next.

DIGESTS. Extracts.

DIGITALIS. A drug that increases the strength of the heartbeat while decreasing the rate.

DILATED FIXED PUPIL. Pupil that does not contract.

DIMELIA. Congenital duplication of a limb.

DIPROSOPUS. Congenital malformation involving duplication of the face.

DISSEMINATED INTRAVASCULAR COAGULATION (DIC). A bleeding disorder characterized by destruction of blood clotting factors and resultant hemorrhage from blood failing to clot.

DISTAL. Farther, more distant.

DIURETIC. Agent that promotes urination.

DOMINANT GENE. One capable of expressing its trait even when carried by only one member of a chromosome pair.

DORSAL. Pertaining to the back.

DUODENUM. First part of the small intestine.

DYSPLASIA. Abnormal development.

DYSPNEA. Difficulty breathing; labored breathing.

DYSTOCIA. Difficult birth.

ECCRINE GLAND. Sweat gland found in the footpads.

ECHOCARDIOGRAPHY. Ultrasonic examination of the heart.

ECLAMPSIA. Milk fever; calcium deficiency in a lactating queen.

ECTOPARASITE. External parasite; fleas, ticks, mites are examples.

ECTOPIC. Not in normal position.

ECTRODACTYLY. Congenital absence of all or part of a digit.

EDEMA. Presence of abnormally large amounts of fluid in the intercellular tissue spaces, usually under the skin; pulmonary edema is fluid in the lungs.

EDEMATOUS. Swollen with fluid.

EFFUSION. Fluid escaping into tissues or a body cavity.

ELASTIN. Protein found in elastic connective tissue.

ELECTROCARDIOGRAPHY (ECG). The process by which there is a graphic tracing of the electrical activity of the heart.

ELECTROLYTE. A molecule that dissociates into ions (atoms having a positive or negative charge due to the addition or subtraction of an electron) in solution.

ELISA. *Enzyme-linked immunosorbent assay*; a color-based test for the presence of either antibody or antigen in the blood.

EMBOLISM. Sudden blocking of an artery by a blood clot, fat, or air.

EMPYEMA. Pyothorax; accumulation of pus in the chest cavity.

ENDOCARDIUM. A thin serous membrane that lines the cavities of the heart.

ENDOCRINOPATHIES. Hormonal disturbances.

ENDOGENOUS. From a source within the body.

ENDOMETRITIS. Inflammation of the lining of the uterus.

ENDOSCOPY. A procedure in which a small tube is inserted into an orifice in order to examine internal portions of a hollow organ.

ENDOSPORE. A type of spore produced in the spherule stage of the fungus *Coccidioides immitis*.

ENDOTRACHEAL TUBE. A plastic tube for breathing, inserted into the trachea during anesthesia.

ENTERIC. Of the small intestine.

ENTERITIS. Intestinal inflammation.

ENTROPION. Turning inward of an eyelid.

ENUCLEATION. Removal of an eye.

ENZOOTIC. A constantly present disease that is widespread but produces disease in relatively few animals.

ENZYMATICALLY. By means of enzymes.

ENZYME. One of a number of different protein substances produced in a cell, which is capable of accelerating one of the cell's various catalytic actions.

EOSIN. Rose-colored stain or dye.

EOSINOPHIL. Granular white blood cell that can be readily stained with eosin; functions in the allergic reaction to parasitic infections.

EOSINOPHILIC GRANULOMA COMPLEX. A disease of unknown (perhaps allergic) origin, characterized by the formation of lesions ranging from well-demarcated, linear, raised plaques on the thighs to erosions, ulcerations, and swellings on the lips, face, and in the mouth; microscopically, eosinophils and cellular components of granulation tissue are seen.

EPIDERMIS. Outer layer of skin.

EPIDIDYMIS. Duct connecting the testis to the vas deferens.

EPILATION OF HAIRS. Removal of hairs by the roots.

EPICARDIUM. Layer of pericardium (serous membrane) on the outer surface of the heart.

EPINEPHRINE. Hormone secreted by the adrenal medulla (the inner portion of the adrenal gland), which elevates blood glucose and increases blood pressure and cardiac output; also called adrenaline.

EPIPHORA. An overflow of tears.

EPISTAXIS. Bleeding from the nose.

EPITHELIUM. Covering of the internal and external surfaces of the body.

EPITHELIALIZED. Having new covering or surface grow back.

EPIZOOTIC. An outbreak of a disease attacking many animals with many sick (high morbidity).

ERYSIPELOID. A deep skin infection caused by a specific bacterium.

ERYTHEMA. Redness.

ERYTHEMATOUS MACULE. A small red spot.

ERYTHEMATOUS PAPULE. A red bump.

ERYTHROCYTE. Red blood cell, the carrier of oxygen in the blood.

ERYTHROPOIETIN. Hormone, produced by the kidney, which stimulates red blood cell production.

ESCHERICHIA COLI. A bacterium normally found in the digestive tract.

ESOPHAGUS. The muscular tube extending from the pharynx to the stomach.

ESTRADIOL. Ovarian estrogen.

ESTRADIOL CYPIONATE (ECP). An estrogen compound.

ESTROGEN. Female sex hormone that stimulates estrus.

ESTROUS CYCLE. The reproductive pattern of the adult female cat, including proestrus, estrus, metestrus, and diestrus.

ESTROUS CRY. Sound given by the queen to indicate that she is in heat and sexually receptive.

ESTRUS. "Heat"; a recurrent period of varying length, during which the female produces a watery secretion from the genital tract, becomes sexually receptive to the male, and ovulates (releases egg from the ovary) if mated.

ETIOLOGY. Origin, cause.

EXCISING. Cutting out; surgical removal.

EXCORIATION. Abrasion; scratch.

EXENCEPHALY. Congenital defect in which the brain bulges through the skull.

EXOGENOUS. From a source outside the body.

EXOSTOSIS. Bony outgrowth.

EXTRACORPOREAL IMMUNOSORPTION. Plasmapheresis; procedure in which plasma extracted from blood is treated and then returned to the host.

EXTRAOCULAR. Outside the eye.

EXUDATE. Material (plasma, cells, cellular debris) deposited in tissues or on tissue surfaces, usually as a result of inflammation.

FADING KITTENS. Kittens that fail to thrive.

FASCIA. Sheet of fibrous tissue that covers muscles or organs.

FAT-SOLUBLE VITAMINS. Vitamins A, D, E, and K.

FEBRILE. Feverish.

FECAL CASTS. Black, comma-shaped, one- to two-millimeter-long granules of waste from adult fleas; "flea dirt."

FELIDAE. Taxonomic family name for cats.

FELINE CALICIVIRUS (FCV). A virus that infects the feline respiratory system.

FELINE ENTERIC CORONAVIRUS. A group of viruses that infect the intestinal tract.

FELINE IMMUNODEFICIENCY VIRUS (FIV). Previously called feline T-lymphotropic lentivirus (FTLV); a virus that attacks the cat's immune system.

FELINE INFECTIOUS ANEMIA. Feline hacmobarto nellosis; a rickettsial disease of the red blood cells.

FELINE INFECTIOUS PERITONITIS (FIP). A coronavirus infection; a relatively uncommon disease in cats but virtually always fatal.

FELINE ISCHEMIC SYNDROME. Constricted or obstructed blood vessels in the brain.

FELINE LEUKEMIA VIRUS (FeLV). The causative agent of the most important fatal infectious disease complex of American domestic cats today; directly or indirectly the cause of a number of feline diseases, among them lymphosarcoma (cancer of the lymphocytes, a type of white blood cell).

FELINE PANLEUKOPENIA (FP). Feline infectious enteritis; feline "distemper"; feline ataxia or incoordination; a highly contagious viral disease of cats characterized by sudden onset, fever, inappetence, dehydration, depression, vomiting, decreased numbers of circulating white blood cells, and often a high mortality rate; caused by a parvovirus (one of a group of viruses).

FELINE SARCOMA VIRUS (FeSV). The causative agent of multiple fibrosarcomas (cancers of connective tissues) in young cats.

FELINE UROLOGIC SYNDROME (FUS). Cystitis, urethritis, or urethral blockage; stone formation.

FELINE VIRAL RHINOTRACHEITIS (FVR). Feline herpesvirus type 1 infection; a respiratory disease.

FETAL RESORPTION. Disintegration of the fetus within the uterus.

FIBRIN. A protein that forms the nucleus of a blood clot.

FIBRINOGEN. Clotting factor in the blood, which is converted into fibrin.

FIBROSARCOMA. Malignant tumor of connective tissue cells.

FIBROUS. Thickened.

FILAMENTOUS. Threadlike.

FLAGELLUM. Long, snakelike projection from a cell, used for locomotion.

FLEHMEN RESPONSE. Response (exposing the teeth by retracting the upper lip) elicited by the odor of urine.

FLUORESCEIN. A dye used to stain and demonstrate ulcerations of the cornea.

FOLACIN. Folic acid; a water-soluble vitamin.

FOLLICLE-STIMULATING HORMONE (FSH). Hormone produced by the pituitary gland that stimulates growth and maturation of ovarian follicles in the female and sperm production in the male.

FOLLICULITIS. Inflammation of hair follicles.

FRACTURE. Breaking of a bone.

FULMINANT. Sudden and severe.

FURUNCULOSIS. Boils.

GAMETES. Reproductive cells; sperm in the male and ova (eggs) in the female.

GANGRENE. Death and decay of tissue, usually resulting from loss of blood supply.

GASTRULA. The early stage of a developing embryo that follows the blastula.

GENOME. The genetic information of an individual cell or virus.

GENOTYPE. The genetic makeup of a given trait.

GERIATRICS. The study of old age and aging.

GESTATION. The full period of pregnancy; period of development from fertilization of the ovum until birth; feline gestation lasts sixty-four to sixty-nine days, with an average of sixty-six days.

GIARDIA LAMBLIA. Protozoan parasite of the intestinal tract.

GINGIVITIS. Inflammation of the gums.

GLANS PENIS. The cap-shaped end of the penis.

GLOBE. The eyeball.

GLOMERULONEPHRITIS. A kidney disease that damages the glomerulus.

GLOMERULUS. One of many tiny tufts of blood vessels in the kidney that separate fluid and cellular components and through which the blood is filtered.

GLUCOCORTICOIDS. Corticosteroids that affect the metabolism of carbohydrates, fats, and proteins.

GLYCOGEN. Animal starch.

GOITER. Enlarged thyroid gland.

GOITROUS. Pertaining to a goiter.

GONADAL HYPOPLASIA. Impaired development of sex glands.

GONADOTROPINS. Hormones that stimulate the sex glands.

GONADS. Testes or ovaries; reproductive glands that produce sperm and ova (eggs) and the steroid hormones testosterone (testes) and progesterone and estrogen (ovaries).

GRANULE. Small particle or grain.

GRANULOCYTE. Type of white blood cell, containing stainable granules.

GRANULOCYTIC LEUKEMIA. Cancer of granulocytes.

GRANULOMA. Lesion with chronic inflammatory response characterized by the accumulation of certain types of white blood cells around some infectious and noninfectious agents, for the purpose of walling off the agent from the rest of the body; may be microscopic in size or visible to the unaided eye as small nodular grains of tissue.

GRANULOSA CELL. Cell type that surrounds the ovarian follicle.

GRISEOFULVIN. Medication for ringworm.

GROSS APPEARANCE. Appearance as seen by the naked eye (as opposed to microscopic appearance).

GROWTH HORMONE (GH). Hormone produced by the pituitary gland which influences growth.

GUARD HAIRS. Coarse, thick, straight hairs that taper to a fine tip.

HAEMOBARTONELLA FELIS. Rickettsial parasite that causes feline infectious anemia.

HAIRBALLS. Entwined accumulations of ingested fur, resulting from self-washing behavior of cats.

HALITOSIS. Bad breath.

HARD PALATE. Bone and tissue separating the nasal cavity from the oral cavity.

HAW. Third eyelid in inner corner of the eye.

HELMINTHIC. Pertaining to parasitic worms.

HEMANGIOMA. Benign tumor of blood vessels.

HEMANGIOSARCOMA. Malignant tumor of blood vessels.

HEMATOCRIT. Percentage of red cells in whole blood.

HEMATOMA. Localized collection of blood, usually due to blood vessel breakage.

HEMATOPOIETIC. Blood cell–forming.

HEMIMELIA. Congenital absence of all or part of the distal portion of a limb.

HEMOGLOBIN. The oxygen-carrying pigment in red blood cells.

HEMOGRAM. Results of blood examination including total and differential white blood cell counts, and packed cell volume.

HEMOLYMPHATIC SYSTEM. The circulatory system and the lymphatic system together.

HEMORRHAGIC PUNCTUM. A small blood-spot.

HEMOTHORAX. Blood in the chest cavity.

HEPARIN. An anticoagulant, which indirectly inhibits the conversion of fibrinogen to fibrin.

HEPATIC ENCEPHALOPATHY. Neurologic abnormalities secondary to liver failure.

HEPATIC LIPIDOSIS. Buildup of fat in the liver.

HEPATOMEGALY. Enlargement of the liver.

HETEROSIS. Hybrid vigor; breed strength gained by crossbreeding.

HERITABILITY. Capability of being inherited.

HERMAPHRODITISM. Presence of male and female sex organs.

HERNIA. Protrusion of an organ or tissue through an abnormal opening; rupture.

HERPESVIRUS. Feline rhinotracheitis virus, a respiratory pathogen.

HETEROZYGOUS. Having two different alleles at a given locus on a chromosome.

HISTAMINE. Substance that affects blood vessels, muscles, and the heart; responsible for many of the unpleasant effects of allergy.

HISTOLOGY. Microscopic examination of tissue.

HOMOGENEOUS. Uniform.

HOMOZYGOUS. Having the same two alleles at a given locus on a chromosome.

HORMONE. A chemical substance produced by an organ or cells of an organ, which has a specific regulatory effect on the activity of some other organ.

HUMAN CHORIONIC GONADOTROPHIN (HCG). Hormone produced by the placenta, which can stimulate ovulation in estrous queens.

HYDROCEPHALUS. Fluid accumulation within the brain.

HYDROMETRA. Collection of watery fluid within the uterus.

HYDROPHILIC. Water-attracting.

HYDROXYUREA. Anticancer drug that interferes with cellular DNA synthesis.

HYPER-. A prefix meaning *above* or *beyond; excessive.*

HYPERADRENOCORTICISM. Cushing's syndrome; overactivity of the adrenal glands.

HYPERAMMONEMIA. High levels of ammonia in the blood.

HYPERESTROGENISM. Excessive secretion of estrogen.

HYPERPIGMENTATION. Darkening of the skin.

HYPERPLASIA. Overgrowth due to an increase in the number of cells in a given tissue; compare to hypertrophy.

HYPERTENSION. Abnormally elevated blood pressure.

HYPERTHERMIA. Abnormally elevated body temperature.

HYPERTHYROIDISM. Overactivity of the thyroid gland.

HYPERTROPHY. Overgrowth due to an increase in the size of cells in a given tissue; compare to hyperplasia.

HYPERVISCOSITY. Thickening of the blood in certain disease states.

HYPO-. A prefix meaning *below* or *under;* deficient.

HYPOADRENOCORTICISM. Addison's disease; insufficient secretion from the adrenal cortex.

HYPOGLYCEMIA. Low blood sugar.

HYPOKALEMIA. A low level of potassium in the blood.

HYPOLUTEOIDISM. Sterility in queens caused by the insufficient secretion of progesterone.

HYPOPLASIA. Underdevelopment of a given tissue.

HYPOPYON. Accumulation of white blood cells (pus) in the anterior chamber of the eye.

HYPOSENSITIZATION. "Allergy shots," intended to reduce an allergic individual's sensitivity to allergens.

HYPOSPADIAS. Congenital defect in males in which the urethral opening develops on the underside of the penis or on the perineum.

HYPOTHALAMUS. Critical portion of the brain concerned with operation of much of the autonomic (unconscious) nervous system; production of certain hormones that are subsequently stored in the pituitary gland; and regulation of body temperature, sleep cycles, and food and water intake.

HYPOTHERMIA. Abnormally low body temperature.

HYPOTHYROIDISM. Decreased thyroid function.

HYPOTRICHOSIS. Sparse hair coat.

HYPOVOLEMIA. Decreased blood volume; can lead to shock.

HYPOXIA. Oxygen deprivation.

I.V. MEDICATION. Intravenous medication.

IATROGENIC. Arising as a complication of medical treatment.

IDIOPATHIC. Of unknown cause.

IDIOPATHIC MEGACOLON. Massive enlargement or dilation of the colon; of unknown cause.

IMMUNE-MEDIATED DESTRUCTION. Damage caused by the response of the host's immune system to a disease agent or drug.

IMMUNIZATION. The process whereby the immune system recognizes the various foreign proteins or antigens present in a vaccine and produces antibodies and immune cells against those antigens.

IMMUNOASSAY. Determination of quantity of specific antigen in the serum; tests such as ELISA and immunofluorescence assay.

IMMUNOFLUORESCENCE ASSAY (IFA). A fluorescent antibody test for the presence of antigen or antibody.

IMMUNOGLOBULIN. An antibody.

IMMUNOPOTENTIATOR. Substance with immune-boosting capabilities.

IMMUNOSUPPRESSED INDIVIDUALS. Those on immunosuppressive drug therapy such as steroids, or with diseases of the immune system.

IMMUNOTHERAPY. Boosting the immune response to assist in the treatment of a disease.

IMPETIGO. Skin pustules caused by bacteria.

IN UTERO. Within the uterus.

IN SITU. At the site.

INACTIVATED ("KILLED") VACCINE. A vaccine in which the infectious agent has been treated in some way (usually by chemicals) so that it no longer can infect and replicate within the host.

INCLUSIONS. Anything that is enclosed within, as within a cell.

INAPPETENCE. Lack of appetite.

INGESTA. Ingested food.

INGUINAL. Between abdomen and thigh; in the groin.

INGUINAL RING. An opening deep within the groin for the passage of the spermatic cord or the round ligament of the uterus.

INNERVATION. The distribution of nerves to a given tissue or body part.

INTEGUMENT. The skin.

INTERESTRUS. Diestrus; the quiescent period tween one estrus and the next.

INTERFERONS. Natural substances that can inhibit virus replication and also the growth of tumor cells.

INTERTRIGO. Skin-fold dermatitis.

INTERSEXUALITY. Having characteristics of both sexes present in the same individual.

INTERVERTEBRAL DISCS. The cartilaginous structures between the vertebrae.

INTOXICATION. Poisoning.

INTRAMUSCULARLY (IM). A route of injection (into the muscle).

INTRANASAL. Within the nasal passage.

INTRANASAL (IN). A route of administration of a vaccine by instilling in the nasal passage.

INTRAVENOUS PYELOGRAM (IVP). Radiograph of the urinary tract after injecting dye for visualization of structures.

INTROMISSION. Insertion, as of the penis.

INTUSSUSCEPTION. Prolapse ("telescoping") of one section of the bowel into another.

INVOLUTION. Return to normal size, as of the uterus after birth.

IONIZE. To separate into ions (charged atoms).

IONIZING RADIATION. Radiation capable of ionizing matter; examples are X rays and radioactive isotopes of the elements radon, strontium, and cesium.

IRIDOCYTES. Cells that produce iridescence (lustrous, changing colors).

IXODID. Belonging to a family of hard-bodied ticks (hard ticks).

JAUNDICE. Yellowing of the mucous membranes.

JEJUNUM. Middle portion of the small intestine.

KELA. A kinetics-based ELISA (enzyme-linked immunosorbent assay); a test for the presence of antigen or antibody.

KERATIN. An insoluble protein synthesized by cells within the skin; it is the principal component of skin, hair, and nails.

KERATITIS. Inflammation of the cornea.

KERATOCONJUNCTIVITIS SICCA (KCS). A lack of tears; dry eyes; dry cornea.

KERATOLYTIC. Able to cause softening and peeling of the outer layer of the skin.

KETONES. By-products of digestion.

KILOCALORIE (KCAL). Unit defined as the amount of heat required to raise the temperature of one kilogram of water one degree Celsius (centigrade); the "large" calorie; commonly called *calorie,* although technically the calorie is the amount of heat needed to raise the temperature of one gram of water one degree celsius. The kilocalorie is 1000 of these small calories. In this book the terms *calorie* and *kilocalorie* are being used interchangeably to mean the large calorie, as is the custom in America.

KILOGRAM. One thousand grams (2.2 pounds).

KNOTT'S TEST. Technique for staining microfilariae in a blood sample when testing for heartworm disease.

L-ASPARAGINASE. An enzyme that kills cancer cells by depleting their supply of the amino acid L-asparagine.

LABILE. Chemically unstable.

LACRIMAL GLAND. Tear gland.

LACTASE. Enzyme that breaks down lactose.

LACTATED RINGER'S SOLUTION. A sterile saltwater solution for injection that includes calcium, potassium, and sodium chloride and sodium lactate.

LACTOSE. Milk sugar.

LAPAROSCOPY. Visual inspection of the interior of the abdomen with an instrument.

LARVAE. Immature forms or stages in the life of small creatures, such as parasites or insects.

LARYNX. Upper part of the respiratory tract between the pharynx and the trachea; having cartilage walls and containing the vocal cards.

LECITHIN. A fatty acid–containing constituent of cell membranes.

LEUKOCYTES. White blood cells.

LEUKOPENIA. Decreased number of circulating white blood cells.

LEUKOTRICHIA. Whitening of the hair.

LICHENIFICATION. Leathery thickening of the outer layer of the skin.

LIGAMENT. Strengthening band of fibrous tissue, for stabilizing joint structure.

LIGATION. Binding or tying off.

LINOLEIC ACID. An essential fatty acid acquired from vegetable sources.

LIPID FILM. A layering of fat.

LIPOSARCOMA. Malignant tumor of fat cells.

LOCHIA. Vaginal discharge that continues after giving birth.

LOCUS (plural: LOCI). Position on the chromosome where a specific gene is located.

LORDOSIS. Downward curvature of the lumbar spine (swayback).

LUMBOSACRAL. Pertaining to the lower back.

LUMEN. Interior or cavity in a tube, or tubular organ.

LUTEAL PHASE. Period during which the ovarian follicle converts to a corpus luteum and secretes progesterone.

LUTEINIZATION. Conversion of the ovarian follicle to a corpus luteum.

LUTEINIZING HORMONE (LH). Hormone, produced by the pituitary gland, which assists in causing ovulation and in production of estrogen by the cells of the ovary.

LUTEINIZING HORMONE-RELEASING HORMONE (LH-RH). Hormone, released from the hypothalamus in the brain, which triggers the release of luteinizing hormone.

LUXATION. Dislocation.

LYMPH. Clear fluid, derived from the tissues, which contains proteins and large molecular particles.

LYMPHADENITIS. Inflammation of lymph nodes.

LYMPHADENOPATHY. Enlargement of the lymph nodes.

LYMPH-NODE ASPIRATE. Sample drawn through a needle from a lymph node.

LYMPHOCYTE. A type of white blood cell capable of responding immunologically to the presence of foreign material.

LYMPHOID CELL. Lymphocyte and plasma cell.

LYMPHOMA. Cancer of lymphoid tissue.

LYMPHOSARCOMA (LSA). Cancer of lymphocytes.

MACERATION. Softening of the skin from overexposure to water or topical medications.

MACROPHAGE. A specialized white blood cell that engulfs and processes antigens such as bacteria, fungi, viruses, parasites, or toxins.

MALIGNANT. Capable of spreading; said of tumors.

MANDIBLE. Lower jaw.

MAST CELL. A connective tissue cell that is involved in the development of allergy.

MASTITIS. Inflammation of the mammary gland.

MATRIX. Intercellular substance of a tissue (as of bone or cartilage); in urinary stones and plugs, the matrix is the mucoprotein base or ground substance.

MAXILLOFACIAL COMPRESSION. Shortening of the lower and upper jaw.

MEDIASTINUM. Median partition separating the two lungs.

MEDULLA. Inner part of the kidney or adrenal gland; part of the brain stem.

MEGAKARYOCYTE. Giant cell of bone marrow which breaks into platelets.

MEGESTROL ACETATE (OvabanR). A synthetic progestin.

MELANIN. Skin pigment.

MELANOCYTES. Cells producing the skin pigment melanin.

MELANOMA. Tumor of pigmented skin cells.

MELANOTRICHIA. Darkening of the hair.

MENINGES. Protective covering surrounding the brain and spinal cord.

MENINGIOMA. Most common tumor of the feline central nervous system; arises from the meninges.

MESENTERIC. Of the mesentery, a membrane covering the abdominal organs and attaching them to the body wall.

METABOLISM. All life-sustaining chemical processes in the body; the conversion of nutrients into energy.

METABOLITES. Products of metabolism.

METASTASIS. Spread of a malignant tumor to other sites.

METESTRUS. The period of subsiding follicular function following estrus.

METHIONINE. A sulfur-containing amino acid.

METRITIS. Inflammation of the uterus.

MICROBE. Any minute living organism, but especially one capable of causing disease.

MICROFILAREMIA. Presence of microfilariae in the blood.

MICROFILARIA. Minute larval stage of the heartworm.

MICROPHTHALMIA (MICROPHTHALMOS). Congenital smallness of one or both eyes.

MICROVASCULATURE. The smallest blood vessels (capillaries).

MILIARY DERMATITIS. Miliary eczema; small, red, crusty skin lesions.

MINERALOCORTICOIDS. Corticosteroids that affect the regulation of electrolyte and water balance.

MIOTIC. A drug that causes the pupil to contract.

MODIFIED-LIVE VIRUS (MLV). Attenuated (altered) virus that no longer produces clinical disease; used as a vaccine.

MONOCYTE. White blood cell capable of responding to the presence of foreign material.

MORPHOGENESIS. The development of form and shape in an organism.

MORPHOLOGY. Form and structure.

MOTILE. Capable of movement.

MOTILITY. Ability to move.

MUCOID. Mucuslike.

MUCOMETRA. Mucus in the uterus.

MUCOSAL-ASSOCIATED LYMPHOID TISSUE (MALT). Lymphoid tissue associated with the lining of the digestive, respiratory, and urogenital tracts.

MUCOUS MEMBRANES. Linings of the interior portions of the body that secrete mucus.

MUCUS. Substance produced by the mucous membranes, containing various secretions, salts, lymphocytes, and cells.

MUTATION. A genetic change.

MYCETOMA. General term for a fungus-induced, tumorlike skin lesion.

MYCOBACTERIUM. A genus of bacteria, members of which are responsible for tuberculosis and leprosy.

MYCOLOGY. The study of fungi.

MYDRIATIC. A drug that dilates the pupil.

MYELIN. Fatty substance forming the outer tunic or sheath around many nerve cells.

MYELOGENOUS. Produced in the bone marrow.

MYELOPATHY. Any degenerative disorder of the spinal cord.

MYELOPROLIFERATIVE DISORDERS. Heterogeneous group of tumors or tumorlike diseases involving cells of the bone marrow.

MYIASIS. Infestation of the body by fly maggots.

MYOCARDIAL DISEASE. Any disease of the heart muscle.

MYOCARDIUM. The muscle layer of the heart.

NANOGRAM. One billionth of a gram.

NASOPHARYNX. Back of the throat, above the soft palate.

NECROPSY. Autopsy; examination of a dead animal.

NECROSIS. Cell death.

NECROTIC. Composed of dead cells.

NECROTIZING. Causing cell death.

NEGRI BODIES. Intracellular inclusion bodies found in brain cells of animals or humans with rabies.

NEMATODE. General term for a roundworm.

NEONATAL. Newborn.

NEOPLASIA. Uncontrolled, progressive proliferation of cells under conditions that normally should be restrictive of cell growth; cancer.

NEOPLASM. Tumor; new growth.

NEOVASCULARIZATION. New blood vessel ingrowth.

Nepeta cataria. The catnip plant.

NEPETALACTONE. The primary constituent of catnip.

NEPHRITIS. Inflammation of the kidney.

NEPHROLITH. Gravel or mineral deposit in the kidney; kidney stone.

NEURULA. An early stage of embryonic development.

NEURON. An individual nerve cell.

NEUTROPHIL. A type of white blood cell important in destroying bacteria.

NEVUS (plural: NEVI). A mole; pigment spot.

NIACIN. Nicotinic acid, a vitamin of the B complex.

NIT. Louse egg.

Nocardia. Genus of bacteria commonly found in soil.

NUCLEIC ACIDS. The genetic material: deoxyribonucleic acid (DNA) and ribonucleic acid (RNA).

NULLIPAROUS. Having never given birth.

NYSTAGMUS. Involuntary, rapid eye movement, most often horizontal.

OBSTIPATION. Obstruction of the digestive tract; intractable constipation.

OCCLUDE. To close off or obstruct.

OCCLUSION. A blockage; relation of the upper and lower teeth when in contact.

OCULAR DISEASE. Any disease of the eye.

OCULOCUTANEOUS ALBINISM. Absence of pigmentation in the iris, skin, and retina.

OMNIVORE. Any organism that eats both plants and animals.

OMPHALOPHLEBITIS. Navel ill; infection of the veins of the umbilical cord.

ONCOGENESIS. Tumor causation.

OOCYTE. Developing egg cell in the female.

OOCYST. An encapsulated ovum (egg) of a sporozoan parasite, such as *Toxoplasma gondii*.

OPACITY. An opaque area or spot.

OPTIC DISC. The portion of the optic nerve visible at the surface of the retina.

OPTIC CHIASM. Location where the two optic nerves cross over each other to the opposite side of the brain.

ORGAN OF CORTI. The organ of hearing within the inner ear.

ORGANOGENESIS. The third stage of embryonic development, in which the organs begin to form.

ORGANOPHOSPHATE. Compounds containing carbon and phosphorus, which are highly toxic to cats.

OROPHARYNX. Back of the mouth; tonsillar area, between the soft palate and the epiglottis.

OSSICLES. The small bones within the ear.

OSTEOBLAST. A bone-forming cell.

OSTEOMALACIA. Disease characterized by softening of bones.

OSTEOMYELITIS. Infection of bone, with pus formation.

OSTEOPOROSIS. Thinning and weakening of bone.

OTITIS EXTERNA. Inflammation of the outer ear.

OTITIS INTERNA. Inflammation of the inner ear.

OTITIS MEDIA. Inflammation of the middle ear.

OVARIAN FOLLICLE. The ovum (egg) and its surrounding cells.

OVARIECTOMY. Removal of an ovary or ovaries.

OVARIOHYSTERECTOMY. Spay; surgical removal of the uterus and ovaries.

OVULATE. To release an egg from the ovary.

OVUM (plural: OVA). Egg.

OXYTOCIN. A pituitary hormone formed in the brain; it stimulates uterine contraction and is of therapeutic value in certain cases of dystocia (difficult birth).

PACKED CELL VOLUME. Volume of red blood cells in relation to the volume of blood fluid; hematocrit.

PALPATE. To examine with the hand and fingers.

PANCYTOPENIA. Condition in which red cell, white cell, and platelet cell are all decreased in number; deficiency of all cell elements of the blood.

PANLEUKOPENIA VIRUS. *See* Feline Panleukopenia.

PAPULE. Tiny, solid elevation in the skin.

PAPULOCRUSTOUS. Characterized by crusty elevations in the skin.

PAPULOPUSTULAR DERMATITIS. Inflammatory skin disease characterized by the presence of pus-filled elevations.

PARASITE. Organism that finds its food source by living in or on a host animal, often to the detriment of the host.

PARASITEMIA. Presence of a parasite in the bloodstream.

PARASITISM. Any parasite infestation or infection.

PARATHYROID GLANDS. Two small pairs of endocrine glands located adjacent to the thyroid glands; they are important in regulation of calcium and phosphorus balance.

PARATHYROID HORMONE (PTH). Hormone secreted by the parathyroid glands that regulates the metabolism of calcium and phosphorus in the body.

PARIETAL PLEURA. Membrane that forms the lining of the chest cavity.

PARONYCHIA. Pus-forming infection of the nail bed.

PARTURITION. The act of labor; birth.

PASTEURELLA MULTOCIDA. Common bacterium found in the feline mouth and upper respiratory tract.

PATELLAR LUXATION. Displacement of the kneecap.

PATENT. Open.

PATENT DUCTUS ARTERIOSUS (PDA). Abnormal persistence of the embryonic blood vessel connecting the pulmonary artery to the aorta.

PATHOGEN. Organism capable of producing disease.

PATHOGENESIS. Mechanism of development of a disease.

PATHOGENICITY. Relative ability of an organism to produce disease.

PEDICLE. A small stalk or stem.

PEDUNCULATED. On a stalk.

PEPTIDE. A short chain of amino acids.

PERCUTANEOUS NEEDLE BIOPSY. Method by which a sample of organ tissue is obtained by passing a biopsy needle through the skin.

PERICARDIUM. Membranous sac that surrounds the heart.

PERINEAL URETHROSTOMY. Surgical removal of the penis and widening of the urethral opening, to relieve urinary blockage in male cats.

PERINEUM. Region around the anus and genitalia.

PERIOCULAR LEUKOTRICHIA. "Goggles"; condition wherein hair grows in lighter around the eyes.

PERIODONTITIS. Inflammation of the tissue surrounding the base of a tooth.

PERIORBIT. Eye socket, including the surrounding tissues.

PERIOSTEUM. Tissue covering a bone.

pH. Measure of the acidity/alkalinity of a solution.

PHAGOCYTIC CELLS. Cells from blood and tissue that surround and ingest foreign material.

PHAGOCYTIZE. To surround and ingest material (said of cells).

PHARYNX. Area extending from the back of the nasal passage to the larynx and the esophagus.

PHENOLS. Toxic compounds derived from coal tar.

PHENOTYPE. Visible, physical expression of a genetic trait.

PHEROMONE. An odorous secretion releasing a specific response in another individual of the same species.

PHOCOMELIA. Developmental abnormality in which the upper part of the limb is absent and the paws are attached to the trunk by a small, abnormally formed bone; "seal-limb."

PHOTOPERIOD. Period of daylight or artificial light.

PHOTOPHOBIA. Hypersensitivity to light.

PHTHISIS BULBI. Shrinking or wasting of the eyeball.

PHYCOMYCOSIS. Disease caused by a number of specific fungi, especially *Rhizopus, Absidia,* and *Mucor.*

PHYSIOLOGY. The study of body functions.

PICOGRAM. One trillionth of a gram.

PILOCARPINE. A drug that stimulates constriction of the pupils and decreases intraocular pressure.

PILOERECTION. Reflex by which the hair "stands" on end.

PINNA. External ear; auricle.

PITUITARY GLAND. Endocrine gland at the base of the brain; secretes hormones that control other endocrine glands.

PLAGUE. Severe, life-threatening illness caused by the bacterium *Yersinia pestis.*

PLAQUE. Any patch or flat area.

PLASMA. Fluid portion of the blood (as opposed to the cellular portion).

PLASMA CELLS. Cells that make antibodies.

PLASMAPHERESIS. Extracorporeal immunosorption procedure in which plasma extracted is treated and then returned to the host.

PLATELET. Blood cell fragment involved in blood clotting.

PLEURA. Membrane that surrounds the lungs and lines the chest cavity.

PLEURAL EFFUSION. The accumulation of fluid within the pleural cavity in the chest.

PNEUMONITIS. Inflammation of the lungs.

PNEUMOTHORAX. Accumulation of air in the pleural cavity, outside the lungs.

POLYDACTYLY. Congenital abnormality characterized by the presence of extra digits (toes).

POLYDIPSIA. Excessive thirst.

POLYHEDRAL. Having many sides.

POLYMORPHONUCLEAR LEUKOCYTE. Type of white blood cell; neutrophil.

POLYP. Protruding growth on the surface of a mucous membrane.

POLYPEPTIDE. Molecule containing more than two amino acids.

POLYURIA. Excessive urination.

PORTOCAVAL SHUNT. Abnormal persistence of an embryonic blood vessel within the liver.

POSTERIOR PARESIS. Partial paralysis of a hind limb or limbs.

PREAURICULAR ALOPECIA. Absence of hair on the side of the head in front of the ear, normal in many breeds of cats.

PREGNANT MARE'S SERUM GONADOTROPHIN (PMSG). Sexual stimulation hormone; a series of doses given intramuscularly can induce estrus in queens.

PREPUBERTAL. Pertaining to the period before sexual maturity.

PREPUCE. Fold of skin covering the penis.

PROESTRUS. The period before estrus.

PROGESTOGEN. Any compound with progesterone-like activity.

PROGESTERONE. Hormone secreted by the corpus luteum, adrenal cortex, and placenta, to prepare the uterus for pregnancy.

PROGESTIN. Progesterone.

PROGNOSIS. Outlook as to outcome.

PROLACTIN. Hormone produced by the pituitary gland that stimulates and sustains lactation.

PROLAPSE. To fall or slip out of place.

PROLAPSE OF THE THIRD EYELID. Condition wherein the third eyelid partially occludes the eye.

PROPTOSIS. Bulging or protrusion of the eyeball.

PROTEOLYTIC. Protein-splitting.

PROTHROMBIN TIME. One measure of the clotting ability of the blood.

PROTOPLASM. The clear fluid, and the substances within it, that makes up all plant and animal cells.

PROTOZOA. Simple organisms that are usually composed of a single cell; some are capable of producing disease in animals and humans.

PRURITUS. Itching.

PSEUDOCOPROSTASIS. False fecal impaction.

PSEUDOPREGNANCY. A condition wherein the queen shows signs of pregnancy after a nonfertile mating.

PTYALISM. Excessive drooling.

PULMONARY EDEMA. Buildup of excessive fluid in the lungs.

PULMONARY EMBOLISM. A detached clot from elsewhere occluding a vessel within the lung.

PUNNETT SQUARE. Checkerboard diagram for delineating possible outcomes of mating two individuals with defined genetic characteristics.

PURULENT. Pus-forming.

PURULENT PERITONITIS. Pus forming inflammation of the lining of the abdomen.

PUSTULAR. Pimply.

PUTREFACTIVE. Refers to decomposition of organic matter by microorganisms.

PYELONEPHRITIS. Infection of the kidney and the kidney pelvis.

PYLORUS. Terminal part of the stomach, connecting with the duodenum.

PYOMETRA. Accumulation of pus within the uterus.

PYOMETRITIS. Purulent inflammation of the uterus.

PYOTHORAX. Empyema; accumulation of pus in the chest cavity.

PYRIDOXINE. Vitamin B_6.

QUATERNARY AMMONIUM COMPOUND (QAC). Chemical structure of a class of compounds used in disinfectants.

QUEEN. Breeding female cat.

RADIOGRAPHY. The making of film records of internal structures by use of X rays.

RAPID EYE MOVEMENT (REM). Type of eye movement during dreaming.

RECESSIVE GENE. A gene that can be expressed *only* when both members of a chromosome pair contain the same allele.

RECOMBINATION. Genetic exchange.

REDUCTION. Setting of a fracture.

REFLEX OVULATOR. Animal species in which ova are released only in response to mating; an example is the cat.

REGURGITATION. Involuntary return of ingested food to the mouth; differs from vomiting in that it is a passive process (i.e., unaccompanied by reflex, propulsive movements).

RENIN. Hormone produced by the kidneys that influences blood pressure.

RENIN-ANGIOTENSIN SYSTEM. Hormone-enzyme system that influences blood pressure by stimulating contraction of blood vessels.

RESORB. Biochemical dissolution of substances or cells; resorption; *see* Fetal Resorption.

RETINOL. Vitamin A.

RETROVIRUS. Virus of the family Retroviridae; examples are feline leukemia virus and feline immunodeficiency virus.

REVERSE TRANSCRIPTASE. Enzyme important in replication of certain viruses, such as the retroviruses.

RHINOTRACHEITIS. *See* Feline Viral Rhinotracheitis.

RIBOFLAVIN. Vitamin B_2.

RIBONUCLEIC ACID (RNA). A nucleic acid occurring in all cells and involved in protein synthesis.

RICKETTSIA. A genus of microorganisms transmitted to animals and man by lice, fleas, ticks, and mites; a specialized bacteria; a species of this genus causes Haemobartonellosis in cats.

SALINE. A salt solution; physiological sodium chloride solution.

SALMONELLA. Common genus of bacteria responsible for a spectrum of maladies ranging from intestinal disease to life-threatening systemic illness.

SARCOMA. General term for cancer of connective tissue cells (those cells within an organ or structure that bind it together and support it).

SCABIES. A specific skin mite infestation.

SCAPULA. Shoulder blade.

SCHIZONT. A development stage of certain protozoa.

SCLERA. White outer covering of the eyeball.

SCLEROTIC. Hardened.

SCROTUM. Pouch of skin containing the testes.

SEASONALLY POLYESTROUS. Experiencing estrous cycles during one part of the year (usually February through October for cats in the Northern Hemisphere).

SEBACEOUS GLAND. Small skin gland, attached to the hair follicle, that secretes sebum.

SEBORRHEA SICCA. Dry, scaly dermatitis; dandruff.

SEBUM. Thick, semi-fluid substance composed of fat and cellular debris, secreted by the sebaceous glands in the skin.

SEMINAL FLUID. A milky white secretion from the prostate and bulbourethral glands of the male.

SEMINIFEROUS TUBULES. Small channels in the testes wherein sperm develop.

SEPTIC ARTHRITIS. Inflammation of the joints caused by an infectious agent.

SEPTICEMIA. Bacterial blood poisoning; presence of bacteria in the bloodstream, accompanied by signs of disease.

SEROLOGY. The use of antigen-antibody reactions to detect antigens and antibodies in serum.

SEROUS MEMBRANE. A lining tissue that produces a watery secretion.

SERUM. Blood plasma minus the clotting factor fibrinogen; the clear liquid that remains after the blood clots; adjectival form is "serous."

SERUM ALKALINE PHOSPHATASE (SAP). An enzyme present in serum that is produced in many tissues but is of greatest diagnostic significance in disease of the liver and bone.

SIGN. A characteristic of a disease; signs are seen by observation, symptoms are characteristics reported by the patient.

SINOATRIAL (SA) NODE. Structure located at the junction of the right atrium of the heart and the vena cava; it is the heart's natural pacemaker.

SINUS HAIRS. Specialized tactile hairs on the cat, found on the muzzle, above the eyes, and on the underside of the forelegs.

SOFT PALATE. Soft, fleshy posterior part of the partition separating the nasal and oral cavities.

SOLAR DERMATITIS. Actinic dermatitis; inflammation of skin induced by sunlight.

SPERMATOZOA. Sperm.

SPHERULE. Parasitic stage of the fungus *Coccidioides immitis,* formed during the organism's growth phase in host tissue.

SPINA BIFIDA. Broad term that includes all failures of the vertebrae to close normally around the spinal cord.

SPLEEN. Abdominal organ that filters senescent (aging) red blood cells and foreign material from the blood.

SPLENECTOMY. Surgical removal of the spleen.

SPONTANEOUS OVULATOR. Animal species in which ova are released periodically, regardless of whether sexual intercourse has occurred.

SPORE. Thick-walled "resting stage," formed by certain bacteria during unfavorable environmental conditions; it germinates quickly once favorable conditions have been restored, to produce a new generation.

SPRAIN. Injury to a joint involving damage to one or more ligaments without ligament rupture.

SQUAMOUS CELL CARCINOMA. A type of skin cancer arising from surface cells.

STAPHYLOCOCCUS. A bacterial genus important in skin infections and other pus-producing processes.

STEATITIS. Yellow fat disease; disease wherein a yellow-pigmented substance is deposited in body fat; the result of a vitamin E deficiency.

STENOSIS. A constriction or narrowing.

STEROID. A common term for corticosteroid; sex hormones also belong to the steriod group; anabolic steroids promote growth and tissue repair.

STOMATITIS. Inflammation of the lining of the oral cavity.

STRABISMUS. Affected individuals are referred to as cross-eyed.

STRANGLES. Contagious streptococcal lymphadenitis; a respiratory disease caused by streptococci.

STRANGULATED. Congested because of a constriction.

STREPTOCOCCUS. A bacterial genus some species of which are of importance in abscesses and other pus-producing processes.

STRONGYLOIDES. A genus of threadworm; small parasitic worms.

STRUVITE. Magnesium-ammonium-phosphate crystals that form in the urinary tract, causing irritation and/or blockage; also called triple phosphate crystals.

STUD TAIL. Excessive oil production by the supracaudal organ of the cat.

SUBCUTANEOUS. Beneath the skin.

SUBCUTANEOUSLY (SC). A route of injection (under the skin).

SUBCUTIS. Layer beneath the dermis and epidermis of the skin, composed of fatty tissue and fibers.

SUBINVOLUTION. Partial involution (return to normal size) as of the uterus after birthing.

SUBMANDIBULAR. Under the lower jaw.

SUCROSE. Table sugar.

SUPERFECUNDATION. Fertilization of ova by separate matings during one ovulatory cycle; thus a litter of kittens may have more than one father.

SUPERFETATION. Fertilization of an ovum occurring when a fetus is already present in the uterus.

SUPPURATIVE. Producing pus.

SUPRACAUDAL ORGAN. Preen gland; large oil glands along the top of the tail.

SUTURE. A surgical stitch.

SYNAPSE. The site at which one neuron connects with another.

SYNDACTYLY. Congenital abnormality wherein adjacent toes are fused.

SYSTEMIC LUPUS ERYTHEMATOSUS (SLE). Rare multisystemic autoimmune disease.

TACHYCARDIA. Rapid heart rate.

TAIL HEAD. Place where the tail joins the body.

TAPETUM LUCIDUM. Specialized reflective layer beneath the retina; makes cats' eyes shine in the dark.

TAURINE. An amino acid essential for cats; required for proper development and functioning of the retina and heart.

TELOGEN HAIRS. Hairs in the resting stage of the hair growth cycle.

TEMPORAL REGION. Area of the head in front of the ears.

TENDON. Fibrous tissue that connects muscle to bone.

TERATOGEN. Any infectious agent or chemical that disrupts normal fetal development.

TERATOLOGY. The study of abnormal development and congenital malformations.

TESTOSTERONE. Male sex hormone, produced in the testes.

TETANY. Muscle spasms.

THALAMUS. Portion of the brain that serves as a conduit for sensory information coming from the rest of the body and for nerve impulses concerned with balance and coordination, arising from the cerebellum.

THERIOGENOLOGY. The study of reproduction.

THIAMINASE. An enzyme that destroys thiamine.

THIAMINE. Vitamin B_1.

THORACIC. Pertaining to the chest.

THORACOCENTESIS. Procedure wherein a needle is inserted into the chest cavity in order to remove accumulated air or fluid.

THROMBOPLASTIN. A protein essential to the formation of blood clots.

THROMBOSIS. Formation of a blood clot (thrombus).

THYMUS. Lymphoid organ located in the chest that regulates the maturation of specialized lymphocytes known as T cells.

THYROIDECTOMY. Removal of the thyroid gland.

THYROID-STIMULATING HORMONE (TSH). Hormone produced by the pituitary gland that stimulates the thyroid gland to produce thyroxine (T_4) and triiodothyronine (T_3).

THYROXINE (T_4). One of two hormones secreted by the thyroid gland that help to regulate the overall cellular metabolism of the body.

TITER. A quantitative measure of the concentration of an antibody or antigen in blood serum.

TOCOPHEROLS. Vitamin E.

TOXEMIA. Presence of toxins in the blood, accompanied by signs of disease.

TOXIC EPIDERMAL NECROLYSIS. Skin condition in which redness and peeling occur over the entire body surface.

TOXOCARA CATI. The cat roundworm, an internal parasite.

TOXOPLASMOSIS. A protozoan disease caused by *Toxoplasma gondii*.

TRACHEA. The windpipe, which is a tube descending from the larynx and branching at the lower end into two bronchi that enter the lungs.

TRACHEOSTOMY. Surgically created opening in the trachea through the skin of the neck.

TRANSPLACENTALLY. By way of the placenta.

TRANSPORT MEDIUM. Material for preserving a specimen until it reaches the laboratory.

TRANSTRACHEAL WASH. Flushing of material from the trachea and bronchi for diagnostic purposes, by needle puncture and aspiration through the tracheal wall.

TREMATODES. Flukes.

TRICHINOSIS. A parasitic disease contracted by eating meat (especially pork) that has not been thoroughly cooked.

TRI-IODOTHYRONINE (T_3). One of two hormones secreted by the thyroid gland that help to regulate the overall cellular metabolism of the body.

TULAREMIA. A plaguelike disease mainly affecting rodents; caused by *Francisella tularensis*.

TURBINATES. Rolled bony structures within the nose that filter, warm, and humidify the inhaled air.

ULCERATIVE KERATITIS. Inflammation of the cornea accompanied by corneal ulceration.

ULTRASONOGRAPHY. Ultrasound; study of the body's interior by means of echo reflections.

ULTRAVIOLET RADIATION. Radiation beyond the violet region of the spectrum; can induce sunburn.

UNICORNUAL UTERINE TORSION. Twisting of one uterine horn.

UNTHRIFTY. Unkempt in appearance and failing to thrive.

URETER. A tube that carries urine from the kidney to the urinary bladder.

URETEROLITH. A stone in a ureter.

URETHRA. A tube that carries urine from the bladder to the exterior of the body.

URETHRAL PLUG. Soft, pastelike, compressible substance blocking the urethra in cases of feline urologic syndrome (FUS).

URETHROLITH. A stone in the urethra.

URETHROSTOMY. *See* Perineal Urethrostomy.

URINALYSIS. Series of physical and chemical tests that aid in the diagnosis of urinary tract disorders.

URINARY CALCULUS (plural: CALCULI). Stone in the urinary tract.

UROLITHIASIS. Formation of urinary stones; disease associated with presence of urinary stones.

URTICARIA. Hives.

UTERINE TUBES. Fallopian tubes.

UTERINE INVERSION. Uterine prolapse; inside-out uterus protruding through the cervix.

UTERUS UNICORNIS. Uterus having only one uterine horn.

UVEA. Layer within the eye that contains the iris, blood vessels, and choroid.

VACCINATION. Process of giving a vaccine; *see* Immunization.

VAGINITIS. Inflammation of the vagina.

VAGINOSCOPIC. By means of visual inspection of the vagina with a speculum.

VALERIC ACID. Substance present in the vaginal secretions of estrous females; stimulates a reaction in the tomcat.

VASCULAR RING DEFECT. Abnormal retention of embryonic blood vessels in the region of the aorta.

VAS DEFERENS. A tube that carries sperm from the testis to the urethra.

VASCULARIZATION. Formation of blood vessels.

VASCULITIS. Inflammation of a blood vessel.

VASODILATION. Dilation of a blood vessel.

VENTRAL. Toward the belly surface.

VENTRICLE. One of two lower chambers of the heart.

VENULE. Small vein.

VESICLE. Blister.

VESICULAR. Fluid-filled.

VESTIBULAR SYNDROME. Incoordination and imbalance related to the inner ear.

VILLI (singular: VILLUS). Fingerlike projections lining the interior of the small intestine.

VIREMIA. Presence of virus in the bloodstream.

VIRILIZING. Producing male characteristics.

VIRULENCE. Disease-producing capacity.

VIRULENCE FACTOR. Any factor that enhances the ability of a pathogen to infect and damage tissue.

VIRUS ISOLATION. Growth of a virus artificially in the laboratory.

VISCERA (singular: VISCUS). The large interior organs of the body.

VISCERAL LARVA MIGRANS. Disease in human beings usually caused by the dog roundworm *Toxocara canis,* and very rarely by the cat roundworm *Toxocara cati.*

VISCERAL PLEURA. Membrane that covers the surface of the organs in the chest.

VITREOUS HUMOR. Fluid within the posterior portion of the eyeball.

VULVA. Entrance to the vagina.

WHEAL. Smooth elevated area in the skin, often itchy and associated with allergy.

WHOLE-BODY HYPERTHERMIA. Anticancer procedure in which the core body temperature of the patient is raised.

YERSINIA PESTIS. The bacterium that causes plague.

ZONA PELLUCIDA. The envelope or casing around an ovum.

ZOONOTIC. Of a disease, having the capacity to spread between animals and man.

ZYGOTE. Fertilized ovum.

Index

·····················

·············